PRODUCTION-INVENTORY SYSTEMS
Planning and control

PRODUCTION-INVENTORY SYSTEMS

Planning and Control

ELWOOD S. BUFFA
University of California, Los Angeles

JEFFREY G. MILLER
Harvard University

THIRD EDITION 1979

RICHARD D. IRWIN, INC.   Homewood, Illinois   60430
Irwin-Dorsey Limited   Georgetown, Ontario   L7G 4B3

ISBN 0-256-02041-8
Library of Congress Catalog Card No. 78–61186

Printed in the United States of America

3 4 5 6 7 8 9 0 MP 6 5 4 3 2 1

To our wives
BETTY and SUE

Preface

IN previous editions of *Production-Inventory Systems*, a broad conceptual framework based on the production planning research and practice of the past two decades was developed. This edition continues and updates this work by incorporating the results of the latest advances in the field. Materials requirements planning systems in particular represent one of the major advances that has drawn the attention of industry over recent years. Much of the new material in this book is directed toward increasing the level of understanding of this topic.

In addition, we have tried to expand upon our conceptual framework by emphasizing to a greater degree the organizational context within which these advances apply, and the practical administrative concerns that they generate. Our concern that these issues be exposed to view has been given impetus by several developments. First, the technical advances in planning and control over the last several decades have, in part, given rise to a new breed of professionals and executives. While planning and control was once perceived to be the domain of clerks in green eyeshades and computer specialists, it is now an area dominated by broad gauge, professional managers and analysts who must deal with production planning problems at the managerial as well as the technical level. Materials managers have risen to vice presidential levels in many organizations, and career paths have been formed to the highest executive offices through materials and production planning organizations. These facts bear witness to the increasing scope of responsibilities and concerns of the area. Moreover, the area remains a key to successful manufacturing management. The operating manager has found that he or she must further develop and maintain knowledge of production planning and control concerns as the technology of this area changes.

The second development is closely related to the first. The increased application of sophisticated, computerized, production planning and inventory control techniques has resulted in a number of instances in which they have failed to live up to their promise, or have failed altogether. Very often, the reasons for these failures are not because of technical insufficiencies, but because the system or technique was inappropriate to the organization's problems, or because it failed in execution, rather than in design. It is our hope that the case studies included in this edition will provide the sense of organizational context and administrative urgency necessary to understand the managerial requirements for executing production planning and inventory control decisions. In addition one should understand how the special problems of a manufacturing concern can be incorporated into the design of a planning and control system.

The organization of the book is derived from the rationale just described. It is divided into five major parts, each comprised of one or more chapters of text, and several case studies. The first part serves as an introduction to the basic elements of production planning and inventory control systems, major types of operating environments, and the functions of inventories. The second part examines the major elements of production planning and inventory control systems in depth. This includes a consideration of forecasting, basic inventory decisions, independent demand inventory systems, aggregate planning and master scheduling, and requirements planning techniques. It also includes a discussion of data requirements for planning and control, and the execution, feedback, and management control aspects of such systems.

The latter half of the book is concerned with the special planning and control problems associated with various kinds of process technologies. Part III contains chapters on planning and controlling continuous processes for high volume standardized products. The chapters in Part IV are concerned with scheduling and capacity and materials control in firms with intermittent production systems such as job shops, and in large-scale projects. The final portion of the book summarizes the technical, strategic, and administrative issues involved in designing and managing production inventory planning and control systems.

In general, the book has been written for the business or engineering student, and for practicing managers in the field of production and inventory control. Some chapters contain technical material and references that presume a basic understanding of more advanced research techniques however. Where possible, we have isolated this advanced material in such a way that the book can be used flexibly depending upon instructors' objectives. Chapter 5, for example, presents the basic logic and some simple techniques for aggregate planning and master scheduling; Chapter 6 contains fairly sophisticated mathematical models for aggregate planning and master scheduling. Other segments of the book which may be selectively employed are Chapters 9 and 10, and portions of Chapters 3 and 4.

Acknowledgments

It is always difficult to account in detail for the ideas which go into a work of this length. The conceptual framework for the book has evolved over a period of years through several editions, and we were undoubtedly influenced by many individuals and their work. We have been meticulous throughout the book in attempting to give original source credit to these individuals. If there are omissions, they are unintentional.

We are indebted to William Taubert, currently vice president of Hunt Wesson Foods, for his contributions as coauthor of the second edition of this book. His current responsibilities precluded his participation in the third edition.

William R. Newell of the University of Washington, Warren H. Hausman of Stanford, and Matthew F. Tuite of Northwestern reviewed the manuscripts for earlier editions and provided the basis for many improvements and additions. John Matthews of the University of Wisconsin and Michael Burstein of Dartmouth reviewed this manuscript, and we are in their debt for their insightful suggestions.

This edition contains case studies. We have a special obligation to recognize the contribution of the companies that cooperated in developing these cases, the authors who wrote them, and the organizations that sponsored their development. We are grateful to them for their contributions to education. Steven Wheelwright of the Harvard Business School wrote the "Corning Glass Company: The Erwin Plant" case. Curtis H. Jones wrote the original version of the "Avalon Machinery" case. Edward Davis of the Darden School of Business, the University of Virginia, wrote the "Markem" case which provides so many rich examples in Chapter 7. All of the cases in this book were

written under the sponsorship of the Division of Research of the
Harvard Business School. Funds for case development were provided
by the Associates of the Harvard Business School and the 1907
Foundation for Transportation and Logistics.

December, 1978   **Elwood S. Buffa**
Pacific Palisades, California   **Jeffrey G. Miller**
and Wellesley, Massachusetts

Contents

PART I

INTRODUCTION

Chapter 1

Production-inventory systems

THE WORD "SYSTEMS" has become an integral part of the language of business. In use, the term is applied to describe a range of activities and relationships. These include the minute procedures involved in a computerized cost control "system," to the more vaguely connected set of relationships implied by a total "systems" approach for designing a business. While the word often carries the impression that things are more precisely defined than they really are, we shall use this term extensively. "Systems" describe the relationships between parts of things and a whole. Such relationships are central to the successful management of a business enterprise, as well as the development of the ideas in this book.

This book is focused on the design and management of two kinds of systems. The first is the physical system for producing and distributing goods and services. The parts of this *production-inventory system* are tangible. They include factories, machines, people, warehouses, and transportation equipment such as trucks and railcars. The "whole" production-inventory system is described by the links between its parts—the way materials are fed to machines, finished products are distributed to warehouses, and the way warehouses provide goods to customers. The second type of system of interest to us is the largely intangible *planning and control system* which is used to guide and coordinate the flow of materials and labor inputs and goods and services outputs through the physical system. The important parts of the planning and control system are the individual bits of data that pass between the people who make decisions, other decision makers, and those who execute them; the methods that are applied in making decisions; and the checks that are made to ensure that things are going according to plan. The whole planning and control system is defined by the way these parts are linked together over time as the business strives to match supply and demand in a changing economic environment.

Of course, our two systems—the production-inventory system and the planning and control system—may also be parts, or subsystems, of a larger whole. They are. Our ultimate purpose is to show how these two parts are related to one another and to the whole business.

We have three basic objectives in this introductory chapter. The first is to expand upon the notion of production-inventory systems, and to classify the many different types into a few meaningful categories. Steel mills, appliance and electronic component manufacturers, banks, and large-scale projects such as building a nuclear-powered ship, each represent unique types of production-inventory systems. Our classification scheme is designed to identify groups of industries whose basic technological and market requirements are similar from a planning and control viewpoint. This scheme is used in the latter half of the book to identify the particular characteristics of planning and control systems that are unique to each group.

The second purpose of this chapter is to demonstrate the ways in which goods and materials flow through productive systems, and the functions of inventories in facilitating this flow. Inventories and the subject of inventory control have received a great deal of attention by both scholars and business leaders. In fact, the voluminous literature on this subject often seems to outweigh the relative importance of the subject to business when one considers that they account for only 20–30 percent of the typical industrial firm's assets. However, this is a superficial view. The real importance of inventories accrues to their role as the lubricant which allows businesses to operate competitively. Their existance either in the form of finished products, work-in-process, or materials is an unavoidable consequence of the flow of production. Inventories impact costs, profits, customer service, and investments in facilities and equipment in important ways. They are extremely visible parts of the physical production-inventory system, and a central concern in planning and control. We focus on them here because we believe that an understanding of their role will provide for a clearer understanding of the relationships between production-inventory systems and planning and control systems.

The third objective is to define the basic elements of a planning and control system, and to illustrate the magnitude of the changes in the economic environment that must be considered in managing this system. In addition to defining the contribution of each of the elements of planning and control to the whole system, we shall define a number of terms that will be used throughout the book.

FOUR MAIN CLASSES OF PRODUCTION-INVENTORY SYSTEMS

Our classification scheme is based on two dimensions which are relevant to all production-inventory systems. The first dimension depends on the characteristics of the producing unit itself. We classify production units into two categories: *continuous systems, and intermittent systems*. This dichotomy is largely a function of process technology, since continuous systems are those that are designed to produce a continuous stream of products, while intermittent systems are geared to producing in batches or lots. Examples of continuous systems include assembly lines, such as those found in the automobile and consumer electronics industries, and the large dedicated factories which produce certain types of chemicals, or pulp and paper products. For convenience sake, we also place pure inventory systems in this category. These are operating units which do not produce, but merely serve as stocking points, such as warehouses or distributors. Intermittent systems are more characteristic of metal, plastic, woodworking, or electronic component industries where products tend to be nonstandard, and are produced in discrete lots or batches. We include in this category the special kind of intermittent system represented by large-scale, one-time projects, such as the manufacture of a large building or a ship, the Polaris missile, or the Gemini or Apollo projects of the U.S. Space Program.

One of the major reasons for differentiating between continuous and intermittent systems is that the mechanisms for adapting production output to changes in demand are largely dependent upon this distinction. For example, consider a firm which employs an assembly line (a continuous system) balanced to produce 1,000 units per month to match a demand for 1,000 units per month. Here, the line is producing at a continuous rate which exactly matches the rate of demand. If the demand increases to 2,000 units per month, production can adapt to this by either increasing the rate at which the line produces, by rebalancing and hiring more people, or by running the line on a second shift. In contrast, an intermittent system might meet a demand for 1,000 units each month by producing a batch of 3,000 units in one month, and depleting the resulting inventory over a three-month period. If the demand in this system leaps to 2,000 per month, we might not see an increase in the daily *rate* of production at all. Instead, we might see this firm producing batches of 6,000 units over a two-month period, and depleting the resulting inventory over three months. As we shall see, there are also other important differences between continuous and intermittent systems.

The second basis for classification depends on whether or not final products are held in inventory for immediate use or sale, or whether goods are produced only after a definite need for them is established. This way of differentiating among systems addresses the issue of *product positioning*, in terms of the elapsed time between the receipt of a customer's order for a product, and the manufacturer's delivery of that product to the customer. While the previous continuous-intermittent classification was based on the characteristics of the production technology a manufacturer uses, the positioning classification scheme is largely a function of marketing policies regarding customer service and response time. It is useful in explaining different approaches to scheduling, and the need for finished goods, as opposed to in-process inventory control.

At one extreme, we find companies who produce in anticipation of customers' orders. They position themselves so that they can deliver a customer's order immediately upon its receipt. This is usually accomplished by holding finished goods inventories; hence, operating systems which are geared to this policy are called *to stock* systems. At the other extreme, we find companies or manufacturing units which produce to order; that is, which procure raw materials and produce products only after they have received a definite commitment from a customer to buy the product. Naturally, firms which follow a "to order" policy cannot ship their products immediately. The time lag between order entry and shipment in such instances must be at least as long as the period of time it takes to acquire materials from vendors, and to process them into finished products.

To illustrate one of the major trade-offs in to stock/to order positioning decisions, consider the case of a company which has a demand for a certain product of 1,000 units per month, and has found it economical to produce it in lots of 2,000 units. If this company chooses to make to stock, it must produce the lot of 2,000 before any customer orders are received. As Figure 1–1 illustrates, the result of

Figure 1–1
Pattern of inventory levels over time with a "to stock" policy (assumes average monthly demand of 1,000 units, spread evenly over the month, and production batch sizes of 2.000 units)

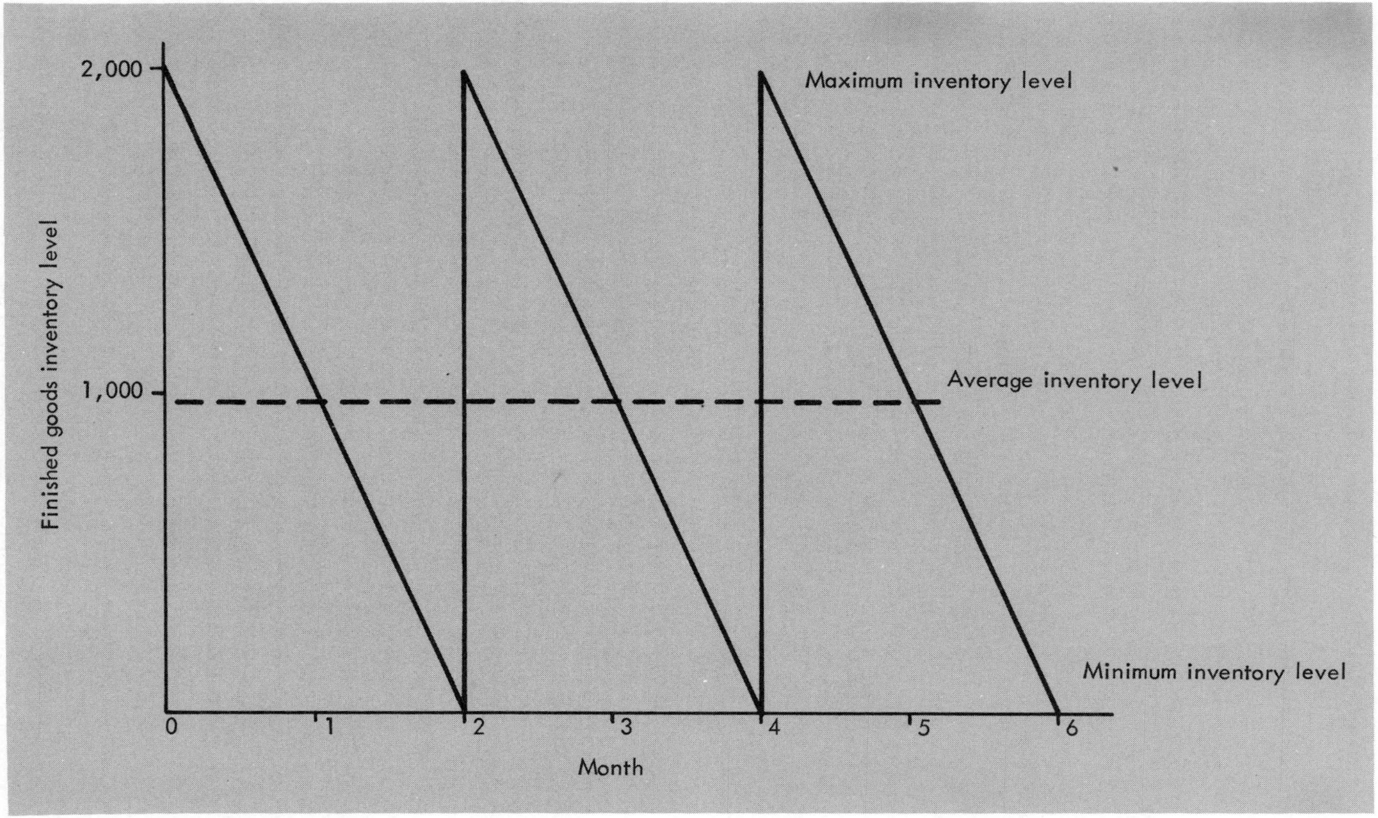

this decision will be an average inventory level of 1,000 units, assuming that demand follows the expected pattern of 1,000 per month. However, in return for the costs of maintaining this inventory, the company will be able to offer its customers immediate delivery, a highly valued feature in many industries. On the other hand, if the time to procure materials and to produce a production lot is negligible, a decision to produce to order will enable the firm to avoid carrying any inventories at all. This policy can be implemented by waiting until the total number of units ordered accumulates to 2,000 units, and then producing and immediately shipping the lot. However, the resulting savings in inventory costs must be balanced against the losses in customer goodwill, and possibly lost sales, that may result from the slower response of the company to customer orders. If the company follows a "to order" policy, customers will have to commit themselves to buying the product as much as two months in advance of delivery. Thus, positioning decisions involve trading off the costs, and risks, associated with holding stocks of finished goods, and the marketing advantages associated with fast response to customer orders.

As in the case of the continuous/intermittent system classification scheme, the to order/to stock dichotomy is often blurred in reality. For example, a machine tool manufacturer may produce machines to order, but produce spare parts for these machines to stock. Other companies produce neither to stock, nor completely to order. These firms, typified by electrical instruments, and many component manufacturers, adopt an intermediate position by keeping stocks of raw materials or semifinished products in anticipation of demand, and awaiting the arrival for firm orders before completing production. Intermediate positioning policies result in somewhat faster response to orders than a pure make to order policy, and somewhat lower inventory levels than a pure make to stock policy.

The four main classes of production-inventory systems can be derived by combining the two classification schemes that we have discussed so far. Figure 1–2 shows the results of this combination, and identifies some of the types of products that tend to fall into each of the four categories. An examination of these product types will show that continuous processes tend to be utilized to produce high-volume products, while intermittent processes are usually associated with relatively low-volume products. Similarly, the more speculative "to stock" positioning policy tends to be utilized where the unit value of a product is low, or where the product is highly

Figure 1–2
The four main classes of production-inventory systems

	Positioning policy	
	To stock	*To order*
Process technology	*Continuous/to stock systems* Office copiers Agricultural chemicals TV sets Vacuum cleaners Calculators Wholesalers Distributors	*Continuous/to order systems* Construction equipment Buses, trucks Some chemicals Some wood and pulp products Wire and cable Textiles Some polyethylene resins Electronic components
	Intermittent/to stock systems Medical instruments Testing equipment Some steel products Electronic components Molded plastic products Spare parts	*Intermittent/to order systems* Machine tools Tools, dies Industrial equipment Nuclear pressure vessels Electronic components Military aircraft, ships Gemini project Construction projects

standardized. The "to order" positioning policy is more closely associated with specialized or relatively high-unit value products.

A continuous/to stock system.   The epitome of continuous/to stock, production-inventory systems is the extended production-distribution network of firms which produce high-volume standardized products, such as hand held calculators. Such systems are typically composed of a number of stages at which inventories are held. Thus, the term *multistage inventory system* is often synonymous with this category. The stages of such systems which do not produce, such as distributors, are called *pure inventory systems* when they are considered in isolation, rather than as a part of a larger system.

Figure 1–3 offers a schematic diagram of a typical *multistage inventory system* showing material and information flow and typical system time delays. Though the time delay values are fictional in Figure 1–3, they are typical of the values one might find in many systems. Demand is generated at the consumer level and draws directly from the retail inventory. When items are available in retail inventory, they are supplied to the customer with a transit time delay of only one day. Every ten days the retailer reviews the stock levels and writes replenishment orders to the distributor, who also maintains an inventory. We assume that it takes an additional three days

Figure 1-3
Schematic diagram of multistage inventory system, material and information flow, typical system time delays, and major problems of inventory management at each stage

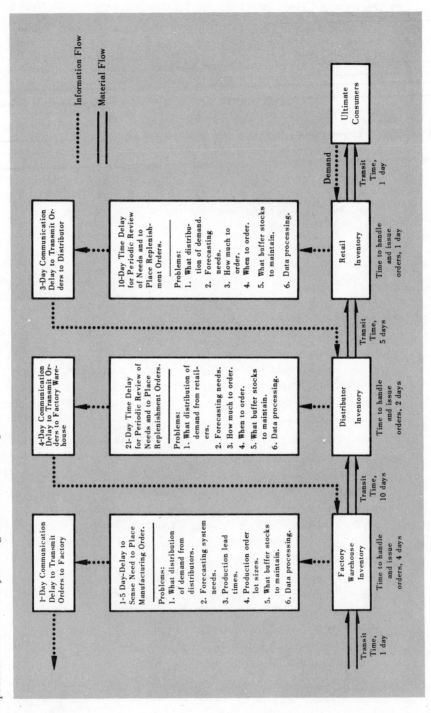

to transmit these orders to the distributor. On receipt of orders the distributor requires two days to handle and issue the orders plus a transit and receipt time of five days, making it seven days before the retailer actually receives the material. The retailer's cycle time for replenishment is, then, a total of (10 + 3 + 2 + 5) = 20 days. The distributor in turn has a similar kind of replenishment cycle, which involves a total of 39 days, and so on back through the system. As we will see later, understanding the dynamics of this time delay system is important if one is to understand the behavior of inventory systems in general. It is also important to understand that the system is interdependent; that is, the retailer's inventory policies and practices are affected by consumer demand, the distributor's policies are affected by the retailer's practices, and so on back through the system. We can also see by virtue of the chain of time delays that a change in consumer demand is felt at the factory warehouse only after considerable delay through the information system shown.

Some of the most important inventory problems for each of the levels are shown in Figure 1–3. Though the problems are similar for each of the levels in the system, they have a somewhat different emphasis. For example, the problem of determining the distribution of demand and forecasting demand is local for the retailer, whereas at the factory warehouse it may be national or international in scope. On the other hand, the factory warehouse may need a data processing system for a relatively few sizes, types, and styles, whereas the distributor and retailer are likely to be dealing with a very much larger number of items.

In Figure 1–4, we have shown a typical continuous *production-inventory system for high-volume standardized products*. In Figure 1–4 we have extended the system of Figure 1–3 two more stages upstream to include the factory and raw material suppliers. We have also changed the focus to the combined problems of production and inventory by drawing a boundary around the factory and factory warehouse, representing the system under managerial control. Obviously, in some instances the company system boundary may extend downstream to include the distributor level or in a very few situations, even the retail level. We see that some of the largest time delays are added by the manufacturing and raw material procurement systems. The major problems of production-inventory systems are summarized in Figure 1–4, and they are in general somewhat more complex than for pure inventory systems. In addition to the multistage inventory systems, we have added the planning and de-

Figure 1–4
System for high-volume standardized products (broad flow of material and information, time delays, and problems)

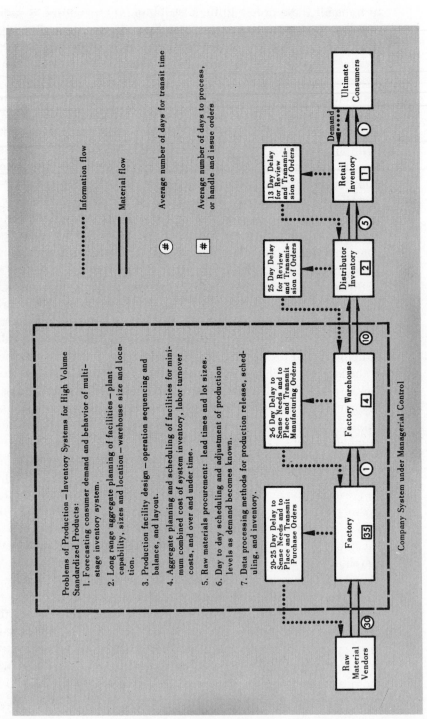

Problems of Production – Inventory Systems for High Volume
Standardized Products:

1. Forecasting consumer demand and behavior of multistage inventory system.

2. Long range aggregate planning of facilities – plant
   capability, sizes and location – warehouse size and location.

3. Production facility design – operation sequencing and
   balance, and layout.

4. Aggregate planning and scheduling of facilities for minimum combined cost of system inventory, labor turnover
   costs, and over and under time.

5. Raw materials procurement: lead times and lot sizes.

6. Day to day scheduling and adjustment of production
   levels as demand becomes known.

7. Data processing methods for production release, scheduling, and inventory.

•••••••••• Information flow

▌▌ Material flow

(#) Average number of days for transit time

[#] Average number of days to process,
    or handle and issue orders

Raw Material Vendors [30]

Factory [35]

20-25 Day Delay to
Sense Needs and to
Place and Transmit
Purchase Orders

(1)

Factory Warehouse [4]

2-6 Day Delay to
Sense Needs and to
Place and Transmit
Manufacturing Orders

(10)

Distributor Inventory [2]

25 Day Delay
for Review
and Transmis-
sion of Orders

(5)

Retail Inventory [1]

13 Day Delay
for Review
and Transmis-
sion of Orders

Demand

(1)

Ultimate Consumers

Company System under Managerial Control

sign of the production facility, which commonly requires a rather large investment. Decision models for planning and scheduling now must consider not only inventory costs but a whole host of other costs, such as labor turnover costs, overtime, undertime, materials, and plant out-of-pocket fixed costs. Though no one would say that the planning and scheduling problems of this type of production facility are simple, they are nonetheless simpler than for intermittent systems.

Intermittent/to order systems. For many intermittent systems, everything is keyed to the basic requirement of holding facilities and labor force "in inventory" to supply the needs of a demand that varies in terms of design, style, and technological requirements. Thus the jobbing machine shop holds in readiness equipment and trained mechanics capable of performing a wide variety of operations on various metals of different sizes, types, and designs. If the number of orders falls temporarily, such an organization does not sell its equipment or fire its skilled machinists, for it is this capability that it has for sale. Similarly, and perhaps even more essential to organizational survival, aerospace companies may stockpile engineering and scientific brains because it is this kind of capability which is crucial in obtaining contracts.

A simple structural model for a job shop is shown in Figure 1–5. Again, broad information and material flow is shown with typical time delays indicated. Though most often the relationships with the customer may be direct, the internal complications are tremendous. These complications arise from the custom nature of the fabrication process, where each item, or order, will require individual planning and scheduling and will follow an unique processing sequence. The typical time delays in the information system are in the bid and order procedure, the special production planning and scheduling requirements, and the special ordering of materials. In the system shown in Figure 1–3, these delays add to a total of 74 days minimum before material starts to flow. The physical flow time then involves 140 days, most of which is consumed in the custom manufacturing process. Obviously, these time delays would vary considerably depending on the specific nature of the products and technology involved. Again, Figure 1–5 summarizes some of the major problems of job shops. The emphasis is somewhat different than for the high-volume standardized system; that is, the inventory problems are largely for raw material and inprocess inventories, and the scheduling problem is focused more on the use of individual pieces of equipment rather than the factory as a whole.

Figure 1-5
System for job shop (information and material flow, time delays, and problems)

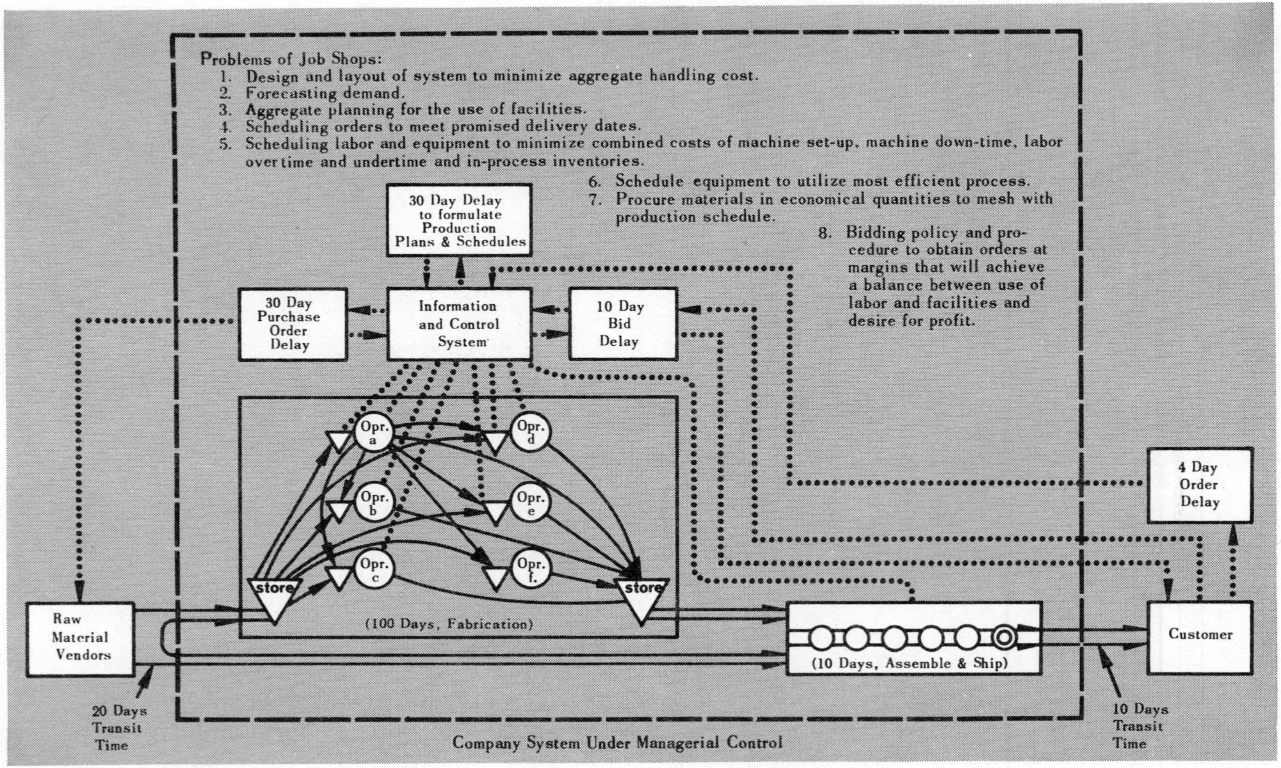

Problems of Job Shops:
1. Design and layout of system to minimize aggregate handling cost.
2. Forecasting demand.
3. Aggregate planning for the use of facilities.
4. Scheduling orders to meet promised delivery dates.
5. Scheduling labor and equipment to minimize combined costs of machine set-up, machine down-time, labor over time and undertime and in-process inventories.
6. Schedule equipment to utilize most efficient process.
7. Procure materials in economical quantities to mesh with production schedule.
8. Bidding policy and procedure to obtain orders at margins that will achieve a balance between use of labor and facilities and desire for profit.

4 Day Order Delay

Customer

10 Days Transit Time

(10 Days, Assemble & Ship)

30 Day Delay to formulate Production Plans & Schedules

10 Day Bid Delay

Information and Control System

30 Day Purchase Order Delay

Opr. d

Opr. e

Opr. f

Opr. a

Opr. b

Opr. c

store

store

(100 Days, Fabrication)

Raw Material Vendors

20 Days Transit Time

Company System Under Managerial Control

The *large-scale one-time project system* might have a structural model which would not be far different from that of the job shop shown in Figure 1–5. The time delays throughout the system are undoubtedly very much longer for the project system because of the immense complexity. Figure 1–6 shows a list of some of the important problems of the project production system in *(A)* and a project graph of activities in *(B)*. Because of the complexity of operations, sequences, and interrelations, some of the most important problems center on the planning and scheduling of this network of operations and finding the maximum time (critical path) through the network. Figure 1–6 represents a very simple network.

The four-way classification scheme shown in Figure 1–2 is a useful way of categorizing the important features of systems for planning and controlling production and inventories. The to order/to stock distinction is important in explaining the type of inventory control, aggregate planning, and master scheduling techniques and methods that are useful in these situations. The continuous/intermittent dichotomy is important in explaining the type of detailed scheduling and control problems that are likely to be encountered in particular situations. In all four categories of productive systems, however, inventories play a crucial part. They leave a trail that marks the flow of goods and materials through the system, and play important roles in allowing these flows to be regulated in an effective manner. Therefore, let us stop to consider the functions that inventories perform, since this will be a very important step toward understanding the nature of both productive and planning and control systems.

FUNCTIONS OF INVENTORY

The physical structures represented by machines, factories, and warehouses, have often been likened to the skeleton of the human body. Building on that analogy, perhaps the flow of goods and materials through the system, marked by the existence of inventories, represents the lifeblood. As a focus for our discussion let us examine Figure 1–7 which has been adapted from Figure 1–4, the production-inventory system for high-volume standardized products. We have rounded some of the time delays and indicated the added information that there are 50 independent distributors, 500 independent retailers, and an average system volume of 2,500 units per week in order to make some rough calculations about inventories.

Figure 1–6

A. Problems of schedules for large-scale one-time projects:

   1. Planning a network of operations to accomplish the desired end result.
   2. Developing schedules of the network of operations such that the critical path schedule of the network meets promised delivery dates.
   3. Allocate the use of limited resources of equipment and/or labor in ways that will not interfere with the critical path schedule through the network.
   4. Procure materials by a schedule that minimizes total inventory costs but meets the needs of the critical path schedule.
   5. Bidding policy and procedure to obtain contracts at margins that will achieve a balance between the use and maintenance of the stockpile of critical resources (engineers, scientists, skilled labor, key facilities, and so on) and the desire for profit.

B. Project graph of activities or operations for a house-building project

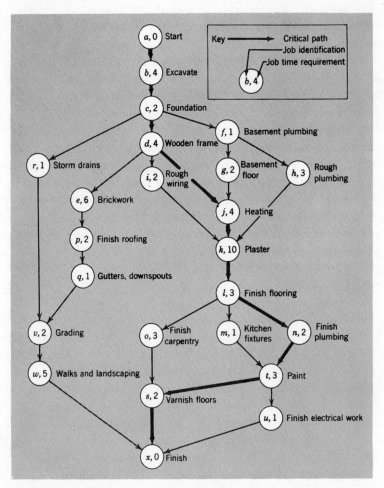

Source: F. K. Levy, G. L. Thompson, and J. D. Wiest, "The ABC's of the Critical Path Method," *Harvard Business Review*, September–October 1963.

Figure 1–7
Production-inventory system adapted from Figure 1–4 (system volume averages 2,500 units per week)

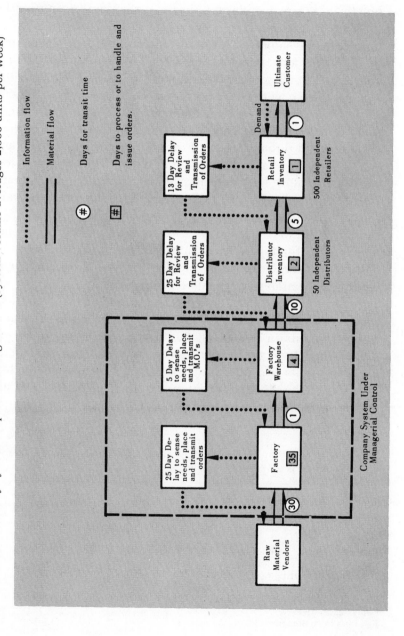

As we examine Figure 1–7, we see that inventories exist continuously throughout the system, not just in the places where we have used the label "inventories." For example, they exist in the *transit pipelines*, as raw material supplies, and as in-process inventories in the factory. At each of the major stages of the Figure 1–7 system we have some inventory by virtue of the fact that it is economical to order in lots, rather than to attempt hand-to-mouth supply, and to be able to give quick service. We call these lot size or *cycle* inventories. Another component of inventories exists because of the random effects of demand, and we call these *buffer stocks*. If demand is seasonal it may be more economical to absorb at least some of the seasonal demand through *seasonal inventories* rather than by attempting to vary production levels to follow the demand curve closely. Finally, inventories serve the function of *decoupling* throughout the entire system; that is, they make it possible to carry on the various activities relatively independently. Let us examine Figure 1–7 more carefully with the objective of assessing the inventory requirements which result from these five kinds of inventory functions.

Pipeline inventories. The supply pipelines of the entire system require in themselves a considerable investment in inventory. If the system volume is 2,500 units per week and it takes one day to transport from the factory to the factory warehouse, then there are 2,500(1/7) units in motion on the average. If the minimum order processing delay at the factory warehouse is four days, then there are 2,500(4/7) units tied up there as a part of the pipeline. Table 1–1 summarizes the pipeline inventory requirements for finished goods for the entire system. Management cannot reduce these inventories

Table 1–1
Summary of pipeline inventory requirements for finished goods (average system volume is 2,500 units per week)

	Average transit or delay time, days	Average pipeline inventory, units (days/7) ×2,500
Factory to factory warehouse	1	357
Delays at factory warehouse	4	1,429
Warehouse to distributors	10	3,571
Delays at distributors	2	714
Distributors to retailers	5	1,786
Delays at retailers	1	357
Retailers to customers	1	357
Total	24	8,571

unless it can reduce the transit times, delays, or handling times; they are a necessary part of the system. Table 1–1 shows that 8,571 units of the total system inventory of finished goods exist solely to fill the pipelines.

Cycle inventories.   If we are going to transport the units from one point to another, then how many do we transport at one time? If the retailer is ordering from the distributor, how many should be ordered at one time? The costs of reviewing the retailer's needs and preparing the order will be the same regardless of the order size. It may also be true that the transport costs are nearly the same for a range of order sizes. The average order size is set by the ordering frequency at each stage. For example, the average retailer orders once each three weeks following a review of sales and projected needs. Once the order is received, there is a two-day order processing delay at the distributor, plus five days for transit and receipt. Thus, when a retailer orders, it must be for a three-week supply just to meet average demand. The average retailer sells 2,500/500 = 5 units per week or 15 during the three-week order period. Therefore, the retailer must have no less than 15 units on hand to sustain sales during the supply cycle, and the average inventory for this purpose is then 7.5 units per retailer or 7.5 × 500 = 3,750 units for the system of retailers.

Table 1–2 summarizes the cycle stock requirements of the system, showing that 16,250 units are required in average inventory just

Table 1–2
Summary of cycle inventory requirements for finished goods
(average system volume is 2,500 units per week)

	Reorder cycle time, weeks	Average cycle inventory, units
500 retailers	3	3,750
50 distributors	4	5,000
Factory warehouse	6	7,500
Total		16,250

because of the reordering cycles. We could reduce this component of inventory by reordering more often, but there are some other costs to consider which would be affected adversely. Determining economical replenishment policies in general is one of the important topics in the study of inventories.

Buffer inventories. Of course, the three stages of the system could not depend on the average demand as a basis for setting inventory levels, because demand may vary widely and be reflected back through the system as variable demand at each point. The result is that an additional inventory over and above the cycle stock must be maintained to provide for the possibility of higher than average demand which may occur from random causes. These buffer inventories which are designed to absorb random variations in demand are determined by estimating the reasonable maximum demand expected. Of course, the reasonable maximum needs to be defined in terms of probability levels; for example, maximum demand might be a demand level which occurs only 5 or 10 percent of the time. Given a definition of this kind let us suppose that maximum demand at the factory warehouse is 19,000 units over the 41-day review plus supply lead time. Average demand during the same period is 14,643 units, and the difference, 4,357 units, is the buffer stock required to ensure an ability to supply the needs of the system. Figure 1–8 shows, the same concept in diagrammatic form for the factory warehouse. In Table 1–3 we see the summary of buffer stock requirements for the

Figure 1–8
Average versus maximum demand at factory warehouse
during supply lead time of 41 days (5.86 weeks—
difference of 4,357 units is required for buffer stock)

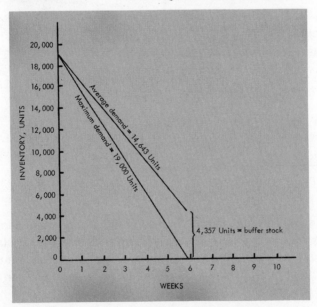

Table 1–3
Summary of buffer inventory requirements for finished goods

	Average demand per week	Lead time, days	Average demand during lead time	Maximum demand during lead time	Average system buffer stock
500 retailers	5	20	14	25	5,500
50 distributors	50	39	279	350	3,550
Factory warehouse	2,500	41	14,643	19,000	4,357
Total					13,407

system. A total of 13,407 units of inventory is required throughout the system just to provide for possible random fluctuations in demand.

Seasonal inventories. We have been assuming that average demand was constant throughout the year in our assessment of requirements for pipeline, cycle, and buffer inventories, but this may not be true. If demand actually follows a seasonal pattern, we can choose to produce according to the expected demand (with suitable lead time) or the opposite extreme; that is, to produce at the average demand level. In the latter case seasonal inventories would accumulate during the slack sales periods and be used to meet the peak sales requirements. Also, of course, one could choose one of the many alternatives which involve some fluctuation in production level and some seasonal inventories. The rational choice, based only on comparative objective costs, would be to achieve a balance between the cost of changing production levels and the costs of holding the seasonal inventory.

For our situation suppose that the seasonal demand curve and production schedule are as shown in Figure 1–9. Inventory begins to accumulate in November and continues through March, at which point demand equals the number of units available from production. The 2,200 units accumulated begin to be used in June for the seasonal demand which will reach its peak in July.

Decoupling function. The existence of inventories at the major stock points throughout the system makes it possible to carry on each of the major activities relatively independently. Of course, there are interactions as we have constantly noted; however, they are not as severe as they would otherwise be if we attempted to operate each of the stages on the basis of a hand-to-mouth supply. If we were

Figure 1–9
Seasonal sales requirements met by a level production plan

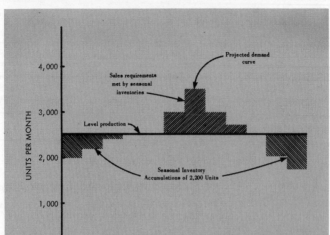

attempting hand-to-mouth supply of each of the stages, any kind of interruption to the flow at any point in the system would very quickly affect all stages downstream. With inventories, however, these interruptions in flow can be absorbed for some period of time by the inventory downstream. This is one of the reasons in-process inventories within the factory serve such an important function. In a production line the decoupling function of inventories is at a minimum, and we know that it is entirely possible that the entire production line may be shut down if we run out of a critical screw.

In our example, we can see that the process of manufacture starts 35 days before a finished product is completed. Thus, to calculate the number of units that we have started in-process (that is, the work-in-process inventory), we have but to multiply the number of days of production (35) by the number of units started in production each day (500). Thus, our decoupling work in process inventory is 17,500 units. We should note that this number is to be treated carefully, since these 17,500 units are in all stages of completion. Thus, the dollar value of a unit of in-process inventory will be somewhat lower than that of a completed unit.

These five basic functions of inventories are fundamental to achieving smooth flow, reasonable equipment utilization, reasonable

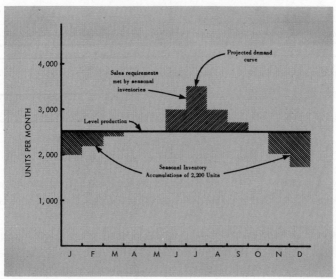

material handling costs, and the maintenance of good customer service. At each stage of both manufacturing and distribution, inventories serve the vital decoupling function between each pair of activities. Thus, when raw materials are ordered, a supply is ordered that is large enough to justify the out-of-pocket cost of putting through the order and transporting the materials. When production orders to manufacture parts and products are released, we try to make them large enough to justify the cost of order writing and setting up machines. Otherwise, these setup and preparation costs might easily become prohibitive. Running parts through the system in lots also tends to reduce material handling costs because parts can be handled in groups. Similarly, in distributing finished products to warehouses and other stock points, freight and handling costs per unit go down if we can ship in quantity. These advantages are partially lost when we are dealing with the job shop and the large-scale one-time project because the order size is dictated by the customer's order. Thus, order writing, material handling, and machine setup costs are just as high for the custom-sized lot as for an economical lot size. Similarly, when the custom order is shipped to the customer, we cannot take advantage of carload or truckload freight rates. If the order is for only one item, then all of these charges must be absorbed by the single unit. It is obvious why low-volume special orders are extremely costly.

For all five of the functions of inventories we were able to make rough computations indicating the component of inventory devoted to each function. Summarizing all of these we have:

	Units
Pipeline inventories	8,571
Cycle inventories	16,250
Buffer inventories	13,407
Seasonal inventories	2,200
Work-in-process inventories	17,500
Total	57,928

These are inventories that are required by the structure of the system. They perform functions vital to its economical operation. Yet, inventories themselves are very costly. Therefore, management will always attempt to design systems and policies which perform the vital functions but do so with minimum inventories.

Dependent versus independent demand

As a final note on the functions of inventory, we will find it useful in the chapters ahead to distinguish between the forces which generate the demands for an item. In general, these are two important types of demands that can be placed on an item—*dependent demands,* and *independent demands.* The distinction between these types of demand is critical in choosing the type of system to be used in controlling an item, whether the item is part of a continuous, intermittent, to stock or to order production system.

An item is said to have dependent demands if the source of the demand for that item is derived from another item that is under the control of the firm. For example, if the company produces a product that is made up of a number of materials and components, we call the demand placed on those materials and components *derived,* or *dependent,* demands, since the demand for them is clearly dependent upon the demand for the end item.

Figure 1–10 illustrates this type of relationship with a *product structure* or *gozinto* chart, showing some of the major parts and components that "go into" the creation of a finished automobile. This illustration graphically demonstrates that the demand for engine blocks, for example, is dependent upon the demand for engine subassemblies, and ultimately, upon the demand for the automobile

Figure 1–10
Partial product structure chart for an automobile (an example of dependent demand items)

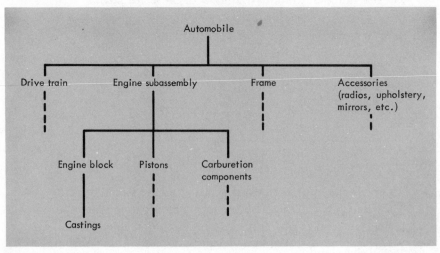

itself. The implications of this dependent relationship are quite important in two respects. First, it is obvious that a forecast of the number of engine blocks can be prepared directly from a forecast of the number of automobiles that are to be produced. Dependent demand item forecasting is thus rather straightforward and simple. Second, the product structure that relates dependent demand items to end products can be exploited by creating inventory control and production scheduling systems that link a manufacturing process together in a manner analogous to the physical linkages that a product structure diagram implies. Such systems are typified by the material requirements planning systems that will be discussed in Chapter 7. These systems enable changes in priorities and schedules for all parts and components at each level in a product structure to be made in a manner that is consistent with new information about supplies of raw materials or demands for end items.

By way of contrast, *independent demand items* are those whose demand originates from a source outside of a company's control. The end item, the automobile in Figure 1–10, is one example of an independent demand item. While an automobile company may be able to exert some control over the market it serves, there is still a great deal of uncertainty about the timing and quantity of demands for autos. Thus, forecasting and control systems for independent demand items must be geared to handle forecasts and inventory control decisions in ways that differ from those used for dependent demand items. In Chapter 4 we shall discuss the nature of systems which are appropriate to the latter task.

THE ELEMENTS OF PLANNING AND CONTROL

Continuing with our analogy of physical facilities to the human skeleton and the flow of goods and materials to the circulatory system, it is obvious that our "body" needs a central nervous system to direct their use. As we have noted several times previously, it is important that this "brain" or planning and control system be matched to the particular needs of the productive system that is to be managed. However, there are some basic "elements" of planning and control systems that are common to most, if not all, production-inventory systems regardless of the process technology or market positioning strategies that are employed. It is important to identify and understand these common functions before progressing to a discussion of the distinctive ways in which planning and control systems are adapted to particular situations.

The purpose of production planning and control systems is to set and monitor the course that a manufacturing unit takes as it moves through time. Were all of the factors that impinge upon manufacturing constant through time, this would not be a difficult task. However, internal factors such as product designs, processes, materials, and even goals, are constantly shifting. Moreover, economic forces constantly change the external environment in which the firm procures inputs and markets its outputs. Figure 1–11 contrasts some of

Figure 1–11
A changing manufacturing environment

	1973–74 *upswing mode*	1974–75 *downswing mode*
Shipments and orders	Increasing	Decreasing
Capacity utilization	High	Low
Production bottlenecks	Many	Few
Manufacturing intervals	Increasing	Decreasing
Procurement lead times for raw materials, components, parts	Increasing	Decreasing
Procurement lead times for machinery and equipment	Increasing	Decreasing
Vendor reliability (ability to meet delivery dates)	Low	High
Production reliability	Low	High
Prices of industrial goods	Rising	Stabilizing (in constant terms)
Interest costs	High	Moderating
New product/model introductions	Many	Few
Availability of skilled labor	Short	Long

the important characteristics of the general manufacturing environment between 1973–74, a period of rapid economic expansion that was disrupted by the Arab Oil Embargo, and 1974–75, a period in which the economy slipped into the deepest recession since the Great Depression of the 1930s. While this comparison is based on a rather dramatic series of events, it emphasizes the degree to which the environment can change, and does change, with time. The impact of these and a multitude of less dramatic changes is that the planning and control system must aim manufacturing at a moving, and quite elusive target. In order to hit the mark more times than it is missed, the planning and control system must provide a firm with the capability of answering the following questions and making the following decisions (among others):

What will demand for the products the firm produces be in the future?

What are current finished goods inventory levels? How much of each product should be produced now? In future periods?

How many people should be hired? Laid off? How many shifts? How much overtime should be worked?

Should assembly lines be rebalanced?

When should we promise to deliver a product to a customer?

What purchased materials and components should we buy? In what quantities? When do we want them delivered? Which jobs in production should be worked on next? On what machines?

Are there any orders for materials or products that should be rushed? Delayed?

What is the current status? Are we implementing our plans as we should be?

This list of questions is hardly exhaustive. Nonetheless, it illustrates several important features of the planning and control function. First, these questions identify some of the major decisions involved in planning and control, and some reflection will reveal that these decisions are major ones indeed. They involve the procurement and use of labor and materials, which comprise the largest variable cost elements of many companies, and inventories and facilities, which often constitute a significant portion of a firm's assets. Second, these questions show that planning and control involves much more than just decision making. In fact, there are at least three important elements of planning and control: *data collection; decision making and planning;* and *implementation, feedback, and control.*

Data collection. Typical of the data that must be collected or generated to properly plan production and control inventories are forecasts of future demands and reports of current inventory status. Such data must be made available to decision makers in order for them to make decisions. Other types of basic data include: *routings,* which show the sequence of manufacturing steps involved in producing a product; *bills of material* which list all of the materials, parts, and components involved in putting products together; *cost data* referring to the labor, materials, inventory, and other costs important in making decisions; *procurement lead times*, that is, the time that elapses between placing an order for material with a supplier or production unit and receiving it; and many more. Obtaining accurate and recent data of the types mentioned above is one of the most important, and often the most difficult and frustrating part, of planning and control. Because of the enormity of the data collection and generation task in many firms, it is frequently computerized.

Decision making and planning. Decision making and planning activities are exemplified by the questions referring to the size of the work force, the sizing and timing of production and materials orders, and machine schedules. Depending upon the characteristics of the operating unit in question, there are a number of different types of planning and control decisions that must be made. In this book, we shall concentrate on the few fundamental types of decisions which are common to a wide variety of situations. These include:

1. *Aggregate planning.* Aggregate plans, sometimes called production budgets, are plans that indicate budgeted levels of finished goods inventories, production backlogs, and work force changes. They are called aggregate plans because aggregated data, rather than specific product data, is usually used to formulate them.

2. *Master scheduling.* At some point in time, an operating unit must decide exactly what it is going to produce in terms of specific end products, and must assign specific dates for the completion of these products. The document containing the results of such decisions is called a master schedule. The master schedule is much more detailed than an aggregate plan, but must reflect the capacity decisions made in it.

3. *Inventory and order promise decisions.* The master schedule must also reflect specific stocking decisions that are made for certain end products. In situations where finished goods are not maintained, but orders are taken for the delivery of products to customers before production begins, decisions about specific delivery date promises are important.

4. *Requirements planning.* Most products are made by combining or assembling a number of raw materials or components that are either produced by the same company or purchased from suppliers. Requirements planning decisions involve deciding when and how much of these materials to order.

5. *Scheduling decisions.* These decisions include the assignment of jobs to machines or assembly lines in a particular sequence, and the assignment of individuals to particular jobs or pieces of equipment. These are among the most detailed types of planning and control decisions.

Implementation, feedback, and control. The final, and in many respects, most crucial kind of planning and control activity is that of implementation, feedback, and control. This includes determining whether or not plans and decisions are being implemented properly, or need changing, and taking corrective action to remedy any problems which occur. Typical of the corrective actions which might take place are reordering the *priorities* which are used as a basis for scheduling work to people or equipment, *expediting* jobs or activities which have fallen behind schedule, and delaying, or *de-expediting* the work that is being done ahead of schedule or that is no longer urgently needed. Moreover, since this set of activities is concerned with implementing plans and decisions, it involves all of the administrative problems associated with communicating with others and motivating them to accomplish the goals established in the decision-making process. In a sense, these activities are the "bottom line" of production planning and inventory control, since they involve the accomplishment of what most productive enterprises set out to do in the first place—get the product out the door and into the customer's hands.

Figure 1–12 illustrates the way in which all of these elements of planning and control relate to one another. When a firm or operating unit has a set of predetermined methods and procedures for accomplishing and interrelating all of these elements of planning and control, we have a *production planning and inventory control system*.

SUMMARY

In this introductory chapter we have discussed three basic classification schemes. The first places production-inventory systems into four main categories, each of which have somewhat unique problems, or require special techniques to accomplish the elements of planning and control. The second classification scheme identifies the basic functions that inventories serve in a variety of production-inventory systems. The third categorizes the basic elements of plan-

Figure 1–12
The elements of planning and control

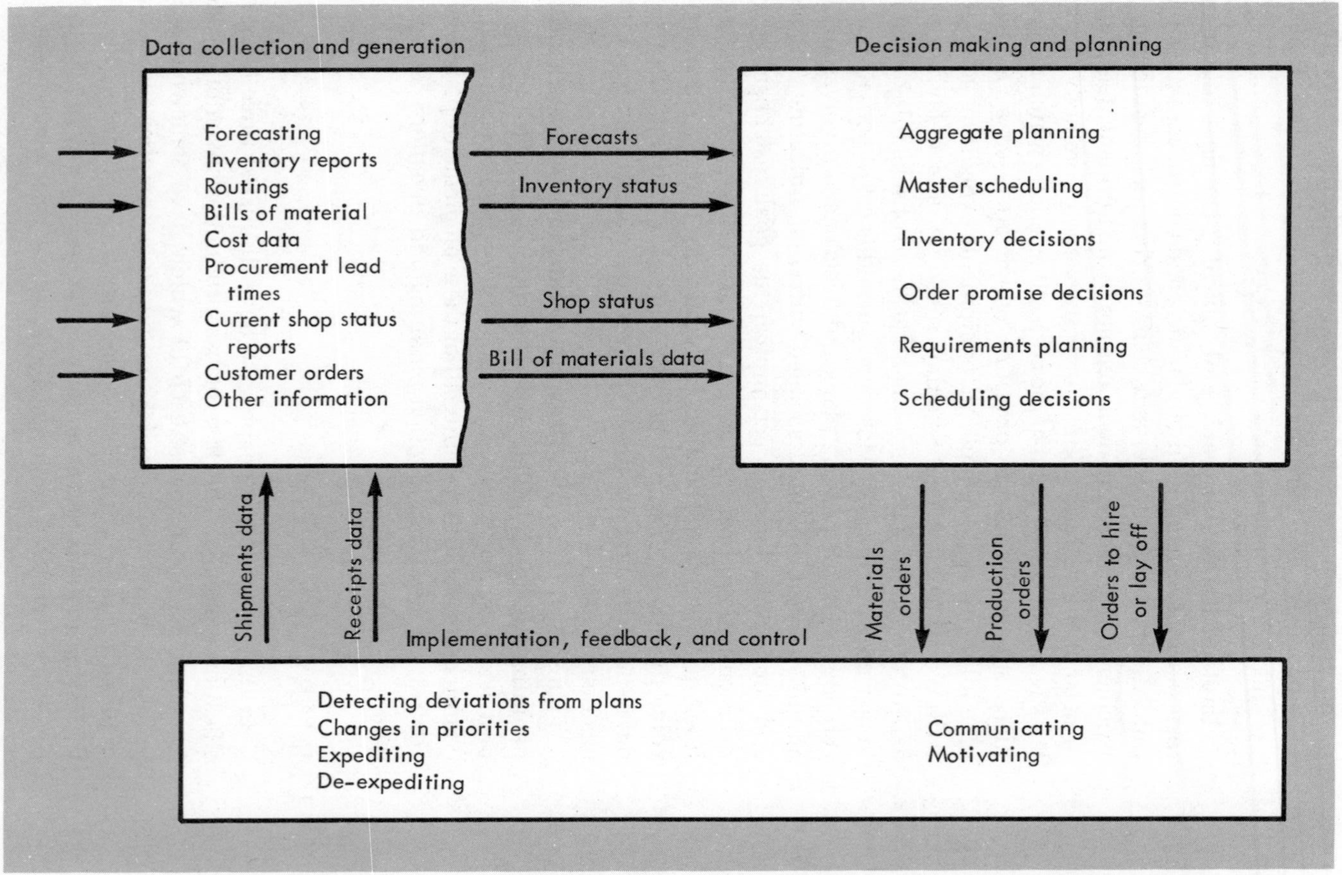

Data collection and generation

Forecasting
Inventory reports
Routings
Bills of material
Cost data
Procurement lead times
Current shop status reports
Customer orders
Other information

Decision making and planning

Aggregate planning
Master scheduling
Inventory decisions
Order promise decisions
Requirements planning
Scheduling decisions

Forecasts
Inventory status
Shop status
Bill of materials data

Materials orders
Production orders
Orders to hire or lay off

Shipments data
Receipts data

Implementation, feedback, and control

Detecting deviations from plans
Changes in priorities
Expediting
De-expediting

Communicating
Motivating

ning and control which are common to most production-inventory systems.

The basic structure of this book is based on the first and last classification schemes. The next major section of the book (Part II) expands upon each of the elements of planning and control that are common to most production-inventory systems. This segment of the book, called "Elements of Planning and Control" is comprised of chapters on "Forecasting for Inventory and Production Control," "Basic Inventory Decisions," "Independent Demand Inventory Systems," "Aggregate Planning and Master Scheduling Decisions and Techniques," and "Requirements Planning: Dependent Demand Systems." The second portion of the book elaborates on the distinctive features of the major categories of production-inventory systems. Part III, "Planning and Scheduling for Continuous Systems" contains chapters which identify the special management problems and techniques associated with aggregate planning, master scheduling, requirements planning, capacity planning, and line balancing in continuous process industries that produce either to stock, or to customer order. In addition to a more comprehensive discussion of the problems and techniques associated with continuous production inventory systems, numerous descriptions of actual systems in use in industry are included. Part IV elaborates on the special problems of intermittent systems. It includes chapters that discuss shop floor control systems, planning and control systems for large-scale projects, and illustrates both infinite and finite capacity loading approaches that may be appropriate to those circumstances. It also uses descriptions of actual systems to demonstrate the ways firms have built them to meet the special challenges that they face.

REVIEW QUESTIONS AND PROBLEMS

1. Select some organization, for example, a company known to you, and classify it according to the four classes of production-inventory systems discussed in the text. It would be preferable if one were to select a system which might not be the pure form of any of the five discussed in the text.

   Develop a flow diagram similar to Figure 1–3 identifying the major raw material, in-process, and finished goods stock points. Describe the inventory replenishment rules used at each point and estimate the time delays for inventory replenishment at each stage. What portion of the overall system is under managerial control? Indicate what is under control by drawing a boundary around the system. What would be the effect on system inventory if management could extend control up-and downstream in terms of ordering and replenishment of inventories?

2. A jobbing printer takes orders for a wide variety of custom jobs such as letterheads, calling cards, leaflets, posters, and so on. He does not have the capability for book printing or other more complex large-volume jobs. He has samples of a wide variety of paper stock, but maintains an inventory of only five types for which he has a substantial demand. All other paper stock he can obtain from a local supplier within one week by normal ordering procedures or within two days if he is willing to make a special pickup. Defining his inventory and usage in terms of pounds of paper, his average usage in pounds per week is:

Paper type	Usage, pounds per week
1	50
2	25
3	75
4	20
5	40
All other	100

Orders for replenishment of the stock papers are placed once each two weeks for the amount actually used and for the nonstock papers orders are placed as needed. All orders are delivered in one week. The ordinary processing of a customer order once placed is as follows:

A. Orders requiring special order paper stock.
   1. Place special order for paper stock and receive; five working days.
   2. Set type required and run proof; one working day.
   3. Hold for customer approval of proof; four working days.
   4. Run job and package for delivery; two working days.
   5. Delay for delivery and receipt of payment, assuming that all jobs are C.O.D.; three working days.

B. Orders requiring stock papers. All time requirements remain the same except for (1) which is zero days since we can assume that the paper stock is immediately available.
   a. What is the average pipeline inventory in pounds? What are the components of pipeline inventory?
   b. Given the replenishment rule stated, what is the size of the cycle inventory for stock items?
   c. Are there any decision variables under managerial control which would allow the owner to reduce inventories?

3. Consider a supply-production-distribution system for a high-volume standardized product, perhaps a small appliance, which has the physical flow, transit, and handling time as indicated in Figure 1–13. The total system volume is 2,000 units per day. Compute the equivalent pipeline inventory required for the system.

Figure 1–13
Supply-production-distribution system for a small appliance showing physical flow, assumed handling and transit times, and major stock points (five company-owner and five independent distributors, 1,000 retailers)

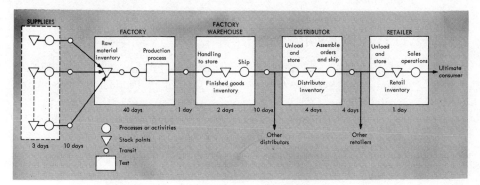

4. Referring to the system shown in Figure 1–13, and discussed in problem 3, list the key elements of a production planning and inventory control system that could be employed to manage it. Identify the kinds of data that would need to be collected, the types of decisions and plans necessary to operate it, and the feedback and control mechanisms that would be needed to replan and implement production.

5. For each of the four major categories of production-inventory systems, identify the major differences between the tasks of data collection, decision making and planning, and implementation feedback and control that are associated with each.

6. A company is faced with the choice of either producing a product to stock in anticipation of demand, or to customer order. The demand for the product is 200 units per week, and management has decided that the product should be produced in lots, or batches. The cost of holding the average unit in inventory per year is $5 times the average inventory level. If the firm produces to order, it must discount its unit price on all sales by $0.25 for each week that the first customer to order has to wait before the product is delivered. Should the firm produce to stock or to order?

7. A firm produces a product which costs $10 at the rate of 14,000 per week. From the time that production is initiated on a unit, it takes three

weeks to complete. The raw material cost per unit is $4. All raw materials are put into process at the time each unit is started. Assuming that labor and overhead value added is added in equal parts over the three-week processing time for each unit, determine the average value of work-in-process inventories for the firm.

8. If sales are seasonal, what are the alternatives available to management as a means of absorbing these seasonal variations in demand? What is the nature of the criterion function which might be appropriate to measure the alternatives for scheduling production in the face of seasonal demand?

SELECTED BIBLIOGRAPHY

1. Alcalay, J. A., and Buffa, E. S. "A Proposal for a General Model of a Production System," *International Journal of Production Research*, March 1963.

2. Buffa, E. S. *Operations Management: Problems and Models*. Chaps. 1 & 2. 3d. ed. New York: John Wiley & Sons, Inc., 1972.

3. Buffa, E. S. *Modern Production Management*. 5th ed. New York: John Wiley & Sons, 1977.

4. Buffa, E. S. *Operations Management: The Management of Productive Systems*. Chaps. 1 & 2. New York: John Wiley & Sons, Inc., 1976.

5. Chase, R. B., and Aquilano, N. J. *Production and Operations Management: A Life Cycle Approach*. Rev. ed. Homewood, Ill.: Richard D. Irwin, Inc., 1977.

6. Eilon, S. *Elements of Production Planning and Control*. New York: The Macmillan Co., 1962.

7. Greene, J. H. *Production Control Systems and Decisions*. Rev. ed. Homewood, Ill.: Richard D. Irwin, Inc., 1974.

8. Holstein, W. K. "Production Planning and Control Integrated," *Harvard Business Review*, May/June 1968.

9. Johnson, L. A., and Montgomery, D. C. *Operations Research in Production Planning, Scheduling, and Inventory Control*. New York: John Wiley & Sons, 1974.

10. Marshal, P. W.; Abernathy, W. J.; Miller, J. G.; Olsen, R. P.; Rosenbloom, R. S.; and Wyckoff, D. *Operations Management: Text and Cases*. Homewood, Ill.: Richard D. Irwin, Inc., 1975.

11. Mize, J. H.; White, C. R.; and Brooks, G. H. *Operations Planning and Control*. Englewood Cliffs, N.J.: Prentice-Hall, Inc., 1971.

12. Orlicky, J. *Material Requirements Planning*. New York: McGraw-Hill Book Co., 1975.

13. Plossl, G., and Wight, O. *Production and Inventory Control: Principles and Techniques.* Englewood Cliffs, N.J.: Prentice-Hall, Inc., 1967.

14. Reisman, A., and Buffa, E. S. "A General Model for Production and Operations Systems," *Management Science*, vol. 2, no. 1 (September 1974).

15. Vollmann, T. E. *Operations Management: A Systems Model Building Approach.* Addison-Wesley Publishing Co., Inc., Reading, Mass.: 1973.

CASE STUDY
PERKIN ELMER INSTRUMENT
DIVISION (Abridged)*

IN OCTOBER 1974, Gaynor Kelley, vice president and manager of
Perkin Elmer Instrument Division, perceived disgruntling differences among three plans central to his division's operations.

The first plan was the division's financial plan. This plan, dated
July 1974, was the result of the division's annual planning activities.
It was based on an anticipated division sales level or "build plan," of
$93.4 million. The second plan had just reached Kelley. It was an
updated forecast of orders received made by the product managers in
early October 1974. It forecast 1974–75 fiscal year orders for instruments and spare parts at $103.1 million. The third plan, also recently
received by Kelley, was a manufacturing plan, which forecast the sales
value of the product which was to be manufactured during the
1974–75 year, and effectively, the total sales of the division. This
updated "build plan" indicated that manufacturing planned to build
$111.8 million worth of product for sale in the year. Inventories and
purchase commitments had already increased since July, because
short-term manufacturing schedules had been increased to the new
higher levels as forecast adjustments were made by product managers and manufacturing personnel in August and September.

Kelley was more troubled by the high volumes indicated by the
latter two plans than by the discrepancies between them. Division

---

* To protect the confidentiality of company data, certain figures in this case have
been disguised.

sales had almost doubled in the previous three years, but signs that the economy was weakening had long been expected and were already appearing in other major industries. Moreover, the corporate financial staff had indicated that they had not planned to provide funds to meet the unexpected surge in business predicted by the marketing and build plans, and that they would have difficulty in obtaining them economically on such short notice.

Company background

Perkin Elmer was an international developer and producer of high technology scientific instrumentation. The company was founded in 1938 to design and produce ultraprecise optical equipment. Growth in this area was rapid as these optical instruments found wide applications in defense and space programs. In the 1970s under the leadership of Chairman Chester W. Nimitz, Jr., and President Robert H. Sorensen, the company began to emphasize the development of other types of laboratory analytical instrumentation, which were marketed to researchers in college and hospital clinical laboratories, and to research and process control groups in a variety of industries. The rapid growth of the Instrument Group, which was responsible for manufacturing and selling these nonoptical instruments resulted in a decrease in the percentage of the company's business that went to U.S. government agencies. This percentage fell to only 27 percent of total sales in 1974. By this time, the Instrument Group's sales accounted for more than one half of the sales of the total company.

The company emphasized research and development to maintain its position as a company on the leading edge of rapidly expanding optical and electrical technologies. In 1974, the company spent $16.7 million on research and development, not counting a much larger amount spent on government contract research (see Exhibit 1 for financial data). Almost 15 percent of the company's 8,600 employees were guaduate scientists and engineers.

The Instrument Group, under the guidance of Senior Vice President Horace McDonell, had sales of $150 million in 1974, a 17 percent increase over 1973 sales levels. This group also emphasized research and development as an integral part of their competitive strategy. Historically, research and development expenses had averaged 8–9 percent of instrument sales. Over 70 percent of the orders taken by the group in 1974 were for products that had not existed in 1969.

Case study

Exhibit 1

PERKIN ELMER INSTRUMENT DIVISION
Ten-year financial summary
($ in 000 except $ per share)

	1974	1973	1972
Financial Operations—Years Ended July 31			
Net sales	$272,042	$233,323	$216,813
Cost of sales	161,524	141,286	136,864
Research and development	16,727	13,120	10,772
Marketing	43,191	35,178	30,240
General and administrative	21,681	17,455	16,365
Interest expense	1,385	919	1,575
Other income—net	(3,082)	(1,867)	(1,912)
Income before provision for income taxes	30,616	27,232	22,909
as a percent of sales	11.3%	11.7%	10.6%
Net income	$ 17,159	$ 15,698	$ 13,133
as a percent of sales	6.3%	6.7%	6.1%
Net income per share	$ 0.98	$ 0.90	$ 0.77
Dividends per share	0.225	0.214	0.206
Return on shareholders' equity at year-end	11.9%	12.4%	11.9%
Financial Condition—At July 31			
Working capital	$109,085	$ 91,233	$ 86,179
Fixed assets at cost	71,206	65,577	58,503
Long-term debt	4,295	5,704	7,072
Shareholders' equity	144,390	126,493	110,814
General			
Average number of common shares outstanding including common stock equivalents (in 000s)	17,667	17,514	17,305
Employees	8,627	7,933	7,334
Shareholders	10,668	10,559	10,087

Consolidated balance sheet
As of July 31

Assets

	1974	1973
Current Assets:		
Cash, including time deposits	$ 7,554,375	$ 9,727,595
Marketable securities, at cost (approximate market)	17,535,029	16,608,661
Accounts receivable, less allowance for doubtful accounts of $608,630 ($583,809 in 1973)	62,787,044	55,732,439
Inventories, at lower of cost or market	75,287,832	54,857,102
Prepaid expenses and other current assets	6,612,049	4,426,662
	$169,776,329	$141,352,459
Marketable securities maturing beyond one year, at cost (approximate market)	$ 5,753,005	$ 6,598,684
Property, Plant and Equipment, at cost:		
Land	$ 4,285,966	$ 4,499,384
Buildings	36,207,139	34,540,674
Machinery and equipment	30,712,593	26,536,833
	$ 71,205,698	$ 65,576,891
Accumulated depreciation and amortization	(34,625,244)	(31,290,702)
	$ 36,580,454	$ 34,286,189
Other Assets:		
Excess of purchase price over net assets of companies acquired	$ 4,207,142	$ 4,194,168
Other investments, patents, deferred charges, etc.	3,534,311	3,873,891
	$ 7,741,453	$ 8,068,059
	$219,851,241	$190,305,391

Source: 1974 Annual Report.

1971	1970	1969	1968	1967	1966	1965
$202,550	$232,948	$227,102	$171,962	$128,542	$103,511	$78,383
129,818	159,049	157,814	114,428	80,199	62,466	46,380
10,076	10,814	10,394	8,869	8,135	6,357	4,747
28,053	27,052	23,751	20,409	18,025	14,878	11,699
14,892	16,197	15,244	13,009	10,546	8,992	7,018
1,443	1,563	1,628	1,564	1,146	732	764
(1,729)	(1,843)	(570)	(541)	(440)	(576)	(613)
19,997	20,116	18,841	14,224	10,931	10,662	8,388
9.9%	8.6%	8.3%	8.3%	8.5%	10.3%	10.7%
$ 10,122	$ 9,647	$ 9,297	$ 6,601	$ 5,193	$ 5,486	$ 4,201
5.0%	4.1%	4.1%	3.8%	4.0%	5.3%	5.4%
$ 0.60	$ 0.58	$ 0.57	$ 0.42	$ 0.34	$ 0.38	$ 0.33
0.15	—	—	—	—	—	—
10.6%	11.1%	12.3%	10.7%	9.9%	12.4%	11.1%
$ 79,548	$ 71,540	$ 60,002	$ 47,368	$ 37,778	$ 29,860	$27,051
57,249	55,284	52,169	47,929	39,181	31,186	24,256
16,015	18,213	19,055	19,718	13,681	8,274	8,605
95,750	86,996	75,858	61,876	52,331	44,318	37,725
16,740	16,621	16,445	15,890	15,081	14,441	12,889
7,509	7,827	8,204	7,623	6,978	5,769	4,417
10,176	10,925	9,562	9,510	8,118	6,427	5,588

Liabilities

	1974	1973
Current Liabilities:		
Loans payable, United States	$ 7,500,000	$ 3,385,994
Loans payable, foreign	7,220,911	3,828,395
Accounts payable, including advances from customers	17,671,796	16,023,352
Accrued salaries and wages	11,347,676	10,041,667
Accrued taxes on income	7,086,132	7,745,084
Other accrued expenses	9,865,276	9,095,211
	$ 60,691,791	$ 50,119,703
Long-Term Debt:		
United States	—	—
Foreign	$ 4,294,631	$ 5,704,420
Other Long-Term Liabilities	8,957,309	6,677,774
Minority Interest	1,517,760	1,310,986
Shareholders' Equity:		
Capital stock		
Preferred stock, $1 par value:		
Shares authorized 1,000,000	—	—
Common stock, $1 par value:		
Shares authorized 20,000,000		
Shares issued 17,435,881 (17,264,034—1973)	17,435,881	17,264,034
Capital contributed in excess of par value	28,386,472	24,284,280
Retained income	98,567,397	84,944,194
	$144,389,750	$126,492,508
	$219,851,241	$190,305,391

The Instrument Division

The Instrument Division, headed by Gaynor Kelley, was the largest organizational entity in the Instrument Group. Kelley had profit and asset responsibility for the marketing and manufacture of eight product lines. Reporting to him were eight product managers, the director of manufacturing, and the technical director who was responsible for engineering and development. Kelley also worked closely with the vice president of the Instrument Group Marketing Division, which was responsible for field sales and service.

Research and engineering. The Instrument Division product engineering group was responsible for designing new products for the Instrument Division. New product ideas were generally stimulated either in response to competitors' actions, or new technological developments. The engineering group worked closely with the product managers in deciding on new product features, and priorities for new products and redesigns within a product group. A high premium was placed on being first in the market with a new or improved laboratory instrument.

Once a new product idea was committed to by the product manager and engineering group, specific dates for introduction were set as goals for the company. These dates were usually timed to coincide with major trade shows. The engineering group then worked to design a working model of the new product. Depending on the complexity of the product, this took from one month to several years of engineering effort.

When a working model was available, other groups were involved. Manufacturing engineering, for instance, was given a set of plans and specifications so they could determine how the parts and components should be manufactured and assembled, and which should be purchased from outside suppliers. Production planning formulated a preliminary production plan which detailed when parts production should commence, and forecast the likely investment in inventories and labor necessary to support the product.

At the stage where the manufacturing groups came into the design process, a phenomenon Perkin Elmer management called "impedence mismatch" occurred. Impedence mismatch referred to the natural conflict brought about by engineering and the product manager's desires to continually revise and improve the product design, and the desires of manufacturing to "freeze" the design so that manufacturing plans could be made and orders placed. The orientation of engineers and product managers was stimulated by their desire to be competitive in the marketplace. Manufacturing responded to the fact that quick design changes often resulted in write-offs of obsolete parts in stock, order cancellation charges from parts suppliers, and the disruption of a smooth flow of work in manufacturing. Resolution of these conflicting desires was achieved through the efforts of a project team, with members from all the concerned areas.

The duties of the product engineering group did not end with the introduction of a new product. Constant changes and improvements were made throughout the product's life. The experience with one of 1974's new products, an automated analyzer, was typical. This product had about 2,200 unique parts and components. Within the first ten months after it was introduced, 600–800 parts change notices were written by engineering. About 600 more had been initiated by quality control to improve the reliability of the instrument. When asked about the risks of obsolescence involved in this, Ralph Scalo, manager of engineering services replied "If we didn't keep the design process rolling, and new improvements coming out continuously, we just wouldn't be doing our job."

Manufacturing.   Instrument Division manufacturing was the responsibility of Mel Redmond, director of manufacturing. He had assumed this position in the spring of 1974 and was responsible for costs, quality, and inventory levels. His staff included the various plant and production department managers, the materials manager, and the manager of manufacturing engineering. Altogether, there were about 800 people in the Instrument Division manufacturing organization who were responsible for acquiring and/or manufacturing some 48,000 parts and their subsequent assembly into 200 major types of instruments, and 1,800 accessory items.

Production was essentially a two-stage process. In the first stage, fabrication, materials were transformed into parts and components in one of five departments, including a general machine shop, a sheet metal shop, an optical facility, a printed circuit board shop, and a finishing shop. About 50 percent of the cost of goods sold were accounted for by parts which were purchased from outside vendors. The remainder were produced in-house. The cost of raw materials for in-house production was about 10 percent of the cost of goods sold. Parts were generally manufactured or purchased in lot sizes recommended by production control and purchasing, and inventoried in the factory.

The second major stage in manufacturing was assembly. Here,

each of the 700–3,000 parts which went into an instrument or an accessory were brought together and assembled. While parts were produced to stock, assembly was initiated by a customer order. Virtually no inventories of finished instruments were maintained. Although general product categories were fairly standardized, each product had a number of options that could be specified by a customer, such as whether the instrument would run on AC or DC current. When options were considered, the number of possible end products went from 200 to thousands.

The Perkin Elmer Instrument Division manufacturing work force was generally highly skilled and highly paid. The average wage in 1974 was about $5 per hour. During October of 1974, the workweek was often as long as 55 hours. As a general rule, it was considered economical to hire an additional worker whenever eight workers were working 50 hours or more, because of the fixed costs of hiring, and because of the generous fringe benefit package. Instrument Division management felt that they should be conservative about hiring, however, because of their long-standing record of never laying off workers due to a drop in business.

The division was able to smooth the work load over the relatively fixed size of the work force by subcontracting more during periods of very high demand. Normally, the company subcontracted about 10 percent of its production, but during slack periods, only 5 percent. When the company subcontracted more than 10 percent of their work, they found that the cost of the parts farmed out over this level was up to 50 percent higher than in-house cost. This occurred because the Instrument Division could produce them more efficiently than subcontractors when they had the capacity. On the other hand, when the level of subcontracting fell below 10 percent, the company found that the cost of affected parts tended to be about 20 percent higher, since more of the parts that Perkin Elmer did not have the equipment to make as efficiently as their subcontractors were brought in-house.

Marketing.   Instrument Division products were sold through the field sales and service representatives of the Instrument Group Marketing Division. These people called on and advised potential customers, attended trade shows, and provided spare parts and technical service advice to users of Perkin Elmer equipment.

Marketing strategy, product line selection, and promotional strategy were the responsibility of the eight product managers in the Instrument Division. Each product manager had profit responsibilty for an entire line of instruments and associated accessory items.

The price of an instrument varied from $3,000–$35,000, while the price range for the accessory items used to operate the instrument was from $200–$5,000. Price was not the primary basis for competition, however. Perkin Elmer's product managers claimed that the most important selling points were the features of their products. Perkin Elmer customers tended to be highly sophisticated from a technological standpoint. Thus, new instruments which could perform new tests or measurements with a high or greater degree of accuracy and reliability were preferred by them. Most major competitors tended to compete on the same basis.

A secondary selling point was delivery time and service. In the words of Jack Kerber, product manager for the atomic absorption instrument line, "A customer may take up to a year deciding whether he needs an instrument or in obtaining funds to purchase it, but once they decide and have the money, they want immediate delivery. And a lot of times, if they can't get it, they'll turn to our competitors if they have a comparable instrument."

Because the mechanical or electrical failure of an instrument could delay the completion of a research project, or shut down the production of industrial customers, rapid delivery of service parts was also felt to be important. To respond rapidly to these customer service needs, over 60 domestic field sales and service offices were maintained by the U.S. Sales Division. Service parts were produced to stock.

The Instrument Division, dealt with delivery lead times for finished instruments in two ways. First, they maintained an informal standard delivery lead time of four to six weeks. In other words, they attempted to maintain enough components in parts inventory or in-process, to be able to assemble, inspect, package, and ship an instrument within four to six weeks after it was ordered. During 1974, the average delivery lead time had slipped to about 12 weeks, however. According to Bill Chorske, general manager, U.S. Sales Division, "We just haven't been able to catch up with our orders. The purchase lead times on some of the critical parts and materials we use have gone out to 10–12 months from an average of 3 months. Add to that manufacturing time required to assemble parts into an instrument and you've got an impossible planning horizon. Couple that with an unexpected increase in demand and the result is inevitable."

The second way that the Instrument Division coped with delivery lead times was to keep the field sales force constantly informed of changes in them. This was partially accomplished with a "Monthly

Export Instrument Shipment Schedule" for export items and sales (see Exhibit 2). In the United States, delivery lead times for an item could be supplied to the field sales force almost instantaneously if they called the Marketing Service Department at Perkin Elmer's home office in Norwalk, Connecticut. Marketing Service representatives queried computerized files from the centralized production control system on video display units to determine if enough parts were on hand to assemble the item immediately, or to determine the length of time required to obtain unavailable parts. This information

Exhibit 2
Monthly export instrument shipment schedule

		Shipment		
	Air freight (weeks)		Ocean freight (weeks)	
Products	60 Hz	50 Hz	60 Hz	50 Hz
Major GC Accessories:				
009-0402 ECD Kit NI63	5	—	7	—
009-0565 through 009-0572				
Model 900 and 990				
Tritium and NI63 ECD Kits	3	3	5	5
045-0166/0171 FID Amp.	5	5	7	7
045-0168/0933 HWD-FID	5	7	7	7
045-0170/0929 ECD Amp	5	5	7	7
045-0470/0469 FID-HWD				
ECD	5	5	7	7
045-0934/0169 ECD Kit	5	5	7	7
051-0054/0128 PEP Interface	5	5	7	7
051-0042 Interface Bd	5	5	7	7
045-0667 Dial-a-Flow	4	4	6	6
228-0301 NPD Kit	3	3	5	5
UV:				
Model 156				
Model 356	9	9	11	11
Model 402	13	13	15	15
Model 241	3		5	
Model 241 MC	9		11	
Fluorescence:				
Model 204	8	5	11	7
Model MPF-3	2	2	4	4
Model MPF-3 with CSA	2	2	4	4
Model MPF-4	7	7	9	9
Model MPF-4 with CSA	13	13	15	15
LM:				
602				
MA:				
Model 240	4	4	6	6
Model DSC-1B with Effl.	5	5	7	7
Model DSC-1B without Effl.	5	5	7	7

Exhibit 2   (continued)

	Shipment			
	Air freight (weeks)		Ocean freight (weeks)	
Products	60 Hz	50 Hz	60 Hz	50 Hz
Model DSC-2				
Subambient	4	4	6	6
Ambient	4	4	6	6
Lab Subambient	4	4	6	6
Model TGS-1 System	3	3	5	5
Model TGS-1 Accessory	3	3	5	5
MA:				
Model UU-1 System	3	3	5	5
Model UU-1 Accessory	3	3	5	5
Model TMS-1	3	3	5	5
Model MC-1	5	5	7	7
Major MA Accessories:				
219-0028 Holder	5	5	7	7
219-0048 Crimper	5	5	7	7
219-0061 Sealer	5	5	7	7
219-0164 Furnace	5	5	7	7
319-0007 Cup	5	5	7	7
A/B:				
AM-2	2	2	4	4
AD-2	2	2	4	4
AR-2	3	3	4	5
Digital:				
DCR-2B	4	4	6	6
Encoders	4	6	6	8
DDR-1C	5	5	7	7
DDR-2C	5	5	7	7
MS:				
Model RM-50				
Model R-12B	13	n.a.	15	n.a.
Model R-24A Standard	9	9	11	11
Model R-24A with Lock Accessory	9	9	11	11
Model R-32	13	13	15	15
LC:				
Model 131	3	3	5	5
Model 151 Still	4	4	6	6
Model 251 Still	4	4	6	6
Model 1220				
Model 1240				
Model 1250				
Glass Stills	5	5	7	7
Model KLA-3B/5				
Model 601	12	12	12	12
Model 604	12	12	12	12
Model 55 Detector	7	7	9	9
LC Accessories:				
Columns	3	3	5	5

n.a. = not available.
Source: Company files.

was relayed to the field representative. If a firm order was made, parts were reserved for that order and an assembly order issued.

The planning process

The total planning process at Perkin Elmer Instrument Divison involved the coordination of the plans of the four major functional entities: engineering, marketing, manufacturing, and finance. The degree of coordination in these individual efforts was most apparent in the annual business and financial planning cycle.

The business plan. The annual business plan started off with a detailed instrument-by-instrument forecast of order receipts. This forecast was made from a "bottom up" sales forecast from the field sales and service personnel in the Instrument Marketing Division, and a "top down" forecast by the product managers. Differences between these two forecasts were resolved by further investigation and negotiation between the two groups. The final forecast specified instrument order receipts by month for the two immediately following quarters, and projected orders by quarter for the last half of the fiscal year (Exhibit 3).

In addition to the forecast of orders for instruments, the sales of spare parts for technical service and accessory items were also forecasted. Since these items were generally stocked in inventory for immediate delivery, sales rather than orders were forecasted. A computer program was used to forecast most of these items. All in all, accessories and spare parts sales accounted for about 20 percent of the division's annual sales. Instruments accounted for only a small percentage of the total number of salable items, but made up to 80 percent of sales.

Yet a third source of forecast information was Gaynor Kelley himself. He reserved the right to make "management stock orders." These were essentially hedges on major products with long lead times. For example, one new product which was still partially in the preproduction design stage was expected to be completely ready for manufacture by February 1975. Since the procurement and manufacturing lead times for this item were in excess of a year, and the company wished to be in a position to promise six weeks' delivery when it was introduced, Kelley, after weighing both the market and engineering risks, might wish to forecast sales for this item in April of 1975. This would serve as an authorization to purchase or start manufacturing the long lead time parts that went into the instru-

Exhibit 3
Instrument orders forecasts

Instrument	1971A*	1972A	1973A	Forecast							
				Aug.	Sept.	Oct.	Nov.	Dec.	Jan.	3d quarter	4th quarter
874X	—	—	78	19	33	51	27	29	48	133	129
90475Z	174	235	153	8	8	18	15	8	14	18	20
9903751	177	122	110	2	3	9	—	2	3	11	—
4753ZY	22	14	15	—	—	2	1	—	1	—	1
976427	3	14	18	—	—	7	1	—	2	1	3
274678	—	4	33	4	7	12	2	6	11	29	26

* Actual.
Source: Company files.

ment. Similarly, if a major sale to a single customer (such as the government) of a particular high value, long lead time instrument was expected (over and above regular sales), a management stock order might be placed to ensure that a reasonable delivery lead time could be offered to the prospective customer, or to make sure that the sale could be made within the current fiscal year.

Management stock orders were collected together in a special Z plan. In general, the Z plan served to ensure that the major risks of the division were handled and monitored by the highest level of management. In July of 1974, the sales value of the instruments in the Z plan that were expected to be sold in fiscal year 1975 was $4.3 million. The July product manager's forecast of instrument orders received plus service parts sales was $80 million, but only $72.2 million of this amount was expected to be actually sold in fiscal year 1975. The beginning backlog of orders brought into fiscal year 1975 to be sold in 1975 was worth $16.9 million in sales.

The three forecasts, the product manager/marketing forecast of major instrument orders, the computer generated forecast of accessory and spare parts sales, and the Z plan for management stock orders were given to manufacturing. Mel Redmond and his production planning group then proceeded to project the manufacturing implications of the forecasts in ways that were meaningful both to the manufacturing function and the business as a whole.

First, the forecasts were used to construct a series of master plans. At least a part of the forecast data was forecasted order receipts. To construct the "exploded"[1] master plan, which showed forecasted shipments and hence, sales, the standard delivery lead times were added to the forecasted order receipt dates. For example, instrument number 874X, had sales orders for 51 systems projected for October. The "exploded" master plan broke this monthly forecast down into a weekly forecast for 13 units in each of the four weeks of the month. Then, since the Instrument Division tried to maintain a four-week position on this part, that is, be able to deliver four weeks after an order, the forecast orders for 13 units in each week in October were translated into forecast shipments of 13 units in each week of November.

Parts and accessories which were stocked for immediate shipment were transposed directly into a "sales" master plan without adding

---

[1] All end items (instruments) which were assembled from many parts were put on the "exploded" master plans since it would be used to derive or "explode" the requirements for these parts.

lead times. The Z plan, which already reflected delivery time hedging was the third type of master plan used by the Instrument Division. The master plans were then used as the basis for projecting capacity needs, production and procurement costs, and sales, and could be used to develop pro forma profit and loss statements for the business plan.

The business plan was formulated in the manner described above at the beginning of each fiscal year. The process was repeated at midyear in what was called the Phase II plan. Thus, the company maintained a rolling six-month plan.

Short-term planning. Between the business planning cycles, forecasting, and replanning was carried out on a continual basis. Sales and orders forecasts for major items were reviewed monthly by product managers. Sales and orders forecasts for less important items were reviewed bimonthly or every quarter. These changes in forecasts meant that changes in the master plans were made monthly. These short-term master plans were used to develop detailed production and procurement schedules, and to make inventory ordering decisions.

Preparing for a business turndown

Gaynor Kelley felt that the differences between the forecasts in the financial plan, the product manager forecast, and the build plan were largely due to differences in the perceptions of the people involved in making these forecasts. The product managers, after having been caught short during the 1974 boom were bullish. Many manufacturing people, and especially the production planners, after having lived through a period of materials shortages, extended lead times, and vendor unreliability, were cautious. They were attempting to gain back the four- to six-week delivery position lost earlier in the year.

Kelly felt that fiscal year 1975 sales would actually turn out to be very close to those projected in the original business or financial plan if a recession did occur. The Instrument Division had generally followed a cyclical pattern close to that of the national company. Some lead times were falling and purchase commitments for the division were rising. Order cancellations threatened in other industries. But, he was at this point undecided as to whether the Instrument Division should position themselves to handle the upside or downside risks.

The upside risks of losing sales and market position would be felt if he did not allow the new forecast and build plan to continue in effect, and a recession did not materialize. The downside risks of large inventories, write-offs of obsolete parts, and a high fixed cost position would be felt if he did allow these new plans to replace the original business plan and the recession did occur.

PART II

ELEMENTS OF PLANNING AND CONTROL

Chapter 2

Forecasting for inventory and production control

WHILE WE CONSIDER THE FORECAST to be critical to the planning and control of production-inventory systems, it is not our purpose here to present an exhaustive treatment of the subject. Forecasting is a subject in itself, and there are a number of books devoted entirely to it [8, 33]. Forecast data will be regarded as an input to models and operating systems for inventory and production control. As such it is important that we state the requirements of these data. If they are to be useful for our purposes, we must understand forecasting systems so that we can make correct interpretations of forecast data.

We will discuss initially the requirements for forecasting systems, as well as the effects of forecasting methods on planning horizon times, market patterns, and production lead times, and analyze forecasting methods when viewed as information feedback systems. In the second major section of this chapter we will break down the forecasting problem into *components* of demand, such as average demand, trend effects, seasonal effects, and noise or random effects, so that we can construct effective statistical methods to deal with these components. In the third major section of the chapter, we will discuss the forecasting methodology known as exponential smoothing. This technique is illustrative of a class of techniques whose purpose is to determine underlying patterns in historical demand data. The fourth section introduces some basic regression techniques for forecasting and discusses both causal and temporal regression models. The chapter will conclude with a discussion of other types of forecasting approaches and how to select the best method for preparing a forecast.

Before we proceed, however, it is important that we distinguish our meaning of "forecasting" from the general definition of the term. In the general sense we would expect that a forecast would represent an estimate of the net result of all factors impinging on the market, but a little thought should tell us that this may be unreasonable. The number of factors which can possibly enter a forecasting model may be enormous. Some of these factors might contribute a great deal to the net effect on demand and some may be quite unimportant. Some of the factors might be quite predictable and some not. Brown [8] states, however, that any factor can be placed in one of two categories: (a) factors that generated demand in past months and are not new to the future, and (b) factors that appear for the first time in affecting total demand:

> There are many industries, and many types of products, for which the factors in the first class have most of the effect on total demand. In such cases, routine methods can be developed to forecast the effect of those factors, leaving management free to predict the effect of the new influences. For other industries by contrast, the future is almost entirely a change from the past; management predictions are more difficult and occupy a more central role.—I use the term "forecast" or "routine forecast" to mean the projection of the past into the future; and the term "predict" to mean management's anticipation of changes and of new factors affecting demand [8].

In this book we shall use this definition of the term "forecast." Forecasting can be systematized for a large number of inventory items based upon some carefully determined model. By these definitions, prediction represents a somewhat higher order of skill and knowledge. It, too, must be done as a function of management whenever a new item is introduced into an organization's product line or whenever it is necessary to establish a strategy in response to real or anticipated changes in the economic and political climate.

Requirements for forecasts

The demand forecasting function is commonly a part of the sales organization, and forecasting data has many important uses in setting sales goals and measuring the effects of promotional programs. It serves many other broad managerial purposes as well. To be useful for inventory and production control, however, it is important that demand forecast data be available in a form which can be translated into demands for specific items of material, demands for time in specific equipment classifications, demands for specific labor skills, and so on. Therefore, forecasts of gross dollar demand, demand by customer classification, or demand by broad product classifications are of limited value for the planning and control of inventories and production programs.

Planning and control for production-inventory systems must necessarily take place at several different levels. Therefore, it is unlikely that one kind of forecast can do the job. To be sure, the immediate problem is always the controlling of inventories, providing raw materials required for current production programs, planning the use of workers and machines on a day-to-day, week-to-week, or month-to-month basis. However, it is important to look somewhat farther into the future to provide for new capacity or a different kind of capacity. The result is that we require forecasts of different time spans to serve as the basis for operating plans of different time spans. These plans are: (1) Plans for current operations and for the immediate future. (2) Intermediate-range plans to provide for the required capacities of workers, materials, and equipment for the next three to five years. (3) Long-range plans for plant and warehouse capacity, plant location, changing product mix, and the exploitation of new products.

Finally, we need to specify a range of possibilities in making forecasts. The common practice is to state a single value for the forecast which represents the average or most likely estimate. But, we know that demand is subject to many random effects which produce variations from the forecast value, and these variations are themselves measurable. The result is that forecasters can make a somewhat more confident statement about a range of values than they can about a specific single number. If forecasts are stated as a range of values, the attention of everyone is immediately focused on the fact that any plans for inventories and for the use of production facilities on the basis of these forecasts ought to be flexible enough to shift up or down in order to accommodate normal forecasting errors. We also need to take account of forecasting errors in order to determine realistic buffer stocks for inventories. We will see later how to account for uncertainty in forecasts.

The planning horizon time

Aside from the comments just made regarding the requirements for forecasts and the need for forecasts of different time spans, there is the question of the appropriate horizon time, particularly for the forecast on which current operating plans are made. We are interested in the two related questions: How far into the future should one look each time he or she wishes to decide what the levels of inventory, production, and employment should be? Into what increments should this planning horizon be divided? These are practical questions for each organization, and the answers depend on such factors as the behavior of markets and raw material suppliers, and the nature of internal operations and controls.

Markets and suppliers.   If the market in which we must compete is seasonal for whatever reason, this factor may dominate in selecting a horizon time for planning. To select a planning period which breaks right into the middle of the peak of the marketing season would undoubtedly make a rational planning process very difficult. But, the peak marketing season for automobiles is somewhat different than for bathing suits. The furniture marketing season is strongly influenced by the annual trade shows, as is true for many other style goods. In some instances the timing of raw material supply may be dominant, as would be true in the canning industry. One must can peas when the crop is ready to be canned, and the period cannot be changed at will.

Effect of internal operations and controls.   The internal nature of one's business or activity can have an important effect on the horizon time. One of the important factors is simply the production lead time. The production lead time varies widely from a few hours in some simple blending operations to weeks and months in homebuilding, shipbuilding, and other complex manufacturing situations. If production lead time is short, then it may be possible to react quickly to changes in external influences such as the market. On the other hand, if production lead time is six months, then it is difficult to envision an increment in the planning horizon time less than this.

The fiscal year is probably the most common planning horizon time because of the requirements of both tradition and the federal income tax. Internal managerial practices can have severe interactions with the problems of planning and control for production-inventory systems. For example, the common practice of inventory reduction just before the end of the fiscal year must be taken into account by those responsible for inventory and production planning.

The information feedback system

It is important to consider not only the information that the forecast contains but also the usefulness of this information in the light of the dynamics of the broad information system and the effects of time lags in the system. If we consider the information system structure of the multistage system indicated in Figure 1–3, we note that a change in demand would be reflected back through a chain of time lags adding to 43 days. Obviously, when a production planner at the factory notes an increase or decrease in demand based on orders from the factory warehouse, the wrong problem is in front of the planner. That problem has already passed in terms of timely action, and by now the situation could have reversed.

One way of short-circuiting the information system is to have the factory respond directly to forecasts of demand instead of through the chain of demand. Of course, there is still a time lag required to make and assemble the forecast, but it is a much shorter time lag. We will have more to say about these system dynamics in later chapters, where we will discuss the scheduling dynamics of a production system imbedded in a multistage production-inventory-distribution system.

Meaning for forecasting. What is the value of this discussion of information feedback systems in connection with forecasting? It is simply that the design of a forecasting system cannot stop with just the design of an excellent statistical model to take account of trends, seasonal, and random effects. To be sure, the technical aspects of the forecasting model are critical, but if a perfect forecast is provided through a system of time lags, the personnel who attempt to plan production and control inventories will think that the forecast is of almost no value. The essence of a forecasting system is in providing feedback information quickly and accurately where it is needed in order to anticipate whenever possible the changes in demand that will be reflected back through the stages of the system.

As we have just noted, the value of a forecasting system is intimately bound up with the overall information system. But, we cannot have good forecasting without careful attention to the statistical details of forecasting models. We will now turn our attention to these problems by examining the components of demand.

Components of demand

Earlier we defined the term "forecasting" to mean the projection of the past into the future. At first glance this seems to be satisfied by almost a "plot-and-draw" technique in which one looks at the immediate past and calculates or draws lines of best fit which indicate by simple extrapolation what to forecast for the next period. Indeed, in the very simplest and statistically most stable situations, the plot-and-draw technique might work. Obviously, it is not that simple, however, or managers would not feel that there was a difficult problem in forecasting, and an important technical field would not have grown up. There are several different kinds of basic situations plus combinations, and it is around these that forecasting methodology has developed. We will refer to these basic situations as the "components of demand." Through the components of demand we can describe any of the combination situations we may encounter. The components are: average demand, trends in the average, seasonal patterns, cyclic patterns, and random variations around the basic pattern characterized by the averages, trends, seasons, and cycles. Cyclic variations, dealing with the concept of the business cycle, are beyond our scope and we will not discuss them.

To illustrate, let us examine the fictional graphs of the demand for three products. They typify the components of demand patterns in a large number of actual instances:

1.   Product A, shown in Figure 2–1, is an item whose demand is affected by a large number of factors the result of which is that there seems to be no particular pattern. The average demand for the five-year record shown is 451 units per month with a maximum demand of 755 units in May 1963, and a minimum of 161 units in October 1966.

2.   Product B, shown in Figure 2–2, is typical of a new introduction, and there is evidence of a relatively stable average growth from 1963 on. The average demand for the entire five-year record is 50.8 units per month, but this seems of little value for projecting into 1967.

3.   Product C, shown in Figure 2–3, may at first seem to be characterized by random variation around its five-year average of 162 units per month. If one examines the timing of the peaks and valleys, however, there appears to be seasonal variation with the minimum values occurring in the summer and the maximum values during the winter.

Figure 2–1
Monthly demand for Product A

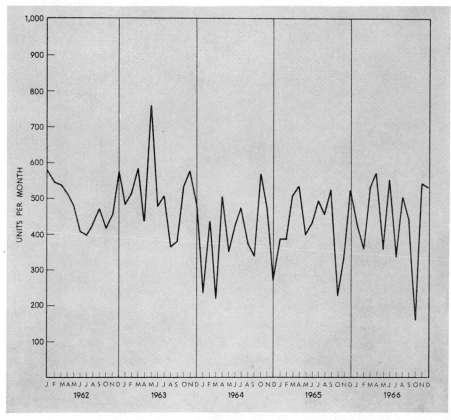

Now let us look a little more closely at the components of demand, keeping in mind our three illustrative products, all of which exhibit a certain amount of random variation but with Products B and C exhibiting trend and seasonality, respectively.

Average demand

Average demand could mean the average of all of the past data, and this might be reasonable as one of the bases for projection if we are dealing with a situation similar to the record of demand shown in Figure 2–1 for Product A. But what about the useful meaning of averages in the situations described in Figures 2–2 and 2–3 for Prod-

Figure 2–2
Monthly demand for Product B

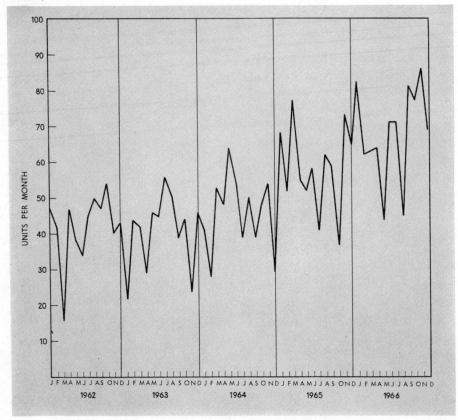

ucts B and C? Obviously, some other kind of average is needed. In
Figure 2–2 the demand for Product B, the overall average of 50.8
units per month is meaningless if we are attempting to project into
1967—the trend is dominant, and we must emphasize the more recent months if we want a meaningful average in this situation. Some
kind of moving average is of more value. For example, the average of
the last six months of the demand for Product B from Figure 2–2 is
71.5, which seems like an obviously more useful figure for projecting
into 1967 than the grand average of 50.8. But, the consistent uptrend
would make us wonder if the six-month average is high enough,
since the average of the last three months is even higher; i.e., 77.3 per
month.

Figure 2–3
Monthly demand for Product C

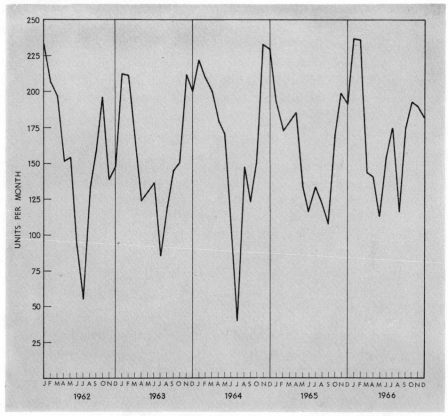

We are on the horns of a dilemma. First, we want to emphasize the more recent data because we feel that it may more accurately portray any recent changes in important demand factors, yet if we reduce the sample size from six to three, we know that the confidence we can have in that average value has declined. Second, it is obvious simply by inspecting the graph of Figure 2–2 that even the three-month average will lag as an estimate on which to base a projection into 1967 because of the trend effect. Therefore, let us agree to separate the trend effect from the problem of determining a useful moving average. We will consider the problem of trend separately in the next section.

We would like to have an average which represents all of the data,

so that it is statistically stable, but which also emphasizes more recent data which we assume is more representative of recent events.
We would also like this average to be easy to compute. The present
best answer to these requirements is the exponentially weighted
moving average.

Weighted averages. Suppose that we simply take a frontal attack
on the problem of weighting the recent data more heavily in a
three-month moving average. We can express a simple three-month
average as follows:

$$\bar{X}_0 = a_0 D_0 + a_1 D_1 + a_2 D_2$$

where D_0 is the present month's demand, D_1 the demand one month
ago, etc., and the a's are weighting constants which equal $\frac{1}{3}$. However, we can still have a true but different average if the a's are not
equal but of decreasing value. The restriction is simply that the sum
of the a's is 1. Suppose we arbitrarily weighted the a's as follows:
$a_0 = 0.6, a_1 = 0.3, a_2 = 0.1$. Using the data for the last three months
of demand in Figure 2–2, then $D_0 = 69, D_1 = 86, D_2 = 77$, and

$$\bar{X}_0 = 0.6 \times 69 + 0.3 \times 86 + 0.1 \times 77 = 74.9$$

For comparison the simple average is 77.3. We can see the effect of
the decreasing value weighting on the latter two months.

We could carry this idea further and develop weights for an average which embraced the entire five years of monthly data from Figure 2–2, weighting the more recent data more heavily. It is easy to
see that if one gave heavy weight to the most recent three to six
months the relative effect of the early data on the resulting average
would be small. Exponential weights do all of these things and in
addition are simple to calculate.

EXPONENTIALLY WEIGHTED AVERAGES[1]

The operation of the simplest exponentially weighted average is
based on a period-by-period adjustment of the latest smoothed average (S_{t-1}) by adding (or subtracting) a fraction (α) of the difference
between the actual demand in the current period (D_t) and the last
smoothed average (S_{t-1}). The result (which involves no extrapolation) yields the new smoothed average in the current period (S_t):

$$S_t = S_{t-1} + \alpha(D_t - S_{t-1}) \tag{1}$$

---

[1] See also Brown [6, 8], Trigg and Leach [32], Winters [35], and Geoffrion [15].

The fraction of the difference between actual demand and the previous period estimate of the average, α, is the exponential smoothing constant. α must be between 0 and 1. Actually, the most commonly used values are between 0.01 and 0.3. By rearranging Equation (1) we have the smoothed average, S_t, in a more convenient form:

$$S_t = \alpha D_t + (1 - \alpha)S_{t-1} \qquad (2)$$

The convenience of Equation (2) is obvious in computing forecasts for a large number of stock items.

The time periods represented by S_t, D_t and S_{t-1} are sometimes confusing. First let us recognize that S_t is not an extrapolation beyond known demand data. Instead, it is the most current smoothed average used to help guide current operations, computed at time t. In the true sense, it is not a forecast at all, but a statement about current demand. How then is S_t different from D_t? The latter figure is raw data available at time t containing components of random variations. The smoothed average figure is smoothed to discount the random variation effect. Thus if $\alpha = 0.20$, then Equation (2) states that the smoothed average S_t in period t is determined by adding 20 percent of the new actual demand information D_t to 80 percent of the last smoothed average S_{t-1}. Thus, 80 percent of the possible random variations included in D_t are discounted. Small values of α will have a strong smoothing effect. On the other hand, large values of α will react more quickly to real changes in actual demand.

Extrapolation from S_t to infer a forecast for the period $t + 1$ is justified since there is nothing in the model to indicate trends or seasonality. Therefore, the forecast for the upcoming period F_{t+1} is taken directly from the computed value of S_t.

Equation (2) is simple enough, but the fact that it embraces all of the past data, emphasizes the most recent data, and is in fact a true average of all past data, is not so obvious. We will now demonstrate that these facts are true. Beginning with Equation (2), we can substitute for the last smoothed average S_{t-1} a similar equation involving the actual demand in that period, D_{t-1}, and the previous smoothed average, S_{t-2} :

$$S_{t-1} = \alpha D_{t-1} + (1 - \alpha)S_{t-2}$$

which can be substituted in Equation (2),

$$S_t = \alpha D_t + (1 - \alpha)[\alpha D_{t-1} + (1 - \alpha)S_{t-2}]$$
$$= \alpha D_t + \alpha(1 - \alpha)D_{t-1} + (1 - \alpha)^2 S_{t-2} \qquad (3)$$

which gives us an equation for S_t in terms of α, D_t, D_{t-1} and S_{t-2}. But S_{t-2} was determined by a similar computation, i.e.,

$$S_{t-2} = \alpha D_{t-2} + (1 - \alpha)S_{t-3}$$

which we can substitute for S_{t-2} in Equation (3) to obtain:

$$S_t = \alpha D_t + \alpha(1 - \alpha)D_{t-1} + (1 - \alpha)^2[\alpha D_{t-2} + (1 - \alpha)S_{t-3}]$$
$$= \alpha D_t + \alpha(1 - \alpha)D_{t-1} + \alpha(1 - \alpha)^2 D_{t-2} + (1 - \alpha)^3 S_{t-3}$$

We now have an equivalent statement for S_t, involving the constant α, the three past actual demands, and the smoothed average three periods ago. We can continue this process of successive substitution for the remaining smoothed average term all the way back through the entire series of data of k periods and end up with the statement:

$$S_t = \alpha D_t + \alpha(1 - \alpha)D_{t-1} + \alpha(1 - \alpha)^2 D_{t-2} + \alpha(1 - \alpha)^3 D_{t-3} +$$
$$\ldots + \alpha(1 - \alpha)^k D_{t-k} + (1 - \alpha)^{k+1} S_{t-(k+1)} \quad (4)$$

Equation (4) now includes all of the actual demands in the data record plus the original smoothed average used $(k + 1)$ periods ago. Since the factor $(1 - \alpha)^{(k+1)}$ becomes very small and approaches 0 as k becomes large, the last term can be ignored. At the same time, the sum of the other coefficients $\alpha(1 - \alpha)^n$ approaches 1, and we have the conditions of a true weighted average. It is also easy to see now that the actual weight given each of the D's depends on the value of α selected and that the most recent demands are given heavier weight. Table 2–1 shows the weights given past data for two values of α.

Table 2–1
Weights given past data of actual demand in exponentially weighted averages for $\alpha = 0.1$ and $\alpha = 0.3$

		Weight in percent	
Period	Formula	$\alpha = 0.1$	$\alpha = 0.3$
t	α	10.0	30.0
t − 1	$\alpha(1 - \alpha)$	9.0	21.0
t − 2	$\alpha(1 - \alpha)^2$	8.1	14.7
t − 3	$\alpha(1 - \alpha)^3$	7.3	9.9
t − 4	$\alpha(1 - \alpha)^4$	6.6	6.9

Now we can return to Equation (2), which is the one we would use for computational purposes. It is deceptively simple, but let us remember that the term S_{t-1} has been generated by a sequential process which in fact represents all of the past actual demands. We have shown that the selection of α, the smoothing constant, can be made in such a way that recent data is emphasized as heavily as desired. A relatively large value of α will cause the smoothed average S_t to respond quickly to changes in actual demand, reflecting a fraction of random changes in demand as well as actual shifts in the average demand. A small value of α will respond more slowly and smoothly. Brown [8] recommends beginning with a smoothing constant of 0.3 and reducing it to 0.1 after six months.

Figure 2–4 shows the exponentially smoothed average of the demand for Product A using a smoothing constant of $\alpha = 0.1$. Note that the smoothed average is stable even though there are wide fluctuations in actual demand but that the average does change gradually when actual demand changes. At the beginning of this section we alluded to the fact that the smoothed average would lag behind an

Figure 2–4
Monthly demand for Product A with exponential average shown

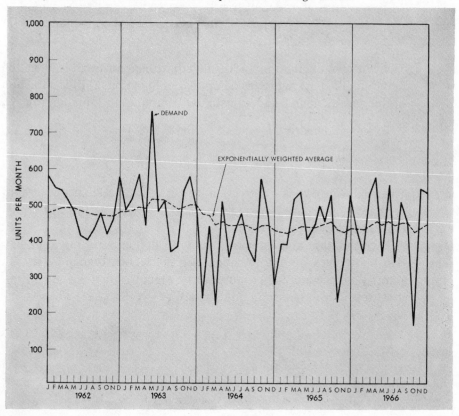

upward or downward trend. We can correct for this lag, and we will discuss the methods for accomplishing this correction by exponential smoothing.

Trend effects

The apparent trend from period to period is simply the difference in the smoothed averages from period to period, $S_t - S_{t-1}$. But this difference is subject to the random variations which occur and can be smoothed exponentially just as the average demand was smoothed. What we want is an exponentially weighted average trend, and the procedure is similar to the procedure for averages. The current apparent trend is simply the differences between the last two smoothed averages, that is,

$$\text{Current apparent trend} = S_t - S_{t-1}$$

The new *average* trend adjustment, $\bar{T}_t$, is then,

$$\bar{T}_t = \alpha(\text{current apparent trend})$$
$$+ (1 - \alpha)(\text{last average trend adjustment})$$
$$= \alpha(S_t - S_{t-1}) + (1 - \alpha)\bar{T}_{t-1} \tag{5}$$

The expected demand including an adjustment for trend is, then, the new smoothed average S_t as computed in Equation (2) plus a fraction of the new average trend adjustment computed in Equation (5):

$$\text{Expected demand for current period} = E(D_t)$$
$$= S_t + \frac{(1 - \alpha)}{\alpha}\bar{T}_t \tag{6}$$

The term $(1 - \alpha)/\alpha$ is a correction for lag in $\bar{T}_t$, in response to a ramp increase or decrease. The lag term is more complex for other functions (see Brown [6, p. 115]).

Extrapolation and forecast. As with the no trend model, Equation 6 involves no extrapolation beyond known demand data. To extrapolate beyond $E(D_t)$ to forecast F_{t+1} requires that we add $\bar{T}_t$, the most recent average trend adjustment,

$$F_{t+1} = E(D_t) + \bar{T}_t = S_t + \frac{1 - \alpha}{\alpha}\bar{T}_t + \bar{T}_t$$
$$= S_t + \frac{1}{\alpha}\bar{T}_t \tag{7}$$

Then to extrapolate or forecast the demand for n periods in the future,

$$F_{t+n} = E(D_t) + n\bar{T}_t$$

$$= S_t + \left(\frac{1}{\alpha} + n - 1\right)\bar{T}_t \qquad (8)$$

As with the computations for the smoothed average, those for the average trend adjustment, the expected demand, and the forecast are simple for either desk or automatic computing.

Computations. A computed example at this point will serve to illustrate the methods for both smoothed averages and average trend adjustment for exponential smoothing. Table 2–2 shows the raw demand data and computations required for Product B. Column (2) gives the raw demand data shown originally in Figure 2–2. Column (3) shows the computed smoothed averages and columns (4) and (5) the two-stage calculation of average trend adjustments. Column (6) shows the result of adding (or subtracting) the trend adjustment to the smoothed average to yield the expected demand. Finally, column (7) shows the computation of a forecast for F_{t+1}. The results of columns (3) and (7) are plotted in Figure 2–5 in relation to the raw demand data. Notice the smoothing effect of the smoothed average and extrapolated forecast series and the fact that the trend adjustment does correct for the lag in the simple smoothed average when there is a trend to cope with. Note that the smoothed average (without trend adjustment) lags the extrapolated forecast curve, being above it when trend is negative and below it when trend is positive.

Seasonal effects

As discussed previously, the demand for some items exhibits a seasonal characteristic for clear-cut obvious reasons such as weather patterns, which may, for example, dominate the demand for winter coats. Other products may be influenced by traditional patterns of style change and promotion programs, such as in automobiles and furniture.

Sometimes the reasons for a seasonal demand pattern are more subtle and must be determined. Brown [8, p. 129] states that the first principle "for deciding to use a seasonal method of forecasting is that there must be a definite, dependable reason that creates heavy demand at one time and light demand another." We will not attempt a

Table 2–2
Computations of smoothed average demand, average trend adjustment, and expected demand for Product B ($\alpha = 0.1$)

(1) Date	(2) Demand, D_t	(3) Smoothed average, $S_t = \alpha D_t + (1-\alpha)S_{t-1}$	(4) Current apparent trend, $S_t - S_{t-1}$	(5) Average trend adjustment, $\bar{T}_t = \alpha(S_t - S_{t-1}) + (1-\alpha)\bar{T}_{t-1}$	(6) Expected demand, $E(D_t) = S_t + \dfrac{(1-\alpha)}{\alpha}\bar{T}_t$	(7) Forecast for period $t+1$, $F_{t+1} = S_t + \dfrac{1}{\alpha}\bar{T}_t$
Initial		40.0		0		
1962:						
January	47	40.70	0.70	0.070	41.33	41.40
February	42	40.83	0.13	0.076	41.51	41.59
March	16	38.35	−2.48	−0.180	36.73	36.55
April	47	39.21	0.87	−0.075	38.53	38.46
May	38	39.09	−0.12	−0.080	38.37	38.29
June	34	38.59	−0.51	−0.123	37.48	37.35
July	45	39.22	0.64	−0.046	38.81	38.76
August	50	40.30	1.08	0.066	40.90	40.96
September	47	40.97	0.67	0.126	42.11	42.24
October	54	42.27	1.30	0.244	44.47	44.71
November	40	42.05	−0.23	0.197	43.82	44.02
December	43	42.14	0.10	0.187	43.82	44.01
1963:						
January	22	40.13	−2.01	−0.033	39.83	39.79
February	44	40.52	0.39	0.009	40.59	40.60
March	42	40.66	0.15	0.023	40.87	40.89
April	29	39.50	−1.17	−0.096	38.63	38.53
May	46	40.15	0.65	−0.022	39.95	39.93
June	45	40.63	0.49	0.029	40.89	40.92
July	56	42.17	1.54	0.180	43.79	43.97
August	50	42.95	0.78	0.240	45.11	45.35
September	39	42.56	−0.40	0.177	44.15	44.32
October	44	42.70	0.14	0.173	44.26	44.44
November	24	40.83	−1.87	−0.031	40.55	40.52
December	46	41.35	0.52	0.024	41.56	

Figure 2–5
Monthly demand for Product B with two exponential averages shown

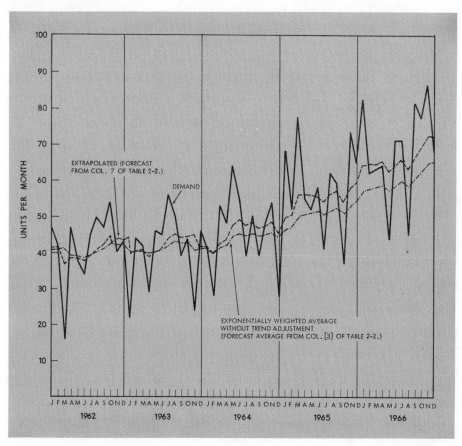

complete discussion of seasonal forecasting methods, but rather will focus our attention on the use of an exponential smoothing technique used when a definite seasonal pattern has been established. We will use the data for Product C as an example.

The basis of the methodology is to develop a base series which represents the seasonal cycle and to compute a demand ratio of actual demand in each period to the base series demand for that period. This demand ratio is then smoothed, correcting for trend, in the same general way as was illustrated in Table 2–2 and Figure 2–5. The result of these operations is an expected demand ratio. Expected demand is computed by the period-to-period multiplication of the base series by the smoothed ratio. Forecast demand is computed as the product of the expected ratio plus trend and the base series. We will discuss these steps in relation to the computed example for Product C shown in Table 2–3 and plotted in Figure 2–6.

Base series.   The base series is usually constructed from last year's experience in some way. If the seasonal pattern is strong and relatively invariant, then the base series could simply be the period-by-period demand for last year. If the peaks and valleys shift forward or backward slightly from year to year, then an averaging process may be used such as a moving average, or an exponentially

Table 2–3
Computations of expected demand for the seasonal Product C using a base series of the average of the surrounding quarter in the same month in the preceding year ($\alpha = 0.1$)

(1)	(2)	(3)	(4)	(5)
				Smoothed average ratio, $\overline{SAR}_t$ $= \alpha DR_t +$ $(1 - \alpha) \times$ $\overline{SAR}_{t-1}$
			Demand ratio $= \dfrac{(col.\ 2)}{(col.\ 3)}$	$= \alpha(col.\ 4) +$ $(1 - \alpha) \times$
Date	Demand, D_t	Base series	$= DR_t$	$\overline{SAR}_{t-1}$
Initial..............				1.000
1962:				
January	232	231.8	1.001	1.000
February	207	211.2	0.980	0.998
March	198	204.6	0.968	0.995
April	152	168.4	0.903	0.986
May	154	155.6	0.990	0.986
June	93	120.3	0.773	0.965
July	56	121.0	0.463	0.915
August	130	116.7	1.114	0.937
September	160	119.7	1.337	0.957
October	197	139.5	1.412	1.021
November	139	150.0	0.927	1.011
December	148	221.5	0.668	0.977
1963:				
January	213	233.5	0.912	0.971
February	212	212.3	0.999	0.973
March	172	185.7	0.926	0.969
April	124	168.3	0.737	0.945
May	131	133.0	0.985	0.949
June	137	101.0	1.356	0.990
July	86	93.2	0.923	0.983
August	120	115.4	1.040	0.989
September	145	162.4	0.893	0.979
October	151	165.3	0.913	0.973
November	212	161.6	1.312	1.007
December	200	166.7	1.200	1.026

smoothed average. In Table 2–3 we have used a three-month moving average centered on the month for which the average is being determined. For example, computing the base series average in February we use the actual last year's demand for January, February, and March. The resulting base series for two of the five years of demand for Product C is shown in column (3).

Demand ratios. The raw data are deseasonalized by computing for each period the simple ratio of actual demand in the current month to the value of the base series for the same month. The results

(6)	(7)	(8)	(9)	(10)
	Average trend adjustment, $\bar{T}_t =$	Expected ratio $= \overline{SAR}_t +$	Expected demand, $E(D_t)$	
Apparent trend of $\overline{SAR}$ $= \overline{SAR}_t - \overline{SAR}_{t-1}$	$\alpha(\overline{SAR}_t - \overline{SAR}_{t-1}) + (1 - \alpha)\bar{T}_{t-1}$ $= \alpha(col.\ 6) + (1 - \alpha)\bar{T}_{t-1}$	$\dfrac{(1 - \alpha)}{\alpha}\bar{T}_t$ $= (col.\ 5) + \dfrac{(1 - \alpha)}{\alpha} \times$ $(col.\ 7)$	$= (expected\ ratio) \times (base\ series)$ $= (col.\ 3) \times (col.\ 8)$	Forecast, F_{f+1} $=[(col.\ 8) + \bar{T}_t] \times$ $[base\ series_{t+1}]$
0	0			
0	0	1.000	231.8	
−0.002	−0.0002	0.996	210.4	211.2
−0.003	−0.00048	0.991	202.8	203.7
−0.009	−0.00133	0.974	164.0	166.8
0	−0.00119	0.975	151.7	151.3
−0.021	−0.0032	0.936	112.6	117.1
−0.050	−0.0079	0.844	102.1	112.9
0.022	−0.0049	0.892	104.1	97.6
0.040	−0.0004	0.973	116.5	106.2
0.044	0.0041	1.058	147.6	135.7
−0.010	0.0026	1.034	155.1	159.3
−0.034	−0.0010	0.968	214.4	229.6
−0.006	−0.0015	0.957	223.5	225.8
0.002	−0.0012	0.962	204.2	202.9
−0.004	−0.0014	0.956	177.5	178.4
−0.024	−0.0037	0.912	153.5	160.7
0.004	−0.0029	0.923	122.8	120.8
0.041	0.0015	1.004	101.4	92.9
−0.007	0.0006	0.988	92.1	93.7
0.006	0.0012	1.000	115.4	114.1
−0.010	0.00003	0.979	159.0	162.6
−0.006	−0.0006	0.968	160.0	161.8
0.034	0.0029	1.033	166.9	156.3
0.019	0.0045	1.066	177.7	172.5

Figure 2–6
Monthly demand for Product C with seasonally adjusted expected demand computed
by exponential smoothing techniques (α = 0.1)

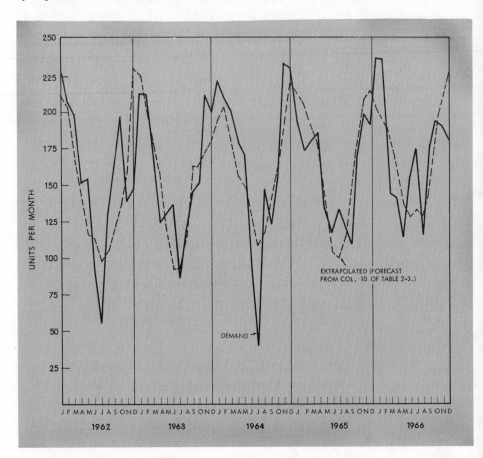

of these computations for Product C are shown in column (4) of Table
2–3. These ratios reflect all of the random variations which might
occur in both the actual demand and the base series, and so the
demand ratio is smoothed by means of an exponentially weighted
average to yield a series of smoothed average ratios ($\overline{SAR}$) as shown
in column (5) of Table 2–3.

Trend adjustments. The trend adjustment process is also identical to the methods shown in Table 2–2 for Product B except that we
are now talking about a trend in the smoothed average ratio. As
before we compute first an apparent trend shown in column (6) and
finally smooth this trend by exponential methods in column (7). A

fraction of the smoothed trend is then added to the smoothed average ratio $\overline{SAR}$, to yield the final expected ratio as shown in column (8).

Expected demand is then computed for each period by multiplying the expected ratio by the base series figure for the same period as shown in column (9) of Table 2–3. The expected demand is then an exponentially weighted and seasonally adjusted average. The extrapolated forecast F_{t+1} is computed in column (10) as

$$F_{t+1} = [\text{Expected ratio}_t + \bar{T}_t][\text{Base series}_{t+1}]$$

The extrapolated forecast is shown plotted in relation to actual demand for the five-year data record of Product C in Figure 2–6.

Random effects and forecast error

We see the random effects occurring in all of the graphs of the demand in each period. These variations are unexplainable or at least unforecastable with the methods that have been applied so far, and may be due to a wide variety of causes, such as reactions to the political and economic climate, the weather, acts of God, and so on. The exponential smoothing systems we have discussed are designed to react slowly to a big change in demand, taking a "wait and see attitude" for fear that the change is only a random variation. If the change in fact reflects a true increase or decrease in demand, it will continue in subsequent periods, and the weighted averages will track the actual demand and respond to it.

Recall that the selection of the value of the smoothing constant, α, will determine the sensitivity of the forecasting system to changes in demand and therefore to random changes as well. A relatively large value of α, perhaps 0.3, will give greater credence to the possibility that an observed change in demand is real and not random and will reflect a larger fraction of the observed change in the forecast. A smaller value of α, perhaps between 0.01 and 0.1, discounts the possibility that a big change is real and tells us to ignore the change as being only random unless it persists into subsequent periods.

While these guidelines may be somewhat useful in determining whether to use a relatively large or small smoothing constant, they are not precise enough to determine exactly what the best value of α should be. The "best" α for an exponential smoothing model can be determined, however, if the user is willing to specify a criterion, and then is willing to use trial and error, or search [4], methods with historical data to see which value of α comes closest to meeting the criterion. The same general approach can be applied to determine which of several techniques or methods should be used to generate forecasts.

We can choose from among at least three widely used criteria for evaluating the usefulness of a forecasting method, or the parameters that are to be used in the context of a particular method, such as exponential smoothing. These measures include average error (AE), mean absolute deviation (MAD) and the mean squared error (MSE). All three of these criteria involve different measurements of forecast error, which is defined as:

Forecast error = Actual demand − Forecast demand

The average error criterion is based on the notion that while it may be unrealistic to expect a forecasting technique to always give perfect forecasts, a good technique will, on the average, exhibit an error that is zero or close to it. Table 2–4 illustrates the calculation of the average error for the simple exponential smoothing model whose results are shown in Table 2–2. Note that the average error of −0.60 which resulted from this calculation meets our expectations in that this value is at least close to zero. Were our sample of forecast and actual demands larger, and were the resulting average error a large positive or negative number, we would have to be concerned that our forecasting method was biased. A positive bias is signified by the fact that the average error is a large positive number, indicating a systematic tendency for our forecasting methods to underforecast demand. Conversely, a negative bias is signified by a large negative average error, and indicates a systematic tendency for our method to overforecast demand. Clearly, neither a positive nor a negative bias is desirable.

The average error contains important data for the forecaster. But, as in the case of the person who drowned crossing a river six inches deep on the average, it obscures the variability associated with a forecasting method or value of α. This occurs because the positive and negative errors summed in calculating the average error cancel one another out so that it is difficult to see how consistent our method is in minimizing forecast errors in individual instances. The mean absolute deviation (MAD) provides an additional criterion that we can use to assess the characteristics of forecast error. As shown in Table 2–4, the MAD is calculated by simply taking the average of the absolute values of the forecast errors using forecasted or simulated data. By using absolute values, we prevent the positive and negative

Table 2–4
Computations of various measures of forecast error

(1) Date	(2) Actual demand	(3) Forecast	(4) Average error (AE) $(2-3)$	(5) Mean absolute deviation (MAD) $\lvert 2-3 \rvert$	(6) Mean squared error (MSE) $(2-3)^2$
1963:					
January	22	40.13	−18.13	18.13	328.69
February	44	40.52	+ 3.48	3.48	12.11
March	42	40.66	+ 1.34	1.34	1.79
April	29	39.50	−10.50	10.50	110.25
May	46	40.15	+ 5.85	5.85	34.22
June	45	40.63	+ 4.37	4.37	19.09
July	56	42.17	+13.83	13.83	191.26
August	50	42.95	+ 7.05	7.05	49.70
September	39	42.56	− 3.56	3.56	12.67
October	44	42.70	+ 1.30	1.30	1.69
November	24	40.83	−16.83	16.83	283.24
December	46	41.35	+ 4.65	4.65	21.62
Total			− 7.15	90.89	1,066.32
Mean			− 0.60(AE)	7.58(MAD)	88.86(MSE)

errors associated with individual forecasts from canceling one another out. Thus, we obtain a much clearer picture of the degree of variability in our forecasting method's ability to yield a good forecast. However, unlike the average error which has an absolute ideal value of zero, MAD is a relative criterion which has little significance until the MAD associated with one method or value of α is compared with that which results when another method or parameter is applied. This suggests that in determining, for example, the best value of α, a number of possible values must be tried on the data, MAD calculated for each, and then the α with the lowest MAD selected for use.

The third criterion, the *mean squared error* (MSE), is often held to be superior to MAD as a method of assessing forecast error variability since it can be used to detect methods or parameters which yield generally low forecast errors, but which occasionally miss by a significant amount. MSE is calculated by squaring the individual forecast errors in a data series and then striking the mean, as shown in the last column of Table 2–4. The act of squaring penalizes large forecast errors much more than relatively small ones, as well as yielding positive forecast error values to avoid the cancellation effect of both positive and negative forecast errors. The former point is particularly important because we might well tolerate a method or α that yielded a relatively high MAD if we could be assured through a relatively low MSE that few extremely bad instances of forecasting would result. The concept of minimizing the mean squared error is also an important one in deriving the regression forecasting methodologies that we will discuss in the latter part of this chapter.

Adaptive response exponential forecasting methods

As we have noted, it is common to use fairly small values of α in exponential smoothing systems in order to filter out random variations in demand. When actual demand rates increase or decrease gradually, the forecasting system can track the changes rather well. If demand changes suddenly, however, a forecasting system using a small value of α will lag behind the actual change substantially. Thus adaptive forecasting systems have been proposed. Trigg and Leach [32] propose to detect sudden changes automatically in computing systems by means of a tracking signal. A subroutine then increases the value of α in order to give more weight to recent data.

Once the system has stabilized, the value of α is reduced again in order to be more effective in filtering out random variations in demand.

The tracking signal proposed by Trigg and Leach is:

$$\text{Tracking signal} = \frac{\text{Smoothed error}}{\text{Smoothed absolute error}}$$

where error is defined as the difference between forecast and actual demand in each period. The two error figures are smoothed by the usual simple exponential methods. If the forecasting system is in control, the tracking signal will fluctuate around zero. If biased errors occur, however, the value of the tracking signal will move toward either plus or minus one. The tracking signal cannot go outside of the range ±1.

In order to adapt the response rate of the forecasting system to changes as measured by the tracking signal, the smoothing constant α is set equal to the tracking signal. Figure 2–7 shows the compara-

Figure 2–7
Comparison of performance of conventional and adaptive exponential forecasting models in response to a step increase in demand

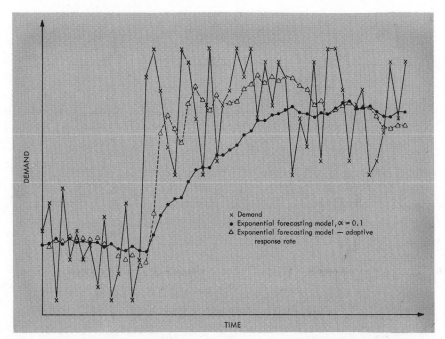

Source: From D. W. Trigg and A. G. Leach, "Exponential Smoothing with an Adaptive Response Rate," *Operational Research Quarterly,* vol. 18, no. 1 (March 1967), pp. 53–59.

tive results of an exponential smoothing model with $\alpha = 0.1$ and one with an adaptive response rate when a step change is introduced into the demand series. The adaptive system follows the demand change quite well while the conventional exponential forecasting system lags behind the step change in demand substantially. After demand has stabilized at the new level, the adaptive system has reduced the value of α and both systems perform similarly.

More sophisticated models involving the adaptive response rate concept are also discussed in [11, 20, 23, 26, 27, 28, 29, 30, 34]. These adaptive systems parallel the conventional exponential models which take account of trend as well as trend in combination with seasonal variations.

LINEAR REGRESSION TECHNIQUES

Exponential smoothing methods in general require the application of one or more smoothing constants which are used to derive revised estimates of demand in future periods. These models are dynamic in that they involve bootstrapping a new forecast out of a continually changing data base. That is, they automatically incorporate new data on forecast errors into their consideration of a new forecast. By way of contrast, another large class of forecasting techniques, many of which rely on linear regression methodologies, usually require the complete reanalysis of all old and new data each time new historical information is to be taken into account in forecasting future demand. The forecasting techniques which rely on linear regression techniques comprise a very important and substantial part of the forecaster's tool kit. These models do require more extensive data manipulation and storage than exponential smoothing (although many hand calculators now contain simple regression routines), but they are also considerably more sophisticated and flexible. They provide the forecaster with the ability to construct forecasting models which explicitly recognize causal or time-related relationships, as well as historical data on demand and forecast errors.

The common denominator among regression techniques for forecasting purposes is the application of the method of least squares to derive expressions, or models, of the average relationship between a *dependent variable*, whose magnitude we wish to forecast, and one or more *independent variables*. Independent variables are variables which the forecaster believes are associated in some way with the dependent variable. Equation (9) illustrates the general form of a *simple linear regression model*, in which the dependent variable Y is expressed as a function of a constant term a, and a parameter b (the slope of the regression line) times a single independent variable X. The linear form of this equation is important since one of the most critical assumptions that must be made in estimating the parameters a and b is that the dependent variable is linearly related to the independent variable(s). Equation (10) illustrates the general form of a *multiple linear regression model*, in which the dependent variable is expressed as a function of several independent variables, X_1, X_2, and X_3.

A simple linear model:

$$Y = a + bX \qquad (9)$$

A multiple linear model:

$$y = a + b_1X_1 + b_2X_2 + b_3X_3 \qquad (10)$$

Our categories of simple and multiple linear regression models can be further refined to reflect the type of independent variables which a forecaster might employ. *Causal* linear regression models employ independent variables which are believed to influence the value of the dependent variable we are attempting to forecast. In other words, such models employ independent variables which the forecaster believes *cause*, or are related to, fluctuations in the dependent variable. For example, a forecaster who is attempting to predict the annual sales of baby food (the dependent variable) may believe that the number of new births in each year partially explains, or causes, rises and falls in baby food sales. A *simple, causal model* which expresses this belief can thus be formulated:

Y	$=$	a	$+$	b_1X_1
(Annual baby food sales in a year)		(Constant)		(Slope times the number of births in a year)

Once the values of the parameters a and b have been estimated for this model, the forecaster can use it to predict the sales of baby formula in a year given any estimate of the number of births in that year. If other factors also influence baby formula sales, such as disposable personal income, a *multiple causal model* can be postulated which includes several independent variables.

A second category of independent variables can be used to differ-
entiate models which attempt to find an underlying pattern in demand over time, rather than a causal relationship. These *temporal*, or
time series linear regression models use time as the independent
variable. For example, a *simple, temporal* linear regression model for
projecting baby formula sales would be:

$$Y \qquad = \qquad a \qquad + \qquad b_1 T_1$$

(Annual baby formula   (Constant)   (Slope times the number of
sales in a year)   the year being forecast)

This simple model, which you may recognize as a *trend* model, can
be used to extrapolate the sales of baby formula in future years, once
the parameters a and b have been estimated, by varying the number
of the year being forecast relative to the base year used in estimating
the parameters. Other underlying components of a demand time
series, such as seasonality and cyclicality, can be accounted for in
multiple temporal models, where additional time-related independent variables are included in the regression model. Thus, regression
models for forecasting purposes can be placed into the four distinct
categories shown below:

Simple causal models

Multiple causal models

Simple temporal models

Multiple Temporal Models

Causal models

The use of regression models in forecasting involves far more than
just specifying the type of model to be used, and running the data
through a hand-held calculator or prepared computer program. As
we discussed earlier, regression models are far more sophisticated in
many ways than the other forecasting techniques we have discussed
up to this point. In general, the preparation of a forecast with regression models involves six distinct steps. These steps include:

1. Specifying the independent variables.
2. Specifying the form of the model.
3. Estimating model parameters.
4. Testing the model.
5. Testing least squares assumptions.
6. Estimating values of independent variables and forecast.

To illustrate the way in which a forecaster must proceed through these steps in developing a causal model, consider the case of a forecaster who wishes to forecast the demand for automobiles.

1. *Specifying independent variables.* The first step for the forecaster involves making some hypotheses about the kind of causal relationships that might exist between U.S. automobile sales and other factors which impinge upon them. This step in formulating a forecasting model is somewhat more of an art than a science, since it requires some understanding of the environment which affects the dependent variable which is to be forecast. In this case, the forecaster may make the hypothesis that automobile sales are dependent upon disposable personal income (DPI). The reasoning the forecaster may apply at this stage is that more automobiles are likely to be purchased when DPI is high; that is, when the amount of wealth consumers have to spend is high, and vice versa. At this point, the forecaster may also wish to specify other independent variables which he or she believes are related to automobile sales, such as Gross National Product (GNP). This could result in a multiple, as opposed to a simple, model. However, for purposes of illustration, we shall assume here that a single independent variable (DPI) has been chosen.

2. *Specifying the form of the model.* All linear regression models have the same form; that is, they all presume a linear relationship between the dependent and independent variables. In this case then, the model must be of the form $Y = a + bX$, where Y is the dependent variable (auto sales) and X is the independent variable (DPI). However, it may well be that the relationship between these two variables is not in fact linear. For example, it may be that the relationship is really of the form $Y = AB^x$, where A and B are constants. If this is the case then, we must perform a *transformation,* which is simply a trick to convert nonlinear equations into the type of linear equation we require for regression. The equation $Y = AB^x$, for example, can be transformed into a linear equation by taking the logarithm of both sides; e.g., $\log Y = \log A + \log B \cdot X$. A comparison of the form of this transformed model will show that it is the same as $Y = a + bX$, except that here, $Y = \log Y$, $a = \log A$, and $b = \log B$.

A simple way to check whether or not such transformations are required can be made by preparing a graph of the independent and dependent variables, such as the one shown in Figure 2–8. If the line which appears to best fit the scatter of points in this graph is curved, then a transformation is required. If, as in this case, the pattern of the

Figure 2–8
Relating auto sales (U.S.) to disposable personal income

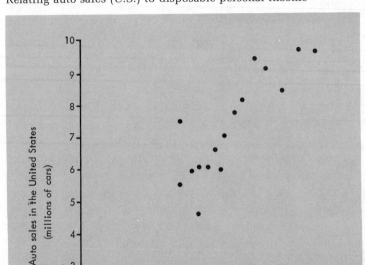

points is reminiscent of a straight line, then a transformation may not
be necessary, and the form of the equation is simply $Y = a + bX$.
The degree to which linear or transformed equations fit can be for-
mally tested as discussed in later sections.

    3. *Estimating model parameters.* Once the independent vari-
ables have been specified, and the form of the relationship of the
dependent and independent variables has been identified, the only
step that remains in deriving a model is to estimate the values of the
model parameters a and b. This can be accomplished by applying the
method of least squares.

    The method of least squares is, in principle, the same for both
simple and multiple models, although the mechanics are consid-

erably more complex in the latter case. It involves deriving estimates of the parameters a and b in such a way that two of the forecasting criteria mentioned in the last section are met, namely:

a. That the parameters will produce a model which yields an un-biased estimate of the dependent variable. In other words, that the *average error* between the observed values of the dependent variable and the corresponding values produced by the linear model is zero (assuming the average is taken over a sufficiently large number of data points).

b. That the linear model will minimize the sum of the squares of the deviations between the observed values of the dependent variable and the corresponding values produced by the linear model. This is equivalent to minimizing the *mean squared* error of the forecasting model.

Given these criteria and some statistical assumptions, elementary calculus and algebra can be used to derive equations which can be used to calculate the parameters for a simple model, as shown below.[2]

$$b = \frac{\Sigma XY - \bar{X}\Sigma Y}{\Sigma X^2 - \bar{X}\Sigma X}$$

$$a = \bar{Y} - b\bar{X}$$

Applying these equations to the data in Table 2–5 yields an estimate of $b = 12.91$, and an estimate of $a = 2,421$. Now, our model can be completely specified as $Y = 2,421 + 12.91\,X$.

As shown in Figure 2–9, this equation gives us the formula for the straight line which passes through our data points in the "best" way. Here, "best" is defined by the criteria we used to derive the method of least squares; that is, the line is one which minimizes the sum of the squared deviations from it, and where the average deviation from the line is zero. Note that the value of a that we derived is the point where our regression line intercepts the Y-axis in our graph, and that b is the slope of this line.

4. *Testing the model.* At this point, having derived a model and specified its parameters, we could quit, and simply use the model to forecast auto sales in future years. However, to do so at this

---

[2] Here, $\bar{Y}$ and $\bar{X}$ denote the average of the values of the dependent and independent variables in the data set. ΣXY denotes the sum of the cross products of the corresponding values of X and Y. ΣY and ΣX denotes the summation of the values of Y and X in the data set, and ΣX^2 denotes the sum of the squared values of X.

Table 2–5
Data for regression analysis: U.S. automobile sales
and disposable personal income

Year	U.S. auto sales*	Disposable personal income†	Period
1954	5,506	247.9	1
1955	7,466	254.4	2
1956	5,942	274.4	3
1957	6,033	292.9	4
1958	4,668	292.8	5
1959	6,100	318.8	6
1960	6,641	337.7	7
1961	5,935	350.0	8
1962	7,092	364.4	9
1963	7,720	385.3	10
1964	8,101	404.6	11
1965	9,332	436.6	12
1966	9,028	469.1	13
1967	8,337	505.3	14
1968	9,656	546.3	15
1969	9,582	590.0	16

* In thousands of cars.
† In billions of 1959 dollars.
Source: Motor Vehicles Manufacturers Association, *1973/74
Automobile Facts and Figures.*

stage would require that we ignore two important questions that the
forecaster should be interested in. The first question is, how reliable
will any forecast derived with this model be? The second question is,
how can we tell whether or not the model is significant? That is, how
much faith should we put in our estimates of reliability? There are a
number of statistical tests which we can apply to help answer these
questions, the mechanics and theory of which are beyond the scope
of this book. Three of these tests are particularly important. Fortunately, most standard computer programs automatically produce
these tests.

The first test involves a number called the *coefficient of determination*, or R^2. The coefficient of determination states the proportion of
the variation in the dependent variable that is explained by the model.
In the case of our automobile sales regression model, the coefficient of determination is 0.743. This means that 74.3 percent of the
variation in automobile sales is explained by DPI, and that (1 -
0.743) × 100 = 25.7 percent is explained by "other" factors which
we have not included in our model. Clearly, if the coefficient of
variation were small, say 0.25, our model would not be doing a very

Figure 2–9
Relating auto sales (U.S.) to disposable personal income:
the regression line

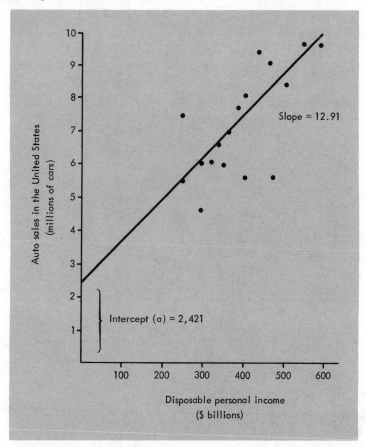

good job of explaining what "causes" automobile sales, and thus may not be very helpful in providing a forecast.

The second test involves a number called the *standard error of the estimate*. This figure indicates the expected range of variation that we would encounter if we were to use the model to make a forecast, assuming that the value of the independent variable is the average of the data used to determine the parameters of the model. In the instance of our auto sales model, the standard error of the estimate is 837.3 thousand. Assuming that the forecast errors are normally distributed, statistical theory indicates that roughly two thirds of the time a forecast made with our model can be expected to be within plus or minus 837,300 automobiles of the true value. Similarly, we can expect that about 95 percent of the time our model will produce a forecast that is in error by no more than two times the standard error of the estimate, or 1,674,600 automobiles. This test should be treated carefully since the standard error of the estimate can only be used to gauge the amount of error that might occur when the value of the independent variable is close to the average of the data used to determine the parameters of the model. In our example, the average value of DPI in the data set is $379.4 billion. If we must estimate a higher or lower value of DPI in making our forecast, the error in our forecast will be larger than that given by the standard error of the estimate.

The third test of our model tests its significance. We have already seen that the coefficient of determination is 0.74, indicating that given our sample data, the model explains 74 percent of the changes in auto sales. But, is it possible that this result could have occurred by chance? Is it possible that the actual coefficient of determination is zero, but that we estimated 0.74 because we just happened to pick a bad data set, to specify the wrong model, or because our sample size was too small? The F test of significance indicates whether or not this might be the case. The F test itself is reasonably complex, even if the computer derives the value of F. Fortunately, however, many computer programs automatically do the F test, and simply compute the probability that the model is *not* significant. In the case of our example auto sales model, the value of F was 40.4, and the probability that the model was *not* significant was computed to be 0.0001. Thus, we are quite well assured that our model is significant, and that it explains a great deal of the variation in the variable we are trying to forecast, although we could have hoped for a smaller standard error of the estimate.

5. *Testing least squares assumptions.* Here again, we could be tempted to use our model in preparing a forecast, armed with the reassurances that our model tests have given us. But, at this critical point in developing a model, we must step back and ask ourselves whether or not we have simply created a house of cards. This is quite easy to do since the foundation of our model derivation, *and our model tests*, rest on the assumptions used to derive least squares estimates of the model parameters. Thus, at this point we must go back to test whether or not these assumptions were indeed valid. These assumptions, which we have not explicitly stated up to this point, are as follows:

a. The dependent variable is linearly related to the independent variables, or that the variables have been transformed so that this is indeed the case.

b. The statistical variance of the errors is constant, where errors are defined as the difference between the actual values of the dependent variable and the estimates produced by the model.

c. The errors that occur from one case to another are independent of one another. In other words, that the error produced by the difference between one actual value of the independent variable and the model's prediction, is independent of the errors produced by the difference between actual and predicted in other instances.

d. The errors are normally distributed.

Normally, the first and last of these assumptions are not too difficult to meet if care has been taken in plotting the relationships between dependent and independent variables, and if the sample size is large enough. There are several tests of these assumptions, however, which are beyond the scope of this book. Several of the references at the end of this chapter give a full explanation of them. The most frequent problems in regression modeling occur with the second and third assumptions regarding the errors produced by the difference between actual values of the dependent variable and the corresponding values produced by the model. The first problem, which occurs when the statistical variance of these errors is non-constant is called *heteroscedasticity*. The second problem, which occurs when errors are not statistically independent of one another, is called *autocorrelation*.

There are several ways of detecting whether or not autocorrelation or heteroscedasticity exist. The first and the most straightforward is to simply plot the residual errors which correspond to values of the dependent variable, as shown in Figure 2–10. If the plot appears to be a random dispersion of data points, then the chances are that no problems exist. If, however, the points in the graph show any kind of pattern, this is evidence that *heteroscedasticity* or *autocorrelation* exist, and that our model, and all of the tests related to it, are invalid. A second test of these problems is indicated by the Durbin-Watson statistic, which is often printed out when standard computer packages are used. While the theory behind this statistic is complicated, suffice it to say that a value of the Durbin-Watson statistic less than 1.5 and greater than 2.5 generally means trouble.

The plot of errors from our auto sales model in Figure 2–10 could be the result of a random pattern, although there does appear to be

Figure 2–10
Plotting residual error values

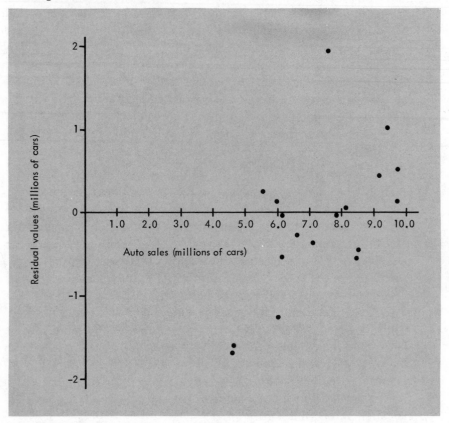

some slight tendency for residuals to rise with higher values of the dependent variable. Thus, even though the Durbin-Watson statistic in this case is 1.6, this information gives us some cause for concern, and makes us wish we had a larger sample size so that we could check to see whether this tendency is a real indication of heteroscedasticity, or just the result of chance. If further checking proved that we were not meeting the basic assumptions of linear regression, then we would have to go back to the beginning and either hypothesize additional, or alternate independent variables, perform some transformations, or otherwise formulate an alternative model.

    6. *Estimating values of independent variables and forecast.* Presuming for the sake of our example that our model has indeed passed all of the tests up to this point, we are at last ready to

prepare a forecast of auto sales in the future. The first thing that we must do to accomplish this, however, is to estimate what DPI will be in the future. In other words, we must prepare another forecast in order to be able to forecast. This presents one of the dilemmas of causal forecasting models, since our forecast of auto sales cannot be any more accurate than our forecast of the independent variable— DPI. However, in a sense, it is also a strength of the technique, since the causal model allows the forecaster to play "what if"; that is, to estimate what auto sales would be presuming different values of DPI. Thus, the weakness in this approach embodies one of its greatest strengths.

If we are able to estimate DPI in the next year as being, say, $610 billion, then the final step, forecasting, is simple. All that we need to do is to use this estimate as the value of the independent variable in our model, as shown in the equation below, to produce a forecast of U.S. auto sales of 10,296.1 thousand cars.

$$Y = 2,421 + 12.91X$$
$$Y = 2,421 + 12.91(610)$$
$$Y = 10,296.1$$

Multiple causal models. In our formulation and testing of the above simple causal model for predicting auto sales, we have had several hints that we may have been better off with a multiple model. First, the coefficient of determination of the simple model of 0.74 showed that while DPI had a strong influence on auto sales, almost 26 percent of the variation was still unexplained. The addition of other independent variables which also have a relationship to auto sales, such as the number of licensed drivers, may have explained more of the variation, and reduced the standard error of estimate, providing us with a better forecasting tool. The second indication that a multiple model may have been more suitable was the plot of the errors. The tendency toward heteroscedasticity shown here indi- cated that our simple model may not have met the strict assumptions under which regression models are formulated, and that we perhaps needed to consider an alternative model.

Had we started off our modeling process by specifying more than one independent variable, the rest of the modeling process, in terms of specifying the model form (making transformations), estimating model parameters, and testing the model and the assumptions would have been virtually the same. In fact, as Figure 2–11 illustrates, even the progression of our thoughts in considering first a single model,

Figure 2–11
Steps in constructing a causal model

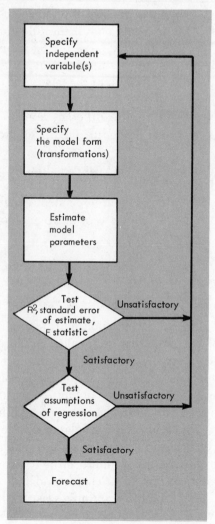

then an alternative single model, then a multiple model would be a normal sequence of events in arriving at a satisfactory causal model. In a sense, much of formulating causal models remains an art in that some trial and error and hunch playing must be combined with sophisticated mathematical techniques before a satisfactory model can be constructed.

Temporal models

In terms of the process of deriving a regression model for forecasting as shown in Figure 2–11, all that applies to causal models also applies to temporal models. The only difference is that in the latter case the independent variables that are specified are related to time, rather than to "causal" phenomena. This is an important difference because in the case of causal models, we are trying to determine cause and effect relationships between sets of externally related data, while temporal models are directed toward determining underlying patterns in demand over time in the same sense as exponential smoothing models do. If there are underlying patterns in demand that tend to repeat themselves over time, temporal models can be very useful in forecasting.

The trend model is perhaps the most frequently applied temporal model. It is based on the presumption that if demand is steadily increasing or decreasing, that it will continue to do so in the future. To illustrate a typical trend model, we can again use the automobile sales data from Table 2–5 as the dependent variable, and specify the time periods denoted in the column named "periods" as the independent variable. The form of the trend model would be $Y = a + bT$, where we have substituted X, normally used to denote causally related independent variables with the variable T, denoting time. All of the other variables in the model equation have the same designation as before. Using the same least squares regression method as we used previously, we can then estimate the parameters; $a = 4,947$, $b = 279.3$, to yield a complete specification of the trend model; $Y = 4,947 + 279.3T$.

Once we have checked the validity of this model, and of the assumptions used to derive it, we can then use it to estimate automobile sales in the next period. Here, we do not have the problem of estimating the future value of the independent variable as we did with causal models. Clearly, if our last time period (year) was denoted as number 16, then the next value of this independent variable must be 17. Hence, automobile sales $(Y) = 4,947 + 279.3(17) = 9,695$ thousand cars. This estimate of auto sales was certainly easy to derive, and it is fairly close to the estimate we obtained with the causal model (10,296 thousand cars). However, it is important to note that our trend model will never predict a decrease in sales, as would almost certainly happen were there a sharp decrease in DPI, while the causal model would predict the decline if DPI was expected to be lower in future years.

An example of a multiple temporal method is given by the technique of Fourier series analysis, which uses various trigonometric transformations of time as independent variables. The mathematical background for this method was established by Joseph Fourier, a French physicist and mathematician, in 1882. Fourier demonstrated that *any* periodic (i.e., seasonal) function which is finite, single valued, and continuous over the period (season) may be represented by a mathematical series consisting of constant term plus the sum of harmonically related sine and cosine terms. The equation for the Fourier series is:

$$F_t = a_1 + b_1 \sin wt + b_2 \cos wt + b_3 \sin 2wt + b_4 \cos 2wt$$
$$+ b_5 \sin 3wt + b_6 \cos 3wt + \cdots$$

Where

F_t = The numerical value of the series computed at time t.

a_1 = A constant term.

$b_1, b_2, \ldots$ = Coefficients defining the amplitude of the harmonics.

$$w = \frac{2\pi}{T} = \frac{6.28318}{T}.$$

T = The length of the period (i.e., the number of forecast intervals per year).

The series is expressed as an infinite series because, in theory, an infinite number of terms are required to duplicate mathematically a given periodic function with complete accuracy. Fourier series techniques are used extensively in engineering and the sciences to represent electrical wave forms, the vibration of mechanical structures, ocean wave motion and so forth. The periodic annual seasonal patterns of many consumer products in a large number of industries provide an obvious opportunity for the extension of this concept to the field of business forecasting.

Extending the Fourier series to business forecasting requires that we add an additional term to the previous equation in order to account for the trend component of demand. With this addition, the forecasting model will provide for three basic components of demand: average demand, trends in the average and seasonal patterns. Random variations around the basic pattern are handled by least squares model fitting. The expanded Fourier Series Business Forecasting Model becomes:

$$F_t = a_1 + b_1 t + b_2 \sin wt + b_3 \cos wt + b_4 \sin 2wt$$
$$+ b_5 \cos 2wt + \cdots$$

The a_1 term represents the average demand exclusive of seasonality or promotional influences. The b_1t term represents the sales trend. The remaining terms handle the seasonal selling pattern and provide a better fit of the model to historical sales data.

The use of least squares methods in estimating the values of the parameters in the Fourier model is straightforward, in that it involves using the multiple regression extension of the simple estimating equations we used in the section on causal models. However, there is a special caution that one must be aware of in formulating this type of multiple model that applies to multiple causal models as well. The problem, called *multicollinearity*, occurs whenever the number of independent variables specified in a model becomes great. Multicollinearity refers to the situation where independent variables are not only highly correlated with the dependent variables, a desirable happenstance, but also with one another. When two or more independent variables are highly correlated (that is, when their corresponding values tend to move together in a predictable way), the least squares technique has a difficult time determining an accurate estimate of the parameters, unless the sample size is very large. The result of multicollinearity tends to be very high values of the coefficient of variation, but little statistical significance.

Fourier models are particularly susceptible to multicollinearity because the theory states that an infinite series of terms (independent variables) is required to duplicate a given periodic function with complete accuracy. Hence, the tendency is to have a very large number of independent variables, and thus, multicollinearity. In fact however, this factor need not inhibit the wise use of Fourier series techniques, since even Fourier models with few independent variables can yield effective models as shown by the computer output (Figure 2–12) of a four-term (independent variable) model that was supplied to the 1962, 1963, and 1964 demand data for Product C given Table 2–3 and Figure 2–6. This model was of the form $F_t = a_1 + b_1t + b_2 \sin wt + b_3 \cos wt$.

A final type of temporal model that is worthy of mention here because of its great power and recent acceptance by business is the general category of Box-Jenkins models [5]. Although regression analysis is but one of the ways of estimating the parameters of Box-Jenkins models (in practice, search techniques are more commonly used), we mention it here because the general form of Box-Jenkins models is linear. Hence, they greatly resemble the linear forms we have already discussed. Moreover, this class of models tends to use historical val-

Figure 2–12
Computer output from four-term Fourier Series Forecasting Model for Product C

```
FORECAST MODEL RESULTS
----------------------

FCST      ACTUAL     FORECAST     FORECAST                              *** ACTUAL            === FORECAST
NO.       DEMAND     DEMAND       ERROR          35        85      135        185        235
                                                 +----+----+----+----+----+----+----+----+----+

 1         232        212          20          1+
 2         207        204           3          2+
 3         198        182          16          3+
 4         152        153          -1          4+
 5         154        124          30          5+
 6          93        104         -11          6+
 7          56         97         -41          7+
 8         130        107          23          8+
 9         160        129          31          9+
10         197        159          38         10+
11         139        189         -50         11+
12         148        210         -62         12+
13         213        217          -4         13+
14         212        208           4         14+
15         172        186         -14         15+
16         124        157         -33         16+
17         131        129           2         17+
18         137        108          29         18+
19          86        102         -16         19+
20         120        111           9         20+
21         145        134          11         21+
22         151        164         -13         22+
23         212        193          19         23+
24         200        214         -14         24+
25         222        221           1         25+
26         207        213          -6         26+
27         202        191          11         27+
28         177        162          15         28+
29         170        133          37         29+
30          85        113         -28         30+
31          40        106         -66         31+
32         147        116          31         32+
33         123        138         -15         33+
34         165        168          -3         34+
35         233        198          35         35+
36         230        219          11         36+
37                    226                      37+
38                    217                      38+
39                    195                      39+
40                    166                      40+
41                    137                      41+
42                    117                      42+
43                    111                      43+
44                    120                      44+
45                    143                      45+
46                    173                      46+
47                    202                      47+
48                    223                      48+


HISTOGRAM OF FORECAST ERRORS
----------------------------


FREQUENCY   1    1    0    1    0    1    1    1    0    3    3    2    3    3    4    2    3    1
          --+----+----+----+----+----+----+----+----+----+----+----+----+----+----+----+----+----+--
     4                                                                      *
     3                                        *    *         *    *    *
     2                                        *    *    *    *    *    *    *    *
     1      *    *         *         *    *    *    *    *    *    *    *    *    *    *    *
          --+----+----+----+----+----+----+----+----+----+----+----+----+----+----+----+----+----+--
CLASS INT   1    2    3    4    5    6    7    8    9   10   11   12   13   14   15   16   17   18

       -63.56    -52.62    -41.68    -30.74    -19.79    -8.85     2.09      13.04     23.98
           -58.09    -47.15    -36.21    -25.26    -14.32    -3.38      7.56      18.51     29.45



CLASS INTERVAL WIDTH =           5.471430
MAXIMUM VALUE        =          37.657242
MINIMUM VALUE        =         -66.299942
MEAN    VALUE        =           0.000604
STANDARD DEVIATION   =          26.961121



DISTRIBUTION OF FORECAST ERRORS
-------------------------------

                        NO. VALUES       PERCENT
MEAN -4 STD DEV              0             0.0
MEAN -3 STD DEV              2             5.6
MEAN -2 STD DEV              4            11.1
MEAN -1 STD DEV             10            27.8
MEAN  1 STD DEV             13            36.1
MEAN  2 STD DEV              7            19.4
MEAN  3 STD DEV              0             0.0
MEAN  4 STD DEV              0             0.0

        TOTAL              36           100.0
```

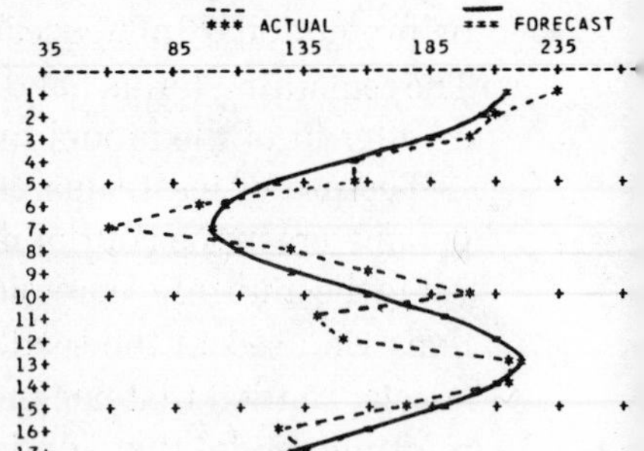

ues of the dependent variable, either lagged through time or weighted in various ways, as independent variables. Therefore, they qualify as temporal models.

The Box-Jenkins approach represents a highly sophisticated general approach to creating a temporal model, largely based on the analysis of autocorrelation in error terms, and successive values of the data. Thus, the technique of constructing one of the basic model forms suggested by Box and Jenkins directly attacks one of the nemeses of other regression models (autocorrelated errors), and in fact uses them to advantage.

Three basic types of models are postulated within the Box-Jenkins framework. The first, called AR, or autoregressive models, use lagged values of the dependent variable itself as independent variables. Interestingly, we have already worked through one type of autoregressive model—exponential smoothing. The second type of model is the MA, or moving average type model. Here, the independent variables are lagged values of the errors produced by using one period's demand as an estimate of the next period's demand. The third type, the ARMA or mixed model, is a combination of the previous two forms. The Box-Jenkins technique itself involves using a specified set of rules for successively building a better and better model, or moving from one type of model form to another. Although this technique has been very successfully applied to forecasting problems where other approaches have been disappointing, the large amount of computer time and the requirements for a skilled user of the technique to apply it correctly, make it an expensive tool to apply, compared to some other approaches we have discussed.

Other Techniques

There are a number of other techniques for forecasting which we will not discuss in this chapter because of their complexity, or their limited usefulness in production-inventory systems. We will mention them here, however, so that interested readers will know that they exist, and can thus pursue them independently if they choose. A good general reference for all of these is Wheelwright and Makridakis [33].

Double exponential smoothing. These techniques are a refinement of the basic exponential smoothing model wherein the smoothed forecast is smoothed again with a reapplication of the exponential smoothing concept. The result is an alternate way of compensating for lag in the simple exponential smoothing model, when a linear trend is present.

Adaptive filtering. These techniques represent an advancement of the concept of "training" or adjusting the weights applied to previous values of the dependent variable as new forecasts are being made. In this sense, they are similar in concept to the Trigg and Leach approach, but are considerably more complex.

Decomposition methods. These techniques are arithmetic, nonstatistical techniques which are useful in deriving the various trend, seasonal, and cyclical components of demand.

Econometric forecasting. These techniques are related to the types of regression methodologies that we have already discussed. The major difference is that a series of equations are developed which represent the cross interrelationships between independent and dependent variables. For example, we assumed that auto sales were a function of DPI in our example of a causal model. An econometrician might see auto sales as a function of DPI and other variables, *and* DPI as a function of auto sales, among other variables. Econometric methods then might be used to simultaneously estimate the relationships between DPI and auto sales since, from the economist's viewpoint, it is not clear which variable is really the causal one.

Choosing and using the right forecasting technique

Even considering the limited number of techniques that we have described in this chapter, it must be readily apparent that there are a vast number of approaches that the forecaster can apply in any one situation. This fact poses the important question, how does one choose which technique to apply? The answer to this question is not easy or straightforward, since there are a number of qualitative judgments that impinge on it. There are, however, a few generalizations that are helpful in sifting through the possibilities.

The most obvious generalization that one can apply is that the cost of developing and using a particular technique should not be greater than the incremental benefits associated with improving forecast accuracy. Thus, we would not expect to find relatively expensive techniques such as Box-Jenkins or causal regression models being used to forecast the demand for 10-cent bolts, nor would we expect to use a moving average or exponential smoothing method to forecast capacity needs for a $50 million plant expansion. But, even as we make this type of generalization, we must plead for caution on the part of the user in drawing hasty conclusions about which techniques are really more expensive than others, for the cost of a technique depends largely upon the situation. For example, the Trigg and Leach adaptive smoothing approach may appear to be more expensive than a simple exponential smoothing technique because the development costs are higher. But when you consider that the adaptive approach is "self-correcting," while the parameters of an exponential smoothing model must be reevaluated and reestimated periodically, the long-run costs of the former may be substantially lower than those of the latter. In another situation, a temporal model such as the Fourier method, may appear to be cheaper than a causal model. But, if the company considering this has not kept data on historical demand for use in the temporal model, a causal model using externally supplied data from trade and government sources may be less costly than trying to reconstruct historical data for the temporal model.

Less obvious generalizations that apply in selecting a forecasting technique revolve around the characteristics of the demand that is being forecast, and the level of sophistication of the organization using the forecast. It should be clear by now that certain types of forecasting methods are more applicable to some types of demand patterns than others. For example, a simple moving average, simple exponential smoothing, or causal regression technique will not normally be well suited to forecasting monthly demand which exhibits strong seasonal effects. None of these methods is readily suitable for this type of situation because they all ignore temporal or seasonal relationships. On the other hand, a large number of temporal models such as seasonal exponential smoothing, Fourier methods, or Box-Jenkins can be used handily. This example illustrates the high premium that is placed on understanding the nature of what you are forecasting before beginning.

In the same way that the forecaster must understand the nature of the demand being forecasted, he or she must also understand the nature of the organization using the forecast. There are few managers who will make important decisions on the basis of data from "mysterious" techniques, unless the technique has a long and successful track record. This emphasizes the point that the user as well as the creator of a forecast must be aware of its value, understand it, and the ways it is to be applied. If the level of sophistication in an organization is such that this understanding is not forthcoming, then the user's sophistication must be upgraded. Alternately, less sophisticated, more intuitively appealing methods must be used in the first place.

Using forecasting techniques

Once a forecasting technique has been selected that has the right cost, the right accuracy, that recognizes the characteristics of the demand situation, and is right for the organization, the forecaster is faced with the problem of actually preparing the forecast. In the hands of a skilled and thoughtful analyst, this will present few conceptual or analytical problems if the data on which the forecast is based is properly prepared. The problem in many situations is finding and conditioning the data. This is often a nontrivial task. It is particularly important that two kinds of data problems be understood from the beginning so that corrective action can be taken, and missteps avoided.

The first data problem occurs when forecasters think they are forecasting one thing, and are actually forecasting another. The cleanest and most common example of this occurs when the forecasters believe they are forecasting *demand*, but are actually forecasting *sales*. In such instances, the forecaster has usually ignored a fundamental business relationship; i.e., Sales = Demand − Stockouts (or backlog). The implications of this equation are obvious. If historical sales are used to predict demand, then that prediction will almost always be understated. In production-inventory systems, the objective is usually to predict demand, and to avoid stockouts or excessive backlogs. Thus, sales data must be conditioned to reflect whatever differences may occur because of stockouts or backlogs if it is to be used in the data base. If the company produces to inventory, historical demand can be derived by summing historical sales and stockouts. If the company produces to order, or backlog, such that the sale occurs, say, three months after the order is taken, then historical demand can be estimated by offsetting sales into the past by three months.

A second common data problem involves the lack of consistency in a data series. As an example, consider the problem of a forecaster who is using a causal model to predict automobile unit sales, with DPI as the independent variable. The number of cars sold is absolute, but DPI is a relative value, depending upon the rate of inflation, government accounting and statistical procedures, and a number of other factors which tend to make the meaning of DPI change over time. Thus, unless relative numbers in a time series like DPI are "conditioned" by stating them in constant dollars and correcting for changes in procedure, spurious and unnecessary forecasting errors will result. This problem also occurs with internal company data which is subject to "drift" as accounting procedures and organizations change over time.

REVIEW QUESTIONS AND PROBLEMS

1. Table 2–6 shows a four-year record of monthly demand for a product which we wish to analyze by exponential smoothing models.
   a. Plot the four-year record on graph paper.
   b. Using a smoothing constant of $\alpha = 0.20$, compute S_t using equation (2) in the text. Plot the results on the same graph as in (a) $S_0 = 65$.
   c. Compute a five-month moving average for the series centered on the third month. Plot the results on the same graph.
   d. Discuss the adequacy of either (b) or (c) as forecasting models for the data given.

2. Using the data of Table 2–6 and the results obtained in Problem 1 for S_t:
   a. Compute $E(D_t)$ and F_{t+1} by Equations (6) and (7) in the text, using $\alpha = 0.20$. $\dot{T}_0 = 0$.
   b. Plot the forecast series on the same graph used in Problem 1.
   c. Discuss the adequacy of this forecasting model for the data given.

3. Using the data of Table 2–6:
   a. Compute $E(D_t)$ and F_{t+1} including seasonal adjustments where the base series is the monthly average of the surrounding quarter demand in the same month in the preceding year. $\alpha = 0.20$. The base series for 1975 and extending into the first two months of 1976, based on 1974 demand data, is:

Month	Base series
1975	
January	46.00
February	65.67
March	93.00
April	118.33
May	130.67
June	128.33
July	123.00
August	110.67
September	101.00
October	93.33
November	86.33
December	79.00
1976	
January	80.33
February	91.00

Table 2–6
Monthly demand for a product

	1975	1976	1977	1978
January	68	76	44	26
February	95	75	75	48
March	110	100	91	80
April	118	136	100	108
May	157	143	115	127
June	176	148	108	134
July	182	122	113	126
August	154	102	104	105
September	120	76	70	79
October	85	56	56	41
November	63	38	36	6
December	60	32	15	4

      b.   Plot the series for F_{t+1} on the same graph used for Problems 1 and 2.

      c.   Discuss the adequacy of this forecasting model for the data given, and compare it to the results obtained in Problems 1(b and c) and 2(a).

4.* Given a record of 24 months' actual demand and an initial smoothed average calculate the smoothed average for each of 24 months, using the "best" value of α in the range of 0.01 to 0.30. To find the best α it will be necessary to perform calculations for a number of different values of α using some criterion such as the following:

      a.   The best value of α is the one which yields the smallest sum of the absolute value of the difference between actual demand in period t and the smoothed average of the preceding period:

$$\sum_{t=1}^{t=24} |D_t - S_{t-1}|$$

      b.   The best value of α is the one which yields the smallest sum of the squares of the difference between actual demand in period t and the smoothed average of the preceding period:

$$\sum_{t=1}^{t=24} [D_t - S_{t-1}]^2$$

The initial forecast is 28 units and actual monthly demands are as follows: 28, 21, 31, 33, 23, 29, 29, 28, 26, 33, 24, 31, 29, 28, 35, 33, 32, 36, 31, 37, 35, 29, and 27.

---

* Problem developed by Professors J. Baker and J. W. Gotcher, Department of Management Sciences, California State College, Hayward, California.

Table 2–7
Differences in actual sales of Cherryoak Company,
1947–70, and sales forecasted by multiple regression
(in $ millions).

Year	Actual sales	Predicted sales	Differences
1947	92.29	93.04	−0.75
1948	122.44	117.72	4.72
1949	125.57	136.91	−11.34
1950	110.46	129.33	−18.87
1951	139.40	128.65	10.75
1952	154.02	154.90	−0.88
1953	157.59	144.88	12.71
1954	152.23	145.17	7.06
1955	139.13	135.64	3.49
1956	156.33	137.44	18.89
1957	140.47	149.27	−8.80
1958	128.24	134.99	−6.75
1959	117.45	123.56	−6.11
1960	132.64	127.31	5.33
1961	126.16	136.52	−10.36
1962	116.99	124.20	−7.21
1963	123.90	125.56	−1.66
1964	141.32	134.79	6.53
1965	156.71	156.61	0.10
1966	171.93	170.59	1.34
1967	184.79	187.90	−3.11
1968	202.70	198.75	3.95
1969	237.34	227.95	9.39
1970	254.93	263.92	−8.99

(1) Perform the necessary calculations to determine the best value of α judged by the two criteria stated in (a) and (b).

(2) What are the best values of α given the criteria stated in (a) and (b)?

(3) Are there criteria other than those stated which should be used to determine α? Why are they appropriate?

5. List the basic assumptions made in regression analysis.

6. Define the following terms: autocorrelation, multicolinearity, heteroscedasticity. Do these phenomena facilitate or defeat attempts to use regression analysis in forecasting? How does one test for their presence?

7. Table 2–7 lists the differences between actual sales of the Cherryoak Company (1947–70) and the sales forecasted by the following multiple regression equation:

$$S_t = -33.51 + 0.373S_{t-1} + 0.033H_{t-1} + 0.672I_t - 11.03T$$

where:

S_t = Gross sales in year t.

S_{t-1} = Gross sales in the previous year.

H_{t-1} = New housing starts in the previous year.

I_t = Disposable personal income during the year t.

T = Time trend (T = 1, 2, 3, ..., n) where T = 1 = 1947.

    a. Is the above regression model a causal or a temporal model?

    b. If S_{t-1} = \$237.34 (in millions); H_{t-1} = 1,524 (in thousands); I_t = \$629.6 (in billions) and T = 24, predict the sales of Cherryoak furniture using the regression equation above.

    c. Using the data in Table 2–7, plot the residual errors (differences) against actual sales on a piece of graph paper. What does the resulting plot indicate?

    d. The regression equation above yields an R^2 (coefficient of determination) of 0.95 and a standard error of estimate of 9.7. What does this indicate?

8. Referring to the data in Table 2–7, formulate a simple trend regression model for forecasting the sales of the Cherryoak Company.

    a. Flowchart the steps you intend to take in formulating and testing this model.

    b. Using a hand calculator with a regression function, or a prepared computer program, determine the parameters of the trend model.

SELECTED BIBLIOGRAPHY

1. Adam, E. E., Jr.; Berry, W. L.; and Whybark, D. C. "Forecasting Demand for Medical Supply Items Using Exponential and Adaptive Smoothing Models." Paper no. 381. Krannert Graduate School of Industrial Administration, Purdue University, Lafayette, Ind., November 1972.

2. Batty, M. "Monitoring an Exponential Smoothing Forecasting System," *Operational Research Quarterly*, vol. 20, no. 3 (1969).

3. Benton, W. K. *Forecasting for Management.* Reading, Mass.: Addison-Wesley Publishing Co., 1972.

4. Berry, W. L., and Bliemel, F. W. "Selecting Exponential Smoothing Constants: An Application of Pattern Search," *International Journal of Production Research*, vol. 12, no. 4 (July 1974), pp. 483–500.

5. Box, G. E. P., and Jenkins, G. M. *Time Series Analysis, Forecasting, Control.* San Francisco: Holden-Day, Inc., 1970.

6. Brown, R. G. *Smoothing, Forecasting, and Prediction.* Englewood Cliffs, N. J.: Prentice-Hall, Inc., 1963.

7. Brown, R. G. *Decision Rules for Inventory Management.* New York: Holt, Rinehart, & Winston, 1967.

8. Brown, R. G. *Statistical Forecasting for Inventory Control*. New York: McGraw-Hill Book Co., 1959.

9. Chambers, J. C.; Mullick, S. K.; and Smith, D. D. "How to Choose the Right Forecasting Technique, *Harvard Business Review*, July–August 1971, pp. 45–74.

10. Chambers, J. C.; Mullick, S. K.; and Smith, D. D. *An Executive's Guide to Forecasting*. New York: John Wiley & Sons, Inc., 1974.

11. Chow, W. M. "Adaptive Control of the Exponential Smoothing Constant," *Journal Industrial Engineering*, September–October 1965.

12. Cogger, K. O. "Extensions of the Fundamental Theorem of Exponential Smoothing," *Management Science*, vol. 19, no. 5 (January 1973), pp. 547–54.

13. Eilon, S. and Elmaleh, J. "Adaptive Limits in Inventory Control," *Management Science*, April 1970.

14. Farley, J. Y., and Hinich, M. J. "Detecting 'Small' Mean Shifts in Time Series," *Management Science*, April 1970.

15. Geoffrion, A. M. "A Summary of Exponential Smoothing," *Journal Industrial Engineering*, vol. 13, no. 4 (July–August 1962).

16. Groff, G. K. "Empirical Comparison of Models for Short-Range Forecasting," *Management Science*, vol. 20, no. 1 (September 1973), pp. 22–31.

17. Huang, D. S. *Regression and Econometric Methods*. New York: John Wiley & Sons, Inc., 1970.

18. Jantsch, E. "Forecasting and Systems Approach: A Frame of Reference," *Management Science*, vol. 19, no. 12 (August 1973); pp. 1355–67.

19. Miller, J. G.; Berry, W. L.; and Lai, C. F. "A Comparison of Alternative Forecasting Strategies for Multi-Stage Production-Inventory Systems." *Decision Sciences*, vol. 7, no. 4 (October 1976), pp. 714–24.

20. Montgomery, D. C. "Adaptive Control of Exponential Smoothing Parameters by Evolutionary Operation," *AIIE Transactions*, September 1970.

21. Moore, J. R., Jr. "Forecasting and Scheduling for Past-Model Replacement Parts," *Management Science*, vol. 18, no. 4 (December 1971), Part 1, pp. 200–13.

22. Nelson, C. R. *Applied Time Series Analysis for Managerial Forecasting*. San Francisco: Holden-Day, Inc., 1973.

23. Nerlove, M., and Wage, S. "On the Optimality of Adaptive Forecasting," *Management Science*, vol. 10, no. 2 (January 1964), pp. 207–24.

24. Packer, A. J. "Simulation and Adaptive Forecasting as Applied to Inventory Control," *Operational Research Quarterly*, vol. 14, no. 4 (July–August 1967) pp. 600–79.

25. Parker, G. C., and Segura, E. L. "How to Get a Better Forecast," *Harvard Business Review*, March–April 1971, pp. 99–109.

26. Raine, J. E. "Self-Adaptive Forecasting Reconsidered," *Decision Sciences*, vol. 11, no. 2 (April 1971).

27. Rao, A. G., and Shapiro, A. "Adaptive Smoothing Using Evolutionary Spectra," *Management Science*, vol. 17, no. 3 (November 1970), pp. 208–18.

28. Roberts, S. D., and Reed, R. "A Development of a Self-Adaptive Forecasting Technique," *AIIE Transactions*, December 1969.

29. Roberts, S. D., and Whybark, D. C. "Adaptive Forecasting Techniques." Paper no. 335. Krannert Graduate School of Industrial Administration, Purdue University, Lafayette, Ind., October 1971.

30. Theil, H., and Wage, S. "Some Observations on Adaptive Forecasting," *Management Science*, vol. 10, no. 2 (January 1964).

31. Torfin, G. P., and Hoffman, T. R. "Simulation Tests of Some Forecasting Techniques," *Production and Inventory Management*, vol. 9, no. 2 (1968).

32. Trigg, D. W., and Leach, A. G. "Exponential Smoothing with an Adaptive Response Rate," *Operational Research Quarterly*, vol. 18, no. 1 (March 1976), pp. 53–59.

33. Wheelwright, S. C., and Makridakis, S. *Forecasting Methods for Management.* rev. ed. New York: John Wiley & Sons, 1976.

34. Whybark, D. C. "A Comparison of Adaptive Forecasting Techniques," *The Logistics and Transportation Review*, vol. 8, no. 3(1972), pp. 13–26.

35. Winters, P. R. "Forecasting Sales by Exponentially Weighted Moving Averages," *Management Science*, vol. 6, no. 3 (April 1960), pp. 324–42.

Chapter 3

Basic inventory decisions

THE GENERAL MODEL shown in Figure 1–12 illustrated three fundamental elements of planning and control: data collection and generation; decision making and planning; and implementation, feedback, and control. In the last chapter, we discussed one of the most important parts of the first element—the forecast. In this chapter, we continue to build upon the general model of the elements of planning and control. We discuss additional data that must be identified, and collected or generated, and begin our discussion of basic inventory decisions that utilize this information, especially in the context of independent demand situations.

Figure 3–1 describes that portion of the general model of the elements of planning and control that will be discussed in this chapter. Recall from our discussion of the functions of inventories in Chapter 1 that we isolated six basic functions: inventories to fill the in-transit and in-process pipelines, cycle inventories, buffer inventories, seasonal inventories, and the decoupling function. The inventory decisions we will discuss here relate to two of these functions; cycle inventories, which are the result of order quantity decisions, and buffer stocks, which are the result of decisions on the level of buffer or safety inventories required in order to achieve a given service level for customers. The fact that inventories serve these functions

Figure 3–1
Some elements of inventory management

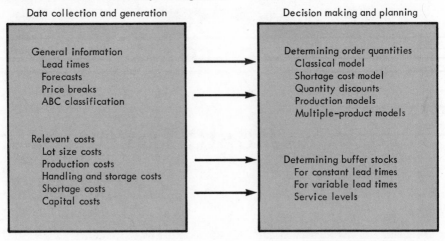

indicates immediately that they have a basic set of values for management. They are not to be minimized; rather we are seeking their correct levels in the context of the requirements of the particular system we may be analyzing or designing. We are seeking a balance between one set of costs or benefits that rise with inventories, and another set of costs and benefits that decline with them. The decision models presented in this chapter comprise a useful set of tools for making some of these trade-offs especially in independent demand situations.

Information for inventory decisions

The data described in Figure 3–1 represents the minimum amount of information required to make the kinds of inventory decisions we are treating. In fact, it represents data that are often found in the "item master" files which computers refer to when they are utilized in inventory control. This information can be divided into two categories. The first category of general information is largely product oriented, in that it contains data such as forecasts, procurement lead times, price breaks, and whether the product is produced or purchased, that spring from the individual product being considered. The second category of information is largely process oriented since it relates to the relevant costs involved in moving a product through the ordering-production/procurement-handling-holding cycle that is characteristic of a particular situation. Much of this data can be extracted from internal accounting systems, although care must be taken to ensure that the information is in the proper form for decision making, as opposed to financial reporting.

Leadtimes. Since one of the most fundamental types of inventory decision involves determining when to order a product or an item, the procurement lead time is a central piece of data. It indicates the length of time that is expected to elapse between ordering and receiving the item. Lead time estimates can be obtained by either examining the history of orders and receipts as it might be kept by a purchasing department, by checking with suppliers, reading the numerous trade publications which report on average lead times, or by obtaining estimates from engineering or production departments.

In using lead time estimates, one can make one of three assumptions about them. The first is that they are constant and deterministic. The second assumption is that they are random variables beyond the control of management, and that they must be described in terms of a statistical distribution. These are the assumptions that are made in the models treated in this chapter. A third assumption is that lead times are in fact controllable by management, and that they can be compressed or expanded at will. In other words, that an item can be obtained in less than the standard lead time (expedited), or that once an item is ordered, its receipt can be delayed, canceled, or rescheduled (de-expedited). Models and systems that make this assumption will be treated in later chapters.

In actual fact, no one of these assumptions about lead times is completely consistent with reality. Some firms may chose to assume that lead times are random variables to avoid the extra administrative costs of expediting, even though this may lead to higher inventories. Conversely, some firms may attempt to compress or extend lead times in order to gain improved control. In this case, the relative purchasing power of a firm is a consideration. A very small firm may have a difficult time in getting a large and powerful supplier to expedite deliveries if their sales represent a very small fraction of the supplier's total. On the other hand, it is difficult to conceive of a small supplier of a large firm saying that they wouldn't at least try to expedite deliveries, although there are physical limits to the amount of time by which lead times can be compressed.

Sources of supply. Since lead times, and their compressibility, often depend on whether an item is manufactured in-house or purchased from a supplier, this information is also frequently maintained in inventory files, as well as the name of the department or vendor from which the item is secured. If nothing else, this information is required to indicate to whom an order should be given. In addition, the make or buy designation may give some indication of the type of ordering rule that is to be applied in determining the order quantity, as we shall see later in this chapter.

Forecasts. We have already discussed the importance of forecasts as an input to inventory decisions. Clearly, since many types of inventories exist because firms anticipate demand, they must have an estimate of how much demand to anticipate in order to make cogent decisions. As we shall see in the latter portion of this chapter, it is also important to have a measure of either the variability in demand, or of forecast accuracy, if buffer stocks are to be determined rigorously.

Price breaks. A fourth category of general information that is important in making inventory decisions when the item is purchased is data about price breaks and minimum purchase quantities. Vendors often price their goods so that small quantities are more costly to order than larger quantities. While the forms in which such price schemes occur are quite varied, their purpose is obviously to take advantage of the economics associated with large lot sizes. Towards the same purpose, many manufacturers also stipulate minimum purchase order quantities. In either case, the implications for inventory management are obvious and important.

ABC Classification. A final piece of general information is whether or not the item has been placed in a predesignated category which indicates the type of inventory decision to be made or the type of model that should be employed in making it. The ABC classification scheme is commonly used to make such designations. An item is classified as being in category A, B, or C depending on whether it is a high-value, high-volume; medium-value, medium-volume; or low-value, low-volume item. Frequently A, B, and C classes are established by ranking the annual dollar volume of the orders for all of the items under control at a single point. The utility of such schemes results from the empirical finding that roughly 80 percent of the dollar value of sales is accounted for by 20 percent of the items in many situations. Thus, one would expect to give much more time and attention to high-valued A items, than to low-valued C items.

Relevant costs

Our ability to quantify and develop rigorous models of most managerial problems is dependent on the determination of the behavior of relevant costs. The practical application of such models is also dependent on our ability to obtain cost data as we have defined it. Most cost accounting data is related to "responsibility centers," and cost data usually represent average product costs or period costs. The process is normally one of grouping individual component costs, which may represent the average of the appropriate variable costs, and by adding in an allocation for joint costs. The result is that in many instances the relevant cost behavior for model-building purposes must be determined by special studies. The following types of incremental or out-of-pocket cost items are commonly relevant: costs which depend on lot sizes, production costs, handling and storage costs, shortage costs, and capital costs.

Costs depending on lot sizes.   There are certain costs which remain the same regardless of the size of the lot purchased or requisitioned. This would be true for the retailer ordering from the distributor, for the distributor ordering from a factory warehouse, for the factory warehouse ordering a new production run from the factory, and for the factory ordering raw materials from vendors. We call these kinds of costs "preparation" or "setup" costs. If we are ordering to replenish supplies at one stock point from another point, our interest is in the incremental clerical costs of preparing orders, following up these orders, expediting them when necessary, and so on. We must take care, however, to be sure that we obtain a true incremental cost of order preparation. It is not correct to derive the figure by simply dividing the total cost of the ordering operation by the average number of orders processed. A large segment of the total costs of the ordering function are fixed, regardless of the number of orders issued. There is, however, a variable component, and this is the pertinent figure for our use. Even then it may be difficult to determine satisfactorily the incremental cost which results from placing one more order. Quantity discounts and handling and shipping costs are other factors which vary with lot sizes.

When the order to be placed is on the factory, then the equivalent decision is in determining the size of the production run. In this instance the preparation costs are the incremental costs of planning production, writing production orders, setting up machines and controlling the flow of orders through the factory. Material handling costs in the plant have an effect on production lot sizes in much the same way that freight costs may affect purchase lot sizes.

Production costs. We have already discussed, in the previous paragraph, the preparation costs of production. There are some other production costs which can have a direct bearing on inventory models, however. These are overtime premiums and the incremental costs of changing production levels, such as hiring, training, and separation costs.

Handling and storage costs. Some incremental costs vary directly with the size of inventories. There are handling costs required to place materials in inventory and to issue them from inventory, and costs associated with storage, such as insurance, taxes, rent, obsolescence, spoilage, and capital costs. If average inventories increase, these costs will also increase and vice versa.

Shortage costs. What costs occur if we run out of stock? It would be difficult to find such an item in accounting records. Nevertheless, a part shortage can be the cause of idle labor on a production line or be the cause of incremental labor costs to perform operations out of sequence. What is the magnitude of the opportunity cost we must absorb if business is lost because of stock shortages?

Capital costs. If average inventories increase, then the capital invested in inventory increases proportionately, and we must assign an opportunity cost. This cost does not appear in the accounting records. In general, the appropriate interest rate to use should reflect the opportunities for investment of comparable funds within the organization. The cost of borrowed funds, or investing extra cash in government securities, might represent lower limits.

DETERMINING ORDER QUANTITIES

The classical inventory model

The earliest derivation of the classical inventory model is due to F. W. Harris [10]. Incongruously, however, this formula is often referred to in the literature as the "Wilson formula." Wilson was a consultant and used such a formula in many company applications. In 1931, F. E. Raymond [17] published the first book-length work on inventory control and attempted to show how the classical inventory model could be extended to account for a wide variety of conditions in industry.

The objective of the classical inventory model is to determine the lot

Figure 3–2
Idealized structure of inventory levels in relation to time in the classical
inventory model

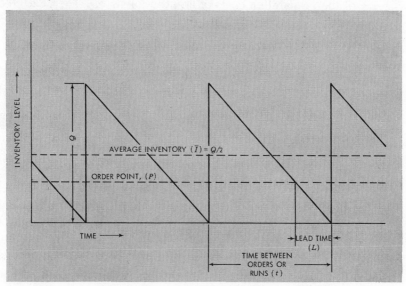

size (Q) under highly idealized conditions. Figure 3–2 shows the
assumed structure of inventory levels in relation to time. Q units are
ordered when the inventory level has declined to the reorder point
(P). The order is placed precisely at this point such that demand
during the procurement lead time (L) will draw the inventory down
to zero. The previous order for Q units is timed to be received exactly
at that point which raises the inventory level to Q and the cycle
repeats itself. Let us establish the following list of symbols:

TIC = Total incremental cost.
TIC_o = Total incremental cost of an optimal solution.
Q = Lot size.
Q_o = Optimal lot size [economic order quantity (EOQ)].
R = Annual requirements in units.
c_H = Inventory holding cost per unit per year.
c_P = Preparation costs per order.
P = Order point.
L = Lead time.
B = Buffer stock.
I = Inventory level.
S = Sales rate.

Objective function. The incremental costs for this simple system are those associated with holding inventory and those associated with the preparation costs of an order of size Q. Therefore, the cost function which we wish to minimize is:

$$TIC = \text{Inventory holding costs} + \text{Preparation costs}$$

The lot size Q is the variable which is under managerial control. We can see from Figure 3–2 that if Q is increased the average inventory level, $Q/2$ will increase proportionately. If the inventory holding cost per unit per year is c_H, the annual incremental costs associated with inventory are:

$$c_H \frac{Q}{2}$$

If we now take a specific example where the inventory holding cost $c_H = \$0.50$ per unit per year, then the inventory holding cost function reduces to $0.50 \, (Q/2) = Q/4$. The graph of the inventory holding cost function appears in Figure 3–3(a).

In a similar way we can make a general statement about the annual preparation cost. These costs depend on the number of times that orders are placed each year and the incremental cost of placing an order. The number of orders written to supply an annual requirement

Figure 3–3(a)

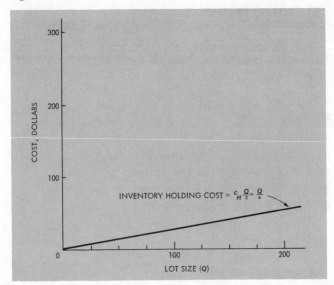

of R will depend on the lot size Q of each order, or R/Q. If the preparation cost is c_P for each order, then the annual preparation costs may be expressed as:

$$c_P \frac{R}{Q}$$

In our example let us assume that R = 250 units per year and c_P = $10 per order. The annual preparation cost function then reduces to 10 (250/Q) = 2,500/Q. The graph for this function is shown in Figure 3–3(b).

Figure 3–3(b)

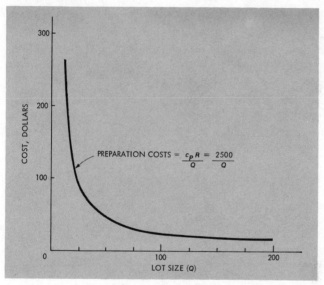

The two components of cost shown in Figure 3–3(a) and (b) are simply added algebraically to form the total incremental cost (TIC) curve shown in Figure 3–3(c). In Table 3–1, we have shown the computed points for all three curves for specified values of lot size. We can see that the minimum cost lot size is Q_o = 100 units by inspection of either Figure 3–3(c) or Table 3–1. The lot size of 100 units is, of course, associated with the total incremental cost of $50 in column (4). What we want is a general solution for all problems of this type.

Derivation of minimum cost formulas. In order to develop formulas for easy computation which are applicable to any set of data

Figure 3–3(c)
Classical inventory model ($R = 250$ units per year, $c_H =$
$0.50 per unit per year, and $c_P = $10 per order)

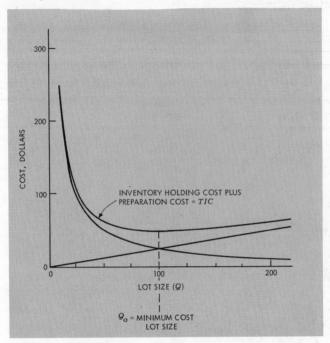

we will start with the general expression for total incremental cost
which we have already developed.

$$TIC = \frac{c_H Q}{2} + \frac{c_P R}{Q} \tag{1}$$

This is an equation for the total incremental cost curve, and we wish
to determine a general expression for Q_o, the lot size associated
with the minimum of the total incremental cost curve. Mathematically, this may be done by finding the value of Q for which the
slope of the total incremental cost curve is zero. Using the elements of simple differential calculus, the first derivative of Equation
(1) with respect to Q is:

$$\frac{d(TIC)}{dQ} = \frac{c_H}{2} - \frac{c_P R}{Q^2} \tag{2}$$

The value of Equation (2) is the slope of the line tangent to the total
incremental cost curve. We wish to know the value of Q when this

Table 3–1
Incremental costs for holding inventory, preparation, and total costs for
curves of Figure 3–3(c) ($R = 250$ units per year, $c_H = \$0.50$ per unit
per year, and $c_P = \$10$ per order)

| (1) | (2) Inventory holding | (3) Preparation costs | (4) Total incremental |
| | | | cost = col. (2) |
Lot size, Q	cost = Q/4	= 2,500/Q	+ col. (3)
25	\$ 6.25	\$100.00	\$106.25
50	12.50	50.00	62.50
75	18.75	33.33	52.08
100 = Q_o	25.00	25.00	50.00
125	31.25	20.00	51.25
150	37.50	16.67	54.17
175	43.75	14.30	58.05
200	50.00	12.50	62.50

slope is zero, therefore, we set Equation (2) equal to zero and solve
for Q:

$$\frac{c_H}{2} - \frac{c_P R}{Q_o^2} = 0$$

$$Q_o = \sqrt{2c_P R/c_H} \tag{3}$$

$\dfrac{CH}{2} = \dfrac{C_P R}{Q_o^2}$

$CH\,Q_o^2 = 2C_P R$

$Q_o = \sqrt{2C_P R / C_H}$ (3)

The cost of an optimal solution computed by Equation (3) may be
derived by substituting the value of Q_o in Equation (1):

$$TIC_o = \sqrt{2c_P c_H R} \tag{4}$$

The optimal number of orders or manufacturing runs per year N_o
and the time between orders or manufacturing runs t_o for an optimal
solution follows:

$$N_o = R/Q_o \tag{5}$$

$Q_o = \dfrac{R}{N_o}$

$$t_o = Q_o/R = 1/N_o \tag{6}$$

$t_o = \dfrac{Q_o}{N_o R}$

Equations (3), (4), (5), and (6) are the ones of possible value in
computations. If we substitute the values for R, c_H, and c_P used in
our specific example we obtain:

$$Q_o = \sqrt{\frac{2 \times 250 \times 10}{0.50}} = \sqrt{10,000} = 100 \text{ units}$$

$$TIC_o = \sqrt{2 \times 10 \times 0.50 \times 250} = \sqrt{2,500} = \$50$$

$$N_o = \frac{250}{100} = 2.5 \text{ orders per year}$$

$$t_o = \frac{1}{2.5} = 0.4 \text{ years between orders}$$

Some simple extensions of the classical inventory model are useful in relaxing some of the assumptions of the model. For example,
the classical model assumes that all demand is satisfied on time. We
can, however, allow back orders to occur through the provision for
shortage costs in the model. The classical model assumes price or
value to be fixed, whereas we know that quantity discounts are a
common practice. The assumption that the entire order is received in
inventory all at one time is often not appropriate, particularly in
production lots where the finished items may be placed in inventory
over a period of time as they are produced. We will discuss these
extensions in this chapter, as well as the removal of the assumption
of constant demand and lead time.

Shortage costs

If we relax the assumption that back orders are not allowed in the
classical model, we have the graphical structure of the model shown
in Figure 3–4. We wish to determine the best order quantity when
shortages, or back orders, are allowed at some definite cost c_S, in
dollars per unit per time unit short. Receipt of the order quantity
raises the inventory level to only I_{max} because the difference $Q - I_{max}$

Figure 3–4
Idealized structure of inventory levels with back orders of $Q - I_{max}$ allowed

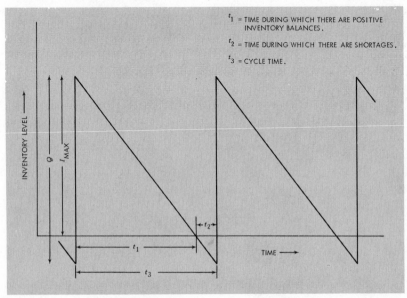

is assumed to meet the back orders instantaneously. We proceed as before to develop an equation for the total incremental cost of the system with components due to ordering, holding inventory, and shortages.

The cost per order is c_P as before. The average inventory cost during the period t_1 when there is an inventory balance is:

$$c_H \frac{I_{\max}}{2} t_1 = c_H \frac{I_{\max}^2}{2R}$$

since

$$t_1 = \frac{I_{\max}}{R}$$

where t_1 is the period during which there is a positive inventory balance. And the average shortage cost during t_2 is:

$$c_S \frac{Q - I_{\max}}{2} t_2 = c_S \frac{(Q - I_{\max})^2}{2R}$$

since

$$t_2 = \frac{Q - I_{\max}}{R}$$

where t_2 is the period during which there is a shortage. Therefore, the incremental cost for one cycle of length t_3 is:

$$c_P + c_H \frac{I_{\max}^2}{2R} + c_S \frac{(Q - I_{\max})^2}{2R} \tag{7}$$

The annual total incremental cost is then obtained by multiplying (7) by the number of orders placed per year, R/Q,

$$TIC = c_P \frac{R}{Q} + c_H \frac{I_{\max}^2}{2Q} + c_S \frac{(Q - I_{\max})^2}{2Q} \tag{8}$$

To obtain optimal values of Q and $I_{\max}$ we take partial derivatives of TIC in Equation (8) with respect to Q and $I_{\max}$, equate to zero, and obtain the following formulas:

$$Q_o = \sqrt{2c_P R/c_H} \sqrt{\frac{c_H + c_S}{c_S}} \tag{9}$$

$$I_{\max o} = \sqrt{2c_P R/c_H} \sqrt{\frac{c_S}{c_H + c_S}} \tag{10}$$

$$TIC_o = \sqrt{2c_H c_P R} \sqrt{\frac{c_S}{c_H + c_S}} \tag{11}$$

Equations (9), (10), and (11) may be used in computations. Note that the effect of including shortage costs is to increase Q_o since annual inventory holding costs are smaller due to the smaller average inventory, and TIC_o is smaller than for the classical model because both inventory holding costs and annual preparation costs are lower.

If we consider shortages in the previous numerical example used for the classical model, where $c_S = \$1$ and the other data remain the same, that is, $c_H = \$0.50$ per unit per year, $c_P = \$10$ per order and $R = 250$ units per year, then:

$$Q_o = 100\sqrt{\frac{0.50 + 1.00}{1.00}} = 122.5 \text{ units}$$

$$TIC_o = 50\sqrt{\frac{1.00}{0.50 + 1.00}} = \$40.83 \text{ per year}$$

and

$$I_{max} = 100\sqrt{\frac{1.00}{0.50 + 1.00}} = 81.65 \text{ units}$$

Note that if $c_S \to \infty$ the term $\sqrt{(c_H + c_S)/c_S}$ in Equation (9) becomes 1 and Equation (3) results, corresponding to a policy of no shortages permitted. If $c_S \to 0$ the term and Q_o become infinity, corresponding to a policy of infinite backordering.

Model for quantity discounts

It is common for suppliers to quote prices that vary with the quantity ordered. These price breaks will, of course, have an effect on the most economical lot quantity in many instances. The effect is directly in terms of differences in total purchase price, ordering costs, and in inventory holding costs. For simple one-price break situations the procedure might be as follows: (1) Compute the Q_o based on appropriate formulas, (2) if Q_o falls above the price break b, then Q_o is indeed the most economical quantity. (3) If Q_o is less than b, then a simple incremental cost study will determine if the savings in purchase and ordering costs overbalance the incremental inventory holding costs. For more complex discount schedules it may be of value to apply a formal decision model.

Decision models for price breaks. The classical inventory model assumes a constant price or value so that in order to develop a decision system which takes account of price breaks, we must modify the classical inventory model to include the price or value of the item as a variable. The total incremental cost equation becomes:

$$\frac{CPR}{Q^2} = \frac{KFH}{2} \qquad \frac{2CPR}{Q^2} = KFH \, Q^2$$

$$TIC = c_P \frac{R}{Q} + kR + k\frac{Q}{2}F_H \qquad (12)$$

where,

$$\frac{\partial\, TIC}{\partial Q} = -\frac{CPR}{Q^2} + \frac{KFH}{2}$$

k = Unit cost or price of item.
F_H = Inventory holding cost as a fraction of inventory value.

Following the previous procedure, Equation (12) is differentiated with respect to Q and the result set equal to zero. The following formulas for computation result:

$$Q_o = \sqrt{2c_P R/(kF_H)} \qquad (13)$$
$$TIC_o = \sqrt{2c_P kF_H R} + kR \qquad (14)$$

Equations (13) and (14) are then employed in a sequential decision system to determine the most economical quantity to produce when price breaks are involved.

The one-price break system is shown in the decision flowchart of Figure 3–5. Figure 3–5 shows the sequence of computations required to determine the Q_o with minimum effort. First, one computes q_{2o}

Figure 3–5
Decision flowchart for inventory model with a price break at the lot size b

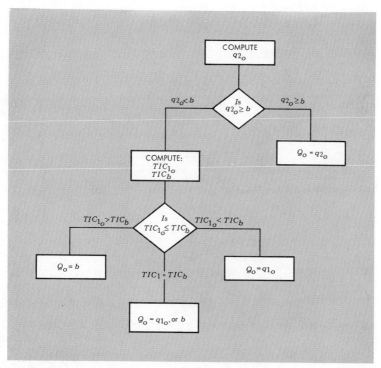

using Equation (13) for the price k_2 for quantities beyond the price break b. The decision will be made at that point if $q_{2o} \geq b$ because the total incremental cost curve for price k_2 will fall wholly below the curve for price k_1 and, if the minimum of the TIC_2 curve is beyond the price break b, then that minimum is the minimum for the price break inventory system. If a decision is not made at this point, however, that is, if $q_{2o} < b$, then we must follow the left branch of the flowchart and compute TIC_{1o} and TIC_b, the costs at the minimum of the k_1 price curve and at the point b on the k_2 price curve. Whichever TIC is smaller then determines the final decision.

Figures 3–6 and 3–7 are illustrative of the effect of changing the location of the price-break quantity in relation to the curve minima.

Figure 3–6
Total incremental cost curves (inventory model with one price break at $b = 250$ units, $R = 500$ units per year, $c_P = \$10$, $F_H = 20$ percent, $k_1 = \$1$, $k_2 = \$0.90$, $Q_o = b = 250$ units)

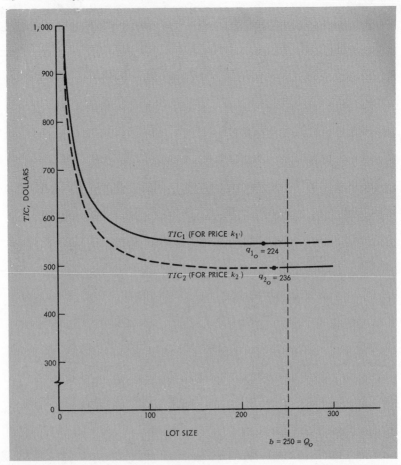

Figure 3–7
Total incremental cost curves (inventory model with one price break at $b = 1,500$ units. Other data same as in Figure 3–6. $Q_o = q_{1o} = 224$ units)

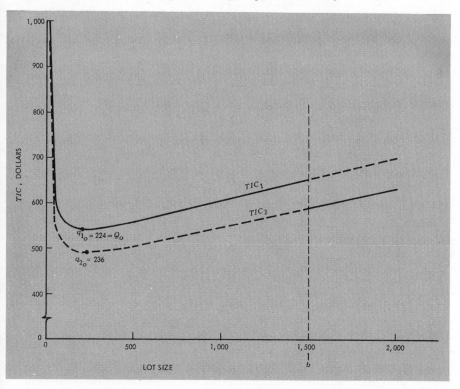

The basic data for both figures is the same. In Figure 3–8 the decision flowchart (as well as inspection of the graphs) would take us to the decision that $Q_o = b = 250$ units. When the price break is moved out to $b = 1,500$ units, however, q_{1o} becomes minimum for the system.

Where *multiple price breaks* are involved, the sequence of computations becomes more complex and a rigorous procedure more valuable. Figure 3–8 is a decision flowchart for a system with three price breaks. By making the computations in the sequence called for in the flowchart it may be possible to come to a decision with relatively few calculations. At least the calculations will be the minimum required for the particular situation.

Figure 3–8 can be used directly for one, two, or three price breaks by truncating the chart. Also, the basic pattern which the chart develops can be generalized, and the chart can easily be extended to a system of more than three price breaks.

Figure 3–8
Decision flowchart for inventory model (three price breaks at quantities b_1, b_2, and b_3)

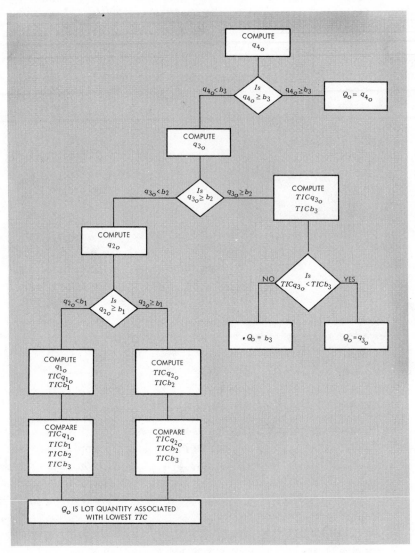

Lot sizes for production runs

The determination of production lot sizes follows the same general concepts as for purchase lot sizes. The preparation costs represent the costs to develop production plans for the item, write shop orders and perform other necessary paperwork, set up machines, and control the flow of the order through the manufacturing facility. If the manufacturing cycle is fairly long and the size or shape of the item such that parts are handled individually or in sublots rather than all in one lot, then the order may go into inventory in smaller quantities as production progresses rather than all at one time. The result is an inventory level pattern similar to that shown in Figure 3–9. If the production

Figure 3–9
Inventory model for production runs when the production lot is received in inventory over a period of time as production progresses

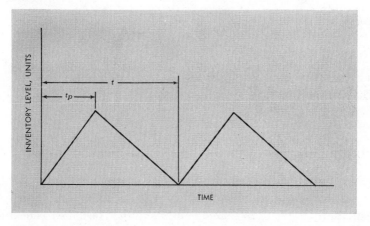

run time is roughly 30 to 60 percent of the total inventory cycle time, then the effect on average inventory levels is likely to be significant, and the inventory model should take account of the changed structure. Referring to Figure 3–9, if r is the daily requirement of usage rate and p is the daily production rate, then during the production period t_p inventory is accumulating at the rate of the difference between the production and requirements rate $p - r$. This assumes, of course, that $p > r$. Inventory will accumulate at this rate for the period t_p and the peak inventory is $t_p(p - r)$, and the average inventory is:

$$\frac{t_p(p - r)}{2} \tag{15}$$

Since Q units are produced in the lot at the daily rate of p for a period of t_p, $Q = pt_p$, and $t_p = Q/p$. Substituting for t_p, the average inventory of the system becomes:

$$\frac{(p - r)Q}{2p} = (1 - r/p)\frac{Q}{2}$$ \qquad (16)

We can now develop an equation for the total incremental costs of the production lot model. The preparation costs are defined as before and the average inventory cost is the product of c_H and the statement of average inventory in Equation (16), or

$$TIC = c_P\frac{R}{Q} + c_H(1 - r/p)\frac{Q}{2}$$ \qquad (17)

This equation for TIC is differentiated with respect to Q and the result set equal to zero. The following formulas can then be derived:

$$Q_o = \sqrt{\frac{2c_PR}{c_H(1 - r/p)}}$$ \qquad (18)

$$TIC_o = \sqrt{2c_Pc_HR(1 - r/p)}$$ \qquad (19)

For production lots it is common to think in terms of the cycling of items so that the optimal number of runs of lot size Q_o is $N_o = R/Q$ and the optimal time between runs is $t = Q/R = 1/N_o$.

Production runs for multiple products

It is not uncommon that the same equipment is used to fabricate or process a large number of different items on a cyclical basis. The availability of the time-shared equipment then becomes a constraint, and the independent determination of production cycles and lot sizes by Equation (18) is not applicable in most situations (unless a great deal of slack time exists).

To illustrate the possible difficulties, let us analyze the situation posed by the data of Table 3–2, which indicates annual requirements, production rates, and cost data for ten products to be manufactured on the same equipment. The requirement rates, production rates, inventory holding costs per unit, per unit time and machine setup costs vary considerably from product to product. On the surface it appears that the equipment has adequate capacity to process all ten products in the annual requirement amounts shown, since the total production days required of 232.3 is less than the normal capacity of 250 production days per year.

In Table 3–3 we compute the lot sizes independently based on the EOQ Equation (18). In Table 3–3 we also compute in column (5) the number of production days required to produce the lot size for each product, and the total of this column, 85.77 days, represents the

Table 3–2
Annual requirements, production rates, and cost data for ten products to be
manufactured on time-shared equipment (based on 250 days per year)

(1)	(2)	(3)	(4)	(5)	(6)	(7)
Product number	Annual requirements, units R_i	Average sales per production day, r_i	Production daily rate, p_i	Production days required	Annual inventory holding cost ($) per unit, c_{H_i}	Setup cost ($) per run, c_{P_i}
1	8,000	32	800	10.0	0.40	36
2	15,000	60	500	30.0	0.02	13
3	7,000	28	700	10.0	0.30	24
4	1,000	4	200	5.0	0.10	14
5	3,000	12	300	10.0	0.35	15
6	10,000	40	200	50.0	0.05	20
7	20,000	80	1,000	20.0	0.10	20
8	5,000	20	150	33.3	0.15	40
9	12,000	48	500	24.0	0.02	45
10	18,000	72	450	40.0	0.05	55
				232.3		$312

actual production cycle required if each product is produced once in
the amount of the computed Q_o. In column (7) of Table 3–3 we have
computed the number of production days required to use up the lot
sizes produced for each product at average demand rates, and we see
that there are five products (nos. 1, 3, 5, 6, and 7) where the lot size
produced is not large enough to last through one complete cycle at
average demand rates. This suggests that while the data of Table 3–2
seems to indicate that capacity is sufficient in an aggregate sense,
there will be conflicts in scheduling if we attempt to produce according to the lot sizes shown in Table 3–3.

What we must do then, is to develop a methodology where the
production runs (lot sizes) of all products are determined jointly so
that scheduling interference is taken into account. Conceptually, the
problem is parallel to the development of production runs for the
one-product case which yielded Equation (18). Now however, we
must determine a cycle length which will minimize total machine
setup costs plus inventory costs for the entire set of products, assuming that each product is produced just once each cycle.

The average inventory for each item is given by Equation (16) as
$(1 - r_i/p_i)(Q_i/2)$. Since $Q_i = R_i/n$, the average annual inventory cost
for an item is:

Table 3–3
Lot sizes determined independently, estimate of production cycle, adequacy of inventory to cover usage during the cycle, and total incremental costs

(1) Product number	(2) Q_{o_i} Computed by Equation (18)	(3) $N_{o_i} = R_i Q_{o_i}$	(4) p_i from Table 3–2	(5) Days required to produce $Q_{o_i}/P_i =$ col. (2)/ col. (4)	(6) r_i from Table 3–2	(7) Days to use up Q_{o_i} at average demand rates, $Q_{o_i}/r_i =$ col. (2)/ col. (6)	(8) TIC_{o_i} Computed from Equation (19)
1	1,225	6.53	800	1.53	32	38.3*	$ 470
2	8,561	1.75†	500	17.12	60	142.7	151
3	1,080	6.48	700	1.54	28	38.6*	311
4	535	1.87†	200	2.67	4	133.6	52
5	518	5.80	300	1.73	12	43.1*	174
6	3,162	3.16	200	15.81	40	79.1*	126
7	2,949	6.78	1,000	2.95	80	36.9*	271
8	1,754	2.85	150	11.70	20	87.7	228
9	7,729	1.55†	500	15.46	48	161.0	140
10	6,866	2.62	450	15.26	72	95.4	288
				85.77			$2,211

* Items where inventory would be used up before end of 85.77-day cycle.
† Candidate for occasional runs.

$$\frac{c_{H_i}R_i}{2n}(1 - r_i/p_i)$$

The annual inventory cost for the entire set of m products is the sum of m such expressions, or:

$$\frac{1}{2n}\sum_{i=1}^{m}c_{H_i}R_i(1 - r_i/p_i)$$

where n is the common number of runs.

The machine setup costs for a given item are c_{P_i} in dollars per production run. The total setup cost per year is nc_{P_i} and the total annual setup cost for m products is

$$n\sum_{i=1}^{m}c_{P_i}$$

The total incremental cost for m products is then the sum of annual machine setup costs and annual inventory holding costs, or:

$$TIC = n\sum_{i=1}^{m}c_{P_i} + \frac{1}{2n}\sum_{i=1}^{m}c_{H_i}R(1 - r_i/p_i)$$

The minimum of the total incremental cost curve with respect to n, the number of production runs, is determined as before, and the following equations result:

$$N_o = \sqrt{\frac{\sum_{i=1}^{m}c_{H_i}R_i(1 - r_i/p_i)}{2\sum_{i=1}^{m}c_{P_i}}} \qquad (20)$$

and

$$Q_i = \frac{R_i}{N_o}$$

The total cost of an optimal solution is determined by substituting the expression for N_o for n in the equation for TIC. Simplification leads to:

$$TIC_o = \sqrt{2\sum_{i=1}^{m}c_{P_i}\sum_{i=1}^{m}c_{H_i}R_i(1 - r_i/p_i)} \qquad (21)$$

The joint determination of the product cycle using Equation (20) is developed in Table 3–4, yielding $N_o = 4$ cycles per year. This means

Table 3–4
Joint determination of production cycle for 10 products from Equation (20)

(1) Product number	(2) Ratio r_i/p_i col. (3)/ col. (4) from Table 3–2	(3) $(1 - r_i/p_i)$	(4) $c_{H_i}R_i =$ col. (2) × col. (6) from Table 3–2	(5) $(1 - r_i/p_i) \times$ $c_{H_i}R_i =$ col. (3) × col. (4)	(6) c_p from col. (7) Table 3–2
1	0.040	0.960	3,200	3,072.0	$ 36
2	0.120	0.880	300	264.0	43
3	0.040	0.960	2,100	2,016.0	24
4	0.020	0.980	100	98.0	14
5	0.040	0.960	1,050	1,008.0	15
6	0.200	0.800	500	400.0	20
7	0.080	0.920	2,000	1,840.0	20
8	0.133	0.867	750	650.0	40
9	0.096	0.904	240	217.0	45
10	0.160	0.840	900	756.0	55
				10,321.0	$312

$$N_o = \sqrt{\frac{10,321}{2 \times 312}} = 4.07 \approx 4$$

$$TIC_o = \sqrt{2 \times 312 \times 10,321} = \$2,538$$

Table 3–5
Lot sizes determined jointly (determination of actual production cycle and adequacy of inventory to cover usage during the cycle)

(1) Product number	(2) Lot size based on joint determination of cycle, $Q_i = R_i/N_o$	(3) p_i from Table 3–2	(4) Days required to produce $Q_i/p_i =$ col. (2)/ col. (3)	(5) r_i from Table 3–2	(6) Days required to use up Q_i at average demand rates = $Q_i/r_i =$ col. (2)/ col. (5)
1	2,000	800	2.50	32	62.5
2	3,750	500	7.50	60	62.5
3	1,750	700	2.50	28	62.5
4	250	200	1.25	4	62.5
5	750	300	2.50	12	62.5
6	2,500	200	12.50	40	62.5
7	5,000	1,000	5.00	80	62.5
8	1,250	150	8.33	20	62.5
9	3,000	500	6.00	48	62.5
10	4,500	450	10.00	72	62.5
			58.08		

that each of the ten products would be produced four times each year in lot sizes equal to one fourth of the annual requirement. In Table 3–5 we develop calculations to show that $N_o = 4$ is feasible. The production days required to produce Q_i is shown in column (4) of Table 3–5 to be 58.08 days. In column (6) of Table 3–5 we see that each lot produced provides three months' supply (62.5 production days), so that the joint cycle accommodates all products.

The total incremental cost of the joint cycling plan is $2,538 as compared with $2,211 if lot quantities and cycles are set independently. The additional cost of $327 is due largely to a higher average inventory requirement, but the joint cycle plan is feasible. In some instances the joint plan reduces the lot size considerably. This is particularly true of products 2, 4, and 9.

Magee and Boodman [12] state a rule of thumb that if "the minimum-cost number of runs for the product alone, for any one or more products is less than half the value for all products, the product is a possible candidate for only occasional runs." In our example $N_o = 4$, and we see in column (3) of Table 3–3 that products 2, 4, and 9 have a number of runs less than $N/2$. Therefore, they might be run independently outside the normal cycle.

DETERMINING BUFFER STOCKS

One of the important components of system inventories is a buffer or safety stock to absorb variations in demand and/or variations in supply lead time. If either or both demand and supply lead time are greater than the constant values indicated in the classical inventory model, we will run out of stock. If the classical lot size structure is superimposed on a planned buffer stock, however, as shown in Figure 3–10, we can reduce the risk of stockout. A *stockout* is here defined as the occurrence of zero inventory level in any order period, and *stockout percentage* as the percent of order periods in which a stockout occurs. Other definitions are used, such as percentage of days out of stock and percentage of units short in relation to demand.

Obviously, the larger the buffer stock the smaller will be the risk of running out of stock. Our problem is to determine concepts and methods which will allow us to set buffer stocks at reasonable levels such that the risk of stockout is acceptable. Better still, we would like to set buffer stock levels such that their cost balances the expected cost of stockout. Thus, an optimum buffer stock level would be one which minimizes combined expected inventory plus stockout cost.

Figure 3–10
Idealized structure of inventory levels in relation to time

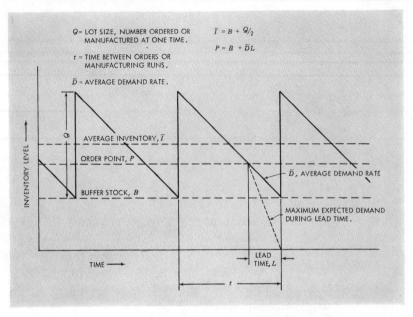

Though it is not difficult to develop a model for buffer stock based on this concept of balancing inventory and stockout cost, more often than not it is difficult or impossible for management to isolate a realistic stockout cost. The result is the common managerial practice of setting a service level which guarantees that average stockouts will not exceed some predetermined level. Therefore, if management states a policy of wishing to maintain a 90 or 95 percent average service level, then some of the procedures which we will discuss can be used to design systems to meet that objective.

In the second cycle diagrammed in Figure 3–11 we have shown that a buffer stock is simply the difference between the number of units used at maximum demand rates, D_{max}, and average demand $\bar{D}$, during the constant lead time L. Since we are now considering demand to be variable, Figure 3–11 is a better representation of the fluctuation of inventory levels. The buffer stock B is then defined as:

$$B = D_{max} - \bar{D} \tag{22}$$

We can see from Equation (1) that B will depend on how we define D_{max} and on the nature of the distribution of the demand function.

Figure 3–11
Structure of inventory levels in a fixed order quantity system when demand
varies

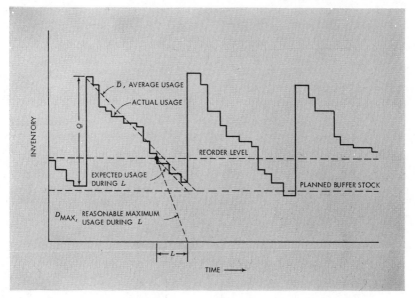

If L is also variable we have additional complications, so we will
discuss first the special case where L is constant.

Buffer stocks for constant lead times.   First, let us examine any
demand frequency distribution, such as that shown in Figure 3–12.
Figure 3–12 represents only the *random variations* in demand for the
item. If there were trends, seasonals, or cycles to contend with, we
assume that these effects have been removed by standard statistical
techniques. We see for this example that weekly demand has been as
low as 10, as high as 110, and has averaged nearly 55 for the 63
weeks recorded in the sample. We would expect demand *during the
lead time* to be 55 units per week, but from the frequency distribution
we can see that a demand of 110 units per week is possible and
actually occurred during one week. Since lead time is one week, then
a buffer stock which would protect us from stockout would be $D_{\max}$
$- \bar{D} = 110 - 55 = 55$ units. But $D_{\max} = 110$ units is actually quite
unlikely, since it occurred in only one week during the 63-week
sample, or approximately 1.6 percent of the time. We must decide
whether or not we are willing to maintain a buffer stock level so high
that based on the sample distribution, we would never run out of

Figure 3–12
Frequency distribution showing random variation of demand during the
lead time of $L = 1$ week

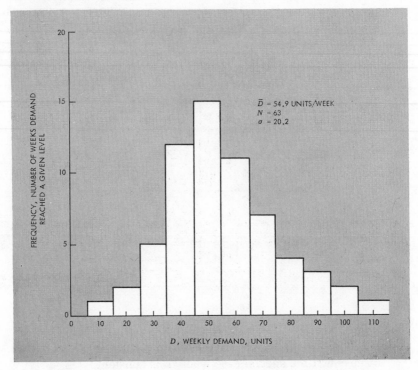

stock. If we maintained a level of $B = 55$ units, we would always at
least meet the needs of the maximum demand recorded in our 63-
week sample. Since the probability of even $D = 110$ units per week is
small, let us examine the effects on buffer stocks of some more reasonable definitions of maximum demand, perhaps a 5 percent risk of
running out of stock.

Figure 3–13 is helpful in examining the effects of various risk
levels for stockouts. Figure 3–13 was constructed from Figure 3–12
by tabulating the number of weeks demand actually exceeded each
of the discrete levels given. The scale of the vertical axis was then
converted to a percentage scale in order to read off risk levels conveniently. Since our data are discrete, we will read off the closest value
of demand associated with given risk levels. We see that if we defined
$D_{\max}$ as 90 units per week, we run the risk of stockouts in about three
weeks in 63, or about 5 percent of the time. A 10 percent risk is
associated with a $D_{\max}$ of about 80 units per week. A 15 percent risk is

Figure 3–13
Distribution of percent of weeks demand exceeded a given level (developed
from Figure 3–12)

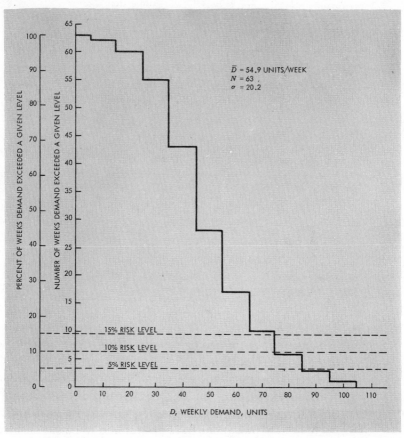

associated with a D_{max} of about 70 units per week. The buffer stocks
required for each of these levels is shown in Table 3–6. We can see
from Table 3–6 that it requires progressively larger buffer stocks to
achieve lower risk levels. The cost of providing progressively higher
service levels (lower risk levels) increases disproportionately, as is
shown in Table 3–7 where we have assigned a value of $100 to the
item and assumed an inventory holding cost of 20 percent of inventory value. The 100 percent service level is, of course, defined only for
the sample distribution based on 63 weeks' experience. The actual
parent distribution would assign a measureable probability for demand above 110 units per week. In fact, the normal, Poisson, and
negative exponential distributions commonly used in inventory

Table 3–6
Buffer stocks required for four risk levels of stockout

Approximate risk level, in percent	Definition of D_{max} associated with risk level, units/week	Buffer stock required $(D_{max} - \bar{D})$
0	110	55
5	90	35
10	80	25
15	70	15

Table 3–7
Cost of providing four levels of service (when the items are valued at $100 each and inventory holding cost is 20 percent)

	Service level			
	85 percent	90 percent	95 percent	100 percent
Reasonable maximum usage......	70	80	90	110
Buffer stock required (from Table 3–6)	15	25	35	55
Value of buffer stock............	$1,500	$2,500	$3,500	$5,500
Inventory cost at 20 percent	$ 300	$ 500	$ 700	$1,100

models have no upper bound so that providing a 100 percent service level theoretically would require an infinitely large buffer stock.

Buffer stock computations are considerably simplified if we are able to justify the assumption that the demand distribution follows some definite mathematical function. The normal, Poisson, and negative exponential distributions have been found to be of considerable value in representing demand functions for inventory management. The general procedure for determining buffer stock levels is similar for all three distributions. The procedure is as follows: (1) Determine whether the normal, Poisson, or negative exponential distribution approximately describes demand during lead time for the case under consideration. This determination is, of course, critically important, involving well-known statistical methodology. (2) Set a service level based on managerial policy or an assessment of the balance of incremental inventory and stockout cost. (3) Using the service level, define D_{max} during lead time in terms of normal, Poisson, or negative exponential demand. (4) Compute the required buffer stock from $B = D_{max} - \bar{D}$, where both D_{max} and $\bar{D}$ are based on a demand distribution over the constant lead time L.

The normal distribution has been found to describe many demand functions adequately, particularly at the factory level of the supply-production-distribution system [4]. Given the assumption of normality and a service level of perhaps 95 percent, we can determine D_{max} by reference to normal distribution tables, a small part of which has been reproduced in Table 3–8. We must know the mean demand

Table 3–8
Area under the right tail of the normal distribution
(showing the probability that demand exceeds $\bar{D} + n\sigma_D$ for selected values of n)

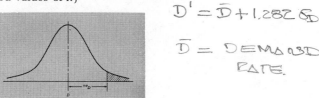

$$D' = \bar{D} + 1.282\, \sigma_D$$

$$\bar{D} = \text{DEMAND RATE}$$

$$\sigma = \sqrt{\bar{D}}$$

D'	Probability
$\bar{D} + 3.090\sigma_D$	0.001
$\bar{D} + 2.576\sigma_D$	0.005
$\bar{D} + 2.326\sigma_D$	0.010
$\bar{D} + 1.960\sigma_D$	0.025
$\bar{D} + 1.645\sigma_D$	0.050
$\bar{D} + 1.282\sigma_D$	0.100
$\bar{D} + 1.036\sigma_D$	0.150
$\bar{D} + 0.842\sigma_D$	0.200
$\bar{D} + 0.674\sigma_D$	0.250
$\bar{D} + 0.524\sigma_D$	0.300
$\bar{D} + 0.385\sigma_D$	0.350
$\bar{D} + 0.253\sigma_D$	0.400
$\bar{D} + 0.126\sigma_D$	0.450
$\bar{D}$	0.500

$\bar{D}$, and the standard deviation σ_D, to completely describe a normal distribution of demand. A service level of 95 percent means that we are willing to accept a 5 percent risk of running out of stock. From Table 3–8 demand exceeds $\bar{D} + n\sigma_D$ by 0.05, or 5 percent when $n = 1.645$. To implement the 95 percent service level, then, we must know $\bar{D}$ and σ_D for the normal distribution. For example, if Figure 3–12 is described by a normal distribution, then $D_{max} = 54.9 + 1.645 \times 20.2 = 88.13$ units per week, and $B = 88 - 55 = 33$ units if $L = $ one week. Obviously, any other service level policy could be implemented in a similar way.

The Poisson distribution has been found to describe retail sales in many situations [4]. Buffer stock determination on the basis of the Poisson distribution is very simple because of the ease of calculating the standard deviation ($\sigma_D = \sqrt{\bar{D}}$). Where the Poisson distribution is applicable, then a knowledge of the average demand, $\bar{D}$, is sufficient to completely describe the demand distribution. Table 3–9 shows data on the right tail of the Poisson distribution for selected values of

Table 3–9
Area under the right tail of the Poisson distribution (showing the probability that demand exceeds a given value D' for selected values of average demand, $\bar{D}$)

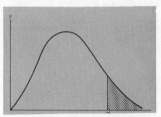

D', demand greater than	$\bar{D}$, average demand									
	2	4	6	8	10	12	14	16	18	20
2	0.323									
3	0.143									
4	0.053									
5	0.017	0.215								
6	0.005	0.111								
7	0.001	0.051	0.256							
8		0.021	0.153							
9		0.008	0.084	0.283						
10		0.003	0.043	0.184						
11		0.001	0.020	0.112						
12			0.009	0.064	0.208					
13			0.004	0.034	0.136					
14			0.001	0.017	0.083	0.228				
15				0.008	0.049	0.156				
16				0.004	0.023	0.101	0.244			
17				0.002	0.014	0.063	0.173			
18				0.001	0.007	0.037	0.118	0.258		
19					0.003	0.021	0.077	0.188		
20					0.002	0.012	0.048	0.123	0.269	
21					0.001	0.006	0.029	0.089	0.201	
22						0.003	0.017	0.058	0.145	0.279
23						0.001	0.009	0.037	0.101	0.213
24							0.005	0.022	0.068	0.157
25							0.003	0.012	0.045	0.113
26							0.001	0.007	0.028	0.078
27								0.004	0.017	0.052
28								0.002	0.010	0.034
29								0.001	0.006	0.022
30									0.003	0.013
31									0.002	0.008
32									0.001	0.005
33										0.003
34										0.001

Handwritten annotations:

$\bar{D} = 2$

RISK $= .05$

$D_{MAX} \approx 4$

$B = D_{MAX} - \bar{D}$

$B = 4 - 2 = 2$

$B = 2$

$\bar{D}$ up to $\bar{D} = 20$, since the Poisson distribution is not commonly applicable to distributions with mean values above 20. Since the risk levels vary slightly for a given multiple of σ_D for different values of $\bar{D}$ in the Poisson distribution, the most satisfactory way of maintaining a preset risk level is simply by reference to the Poisson tables. For example, if average demand is $\bar{D} = 2$ per week, and we wish to hold the risk of stockout to about 5 percent, then from Table 3–9, $D_{\max} \approx 4$ per week and $B = 4 - 2 = 2$ units if L is one week. Similarly, if $\bar{D} = 14$ units per month, then from Table 3–9 $D_{\max} \approx 20$ units per month if we wish to maintain a 5 percent risk level and $B = 20 - 14 = 6$ units if L is one month.

The *negative exponential distribution* has found application in inventory management as a good approximation to demand in some retail and wholesale situations [4]. As with the Poisson distribution, the negative exponential distribution is completely defined by a knowledge of its mean value, since the standard deviation is equal to the mean. Table 3–10 shows data on the unitized negative exponen-

Table 3–10
Unit negative exponential distribution of demand $\bar{D} = 1$, $\sigma_D = 1$ (values indicate the probability that given demands will be exceeded)

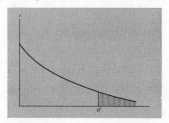

Unitized demand, $D/\bar{D}$	Probability that demand exceeds D'	Unitized demand, $D/\bar{D}$	Probability that demand exceeds D'
0.00	1.000	1.50	0.223
0.50	0.951	2.00	0.135
0.10	0.905	2.50	0.082
0.15	0.861	3.00	0.050
0.20	0.819	3.50	0.030
0.25	0.779	4.00	0.018
0.50	0.607	4.50	0.011
0.75	0.472	5.00	0.007
1.00	0.368	6.00	0.002

tial distribution which is useful in implementing a given risk level. Since $\sigma_D = \bar{D}$, then $\bar{D} + n\sigma_D$ can be stated as simply $(n + 1) \bar{D}$. Thus from Table 3–10 a 13.5 percent risk level is associated with $2 \bar{D}$, a 5 percent risk level with $3 \bar{D}$ and a 1.8 percent risk level with $4 \bar{D}$.

As a specific example, let $\bar{D} = 10$ units per week, given a negative exponential distribution. Then, in order to hold the risk of stockout to 5 percent, $D_{max} = 3\bar{D} = 30$ units per week, and $B = 30 - 10 = 20$ units.

Relation of buffer stocks to average demand. Our discussion of buffer stocks should make it possible to appraise the common business and industrial decision rule for setting buffer stocks as a given number of days' or weeks' supply. This decision rule sets buffer stock as some proportion of average demand. We can see easily, however, that buffer stocks by our methodology might vary as the square root of average demand since:

$$B = D_{max} - \bar{D} = n\sigma_D \tag{23}$$

since

$$D_{max} = \bar{D} + n\sigma_D$$

If a distribution of demand follows either the normal or Poisson distributions then buffer stocks are proportional to the square root of demand since the computation of σ_D in both cases involves the square root of $\bar{D}$. Thus, if $\bar{D}$ increases or decreases, reserve stocks should not change in direct proportion. There is an economy of scale involved and a larger demand can be accommodated by a less than proportional buffer stock. Following the common practice of holding a given "time supply" as a buffer is not only an expensive buffer stock policy but in addition contributes to the instability of a multistage production-inventory system. Such a policy increases buffer stocks too much for a given increase in demand (or decreases them too much for a decrease in demand) because a change in demand requires that we not only respond to the real demand change but to a partially illusory need to alter buffer stocks.

Of course, if demand follows the negative exponential distribution then $\sigma_D = \bar{D}$ and the time supply rule for buffer stocks is valid if properly determined. This rule would be simple and appropriate for use in many wholesale and retail inventory situations. Thus, if a 95 percent service level were appropriate and $\bar{D} = 5$ units per week ($L = 1$ week), from Table 3–10, $D_{max} = 15$ units and $B = 10$ units, or two weeks' supply. If $\bar{D}$ doubled to 10 units per week then the appropriate buffer stock is 20 units which is also two weeks' supply at the new demand rate.

Buffer stocks for variable lead times. When both demand and lead time are variable, the problem of determining buffer stocks becomes somewhat more complex. With constant lead times, the relationship between stockouts and buffer stock was simple and direct. When lead times are also variable, we are faced with an interaction between fluctuating demand and fluctuating lead times similar to the structure of the graphical model shown in Figure 3–14. Nevertheless,

Figure 3–14
Structure of inventory balance when both demand and lead times vary and the quantity Q ordered when inventory falls to the reorder point P

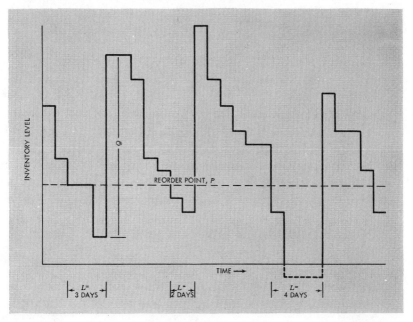

buffer stocks may be determined by a Monte Carlo simulation. To carry out such a simulation we need data on both the demand and lead time distributions. With this distribution data, we can simulate demand during lead time and finally develop buffer stock requirements for various risk levels of stockout. As previously, then, we can implement whatever risk level we choose by selecting the corresponding buffer stock.

An example.[1]   Let us illustrate the methodology with an example that is simple enough that we can see how to compute a resulting probability distribution of demand during lead time from the two

---

[1]For a complete description including programming details, see C. McMillan and R. F. Gonzalez, *Systems Analysis: A Computer Approach to Decision Models*, rev. ed. (Homewood, Ill.: Richard D. Irwin, Inc., 1968).

Table 3–11
Distribution of demand for an
electronics component

Table 3–12
Distribution of supply lead
time for an electronics
component

Daily demand	Probability
0	0.40
1	0.30
2	0.20
3	0.10
	1.00

Days lead time	Probability
1	0.25
2	0.50
3	0.25
	1.00

independent distributions of demand and lead time. Let us assume from past known data the demand and lead time distributions for an electronics component as shown in Tables 3–11 and 3–12.

From Tables 3–11 and 3–12 we need to construct a joint probability distribution of demand during lead time. From the tables we can see that demand during lead time could be as high as nine (a demand of three units on each of the three days of a total lead time of three days) or as low as zero. The probability that a demand during lead time of nine units will occur is easily computed as the joint probability that lead time will be three days and that a demand of three units per day for three successive days will occur. From Table 3–12 the probability of a three-day lead time is 0.25, and from Table 3–11 the probability that a demand of three units per day will occur for three successive days is $0.10 \times 0.10 \times 0.10$. Then the joint probability of a nine-unit demand during lead time is $0.25 \times 0.10 \times 0.10 \times 0.10 = 0.00025$.

Similarly, we can compute the probability of an eight-unit demand during lead time as shown in Table 3–13. By examining Tables 3–11 and 3–12, we can see that the only way we can accumulate an eight-unit demand during lead time is with a three-day lead time. Table 3–13 shows, then, the computations for the three possible combinations of demand with a three-day lead time that will produce a demand during lead time of eight units.

We could, of course, proceed in this way to develop the entire table of the distribution of demand during lead time, but the enumeration approach is quite laborious, particularly for more extensive distributions of demand and lead time. A simpler way would be to develop the distribution of demand during lead time through Monte Carlo sampling from the two distributions of Tables 3–11 and 3–12. A

Table 3–13
Computation of the probability of the demand of eight units during lead
time for an electronics component

Ways in which demand for eight might occur	*Probability of the joint event*
1. First day, 3 demanded Second day, 3 demanded $\Big\}$ .... Third day, 2 demanded	$(0.25 \times 0.10 \times 0.10 \times 0.20) = 0.0005$
2. First day, 3 demanded Second day, 2 demanded $\Big\}$ .... Third day, 3 demanded	$(0.25 \times 0.10 \times 0.20 \times 0.10) = 0.0005$
3. First day, 2 demanded Second day, 3 demanded $\Big\}$ .... Third day, 3 demanded	$(0.25 \times 0.20 \times 0.10 \times 0.10) = 0.0005$
Total	0.0015

Monte Carlo sampling to develop the distribution of demand during
lead time has been done for this example by McMillan and Gonzalez
[13] and Table 3–14 is the result.

Table 3–14
Distribution of demand during lead time developed by
Monte Carlo sampling (for an electronics component.
$\bar{D}$ = 2 units)

Possible demand, units	*Probability*	*Cumulative probability**
0.............................	0.1960	0.8040
1.............................	0.2310	0.5730
2.............................	0.2260	0.3470
3.............................	0.1797	0.1673
4.............................	0.0935	0.0738
5.............................	0.0477	0.0261
6.............................	0.0190	0.0071
7.............................	0.0053	0.0018
8.............................	0.0015	0.0003
9.............................	0.0003	0.0000

* Probability that demand will exceed levels given.

Table 3–14 gives us directly the data we need to set buffer stocks.
The average demand during lead time from Table 3–14 is $\bar{D} = 2$
units. Reasonable maximum demand can now also be defined depending on desired risk levels. Table 3–15 shows buffer stock requirements for four possible definitions of D_{max} and the associated
risk levels. Where D_{max} is defined as reasonable maximum demand
during lead time as we have used it, it is, of course, the reorder point
P.

Table 3–15
Buffer stocks and risks levels for four
possible definitions of $D_{\max}$, (based on data
from Table 3–14)

D_{max}, units	Buffer stock, units $B = D_{max} - \bar{D}$	Risk of stockout
3	1	16.7%
4	2	7.4
5	3	2.6
6	4	0.7

One might well question the use of the foregoing simulation methodology for determining buffer stock as a managerial technique. Is it feasible for a system involving large numbers of items? The use of the technique would be feasible only with automatic data processing systems where buffer stock computations could be incorporated as a subroutine. If average demand changes, the subroutine could be called to compute a new reorder point P based on a newly generated distribution of demand during lead time and established risk levels for stockout. A classification of suppliers and/or items into categories of constant and variable lead time based on some arbitrary cutoff on the coefficient of variation of lead time would reduce considerably the volume of items for which the more time-consuming buffer stock computations would be required.

Service levels

Recall from Equation (2) that buffer stock requirements may be expressed as $B = n\,\sigma_D$, where n is a safety factor. For a given value of n and a specified distribution, we can state the service level, or conversely, the chance that a stockout will occur. For example, if $n = 1.282$ in a normal distribution and the service level is 90 percent, the chance of a stockout is 10 percent, from Table 3–8. There is one chance in ten that demand during lead time will exceed the buffer stock on any of the occasions of exposure to risk, but this does not mean that 10 percent of the demand is unsatisfied. It does mean that demand during lead time will be expected to exceed buffer stock for 10 percent of the orders. Stated differently, the chance that demand will exceed the buffer stock for any given order is 10 percent. A question of considerable interest then is, "if demand during lead time exceeds the buffer stock, what is the probable amount of the shortage?" There is also an interaction with order size, or conversely, the number of orders per year. If we ordered 10 times per year, we would expect some shortages to occur an average of once per year. However, if we ordered in lots of $2Q$ (five times per year), we would expect some shortages to occur an average of only once every other year. Larger orders definitely provide less exposure to risk, and as we shall see, they result in a smaller average annual quantity short, even though service levels as we have defined them, remain the same.

Expected quantity short. Given the occurrence of a shortage then, we may be short 1, 2, 3, . . . k units. For a given safety factor and distribution of demand during lead time, we can determine the average quantity of shortages to expect. Let us assume a normal distribution with average demand during lead time of $\bar{D} = 25$ and $\sigma_D = 5$. Following the methods of Brown [3, pp. 88–94] let us compute the expected quantity short for service levels of approximately 90 and 95 percent. From Table 3–8 the safety factors are $n_1 = 1.282$ and $n_2 = 1.645$, respectively. Then, $B_1 = 1.282 \times 5 = 6.410$, or approximately 6 units, and $B_2 = 1.645 \times 5 = 8.225$ or 8 units. These values of B approximate the stated service levels giving service slightly below the stated nominal levels.

If actual demand during lead time were $25 + 6 = 31$ units, then we have 0 units short for the 90 percent service level policy. The exact chance of exceeding a demand of 31 units is 0.1151 from normal tables (convert to normalized demand in standard deviation units, $(31 - 25)/5 = 1.20$, and look up associated probability). The chance of exceeding a demand of 32 units is 0.0808. Therefore, the chance of a demand of exactly 31 units (no shortage) is the difference, $0.1151 - 0.0808 = 0.0343$. Table 3–16 shows calculations of this type for the two service levels from which we compute the expected quantity short for both policies. The expected quantity short is the sum of the products of the number short times the probability of exactly the associated demand occuring. These sums are shown at the bottom of Table 3–16. The series was cut off at a demand of 42 units since the additional contribution to the expected short figure is extremely small beyond that demand level.

Now, let us examine the significance of the figures we have computed for the two policies in terms of their impact on actual service. Suppose that annual supply for the example item was in 10 orders of 50 units per order. Under a 90 percent policy we expect shortages to occur in one of these order cycles during the year as noted previously. Another view of the service policy, however, is

Table 3–16
Calculation of expected quantity short for two service levels (average demand during lead time = 25 units, standard deviation = 5 units, normal distribution)

(1) Demand	(2) Normalized demand	(3) Chance of exceeding	(4) Chance of equaling	(5) Quantity short (90% policy)	(6) Col. (4) × col. (5)	(7) Quantity short (95% policy)	(8) Col. (4) × col. (7)
31	1.2	0.1151	0.0343	0	0	—	—
32	1.4	0.0808	0.0260	1	0.0260		
33	1.6	0.0548	0.0189	2	0.0378	0	0
34	1.8	0.0359	0.0131	3	0.0393	1	0.0131
35	2.0	0.0228	0.0089	4	0.0356	2	0.0178
36	2.2	0.0139	0.0057	5	0.0285	3	0.0171
37	2.4	0.0082	0.0035	6	0.0210	4	0.0140
38	2.6	0.0047	0.0021	7	0.0147	5	0.0105
39	2.8	0.0026	0.0012	8	0.0096	6	0.0072
40	3.0	0.0014	0.0007	9	0.0063	7	0.0049
41	3.2	0.0007	0.0004	10	0.0040	8	0.0032
42	3.4	0.0003	0.0001	11	0.0011	9	0.0009
Expected quantity short per order:					0.2239		0.0887

given by the expected quantity short calculated in Table 3–16. The expected quantity short per order is 0.224 units, or for the year, $10 \times 0.224 = 2.24$ units short. Thus, the service offered under the 90 percent policy in terms of the percent of units short is $2.24/(10 \times 50) = 0.45$ percent, not 10 percent. Similarly, the 95 percent policy has service of only 0.18 percent units short. If the order quantities were doubled to 100 units per order, only five orders per year are required and the annual units short as well as the percentages are cut in half. Thus, while the general service policy may seem relatively loose at the 90 percent level, it holds fairly tight control in terms of the actual number of units short.

Cost effects. Now let us illustrate the possible range of economic effects where we are able to place dollar values on inventory connected costs. Filling in additional data concerning the example with which we have been dealing, let us assume that $c_P = \$25$, $c_H = \$10$, $c_S = \$20$ per unit short, and $Q = 50$ units. We show comparative incremental costs in Table 3–17 for the two service policies and the two order quantities discussed. For the particular situation described by the example, the 95 percent service policy with $Q = 50$ units has the lowest combination of costs.

Table 3–17
Comparative incremental costs for two service policies and two order quantities (R = 500 units per year, c_H = \$10 per unit per year, c_P = \$25 per order, c_S = \$20 per unit short)

	Service policy = 90%		Service policy = 95%	
Incremental costs	$Q = 50$	$Q = 100$	$Q = 50$	$Q = 100$
Cycle inventory:				
Holding costs*	$250.00	$500.00	$250.00	$500.00
Ordering costs†	250.00	125.00	250.00	125.00
Buffer inventory costs‡	60.00	60.00	80.00	80.00
Shortage costs§	44.78	22.39	17.74	8.87
Total..................	$604.78	$707.39	$597.74	$713.87

    * $(Q/2) \times 10$.
    † $(500/Q) \times 25$.
    ‡ $(B) \times 10$.
    § (Expected annual shortages) $\times$ 20 = (Expected short per order) $\times$ (Number of orders per year) $\times$ 20.

Brown [2] has shown that the expected quantity short is the product $\sigma_D E(k)$ where $E(k)$ is the partial expectation for a distribution with unit standard deviation. The partial expectation is the expected value of occurrences (demands) beyond some specified value. He has

Figure 3–15
Graph for determining the expected quantity short
per order, given the safety factor n

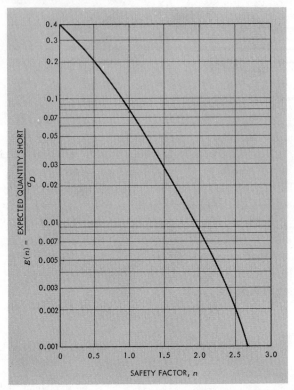

Source: From R. G. Brown, *Statistical Forecasting for Inventory Control,* used by permission of McGraw-Hill Book Co., 1959, Figure 4.1, p. 109.

developed tables and graphs of partial expectations [1, 3] for the normal distribution which are reproduced in Figure 3–15. Rough estimates of the expected quantity short can be obtained from Figure 3–15 for a given safety factor which in turn is associated with a given service level. Table 3–18 gives more precise values for certain points on this graph. Using the previous example for a 90 percent service policy, the safety factor is 1.282. Reading approximately from the graph, $E(k) = 0.046$ (or interpolating in the tables of [1], 0.047300), and for the example computed in Table 3–16 with $\sigma_D = 5$, we obtain an estimate of the expected quantity short per order of $5 \times 0.046 = 0.230$ units which compares closely with value of 0.2239 computed in Table 3–16. Note that we should expect the

Table 3–18
Expected quantity short per order for values of
the safety factor n, corresponding to the selected
points on the graph in Figure 3–14

Safety factor, n	Service level, percent	$E(k)$, expected quantity short/σ_D
3.090	99.9	0.00028
2.576	99.5	0.00158
2.236	99.0	0.00441
1.960	97.5	0.00945
1.645	95.0	0.02089
1.282	90.0	0.04730
1.036	85.0	0.07776
0.842	80.0	0.11156
0.674	75.0	0.14928
0.524	70.0	0.19050
0.385	65.0	0.23565
0.253	60.0	0.28515
0.126	55.0	0.33911
0.0	50.0	0.39894

value computed in Table 3–16 to understate the true value since we
cut off calculations at a demand of 42.

SUMMARY

Our discussion of basic inventory decisions has revolved around
three basic questions that must be answered by the managers of any
system utilizing inventories for finished goods and independent demand items. The first question that we addressed was, what information is needed to make inventory decisions? Our answer was a listing
of a number of important parameters that must be determined in
order to make inventory decisions intelligently. It included information about lead times, sources of supply, price breaks, forecasts, ABC
classifications, and relevant costs.

The second important inventory question was, how much should we
order? The segment of this chapter that discussed various models for
determining order quantities illustrated that there are a number of
different ways of approaching this question, all dependent upon the
particular situation at hand. The classical model, for example, is
appropriate where demand and lead times are constant and inventory holding costs must be traded off against setup and ordering

costs. Other approaches are appropriate when shortage costs, quantity discounts, long-production runs or multiple-product interactions must be considered.

The third question was how much buffer or safety stock should be used to protect against stockouts during replenishment cycles when both demand and lead times are uncertain. The techniques discussed in the latter portion of the chapter illustrate that the appropriate use of statistical methods, coupled with management policy decisions about desired service standards, provides a rational approach for answering this question.

The answers to these three questions, what information, what order quantity, how much buffer stock, are important to the effective management of inventories. However, they do not in themselves comprise a system for managing inventories over time. In the chapters that follow, we will illustrate how these approaches fit into systems for planning and controlling both dependent and independent demand items.

REVIEW QUESTIONS AND PROBLEMS

1. How sensitive are lot size decisions and costs to changes in $c_P, c_H, c_S, R, r/p$?

2. If management is attempting to adhere reasonably closely to an economic order quantity purchase policy, which parameters should it monitor most closely? Why?

3. The following are data concerning the purchase of an item with a discount schedule involving three price breaks. Determine Q_o in the minimum number of steps following the rationale of the decision flowchart of Figure 3–8. $R = 500$ units per year, $c_P = \$10$, $F_H = 20$ percent.

Quantity	Price per unit
0–49	$1.00
50–99	0.90
100–299	0.80
300 or more	0.75

4. * The following are data involving the purchase of an item having a price discount schedule: $c_P = \$100, F_H = 20$ percent. The price discount schedule is as follows:

---

* Problem developed by Professors J. Baker and J. W. Gotcher, Department of Management Sciences, California State College, Hayward, Calif.

Quantity	Price per unit
0–99	$100
100–999	$ 85
1,000–9,999	$ 75
10,000 or more	$ 65

Annual requirements could vary widely depending on whether or not certain contracts are actually awarded. Therefore, management wishes to know the optimum purchase quantity under three different conditions for R: 24, 1,000, and 60,000 units per year.

a. Write a computer program which can be used to solve problems of this type.

b. What are the optimum purchase quantities for the three alternate values of R?

5. A company manufactures a line of four detergents which are processed on common equipment through a cycling schedule. The aggregate demand for each of the four detergents is growing and forecastable within reasonably close limits, though demand for various sizes of boxes and special promotions are much more erratic. Based on new forecasts of demand for the coming year production lots and product sequencing are being revised. The plant works eight hours per day, 240 days per year.

Preliminary calculations indicated production runs for each product in the following case lots: Wave, 25,000 cases; Ozone, 13,000 cases; Tornado, 8,000 cases; and, Zap, 9,000 cases. A case is a standard measure involving the same amount of detergent regardless of individual box sizes. These case lot sizes would require 12 production runs of Wave per year, 10 of Ozone, 8 of Tornado, and 2 of Zap to meet the overall requirements for each product. The scheduler had developed a cycling sequence that met aggregate sales requirements as follows, coding the products by number as listed in Table 3–19: 1234, 123, 123, 13, 12, 12, 14, 12, 123, 123, 123, 123. Each changeover requires four hours for cleaning and other preparations for the next product.

Table 3–19
Data on four detergents

Product	Forecast (cases per year)	Daily production rate	c_H (dollars/ year/case)	Changeover cost (dollars)
1. Wave	300,000	2,500	0.45	400.00
2. Ozone	140,000	2,500	0.45	400.00
3. Tornado	64,000	2,500	0.45	400.00
4. Zap	18,000	2,500	0.45	400.00

Production was started according to the plan, but before the end of the first cycle the inventory of Wave (Product 1) had been exhausted by sales requirements. More trouble developed as the schedule progressed into the second cycle—the inventory for Ozone was also exhausted. The production foreman urged larger lots to build up larger cycle inventories. The scheduler stated that this would only magnify the problem and that his lot sizes were close to economic quantities and the system should work if given a chance.

a. Why is the scheduler's plan not working?
b. Derive a production plan which will circumvent the problem and show that your plan will work.
c. What is the total incremental cost of your plan? Is your plan more economical in terms of total incremental cost than the scheduler's plan?

6. An organization is attempting to assess the cost of increasing its service level which is currently set at only 80 percent. Average demand during lead time is 18 units and demand is reasonably well described by the Poisson distribution. Inventory holding costs are approximated by $c_H = \$10$ per unit per year. Calculate the buffer inventory costs required for service levels of 80, 90, 95, and 99 percent. What are the comparative costs if the distribution of demand during lead time follows the negative exponential distribution? The normal distribution with $\sigma_D = 2$, 4, and 6 units?

7. * Following are actual demands for 20 periods: 50, 51, 49, 47, 46, 48, 45, 49, 51, 56, 57, 54, 56, 55, 49, 43, 44, 50, 52, and 48. Compute the average demand for the series. Determine the level of buffer stocks necessary to prevent demand from exceeding total supply on hand in 70, 80, 90, and 100 percent of the 20 periods under consideration, assuming that the inventory is returned to the maximum level (average demand plus buffer stock) at the beginning of each period. Find the total dollar sales, total holding cost of all inventory, total shortage cost, and the contribution for each of the service levels indicated. Contribution is here defined as being total sales less holding and shortage costs. Assume that average inventory for each period is equal to one-half the sum of the beginning and ending inventories.

Selling price = $10 per unit; holding cost per unit = $1 per period; shortage cost = $3 per unit of unmet demand.

Hint: Notice that the sequence of the data has no effect on the result of the computations. By sorting the demands into ascending order, one can easily discover the total beginning inventory level needed for each

---

* Problem developed by professors J. Baker and J. W. Gotcher, Department of Management Sciences, California State College, Hayward, Calif.

service level. For example, the demand for the 14th ranked period will be the 70 percent service level inventory, the 16th ranked period provides the 80 percent service level, etc.

8. The organization which manufactures the product for which Figure 1–7 represents the production-inventory system is the subject for this question, including the various time delays and decision rules which define the system. Management is facing the gloomy prospect of a 50 percent forecasted reduction in retail demand from the previous level of 2,500 units per week, and is attempting to plan future operations to take the catastrophe into account.

Among the many proposals to meet the crisis is one to "cut inventories to the bone." Finished goods inventories were felt to be of first importance so the president asked for a status report. The status report was in one sense encouraging because it noted initially that simply because of a happy coincidence with the seasonal cycle, seasonal inventories were at a minimum. Otherwise, finished goods inventories were said to be "normal" for the current operations based on an average retail demand of 2,500 units per week. The report indicated total finished goods inventories of 13,643 units within the factory—factory warehouse system. The report also estimated ominously that there were another 23,328 units "out there" in the distribution system, but this figure was also normal for the present level of operations.

Being a decisive person, the president stated a goal for inventory reduction: "I assume that there is some 'fat' in that figure of 13,643 units for our current operations. Taking this into account as well as the projected decline in demand I want our finished goods inventories reduced to 40 percent of present levels (approximately 5,000 units) within six months." The vice president of operations objected stating that there was no fat in the current inventory—it was minimum for the current level of operations, and that the company was just lucky to be at a point in the seasonal cycle when inventories were low. The president, however, was adamant and ordered production plans to be made to implement the new goal. The operations vice president said that to implement the goal would require a drastic change in service policy, stating that the company now maintains inventories sufficient to offer service 95 percent of the time. Furthermore, it would be uneconomical to change the current "manufacturing order" procedure which was based on the factory cycle time. This produced the rejoiner from the president, "I have always told you that you should be using an *EOQ* system. Perhaps this is the time to install it!"

The issues were finally resolved as follows: The vice president of operations was to present two plans for projected finished goods inventories six months hence. One plan was to implement the president's goal and the second was to be one which he thought was most economical for the projected new demand rate. Comparative costs and other measures of effectiveness were also to be included.

Develop these two plans. Which one would you choose and why? How do system finished goods inventories vary with changes in average demand for this production-inventory system?

Additional data are:

a. Demand during lead time is adequately described by the normal distribution with $\bar{D} = 12,850$ units per 41 days. $\sigma_D = 1,920.7$, or 15 percent of $\bar{D}$. Based on past experience concerning the relationship between the coefficient of variation and demand during lead time, it is expected that $\bar{D}$ will be 6,425 and the coefficient of variation 20 percent. There is a five-day workweek.

b. The review and ordering process is expensive in that a careful assessment of inventory position and forecasted demand is involved. Therefore, $c_P = \$100$. Also, $c_H = \$0.10$ per unit per year.

9. Referring to the situation described in Problem 8, what is the possible impact on the production-inventory system of the estimate of 23,328 units in the distribution system downstream from the factory warehouse?

10. A consultant investigating the inventory policies and procedures of a finished steel products company is attempting to define a stockout policy for the organization. The company maintains stock on 250 standard products for which average inventory holding costs have been determined to be $1 per unit per year. The cost of placing an order for inventory replenishment averages $10 per order.

The company has built its reputation on excellent service so the question of an appropriate risk of stockout became a very emotional issue. Anything but perfect service was unthinkable—"Sure, we might miss once in awhile, but to have a policy which plans to run out of stock a certain percent of time seems almost a dishonest policy. Not only that it costs us a great deal in terms of customer goodwill, lost sales, and special handling of back orders every time we accidentally run out." Taking up the rationality of the last statement, the consultant replied coolly, "Yes, our study indicates that the average cost of shortages is about $10 per unit and our suggestion is that a service level of approximately 90 percent would be appropriate."

Management exploded at the thought of 10 percent stockouts so the consultant retreated to his ultimate weapon with, "How much are you willing to spend per year to offer a service level of 99.5 percent over and above the costs of our proposed 90 percent? The 99.5 percent level represents virtually perfect service!" After a great deal of thought, management placed a value of $50,000 per year on a service level of 99.5 percent. The consultant was astounded that they were willing to spend so much for excellent service, but agreed to make the comparative calculation.

How much will it cost to implement management's policy?

Demand during lead time for a "typical" item is well described by a normal distribution with $\bar{D} = 2,000$ units and $\sigma_D = 200$ units, and annual requirements for the typical item total 12,500 units.

11. Referring to Problem 10, a controversy has developed between two individuals on the consultant's staff concerning the best way to allow for buffer stocks. One person states that the entire problem can be handled by the quantity Q ordered at one time and that the "shortage cost model" given as Equation (9) in this chapter will provide orders of such size to cover both cycle and buffer stock requirements. His opponent states that she was taught to compute buffer stocks by Equation (23) with lot sizes being computed by the standard EOQ formula. Compare decisions made by each method. Which should be used and why?

SELECTED BIBLIOGRAPHY

1. Brown, R. G. *Statistical Forecasting for Inventory Control.* New York: McGraw-Hill Book Co., 1959.

2. Brown, R. G. *Smoothing, Forecasting and Prediction.* Englewood Cliffs, N.J.: Prentice-Hall, Inc. 1963.

3. Brown, R. G. *Decision Rules for Inventory Management.* New York: Holt, Rinehart & Winston, Inc., 1967.

4. Buchan, J., and Koenigsberg, E. *Scientific Inventory Mangement.* Englewood Cliffs, N.J.: Prentice-Hall, Inc., 1963.

5. Eilon, S. *Elements of Production Planning and Control.* New York: Macmillan Company, 1962.

6. Fetter, R. B., and Daleck, W. C. *Decision Models for Inventory Management.* Homewood, Ill.: Richard D. Irwin, Inc., 1961.

7. Greene, J. H. *Production Control: Systems Decisions.* rev. ed. Homewood, Ill.: Richard D. Irwin, Inc., 1975.

8. Hadley, G., and Whitin, T. M. *Analysis of Inventory Systems.* Englewood Cliffs, N.J.: Prentice-Hall, Inc., 1963.

9. Hanssmann, F. *Operations Research in Production and Inventory Control.* New York: John Wiley & Sons, Inc., 1962.

10. Harris, F. W. *Operations and Cost.* Factory Management Series. Chicago: A. W. Shaw, Co., 1915, pp. 48–52.

11. Magee, J. F. *Industrial Logistics.* New York: McGraw-Hill Book Co., 1968.

12. Magee, J. F., and Boodman, D. M. *Production Planning and Inventory Control.* 2d ed. New York: McGraw-Hill Book Co., 1967.

13. McMillan, C., and Gonzalez, R. F.   *Systems Analysis: A Computer Approach to Decision Models*. rev. ed. Homewood, Ill.: Richard D. Irwin, Inc., 1968.

14. Moore, F. G., and Jablonski, R.   *Production Control*. 3d ed. New York: McGraw-Hill Book Co., 1969.

15. Naddor, E.   *Inventory Systems*. New York: John Wiley & Sons, Inc., 1966.

16. Peterson, R., and Silver, E. A.   *Decision Systems for Inventory Management and Production Planning*. New York: John Wiley & Sons, Inc., 1979.

17. Raymond, F. E.   *Quantity and Economy in Manufacture*. Princeton, N.J.: D. Van Nostrand Co., Inc., 1931.

18. Starr, M. K., and Miller, D. W.   *Inventory Control: Theory and Practice*. Englewood Cliffs, N.J.: Prentice-Hall, Inc., 1962.

19. Veinott, A. F.   "The Status of Mathematical Inventory Theory," *Management Science*, vol. 12, no. 11 (July 1966).

20. Voris, W.   *Production Control: Text and Cases*. 3d ed. Homewood, Ill.: Richard D. Irwin, Inc., 1966.

21. Wagner, H. N.   *Statistical Management of Inventory Systems*. New York: John Wiley & Sons, Inc., 1962.

22. Whitin, T. M.   *The Theory of Inventory Management*. Princeton, N.J.: Princeton University Press, 1953.

23. Zimmerman, H. J., and Sovereign, M. G.   *Quantitative Models for Production Management*. Englewood Cliffs, N.J.: Prentice-Hall, Inc., 1974.

Chapter 4

Independent demand inventory systems

THE TECHNIQUES AND INFORMATION REQUIREMENTS discussed in the last chapter provide a sound basis for making inventory decisions under various sets of conditions. A glance at Figure 3–1, however, will show that these data and techniques do not in themselves comprise an inventory management system. As Figure 4–1 illustrates, a complete system must make provisions for implementing inventory decisions, and for feeding back the impact of these decisions, and the course of subsequent events (withdrawals and receipts to inventory) into the data base so that new decisions can be made. In other words, an effective system must have a way of "closing the feedback loop" so that subsequent inventory management decisions can be implemented. Moreover, a complete inventory management *system* must operate under a prescribed set of operating rules that indicates exactly how inventory decisions are to be made over time. This implies that the system needs more structure than a mere kit bag of loose tools for determining order quantities and buffer stocks can provide.

Independent demand inventory systems are systems which are designed to control items whose demand is created by forces outside the control of the production-inventory system under consideration. In contrast to the dependent demand inventory control systems dis-

Figure 4–1
Inventory systems for independent demand items

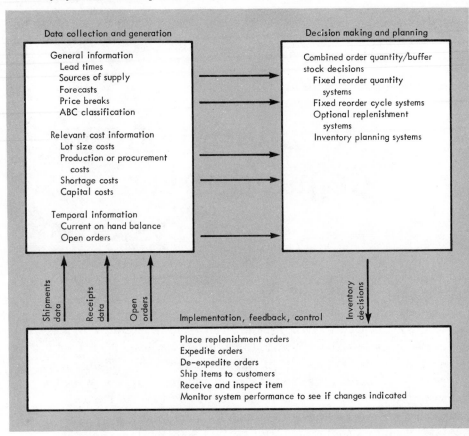

cussed in Chapter 7, independent demand systems are appropriate for items such as spare parts, some supplies and maintenance items, and finished goods. In this chapter, four more or less complete systems for managing independent demand items are introduced and discussed. The first three types of systems, fixed reorder quantity, fixed reorder cycle, and optional replenishment, share a common philosophy in that they are *reactive* systems. While the mathematics involved in deriving the operating rules employed in these systems are fairly complex, they are quite simple to use since they are designed to *react* to a given change in inventory levels, the passage of time, or both, by placing replenishment orders. By way of contrast, *inventory planning systems*, also called *time phased reorder point systems*, are *proactive*. They are not designed to simply react to the current state of inventory affairs. They are designed to plan ahead so that action can be taken before problems arise. The mathematics involved in inventory planning systems are quite straightforward, but here, the operating task is significantly greater than with reactive systems.

Requirements of managerial inventory systems

It is worthwhile to consider the minimum or basic requirements we might impose on practical systems today. In terms of the models being applied, it is paramount, of course, that the models describe the behavior of the most important variables operating in the situation. This may involve the assessment of appropriate costs, such as capital, storage, preparation, freight, shortages, and so on. The system must recognize the inherent variability of demand and perhaps of supply lead times, and forecast how buffer, cycle, and transit inventories should vary with changes in demand. A managerial control plan needs to have clearly recognized that a rational system will involve some shortages, lost sales, or back orders unless an infinite shortage cost can somehow be justified.

One of the significant problems involved in the application of rational models is in adapting them to use with a very large number of inventory items. Here, of course, modern data processing methods can rescue for practical use what might otherwise be a model of only theoretical interest. But it is often possible to simplify the data processing problem through classification of whole groups of items whose demand distribution may be adequately described by one of the standard distributions, such as the normal, Poisson, or negative exponential distributions. Also, good managerial practice would not give the same time and attention to the control of all items. Another kind of classification of items by their total inventory value or otherwise critical nature may make it possible to establish progressively tighter control over higher valued critical items and relatively simple and loose controls over inexpensive and/or noncritical items.

Managerial systems of inventory control also need to recognize that inventories are usually embedded in larger systems and that often other considerations than just those connected with inventory may enter or even dominate. For example, if a large number of items are regularly ordered from one supplier, it may be worthwhile to abandon an order point system and place orders for all items by some regular schedule in order to take advantage of carload freight rates.

Or, a system optimum may call for the use of larger inventories as a trade-off to level production and avoid possibly larger costs associated with overtime premiums, hiring and training, separation, and extra subcontracting.

Finally, systems for inventory control need to recognize the importance of crisp execution of the inventory decisions that have been made, and of the importance of feeding back and controlling exceptions, current status information, and measures of system performance. This formal requirement is a recognition of the importance of the implementation, feedback, and control element of planning and control shown in Figure 4–1.

All four of the types of systems described in this chapter are designed to march through time. That is, they are intended for use in making, implementing, and controlling a series of inventory decisions over a period of time beginning when an item is placed under the system's control, and ending when it is taken off. Over this extended period, which may last for years, we can expect the system structure to remain constant. But, the need to change or update data inputs to the system will arise, in some cases occasionally, and in others frequently.

Those classes of information which change slowly with the passage of time and thus need only occasional changes are called *semipermanent* data. One of the functions of the feedback and control element is to determine when these data require updating, by either monitoring the environment for changes, or monitoring the performance of the system. Often, poor system performance is an indication that the semipermanent data base has become obsolete. Those information inputs which require updating each time a new inventory decision is to be made are called *temporal data*, since this information tends to change almost continuously with the passage of time. Temporal data include current on-hand inventory balances and forecasts. They change as a result of the implementation of prior inventory decisions and the flux of supply and demand forces.

Much of the data that we would classify as semipermanent was identified at the beginning of the last chapter as general and relevant cost information. General information includes such data as lead times, sources of supply, price break data, and ABC classifiers. It is not difficult to understand the reasons why this type of data changes over time as new process technologies are employed, new vendors are selected, and as inflationary and market forces change the costs of capital, production, and procurement. Part of the problem with making changes in the semipermanent data base is that those functions which are routinely involved in making sourcing, technology or cost changes; e.g., purchasing, engineering, and finance may not notify those involved in inventory control that they have been made. This is an especially easy oversight since such changes occur sporadically or infrequently. Obviously, notification is a prerequisite for updating the semipermanent data base, and it is important that the implementation, feedback, and control subsystem contain provisions or procedures for obtaining current data on such information. Naturally, temporal data change very quickly with the passage of time. Since the on-hand balance of an inventory changes every time that a withdrawal is made or an order is received, we could expect this class of data to change almost continually, and it does. Similarly, open order data, which indicates the amount that has been ordered but not yet received, changes frequently as orders are placed and then arrive.

Normally, there are well-established procedures for obtaining, recording, and updating temporal data in most firms. Because of the frequency with which such information changes, and because receipts and withdrawals from inventory must usually be recorded for accounting (invoicing and payables, cost control) purposes anyway, there are few problems that result from a lack of notification. The major problem here is one of data accuracy resulting from the increase in complexity involved in recording temporal changes. Thus, a second function of the implementation, feedback, and control element of inventory management is monitoring the system for errors.

The third function of the feedback and control element of a planning and control system is the execution of the decisions that are made within the context of the system. To understand the importance of this followthrough element, consider what will happen when an item hits a reorder point, signaling the need to reorder, and the orders to do so sit in an out basket for two weeks before the replenishment order is actually placed. The result will likely be a stockout, and a defeat of the purpose of the entire notion of controlling inventories. The same result can occur if there are delays in posting current withdrawals and receipts to stock. Thus an effective managerial inventory control system must include people considerations, and controls to ensure that they play their part in executing inventory decisions and recording their actions on a timely basis. As we discuss the four types of independent demand systems, we shall draw attention to these issues by discussing the records, reviews, and forecasts necessary to run them.

Inventory transactions management. Maintaining accurate and timely inventory records and managing inventory transactions effectively are crucial activities in implementing and controlling the decisions made within the context of an inventory system. However, as we shall see in the balance of this chapter, some types of systems require different approaches to inventory transactions management.

The heart of inventory transactions management involves obtaining an accurate count of on-hand inventories so that the current status of the production-inventory system can be ascertained. Some systems require that a *perpetual inventory record* be maintained so that the physical inventory balance can be quickly obtained at any time. Perpetual inventory records require that each receipt or disbursement of materials be recorded as an addition to or deduction from stock. While such transactions reporting is simple enough in principle, it is quite difficult to attain a level of operations in which they are reported on a timely and accurate basis. At a minimum, accurate and timely perpetual records demand that the firm have a system for identifying items, a numbering system for referring to them quickly, a method of determining where items are located, and an authorization procedure that ensures that materials are only withdrawn for valid purposes, and that such withdrawals are recorded. Moreover, since inventory records are only valid if they account for *good* items, a provision must often be made to ensure that newly received goods are inspected before being physically placed "in stock," and recorded as being available for use.

Even with effective controls over numbering systems, stock locations, receiving and inspection, and withdrawal authorizations, human error can result in large perpetual inventory record errors. Consider the case of a typical firm with 10,000 inventoriable items, where the average item is received once a month, and has a withdrawal from stock once every two days. In a normal working year with 250 days, this firm will have to record $10,000 \times (12 + 250/2) =$ 1,370,000 transactions to keep perpetual records up to date. If the human error rate in counting and recording is only 1 error per 100 transactions, 12,700 errors will have crept into the system by the end of a year—more than one for every item in stock. Since a common rule of thumb has it that perpetual inventory records should be at least 95 percent accurate in order for most systems to work effectively, normal human error alone can effectively sabotage the best system. To counteract such effects, many firms employ *cycle counting* to check on and correct perpetual inventory balances.

Cycle counting involves continuously taking a physical count of some portion of the items in stock each day or week. Often, full-time cycle counting specialists are employed to perform this function. Their job involves determining where and how errors in perpetual inventories arose, as well as counting and checking actual inventory balances against those indicated in records. Tersine [14] has noted five different procedures for determining the frequency with which particular items are cycle counted:

1. ABC system.   Stratify items on the ABC principle with the highest frequency on A items and the lowest on C items.
2. Reorder system.   Count items whenever they are reordered.
3. Receiver system.   Count items whenever a replenishment order is received.
4. Zero-balance system.   Count items when the balance on hand falls to zero or negative.
5. Transaction system.   Count items after a specific number of transactions have been recorded.

Some systems, such as the fixed reorder interval system described later in this chapter, do not require that perpetual inventory records be maintained. Here, *periodic physical inventories* can be performed to determine the on-hand status of the items in stock. Most firms are familiar with periodic physical inventories, since accountants often insist on annual physical counts of all of the items in stock for reporting purposes. Periodic physicals often involve shutting down the entire operation and suspending all transactions while numbers of people count everything in stock. While physical inventories of this type can be quite disruptive, they do allow a firm to avoid heavy transactions reporting expenses. Sometimes, low-valued items are physically counted periodically, while perpetual records are maintained on higher valued items.

REACTIVE INVENTORY SYSTEMS

Fixed reorder quantity systems

The fixed reorder quantity system is based on an order point P as an inventory level trigger to place orders for some predetermined quantity Q, as shown in Figure 3–2. The determination of Q may be based on any of the EOQ formulas that are appropriate to the situation or could be based on judgment. Buffer stocks are determined by setting risk levels and computing D_{max} during the lead time and $B = D_{max} - \overline{D}$ in a conceptual sense. But by recognizing that $P = D_{max}$ we see that we need not make the separate computation of B nor segregate B in records or physically, since the proper determination of P takes buffer stocks into account. The order point P could be determined for constant or variable lead times by the methods discussed previously.

Records, reviews and forecasts. The operation of the fixed order quantity system (alias the order point system, or the two-bin system) depends on the maintenance of a *perpetual inventory record* of some kind so that when inventories on hand and on order fall to the order point P, action is taken to replenish supplies. If the lead time is long (three months, for example) and the typical order quantity is equivalent to a somewhat shorter time period, perhaps a one-month's supply, we would not place a new order when the amount on hand drops to the order point P, since we normally expect to receive outstanding orders once per month on the average. The result is that normal practice is to trigger the system only when the amount on hand plus the amount on order falls to the reorder level.

Figure 4–2 shows an example where the lead time is three weeks and the lot size $Q = 20$ represents a supply of only two weeks at average demand rates. We derive the reorder point P in the usual way and find D_{max} during the three-week lead time to be 36 units. Reasonable maximum demand during the relatively long lead time then places P somewhat above the levels of actual inventory on hand.

When the lead time is short compared with the time between orders, it is assumed that a new order is immediately available, and it is in fact added to inventory available at the time the order is placed. The perpetual inventory record could be maintained on inventory cards in a manual system or in the data bank of an automatic data processing system. The term "two-bin" system comes from the practice of physically segregating an amount equal to the order point level P to provide for D_{max} during lead time. When the inventory in the first bin is used up, P has been reached and the system triggered for replenishment. Usage then continues from the second bin during the lead time until the replenishment order is received. The second bin is then loaded up to P units and the balance placed in the first bin from which usage continues, beginning the next cycle. The two-bin system when rigorously followed provides excellent control with minimum record keeping.

Figure 4–2
Inventory balance for a fixed reorder quantity system where lead time is
long compared to the time between orders (system triggered by "on hand
and on order")

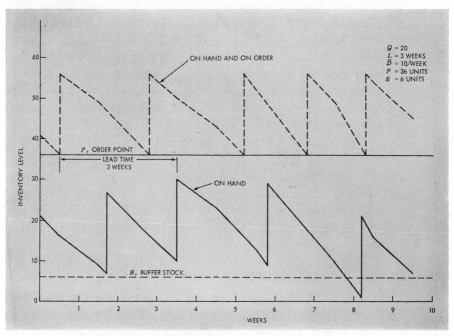

Review of requirements and system parameters. When the system has been triggered, the usual action would be to prepare an order for replenishment of predetermined size Q. But a *periodic review* of requirements is also an integral part of the system and is one of the important parameters which defines the degree of control which can result. Obviously, if requirements are reviewed only annually and new system parameters Q's and P's determined, actual demand might have changed considerably, and the control system would not be very responsive to the new changes. If demand had actually increased since the last review of requirements, then the control system will have responded by more frequent ordering and resultant larger annual ordering costs. Inventory holding costs would remain about the same, since the cycle inventory component is related to Q and the buffer inventory component is related to P, both of which had remained constant. The frequency of stockouts however should increase, since $D_{\max}$ actually would have increased. A decrease in demand since the last review would decrease the annual ordering cost but maintain cycle and buffer inventories that were larger than required for the preset risk levels.

If the requirements review period were reduced to six months, or three months, the responsiveness of the system to changes in demand would, of course, be improved. Ideally, the review would be carried out as a part of *periodic forecasting*, which would update expected demand for the upcoming forecasting period with updated Q's and P's being simply a part of the process. As we discussed in Chapter 2, an exponentially smoothed forecasting system is simple to use and is very well adapted to automatic data processing systems. If inventory records were maintained, a periodic forecasting subroutine could update the forecasted annual requirements R, and compute a new order quantity Q or Q_o as well as a new order point P for all items. Then, as inventory balances are updated routinely by stock receipts and withdrawals, procurement action would be triggered by stock levels falling below the latest P in the record and an order for the updated Q units prepared, based on the latest forecasted demand.

Fixed reorder cycle systems

The key difference in the fixed reorder cycle system compared to the fixed order quantity system is that action is triggered periodically rather than by an order point. The quantity ordered, however, varies depending on usage in the immediate past period. Thus with the fixed reorder cycle system (often called the replenishment system) we place orders of varying size by a fixed periodic cycle, whereas with the fixed reorder quantity system we place orders of fixed size on a variable time cycle.

Figure 4–3 shows the graph of inventory balances for a fixed cycle system with a one-week cycle between orders, which we will term the "review period," R, and a supply lead time of $L = \frac{1}{2}$ week. The solid line shows the fluctuation of physical inventory on hand and the dashed line the sum of inventory on hand and on order. Note that orders are placed each week in an amount equal to usage in the previous week. (There are, of course, other possibilities such as an average of previous periods.) More simply, however, the order size is the difference between inventory on hand and a preset level M, the maximum of inventory on hand and on order. Obviously, the selection of M and R are the critical determinants of the system.[1] The

---

[1] Just as with lot size models, it is possible to derive optimal relationships for specific cases. In periodic models we seek optimal periods instead of the optimal lot size. See E. Naddor. *Inventory Systems* (New York: John Wiley & Sons, Inc. 1966).

Figure 4–3
Inventory balance for a fixed reorder cycle system where $L < R$ (system is triggered once per week)

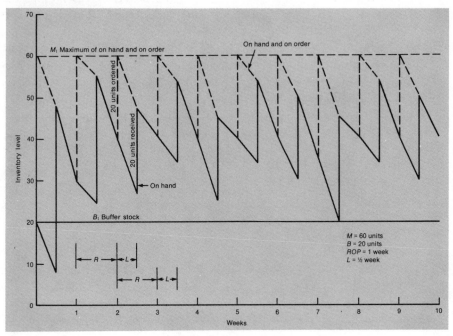

closeness of control is determined by the frequency of review and the action taken to replenish stocks.

An estimate of the optimal review period is simply $R = 1/N_0$ as computed by the *EOQ* formulas. For individual items, of course, the more precise mathematical methodologies found in the literature would make it possible to determine R_o more carefully. An important part of the advantage of using periodic systems would be defeated, however, if we were to determine individual review periods for each item. The result is that review periods will ordinarily be set for all items (or classes of items) based on other considerations such as the time required to perform a review, or the usual time required to accumulate orders for suppliers of sufficient size to take advantage of carload or truckload shipping rates.

The buffer stock protection is determined by the level at which we set M. The determination of M is related to demand during the replenishment cycle $(R + L)$. One can see by examining any of the $(R + L)$ cycles in Figure 4–3 that only one decision which can alter events is made in each cycle, and that decision is the order placed at the beginning of the cycle and received L time units later. If a stockout is to occur during that cycle, it could occur just before the receipt of the order L time units after placing the order, or just before the receipt of the next order $R + L$ time units later. Though a second order is placed R time units after the first, it does not change the possibility of a stockout during $R + L$, since it will not be received until the end of the cycle. The second order affects only the chance of a stockout during the following (but overlapping) $R + L$ cycle. The level of M must then provide for reasonable maximum demand during $R + L$. The data for Figure 4–3 were drawn from a normal demand distribution over the 1½-week $R + L$, with $\bar{D} = 40$ units per period and $\sigma_D = 10$ units per period. Providing a service level of approximately 97 percent, or a risk of stockout of about 3 percent, would define D_{max} as $\bar{D} + 2\sigma_D = 40 + 2 \times 10 = 60$. Then $M = D_{max} = 60$. This level of M provides a buffer stock of $B = D_{max} - \bar{D} = 20$ units as shown in Figure 4–3. The maximum on-hand and on-order inventory is then,

$$M = B + \bar{d}(R + L) \tag{1}$$

where $\bar{d}$ is average daily demand. The average inventory in the system is,

$$\bar{I} = B + \tfrac{1}{2}(\bar{d}R) \tag{2}$$

which is most easily seen for constant demand where inventory varies from a maximum of $M - \bar{d}L$ at the point where an order has just been received to a minimum of B just before the receipt of the next order. The difference between the peak and valley is $\bar{d}R$ and the average inventory is then one-half this amount added to the buffer as stated in Equation (2). Combining Equations (1) and (2),

$$\bar{I} = M - \bar{d}\left(\frac{R}{2} + L\right) \tag{3}$$

When $L < R$ as in Figure 4–3, the curves for inventory on hand and inventory on hand and on order are identical at the time an order is placed. This is not true when $L > R$, and it becomes important to recognize that in all cases the order quantity is determined by the contrast between M and inventory *on hand and on order* at the time of review, or,

$$Q = M - I - O \tag{4}$$

where O is the total on order but not yet received. This is shown in

Figure 4-4
Inventory balance for a fixed reorder cycle system where $L > R$ (system is triggered once per week)

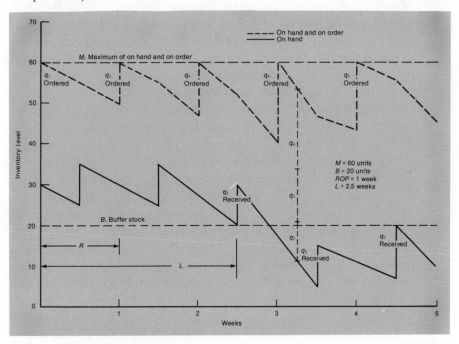

Figure 4-4 for a system where $R = 1$ week and $L = 2.5$ weeks, and the amount ordered each period is determined by the curve of inventory on hand and on order.

The determination of M in the $L > R$ case is the same as for the $L < R$ case. M is the level equal to the maximum demand at defined stockout risk levels over the $R + L$ period. As before, only one decision is made in any $R + L$ period which can alter the prospect of stockout during that span of time. That decision is the amount ordered at the beginning of the period. To be sure, other orders are received during $R + L$ but based on decisions previously made. In Figure 4-4, for example, q_3 is ordered at week 2 to be received at week 4.5. In the meantime, q_1 and q_2 are received, but their receipt did not alter the risk of stockout from the known conditions that existed at the time that q_3 was ordered.

Records, reviews, and forecasts. The presumption in a fixed reorder cycle system is that some sort of physical assessment of inventory, such as an actual count, is made at the time of review. In many instances records of transactions exist such as sales slips, and so on, but the accuracy of the information system may still require an actual count or verification for decision purposes. With the continued development of automatic data processing systems adapted to specific local problems, the maintenance of perpetual inventory records is increasingly used as a basis for decision at the time of reviews. The cost of making the periodic reviews is an incremental cost in deciding on the frequency of reviews.

Just as with fixed order quantity systems, there is a periodic requirements review which may result in a change in M and/or R in response to demand shifts. Of course, the control system will respond to demand changes even if M and R have not been changed. An increase in demand would result in larger orders being placed each order period and a greater likelihood of stock shortage, since D_{max} would have also increased. A decrease in demand would result in smaller orders each period and a larger average inventory. Requirements reviews again would logically be tied in with a periodic forecasting system with automatic data processing techniques being as applicable here as with the fixed order quantity system.

The *information feedback characteristics* of the fixed reorder cycle system on the surface appear to be the same as for the fixed quantity system. Yet there is a fundamental difference which should be noted. The reorder cycle system normally provides more frequent information, and the operation of the entire system is constantly focused on *demand rates*; and its response is obviously and directly to usage in the immediate past period. Therefore, changes in demand are constantly under surveillance, since the review periods are regular and usually frequent. The danger in these facts is that in manual systems the people involved often will not let the control system do its job but attempt to outguess the random processes which control demand. Because of a large demand or usage last period, they may be tempted to order more than the control system calls for or do the reverse for opposite conditions. Such action, of course, not only defeats a rational system but amplifies the effects of both actual demand changes and random variations in demand.

Optional replenishment system

The optional replenishment system, commonly referred to in the literature as the (s, S) system, combines the essential control mechanisms of both the fixed reorder quantity and fixed reorder cycle systems. The optional replenishment system establishes a maximum on-hand and on-order inventory level S (M in our notation), a periodic review R, as well as a reorder point s (P in our notation). The decision rules for ordering are then as follows: (1) At the time of each review determine if inventory on hand and on order is less than the order point P. (2) If the order point has been reached, order the quantity which will bring inventory on hand and on order up to the replenishment level M, that is, $Q = M - I - O$. (3) If the order point has not been reached, no order is placed, and a reexamination occurs at the time of the next review with the same decision rules holding at that time.

The optional replenishment system in effect places a lower limit on the size of an order which can be placed yet maintains the close surveillance over inventory levels and demand rates associated with the fixed reorder cycle system. Buffer stocks can be approximated by examining the demand distribution over the time span $(R/2 + L)$.

Choice of a reactive system

All three of the systems discussed occur with a multitude of minor variations, which we will not attempt to appraise in discussing the basis for choosing a particular system. In general, the fixed order quantity system finds its largest application where close control is not necessary because of low activity and/or the value of the item is low. With low activity the fixed reorder quantity system defers action until an order of reasonable size (perhaps the economical order quantity) can be placed, thus recognizing the possible importance of incremental ordering costs. The fixed order quantity system requires an accurate perpetual inventory record or its equivalent so that it is possible to determine when the order point has been reached without significant delay. Where suppliers require some minimum-size total order or package quantity restrictions, we have some difficulty with the fixed order quantity system, since it treats each inventory item individually as order points are reached. The result is that though many different orders (for different items) may go to the same supplier over a period of time, they are seen as relatively small individual orders shipped individually at relatively high freight cost.

The fixed reorder cycle system makes it possible to group orders for a number of individual items from one supplier and possibly take advantage of low shipping cost with carload lots. The fixed cycle system has a quick response to demand changes and is in general applicable for high-activity situations where close surveillance over both demand and inventory levels is of importance. On the other hand, the fixed reorder cycle system requires larger safety stocks, since we must provide for the possibility of stockout over the longer $(R + L)$ period instead of only L as in the fixed order quantity system. In general, the costs of maintaining the fixed reorder cycle system will be higher because of the larger buffer stock and the cost of making the periodic reviews. While it is possible to determine optimal review periods for each item, it will normally be advantageous to set a common review period for all items or for classifications of items in order to gain the advantages of grouping orders to common suppliers. The result is that little attention is given to optimal review periods. Instead, review periods are set based on other considerations.

The optional replenishment system seems to combine the significant advantages of the other two systems. It has probably not gained predominance in practice because the mathematical analysis is very complex and somewhat more information is required to operate such a system.

Eilon and Elmaleh [6] carried out a comparative evaluation of five systems including the fixed quantity and fixed cycle systems, using a simulation methodology. Their results favored a combination system involving both a periodic review at which time an order was placed, as well as an order point, similar to the optional replenishment policy discussed earlier. This policy performed best both in terms of average inventory levels and incremental costs for service levels of 90 and 95 percent.

Adaptive control limits. In conventional systems for inventory control, inventories are allowed to fluctuate between two prescribed limits—a lower limit corresponding to a buffer stock and an upper limit to which inventories are replenished. Such fixed limits are characteristic of all "reactive" systems. In another set of experiments Eilon and Elmaleh [5] experimented with adaptive control limits based on a forecasting procedure which took account of seasonal fluctuations and trends. By taking the course of future demand into account and constantly changing or adapting the control limits, they created a proactive rather than a reactive inventory system. The system used as a vehicle for the study was the combination system described in the preceding paragraph. The inventory system was applied to three stages of inventories in series, raw materials, work-in-progress, and finished goods. In general, adaptive control systems outperformed fixed limits systems for the systems compared, both in terms of total costs and service level provided.

While the experiments performed by Eilon and Elmaleh used only one particular inventory replenishment system, it seems logical and safe to project that the general results would apply to all inventory replenishment systems. Since large-scale computing systems are now widely available and used, the adaptive limits concept (embodied in all proactive systems) of frequently updating system parameters can be incorporated as a part of inventory control systems. The domain of fixed limits, or reactive, systems then becomes small-scale inventory control systems where computers cannot be justified and situations where a stationary demand pattern can be assumed to persist.

INVENTORY PLANNING SYSTEMS

In contrast to the reactive type systems which have been discussed, proactive inventory planning systems attempt to plan inventory levels and decisions into the future. Thus, inventory planning systems in general are adaptive in the same sense as Eilon and Elmaleh [5] used the term. Inventory planning is a substantially different approach from that taken by fixed reorder quantity, fixed reorder period, and optional replenishment systems which base their decisions on what is happening at present (in terms of current inventory levels) rather than in the future.

To understand why inventory planning methods are useful, it is necessary for us to examine the basic assumptions behind most reactive models since the advantage of inventory planning methods is that such assumptions are not necessary. The first assumption of reactive models in general is that average demand is continuous and constant over time, and that the deviations from the average are described by a single distribution that does not change, regardless of the length of time over which the average demand is projected. We have seen several examples of this kind of demand pattern in Chapter 2, where the average demand was say ten units per month, and the standard deviation of demand was say two units. Such an assumption might well describe the situation depicted in demand pattern 1 in Figure 4–5. Needless to say, however, this assumption will not hold true when there is trend, seasonality, or "lumpiness" in the demand pattern as shown in patterns 2, 3, and 4, respectively (Figure 4–5). In these cases, systematic (and therefore predictable) variations in demand occur that one may want to take into account in lot sizing decisions. The only way to accomplish this is to forecast demand in future periods and "plan" inventory decisions.

The second assumption of most reactive models is that procure-

Figure 4–5
Types of demand patterns encountered in inventory control

Demand pattern (unit)	Time period								
	1	2	3	4	5	6	7	8	9
1	8	11	10	9	12	9	10	11	10
2	8	10	11	13	16	18	19	22	24
3	6	8	10	8	6	4	2	4	6
4	0	0	0	0	54	0	0	31	0

ment lead times are either constant, or that they can be statistically described by a mean and a standard deviation. However, we have already discussed the fact that lead times can in fact be "controlled," and that they are rarely constant. That is, lead times can often be compressed or extended by a mutual agreement between the supplier and the customer. Reactive systems not only assume that such "expediting" or "de-expediting" activity does not take place, but they also do not provide the information required to indicate when, and whether it is necessary. Thus, inventory planning systems are most useful when expediting or de-expediting activities are frequent and necessary, and/or when the demand pattern is perturbed.

The first step in developing an inventory planning system is to define the basic unit of time within which inventory plans will be laid. This unit of time is called a period and can designate a day, week, or a month. The amount of time in a period depends on the characteristics of the business involved; that is, the amount of detail required to operate in a given industry. For example, a grocer that receives daily deliveries from a bakery, and makes daily deliveries to its customers, might want to define a period as being one day because of the short shelf life of the product. On the other hand, a distributor of construction machinery who receives monthly shipments from the manufacturer and sells but two units a month might find that planning inventories in less than monthly periods is useless.

After the length of a period is defined, the planning horizon, that is, the number of periods to plan, must be determined. The most important factor affecting the selection of a planning horizon is vendor or manufacturing lead times. For example, in the case of the grocer the planning horizon might only be a few days since all bread must be purchased and sold before it becomes stale. However, the construction machinery distributor might want to plan for a full fiscal year (12 monthly periods), because of the long delivery lead time from the manufacturer. In order to make inventory planning effective the planning horizon should never be less than the lead time offered by the supplier of a product. A good rule of thumb is that the planning horizon should be two to four times the delivery or manufacturing lead time of the item in question. Special lot size or other planning considerations may dictate even longer planning horizons.

The third step in the development of an inventory planning system is the design of a control document. Figure 4–6 is a commonly used inventory planning format covering a planning horizon of 13 weekly periods. The columns corresponding to each period are commonly called *time buckets*, emphasizing the fact that inventory planning recognizes possible differences in demand over time. The first time bucket is called the *"action bucket,"* since a planned order in this column signals that it is time to place an order, or to take other actions necessary to control the flow of materials.

Figure 4–6
Inventory planning control document

Period (weeks)	1	2	3	4	5	6	7	8	9	10	11	12	13
Forecast													
Scheduled receipts													
On hand														
Planned orders													

The first line on Figure 4–6 designates the individual periods in the planning horizon. The second line is for a period-by-period sales forecast. The third line indicates the scheduled receipts in inventory of replenishment orders; that is, the scheduled receipt dates of orders that have been placed in previous periods. The fourth line indicates the ending on-hand balance (beginning inventory − period sales + period receipts = ending inventory). The fifth line shows the planned orders for the item that, once ordered, become scheduled receipts. For example, if the on-hand balance was projected to be negative in period 5 and the item in question had a three-period delivery lead time, then an order would be planned in period 2 for receipt in period 5.[2]

---

[2] Throughout this book the simplifying "midperiod" convention will be used. With it, all orders are assumed to arrive at the beginning of a period and all usage occurs in the middle of the period. On-hand balances refer to the amount on hand at the *end* of the period.

Using an inventory planning system. To illustrate the way in which inventory planning systems for independent demand items operate, consider Company A, a paint distributor that sells paint to hardware and paint stores. Company A orders paint from Company B; an order takes two weeks in the mail to get to Company B. Company B produces the paint to order with a two-week lead time. The paint also spends one week in transit being shipped to Company A, thus, the total procurement lead time for Company A is five weeks. Figure 4–7 represents this relationship and also shows the annual de-

Figure 4–7
An example of a production-inventory system
(Company A)

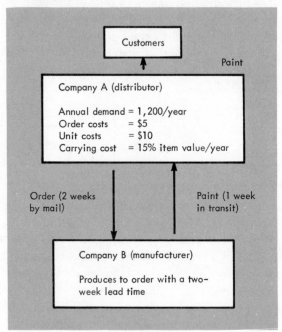

mand for paint, the cost of issuing an order to Company B for paint, the cost of a can of paint, and Company A's estimated annual inventory carrying costs.

Company A probably knows that their annual sales will be around 1,200 cans of paint a year and might therefore decide to forecast sales of 25 cans per week. Given a beginning inventory of 150 cans of paint (enough to cover sales for six weeks), Figure 4–8 represents the projected paint inventory position by period given Company A's

Figure 4–8
Forecasting inventory balances for Company A

Period		1	2	3	4	5	6	7	8	9	10	11	12	13
Forecast		25	25	25	25	25	25	25	25	25	25	25	25	25
Scheduled receipts														
On hand	150	125	100	75	50	25	0	(25)	(50)	(75)	(100)	(125)	(150)	(175)
Planned orders														

sales forecast. Notice that this inventory plan presumes a period of one week in duration, and a planning horizon of 13 weeks. The control document is used to project (forecast) the inventory balance over the planning horizon by using the simple relationship:

Projected on-hand balance
at the end of period t = Balance in period $t - 1$
+ Scheduled receipts in period t
− Forecasted sales in period t

Company A might realize after planning their inventories in this way that because of the customary five-week lead time, they will need to place an order in period 2 for delivery in period 7 in order to have paint available for period 7 sales. The need to place or plan an order is indicated by the first period in which the projected on-hand balance falls below zero (indicated by parentheses). The period in which the replenishment order is to be placed is determined by counting backward from the desired period of order receipt the number of periods assumed in the order lead time. This simple procedure is analogous to that employed in reorder point systems, in that it indicates when orders should be placed. For this reason, inventory planning is sometimes called the "time phased order point" method.

Lot sizing with inventory planning systems

Once the need to place an order has been established, the size of the order, or the order quantity, must be determined. In principle, the trade-offs, and even some of the lot sizing techniques that are used in inventory planning are analogous to those used with reactive systems. Inventory lot sizing methods, however, must be adapted to use with the time phased orientation of such systems. Lot sizing decision rules that can be used with inventory planning systems include lot-for-lot, economic order quantities, periodic order quantities, least total cost, least unit cost, and the Wagner-Whitin algorithm.

Lot-for-lot. The lot-for-lot order quantity decision rule is the simplest. It minimizes inventory levels, but ignores the fixed costs of placing an order. With the lot-for-lot technique, orders are generated for a period based on the sales requirements for that period. In Company A's case (Figure 4–8), a lot-for-lot rule would find a requirement for 25 cans of paint in period 7. It would then schedule the receipt of 25 cans of paint in period 7 and plan an order corresponding to that receipt in period 2. In other words, the sales requirement becomes the order quantity and the order itself is offset by the lead time for the item. Figure 4–9 shows Company A's inventory plan assuming that a lot-for-lot order quantity rule was applied. The arrow in Figure 4–9 shows the relationship between the planning of an order in period 2 and the scheduling of a receipt for that order in period 7. The circled numbers in the scheduled receipts, on-hand balance, and planned order rows emphasize that these figures are only the results of *planned* orders, not orders that have actually been released.

Figure 4–9
An application of the lot-for-lot technique

Period		1	2	3	4	5	6	7	8	9	10	11	12	13
Forecast		25	25	25	25	25	25	25	25	25	25	25	25	25
Scheduled receipts								(25)	(25)	(25)	(25)	(25)	(25)	(25)
On hand	150	125	100	75	50	25	0	(0)	(0)	(0)	(0)			
Planned orders		0	(25)	(25)	(25)	(25)	(25)	(25)	(25)					

Economic order quantity (EOQ). An EOQ policy is based on the assumption of continuous demand at a fixed rate, as discussed in the previous chapter. This rule attempts to trade off inventory carrying costs against the fixed costs of releasing an order. Our example Company A would calculate their economic order quantity as follows:

$$\text{Setup cost } (c_P) = \$5$$
$$\text{Unit cost } (c) = \$10$$
$$\text{Carrying cost } (c_H) = 15\% \text{ per annum} \times 10 = \$1.50$$
$$\text{Annual usage } (R) = 1,200 \text{ cans of paint}$$

$$Q = \sqrt{\frac{2c_PR}{c_H}} = \sqrt{\frac{2 \times 1{,}200 \times 5.00}{1.50}} \approx 90$$

Using the previously stated demand pattern and beginning inventory levels, Figure 4–10 represents Company A's inventory plan using a lot size determined by an EOQ analysis.

Figure 4–10
An application of the economic order quantity technique

Period		1	2	3	4	5	6	7	8	9	10	11	12	13
Forecast		25	25	25	25	25	25	25	25	25	25	25	25	25
Scheduled receipts								90			90			
On hand	150	125	100	75	50	25	0	65	40	15	80	55	30	5
Planned orders			90			90								

Period order quantity. An examination of Figure 4–10 shows that the EOQ of 90 includes a "remnant" of 15 cans of paint that will be carried in inventory in periods 7 through 9, and 30 cans in periods 10 through 12, to no purpose. These remnants are the result of the fact that the order quantity is not a multiple of the average period's requirements. A method of eliminating these "remnants" is to use the period order quantity (POQ) lot sizing technique. This technique results in order quantities based on a predetermined number of periods for which replenishment orders supply goods. The POQ is determined by calculating the number of weeks between orders that would result from the use of an economic order quantity, and rounding the result to the nearest integer. For example:

$$EOQ = 90$$
$$\text{Number of periods in year} = 52$$
$$\text{Annual demand} = 1{,}200$$
$$\frac{1{,}200}{90} = 13.3 \text{ orders per year}$$
$$\frac{52}{13.3} = 3.91 \text{ week order interval, or approximately 4 weeks}$$
$$POQ = 4 \text{ weeks' supply}$$

Figure 4–11 shows an inventory plan for Company A that is based on the application of a four-week POQ. The ordering rule here was to order enough to satisfy the next four periods of demand that were not already covered by existing inventories or scheduled receipts.

Figure 4–11
An application of the period order quantity technique

Period		1	2	3	4	5	6	7	8	9	10	11	12	13
Forecast		25	25	25	25	25	25	25	25	25	25	25	25	25
Scheduled receipts								100				100		
On hand	150	125	100	75	50	25	0	75	50	25	0	75	50	25
Planned orders			100				100							

Although the logic behind POQ lot sizing techniques is almost identical to that of the EOQ methods, it is considerably more effective than EOQ if demand is discontinuous, seasonal, or nonuniform. This is true because, with POQ, an order is always equal to an even number of periods sales requirements and thus, there can be no unnecessary remnants of inventory. The POQ technique also has the advantage that the lot size fluctuates in accordance with seasonal or other fluctuations in demand. Unlike EOQ, POQ avoids placing added orders during seasonal peaks, and overlarge inventories during troughs. Figure 4–12 illustrates the difference between the EOQ and POQ methods in a seasonal environment. Note from period 7 through

Figure 4–12
EOQ versus POQ in a seasonal environment

EOQ

Period		1	2	3	4	5	6	7	8	9	10	11	12	13
Forecast		50	15	10	0	25	50	10	10	10	40	60	30	5
Scheduled receipts								90				90		
On hand	150	100	85	75	75	50	0	80	70	60	20	50	20	15
Planned orders			90				90							

POQ

Period		1	2	3	4	5	6	7	8	9	10	11	12	13
Forecast		50	15	10	0	25	50	10	10	10	40	60	30	5
Scheduled receipts								70				95		
On hand	150	100	85	75	75	50	0	60	50	40	0	35	5	0
Planned orders			70				95							

period 13 the average inventory carried by the *EOQ* system is 45 per week while it is only 27 per week with the *POQ* lot sizing technique.

Least total cost and least unit cost. One of the reasons that the *POQ* often outperforms the *EOQ* technique in inventory planning is that it relaxes the restriction that the order quantity is fixed. Thus, it makes sense that a technique which relaxes the remaining *POQ* restriction, that the reordering interval is constant, will do even better. This assumption is the basis for the least total cost (LTC) method of inventory planning.

In determining the lot size for an order, the LTC procedure tries to equate the total cost of placing orders and carrying inventories for individual sets of planning periods. The technique can be illustrated by considering the alternative lot size choices that can be made for period 7 in our example from Figure 4–12. The first alternative is to order only enough to satisfy the period 7 demand of ten units. Using the common assumption that inventory carrying costs are charged only on the ending inventory balance, this alternative would result in zero inventories at the end of period 7, and thus in inventory carrying costs of $0. The second alternative would be to order enough for periods 7 and 8 combined, or 20 units. Since this alternative would result in 10 units of inventory at the end of period 7 and 0 units at the end of period 8, the inventory carrying costs associated with it would be:[3]

Week 7: 10 units × $0.029/unit/week = $0.29
Week 8: 0 units × $0.029/unit/week = $0
Total inventory carrying costs: $0.29

The inventory carrying costs for other alternative ordering patterns can be computed in a similar way. These alternatives, including those already discussed, are shown in Table 4–1.

Since the ordering costs in our example are $5 per order, the alternative ordering pattern that comes closest to accomplishing the LTC objective of balancing ordering and holding costs is *d*. Thus, this method would result in a period 7 order of 70 units. Orders for subsequent periods (from period 11 on) can be planned by reapplying the LTC logic.

---

[3] The unit inventory carrying cost per weekly period for our example problem can be calculated by dividing the $1.50 annual carrying cost by 52 weeks, or, $1.50/52 = $0.029 per unit per week.

Table 4-1
Evaluating alternative ordering decisions with the least total cost technique

Ordering pattern	Inventory carrying costs
a. Period 7 only.....................	$0.029 × 0 = $0
b. Periods 7 and 8 only	$0.029 (10 + 0) = $0.29
c. Periods 7, 8, and 9 only	$0.029 (20 + 10 + 0) = $0.87
d. Periods 7, 8, 9, and 10 only	$0.029 (60 + 50 + 40 + 0) = $4.35
e. Periods 7, 8, 9, 10, and 11 only	$0.029 (120 + 110 + 100 + 60 + 0) = $11.31

A closely related lot sizing technique is the least unit cost (LUC)
method. With it, the unit cost of alternative ordering quantities is
calculated as shown in Table 4-2. The lot size that is chosen is the
one that results in the *least* unit cost. Conceptually, this approach is
superior to the LTC method because it does not make the assumption
that the best order quantity occurs at the point where ordering costs
are equal to total carrying costs, an assumption that only holds true
when demand in each period is the same.

Table 4-2
Applying the least unit cost technique

Ordering pattern	Inventory carrying costs*	Order cost	Total cost	Quantity ordered	Unit cost
a. Period 7 only....................	$ 0.0	$5	$ 5.00	10	$0.50
b. Period 7 and 8 only	0.29	$5	$ 5.29	20	$0.26
c. Periods 7, 8, and 9 only	0.87	$5	$ 5.87	30	$0.20
d. Periods 7, 8, 9, and 10 only	4.35	$5	$ 9.35	70	$0.13
e. Periods 7, 8, 9, 10, and 11	11.31	$5	$16.31	130	$0.12
f. Periods 7, 8, 9, 10, 11, and 12 ...	15.66	$5	$20.66	160	$0.13

* From Table 4-1.

While the LUC technique often results in lower cost ordering
decisions than some other kinds of ordering rules, it does not always yield the optimal solution. It does not consider all of the
alternatives. The alternatives considered with the LUC method are
single sequences of periods, such as ordering for periods 7, 8, and 9
only, *or* 7, 8, 9, and 10 only. The technique does not consider multiple sets of sequences, such as, order in period 7 for periods 7 and 8,
and reorder in period 9 for periods 9 and 10. The determination of
the optimal solution requires that all the alternatives either explicitly

or implicitly be considered, and this requires a more powerful technique, such as the Wagner-Whitin algorithm.

The Wagner-Whitin algorithm. The lot-for-lot, EOQ, and POQ
approaches only yield optimal inventory ordering decisions in certain, very limited, situations. More often, they are used to yield
"good" as opposed to optimal solutions because they are easy to use,
and because they are relatively easy to understand. Optimal inventory planning decisions can only be guaranteed when relatively more
complex methods such as dynamic programming, of which the
Wagner-Whitin algorithm is an example, are applied.

The Wagner-Whitin algorithm, like any of the decision techniques
we have described, was derived under a certain set of assumptions:

1. Demand forecasts are available for N periods in the future.
2. Stockouts are not planned. That is, all forecasted demand will be
   met.
3. An ordering cost (c_P) is charged each time an order is made. This
   ordering cost *may* vary from period to period.
4. Orders may be made only at the beginning of each period and
   they are received instantaneously (zero lead time). In more complicated versions, this assumption may be relaxed.
5. An inventory holding cost per unit (c_H) is charged at the *beginning of each period* for each unit carried forward from the previous period.

These assumptions are not very restrictive, but they are important
since they help to form the basis on which a total cost objective
function can be formulated as shown below:

$$TIC_N = c_H I_1 + c_P \delta_1(x_1) + c_H(I_2) + c_P \delta_2(x_2) + \ldots$$
$$+ c_H(I_N) + c_P \delta_N(x_N).$$

TIC_N = The total cost of an N period plan.

$\quad c_H$ = The holding cost.

$\quad c_P$ = The order cost.

$\quad I_t$ = The inventory brought into period t (I_1 is the initial inventory level).

$\quad x_t$ = Amount ordered at the beginning of period t.

$\delta_t(x_t) = \begin{cases} 0 \text{ if } x_t = 0 \\ 1 \text{ if } x_t > 0 \end{cases}$

$\quad r_t$ = Forecast demand during period t.

Since it is obvious that $I_t = I_{t-1} + x_{t-1} - r_{t-1}$, the objective function
may be rewritten as (assuming a known initial inventory I_1):

$$TIC_N = c_H(I_1) + c_P\delta_1(x_1) \ldots \ldots \ldots \ldots \text{cost in period 1}$$
$$+ c_H(I_1 + x_1 - r_1) + c_P\delta_2(x_2) \ldots \ldots \ldots \text{cost in period 2}$$
$$+ c_H(I_1 + x_1 - r_1 + x_2 - r_2) + c_P\delta_3(x_3) \ldots \text{cost in period 3}$$

$$+ c_H(I_1 + x_1 - r_1 + x_2 - r_2 + \ldots + x_{N-1} - r_{N-1}) + c_P\delta_N(x_N)$$

In this cost expression, we know I_1, the initial inventory, and the demand forecast given by the r_t. The problem is then one of determining the set of x_t variables, $t = 1, \ldots, N$ which minimize the expression. Table 4–3 shows how this cost expression is used to evaluate an inventory plan.

Table 4–3

$r_1 = 10$	$r_2 = 20$	$r_3 = 30$	$r_4 = 10$
$N = 4$			
$c_H = \$1.00$	$c_P = \$15$	$I_1 = 0$	

Inventory plan: $x_1 = 10, x_2 = 60, x_3 = 0, x_4 = 0$

Period 1	Period 2	Period 3	Period 4
$r_1 = 10$	$r_2 = 20$	$r_3 = 30$	$r_4 = 10$
$x_1 = 10$	$x_2 = 60$	$x_3 = 0$	$x_4 = 0$
$I_1 = 0$	$I_2 = I_1 + x_1 - r_1 = 0$	$I_3 = I_2 + x_2 - r_2$ $= 0 + 60 - 20 = 40$	$I_4 = I_3 + x_3 - r_3$ $= 40 + 0 - 30 = 10$
$c_H I_1 = 0$	$c_H I_2 = 0$	$c_H I_3 = \$40$	$c_H I_4 = \$10$
$c_P\delta_1(x_1) =$	$c_P\delta_2(x_2) =$	$c_P\delta_3(x_3) =$	$c_P\delta_4(x_4) =$
$\$15 \times 1 = \$15$	$\$15 \times 1 = \$15$	$\$15 \times 0 = \$0$	$\$15 \times 0 = \$0$
$\$15$	$\$15$	$\$40$	$\$10$

The total cost of the plan in Table 4–3 is \$80. Note however, that only one plan has been evaluated in this example. Many alternative inventory replenishment plans exist, such as:

$$(a) \ x_1 = 15, x_2 = 15, x_3 = 40, x_4 = 0$$
$$(b) \ x_1 = 10, x_2 = 20, x_3 = 30, x_4 = 10$$

etc.

Clearly, one way to find the lowest cost inventory plan, given a forecast, is to enumerate and evaluate all possible plans. This would certainly be a tedious process. The Wagner-Whitin algorithm provides a simple means of determining an optimum plan while enumerating only a few of the possible plans. This technique is based on five propositions which greatly reduce the number of plans which must be considered:

Proposition 1. $I_t x_t = 0$; that is, one would never plan to carry inventory into a period in which an order is planned. In other words, orders that result in uneven remnants need never be considered. Note also that if inventory is zero, an order *must* be placed since stockouts are not permitted (assuming $r_t > 0$).

Proposition 2. There exists an optimal plan such that for all periods $x_t = 0$ or $x_t = \sum_{j=t}^{k} r_j$ for some k, $t \leq k \leq N$. This proposition, which follows from the first, states that orders in a period t will either be for 0 units, or for the total requirements for period t, or for the total requirements for period $t + 1$, or for the total requirements for t, and $t + 1$, and $t + 2 \ldots t + k$, etc. This means that schedules such as (a) need not be considered, because they cannot be a part of an optimal sequence.

Proposition 3. If requirements in period $t = k$ are satisfied from an order in period $k - z$, then the requirements in all intervening periods $k - z + 1$, $k - z + 2$, . . . , $k - 1$ are also satisfied by the order in period $k - z$ for some optimal inventory plan.

Proposition 4. Given an optimal plan for the first n periods of an N period problem in which $I_t = 0$ for $t < n$, one can determine the optimal plan for the rest of the periods without considering any other alternatives to the first $t - 1$ periods.

Proposition 5. Given an optimal plan for the first n periods of an N period problem in which $x_n > 0$, one does not need to consider periods 1 through $n - 1$ in formulating the rest of the plan. (This is called the planning horizon theorem and is a slightly stronger variation on Proposition 4).

In the Wagner-Whitin algorithm, these propositions are used to determine first an optimal one-period plan, then an optimal two-period plan, then an optimal three-period plan, and so on until the optimal N period plan is derived. They are also used to eliminate nonoptimal alternatives, thus reducing the amount of analysis needed to find an overall optimum. The example problem from Table 4–3 will be used to illustrate this process, in conjunction with the flowchart shown in Figure 4–13.

First, an optimal plan considering only the first period must be derived. This plan is simple to derive since the only alternative is to order 10 units in period 1 (i.e., $x_1 = 10$). This partial plan costs \$15,

Figure 4–13
A Flowchart of the Wagner-Whitin algorithm

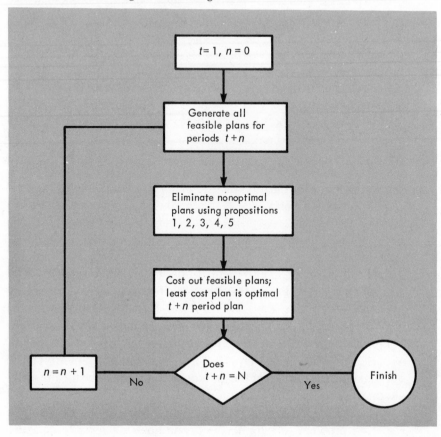

the order cost, since no inventories are carried into the first period
($I_1 = 0$).

Next, we derive an optimal two-period plan. In this case we have
two alternative plans to consider (using Propositions 1 and 2). The
first alternative is to order enough in period 1 for both periods one
and two (this alternative is designated by (1,2)). The second alternative is to order the requirements for period one in period one and the
requirements for period two in period two (this alternative is designated by (1)(2)). In other words, alternative one is $x_1 = 30, x_2 = 0$ and
alternative two is $x_1 = 10, x_2 = 20$. We may then cost out these two
plans:

$$TIC_2 = c_H(I_1) + c_P\delta_1(x_1) + c_H(I_1 + x_1 - r_1) + c_P\delta_2(x_2)$$
$$TIC_{(1,2)} = 0 + \$15 + \$1(0 + 30 - 10) + \qquad = \$35$$
$$TIC_{(1)(2)} = 0 + \$15 + \$1(0 + 10 - 10) + \$15 = \$30$$

Thus, the best two-period plan is (1)(2). In tabular form, we have evaluated plans for two periods as shown in Table 4–4.

Table 4–4

Period	1	2
Plans	(1) $15	(1,2) $35 (1)(2) $30
Minimum cost	$15	$30
Best policy so far	(1)	(1)(2)

Now, considering the best three-period policy, there are four alternative plans if we consider only Propositions 1, 2, and 3. These plans are:

a. (1,2,3) i.e., $x_1 = 60$, $x_2 = 0$, $x_3 = 0$
b. (1)(2)(3) i.e., $x_1 = 10$, $x_2 = 20$, $x_3 = 30$
c. (1)(2,3) i.e., $x_1 = 10$, $x_2 = 50$, $x_3 = 0$
d. (1,2)(3) i.e., $x_1 = 30$, $x_2 = 0$, $x_3 = 30$

However, we know that we do not need to consider alternatives a and d because of Propositions 4 and 5. Thus, we only need to determine the costs for the two possibly optimal three-period plans:

$$TIC_3 = c_H(I_1) + c_P\delta_1(x_1) + c_H(I_2) + c_P\delta_2(x_2) + c_H(I_3) + c_P\delta_3(x_3)$$
$$TIC_{(1)(2)(3)} = 0 + \$15 + 0 + \$15 + 0 + \$15 = \$45$$
$$TIC_{(1)(2,3)} = 0 + \$15 + 0 + \$15 + \$1(30) + 0 = \$60$$

Alternative b yields the best three-period plan. Continuing in a similar manner, we can arrive at the best four-period plan as shown in Table 4–5.

Choice of lot sizing method

On the basis of the logic behind the lot sizing rules for inventory planning that we have discussed, one might predict that the

Table 4–5

Period	1	2	3	4
Plans	(1) $15	(1,2) $35 (1)(2) $30	(1)(2)(3) $45 (1)(2,3) $60	(1)(2)(3)(4) $60 (1)(2)(3,4) $55
Minimum cost	$15	$30	$45	$55
Best policy	(1)	(1)(2)	(1)(2)(3)	(1)(2)(3,4)

Wagner-Whitin algorithm would produce the best ordering decisions (based on the minimization of ordering and inventory holding costs), followed in rank order by the least unit cost, least total cost, period order quantity, and lot-for-lot methods. Indeed, Berry [1] has provided experimental evidence that this rank ordering is appropriate. However, such generalizations must be treated carefully since there are certain conditions and other criteria which can change or nullify them. For example, Berry [1] and Kaimann [8] have shown that when demand is uniform over the periods of an inventory plan and when the EOQ is an integer multiple of the uniform period demand, this rule will equal the performance of the Wagner-Whitin algorithm.

Of more importance, however, is the impact of other criteria on the choice of lot sizing rules. For example, the period order quantity is quite often selected over the Wagner-Whitin algorithm and part-period balancing methods because the criteria managers use to select ordering rules often weigh simplicity and minimizing computer time over optimality. Similarly, the lot-for-lot technique is often used because it results in a smoother flow of orders than the other rules which tend to bunch them into large lots. This may be desirable where smoothing the work load has important cost advantages that outweigh setup costs. Such considerations illustrate that optimality in the theoretical sense can be an elusive criterion, and that the whole system and its needs must be considered in selecting a lot sizing technique for use in inventory planning.

Inventory planning under uncertainty

In our discussions of inventory planning systems to this point, we have presumed that our forecasts of demand and our lead time values were certain. However, it goes without saying that uncertainty is a persistent characteristic of the industrial world, and that any realistic system must incorporate methodologies for handling it. Notwithstanding the various combinations of methods that inventory planners use, there are three basic approaches for handling uncertainty in inventory planning systems. The first is to employ safety or buffer stocks, in much the same way that they were employed in reorder point and other reactive systems that we have discussed. The second approach involves the use of "safety lead times." Safety lead times are extra time periods added on to the expected lead time in anticipation of poor deliveries or forecasts. The third approach involves what we have termed expediting and de-expediting, or controlling demand. This approach is based on the use of managerial muscle to either slow down the arrival of an order when poor forecasts or quick deliveries result in high inventories; to speed up the delivery of materials in less than the normal lead time when shortages are imminent; or to negotiate the delivery date of orders or partial shipments of orders with customers.

To illustrate the use of these techniques for protecting against uncertainty, consider the inventory plan shown in Figure 4–14. It

Figure 4–14
An unbuffered inventory plan

Period		1	2	3	4	5	6	7	8	9	10	11	12	13
Forecast		50	15	10	0	25	50	0	10	10	40	60	30	15
Scheduled receipts									60			105		
On hand	150	100	85	75	75	50	0	0	50	40	0	45	15	0
Planned orders				60			105							

was derived with the use of a period order quantity of three weeks' supply, and the assumption of a five-period lead time. It is completely unbuffered from the uncertainty stemming from either a poor forecast, or from unreliable deliveries. Figure 4–15 shows the same situation in which a safety stock of 50 units has been employed. Here, inventory planning proceeded as in the first case, with the exception that a planned order was triggered when the projected on-hand balance fell below 50 rather than zero units. The safety stock of 50 could have been derived by using the same statistical

Figure 4–15
Safety stock of 50

Period		1	2	3	4	5	6	7	8	9	10	11	12	13
Forecast		50	15	10	0	25	50	0	10	10	40	60	30	15
Scheduled receipts							60			110			45	
On hand	150	100	85	75	75	50	60	60	50	150	110	50	65	50
Planned orders		60			110			45						

techniques as those employed in determining buffer stocks in Chapter 3.

Safety lead times imply that additional time has been added to the lead time to protect against uncertainties in supply. Figure 4–16 shows an inventory plan similar to that shown in Figure 4–14, except that a seven-week lead time was used instead of a five-week lead time. If in spite of the assumption of a seven-week lead time, goods arrive five weeks after the order is placed, the safety lead time will in fact result in extra inventories as shown in Figure 4–17, thus effectively buffering the system against both supply and demand uncertainty in much the same way that safety stocks do.

Figure 4–16
Seven-week lead time

Period		1	2	3	4	5	6	7	8	9	10	11	12	13
Forecast		50	15	10	0	25	50	0	10	10	40	60	30	15
Scheduled receipts									60			105		
On hand	150	100	85	75	75	50	0	0	50	40	0	45	5	0
Planned orders		60			105									

Whybark and Williams [16] have studied the use of safety stocks and safety lead times in order to determine the most effective technique under various types of operating conditions. They classified uncertainty into four different categories, according to the source of the uncertainty (demand or supply), and the type of uncertainty

Figure 4–17
Seven-week planned lead time (actual lead time five weeks)

Period		1	2	3	4	5	6	7	8	9	10	11	12	13
Forecast		50	15	10	0	25	50	0	10	10	40	60	30	15
Scheduled receipts							60			105				
On hand	150	100	85	75	75	50	60	60	50	145	105	45	15	0
Planned orders		60			105									

Table 4–6
Categories of uncertainty in MRP system

	Sources	
Types	Demand	Supply
Timing	Requirements shift from one period to another	Orders not received when scheduled
Uncertainty	Requirements for more or less than planned	Orders received for more or less than planned

Source: D. Clay Whybark, and J. Gregg Williams, "Material Requirements Planning under Uncertainty," *Decision Sciences*, vol. 7, no. 1
(October 1976), pp. 595–606.

(timing or quantity) as shown in Table 4–6. Their hypothesis was
that there would be a preference for either safety lead time or safety
stock under each category of uncertainty. Using a simulation model,
they tested the effect of the two strategies on service levels and average inventory levels under widely varying conditions. Their conclusions were that under conditions of uncertainty in *timing* (either in
the arrival of supplies or demands) safety lead time is the preferred
technique. Conversely, when either the *quantity* demanded or
supplied was uncertain, safety stock was the preferred technique.

Management action. The use of safety stocks or safety lead times
in conjunction with an inventory planning system for independent
demand items results in systems with characteristics similar to those
of the reactive systems that were discussed earlier in this chapter. For
example, the system becomes attuned to at least one "fixed limit";
the safety stock or the safety lead time. In such instances the advantages of planning inventories over reacting to the fixed parameters of

a reactive model are diminished. Inventory planning systems are most effective in the independent demand context when they are used to provide more information for management action than simply when and how much to order. Inventory planning systems also provide information about when and how much material is to be expedited or rescheduled, thus providing extra data that can be used to manage uncertainty.

To illustrate the use of expediting and rescheduling with an inventory planning system, consider the sequence of plans shown in Figures 4–18, 4–19, and 4–20. The inventory plan shown in Figure

Figure 4–18
Original plan and forecast

Period		1	2	3	4	5	6	7	8	9	10	11	12	13
Forecast		50	15	10	0	25	50	0	10	10	40	60	30	15
Scheduled receipts									60		105			
On hand	150	100	85	75	75	50	0	0	50	40	0	45	15	0
Planned orders				60			105							

Figure 4–19
New forecast and old plan

Period		2	3	4	5	6	7	8	9	10	11	12	13	14
Forecast		70	10	0	25	50	0	10	10	40	60	30	15	25
Scheduled receipts								60			105			
On Hand	95	25	15	15	(10)	(60)	(60)	(10)	(20)	(60)	(15)	(45)	(60)	(85)
Planned orders			60			105								

4–18 is the same unbuffered plan that we have treated in previous examples. It reflects the current position of a company in terms of on-hand inventory and the best forecast available at the beginning of period 1. The projected on-hand balance, scheduled receipts, and planned orders are the result of inventory planning decisions made at the beginning of period 1. Assuming that this plan has been

Figure 4–20
New forecast and new plan

Period		2	3	4	5	6	7	8	9	10	11	12	13	14
Forecast		70	10	0	25	50	0	10	10	40	60	30	15	25
Scheduled receipts							80			130			40	
On hand	95	25	15	15	(10)	(60)	20	10	0	90	30	0	25	0
Planned orders		80			130			40						

adopted, management would take no action at the beginning of period 1. The plan shows that action will not be called for until the beginning of period 3, when an order for 60 units must be released for delivery during period 8.

During the course of week 1, the following information is representative of what might be recorded and determined:

a. Actual demand was 40 units, not 50 units as predicted.
b. After a physical inventory, it was determined that the actual on-hand balance at the beginning of period 1 was 135 not 150, because of recording errors, and the failure of some parts to pass inspection.
c. A new forecast was made at the end of period 1 on the basis of new marketing information.

These transactions and the new forecast substantially change the planned availability of materials in future periods as shown in Figure 4–19. Since the old plan was unbuffered, the result will be stockouts, predicted for periods 5 through 14. To avoid the projected stockouts, the inventory manager must replan and adjust planned orders to cover demand. A new inventory plan using the standard lead times that have been assumed in this example is shown in Figure 4–20. This plan illustrates one of the alternative courses of action that the manager can take; ordering 80 units as soon as possible to cover demand in periods 5 through 9, anticipating that the demand in periods 5 and 6 can be backordered and filled in period 7 when the material arrives. This plan will work if customers will wait an extra two weeks for their order to be completely filled, and if the costs of a stockout are relatively low, or at least negotiable.

Figure 4–21
New forecast and an expedited plan

Period		2	3	4	5	6	7	8	9	10	11	12	13	14
Forecast		70	10	0	25	50	0	10	10	40	60	30	15	25
Scheduled receipts					60			60			105			?
On hand	95	25	15	15	50	0	0	50	40	0	45	15	0	
Planned orders		60	60			105								

A second alternative plan that an inventory manager might create is shown in Figure 4–21. This plan might be preferable if the costs of stocking out or backordering were perceived to be high. It involves expediting an order of 60 units immediately for delivery in less than the standard lead time of five periods. Expediting would involve recognition of the fact that standard lead time estimates reflect a certain "normal" way of doing business, but that "abnormal" methods can be applied to change them. For example, Figure 4–7 shows that the normal way for Company A to order involves two weeks of paper work and mail time, two weeks (usually) for the vendor to fill the order, and one week for the order to be shipped to Company A, say by truck. Methods of expediting the order might involve the "abnormal" actions associated with (a) placing the order by phone, (b) using influence or even extra payments to encourage the vendor to fill the order quickly, or (c) having the order delivered by air rather than truck.

This example of the use of management action to handle uncertainty illustrates several important features of systems based on such methods. The first is that such techniques offer the manager wide latitude in terms of taking creative steps to solve operating problems, while the use of buffers such as safety lead times or safety stocks yield much more straightforward, formal, but limited opportunities for management. The second major feature is that in a sense, management action is used in lieu of buffer inventories to handle uncertainty. This observation provides an important clue for determining when it should be used instead of safety stock or safety lead time in independent demand systems. When the cost of extra inventory to handle uncertainty is less than the expected management time and other penalties associated with expediting or rescheduling

$$Q_0 = \left[\frac{2 C_p L}{C_H (1 - Y/p)} \right]^{1/2}$$

IF $C_{p1} = 10$, $\quad$ { EVERYTHING ELSE IS
$C_{p2} = 12$. $\quad$ CONSTANT

$$\frac{Q_{01}}{Q_{02}} = \sqrt{\frac{21}{10}}$$

$$Q_{01} = Q_{02} \sqrt{\frac{21}{10}}$$

$$Q_0 = 1000 \text{ units.}$$
$$TIC_0 = \$500$$
$$C_p = \$10$$

$$\frac{Q_{O_1}}{Q_{O_2}} = \frac{\sqrt{\dfrac{1}{1-\dfrac{z_i}{P_1}}}}{\sqrt{\dfrac{1}{1-\dfrac{r_2}{P_2}}}} = \sqrt{\left[\dfrac{1}{1-\dfrac{r_i}{P}}\right]\left[\dfrac{1}{1-\dfrac{r_2}{P_2}}\right]} = \sqrt{\dfrac{1-\dfrac{r_2}{P_2}}{1-\dfrac{r_1}{P_1}}}$$

(phone bills, premium freight, payments to vendors), buffering methods should prevail. Conversely, when the average cost of expediting or rescheduling is less than the average cost of the buffer inventory associated with safety stocks or safety lead time, management action is the most appropriate method of managing uncertainty.

SUMMARY

Independent demand inventory systems must include all of the three basic elements of a planning and control system: data collection and generation, decision making and planning, and implementation, feedback, and control. In this chapter we have illustrated four different types of independent demand inventory systems, each of which implies a different definition of these three activities.

Fixed reorder quantity systems generally require the maintenance of a perpetual inventory record, and rely upon fixed reorder quantities (EOQs) and statistical reorder points as operating parameters. From an operating standpoint, the most critical variables in this type of system are the accurate definition of order points and order quantities, and accurate and timely reporting of inventory transactions into a perpetual inventory record. Fixed reorder quantity systems have their greatest application in controlling relatively low-volume items where lot size economies are great.

Fixed reorder cycle systems rely on the maintenance of a fixed period of time between the issuance of orders of unequal size. This approach has certain advantages, including the fact that it demands a periodic reassessment of demand rates, and that perpetual inventory record keeping is not necessary. The main disadvantage is that the notion of a fixed reorder cycle can result in a slow response to rapid changes in inventory positions and demand rates. A major advantage of fixed reorder cycle systems is that they allow for the grouping of orders of different items for transportation or supplier economies.

The optional replenishment type system has the advantage that both order quantities and reorder intervals can vary over time. Thus, it embodies the advantages of both the fixed reorder cycle and fixed reorder quantity systems. It also shares in the common disadvantage of both of these alternatives as well. In practice, all three of these types of systems are reactive to one or at most two fixed parameters. When the distribution of demand and lead times are stable, this does not offer great problems. However, when demand is seasonal, has a strong trend, or is "lumpy," the use of fixed parameters leads to poor inventory decisions. In such situations, the use of these systems with "adaptive" parameters, or inventory planning, usually proves to be superior.

Inventory planning methods are generally suited for items which should be very tightly controlled. In the technical sense, these systems are quite easy to operate and to understand, although some of the lot sizing methods that can be used in conjunction with them, such as the Wagner-Whitin algorithm, are fairly complicated. Operationally, however, inventory planning or "time phased reorder point" methods are quite demanding. They demand timely, accurate perpetual inventory balances, for example. But, the greatest demands that they place on operations are managerial in nature. The capability of projecting inventory shortages and overages requires managers to be creative in considering a wide range of options including stocking out, expediting, backlogging, or rescheduling, and in negotiating with customers and vendors to implement these plans. As we shall see in Chapter 7, they are also important because inventory planning methods form the basis for material requirements planning systems.

REVIEW QUESTIONS AND PROBLEMS

1. A firm has 14,000 items. One thousand of the items are classed as A items. On the average, each A item stock is replenished once a week, and each item has three withdrawals from stock each day. Four thousand of the items are B items; they average one replenishment every two months for each item, and withdrawals for each item average two per week. The balance of the items in stock are C items; they are replenished once every six months and average one withdrawal from stock per month for each item. A study of past inventory transactions activity has shown that an error is made in counting or recording 1 out of every 50 inventory transactions.

    a. If management wishes to maintain at least 95 percent inventory record accuracy, how frequently should the A items be cycle counted? The B items? The C items? (Assume 52 weeks per year, 260 working days per year.)

    b. Create a schedule indicating how many A, B, and C items should be counted each week.

2. For each or the cycle counting methods listed in this chapter, compare the advantages and disadvantages of each with respect to:

    a. The number of items that must be counted to validate perpetual records.

  b.   The evenness of the work load on cycle counting specialists.
  c.   The ease with which these methods can be administered without disrupting ongoing operations.
3.   A firm has an item with the following characteristics:
     Unit cost: $9
     Inventory carrying cost (as a percent of item value): 20% per year
     Demand: 200 per week (10,000 per year)
     Ordering cost: $15
     Lead time: 2 weeks (constant)
     Demand variability: Demand over the lead time is normally distributed with a mean of 400 and a standard deviation of 25 units.

  a.   Determine the order quantity and order point assuming a fixed reorder quantity system, and a 95 percent service level.
  b.   How large is the buffer or safety stock given the order point you computed in (a) above? What average level of inventory will result from the use of this system?
  c.   Construct a flowchart identifying the key elements of the fixed reorder quantity system required to control the item.
4.   Given the data in Problem 3, determine the parameters of a fixed reorder cycle system that yield a 95 percent service level. (Note: The average usage over the lead time (L) plus review period (R) is equal to 200 $(R + L)$. The standard deviation of demand over this period of time is equal to $(R + L) \times 12.5$.
  a.   What average inventory will result from the use of this system? Why is it different from that obtained in answer to Question 3(b)?
  b.   Double the reorder cycle interval used in answer to 4(a), and recalculate the buffer stock necessary to operate with 95 percent service given this cycle interval? Why is it larger than the buffer stock resulting from the answer to 4(a)?
  c.   What does the answer to 4(b) indicate about the relationship between order quantities or order cycles and the buffer stock required to maintain a given level of service?
  d.   Construct a flowchart identifying the key elements of a fixed order cycle system. How does this differ from the result of Question 3(c)?
5.   A firm has an item with the following characteristics:
     Unit cost: $12
     Inventory carrying cost (as a percent of item value): 25 percent per year
     Ordering cost: $15
     Lead time: 3 weeks
     Beginning inventory: 655 units
     Demand forecast for the next 12 periods: 150; 160; 170; 180; 190; 200; 250; 350; 300; 200; 200; 180.

     Using the inventory planning format described in Figure 4–6, plan your inventories and inventory decisions for the next 12 periods using the following lot sizing rules:

    a. Lot-for-lot.

    b. Economic order quantity.

    c. Period order quantity.

    d. Least total cost.

    e. Least unit cost.

    f. The Wagner-Whitin algorithm.

6. How would the inclusion of a buffer stock of 100 units change the plans laid in response to Question 5(c)?

7. How would a two-week safety lead time change the plans laid in response to Question 5(c)?

8. When is safety lead time more desirable than safety stock in inventory planning?

9. Construct a flowchart identifying the key elements of an inventory-planning system using the period order quantity lot sizing technique and safety lead times. How might this flowchart change if expediting and de-expediting are used in lieu of safety lead times?

SELECTED BIBLIOGRAPHY

1. Berry, W. L. "Lot Sizing Procedures for Requirements Planning Systems: A Framework for Analysis," *Production and Inventory Management*, vol. 13, no. 2 (1972), pp. 19–34.

2. Brown, R. G. *Decision Rules for Inventory Management.* New York: Holt, Rinehart & Winston, Inc., 1967.

3. Buchan, J., and Koenigsberg, E. *Scientific Inventory Management.* Englewood Cliffs, N.J.: Prentice-Hall, Inc., 1963.

4. Eilon, S. *Elements of Production Planning and Control.* New York: Macmillan Co., 1962.

5. Eilon, S., and Elmaleh, J. "Adaptive Limits in Inventory Control," *Management Science*, vol. 16, no. 8 (April 1970), pp. 532–48.

6. Eilon, S., and Elmaleh, J. "An Evaluation of Alternate Inventory Control Policies," *International Journal of Production Research*, vol. 7, no. 1 (1968), pp. 3–14.

7. Greene, J. H. *Production Control: Systems and Decisions.* rev. ed. Homewood, Ill.: Richard D. Irwin, Inc., 1974.

8. Kaimann, R. A. "E.O.Q. vs. Dynamic Programming: Which One to Use for Inventory Ordering?" *Production and Inventory Management*, vol. 10, no. 4 (1969), pp. 66–74.

9. Naddor, E. *Inventory Systems.* New York: John Wiley & Sons, Inc., 1966.

10. Orlicky, J. *Material Requirements Planning*. New York: McGraw-Hill Book Co., 1975.

11. Peterson, R., and Silver, E. A. *Decision Systems for Inventory Management and Production Planning*. New York: John Wiley & Sons, Inc., 1979.

12. Plossl, G. *Manufacturing Control: The Last Frontier for Profits*. Reston, Va.: Reston Publishing Company, 1973.

13. Plossl, G., and Wight, O. *Production and Inventory Control: Principles and Techniques*. Englewood Cliffs, N.J.: Prentice-Hall, Inc., 1967.

14. Tersine, R. J., and Campbell, J. H. *Modern Materials Management*. New York: Elsevier North-Holland, Inc., 1977.

15. Wagner, H. J., and Whitin, T. M. "Dynamic Version of the Economic Lot Size Model," *Management Science*, October 1958.

16. Whybark, D. C., and Williams, J. G. "Material Requirements Planning under Uncertainty," *Decision Sciences*, vol. 7, no. 1 (October 1976), pp. 595–606.

17. Wight, O. W. *Production and Inventory Management in the Computer Age*. Boston: Cahners Publishing Company, 1974.

CASE STUDY
AVALON MACHINERY
COMPANY (R)

PAUL WILLIAMS, president of the Avalon Machinery Company, decided to review his company's inventory policies "to see if scientific inventory control will produce substantial savings for our company." Because the principal inventory category at Avalon was machined parts, he selected two parts from one of the company's products for detailed study—a presser foot and a roller cam from a border machine used in stitching the vertical border of mattresses.

Company background

Employing 300 office and factory workers, Avalon was one of two large American manufacturers of bedding equipment machinery. The company produced 17 basic types of machines consisting of quilting machines, lace tufters, border machines, tape edging machines, mattress packaging equipment, and other machines used in manufacturing mattresses and innersprings. While the machine designs permitted customers to select various options and add features, most of the machines were designed and fabricated as standard products.

Avalon's primary manufacturing facility was a large, varied array of machine tools, including lathes, automatic screw machines, milling machines, grinders, and drill presses. The machine tool section and an area for assembly were contained in a one-story building. Connected to this plant was a new 100-foot by 120-foot one-story warehouse completed early in 1973 to replace three widely separated storage facilities. At a cost of $480,000 to build, the new warehouse completely eliminated the costs of moving parts to and from the distant warehouses. The new building also provided easier materials handling and better material control because all parts were centrally located, in close proximity to the places where they were made and used.

Planning and scheduling

Because Paul Williams was unwilling to assemble machines for stock, there was no system of annual production budgets or monthly production bogies. Jim Williams, the president's son, scheduled the assembly of machines whenever orders for machines had accumulated to the point at which he felt he had a production lot. For economies in assembly, machines were scheduled in lots of six or more. (A careful analysis of the assembly costs had led Jim Williams to estimate that a machine would cost 33 percent more if assembled in a lot of one rather than a lot of six.) When selling at its peak, a machine might be scheduled in lots of 24; but later, when demand was only for replacement machines, the lot size might be 6. If a customer or a salesman exerted great pressure for a quick delivery, Jim Williams started an assembly lot, even though not all the machines had been ordered. The remaining machines were usually ordered before the lot was completed; but in a few rare cases, unsold, completed machines were placed into a finished goods inventory. Although there was no formal program of budgeting the total number of machines to be manufactured or of keeping track of the load in the shop, Jim Williams informally considered the amount of business in the shop in determining when a new lot should be started and when it could be completed. In general, he expected completion of orders in three months but actual completion might vary by as much as one month either way from this expectation.

Delivery promises were of considerable concern to Paul Williams and other Avalon managers. They were convinced that the quality of Avalon machines was superior to others, and that most Avalon customers were willing to wait in order to get Avalon machines. The principal competitor, however, was building standard machines for stock and providing prompt delivery. Avalon salesmen stated that some customers were citing delivery as the reason they selected this competitor's machines. Since most customer orders waited until additional orders were received to make an assembly lot, customers usually faced a lead time of over four months.

A copy of the order for an assembly lot was sent to Spence Larrimore in the warehouse, whose job it was to "explode" the order into detailed parts requirements. For items which had to be purchased and required raw materials, he worked with the purchasing department to insure that the necessary parts and materials would be on hand. On parts manufactured at Avalon, he checked requirements against inventory; when the quantity of parts on hand minus the number to be used in this assembly lot fell below the reorder point, he sent an order to the machine tool section for a new lot of parts.

An order to the machine tool section for parts was triggered also by a customer's order for a spare part if it reduced the inventory to or below the reorder point. Customer orders for spare parts consumed a significant portion of the parts in stock. Orders for spare parts for border machines alone totaled $64,000 in 1973 and $72,000 in 1974.

The economic lot size and the reorder point were established when the company began using the new warehouse. The basic rule of thumb was that delivery from the machine tool section might take two months, and production lots should be large enough to avoid having two orders for the same part outstanding at any one time.

In the machine tool section, a clerk pulled from the files the operation card for each part ordered. From these were made perforated job tickets for all operations. When each operation was completed, the pertinent ticket was torn from the rest and returned to the office. (Samples of these tickets are shown in Exhibit 1.) The tickets provided cost accounting and wage incentive information in addition to notifying the office of the up-to-date status of each lot. Jim Williams estimated that the paperwork on one order required one hour's time valued at $5 an hour.

The scheduling of parts on specific machines was done by a leadman for each group of machines and workers. In selecting the item to be processed next from among the jobs ready for work in his department, the leadman was influenced by these factors:

1. He attempted to combine orders having similar or identical operations in an effort to reduce or eliminate setup times.
2. He attempted to give priority to items on the shortage list for assembly.[1]
3. He attempted to give priority to items on the shortage list for spares.

---

[1] Several weeks before a machine lot was scheduled for assembly, Spence Larrimore started checking to see if all the required parts were available. Any parts missing were listed on a shortage list distributed throughout the plant. Orders for spare parts not in stock were also shown on the shortage list.

Exhibit 1
Operation job tickets, Part BM–134, Order No. 7398

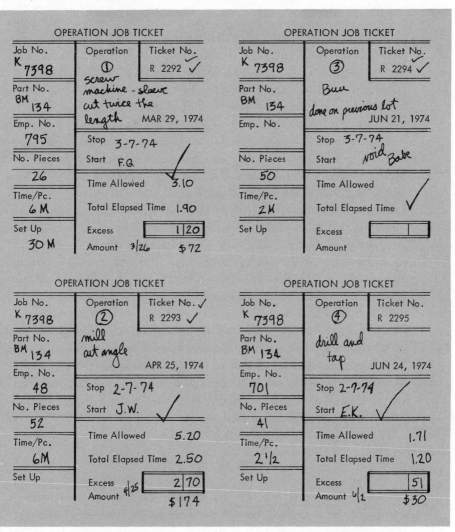

4. Jim Williams suspected that the typical leadman was influenced by his workers' desires for high wages, which could be met by working on orders where the standards were loose.

5. He was expected to respond to requests from leadmen in departments following his who requested certain kinds of work.

6. He necessarily had to take account of any possible bottlenecks in his own department. If particular machines or workers were ex-

pected to be limiting factors, he had to make sure that these machines and workers were used to the maximum extent possible on items requiring their special capabilities.

There was no system of machine loading but, as Jim Williams pointed out, machines were almost never bottlenecks, the company having more machine tools than it could use. Occasionally a worker, possessing skills not possessed by other workers, became a bottleneck. The company had no formal means of keeping track of the load on such a worker.

If the production load built up, the leadman exercised his judgment in determining whether he was falling farther and farther behind the production demanded of his machines and men or if this was a temporary overload which could be overcome. In some instances, a leadman asked Spence Larrimore if Spence had any parts orders which could be ordered a little early to provide work for available machines or workers. If it seemed desirable to the leadman, he might ask the production foreman for approval to work overtime or short time. If a change in the number of hours did not appear sufficient to meet the problem, or if the problem seemed of a long-term nature, a leadman might ask the production foreman to ask the plant management for approval to hire or lay off employees. The production foreman would, of course, evaluate the possibility of transferring men between groups of machines before passing on the request to hire or lay off. In evaluating a request for hiring or layoffs, Avalon management was influenced by its estimation of the expected duration of the production rate changes.

Inventories

Very few raw materials were carried in inventory. Most raw materials were basic rod, bar, or sheet metals, and could be obtained on overnight delivery from nearby metal supply houses. The basic castings, forming the large parts of the frame, were not stocked but rather were ordered for each assembly. Since frame parts rarely broke in usage, there was almost no demand for them as spares. When the castings arrived at the plant, they were taken to the assembly area, or to the machine tool section if machining was required. A few parts not manufactured by Avalon had long lead times. Particular kinds of needles, for instance, required three months for delivery. On these items, Avalon *did* carry an inventory intended to meet all demand until the next order was placed and the parts received.

The largest part of the inventory was machined parts. The warehouse contained 8,000 different parts valued at $1,000,000. These parts, typically small, were contained in wooden boxes on metal shelves lined up in rows in the warehouse. The parts were described by a two-letter prefix indicating the type of machine (e.g., BM stood for border machines) and an identification number (ranging from 1 up to the number of parts required for the machine). If an identical part was used in more than one machine, the inventory was carried at only one point. In the section of the shelves devoted to the second machine, there was a card referring the warehouseman to the equivalent part number for the first machine. A typical machine had over a hundred parts, all found on one row of shelves.

A section of the warehouse enclosed as an office contained file cards providing the records of each part. Each card showed replacement orders sent to the machine tool section, withdrawals for assembly or for spares, and receipts of parts from the machine tool section. In addition, each card carried the reorder point and the order quantity, which the warehouse superintendent had the authority to change when experience and his judgment indicated these numbers to be too high or too low. In determining the order point and order quantity, he drew on the card information showing the dates recent orders were placed on the machine tool section, the dates they were received, and the usage of the part.

Data on expected sales

Both of the parts selected by Paul Williams for study were used in the border machine (see Exhibit 2). This machine prepared a strip of cloth which became the vertical side of a completed mattress. The strip could be quilted with felt or other backing in a variety of patterns, edge hemmed, and if desired receive ventilation holes. One person could operate two or three machines, and each machine could stitch 12 feet of border per minute. The machine, one of the basic items in the Avalon line, was designed in the late 1950s and had been a consistent seller since then. Although some minor parts had been redesigned in response to customer problems, the basic machine was unchanged from its original design. Jim Williams believed that this machine had passed its peak sales around 1960 and was now pretty well stabilized.

There was no particular seasonal pattern to the sales of border machines or other mattress manufacturing equipment. In the early

Exhibit 2
Photograph of a border machine

Vertical stitch borders are increasingly popular. They add height and beauty to mattresses,
therefore make the mattresses easier to sell.
The Avalon Vertical Border Machine is best for
making these very popular borders because it
is designed and manufactured by mattress machinery experts, for maximum border yardage.
Its extremely rugged, yet simple design makes
it easy to operate. More than 500 machines
are in use, in both large and small bedding
plants, all over the world.

You can make your Vertical Stitch Borders
for about half the cost of buying them.
You can give your customers faster service,
by getting the borders in the particular
material you want at once, and have less
money tied up in inventory.

One person can keep 2 or 3 Avalon machines in operation.
The standard machine is easily adjustable for any border
from 4" to 7". Cams are available for 3 1/2" to 5" borders and 7" to 10" borders. The width between vertical
stitchings is adjustable from 1 1/8" to 2". The Avalon
automatically turns and sews as it hems (sews double
lock stitch, U.S.#401) thereby saving you labor, time,
thread, and eliminating prehemming operation.

1960s, sales tended to peak after the equipment convention held at
Thanksgiving time, but the industry change to an Eastertime convention seemed to have leveled sales seasonally.

The inventory cards used in the warehouse showed the sales history since May 1973, when the records were transferred to the new
procedures and facilities. The information on the cards for the two
parts selected by Paul Williams is summarized in Exhibits 3, 4, and 5
of this case. The cards carried the order number for each withdrawal
and indicated if the withdrawal was for a customer spare part order,
for a border machine assembly lot, for assembly into some other
machine, or for insertion into the kit of one of the six Avalon repair-
men who provided service on Avalon machines. Jim Williams, knowing of no changes in the design for either of these parts, could not
explain the fluctuation in the consumption of spares. Some of the
increase might have been caused by scare buying by Avalon customers. In November 1973, hints of material shortages had seemingly

prompted many customers to rush in large orders for spares. The recent increase in purchases of machinery by foreign manufacturers also might have increased purchases of spares, because a number of these manufacturers, unable to afford having their machines idle while spares crossed the ocean, purchased larger quantities of spares with the original equipment.

Costs and standards

Time standards for machining parts were established for all the Avalon machines in the 1950s and were carried on the operations cards. The card listed the operations for the part and showed the time for each piece for two different size lots. The standard times from two such cards are shown in Exhibits 6 and 7.

Since the time the standards were established, there were many changes in machines and methods, and by late 1974, the workers were able to do significantly better than the standard times on most operations. Since the scheduling was done by leadmen familiar with the actual times required to perform operations, the schedulers could make mental corrections of the standard times to arrive at estimated actual times.

Increases in wage rates occurring since the establishment of standards were paid as cents per hour. As a result, the bonus for above-standard performance had become a smaller portion of the total wage. The average incentive bonus was 20 cents per hour, and in 1974 the average take-home pay including bonus was $5.30 per hour.

Parts were transferred into inventory at a transfer price set at material cost plus $14 for each man-hour worked on the order. At the conclusion of each run, the value of the actual time charged to the order at $14 an hour plus the actual material cost was checked to see if the costs so figured were still equal to the existing transfer price. If two consecutive lots showed a sizable deviation from the set standard transfer price, the transfer price usually was adjusted. The $14 per hour figure was checked at the end of each year to see if it still covered the costs of plant operations. The $14 figure had been valid for the last four years.

The company did not use machine-hour costs. Because of the large idle machine capacity, the company had found it more helpful to control the labor-hours than the machine-hours. Thus, an hour spent working with a hand file was costed as equal to an hour spent working with an automatic screw machine.

Exhibit 3
Summary of stock records for BM–19, roller cam

Date	Balance	Note*	Date	Balance	Note*	Date	Balance	Note*
5/26/73	45	2	11/23/73	29	1	5/13/74	2	2
5/29/73	44	2	11/27/73	28	2	5/13/74	0	6
6/11/73	42	2	11/27/73	27	1	5/21/74	53	5
6/11/73	40	2	12/ 3/73	26	1	5/24/74	51	2
6/11/73	34	2	12/24/73	25	1	5/27/74	49	2
6/18/73	16	3	1/11/74	7	3	6/ 3/74	45	2
6/19/73	67	5	1/18/74	4	2	6/ 4/74	39	2
6/25/73	66	2	1/18/74	6	6	6/ 4/74	33	2
7/10/73	60	4	1/19/74	0	4	6/ 4/74	30	1
7/25/73	59	2	1/19/74	56	5	6/ 7/74	24	2
7/30/73	57	2	1/23/74	55	2	6/17/74	22	2
8/ 6/73	56	2	1/25/74	52	2	6/17/74	21	2
8/13/73	52	2	1/30/74	50	2	6/24/74	20	2
8/22/73	49	2	1/31/74	47	2	6/24/74	17	2
8/22/73	48	1	2/13/74	41	4	7/ 1/74	15	2
8/24/73	45	2	2/14/74	40	1	7/11/74	12	1
8/24/73	44	1	2/18/74	38	2	7/11/74	11	2
8/24/73	38	3	2/28/74	34	2	7/10/74	5	2
8/29/73	36	2	3/ 1/74	33	1	7/31/74	3	2
9/11/73	35	2	3/ 6/74	27	4	8/ 2/74	0	6

Date	Qty	Note	Date	Qty	Note	Date	Qty	Note
9/17/73	34	2	3/ 7/74	23	2	8/ 6/74	54	5
10/10/73	33	2	3/ 9/74	21	1	8/ 6/74	51	2
10/16/73	30	3	3/12/74	22	7	8/ 7/74	48	1
10/19/73	29	2	3/14/74	4	3	8/17/74	46	2
10/29/73	27	2	3/31/74	3	5	8/19/74	44	1
10/31/73	25	2	3/21/74	54	5	8/30/74	42	2
11/ 6/73	10	3	3/25/74	48	4	9/ 3/74	40	2
11/ 6/73	7	2	4/ 8/74	47	2	9/ 6/74	39	2
11/ 6/73	4	2	4/18/74	45	2	9/ 6/74	38	2
11/ 6/73	3	2	4/22/74	44	2	9/ 6/74	36	2
11/ 8/73	2	2	4/24/74	26	3	9/18/74	32	2
11/ 9/73	3	6	5/ 2/74	20	4	9/18/74	31	2
11/ 9/73	0	2	5/ 6/74	19	2	9/19/74	29	2
11/16/73	53	5	5/ 6/74	15	4	9/24/74	28	2
11/16/73	50	2	5/ 7/74	14	1	10/ 4/74	10	3
11/20/73	32	4	5/ 7/74	12	2	10/ 5/74	9	1
11/23/73	31	1	5/ 8/74	10	2	10/17/74	7	2

Totals

23	
160	
114	
58	
318	
-2	
1	

* Notes:
1. Withdrawal for repairman's kit
2. Withdrawal for spare parts order
3. Withdrawal for border machine assembly
4. Withdrawal for lace tufter assembly
5. Receipt of manufactured part
6. Inventory correction
7. Returned part

Exhibit 4
Summary of stock records for BM-134, presser foot

Date	Balance	Note*	Date	Balance	Note*	Date	Balance	Note*
5/28/73	108	2	11/19/73	58	2	5/13/74	12	2
6/ 4/73	107	2	11/20/73	55	2	5/16/74	11	2
6/14/73	106	2	12/ 3/73	54	2	6/ 7/74	8	2
6/14/73	104	2	12/ 6/73	53	2	6/14/74	7	2
6/18/73	103	2	12/17/73	51	2	6/17/74	5	2
7/ 3/73	102	2	12/31/73	53	6	6/18/74	4	2
7/ 9/73	94	3	1/ 4/74	52	2	6/20/74	3	2
7/23/73	90	2	1/ 8/74	51	3	6/20/74	4	6
7/23/73	88	2	1/10/74	45	2	6/20/74	2	5
8/ 1/73	87	2	1/18/74	43	2	7/ 2/74	43	2
8/ 3/73	84	3	1/23/74	42	2	7/ 2/74	41	2
8/ 3/73	82	2	2/13/74	41	2	7/ 3/74	40	2
8/ 6/73	81	2	2/14/74	40	2	7/11/74	38	2
8/ 6/73	80	2	2/14/74	39	2	7/16/74	37	2
8/14/73	79	2	3/ 1/74	38	2	8/14/74	36	2
9/ 7/73	78	2	3/ 6/74	32	3	8/22/74	35	2
9/11/73	77	2	3/14/74	30	2	9/ 3/74	32	2
9/12/73	76	2	3/21/74	29	2	9/20/74	31	2
9/14/73	74	2	3/21/74	28	2	9/20/74	29	2
9/28/73	73	2	3/28/74	27	2	9/24/74	28	2
10/ 1/73	71	2	4/ 1/74	26	2	9/24/74	26	2
10/ 3/73	69	2	4/ 1/74	25	2	9/25/74	24	2
10/17/73	68	3	4/ 8/74	24	2	9/27/74	23	2
10/19/73	67	2	4/18/74	18	3	9/27/74	22	2
10/22/73	65	2	4/19/74	17	2	10/10/74	21	2
11/19/73	60	3	4/29/74	13	2			

Totals
96
35
41
3

*Notes:
2. Withdrawal for spare parts order
3. Withdrawal for border machine assembly
5. Receipt of manufactured part
6. Inventory correction

Exhibit 5
A. Summary of usage of parts BM–19 and BM–134

| | | BM–19 | | | BM–134 |
| | | | | | |
Year	Spares	BM assembly	LT assembly	Spares	BM assembly
1960	35	255		3	90
1961	41	111		6	42
1962	102	135		14	42
1963	127	87		28	30
1964	132	153	3	40	54
1965	93	99	24	36	33
1966	171	114	60	42	36
1967	215	132	45	63	42
1968	143	147	36	58	48
1969	208	102	48	66	33
1970	199	75	72	70	24
1971	161	84	42	59	30
1972	105	72	30	58	27
1973	105	75	42	94	24
1974*	127*	72*	24*	57*	18*

* 1974 usage figures show usage only through October 17.

B. Recent production orders for parts BM–19 and BM–134

Part no.	Order placed	Order quantity	Order received	Quantity received
BM–19	5/11/73	50	6/19/73	51
BM–19	10/31/73	50	11/16/73	53
BM–19	11/28/73	50	1/19/74	56
BM–19	2/18/74	50	3/21/74	51
BM–19	4/25/74	50	5/21/74	53
BM–19	6/18/74	50	8/ 6/74	54
BM–19	9/ 3/74	80		
BM–134	2/28/74	40	7/ 2/74	41
BM–134	9/24/74	50		

The costs of operating the new warehouse had been established. The building cost $480,000 and contained an inventory of parts worth $1,000,000. The building was being depreciated on a 20-year basis. The main yearly operating costs were as follows: taxes $8,270; insurance on building and contents $2,000; heat $12,000; electricity $3,000; and labor (superintendent, clerk, two material handlers, one half-time janitor) $70,000 (including a 50 percent overhead charge). These costs did not include general and administrative charges.

Exhibit 6
Production charges for BM–134, presser foot

A. Materials
     Bar stock . . . . $ 3.12

B. Direct labor

| | | Job sheet standard times | | | | | |
| | | Per piece in lots of | | Job tickets on lot received on 7/2/74 | | | |
	Setup hrs.	50–100 hrs.	14 hrs.	Standard hrs.	Actual hrs.	Pieces	Date
1. Screw machine . . . . Cut two parts at one time	0.50	0.10	0.125	3.10	1.90	26	3/29
2. Mill: cut angles	—	0.10	0.125	5.20	2.50	52	4/25
3. Burr	—	0.033	0.042	void*			
4. Drill and tap	—	0.042	0.05	1.71	1.20	41	6/24
5. Weld shop: solder	—	0.083	0.10	3.42	5.50	41	6/24
6. Bench	—	0.017	0.025	0.68	0.80	41	6/24
7. Retap and check . . . . :.	0.33	0.017	0.025	1.36	1.60	41	7/2
	0.83	0.392	0.492		13.50		

C. Cost summary
1. 13.50 hours
     at $14.00 . . . . $189.00
2. Plating done
     by outside firm 40.60
3. Punching done
     by outside firm 13.12
4. Materials 3.12
                                                                                        $245.84

D. Transfer pricing
     41 units at $6.30 . . . . . . $258.30

* No times were recorded for this operation on this lot because the operator's time was still recorded on the preceding lot while he was working on this lot.

Cost data not provided by accounting records

Spence Larrimore and Jim Williams did not feel that obsolescence was a significant cost in their business. The large number of parts used for spares meant that even if the company discontinued manufacturing a particular machine,[2] the demand for spares could consume a considerable number of parts. Occasionally, customer ex-

[2] In many cases, the company could not immediately discontinue a machine. When the lace tufter was developed, for example, it made the button tufter obsolete for most customers. However, ten years later Avalon still received an occasional order for a button tufter.

Exhibit 7
Production charges for BM–19, roller cam

1. Materials
   Bar stock . . . . $ 19.80

2. Direct labor

		Job sheet standard times			Job tickets on lot received on 8/6/74			
		Per piece in lots of						
	Setup hrs.	130–200 hrs.	60–100 hrs.	Standard hrs.	Actual hrs.	Pieces	Date
Screw machine	1.0	0.10	0.167	10.17	8.50	55	7/15
Grinder	—	0.067	0.067	3.67	0.60	55	7/31
Bench	—	0.05	0.075	4.13	3.10	55	8/1
Harden and draw	—	—	—	3.60	0.90	54	8/6
	1.0	0.217	0.309		13.10		

   Cost summary
   13.10 hours at $14.00 . .   183.40
   Materials 19.80
                                                                       $203.20

3. Pricing
   54 Roll cams at $3.90 . . $210.60

perience indicated that a particular part should be redesigned. If such a part was redesigned, Avalon sent a flyer to all customers ordering these parts, suggesting that they buy newly designed parts. Despite this notice, orders continued to be received for the obsolete parts. Jim Williams recalled that there had been some large-scale scrapping of parts acquired when the company took over the name and inventory of the Simon & Selig Company, a small manufacturer of similar products. In that case, the inventory of parts was too large for the rate of spare parts consumption. After some discussion, Spence and Jim estimated that 1 percent to 3 percent of the parts put into inventory might eventually be declared obsolete and be scrapped, but both men pointed out that this was only a seat-of-the-pants estimate with no scientific basis.

Paul Williams recognized that EOQ formulas (economic order quantity) required an interest cost or a cost of capital; but since Avalon had a policy of not borrowing money, no interest charge could legitimately be tied to the inventory. Ideally, he would use the return which the firm could have realized on alternative investments, but he did not have up-to-date, carefully calculated returns on the various ideas for new production equipment, new investments in mattress machinery design, or new sales campaigns which flowed through his office. Over the past several years, the company averaged less than a 9 percent return before taxes on its invested capital. Paul Williams hoped to improve this return.

Some mathematical formulations of inventory models required a figure for the cost of being out of stock. Because the Avalon management appreciated the importance of continuity of operation for its customers, it tried to maintain stocks of all parts tending to wear or break. In addition to the plant inventory, some parts were stocked by the company's distributors in Chicago, Los Angeles, and England. The amount of money that the Avalon management would be willing to spend to make a prompt correction in an out-of-stock position for a spare part order depended on the customer and the urgency of his situation. The amount of money required to make such a correction depended on the part, its availability at other locations, and the status of production orders inside the plant. If the lack of a part actually forced assemblers to sit idle, the cost of an out-of-stock position could be calculated. Out-of-stock positions were, however, usually found sufficiently early that something could be done about it before assemblers sat idle.

Chapter 5

Aggregate planning and master scheduling

SYSTEMS FOR PLANNING AND CONTROLLING the output of manufacturing enterprises are substantially different from those engaged in procuring independent demand items and selling or transferring them to other parties. While much of what we have discussed in Chapter 4, "Independent Demand Inventory Systems," does apply to manufacturing settings, our requirements for effective manufacturing control systems are much greater. Perhaps the most important additional factor that must be considered in manufacturing is capacity. We must be concerned with scheduling equipment and a work force in manufacturing systems, in addition to managing inventories and material flows. In most productive systems, the decision points at which all of these factors of production are considered involve aggregate planning and master scheduling. Aggregate plans and master schedules provide common points at which capacity and inventories can be jointly considered in the light of a firm's long-range plans and strategies, and provide inputs to financial plans and related dependent demand inventory and detailed scheduling decisions. Aggregate plans and master schedules are thus the starting points for most manufacturing control systems.

The economic significance of aggregate planning and master scheduling is by no means minor, for we are confronted with broad basic questions such as the following: To what extent should inventory be used to absorb the fluctuation in demand that will occur over the next 6 to 12 months? Why not absorb these fluctuations by simply varying the size of the work force? Hire and fire as demand increases or decreases. Why not maintain a fairly stable work force size and absorb fluctuations through changing production rates by resorting to overtime or shorter hours? Why not maintain a fairly stable work force size and production rate and let our subcontractors wrestle with the problems of fluctuating order rates from us? Should we purposefully not meet all demands? In most instances it is probably true that any one of these pure strategies would not be as effective as a balance between them. There are costs associated with each strategy, so what we seek is an astute selection of a combination of the alternatives.

If we use inventories to absorb seasonal changes in demand, capital and obsolesence costs as well as the costs associated with storage, insurance, and handling will all tend to increase. Beyond the question of seasonal factors the use of inventories to absorb short-term fluctuations will incur increases in these same costs compared to some ideal or minimum inventory level necessary to maintain the production process. When inventories fall below this ideal or minimum level, stockout costs will increase, as will all of the costs associated with short runs.

Changes in the size of the work force affect the total costs of labor turnover. When new workers are hired, there are costs of selection, training, and lower production effectiveness. The separation of workers may involve unemployment compensation or other separation costs as well as an intangible effect on public relations and public image. If changes in the size of the work force are large, it may mean adding or subtracting an entire shift. The incremental costs involved here are shift premiums as well as incremental supervision and other overhead costs. If we absorb fluctuations through changes in the production rate, we will absorb overtime premium costs for increases and probably idle labor costs (higher average labor cost per unit) for decreases. Usually, however, managers will try to maintain the same average labor costs by reducing the hours worked below normal levels. Where undertime schedules persist, labor turnover and the costs attendant to it are likely to increase. Many of the costs affected by aggregate planning and master scheduling decisions are difficult to measure and are not segregated in accounting records.

Some are alternative costs of opportunity, as with interest costs on inventory investment, and some costs are not measurable, such as those associated with public relations and public image. However, all of the costs are real and bear importantly on a number of management decisions.

Aggregate production plans

As an introduction to aggregate planning let us take the data of Table 5–1, which states the expected production requirements by

Table 5–1
Forecast of production requirements for a seasonal product

Month	Production requirements		Required buffer stocks	Production days	Cumulative days
	Expected	Cumulative			
January	700	700	300	22	22
February	900	1,600	340	18	40
March	1,100	2,700	375	22	62
April	900	3,600	340	21	83
May	650	4,250	290	22	105
June	600	4,850	275	21	126
July	550	5,400	265	21	147
August	400	5,800	230	13	160
September	400	6,200	230	20	180
October	300	6,500	195	23	203
November	300	6,800	195	21	224
December	400	7,200	230	20	244

month for a small appliance manufacturer, together with required buffer stocks and available working days. The seasonal requirements are already phased forward from seasonal sales requirements to take account of production and distribution lead times so that the requirements are those that the factory must meet. We are interested in some of the alternate ways that can be used by the manufacturer in meeting the requirements. First, the requirements by month as stated in Table 5–1 appear somewhat differently when related to available production days. Figure 5–1 shows production requirements per production day, which reveals a less smooth pattern of demand on the production facilities because of the variation in days available in given months and particularly the problem of the vacation period in August, when the entire plant shuts down for two weeks. While the pronounced seasonal pattern seems to be 1,100/300 = 3.67 (peak in March, 1,100, and valley in October and November, 300), actually, of

Figure 5–1
Production requirements per production day

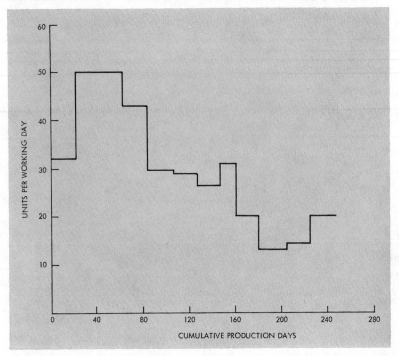

course, we see from Figure 5–1 that the ratio of peak to valley is really 50/13 = 3.9.

In Figure 5–2 we show a graphical technique by which feasible alternate plans can be developed. The procedure is, first, to plot the cumulative production requirements, followed by the curve for cumulative maximum requirements. The latter curve simply requires the addition of buffer stocks for each period. The cumulative graph of maximum requirements can then be used effectively to compare alternate ways of meeting requirements and still provide the desired protection against stockouts. Any production program that is feasible in this sense must fall entirely above the cumulative maximum requirements line. The vertical distances between production programs and the cumulative maximum requirements curve represent seasonal inventory accumulations for the plan in question.

We have plotted three alternate production programs in Figure 5–2. Plan 1 proposes level production and requires a beginning inventory of 1,650 units in order to be feasible, as shown by the y

Figure 5–2
Cumulative requirements with three alternate programs that meet maximum
requirements

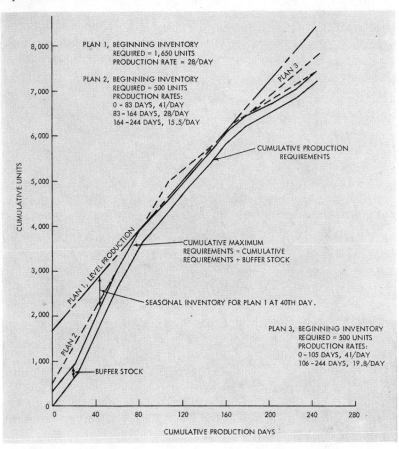

intercept of the Plan 1 line. Plan 2 follows requirements somewhat
more closely by changing production rates three times during the
year (including the change at the end or the beginning of the year).
Plan 2 obviously requires somewhat smaller seasonal inventory accumulations than Plan 1 but involves other cost disadvantages because of needed hiring and separation, overtime pay rates, and some
subcontracting costs. Plan 3 involves only two changes in production level (including the change at the beginning or the end of the
year) but accumulates more seasonal inventory during the middle of
the year.

The timing of the changes in production rates for the three alternate plans are shown in relation to forecasted production requirements in Figure 5–3. Here we see also that normal plant capacity
without overtime is 30 units per day and with overtime 36 units per

Figure 5–3
Comparison of three production programs that meet requirements

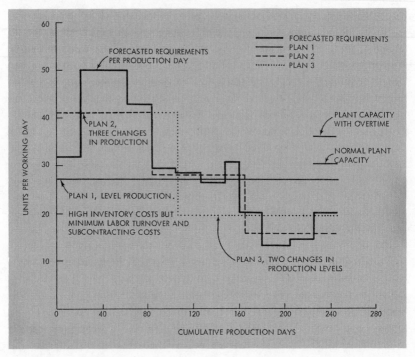

day. Requirements beyond the 36-unit-per-day maximum must be
met either with accumulated seasonal inventories or by resorting to
outside subcontracting. We see that in order to meet requirements
both Plans 2 and 3 must resort to both overtime and some outside
subcontracting. Table 5–2 summarizes the comparative incremental
costs for the three programs, the unit costs of each of the four modes
of providing seasonal capacity being indicated in the footnotes to the
table. In this instance we see that Plan 2 yields the lowest cost of the
three plans. Obviously, many other alternate proposals could be
evaluated in a similar way. Plan 2 is very likely not the minimum-
cost plan possible.

One of the difficulties with this kind of graphical approach is that
it does not generate alternative proposals nor is it in any sense an

Table 5–2
Incremental costs for three alternate production programs

	Plan 1	Plan 2	Plan 3
Seasonal inventory*	$99,960	$24,480	$ 44,880
Changes in work force†	0	48,000	40,800
Overtime costs‡	0	8,300	10,500
Subcontracting costs§	0	12,450	15,750
	$99,960	$93,230	$111,930

* Inventory carrying cost is at $240 per unit per year.
† A change in production level of 10 units per day (not including overtime production rate increases) requires the hiring or separation of 100 employees at a cost of hiring, training, and separation of $200 per person.
‡ Units produced at overtime labor rates cost $20 per unit extra.
§ Units produced by subcontracting cost $25 per unit extra.

optimizing approach. Perhaps even more important, however, is the fact that the technique is static in character and seems to develop a plan which takes no account of the need for flexibility in changing the plan as the year grinds on and we obtain actual data on the progress of demand. Some of the mathematical and heuristic methods which we will develop later tend to meet these objections.

Nature of aggregate planning

We have been using the term "aggregate" without defining it in relation to the production planning and scheduling problem. Holt, Modigliani, and Simon [12] defined it as:

. . . a measure of production per unit of time (per week or per month, for example). Most factories produce many products rather than just one; hence, a common unit must be found by adding quantities of different products. For example, a unit of weight, volume, work required, or value might serve as a suitable common denominator. (Aggregate) work force refers to the number of employees to whom there shall be a company commitment to supply regular work for one unit of time.

From the time of the publication of the pioneering papers by Holt, Modigliani, and Simon, [12] aggregate planning and scheduling has been considered to be the setting of aggregate production rate and size of work force in a factory resulting in the simultaneous determination of the amount of overtime and the projected size of inventories. In conceptualizing the problem we would like to add as another variable the aggregate amount of subcontracting, since for many manufacturers the use of subcontracting represents a logical strategy for the absorption of fluctuations in demand.

There are recognized interactions between the decision variables and other factors, such as product and labor mix. For example, the number of workers needed may depend on the number of different products to be produced as well as on the aggregate production rate, but many techniques do not attempt to take such interactions into account, using instead an average number of workers in relation to production rate. The reason for these assumptions is simply model complexity and the difficulty of obtaining solutions to the more complex model in relation to possible benefits in terms of improved solutions.

The alternatives open to an executive in attempting to adjust to fluctuations in demand are as follows: (1) adjust to the size of the work force by hiring and firing in response to fluctuations; (2) adjust the production rate by working overtime or undertime with the same work force; (3) absorb fluctuations through fluctuations in inventory, backlog of orders, or lost sales; (4) increase or decrease the aggregate amount of subcontracting to absorb the fluctuation in demand; (5) vary the allocation of resources to the marketing function to attenuate fluctuations in demand (see Holloway [11, pp. 50–66]); and (6) combinations of the five pure strategies.

Responding by any of the five basic modes will involve cost penalties. Changing the size of the work force requires hiring or firing and the attendant costs involved. If a large change is contemplated, involving the addition or elimination of a shift, the cost effects are more complex, involving shift premiums and some variable overhead. The second alternative of adjusting production rates may involve overtime premiums, on the one hand, and the penalty of idle labor for undertime, on the other. Using inventories to absorb fluctuations involves the usual inventory holding costs for increased inventories and the costs of back orders, possible lost sales, and the intangible costs of poor service to customers if inventories are reduced. Absorbing fluctuations through subcontracting will involve other costs; the cost behavior may be complex depending on whether the subcontractor is more or less efficient than the prime contractor. If the subcontractor is more efficient, there will be a cost to return subcontracted work to the home plant and vice versa. In addition, there are costs involved in supervising and coordinating subcontracted work. Finally, attenuating fluctuations in demand through the marketing function involves the costs of compensatory promotion or smaller revenues per unit if price variations are used.

One of the important aspects of the aggregate planning and

scheduling problem is the dynamic nature of the decision process involved. The current decision is merely one of a sequence of decisions and therefore does not make a commitment for all time. An error in the forecasts made for the past period in which decisions were based can be compensated for in the decisions made for the current period. Therefore, a decision is a commitment only until the time of the next decision.

Costs of changing production levels

Though aggregate programming and master scheduling techniques generally treat the work force and production rate decisions as separate and independent, it is perhaps useful to talk about the interrelationships and look at the structure of costs involved in changing production levels (both work force and rate). Our objective will be to try to gain a better insight into what actually happens when production levels are changed. We are interested in the incremental cost effects of a decision to change production levels. We may divide these incremental cost effects into the one-time costs of carrying out the decision and the incremental direct costs incurred during the period that the new production level is in effect. McGarrah [15] suggests three critical factors as determinants of the total incremental costs of changing production and employment levels:

1.   The production output rate and inventory level of the program about to end, that is, the *point of departure.*
2.   The *magnitude of the change* in output level and/or inventory level.
3.   The *length of the period* of the production program.

He goes on to say:

The influence of the current production rate is fairly obvious. If the firm has been operating at 80 percent of normal capacity (single-shift operation), an increase in output could be effected without additional costs of overtime or second-shift premiums. A decrease in output might necessitate laying off key personnel who would be difficult to replace. However, if the plant has been operating at 100 percent of normal capacity for single-shift operation, an increase may very likely involve overtime costs, or second shift premiums, and extra supervision. A decrease in production could be effected by reducing the work week or by laying off personnel with the lowest seniority and least skill; these costs would not be so great as a lay off when the plant was at 80 percent of normal capacity.

The effect of the magnitude of the change in the current operating or inventory level is also obvious. Hiring or laying off fifty employees is more costly than changing the payroll by only five employees. Similarly, a large boost in the inventory level may require additional warehouse space, and a large reduction in inventory may necessitate abandoning some of it. The magnitude of any maximum change in the output rates of sequential programs is likely to be restricted because the supply of skilled labor in the local labor market may be limited. Also, because of complicated seniority clauses, the union contract may indirectly restrict the rate at which employees can be laid off.

The length of the programming period will affect the costs of changing production programs. An increase in output in a sustained overtime operation will obviously require summing the overtime premium expenses over the period of the new program. Overtime premium costs would be greater for a six-month period than for one of six weeks. The choice of the programming period will depend on the expense of forecasting, the errors in the forecast, the time to consolidate and study new market information to improve the forecast previously made, and the cost of making changes in the detailed manufacturing schedules already released to the factory.

The three proposed determinants of the cost of changing production, employment, and inventory levels are not mutually exclusive. More new employees can become effective in six months than in six weeks. And if the current program has been at 80 percent of normal capacity, new employees can be expected to boost production to 100 percent of capacity more readily than if the current program had been at 100 percent and output was to be boosted to 120 percent. Hence the period of the program, the magnitude of the change in output, and the "point of departure" are interrelated [15].

It is unlikely that the costs of increasing and decreasing production and employment levels would be quantitatively the same. Table 5–3 shows lists of typical items involved in both increasing and

Table 5–3
Cost items involved in changing production levels (work force and rate)

Cost of increasing levels	Costs of decreasing levels
1. Employment and Training: (a) Interviews and selection, (b) New personnel records, physical examinations, payroll setup, (c) Training new workers.	1. Unemployment compensation insurance.
2. Service and Staff Functions: (a) Production and inventory control, (b) Purchasing, receiving, inspection, and materials handling.	2. Contributions to union funds.
3. Added Shifts: (a) Supervision. (b) Shift premium.	3. Costs of employee transfer and retraining.
4. Overtime costs related to the increased level.	4. Intangible effects on public relations.
	5. Production and inventory costs of revising schedules, order points, etc.
	6. Idle time costs due to lags in decisions and action.

decreasing levels and we see that the lists are quite different. The resulting aggregate cost functions we would also expect to be different.

Cost functions for changes of level. Based on the first two of the determinants of incremental costs of changing production and employment levels (that is the point of departure and the magnitude of change), we can postulate the shapes of a family of cost curves which relate to them. Figure 5–4 shows samples of three such curves for

Figure 5–4
Sample change cost curves for three present output rates (points of departure)

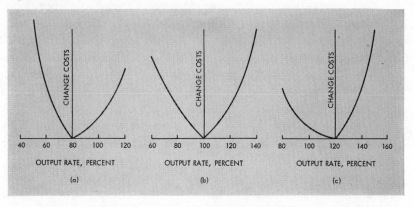

three different points of departure. Assume, for example, that 100 percent output is considered to be normal capacity for one-shift operation, and curve (b) is a sample curve for this point of departure. The curves are concave upward because management will resort to increasingly costly combinations of methods to obtain different degrees of change in level. For example, in curve (a), with a point of departure of 80 percent, increases in output up to 105 percent are probably obtained mainly by hiring, but beyond that point management resorts largely to overtime and/or subcontracting involving a substantially different cost, thus the increasing slope of the cost curves. In curve (b), increases above the 100 percent point of departure may be obtained with overtime and/or subcontracting, but beyond some point, perhaps 120 percent, a second shift is invoked. Decreases below 100 percent down to perhaps 75 percent may be achieved by layoffs and separations, but below that point, perhaps, idle labor costs dominate, because management wishes to retain the core of its most skilled labor force. Curve (c) has a point of departure of 120 percent and presumably is already operating with a second shift.

The nature of the production system may emphasize or deemphasize discontinuities in the curves; that is, production capacity is not necessarily available in continuously varying amounts. Capacity tends to be available in "chunks" i.e., whole machines. For example, the usual production line can only vary output continuously by varying hours worked. In order to employ a larger or smaller labor force for a standard workday, the entire line must be rebalanced at a different output rate.

Linear segments may represent quite reasonable approximations over limited ranges for the change-of-level curves. There are two reasons for assuming linearity. The first is our limited ability to measure the actual subleties of the cost functions over the limited ranges. The second reason is that in one of the prominent mathematical models proposed for the aggregate scheduling problem, linear programming, linearity is required for solution.

Since it is difficult to measure as a separate entity a total incremental change cost, the more usual approach would be to measure and establish the behavior of the components of change cost and add the components to estimate the total change cost function. The general shapes of functions of four of the five components are shown in Figure 5–5. (There may also be additional components.)

The first component is the hiring and layoff-separation function in (a), which incurs costs by changes in work force size, either positive or negative. There is no good reason why the curve should be symmetrical, and one could argue, particularly for specific firms, for either increasing or decreasing slopes of the two curve segments. The overtime function is shown by (b). The approximate maximum that can be produced with a given work force without overtime is near the heel of the curve. As the limit of output with the assigned work force is approached, some workers on bottleneck operations are assigned overtime, and beyond that point overtime cost per period increases at an increasing rate. The general shape of the cost curve for the installation of a new shift is shown by (c). The step in the curve represents new supervision and other overhead costs required to put on a new shift, and the variable portion of the curve represents payroll costs at augmented multiple-shift rates. Shown in (d) is an estimate of subcontracting costs which involve a step increase for new administrative costs of supervision and coordination of subcon-

Figure 5-5
Form of cost functions for components of total incremental change cost

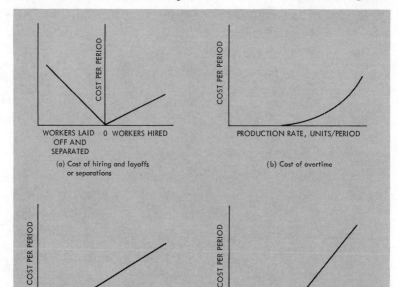

(a) Cost of hiring and layoffs or separations

(b) Cost of overtime

(c) Cost of new shifts

(d) Cost of subcontracting

tracting and a variable portion which may not be linear. The step increases in both the new shift and subcontracting curves would introduce discontinuities in the total change cost curves of Figure 5–4.

The fifth component, not shown in Figure 5–5, is the cost of undertime, which is a derived function based on the actual work force, production rates, and subcontracting assigned by the programming system. If the programming system assigns a work force larger than necessary in relation to the production rate assigned, at average productivity rates, then, in effect, idle labor has been assigned, and the cost of this labor is undertime cost.

Inventory and shortage costs for aggregate planning

Our discussion of inventory costs, shortage costs, and buffer stocks in Chapters 3 and 4 is in general pertinent here, and we will not repeat it. At this point, however, we are interested only in aggregate inventories and the cost of carrying them, and in aggregate shortage costs, and in how both vary with varying levels of aggregate inventories. In general, the costs of holding inventory are regarded as being linear over a fairly broad range with possible discontinuities at very high inventory levels as management must resort to inefficient storage capacity or inefficient storage locations to accommodate extremely large inventories. For example, the handling costs in and out of storage might be somewhat larger if it were necessary to invoke

Figure 5–6

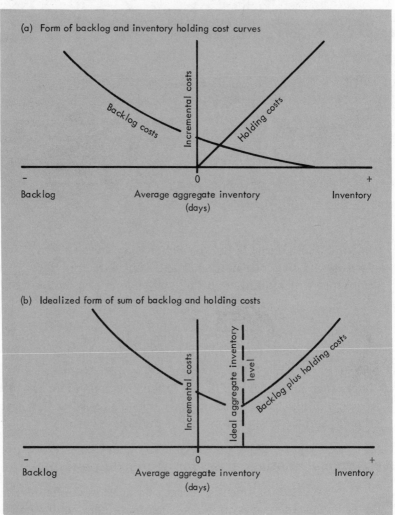

(a) Form of backlog and inventory holding cost curves

Incremental costs

Backlog costs

Holding costs

–
Backlog

0
Average aggregate inventory
(days)

+
Inventory

(b) Idealized form of sum of backlog and holding costs

Incremental costs

Ideal aggregate inventory level

Backlog plus holding costs

–
Backlog

0
Average aggregate inventory
(days)

+
Inventory

inefficient warehouses and warehouse locations. The inventory holding cost curve in Figure 5–6 reflects one such possible discontinuity.
This cost curve is defined in terms of days' supply of inventory or
days of backlog, since negative inventories or backlogs are usually
expressed in terms of the number of days of work at capacity that it
takes to complete all unfilled orders. In this case then, a positive
inventory expressed in days is the number of days that it would take
to produce an amount equal to what is being held in inventory.

Figure 5–6 also illustrates that there are costs associated with
backlogs, or negative inventories. These costs are incurred whenever
a firm produces to order, such as the shoe manufacturer, rather than
to stock. While such costs are difficult to measure, they are very real,
reflecting customer needs for fast response times from their vendors.
In some businesses, such as farm implement spare parts manufacture, customers need the product immediately lest their equipment
become unproductive. In this case there would be a very high penalty for backlogging, and thus a great incentive to have a positive
ideal aggregate inventory with high service levels of up to say 99
percent. In the nuclear pressure vessel industry, the extremely high
inventory holding costs that accrue because of the rapid obsolescence and high cost of these items, coupled with the fact that none of
the competitors in the industry produces to stock, results in a negative ideal inventory level; that is, backlogging so that customers have
to wait up to three years to receive these goods. The diagram in
Figure 5–6(a) indicates that the ideal aggregate inventory level can
be defined by the minimum point on the curve defined by the sum of
the backlog plus holding cost curves. Figure 5–7 defines the cost
penalty curve associated with deviating from the ideal aggregate
inventory level that is derived from Figure 5–6(a). In terms of aggregate inventory planning and scheduling then, this curve defines the
incremental costs of interest to us. Inventory levels below the ideal or
optimal aggregate level will incur the cost of shortages, stockouts or
excess back ordering, and inventory levels above the optimal level
will incur the added costs of holding inventory. The curve might be
segmented as in Figure 5–7 as an approximation.

Different solutions for different cost structures

Gordon [8], as a part of his study of aggregate planning, inter-
viewed executives in widely differing firms concerning the nature of
their solutions to aggregate planning and scheduling problems and

Figure 5–7
Idealized cost penalty curve for aggregate inventories above or below ideal
levels

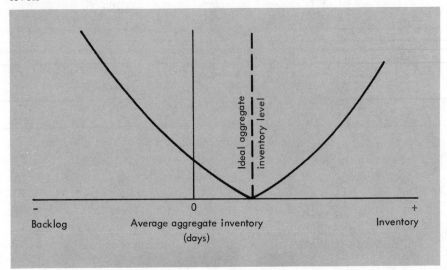

the variables which seem to dominate. The following five cases summarized by Gordon indicate the wide range in the balance of managerial alternative solutions which a given industry or firm cost structure will produce.

In a men's shoe manufacturing firm in a small New England community, it was found that inventory was used as the key variable in absorbing demand fluctuations throughout the year. As these fluctuations were relatively pronounced, it meant that the inventory varied by almost 50 percent during the course of the year. In the extreme condition of peak sales, negative inventory was used in the sense of permitting back orders to build up and increasing delivery times. The reasons behind this policy were that the labor force was a critical variable in short supply and an instability in employment would lead to further depletion of an already scarce resource to the major urban centers. In addition, the firm had a well-established brand name and felt the consumer was willing to wait for the product. Storage space was not a critical variable but inventory control was becoming a major issue as well as the capital tied up in inventory. Capacity utilization was also aided by inventory policy.

A major dairy products producer was faced not only with a seasonal pattern in demand with respect to product mix, but by long-term contracts on the supply side which meant that all the output of the suppliers had to be absorbed. As the supply also fluctuates with the season, the problem finds its solution not only in the gross quantity of inventory but also in the form of the inventory. As some dairy products require different quality characteristics than others and have different shelf-life characteristics, much of the excess supply can be processed as cheese, butter and ice cream which can be stored for the peak season. As some wastage is involved in using the total supply for these products, a trade-off must be made in terms of the split-off criteria in processing decisions.

In a very large container plant which supplies the beverage industry, the demand for cans is derived from the demand for the beverages. As the production of tin cans may be typified as a three-stage process, sheeting-printing-forming, it is possible to use a combination of in-process buffer inventory and production rate fluctuations to serve the beverage industry. As the container industry is extremely competitive, it is considered essential to offer very quick service to major customers. To do this and avoid the space requirements necessary to store large quantities of empty cans, it is common to complete the first two stages of the process and then hold printed plate in inventory. When an actual delivery order is received it is possible to form and ship the required cans quickly by using overtime in the forming stage. The degree of mechanization involved in the process of manufacturing limits the amount of work force fluctuation possible.

In a medium-sized candy and chocolate producer, which experiences very pronounced fluctuations in demand during the year, work force variations were used extensively to absorb peaks and valleys. As the process requires a high labor content with a low skill level, it was possible to obtain the necessary workers in an urban center without much difficulty. The policy was actually dictated by the shelf-life restrictions on chocolate which could only be stored for a short time before it began to deteriorate. This meant that inventory had a limited range of usefulness in meeting demand fluctuations. A technological breakthrough in the area of refrigerating chocolates is presently forcing a rethinking of the policy of work force fluctuations versus inventory. The economics associated with each policy will obviously play a major role in the resultant aggregate scheduling policy.

Finally, in the case of a major producer of outboard motors the policy of acquiring and developing complementary products was used. Although not previously mentioned, this policy has long been an accepted answer to the seasonal demand situation. In the case of outboard motors, the equipment, skill and inventory involved are all of high value and pressure exists to maintain high utilization. The obvious conclusion is to keep all of these resources busy throughout the year rather than using any one of them to absorb demand fluctuations. As a result the firm initially acquired a successful but small producer of power saws which required the same skills as outboard motors as well as the same type of equipment. The demand for power saws does not occur at the same time as that for outboard motors, therefore allowing increased utilization of the resource base. Finally, to further increase this utilization the company developed a line of snowblowers

Table 5-4
Summary of dominant mode for absorbing demand fluctuations for five companies in Gordon's study [8]

Type of company and dominant reasons for policy	Inventory	Backlogs (negative inventory)	Work force size	Production rate*	Complementary products	Subcontracting†	Expanded planning horizon†
Shoe—Labor in critical short supply. Had established brand name and felt customers would wait		X					
Dairy products—Fixed supply contracts for milk. Excess raw material could be processed further to items with longer shelf life	X						
Container—Mechanization limits work force fluctuations. Quick service required to hold market share in competitive market	X			X			
Candy and chocolate—Shelf life of chocolate limits use of inventory. Ample supply of low-skilled labor	In-process		X				
Outboard motor—Seasonal demand with high valued equipment and highly skilled labor					X		

* Overtime and undertime.
† Not included in Gordon's study but shown here as examples of additional variables appropriate to some cases.

for domestic use thus significantly smoothing the demand for their productive resources.

If we reexamine the statements for these five companies, it seems that usually one mode for handling the fluctuation of demand problem was dominant. This is shown in Table 5–4. The reasons for the policy applied in each case, suggest the rationale used to back up the policy. It is not possible to say without further extensive analysis whether some balance or combination of the managerial variables would have produced superior results, but it is perhaps worth observing that without a carefully constructed model of the aggregate planning and scheduling problem management tends to use some dominant mode. It seems unlikely, however, that the use of a single mode for absorbing demand fluctuations would ordinarily be optimum when there are costs associated with all of the modes or variables. Note also, though they were not mentioned as variables in any of the five cases summarized by Gordon, that we have included subcontracting and expanded planning horizons in Table 5–4 as additional variables which might be appropriately used in specific cases. Subcontracting is a common source of capacity in the aerospace industry and could be used as one of the bases for absorbing demand fluctuations. Also, a short planning horizon time could limit the utility of the other modes for absorbing demand fluctuations. For example, by expanding the planning horizon time, one might very well hold the size of the work force constant in the face of declining demand in the nearer term in order to prevent hiring and training costs required by an anticipated increase in demand in the future.

Master scheduling

The output of the aggregate planning process is a set of parameters indicating aggregate inventory or backlog levels, the number of shifts to be operated, the number of employees to be hired or laid off, the anticipated amount of subcontracting, and the aggregate amount that is to be produced within certain time periods. This information is necessary to the smooth functioning of any manufacturing operation, but, because of its aggregated nature, it is not enough to fulfill a basic requirement for plans stated in terms of individual products that are to be produced in certain quantities by certain times. When a manufacturing operation begins its planning process with an aggregate plan, the process of deriving a master schedule that contains this additional information is called *disaggregation* [13]. This term arises because the aggregate plan is stated in aggregate terms, while master schedules must be stated in specific terms, yet be consistent with the overall aggregate plan from which it was derived.

To illustrate the process by which aggregate plans are disaggregated into more detailed master schedules, we shall refer again to the planning problem we discussed earlier in this chapter for which three alternative aggregate plans were derived (Figure 5–3). Let us assume that aggregate Plan 2, which had the lowest costs (Table 5–2), has been adopted by management. Let us also assume, however, that this plan does not completely specify what the plant is to produce because it is stated in aggregate units, while the plant in fact produces three separate but similar products, only one of which can be produced at a time. Table 5–5 specifies the planning variables that are relevant to the process of master scheduling these three products. Some of the data in this table were derived from the aggregate plan, others are unique to each of the

Table 5–5
Master scheduling input data

Data from the aggregate plan:

	January				February				March			
	1	2	3	4	5	6	7	8	9	10	11	12
Aggregate forecast (a)	159	159	159	159	214	250	250	250	250	250	250	250
Production (b)	205	205	205	205	205	205	205	205	205	205	205	205
Aggregate inventories (c)	546	592	638	684	675	630	585	540	495	450	405	360

Additional data by product line:

	Week												
	1	2	3	4	5	6	7	8	9	10	11	12	Total
Forecast:													
Product 1*	70	70	70	70	70	80	80	80	80	80	80	80	910
Product 2	39	39	39	39	94	120	130	130	130	130	130	130	1,150
Product 3	50	50	50	50	50	50	40	40	40	40	40	40	540
Total	159	159	159	159	214	250	250	250	250	250	250	250	2,600

(a) From Table 5–1, converted from daily to weekly basis assuming a five-day week.
(b) At 41 units per day.
(c) Excess of production over demand, plus 500 units of beginning inventory.
* Forecast units are equivalent units that take up equivalent amounts of capacity.

	Beginning inventory units
Product 1	350
Product 2	100
Product 3	50
	500 units

three products. For the sake of this example, we shall assume that the relevant planning horizon for the master schedule encompasses the first three months of the year as presented in Table 5–1. Because master schedules must be stated in more detailed terms so that plant personnel can see when to set up equipment and order material, however, the master production schedule will be stated in weeks rather than months.

Table 5–6 shows a master schedule that has been formulated using the data in Table 5–5 by the "cut and fit" method. This method, commonly found in industry, involves trying out various allocations of capacity for the products in the line until a satisfactory combination is determined. In several respects, the master schedule shown in Table 5–6 is satisfactory. In several others, however, it is not. The schedule is satisfactory in that it indicates when the plant should plan to start and stop the production of individual items. This information is invaluable to supervisors who must plan their setups and to procurement personnel, who must ensure that the materials needed to support the planned production are available. The schedule is also satisfactory in the sense that the total amount of capacity required to support it is consistent with the capacity (and hence the daily production rate) that the higher level aggregate planning process has indicated is appropriate. There is no indication as to whether the schedule is satisfactory in terms of the number of setups and the associated setup costs for the production line, however. Only the use of optimizing methods or the examination of numerous alternative master schedules can guarantee that the master schedule is appropriate in this regard.

A further examination of the consequences of the master schedule in Table 5–6 will show that it is unsatisfactory in several other respects as well. Table 5–7 shows the profile of inventories that will result from the use of the master schedule. It was derived by using some of the techniques of inventory planning that were discussed in the last chapter; namely, the fundamental relationship: ending inventories equal beginning inventories plus production minus sales. The individual product inventory profile shows that the master schedule will result in total inventory balances that are inconsistant with those called for by the aggregate plan. For example, actual inventories in period 3 will be 642 units rather than the 592 units the plan indicates. The second problem with our master schedule is that it will result in backlogged demand for Product 3 in periods 2 and 3. While this is not necessarily a serious problem if customers are used to waiting up to two weeks for their order to be filled, it is likely that

Table 5–6
A master schedule

Production	1	2	3	4	5	6	7	8	9	10	11	12
Product 1						205	205	150				
Product 2	205	205	205					55	205	175		
Product 3				205	205					30	205	205
Total production	205	205	205	205	205	205	205	205	205	205	205	205
Aggregate plan capacity	205	205	205	205	205	205	205	205	205	205	205	205
Deviation (production from capacity)	0	0	0	0	0	0	0	0	0	0	0	0

Week

◪ denotes a period in which production is split between several products.

Table 5–7
Individual product inventory profile associated with master schedule*

Inventory	Week											
	1	2	3	4	5	6	7	8	9	10	11	12
Product 1	280	210	140	70	0	125	250	320	240	160	80	0
Product 2	266	432	598	559	465	345	215	140	215	260	130	0
Product 3	0	(50)	(100)	55	210	160	120	80	40	30	195	360
Total inventory	546	642	738	684	675	630	585	540	495	450	405	360
Aggregate plan	546	592	638	684	675	630	585	540	495	450	405	360
Deviation (Total inventory − Inventory from aggregate plan)		+50	+100	0	0	0	0	0	0	0	0	0

* Ending inventories.

in this instance backlogs are undesirable, or else management would not have chosen to keep buffer stocks or inventories in the aggregate plan.

The disadvantages of the master schedule that has been derived are probably serious enough to cause a reevaluation of the aggregate plan, so that it is no longer out of step, or the formulation of a new master schedule that is more in line with the existing aggregate plan. The second course of action is more likely since improvements in the master schedule are possible. For example, we see that the current schedule calls for the production of Product 2 first and Product 3 second, even though the beginning inventory of Product 3 will last fewer periods than that of Product 2. A reversal in the sequence in which these products are produced is much more likely to yield a plan that is consistent with the aggregate plan, and which also avoids backlogs. A heuristic procedure based on this type of logic has been suggested by Vollmann [19]. He suggests that the weeks of supply in beginning inventory for all products be calculated, and that the resulting figures be used as a priority index, with the product with the fewest weeks supply being produced first. Alternatively, a master schedule could be produced using optimizing techniques. These techniques, which are discussed in the next chapter, offer powerful alternatives to heuristic or "cut and fit" procedures.

The structure of the master scheduling problem. Our example problem has revealed much of the structure of the disaggregated master scheduling problem in the context of aggregate planning. We have seen that an effective disaggregated master schedule should be consistent with the aggregate plan both in terms of adherence to predetermined capacity limitations, and desired inventory levels. We have also seen that other criteria are important in formulating a master schedule, such as minimizing the number of setups and backlogs or stockouts. It is worthwhile expanding on the latter point. In previous chapters, we have often traded off the costs of setting up or the costs of stocking out with inventory holding costs. We must take a different point of view in the disaggregation process. Here, the level of inventories has been predetermined by the aggregate plan. Thus, trade-offs with setup costs, for example, are in a sense irrelevant. The problem structure changes from one of determining the lot size which jointly minimizes setup and inventory costs to that of choosing a lot size which minimizes setups, subject to the constraint that a certain predetermined inventory level results.

Such changes in problem structure from the traditional ones that we have discussed in earlier chapters on inventory theory derive from the presumption of a hierarchy of plans that consider various aspects of a total problem in rank order of their importance. A hierarchical relationship can be seen, for example, between aggregate plans and disaggregated master schedules. Aggregate planning considers high-level problems such as work force and capacity additions, and total inventory requirements, while less important decisions which consider setup costs, for example, are relegated to a lower level in the hierarchy, master scheduling. Hax [10], whose work we shall explore in the next chapter, has described such decision hierarchies in detail. When hierarchical decision structures are utilized, as in aggregate planning/disaggregated master scheduling, the matter of consistency between plans is of utmost importance. This derives from the fact that plans serve as communicative and integrative devices to other functions in an enterprise besides production. An aggregate plan for example, may be used by finance to plan cash needs for inventories. If a master schedule is derived which is inconsistent with the aggregate plan because it yields higher inventories than anticipated, the firm may be caught short of cash, or other serious financial costs may be incurred.

The issue of consistency between aggregate plans and master schedules raises an important question. Why bother with a top down approach in which aggregate plans are formulated and then master schedules disaggregated from them? Why not instead have just one plan, a master schedule, in which all of the decisions (work force levels, product mix, capacity, setups, stockouts, and so on) are considered simultaneously? This approach would make consistency a moot issue, and might also result in better decisions since hierarchical structures are bound to result in suboptimal decisions in the theoretical sense. The answer to this question is that simultaneous aggregate planning/master scheduling is often more effective when it can be done; when there are few product lines or pieces of equipment, for example. The problem is that a simultaneous procedure is often too complex and time consuming to complete. Hierarchical planning procedures allow analysts to break very large, complex, sometimes insoluble problems, into smaller, simpler and solvable problems with (hopefully) only a small sacrifice in the efficacy of the resulting decisions.

Planning spans and horizon times

As we commented in Chapter 2 on forecasting, there is ordinarily a need for forecasts of different time spans for at least three distinct levels of production plans. Immediate operating plans, and aggregate plans and master schedules, plan the use of capacity in the period six months to one year in advance; and long-range plans are needed for facilities and their locations. The plans and forecasts are interrelated, and their details may depend upon such factors as the behavior of markets and raw material suppliers, and the nature of internal operations and controls. If the market in which we must compete is seasonal for whatever reason, this factor may dominate in selecting a horizon time for planning. To select a planning period which breaks right into the middle of the peak of the marketing season would undoubtedly make a rational planning process very difficult. Thus the peak marketing season for automobiles is somewhat different from that for bathing suits. The furniture marketing season is strongly influenced by the annual trade shows, as is true for many other style goods. Aggregate plans need to take account of seasonal timing. In some instances the timing of raw material supply may be dominant, as would be true in the canning industry.

The internal nature of one's business or activity can have an important effect on the horizon time. One of the important factors is simply the production and procurement lead time. Production and procurement lead times vary widely from a few hours in some simple blending operations to weeks and months in home building, shipbuilding, and other complex manufacturing situations. If the lead time is short, then it may be possible to react quickly to changes in external influences such as the market. On the other hand, if lead time is six months, then it is difficult to envision an increment in planning horizon time less than six months. The fiscal year is probably the most common planning horizon time because of the requirements of both tradition and the federal income tax. Internal managerial practices can have severe interactions with the problems of planning and control for production-inventory systems. For example, the common practice of reducing inventory just before the end of the fiscal year must be taken into account by those responsible for inventory and production planning.

Horizon times are commonly associated with three different levels of planning: long-range plans, aggregate plans, and master scheduling. Table 5–8 summarizes in general the inputs required, the nature of the plans which are the outputs, and the variables which are under managerial control associated with each of the three planning levels. The planning horizon times are, of course, representative rather than specific and rigid. The longest horizon time associated with long-

Table 5–8
Summary of inputs, outputs, and variables under managerial control for three common levels of horizon time

	Several years	One month to several years in advance	One day to several months in advance
Horizon time			
Inputs	Forecasts of: Economic trends Population trends Social and political changes Competitive factors Production and distribution cost patterns Technological innovations Capital constraints	Forecasts of: Amount and timing of sales Costs Supply Policies and constraints on: Overtime Hiring and firing Inventories Capital Long-range plans Backlogs	Progress of actual sales in relation to demand forecasts Aggregate plans and schedules Current inventory position Outstanding orders backlogged
Outputs	Long-range plans for facilities and their·locations	Aggregate plans for the use of various sources of capacity	Detailed master schedule of product mix assignments
Variables under managerial control	Allocation of resources for plant and equipment, engineering and marketing Determination of size and location of plants and warehouses Development of complementary products	Size of work force Production rate Inventory Subcontracting Size of backlogs	Production rate Changes in employee and machine assignments Size of work force (overtime) Changes in product mix/timing

range plans for facilities and their locations involve major capital expenditures, and while they are not irreversible, they do involve critical commitments which may not be easy to change. The forecasts on which they are based involve many assumptions and are the least accurate. Yet the long-range plans may be the most critical in determining the future and possibly even the survival of an organization. Long-range planning is not the subject of this book, but it is regarded as an important input to aggregate planning and scheduling. The literature of long-range planning and technique is a growing and important one [1, 2, 5, 14].

The basic physical capacity for the intermediate term will have been established through previous long-range plans. Nevertheless, even though physical capacity has been relatively fixed, it is still possible to make changes and adjustments which will have an effect on the *actual* output possible within some restricted range. The intermediate range of horizon times with which aggregate plans are associated still leave under managerial control variables such as the size of the work force, production rate, inventory, and possibly outside subcontracting as summarized in Table 5–8. Demand is somewhat more predictable in this intermediate term, and it is likely that past experience will have revealed whatever pattern of seasonality that may exist. Also, forecasts of cost and supply patterns should be somewhat more accurate than would be possible in long-range forecasts so that it is possible to weigh and decide between the several variables of work force size, production rate, inventory level, and subcontracting which management can use to achieve an appropriate plan and schedule.

Finally, detailed master schedules and machine assignments are associated with the shortest horizon time. Actual orders or demand should be well established in this shortest horizon time, but there still may be some flexibility left in the way in which we meet these demands and commitments. Typically, emergency needs for extra capacity are met through overtime, and demand for particular classes of labor and equipment are smoothed through adjustments in employee and machine assignments. Though it is still possible to vary the size of the work force in response to demands which had not been forecast, this is probably the least usable controllable variable.

SUMMARY

The aggregate planning and master scheduling problem has considerable economic significance because it deals with management's attempt to utilize its various sources of capacity in the most effective way. Though there is evidence that current practice tends to focus on a dominant mode within organizations for absorbing fluctuating demand, nevertheless some organizations have recognized that the best solutions to aggregate scheduling problems may be found in a combination of available decision variables. One of the past difficulties in management's use of more advanced methodology has been the elusiveness of the cost data related to the change of production levels. The behavior of costs in relation to changes in level is becoming more apparent and seems to be generally dependent on the existing production level and the magnitude of the contemplated change. Although the graphic models are static, cumbersome, and nonoptimizing, they raise the issues of alternate plans in a way which is easy to visualize. If other methods can do significantly better, then they have a real managerial value. If the more sophisticated techniques cannot improve on present practice, then they may be of interest only in terms of theoretical insight into the aggregate scheduling problem and as stepping-stones to more effective methods. We shall attempt to answer this in the next chapter.

REVIEW QUESTIONS AND PROBLEMS

1. * Consider a situation where the organization wishes to look back over the last 24 periods to see what would have been the effects of a level production policy with the smallest possible production rate. Assume that all production is available only at the end of the period at which it is produced. Also, determine the total storage cost if $c_H = \$1$ per unit per period, assuming that there is no storage cost on units produced within the period and that units sold within the period are stored for one half of the period. In essence, the problem is one of determining the minimum level production rate per period and reduces to finding the period during which inventories would be exhausted. Actual demands for the 24 periods are:

5,000	4,600	5,600	5,200
5,100	4,900	5,500	4,800
4,900	5,100	4,900	5,000
4,700	5,600	4,300	5,100
4,600	5,700	4,400	4,400
4,800	5,400	5,000	5,000

2. An organization is nearing the end of the year, and is making plans for the coming year. It can, through minor adjustments in production rate,

---

* Problem developed by Professors J. Baker and J. W. Gotcher, Department of Management Sciences, California State College, Hayward, California.

end the year with any final inventory between 150 and 1,500 units. The minimum buffer stock is 150 units. What combination of ending inventory (beginning inventory for the new year) and level daily production rate should be used if the criterion for good performance is to minimize the weighted average seasonal inventory cost, where $c_H = \$100$ per unit per year? Suggested procedure: Plot cumulative maximum requirements in relation to production days and compute the costs for two alternate plans which seem logical to you. Cumulative maximum requirements by months are as follows:

Month	Production days	Cumulative maximum requirements
January	22	550
February	18	1,075
March	22	1,575
April	21	2,075
May	22	2,700
June	21	3,530
July	13	4,450
August	21	5,100
September	20	5,700
October	23	6,175
November	21	6,550
December	20	6,950

3. An organization has forecasted maximum production requirements for the coming year as follows:

January	400	July	580
February	510	August	600
March	400	September	300
April	405	October	280
May	460	November	440
June	675	December	500

The present labor force can produce 470 units per month. An employee added or subtracted from the labor force affects the production rate by 20 units per month. The average salary of employees is $660 per month and overtime can be used at the usual premium of time and one-half pay up to 10 percent of time for each employee. Therefore, an employee, working the maximum overtime, could produce the equivalent of an additional two units per month. Hiring and training costs are $100 per employee, and layoff costs are $200 per employee. Inventory holding costs are $10 per month per unit, and shortages cost $50 per unit short. Changeover costs for any increase or decrease in production rate are $3,000 per changeover over and above pertinent hiring and layoff costs. These costs include replanning and rebalancing of production lines and so on. No change cost is appropriate when added production is achieved through the use of overtime. What plan do you recommend? What is the incremental cost of your plan?

4. Given the data in Table 5–2:
   a. What value of c_H would make Plans 1 and 2 equally desirable?
   b. What hiring-layoff cost makes Plans 1 and 2 equally desirable?
   c. What subcontracting extra cost makes Plans 1 and 2 equally desirable?

5. Conceivably, a production-oriented organization has at its disposal a number of possible responses to anticipated changes in demand in developing an aggregate plan. Among the possible responses are production rate changes, inventory fluctuations, changes in employment level, the use of overtime or undertime, back ordering or the absorption of lost sales, and subcontracting. Why then does it seem relatively difficult for organizations to develop rational modes for aggregate production scheduling?

6. Referring to Figure 5–4:
   a. Why should change costs increase at an increasing rate rather than linearly?
   b. Why should a decrease in production rate from a point of departure of 120 percent be somewhat more modest than for a point of departure of 100 percent? (Compare the curves for [b] and [c] of Figure 5–4.)

7. Referring to Tables 5–5, 5–6, 5–7, and aggregate plan number 2 (Table 5–2), create an improved master schedule over the one shown in Table 5–6.

8. State explicitly the criteria one should apply in determining whether or not a master schedule is good.

SELECTED BIBLIOGRAPHY

1. Bowman, E. H. "Scale of Operations—An Empirical Study," *Operations Research*, June 1958.

2. Bowman, E. H., and Fetter, R. B. *Analysis for Production and Operations Management*. 3d ed. Homewood, Ill.: Richard D. Irwin, Inc., 1967.

3. Buffa, E. S. "Aggregate Planning for Production," *Business Horizons*, Fall 1967.

4. Buffa, E. S. *Modern Production Management*. chap. 17. 5th ed. New York: John Wiley & Sons, Inc., 1977.

5. Buffa, E. S. *Operations Management: Problems and Models*. chaps. 12 and 13. 3d ed. New York: John Wiley & Sons, Inc., 1972.

6. Calica, A. B. "Fabrication and Assembly Operations: Part II, Long-Range Planning Techniques," *IBM Systems Journal*, vol. 4, no. 2 (1965).

7. Fetter, R. B.   "A Linear Programming Model for Long-Range Capacity Planning," *Management Science*, vol. 7, no. 4 (July 1961), pp. 372–78.

8. Gordon, J. R. M.   "A Multi-Model Analysis of an Aggregate Scheduling Decision." Unpublished Ph.D. dissertation, Sloan School of Management, Massachusetts Institute of Technology, 1966.

9. Hax, A. C.   *Integration of Strategic and Tactical Planning in the Aluminum Industry*. Technical Report No. 86. Operations Research Center, MIT, 1973.

10. Hax, A. C., and Meal, H. C. "Hierarchical Integration of Production Planning and Scheduling" in M. A. Geisler, ed., *Studies in the Management Sciences, V.I., Logistics*. North Holland American Elsevier, 1975.

11. Holloway, C. A.   "A Mathematical Programming Approach to Identification and Optimization of Complex Operational Systems, with the Aggregate Planning Problem as an Example." Unpublished Ph.D. dissertation, University of California, Los Angeles, 1969.

12. Holt, C.; Modigliani, F.; and Simon, H. A.   "A Linear Decision Rule for Production and Employment Scheduling," *Management Science*, vol. 2, no. 1 (October 1955), pp. 1–30.

13. Krajewaski, L. J., and Ritzman, L. P.   "Dissaggregation in Manufacturing and Service Organizations: Survey of Problems and Research." *Proceedings of the Problems of Disaggregation in Manufacturing and Service Operations Conference*, Ohio State University, 1977, pp. 1–9.

14. Magee, J. F.   *Industrial Logistics*. New York: McGraw-Hill Book Co., 1968.

15. McGarrah, R. E.   *Production and Logistics Management: Text and Cases*. chap. 5. New York: John Wiley & Sons, Inc., 1963.

16. Silver, E. A. "A Tutorial on Production Smoothing and Work Force Balancing," *Operations Research*, vol. 15, no. 6 (November–December 1967) pp. 985–1010.

17. Steiner, G. A., ed. *Management Long-Range Planning*. New York: McGraw-Hill Book Co., 1963.

18. Tuite, M. F.   "Merging Marketing Strategy Selection and Production Scheduling: A Higher Order Optimum," *Journal of Industrial Engineering*, vol. 19, no. 2 (February 1968), pp. 76–84.

19. Vollmann, T. E.   *Operations Management: A Systems Model Building Approach*. Reading, Mass.: Addison-Wesley Publishing Co., Inc., 1973.

CASE STUDY
THE MASTER SCHEDULING
GAME

YOU ARE the president of the Screw-Ball Shot Company, a small firm which produces balls for use in ball bearings and other industrial products. Since your company is small, you personally make out the firm's master schedule each month, and from it, derive a detailed production schedule.

Company background

Screw-Ball has a single shot shooter (a machine for making balls) which is run by one operator on each of three shifts. Company policy is to run the machine three shifts a day, for five days a week. If there is insufficient business to keep the machine busy, the worker(s) are idle since Screw-Ball has made a definite commitment to never fire or lay off a worker. By the same token, the firm has a policy of never working on weekends. Thus, the capacity of the machine (assuming four-week months) is 4 weeks × 5 days × 24 hours = 480 hours per month. Since the hourly wage is $5 per hour, this commits the firm to a fixed labor cost of $5 × 480 = $2,400 per month. Once the machine is set up to make a particular kind of ball, it can produce them at the rate of 5 per hour, regardless of ball type. The process is quite stable. The material content of each ball type is the same, since the balls vary only in shape (spherical balls, square balls, elliptical balls, and so on). The cost of the material in each ball, regardless of type, is $4. Raw materials are never a problem, and can be obtained overnight.

Screw-Ball has divided its product line into three categories: A-Balls, B-Balls, and Odd-Balls.

245

A-Balls

There is only one type of ball in this category. The company has decided to produce this A-Ball to stock, because it is sold to a large number of distributors who require immediate shipment at the end of each month. A-Balls sell for $8 each. If A-Balls are not in stock when demanded, the distributors buy from other sources, and Screw-Ball's penalty is a lost sale. Historically, the demand for A-Balls has averaged 700 per month. However, sales are usually somewhat seasonal. The following demand for these items has been forecasted:

Month	Demand	Month	Demand
1*	500	7	900
2	500	8	900
3	600	9	800
4	700	10	700
5	800	11	600
6	900	12	500

* In other words, the company expects to sell 500 A-Balls at the end of month 1.

It takes 40 hours to set up the shot shooter to make A-Balls. Screw-Ball has found that its forecasts are accurate to within ± 200 units per month.

B-Balls

As with A-Balls, there is only one product type in the B-Ball category, these are called Bean-Balls because of their elliptical shape. Bean-Balls are manufactured to order for a large original equipment manufacturer (OEM); Screw-Ball's price to this company is $7 per ball. The customer usually places "blanket" orders three times a year. When it places these orders, it specifies the delivery of certain quantities in each of the next four periods. The customer has already ordered 2,400 units with delivery of 600 at the end of periods 1, 2, 3, and 4. The company is expected to specify the quantities it requires for periods 5, 6, 7, and 8 at the beginning of period 4. The delivery schedule containing the orders for months 9, 10, 11, and 12 is expected to arrive at the beginning of period 8. The customer has estimated its average monthly needs over the year to be 600 per month, although their estimates are often considerably in error.

Because of the importance of this large customer to Screw-Ball, they always try to satisfy their needs. The company feels that if they ever refuse to accept an order from this company, they will lose their business. Under the terms of their sales contract, Screw-Ball has agreed to pay this customer $1 for every unit not shipped on time for each month that a unit's shipment is delinquent. *Delinquent shipments must be made up.* It takes 30 hours to set up the shot shooter to make Bean-Balls.

Odd-Balls

Odd-Balls are made only to customer order because of their low volume and specialized nature. The company has found that there are three kinds of Odd-Balls that are ordered: Ski-Balls, Ner-Balls, and Snow-Balls. All types of Odd-Balls are sold to distributors at $10 per ball. When a distributor places an order for one, they specify the quantity and the period during which they want them delivered. Screw-Ball looks to see if they can fit these orders into their schedule, and either accepts or rejects the order. If Screw-Ball accepts an order for delivery at the end of a certain period, and fails to meet this commitment, they pay a penalty of $2 per unit for each period delivery is delayed. This penalty is incurred in each period until the delinquent order is delivered. It takes 40 hours to set up the shooter to make one of the various types of Odd-Balls. Exhibit 1, Screw-Ball's open order file, shows the orders they have already promised to deliver in future periods. The company has tried to forecast the de-

Exhibit 1
Screw-Ball Open Order File* (end of period 0)

Month	Product type	Quantity
1	Bean-Balls	600
	Ski-Balls	1,000
	Ner-Balls	200
	(past due from	
	previous period)	
2	Bean-Balls	600
	Snow-Balls	400
	Ner-Balls	200
3	Bean-Balls	600
4	Bean-Balls	600

* All orders are to be delivered at the *end* of the month indicated, after all production for the month has been completed, and before the new month's production is started.

mand for the different types of Odd-Balls, but has given up in disgust.

Master scheduling

Master scheduling at Screw-Ball is done once each month, after production for the month is completed and shipped and new orders from customers arrive, and before production in the next month starts. The master scheduling effort results in two documents. The first is a P&L statement for the month. Exhibit 2 shows that this document factors in sales and production costs, including penalty charges and inventory carrying costs. The inventory carrying cost for *any type of product* is $0.10 per unit per month left in inventory after shipments for the month have taken place.

The second document the company produces is a master schedule as shown in Exhibit 3. This shows what Screw-Ball wants its factory to produce in each month in the future. Since the master schedule loses validity (because of uncertainty) the further into the future that it is projected, it is reformulated each month. Note that the master schedule specifies two things that are important in the "action" bucket (the next period for which definite, *irrevocable* commitments must be made). The first is the number of hours (setup + run) that are allocated to each product to be produced. These can be calculated by adding the setup time to the number of units to be produced divided by 5. The total of all of these times in a month *cannot exceed 480 hours*. The second important piece of data is a circled number indicating the sequence in which products are to be produced on the machines. This is important because at the end of a month, the machine will be set up for the last product produced. If a continuation of this product run in the next month is desired, no new setup will be required as indicated by this number sequence.

The game

You will be asked to play the role of the president of Screw-Ball in class. You should arrive in class with a master schedule for the company (use Exhibit 3). It is up to you to decide how far into the future to plan, but you must be sure to at least have the next action bucket filled in as specified. (Don't forget that you are already 200 units past due on Ner-Balls and the machine is currently set up to run them.) In class, the game will proceed as follows:

Exhibit 2
P&L statement (period 0)

(1) Product	(2) Price	(3) Beginning inventory* (past due)	(4) Production	(5) Available†	(6) Demand	(7) Sales‡	(8) Ending inventory* (past due)	(9) Inventory costs§ (past due cost)
A-Balls	$ 8	750	950	1,700	500	$ 4,000	1,200	$120
Bean-Balls	7	—	600	600	600	4,200	0	0
Ski-Balls	10	—	—	—	—	—	0	0
Ner-Balls	10	—	200	200	400	2,000	(200)	400
Snow-Balls	10	—	—	—	—	—	0	0
Totals			1,750			$10,200		$520

Sales (total of column 7) $10,200
Costs:
Labor $2,400
Materials (total of column 4 × $4) 7,000
Inventory/past due (total of column 9) 520
                                          ————
Total cost $9,920
Contribution to profit 280
Cumulative contribution .... 280 (add to next period's contribution)

* Past due refers to the quantity of units not shipped as promised.
† Available = Column 3 + Column 4
‡ Sales = Column 6 × Column 2 when demand < available; column 5 × column 2 otherwise.
§ Inventory cost = 0.10 times number of units in ending inventory. Past due cost equals number of units not shipped when promised times the penalty ($1 for Bean-Balls; $2 for the Odd-Balls).

Exhibit 3
Master schedule (period 0)

Product	Month 0	1	2	3	4	5	6	7	8	9	10
A-Balls	950 ①										
Hours	230										
Bean-Balls	600 ②										
Hours	150										
Ski-Balls											
Hours											
Ner-Balls	200 ③										
Hours	80										
Snow-Balls											
Hours											
Total hours scheduled											

1. You will be supplied with a form specifying (a) actual demand in month one, and (b) any new order requests for Odd-Balls or Bean-Balls.
2. You will then derive a P&L statement for month one, assuming you made what you specified in your master schedule, and that demands are as given.
3. You should then look at your order requests, and accept those you want and reject the rest. Those you accept for delivery in future periods should be added to your open order file (you may use Exhibit 1). You are then irrevocably committed to them or their consequences.
4. You should then make out a new master schedule, specifying *at least* what you want your factory to do in the next "action bucket" (it will be for month 2 at that time). *You will find it helpful to have thought out a strategy for your master scheduling activities in advance of class.* Extra master scheduling forms will be provided.
5. We will then cycle back through the game.

Chapter 6

Aggregate planning and master scheduling: Techniques

THE APPLICATION OF MATHEMATICAL TECHNIQUES to aggregate planning began during the great post-World War II management science movement. Since then work has continued at an accelerated pace motivated in part by the tremendous economic consequences of aggregate decisions and aided by the concurrent development and improvement of research methodologies in the management science field. The initial thrust of this work was to use mathematical optimizing techniques such as differential calculus and linear programming to solve necessarily simplified aggregate planning cost models. Solving the models yielded a set of decisions, or decision rules, which produced mathematically optimum results with respect to the cost model.

More recent formal approaches to developing aggregate plans and master schedules have taken the form of decision rules which are based on heuristic problem-solving approaches, computer search methods, and on the problem of dissaggregating aggregate plans into master and other more detailed schedules. The objective of these newer methodologies is to enable the model builder and decision maker to introduce greater realism into the techniques they apply. This added realism should, hopefully, more than compensate for the fact that heuristic and computer search techniques do not guarantee mathematically optimum decision rules. Advocates of heuristic, search, and disaggregate or hierarchical decision rule approaches argue that since the decisions produced by a model can be no better than the model itself, it follows that greater realism should produce better overall results. All four approaches have one thing in common—they address one of the most exciting, challenging, and potentially rewarding problems in industry today. Our discussion will present an overview of model formulation and the solution methodologies. From this frame of reference we will view the work in this field in terms of the decision rules they utilize.

MODEL FORMULATION

The materials of Chapter 5 served to define the aggregate planning/master scheduling problem in terms of its general nature, the costs affected, and the general structure of these costs. Now, in order to deal with this problem we must consider how a model should be formulated and, once formulated, how it should be solved. Neither the model formulation process nor the model solution process is mechanical. Insight is required to avoid building a highly realistic but computationally infeasible model on one hand, or a feasible, but greatly oversimplified model on the other. In addition, self-discipline must be continually exercised by the model builders to prevent their enthusiasm for a particular solution technique from leading them to model the problem to fit the solution technique. Thus it is clear that the creation of decision models for aggregate planning and master scheduling is, at the present time, an art involving a careful match between the real world, the model, and the solution technique.

Model building considerations

One of the most critical decisions in model building concerns how to structure the problem since it is usually the structure that determines the method of solution. Careful thought must be given as to whether the problem will be considered to be:

Linear or nonlinear.

Steady state or dynamic.

Continuous time or discrete time.

Continuous value or discrete value.

Deterministic or stochastic.

Single stage or multistage.

Once these decisions have been made, a model can be structured in one of two general ways:

Model structure as a set of mathematical fuctions. This structure uses closed-form mathematical equations to describe the system under study. It has the advantage that, provided the simplifying assumptions do not make the model too unrealistic, it can be effectively used to facilitate rapid and optimal solutions by conventional analytic techniques, such as differential calculus, linear programming, dynamic programming, integer programming, and so on. The main disadvantage is that the mathematical structure may become too complex to solve. In addition, some care is required to select the right equation forms and blend them into a cohesive model.

Model structure as a computational algorithm. This structure can be considered as a "black box" which produces single-valued outputs for given input settings of decision variables. The contents of the black box might include: a table of numbers, a set of graphs, a computer program, decision tables, and so on. This representation is valuable when an analytic expression is either unavailable or too complicated to manipulate. Furthermore, it may enable the analyst to describe the problem more precisely. Nevertheless, it has the disadvantage that the greater the complexity of the algorithm, the lower the probability of finding the global optimum aggregate plan or master schedule.

SOLUTION METHODOLOGIES

In this section we will briefly summarize and classify the solution methodologies which have proved effective in dealing with aggregate planning/master scheduling decisions. The interested reader should refer to references [6, 52] for excellent technical descriptions of optimization methodology.

The solution methodologies that have been applied to this problem can be divided into those which are guaranteed to produce mathematically optimal decision rules with respect to the model and those that do not. Examples of the former include linear programming (both the distribution and standard simplex methods), differential calculus, dynamic programming, and an application of the discrete and continuous maximum principle. Other mathematical programming optimizing techniques will undoubtedly be applied in the future as research in the nonlinear programming field progresses.

The decision rules which do not guarantee mathematically optimum solutions with respect to the model are of three general types. The first is heuristic in nature and hypothesizes that decision rules can be represented by heuristically derived equations. The numerical values assigned to the coefficients of the equations are obtained in two ways. Bowman [4], in his management coefficients approach, performs a regression analysis of historical management decisions to obtain coefficients. Jones [33], in his parametric production-planning approach, builds a forward-looking multistage cost model and simulates the operation of the model by plugging in trial values of the coefficients. The simulation takes the form of a coarse grid search based on systematically evaluating certain combinations of coefficient values. At the conclusion of the coarse grid search the best set of coefficients is selected for use in the heuristically postulated decision rules.

The second major solution methodology of this type does not postulate the form of the decision rule equations but rather obtains specific numerical values associated with various decisions by climbing, or searching, the mathematical response surface formed by the criterion function of the model. This approach combines the advantage of realistic model representation by means of a computational algorithm (computer program) with newly developed computer routines which search for the optimal point, or points, on a mathematical response surface. This approach is termed the search decision rule approach.

The third major solution methodology that seeks good, but not necessarily optimal solutions are those that rely on hierarchical decision structures for disaggregating master schedules or other more detailed schedules from aggregate plans. Some mathematically optimal methods have been applied to the combined problem of determining optimal aggregate plans and master schedules simultaneously. By way of contrast, hierarchical methods seek solutions to

Figure 6-1
Comparison of decision rule approaches to aggregate planning/master scheduling

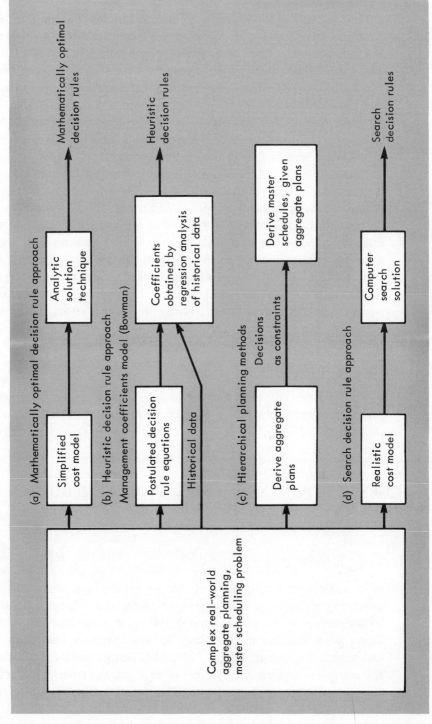

various aspects of the aggregate planning problem sequentially. For example, an optimal aggregate plan may be derived first, resulting in decisions on work force and aggregate inventory levels. Then, a second master scheduling problem may be solved, using as constraints the decisions contained in the optimal aggregate plan. Hierarchical methods, do not necessarily guarantee optimal solutions to the total problem, but, if the hierarchy is cleverly constructed, good solutions may result. Figure 6–1 summarizes all three approaches to the aggregate planning/master scheduling problem.

In dividing the solution methodologies into those which guarantee a mathematical optimum with respect to a particular aggregate planning/master scheduling model and those which do not, we do not intend to imply that one method is necessarily better than the other. The guarantee of optimality may or may not have value depending on how well the model captures the relevant aspects of the problem. Obviously, there is little point in optimizing a model which does not describe what is actually happening. As noted earlier, the solution to aggregate planning problems is an art involving a careful match between the real world, the model, and the solution methodology. This then, is the nature of the challenge that must be faced in creating decision models for aggregate plans and master schedules.

The balance of this chapter deals with alternate aggregate planning/master scheduling solution techniques which have been proposed.

AGGREGATE PLANNING AND MASTER SCHEDULING METHODS USING MATHEMATICALLY OPTIMAL DECISION RULES

Linear programming methods

Linear programming methods have been applied in a variety of ways to generate optimal aggregate plans and master schedules under certain assumptions. One of the earliest applications of the linear programming methodology in this area was Bowman's [4] transportation formulation in 1956. This simple model focused on the assignment of various sources of productive capacity in such a way that combined production and inventory costs are minimized, subject to the constraints that all demands are met, and that capacity limitations are not violated. Some of the types of productive capacity that this model is capable of dealing with include regular time production, overtime production, and subcontracting. While Bowman's model is flexible enough to handle individual products as well as aggregated data, thus making it a feasible method of master scheduling as well as aggregate planning, its basic drawback has been that it doesn't consider the costs of changing production capacity levels. In a sense then, it presumes that capacity levels have already been determined by a higher order process. This disadvantage has been overcome by later linear programming approaches.

Since the time that Bowman's model was introduced, a number of linear programming formulations to aggregate planning/master scheduling have been developed. Many of them take various refinements and special conditions into consideration, and most of them can be viewed as variations on the general linear programming formulation shown in Equations (1)–(5).

Minimize

$$Z = \sum_{t=1}^{T} (c_t X_t + \ell_t W_t + \ell_t' O_t + h_t I_t^+ + \pi_t I_t^- + e_t w_t^+ + e_t' w_t^-) \quad (1)$$

subject to, for $t = 1, 2, \ldots, T$

$$I_t = I_{t-1} + X_t - D_t \quad (2)$$
$$I_t = I_t^+ - I_t^- \quad (3)$$
$$W_t = W_{t-1} + w_t^+ - w_t^- \quad (4)$$
$$O_t - U_t = m X_t - W_t \quad (5)$$

$X_t, I_t^+, I_t^-, W_t, w_t^+, w_t^-, O_t, U_t$ all ≥ 0

Where:

W_t = Work force level in period t, measured in regular time hours.

w_t^+ = Increase in work force level from period $t - 1$ to t (in hours).

w_t^- = Decrease in work force level from period $t - 1$ to t (in hours).

O_t = Overtime scheduled in period t (in hours).

U_t = Undertime (unused regular time capacity) scheduled in period t (in hours).

X_t = Production scheduled for period t (in units of product).

I_t^+ = On-hand inventory at the end of period t.

I_t^- = Back order position at the end of period t.

m = Number of hours required to produce one unit of product.

ℓ_t = Cost of an hour's worth of labor on regular time in period t.
ℓ_t' = Cost of an hour's worth of labor on overtime in period t.
e_t = Cost to increase the work force level by one hour in period t.
e_t' = Cost to decrease the work force level by one hour in period t.
h_t = Inventory carrying cost, per unit held from period t to $t + 1$.
π_t = Back order cost, per unit carried from period t to $t + 1$.
c_t = Unit variable production cost in period t (excluding labor).

This general linear programming model considers most of the costs that we discussed in Chapter 5. An examination of the objective function (Equation 1) shows that regular production costs, overtime, and regular time labor costs, inventory and backlogging costs, and work force change costs are considered. Equation (2) constrains the solution in such a way that current inventories reflect prior inventories, sales, and production. It effectively means that all demands must be satisfied from inventory, from current production, or backlogged. Equation (3) defines finished goods inventories in terms of its positive (inventory) and negative (backlog) components. Equation (4) is a "trick" equation that allows work force changes to be explictly expressed in the formulation. It merely states that the change in work force levels (positive or negative) is a function of the work force level in the last period and that in the current period. The final Equation (5) ensures that all output is produced either on regular time or on overtime. The undertime variable (U_t) is included as a slack variable, which recognizes that a work force may not be fully utilized during some time periods.

The linear programming formulation shown in Equations (1)–(5) is quite flexible and adaptable. For example, a policy decision to always use the work force to the fullest extent can be incorporated by changing Equation (5) by eliminating the slack variable U_t. Similarly, a decision to disallow backlogging or inventorying can be incorporated by eliminating the variable I_t^-, and Equation (3). In fact, one can also manipulate this basic formulation to create Bowman's transportation model by eliminating all of the variables except X_t, O_t, and I_t, eliminating Equations (3) and (4) and modifying Equation (5) to reflect capacity constraints. Further redefinitions can then be employed to get the model in a form suitable for the employment of the transportation algorithm. Multiple products, and hence master scheduling, can also be handled by adding decision variables $(X_{it}, I_{it}^+, I_{it}^-, M_i)$ specific to additional products $i = 1, \ldots N$.

Much of the work that has been done in developing linear programming models for aggregate planning and master scheduling has involved modifications to general models of the types that we have illustrated above, although these modifications and extensions are often quite sophisticated. For example, McGarrah [37] formulated a linear program that used piecewise linear functions to approximate the nonlinear types of work force change costs postulated in Chapter 5 and shown in Figure 6–2. This circumvented one of the most

Figure 6–2
Piecewise linear approximations of a
nonlinear function

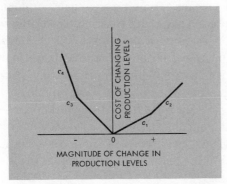

restrictive assumptions of linear programming models; namely, that the functions expressed in it are linear. However, the increased complexity and size of such sophisticated models has precluded their widespread use.

Several applications of linear programming to aggregate planning and master scheduling have been reported by Eisemann and Young [13] in the textile industry; Green, Chatto, Hicks, and Cox [21] in the packing industry; and by Fabian [15] in blast furnace production. These successes, and others, bear witness to the importance of this approach as a decision tool, as well as a means of gaining insights into the nature of the problem.

Linear programming formulations do have several disadvantages however. First, the assumption of linearity is restrictive. When linear functions are forced in practice, linear programming models can fail to capture true cost functions, many of which are nonlinear or discontinuous. Second, even when nonlinear approximations are made with piecewise linear functions, the size and complexity of the resulting formulation can limit their practical use. Third, integer variables cannot be employed. This means that lot size considerations, for example, cannot be incorporated into the decision model. Some of these problems can be avoided by employing alternative techniques, such as the Linear Decision Rule (discussed next), or integer programming (discussed later in the chapter in the context of hierarchical methods).

The Linear Decision Rule (LDR)

The Linear Decision Rule (LDR) was developed by Holt, Modigliani, Muth, and Simon as a means of making aggregate employment and production rate decisions. The model was first tested in a paint factory [29, 30]. The Linear Decision Rule is based on the development of a quadratic cost function with cost components made up of regular payroll, hiring, layoff, overtime, inventory holding, back ordering, and machine setup costs. The quadratic cost function is then used to derive two linear decision rules for setting work force levels and production rates for the upcoming period based on a forecast of aggregate sales for 12 periods ahead. We will summarize the structure of the model as tested in the paint factory, as well as the results obtained by the application.

Regular payroll, hiring, and layoff costs. The LDR model calls for adjustments in the size of the work force once each month with the implied commitment to pay the employees at least their regular time wages for the month. Figure 6–3 shows this relationship as a

Figure 6–3
Regular payroll cost function

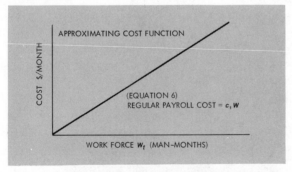

Source: From C. C. Holt, F. Modigliani, and H. A. Simon, "A Linear Decision Rule for Production and Employment Scheduling." *Management Science*, vol. 2, no. 2 (October 1955), p. 10–30.

Figure 6–4
Hiring and layoff cost function

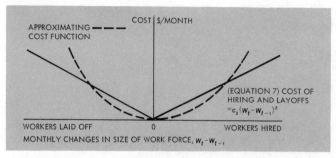

Source: From C. C. Holt, F. Modigliani, and H. A. Simon, "A Linear Deci-sion Rule for Production and Employment Scheduling," *Management Science*, vol. 2, no. 2 (October 1955), pp. 10–30.

linear cost function defined by Equation (6). (The c's in the equations represent constants which will be given values for the paint company example at a later point in our discussion.)

The costs shown in Figure 6–4 are the costs of labor turnover resulting from increasing the size of the work force by hiring or reducing the size of the work force by layoffs. Both hiring and layoff costs will increase with the number of employees affected, and the model approximates these costs with the quadratic function described by Equation (7). The basic model does not require that the costs be symmetrical as shown. With regard to the shape of the cost function the authors comment as follows:

Whether these costs actually rise at an increasing or decreasing rate is difficult to determine. It can be argued that reorganization costs are more than proportionately larger for large layoffs than for small layoffs; and similarly the efficiency of hiring, measured in terms of the quality of the employees hired, may fall when a large number of people are hired at one time. If this argument holds, then the quadratic curve is especially suitable. But if not, the quadratic still can give a tolerable approximation over a range.

Overtime and Undertime costs. If the size of the work force is held constant, then changes in production rate can be absorbed by overtime or undertime. Undertime is the cost of idle labor at regular payroll rates. The overtime cost depends on the size of the work force, W, and the aggregate production rate, P. The form of the overtime-undertime cost function shown in Figure 6–5 is rationalized as follows: "Since workers are each somewhat specialized in function, it is likely that a small increase in production would

Figure 6–5
Overtime cost function

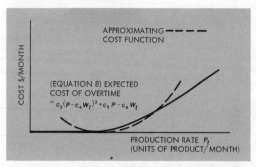

Source: From C. C. Holt, F. Modigliani, and H. A. Simon, "A Linear Decision Rule for Production and Employment Scheduling," *Management Science,* vol. 2, no. 2
(October 1955), p. 10.

require only a few employees who work in bottleneck functions to
work overtime. As production is increased further, more and more
employees are required to work overtime until the whole work force
is doing some overtime work." Thus the upsweeping solid line in
Figure 6–5 approximated by the quadratic cost function of Equation
(8). "As production rate P exceeds c_4W_1, a level set by the size of the
work force, overtime costs increase. The linear terms, c_5P and c_6W,
are added to improve the approximation." Equation (8) takes into
account the point of departure through the specification of W_1, the
present size of the work force at the time decisions are to be made for
the upcoming period.

Thus we have a family of overtime cost curves obtained by substituting various values for W_1 in Equation (8). Whether overtime or
undertime costs will occur for a given decision will depend on the
balance of costs defined by the horizon time. For example, in responding to the need for increased output, the costs of hiring and
training must be balanced against the overtime costs, or conversely
the response to a decreased production rate would require the
balancing of layoff costs against the costs of undertime.

Inventory, back order, and setup costs. When inventories deviate from an ideal or optimal level, either extra inventory costs, or
costs of back ordering or lost sales will occur. In the LDR the optimal
aggregate inventory level is defined by the sum of the optimal average safety stock plus one half the optimal batch size for each paint.
The optimal batch size for each paint is determined by usual economic order quantity formulas. Thus, one of the costs which will

vary with changes in aggregate inventory is machine setup cost. For example, as aggregate inventory is reduced, the average production batch size will be decreased in order to maintain a balanced inventory, and additional machine setups will be required. In the LDR we deal with "net inventory," meaning inventory minus back orders.

Thus, the inventory costs form a U-shaped curve, as shown in Figure 6–6, which has been approximated by the quadratic cost function of Equation (9).

Figure 6–6
Inventory, back order, and machine setup cost function

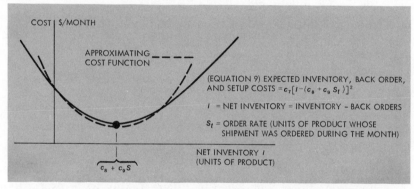

Source: From C. C. Holt, F. Modigliani, and H. A. Simon, "A Linear Decision Rule for Production and Employment Scheduling," *Management Science*, vol. 2, no. 2 (October 1955), p. 13.

The total incremental cost function for the paint factory has the components specified by Equations (6), (7), (8), and (9) indicated on the graphs. For any particular period t the sum of these component cost functions represent a function to be minimized, but each month's decision has cost effects which extend out to the planning horizon time. Therefore, we need a cost criterion function which adds the component costs for each month and in addition adds these monthly costs over the period of the horizon time. The problem is then to minimize monthly costs over N periods, or:

$$C_N = \sum_{t=1}^{N} C_t \qquad (10)$$

and

$$C_t = [(c_1 W_t) \qquad \text{Regular payroll costs from Equation (6)}$$

$$+ c_2 (W_t - W_{t-1})^2 \qquad \text{Hiring and layoff costs from Equation (7)} \qquad (11)$$

$+ c_3 (P_t - c_4 W_t)^2 + c_5 P_t - c_6 W_t$ Overtime costs from
                                          Equation (8)

$+ c_7 (I_t - c_8 - c_9 S_t)^2]$ Inventory-connected costs
                                          from Equation (9)

subject to the restraint,

$$I_{t-1} + P_t - S_t = I_t \quad t = 1, 2, \ldots N \tag{12}$$

The total cost for N periods is given by Equation (10) and the monthly cost, C_t, is given by Equation (11). Equation (12) states the relationship between beginning inventory, production, and sales during the month, and ending inventory.

Equations (10), (11), and (12) are general and applicable to a broad range of situations. By estimating the values of the c's a specific factory cost structure can be specified. For the paint factory, Equation (13) is the result:

$$C_N = \sum_{t=1}^{N} \{[340 W_t] + [64.3(W_t - W_{t-1})^2]$$
$$+ [0.20(P_t - 5.67 W_t)^2 + 51.2 P_t - 281 W_t] \tag{13}$$
$$+ [0.0825(I_t - 320)^2]\}$$

Optimal decision rules for the paint factory. A solution to Equation (13) was obtained by differentiating with respect to each decision variable. The mathematical derivation is contained in a sequel paper by Holt, Modigliani, and Muth [28]. The result for the paint factory is contained in Equations (14) and (15):

$$P_t = \begin{cases} +0.463\, F_t \\ +0.234\, F_{t+1} \\ +0.111\, F_{t+2} \\ +0.046\, F_{t+3} \\ +0.013\, F_{t+4} \\ -0.002\, F_{t+5} \\ -0.008\, F_{t+6} \\ -0.010\, F_{t+7} \\ -0.009\, F_{t+8} \\ -0.008\, F_{t+9} \\ -0.007\, F_{t+10} \\ -0.005\, F_{t+11} \end{cases} + 0.993\, W_{t-1} + 153 - 0.464\, I_{t-1} \tag{14}$$

$$W_t = 0.743\, W_{t-1} + 2.09 - 0.010\, I_{t-1} + \begin{cases} +0.0101\, F_t \\ +0.0088\, F_{t+1} \\ +0.0071\, F_{t+2} \\ +0.0054\, F_{t+3} \\ +0.0042\, F_{t+4} \\ +0.0031\, F_{t+5} \\ +0.0023\, F_{t+6} \\ +0.0016\, F_{t+7} \\ +0.0012\, F_{t+8} \\ +0.0009\, F_{t+9} \\ +0.0006\, F_{t+10} \\ +0.0005\, F_{t+11} \end{cases} \tag{15}$$

Where:

P_t = The number of units of product that should be produced during the forthcoming month t.

W_{t-t} = The number of employees in the work force at the beginning of the month (end of the previous month).

I_{t-1} = The number of units of inventory minus the number of units on back order at the beginning of the month.

W_t = The number of employees that will be required for the current month t. The number of employees that should be hired is therefore $W_t - W_{t-1}$.

F_t = A forecast of number of units of product that will be ordered for shipment during the current month t.

F_{t+1} = The same for the next month, $t + 1$, etc.

Equations (14) and (15) would be used at the beginning of each month. Equation (14) determines the aggregate production rate and Equation (15) the aggregate size of the work force. Though the equations look formidable, they are actually simple to compute, and the computations can be accomplished easily by a trained clerk. Both equations involve a weighted forecast of sales as well as beginning work force and inventory levels.

Paint factory application. The derived decision rules of Equations (14) and (15) were applied to a past six-year period for which there was a known record of decisions. Two kinds of forecasts were used as inputs to the new decision system, a perfect and a moving average forecast. The actual order pattern was extremely variable and in addition involved the 1949 recession and the Korean War.

The graphical record showing actual factory performances compared with the simulated performance of the LDR with the two different forecasts is shown in Figures 6–7, 6–8, 6–9, and 6–10. Figure 6–7 shows the response of the production rule with either forecast to be somewhat smoother than was true for actual factory performance. Actual factory performance involved a number of drastic changes in production rate.

An examination of Figure 6–8 shows that the basic size of the work force was held at roughly the same average levels during the last three years of the study even though average production rates were falling as seen in Figure 6–7. The work force rule, through its interaction with production rate, however, responds and the size of the average work force declines during the same period.

Figure 6–7
Production rule in relation to actual factory performance

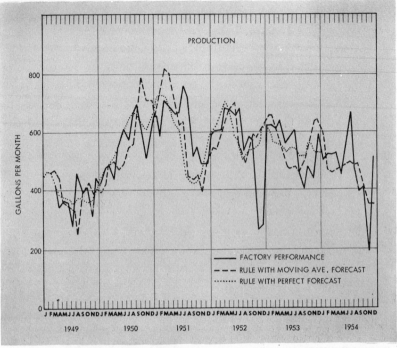

Source: From C. C. Holt, F. Modigliani, and H. A. Simon, "A Linear Decision Rule for Production and Employment Scheduling," *Management Science*, vol. 2, no. 2 (October 1955), p. 21.

The overtime hours graph of Figure 6–9 shows a very large peak of overtime called for by the LDR with the moving average forecast during the latter part of 1950. The moving average forecast, of course, was unable to foresee the sudden Korean War induced orders and so had to compensate through the use of large amounts of overtime work.

The inventory record in Figure 6–10 shows that the surge of orders which caused the overtime peak in 1950 also caused a sharp decline in inventories for both the actual factory performance and the LDR with the moving average forecast followed by a compensatory buildup of inventories.

Cost comparisons. In order to make cost comparisons between the three alternate modes of operation, costs were constructed for the six-year period of actual operation and projected for the decision rules based on the nonquadratic cost structure originally estimated

Figure 6–8
Work force rule in relation to actual factory performance

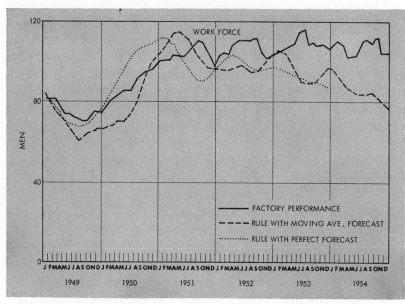

Source: From C. C. Holt, F. Modigliani, and H. A. Simon, "A Linear Decision Rule for Production and Employment Scheduling," *Management Science*, vol. 2, no. 2 (October 1955), p. 22.

Figure 6–9
Overtime hours

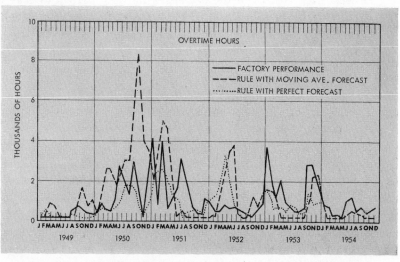

Source: From C. C. Holt, F. Modigliani, and H. A. Simon, "A Linear Decision Rule for Production and Employment Scheduling," *Management Science*, vol. 2 no. 2 (October 1955), p. 23.

Figure 6–10
End-of-month inventories

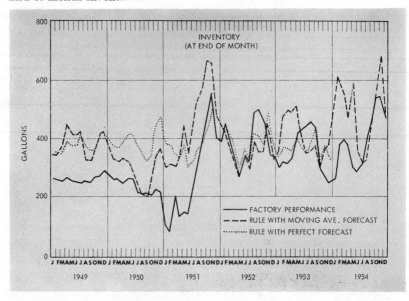

Source: From C. C. Holt, F. Modigliani, and H. A. Simon, "A Linear Decision Rule for Production and Employment Scheduling," *Management Science*, vol. 2, no. 2 (October 1955), p. 24.

from factory data. Table 6–1 shows the summary comparisons. The lowest total cost is for the decision rule with perfect forecasts. The difference between the costs for the perfect forecast and the moving average forecast under decision rule operation is due to better forecasting. The cost difference between the actual company performance and the performance of the decision rule with the moving average forecast amounted to $173,000 per year.

Table 6–1
Cost comparisons for 1949–53 (dollar amounts in thousands)

		Decision rule	
Type of cost	Company performance	Moving average forecast	Perfect forecast
Regular payroll	$1,940	$1,834	$1,888
Overtime	196	296	167
Inventory	361	451	454
Back orders	1,566	616	400
Hiring and layoffs	22	25	20
Total cost	$4,085 (139%)	$3,222 (110%)	$2,929 (100%)

Linear Decision Rule extensions. As in the case of linear programming models for aggregate planning and master scheduling, the LDR approach spawned a number of extensions and refinements. They include LDR models that consider plant capacity [3], multiple products [8], and revenues as well as costs [1].

Sypkens [46] developed an extension of the LDR model which identifies plant capacity as a decision variable in addition to W and P. While we recognize that the short-range capacity of a system is set in the conventional LDR model through the determination of the work force, W, there are some instances where fundamental physical capacity adjustments can also be made. Examples include trucking firms, where trucks can and must be added at some point to vary the capacity to haul goods.

Comparative studies showed that the variable capacity model could yield costs 3 to 5 percent lower than the comparable fixed capacity model when the production process was characterized by low-capacity changeover costs and by systems where variable unit costs were highly sensitive to P. The cost reductions noted were in two rather different areas. The first, as expected, was a result of the fixed capacity model not producing optimally compared to the variable capacity model. The second area of cost reduction, however, was nearly as large as the first and was unexpected since it involved reduced inventory holding costs. The apparent reason why the variable capacity model was sensitive to inventory holding costs was that production could follow demand more closely due to capacity adjustments and therefore, aggregate inventories could be maintained somewhat closer to their optimal values. Cost reductions were, of course, partly compensated for by increased capacity changeover costs. In addition, hiring and layoff costs were increased in the variable capacity model because the work force size, W, more closely followed production requirements.

Chang and Jones [8] generalized the LDR methodology to yield both aggregate plans and master schedules in a multiproduct environment and extended the conceptual framework to handle situations where production cannot be started and completed in the same period. Production start and completion in one period is realistic for bulk processing (paint, for example) and for small products, but not for such products as aircraft, ships, and steam turbines, which involve extensive fabrication, assembly, and test cycles. The Chang and Jones approach involves using a labor distribution matrix D_{it}, which specifies the fraction of the total labor effort required for product i in month t of the production cycle. Conceptually, the method assumes that product i is ready for sale in one period, period k, for example, and then computes the labor requirements for periods $k, k - 1, k - 2$, etc., using the matrix D_{it}. The model provides for the following costs: hiring-layoff, payroll, idle time, overtime, and inventory. The costs elements are assumed to be quadratic thereby permitting the model to be solved using differential calculus combined with a library computer program which solves simultaneous linear equations.

Bergstrom and Smith [1] extended the basic LDR model to one involving both multiproducts and the inclusion of a revenue term (see also Peterson [41]). The objective function of their model therefore becomes one of maximizing contribution to fixed costs and overhead. Their approach includes a crucially different concept with respect to the demand function. In the original LDR formulation and all of the other modifications, the demand forecast has been fixed and specified. Instead, Bergstrom and Smith propose estimating revenue versus sales curves for each product in each time period. The amount to be sold is considered as a decision variable and is dependent on price and possibly other parameters; for example, differential promotional budgets. The total revenue for any volume of output is the product of that volume and the price at which it can be sold as determined from the demand curve.

Hausman and McClain [25] demonstrate that the Bergstrom and Smith deterministic multi-item model can, with some reinterpretation, be used to solve two related stochastic multi-item production planning problems. Specifically, they show that the benefits of individual item-by-item treatment and diminishing marginal revenue contained in the Bergstrom and Smith model can be obtained when future sales are stochastic and uncontrollable, or stochastic but with mean value under the control of the firm. They demonstrate that under both of these situations the certainty-equivalence property holds, thereby reducing the two stochastic problems to two related deterministic problems.

Other mathematically optimal approaches

In addition to the linear programming and Linear Decision Rule approaches to aggregate planning and master scheduling, a number of other optimizing procedures have been applied. For the most part, they are of theoretical rather than practical interest. They include dynamic programming and network models [2, 22, 45, 53, 54], and various other rather exotic techniques such as the maximum principle [32]. A basic difficulty with these approaches is that their usefulness is sharply restricted as additional realism is introduced by increasing the number of constraints and decision variables. Even though computers are much faster now than they were in 1964, Hadley's quote [22] at that time is still partially relevant:

> The numerical difficulties involved in solving dynamic programming problems increase with incredible rapidity as the number of state parameters is increased. This is true even if there is only a single control variable to be determined at each stage. It is equally true that the computational problems can quickly become overwhelming as the number of control variables to be determined at each stage increases, even if only a single state parameter is needed, . . . Problems involving two state parameters can usually be solved, but may easily require 100 times as much computer time as a corresponding problem with only a single state parameter. . . . Problems involving four or more state parameters are almost always beyond the computational abilities available at present.

In spite of the computational difficulties associated with these approaches however, they have been very useful in the theoretical sense as a means of gathering insights into the properties of optimal solutions. These insights can be used to develop other more efficient solution procedures, and heuristics.

AGGREGATE PLANNING METHODS USING HEURISTIC DECISION RULES

The management coefficients model

Bowman [5] has proposed a different approach to many managerial problems and has used the aggregate planning problem as a vehicle for study and demonstration of his proposed approach to managerial decision making. His methodology utilizes the past average managerial coefficients for given decision rules but applies the rules with consistency.

Bowman proposes to establish the *form* of decision rules for aggregate planning through rigorous analysis but to establish the *coefficients* for the decision rules through statistical analysis of management's own past decisions. This is in contrast to the LDR where both the form and the coefficients were determined by mathematical analysis. For example, in the production rule of Equation (14), not only the form of the rule but the values of the coefficients which weight forecasted sales and the 0.993, 153, and -0.464 values were all mathematically determined. In a comparable rule Bowman would determine such coefficients by regression analysis on management's past actual decisions.

The theory behind Bowman's rule is rooted in the assumption that management is actually sensitive to the same criteria used in analytical models and that management behavior tends to be highly variable rather than off center. In terms of Bowman's theory then, management's performance using the decision rules can be improved considerably simply by applying the rules more consistently, since in terms of the usual dish-shaped criterion function, variability in applying decision rules is much more costly than being slightly off center from optimum decisions, but consistent in those decisions.

In a study of a chocolate company a least squares regression of the company's actual scheduling behavior against the LDR was made. For the W_t rule a multiple correlation coefficient of $r = 0.971$ was obtained and for the P_t rule a multiple correlation coefficient of $r = 0.87$ was obtained. "In other words, the *form* of these rules gave a pretty fair indication of the chocolate company managers' decisions. That is, the managers were sensitive to the same variables in their decision behavior." [5]

Applications. Bowman reports four comparative studies where costs were computed comparing LDR performance with both the perfect and moving average forecasts, actual company performance and the performance of a management coefficients model. Table 6–2 summarizes the comparative cost data and the correlation coefficients between the management coefficients model and actual managerial performance for the work force rule and the production rate rule.

As can be seen from the table, in all cases but the candy company, using the decision rules with the coefficients supplied by regression of management's own behavior, and a rather simple estimating scheme for future sales (moving average forecast), the costs would have been less than the company's actual behavior. In the ice cream company and the chocolate company it would have been even cheaper than the decision rule derived from the standard quantitative analysis and the same sales forecasting scheme.

Since the LDR is optimal for its model the lower costs achieved by the management coefficients model suggests that the approximating

Table 6–2
Summary cost comparisons between management coefficients model and LDR models, and company performance

	Company product			
	Ice cream	Chocolate	Candy	Paint
Linear Decision Rule (perfect forecast)	100.0%	100.0%	100.0%	100.0%
Linear Decision Rule (moving average forecast)	104.9%	102.0%	103.3%	110.0%
Actual company performance	105.3%	105.3%	111.4%	139.5%
Management coefficients model (moving average forecast)	102.3%	100.0%	124.1%*	124.7%†
Correlation: $W_b r$ = 0.78		0.57	0.73	0.40
$P_b r$ = 0.97		0.93	0.86	0.66

* Using the perfect forecast would have reduced this to 112.5 percent.
† This figure must be viewed with some reservation since the data was obtained from that available in the publications and working papers concerning the LDR, rather than the actual basic data. It was not possible to reconstruct some of the paint company costs, and the five-years' record used was 1950–54 rather than 1949–53, though both cover the extreme years of the Korean War.
Source: From E. H. Bowman, "Consistency and Optimality in Managerial Decision Making," *Management Science*, vol. 9, no. 2 (January 1963).

cost functions used in the LDR model for the ice cream and chocolate companies may not have been very good approximations of the actual costs.

Bowman's explanation of managerial behavior and of why the management coefficients model may perform well follows:

It seems useful to attempt an explanation of why decision rules derived from management's own average behavior might yield better results than the aggregate behavior itself. Man seems to respond to selective cues in his environment—particular things seem to catch his attention at times (the last telephone call), while at other times it is a different set of stimuli. Not only is this selective cueing the case, but a threshold concept seems to apply. He may respond not at all up to some point and then overrespond beyond that. It is this type of behavior which helps explain the variance in the organization's (or its management's) behavior. Departures of the decision-making behavior of management from the preferred results, in this case then, can be divided or factored into two components, one which in the manner of a grand average departing from some preferred figure, we call bias (which causes a relatively small criteria loss due to the dish-shaped bottom of the criteria surface), and one which representing individual occurrences of experience departing from the grand average, we call variance (which causes large criteria losses due to the individual occurrences up the side of the criteria dish-shaped surface). It is the latter and more important component which seems to offer the tempting possibility of elimination through the use of decision rules incorporating coefficients derived from management's own recurrent behavior.

Later research by Gordon [20], Moskowitz and Miller [39], Ebert [12], and others have served to confirm these hypotheses.

Parametric production planning model

Jones [33] developed a heuristic approach to aggregate planning which is dependent on two linear feedback decision rules, one for size of work force and one for production rate. The specific equation defining each rule is postulated heuristically by Jones. Each decision rule has two parameters which define them so that we have a four-dimensional space in which we wish to find, for a particular firm, the combination of parameters which is associated with minimum cost operation. Jones's approach, then, is to evaluate alternate sets of parameters by the unique cost structure of a firm in order to select that set which yields minimum cost for at least the planning horizon time. There are no limitations in mathematical form to the cost functions; rather they should simply be the best estimates of the cost functions which can be constructed. The selected parameters are incorporated into the two decision rules to make the rules specific for a given firm. Thus, while the decision rules are not optimal in the sense of a mathematically provable optimum, the procedure introduces aggregate production plans involving costs which will not be easily reduced.

While the parametric production planning approach can result in effective low-cost decisions, and is not hindered by the presumption of particular cost structures or equation forms, it is unlikely that it is as flexible as other approaches that we will discuss, or as intuitively appealing as Bowman's management coefficients method. This hypothesis is rooted in the belief that any approach that is directly based on actual cost structures or management beliefs, must be superior to those which take such costs and beliefs into account on an indirect basis.

Summary of heuristic approaches. In reviewing the heuristic approaches that have been applied to aggregate planning/master scheduling, we can see several of their main advantages. First, they are not restricted to specific funtional forms that relate cost structures to management decisions. That is, bothersome assumptions about linearity or quadratic forms do not provide difficulties. Second, at least in the case of Bowman's approach, they take into account the wisdom and experience of managers. Thus, they can embody gut feelings about policies and intangible costs that may be difficult to model in the formal sense. Third, once the decision rules have been developed, they are quite easy to apply. They do not carry the computational burden associated with some analytical methods that can effectively preclude their use in practice.

The disadvantages of these methods can be serious however. First, they do not provide optimal solutions. This is certainly not the most serious problem in many of today's manufacturing environments where a *feasible* solution to such complicated problems is often more than a manager can hope for. The more serious problem with these approaches is that they use historical data and/or decisions to derive the decision rules that are applied to future periods. Thus, they are either not dynamic, or the difficulty in deriving and rederiving decision rules to fit a dynamic environment can become overly burdensome. This may explain why these procedures are not found in wide use today, some years after their development. The contribution of these approaches to our understanding of the nature of decision making in aggregate planning and master scheduling has been considerable however.

SEARCH DECISION RULE (SDR) METHODOLOGY

General concepts

The SDR approach was developed in an attempt to overcome the dilemma one faces in attempting to expand the realism contained in mathematically optimum aggregate planning models. Small incremental improvements in model realism seem to require almost exponential increases in mathematical complexity. Thus it may be concluded that the lack of realism exhibited by cost models of this type is not generally due to a lack of mathematical sophistication on the part of the model builder. Rather, it appears to be an inevitable consequence of the limitation of the solution methodologies themselves. In order to use most of the common optimal solution techniques, the model builder is forced to design the cost model so that it precisely matches the requirements of the particular solution technique. This forced fit generally involves reducing the number of cost relationships, decision variables, and/or assuming that they are linear, quadratic, or some other specified shape. The net result is usually a mathematically optimum solution to a grossly over-simplified cost model. It is not surprising, therefore, that there has been a lack of actual industrial application. Firms have preferred to rely on the judgment of a manager, or executive committees for such decisions. Most managers agree that the techniques are "interesting" and "promising." However, upon closer examination, they typically conclude that the techniques and their associated cost models simply do not adequately represent the realities of their particular operation. In short, most managers have decided to continue to use heuristic, or intuitive, decision rules which do not guarantee mathematical optimality.

The SDR approach does not guarantee optimality either, but it does offer a way of breaking through the restrictive barrier imposed by the analytic model—optimal solution methodologies. In essence, the approach proposes building the most realistic cost or profit model possible and expressing it in the form of a computer subroutine which has the ability to compute the cost associated with any given set of decision variable values. Mathematically, the subroutine defines a multidimensional cost response surface with a dimensionality determined by the number of decision variables and the number of time periods included in the planning horizon. In short, the cost model forms a multistage decision system model where each stage represents the cost structure of the operation at the point in time when decisions are made, such as monthly and quarterly. A computerized search routine is then used to systematically search the response surface of the cost model for the point (combination of decisions) producing the lowest total cost over the planning horizon. A mathematically optimum solution is not guaranteed, but as we shall see, the method finds solutions which cannot be easily improved. This methodology is termed the Search Decision Rule, or SDR for short, in recognition of the fact that the decisions are obtained by searching the cost response surface.

Multistage model development and optimization

The basic building block of the SDR approach is a one-stage decision model. This model is constructed in the form of a computer subroutine to represent the cost or profit structure of the firm at the particular point in time when decisions are to be made. This is usually, but not necessarily, monthly. Figure 6–11 portrays the one-

Figure 6–11
One-stage SDR decision model

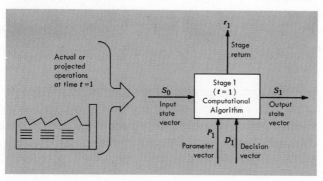

stage model construction process and identifies state and decision vector inputs, stage returns, and state vector outputs. These terms are explained as follows:

Stage. A conceptual device used to represent any real or abstract entity in which a transformation takes place. In the context of the aggregate planning problem a stage represents the point in time when decisions are made concerning the operation of the system. At each stage a decision (D) creates a return (r) and places the system in a new state (S).

Input state vector S_0. A j component vector $S_0 = (s_{01}, s_{02}, \ldots, s_{0j})$ which transmits information to stage 1 and serves to describe the state of the system at the beginning of the stage 1 transformation.

Output state vector S_1. A j component vector $S_1 = (s_{11}, s_{12}, \ldots, s_{1j})$ which transmits information to stage 2 and serves to describe the state of the system at the end of the stage 1 transformation. The functional relationship is given by $S_1 = t_1 (S_0, D_1, P_1)$ where t_1 is a single-valued transformation serving to couple stage 1 to the next stage.

Parameter vector P_1. An i component vector $P_1 = (p_{11}, p_{12}, \ldots, p_{1i})$ of those factors that affect the stage return r_1 and output state vector S_1 and which must be specified to make the problem definitive. In other words the parameter vector contains those factors which affect the outputs, but are not controllable. For example, cost coefficients used in the model, the estimate of demand, etc.

Decision vector D_1. A k component vector $D_1 = (d_{11}, d_{12}, \ldots, d_{1k})$ which controls the operation of stage 1, given S_0 and P_1. The components of the decision vector are commonly referred to as independent variables.

Stage return r_1. A scalar variable used to measure the utility of the stage as a single valued function of the input state, parameter and decision vectors $r_1 = f_1 (S_0, D_1, P_1)$. Utility may be measured in many ways including cost, profit and rate of return.

A one-stage decision system model is constructed for each month in the N month planning horizon. The models are then joined together by means of state vectors to form a serial multistage decision system as shown in Figure 6–12. The serial multistage decision sys-

Figure 6–12
Multistage SDR decision system

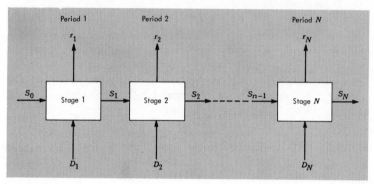

tem is termed *homogeneous* if the cost functions of the individual stages are identical, and termed *heterogeneous* if they are not. A heterogeneous decision system is produced when the firm plans a reorganization, the installation of new equipment, the introduction of a new product or the revision of wages rates, or resource costs, at some point in the planning horizon. The importance of heterogenous model construction cannot be overemphasized because, as noted earlier, it is the essence of the aggregate planning problem. The SDR handles this situation by simply using a different subroutine to represent the cost function of each stage.

The SDR technique for optimizing the return from the multistage decision model is shown in Figure 6–13. It can be seen that the SDR approach uses the same conceptual problem structure as the mathematically optimum approaches. In Figure 6–13, the state vector S_0 establishes the initial conditions at the start of the first time period.

Figure 6–13
SDR method for solving a multistage decision system

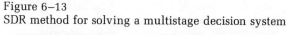
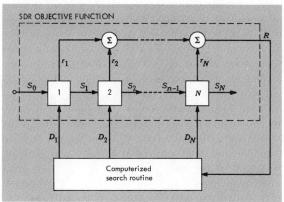

The parameter vectors P_1, P_2, . . . P_N which typically contain the forecast information for each stage are omitted from Figure 6–13 for clarity. The computer search routine attempts to optimize all stages simultaneously and consequently must deal with a response surface whose dimensionality is determined by the product of the number of decisions per stage (K) times the number of stages (N) in the planning horizon. To do this, the search routine measures its progress with reference to the total return (R) produced by summing the returns r_1, r_2, . . . r_N from each stage in the multistage system. The total return (R) need not be linearly additive as shown in Figure 6–13. It might consist of a weighted sum if, for example, present value discounting techniques were used. It might consist of a complex formulation based on utility concepts. The SDR approach provides great flexibility in this respect.

The computer search solution to the SDR model provides decisions for each month of the N month planning horizon. By design, the decisions provided for each stage are optimal with respect to the entire N stage system rather than optimal with respect to the particular stage. Decision vector D_1 contains the decisions for implementation during the current period (month 1). Decision vectors D_2, D_3, . . . D_N provide a forecast of possible actions in succeeding months, but their operational value is limited since they are based on successively shorter planning horizons. Consequently, when it is time to make decisions for the next month, the model is updated with new sales forecast data, new initial conditions, and optimized again.

Figure 6–14
Information flow in a typical SDR monthly updating cycle

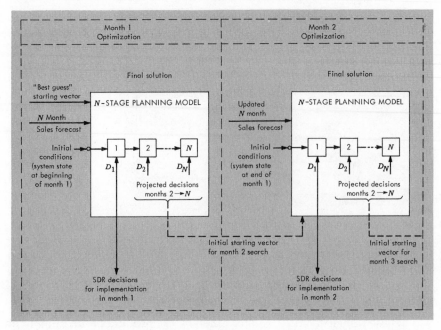

The information flow in this SDR monthly updating cycle is shown in Figure 6–14. It can be seen that following the month 1 optimization of the model by the search routine the decisions contained in D_1, the month 1 decision vector, are reviewed and implemented by management. The projected decision information for the remaining months in the planning horizon $(D_2, D_3, \ldots D_N)$ is not discarded, but is used to form the SDR starting vector for the month 2 search. In this way, the search routine does not have to start all over again from a randomly selected starting point in multidimensional space. Use of the SDR computed starting vector sharply reduces the search time, and hence the cost of computing subsequent decisions.

SDR programming system

The complete SDR programming system consists of a main program and two subroutines containing the search routine and the cost model. The operating sequence of the system is shown in Figure 6–15. The main program initializes all variables and reads in the sales forecast, the initial starting decision vector, and the initial state

Figure 6–15
SDR programming system

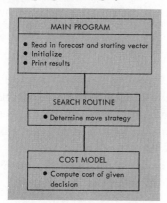

vector. The main program then calls the search routine which, in turn, systematically explores the response surface of the cost model until either the limit on the number of cost model evaluations is reached or a better point cannot be found. The search routine continuously varies the decision vector components in an attempt to minimize the total cost of operation over the entire planning horizon. At the conclusion of the search, control is returned to the main program for printing out the final decision vector and other information relating to the operation of the cost model. Typical computer times for a complete SDR search range from 3 seconds to 2 minutes on most medium-size computers, depending upon the complexity of the cost model.

The heart of the SDR approach is the computerized search routine. A large number of search routines have been developed during the past ten years and vary in design from traditional gradient "hill-climbing" approaches to rather exotic heuristic programs [31]. Regardless of the particular design all search routines may be understood and, in fact, classified by the way they answer two basic questions. Assuming that the routine has selected a particular point on the response surface by specifying the decision vector, then the two key questions are:

1. What is the next direction of movement?
2. How far should the movement be in the given direction?

The direction of movement may be along the gradient, along a deflected gradient, along each of the axes of a basic vector set, or in a randomly selected direction. Once the direction has been determined one step, several steps, or a one-dimensional line search may be made. In quantitative terms the questions are answered by the following iterative equation:

$$D_{i+1} = D_i + \lambda_i P_i$$

where D_i is an n-dimensional decision vector with components $D = (d_i, d_2, \ldots d_n)$ representing the trial point for the ith trial or iteration λ_i is a positive constant and P_i is an n-dimensional direction vector evaluated at the ith iteration. The vector P_i answers the first question by specifying the direction to be taken in moving away from point D_i and the magnitude of λ_i answers the second question by specifying how large a step is to be taken in that direction.

Figure 6–16 is a flowchart illustrating the major elements of a comprehensive search routine. The routine starts by selecting the initial starting vector for the search (see box 1). In the case of the SDR, this vector is based upon the ending solution vector from the previous months SDR optimization as illustrated in Figure 6–14. If this is not available as, for example, in first starting the SDR method, then a "guess" is made and this value is used as the starting point for the search.

Boxes 2, 3, 4, 5, and 7 constitute what is frequently called the search code, or search algorithm. Collectively they determine the location of the next point, evaluate the response surface at that point, determine the best direction of movement and, at the same time, monitor the progress to see if any action need be taken to speed up the rate of progress, or convergence.

Box 6 contains appropriate logic to check if the search code has moved the search outside of the feasible region and, if so, it computes the necessary step size and direction required to bring it back. There are a large number of highly sophisticated techniques available for use here but most require the solution of bounding problems that are almost as complicated as the objective function itself. As a result, many users prefer to transform the problem to one without constraints. This transformation is done by adding penalty functions to the original objective function and then optimizing the model as if it were unconstrained.

Box 8 represents the logic used to determine if the routine has become stuck on a relatively flat portion of the response surface. Typical tests include either random or systematic spot checks at various trial points in the neighborhood of the suspected stationary

Figure 6–16
Flowchart showing the general features of the operation of search
routines

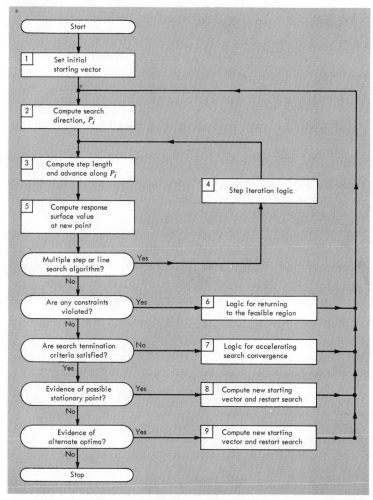

point. If no improvement is noted, the routine moves to the final test
for alternate optima. If a better point is found, the search is restarted
using the location of the new point as the starting vector.

No known search routine can guarantee with certainty that a
global optimum has been found. Therefore, it is essential to conclude
any computerized optimization program with a test for alternate
optima (see box 9). This test is conducted by restarting the search
from different locations on the response surface. If they all converge

to the same point (solution) there is an increased probability that the global optimum has been found.

An extraordinary number of search routines have been developed and published during the past ten years. The interested reader will find the operating characteristics of most of the published search routines classified in reference [48] along with FORTRAN listings of several of the better performing routines. Unfortunately, one cannot predict, before hand, which search routine will give the best performance on a particular response surface. Nevertheless, Taubert has developed a routine [48] which gives consistently good performance on a wide variety of response surfaces. This approach is known as adaptive pattern search and has been used for the bulk of the work reported in references [7, 43, 47, 48, 49].

Search Decision Rule applications and extensions

The SDR methodology has been validated against the known optimum solution of the paint company and extended in terms of horizon and certain stochastic effects in that environment. It has also been applied in additional situations representing increasing complexity in the cost model and involving additional independent decision variables.

The paint company—A single-shift manufacturing facility

Recall that in 1955, Holt, Modigliani, Muth, and Simon published an important series of papers in which they presented a cost model of an actual paint company and a mathematical technique, called the Linear Decision Rule (LDR), which computes aggregate scheduling decisions that are mathematically optimal with respect to their cost model. The paint company was analyzed by Taubert [47] in terms of the production organization shown in Figure 6–17. Other factors such as the indirect work force and second-shift operation were not included in the model in order to permit solution by the LDR technique. The aggregate direct work force level (W_t) and production rate (P_t) were selected as the key decision variables with decisions made monthly, based on a sales forecast planning horizon of 12 months. Cost relationships were restricted to linear and quadratic forms so that a mathematically optimum solution could be developed for the model.

Figure 6–17
Simplified paint company organization
showing aggregate decision variables

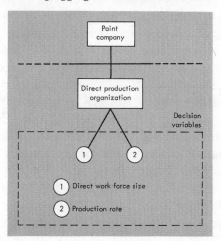

SDR cost model. The total cost equation for this model given by Equation (13) is:

$$C_N = \sum_{t=1}^{N} \{[340W_t]$$

$$+ [64.3(W_t - W_{t-1})^2]$$

$$+ [0.2(P_t - 5.67W_t)^2 + 51.2P_t - 281W_t]$$

$$+ [0.0825(I_t - 320)^2]\}$$

Direct payroll	
Hiring/layoff	
Overtime	
Inventory related	

where $N = 12$

$$I_t = I_{t-1} + P_t - S_t$$

S_t, the unit sales in month t, are deterministic and known.

Transferring this problem into an SDR format is straightforward. I_t in the inventory-related cost expression can be eliminated by substituting the recursive relationship defining I_t as a function of I_{t-1}, P_t, and S_t. The inventory-related cost expression becomes 0.0825 $(I_{t-1} + P_t - S_t - 320)$. As a result of this substitution, C_N, the total cost expression, becomes a function of $C_N = f(W_t, P_t, W_{t-1}, I_{t-1}, S_t)$. W_t and P_t are independent decision variables and become the components of the decision vector. W_{t-1} and I_{t-1} serve to transmit information from the previous time period (stage) and therefore become components of the state vector. The sales forecast, S_t, and the numerical coefficients of the model, 340, 64.3, 0.2, and so on, become components of the parameter vector. With this simple change the model has been converted into a 12-stage decision model. The stages are considered homogeneous as the coefficients and structure of the cost equations governing payroll, hiring and firing, overtime and inventory-related costs do not change from stage to stage. Since two decisions are made at each stage, the dimensionality of the model's response surface is $2N$, or 24.

Comparison of SDR to LDR results. The SDR programming system was established by Taubert following that of Figure 6–15. An early version of the pattern search routine was used requiring the planning horizon to be limited to ten months (20 independent variables). Beginning inventory, work force levels, and monthly sales were taken from the data given in the original LDR paper. The search program was set to end whenever, in exploring the response surface, the program could find only cost improvements which were less than $0.5 \times \$10^{-6}$ dollars. After computing a set of decisions for the first month, the program automatically updated the sales forecasts over the planning horizon of 10 months and reset the initial starting vector so that an entire 24-month sample could be computed in one continuous run. This method is illustrated in Figure 6–14. In order to restrict the search, two constraints were added restricting production rates to 1,000 gallons per month and the work force to 150 employees.

Table 6–3 shows a sample of the SDR output for the first month of factory operation. This output corresponds to the result of the multistage optimization process shown in Figure 6–12. The computer output gives the first month's decision ($P_t = 471.89$ gallons, $W_t = 77.60$ employees) as well as an entire program for the planning horizon of ten months. In the lower half of the table the program prints out the component costs of payroll, hiring and firing, overtime, inventory, and total for the entire planning horizon.

Table 6–4 gives a month-by-month comparison for the first 24 months between the results obtained by the SDR compared to the use of the two optimum decision rules of the LDR. The month-by-month decisions are not identical but are very close to each other and the 24-month production totals differ by only 2 gallons. The total cost of the SDR plans and schedules exceeds the LDR total by only $776 (0.11 percent). This difference may be partially accounted for by the fact that the SDR used a planning horizon of only 10 months as compared to the 12-month horizon used by the LDR.

Table 6–3
Computer output for the first month of factory operation (perfect forecast)

A. Pattern search decisions and projections

Month	Sales (gallons)	Production (gallons)	Inventory (gallons)	Work force (men)
0			263.00	81.00
1	430	471.89	304.89	77.60
2	447	444.85	302.74	74.10
3	440	416.79	279.54	70.60
4	316	380.90	344.44	67.32
5	397	374.64	322.08	64.51
6	375	363.67	310.75	62.07
7	292	348.79	367.54	60.22
8	458	358.63	268.17	58.68
9	400	329.83	198.00	57.05
10	350	270.60	118.60	55.75

B. Cost analysis of decisions and projections (dollars)

Month	Payroll	Hiring and firing	Overtime	Inventory	Total
1	26,384.04	743.25	2,558.82	18.83	29,704.94
2	25,195.60	785.62	2,074.76	24.57	28,080.55
3	24,004.00	789.79	1,555.68	135.06	26,484.53
4	22,888.86	691.69	585.21	49.27	24,215.05
5	21,932.79	508.43	1,070.48	0.36	23,512.06
6	21,102.86	383.13	1,206.90	7.06	22,699.95
7	20,473.22	220.51	948.13	186.43	21,828.29
8	19,950.99	151.70	2,007.33	221.64	22,331.66
9	19,395.30	171.76	865.74	1,227.99	21,660.79
10	18,954.76	107.95	−1,396.80	3,346.46	21,012.37
					241,530.19

Source: From W. H. Taubert, "A Search Decision Rule for the Aggregate Scheduling Problem," *Management Science*, vol. 14, no. 6 (February 1968), pp. 343–59.

Other SDR applications. The promise shown by the initial applications of the SDR methodology have led to a number of other applications and experiments. This additional work has continued to show the versatility and flexibility of this tool.

Taubert extended his work on the application of SDR techniques to the paint company problem by examining the horizon time versus computing time trade-off. He found that the increase in total cost associated with reducing the planning horizon from ten to fifteen months resulted in increases in total costs of only 1.28 percent; however, it also resulted in a reduction in computing time by a factor of 3.

Sikes [43] experimented with several approaches to reducing the cost impact of a reduced planning horizon. He discovered that by

Table 6–4
A comparison of LDR and SDR decisions for the first 24 months of operation with the perfect forecast

Month	Monthly sales (gallons)	Production (gallons) LDR	Production (gallons) Search	Work force (employees) LDR	Work force (employees) Search	Inventory (gallons) LDR	Inventory (gallons) Search	Monthly cost (dollars) LDR	Monthly cost (dollars) Search
0				81	81	263	263		
1	430	468	472	78	78	301	305	29,348	29,705
2	447	442	443	75	74	296	301	27,797	27,930
3	440	416	418	72	71	272	279	26,294	26,460
4	316	382	385	69	68	337	348	24,094	24,415
5	397	377	376	67	66	317	327	23,504	23,436
6	375	368	366	66	64	311	318	22,879	22,672
7	292	360	360	65	63	379	386	22,614	22,539
8	458	382	382	65	63	303	309	23,485	23,382
9	400	377	379	66	64	280	288	23,367	23,331
10	350	366	366	67	64	296	304	22,846	22,569
11	284	365	359	69	67	377	379	23,408	23,004
12	400	404	401	72	70	381	380	25,750	25,654
13	483	447	447	75	74	345	344	28,266	28,367
14	509	477	479	79	78	313	314	30,180	30,408
15	500	495	498	83	81	307	312	31,310	31,479
16	475	511	510	87	86	343	348	32,422	32,481
17	500	543	547	91	90	386	394	34,858	35,074
18	600	595	592	96	94	380	387	38,119	38,216
19	700	641	642	100	98	321	328	40,849	41,110
20	700	661	659	103	101	282	287	41,848	41,898
21	725	659	658	105	103	216	220	41,945	41,981
22	600	627	624	106	105	244	245	39,074	38,910
23	432	605	601	107	106	417	413	38,134	37,928
24	615	653	655	109	108	455	454	41,785	42,003
Totals		11,621	11,619	2,053	2,017	8,122	8,233	734,176	734,952

Source: From W. H. Taubert, "A Search Decision Rule for the Aggregate Scheduling Problem," Management Science, vol. 14, no. 6 (February 1968), pp. 343–59.

increasing the magnitude of inventory related costs as the planning horizon is approached, the cost penalty associated with running the model in a reduced planning horizon mode could be cut substantially. Similarly, Sikes found that the costs associated with SDR decisions for the paint company were relatively insensitive to forecast errors. While the applicability of this finding is restricted to firms with cost and demand profiles similar to those of the paint company, it suggests that better forecasts are not always the panacea that some managers hold them to be.

Taubert also developed an aggregate planning cost model for SDR solution for an applied research laboratory of a large aerospace firm [48]. The lab employed a staff of 400, approximately 300 of whom were direct technical employees, the balance being indirect administrative support personnel. The application of this model to actual data showed that the costs resulting from SDR decisions compared to actual management decisions would have produced significant savings. Over the five-and-one-half-year test period, the annual SDR advantage ranged from a high of 19.7 percent to a low of 5.2 percent.

Following the initial successful application of SDR to the aggregate planning problems of the laboratory, Taubert increased the complexity of the problem by disaggregating the decision variables for the size of the scientific staff into three and then six different departments recognized by the lab organization. The models recognized that a limited number of scientists could be transferred between departments. These latter applications of the SDR approach showed that it could effectively handle the disaggregation problem. It also shows that the approach is useful in nonmanufacturing organizations.

Advantages and disadvantages of the SDR

In concluding this section on SDR methodology, we are in a position to summarize the relative advantages and disadvantages of the SDR approach compared to the optimal solution approaches.

SDR advantages

1. Permits realistic modeling free from many restrictive assumptions, such as closed form mathematical expressions and linear/quadratic cost functions.
2. Permits a variation in mathematical structure from stage to stage

(heterogeneous stages) so that anticipated system changes such as the introduction of new products or production equipment, reorganizations, and wage increases can be considered.

3. Provides the operating manager with a set of current and projected decisions.

4. Permits optimized disaggregate decision making.

5. Lends itself to evolutionary cost model development and provides solutions at desired points in the iterative process.

6. Facilitates sensitivity analysis and provides sensitivity data while the search routine is converging on a solution.

7. Easily handles cash flow discounting, nonlinear utility functions, multiple objective functions, and complex constraints.

8. Offers the potential of solving many otherwise impossible operations planning problems.

9. The methodology is general and can be applied to single or multi-stage decision problems which are not related to aggregate planning. For example, determining the optimal capital structure of a firm given a forecast of interest rates, stock performance, and so on, or determining a least cost allocation of labor force to activities defined by a critical path network.

SDR disadvantages

1. Optimization using computer search routines is an art and it is currently impossible to state, a priori, which search routine will give the best performance on a particular objective function.

2. Decisions made by this methodology may not, and in general, will not, represent the absolute global optimum.

3. Response surface dimensionality appears to be a limiting factor.

HIERARCHICAL PLANNING AND DISAGGREGATION

In Chapter 5 we discussed the fact that aggregate plans represent an important decision process in most manufacturing enterprises. We also noted that aggregate plans in and of themselves were insufficient for planning production where a number of products were to be produced or where the production process was composed of a number of distinct stages. In these cases, aggregate plans must be disaggregated to the product level so that plant managers, supervisors, and purchasing agents and others involved in the manufacturing process will know when to initiate the production of a manufacturing lot, how large it should be, when to procure the materials necessary to produce it, and how requirements at other stages of the manufacturing process are affected.

In general, there have been two solution approaches to the disaggregation problem. The first has been to create more complex aggregate planning models which simultaneously derive an aggregate plan and allocate production capacity to individual product lines, or which simultaneously consider other stages in the manufacturing system. The work of Chang and Jones [8] and Bergstrom and Smith [1] in extending the Linear Decision Rule (LDR) methodology, and Taubert's extension of the SDR approach to multiple departments in the research lab, provide examples in this chapter of such solution approaches.

The second approach to the disaggregation problem, and one that is increasingly drawing the attention of researchers, is to create hierarchical planning systems. Hierarchical system approaches avoid the complexity inherent in creating very large, comprehensive models of a production system by breaking the decision problem into a series of component problems that are at once more tractable, and easy to formulate. Of course, the prime example of a hierarchical system is one in which aggregate plans are first formulated, enabling the firm to make decisions about capacity levels overtime, work force level changes, and aggregate inventory levels. The second step in the hierarchical process is to allocate individual product production to distinct periods in time, subject to the constraints that the resultant detailed schedule is consistent with prior aggregate capacity and inventory decisions. This archetypical form of the disaggregation problem was presented in Chapter 5.

The main disadvantage of hierarchical planning methods is that they are likely to result in nonoptimal solutions. It is clear that the solution to any problem that is obtained by solving parts of it in sequence can never be better than a solution obtained by simultaneously seeking the global optimum. This disadvantage is offset by three extremely important factors. First, when the decision hierarchy is cleverly constructed, the cost disadvantage of hierarchical approaches compared to overall optimum approaches is usually small. Second, the information and computational requirements of overall optimum approaches are often so great that their use in real production settings is prohibitive. Third, we often find that various types of production planning decisions are made at different organizational levels. Hiring and firing decisions may be of interest to the highest levels of management, and detailed scheduling decisions at lower

levels within the organization. Thus, hierarchical production planning systems can be constructed that are consistent with the level of
responsibility of the managers that must make the decisions.

Solution methods

Solution methodologies for disaggregating aggregate plans into
master schedules vary according to the specific design of the particular hierarchical process of concern. In general, however, they can be
classified into heuristic and optimum-seeking approaches. Heuristic
methods, such as the cut and fit, or trial and error approach introduced in Chapter 5 may provide good, but not necessarily optimal
solutions to disaggregation problems. Optimum-seeking methods do,
of course, provide optimal solutions at each stage in the hierarchy of
decisions. But as we have already noted, their use does not guarantee
an optimal solution for the total production planning problem.

A number of formulations of the disaggregation problem have
been proposed to which optimum-seeking methods have been
applied. Most of these formulations, such as those of Dzielinski, and
Gomory [11], have used zero-one integer programming problem
structures and methods, or continuous approximations of them.
Newson [40] has presented a formulation which captures the essential features of most of these approaches when only the disaggregated
master scheduling problem is considered:

Minimize $\qquad f_A(\chi) = \Sigma_i \Sigma_t [s_i \delta(\chi_{it}) + v_i \chi_{it} + h_i I_{it}]$ $\qquad$ (16)

subject to:

$$I_{i,t-1} + \chi_{it} - I_{it} = d_{it} \qquad \begin{aligned} i &= 1, \ldots, N \\ t &= 1, \ldots, T \end{aligned} \qquad (17)$$

$$\Sigma_i [r_{ik}^\delta \delta(\chi_{it}) + r_{ik}^x \chi_{it}] \le R_{kt} \qquad \begin{aligned} k &= 1, \ldots, K \\ t &= 1, \ldots, T \end{aligned} \qquad (18)$$

$$\chi_{it}, I_{it} \ge 0 \qquad (19)$$

$$\begin{aligned} \delta(\chi_{it}) &= 0 \qquad \text{if } \chi_{it} = 0 \\ &= 1 \qquad \text{if } \chi_{it} > 0 \end{aligned} \qquad (20)$$

Where:

χ_{it} = Production of product i in period t. It is not constrained to be
$\qquad$ integral in this formulation.
I_{it} = Inventory level of product i at the end of period t.

$\delta(\chi_{it})$ = Variable assigning setup cost for product i to period t when $\chi_{it} > 0$.

h_i = Per period unit holding cost for product i.

v_i = Per unit production cost for product i. Note that the variable cost of production $(v_i, i = 1, 2, \ldots N)$ will not enter into the optimization process if, for any specified product, that cost is constant over the planning horizon. A constant v_i is a reasonable assumption if the total production is constant over the planning horizon for any feasible (or at least any optimal) plan, and if discounting is not considered.

s_i = Setup cost for product i.

d_{it} = Demand for product i in period t.

r_{ik}^{δ} = Capacity absorption for one setup of product i on resource k.

r_{ik}^{r} = Per unit capacity absorption of product i on resource k.

R_{kt} = The level of resource k available in period t.

K = The number of resources.

T = The number of periods (horizon).

N = The number of products.

This formulation of the disaggregated master scheduling problem can be considered to be appropriate when the level of each of the k resources has been preestablished for each time period (t) over the duration of the plan. These resource limitations or capacities (R_{kt}) can be interpreted as the aggregate production, work force, capacity, and inventory levels that were established in the aggregate planning process. Note that if desired aggregate inventory levels in units are one of the constraints, the term $h_i I_{it}$ can be omitted from the objective function without loss of optimality. The constants r_{ik}^{s} and r_{ik}^{r} are determined for each product i that can be produced, and indicate the amount of each resource that is used up when the product is produced by setting up equipment, and making a run, respectively. Equation (17) is the inventory balance constraint that ensures that the demand in each period is met from beginning inventories plus production during the period, and that production excesses are returned to be counted as inventory at the end of the period. In this formulation, production back orders (negative inventories) are not permitted. The output of this formulation when integer programming solution methodologies are applied are a series of values of χ_{it}. That is, a value indicating the optimal amount of each product to be produced in each time period. The output is, then, a master schedule.

Newson [40] has also developed a heuristic approach to developing a master schedule within the context of the disaggregation problem presented in Equations 16–20. His heuristic approach is based on the rationale that a lower bound solution to the problem can be obtained by applying the Wagner-Whitin algorithm (see Chapter 4) to each of the products individually. This approach will provide a lower bound solution in the sense that the costs associated with the resulting master schedule (excluding the costs of changing production levels) will be at a minimum. The solution is likely to be infeasible, however, because the Wagner-Whitin algorithm will tend to produce large lot sizes during seasonal peaks, and little if any during troughs, thus violating the capacity or inventory constraints determined in aggregating planning. The heuristic is based on the rationale of trying to shift the low-cost Wagner-Whitin derived schedule around until a feasible solution is obtained. Newson uses the concept of a "next best path" to determine which schedules should be adjusted. A "next best path" is defined as an alternate schedule defined in the Wagner-Whitin solution process which relieves some infeasibility at the least marginal cost. The heuristic proceeds by identifying those time periods in which the initial Wagner-Whitin approach has resulted in an infeasibility; that is, where capacity limits are exceeded. It then computes the ratio of the marginal increase in costs associated with the next best path for each product in the schedule to the marginal increase in capacity that results from using the next path. The algorithm terminates when a completely feasible solution is formed.

In a series of experiments with this heuristic method, Newson found that master schedules derived with this heuristic resulted in a 10 percent cost premium, but that the solution only took 30 percent of the computational effort required of a procedure that simultaneously solved the aggregate planning/master scheduling problem. Newson also developed a heuristic method for simultaneously solving the aggregate planning/master scheduling problem that was roughly equal to the heuristic disaggregation approach in terms of computational effort, but which resulted in much lower costs. This latter work illustrates the promise of continuing efforts in developing more efficient algorithms for the overall aggregate planning/ master scheduling problem.

Hierarchical system design

At this point in time, the hierarchical system concept represents one of the most promising areas in production-inventory control. The analytical implications of disaggregation are becoming understood and a number of general solution methodologies have been proposed. However, in practice the steps involved in designing a hierarchical system for a particular firm and process technology are still somewhat obscure. We have noted that the clever design of such hierarchical systems can reduce the impact of suboptimality; the question that still seems to be begging is how does one become clever? The framework suggested by the application of the hierarchical systems approach by Hax and Meal [26] in the process industries provides important clues and directions.

The situation described by Hax and Meal was a firm whose process technology was analogous to that of a batch chemical plant or steel mill. The exact nature of the firm was not divulged in order to protect its anonymity. The firm had four nearly identical plants, geographically separated in order to service different market areas in the country. Manufacturing and transportation costs were such that some products could be made in only one plant, and others in more than one plant. The assignment of products to plants was an important problem faced by management.

The individual products produced by the plants had some natural groupings in manufacturing. The groups were defined by products that could be easily changed over from one to the other with minor setup costs. The setup costs incurred from changing over equipment to make a different grouping of products were quite high. The demand for the company's products was highly seasonal. Three distinct seasonal demand patterns were apparent. Some products were characterized as "winter season" products and others as "summer season" products, with significant differences in the size of the two markets. The third demand pattern was exhibited by products whose demand fluctuated throughout the year.

Management considered a level manufacturing rate throughout the year to be very important for two reasons. First, the capital cost of equipment was very high compared with shift premiums. Normally, three shifts were worked five days a week. Sixth and seventh days were worked occasionally. Second, the labor union was strong, and demanded that production levels be kept nearly constant throughout the year.

Prior to the work of Hax and Meal, the production control system was typified by the existence of reorder points for each of the products. When reorder points were triggered (typically at the peak of a season) a production lot was scheduled. But, because the demands for production were batched together at seasonal peaks, the capacity of the plant was insufficient. The company reduced lot sizes to stay within capacity limits, but even so, three significant symptoms persisted: poor customer service, high inventories, and high production costs.

In planning their approach to the design of a system for this firm, Hax and Meal considered the following:

We decided upon a hierarchical system, one which makes decisions in sequence, with each set of decisions at an aggregate level providing constraints within which more detailed decisions must be made. We did this because we found that we could not, with available analytic methods and data processing capability, develop an optimization of the entire system. *However, even if the current state of the art allowed solution of a detailed integrated model of the production process we would have rejected that approach because it would have prevented management involvement at the various stages of the decision-making process.* A model that facilitates overall planning can only become effective if it helps in establishing at the various organizational levels subgoals which are consistent with the management responsibilities at each level. The model should allow for corrections to be made to these subgoals by the managers at each level, and for coordination among the decisions made at each level. This is the essential characteristic of hierarchical planning.

Moreover, each hierarchical level has its own characteristics including the type of manager in charge of controlling the execution of the plan, the scope of the planning activity, the level of aggregation of the required information (and the form in which the information should be disaggregated when transferred to lower levels) and the time horizon of the decision. The lower one gets in the hierarchy, the narrower is the scope of the plan, the lower is the management level involved, the more detailed is the information needed, and the shorter is the planning time horizon. Each level of planning has its own objectives and constraints in which decisions have to be made. It is only natural, therefore, that a system designed to support the overall planning process should correspond to the hierarchical structure of the organization.

Finally, as Emery [14] points out, when a high-level plan significantly restricts the options available at lower levels the plan becomes centralized. This can only be justified if centralization improves the overall performance of the organization, by recognizing broader objectives which cannot be perceived at lower organizational levels. This is particularly true when the degree of interaction existing among subunits is critical, as is usually the case when dealing with production and transportation decisions in a multiplant-multiproduct corporation.

In spite of the importance that this hierarchical approach has in production planning, very few integrated solutions to this problem have been reported. Most of the published efforts have concentrated on analysis of individual components of the overall problem. Although it is theoretically possible to develop iterative procedures which converge to an optimum final plan, by sequential adjustment of lower level actions [1], this approach is not computationally feasible.

Prior to designing the hierarchical system we are about to describe, we considered the attractiveness of using other approaches, primarily those of Lasdon and Terjung [35], Connors [9], Zangwill [54], and Zoller [55]. We found, however, that those approaches were either difficult to implement or they were based on a given level of aggregation, ignoring the problems associated with detailed scheduling. We decided, therefore, to construct our own hierarchical system, making full use of the idiosyncracies of our particular problem. In taking this pragmatic approach we recognized there was a risk of arriving at planning and scheduling decisions that were not optimal. We are confident, however, that the reasons for isolating and linking manageable portions of the overall decision were sound enough to prevent major deviations from optimality and that we reached our goal of maintaining a simple design, relatively easy to implement.

To decompose the overall problem we examined the extent to which the various aspects of planning and scheduling are coupled. If two sets of decisions were independent we could totally separate them in structuring the hierarchy of decisions.

Starting at the most detailed level, we found that Items sharing a major setup cost had to be scheduled jointly. If these Items are grouped into a Family, the production cost is substantially reduced relative to independent scheduling. Thus, the scheduling decisions for the Items in a Family are strongly coupled. On the other hand, the coupling between the schedules of Items in different Families is very weak. Items produced in one plant are produced with the same equipment and therefore compete for capacity, but otherwise are completely decoupled.

We also found that the scheduling decisions for a Family in one time period are strongly coupled to the scheduling decisions for the same Family in other time periods. This is a consequence of the need to accumulate seasonal stock in most Families of Items, due to the competition among Families for scarce capacity. If this were not so the Families could be scheduled independently and no seasonal stock would have to be accumulated. Furthermore, since we have batch production there is a potential coupling between the Family run length and the season stock accumulation.

The latter coupling was removed by finding the optimum seasonal stock accumulation pattern for all Families simultaneously, under the assumption that the unit cost of production in accumulating seasonal stocks was independent of run length. In effect, we ignored run length economics in developing the Family seasonal stock accumulation pattern. However, we treated explicitly the coupling among Families in competing for capacity and the coupling among Family schedules in different time periods.

Ignoring run length economics in accumulating seasonal stocks is valid if the seasonal stock accumulation quantities do not influence the unit cost of production. This can be accomplished by neglecting the seasonal peak in calculating the economic run length for each Family and then extending the run length each time a batch is run to accumulate the seasonal stock needed without incurring an extra setup charge.

We found that the approaches which integrate production planning and economic lot sizes are impractical because they lead to evaluation of a large number of production sequencing alternatives, present difficulties in aggregating and disaggregating information, and are computationally expensive for a problem of this size.

Families were aggregated into Types in performing the seasonal planning since this made the seasonal planning computations much simpler and also facilitated the development of the Family and Item schedules. Families which have the same seasonal pattern and the same production rate (measured by inventory investment produced per unit time) are indistinguishable from a seasonal planning point of view. If the cost to carry the inventory is the same for two Families in a Type, only the total accumulation for the two Families (or all Families in the Type) need be considered in developing the plan. The schedules of the Families in the Type are coupled only in that the total of the Family schedules must add up to the Type total as given by the seasonal plan.

Having several Families in which a given seasonal stock can be accumulated simplified short-term scheduling. It reduces the danger of too many Items running out at the same time and allows a general lengthening of runs relative to the constant demand economic run length, without inventory penalty.

Thus, the coupling between Family run lengths and the Family seasonal plans is removed by setting up a seasonal plan which assumes no incremental setups are incurred to accumulate seasonal stock and then accumulating the seasonal stock by extending runs which were scheduled to meet the current demand.

Finally, the schedule for a Family in one plant may be coupled to the schedules for the same Family in the other plants where the same Families can be produced. These schedules will be coupled only if it is desirable to produce in one plant to satisfy demand in another plant's territory and if transshipment is cheaper than seasonal stock accumulation as a means of dealing with the shortage. Since, in this case, it is always cheaper to carry the inventory than it is to ship the product, the plants are decoupled and may be scheduled independently. If there were a net annual shortage in one plant and an excess in another, the territories should be redefined or capacity adjusted by transfer of equipment.

The decoupling approach followed by Hax and Meal led them to construct a hierarchy composed of four levels of decision making, as shown in Figure 6–18. The first step in this hierarchy was the assignment of items and families to plants. The subsystem for deter-

Figure 6–18
Hierarchical decision process

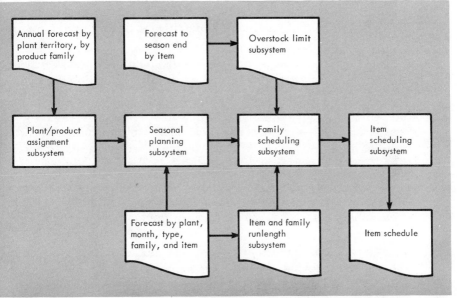

Source: Arnold C. Hax and Harlan C. Meal, "Hierarchical Integration of Production Planning and Scheduling," in M. A. Geisler, ed., Studies in the Management Sciences, vol. I, Logistics (New York: North-Holland Publishing Co., 1975).

mining these *plant assignments* considered the forecasts of annual demand for each plant, and the additional capital investment that would be required to produce a product family at a plant that had not produced it before. The second level of the hierarchy was a *seasonal planning subsystem*. Given the assignment of each product family to a plant, a monthly demand forecast for each product type, and the available production capacity at each plant, the seasonal planning subsystem defined a monthly production plan and a seasonal inventory accumulation strategy for each product plant at each plant location. The seasonal plan was updated monthly to reflect actual demands and new forecasts, while the plant assignments were made annually.

The third subsystem in the hierarchy was the item and family run-length subsystem. This module developed nominal minimum run quantities for all items and families, it also imposed upper limits on the accumulation of seasonal stocks for any one item based on the costs and risks of understocking and overstocking. The heart of this subsystem, and for that matter, the entire system, was the family scheduling subsystem. This subsystem used the results of the seasonal planning system, together with the family run lengths previously determined to find the run quantities to be produced for each family in a forthcoming month.

The fourth and final element of the hierarchy was the item scheduling subsystem. It allocated the family production run quantity among the items in the family. This system was used monthly, immediately following the preparation of the family schedule, which was also prepared each month. This final level of decision making resulted in a master schedule that indicated when particular products should be produced at each plant, and the run quantity.

The solution methodologies employed by Hax and Meal varied according to the particular subsystem. The plant/product assignment subsystem used a zero-one integer programming model to allocate products to plants. This model minimized the sum of the capital investments and manufacturing and transportation costs subject to the constraint that all demands were met. The model did not consider capacity explicitly. If it resulted in assignments which exceeded annual plant capacities, a procedure for reallocating assignments within plant capacities developed by Hax was employed.

The seasonal planning subsystem was designed to create an aggregate plan for each plant, to use the terminology that we have employed in this book. The technique employed to derive this plan was a linear programming approach similar to those plans developed by Hanssmann and Hess [23], and Bowman [4], and described earlier in this chapter. Plant capacities and the product assignments derived in the previous step were explicitly recognized in the formulation of this model, which was run four times, once for each plant.

The seasonal planning subsystem determines the production hours to be used for each product type, which is a group of families with similar seasonal demand patterns. The item/family scheduling subsystem must schedule just enough production in the families in the product type to use all the time available to the type in order to preserve the "optimality" of the aggregate plan, while maintaining customer service levels and minimizing setups. This is accomplished with a heuristic approach that bears some conceptual similarity to both the "runout date" heuristic proposal in Chapter 5, and Newson's approach. The item scheduling subsystem reapplies a similar heuristic approach in allocating item runs to family runs.

In describing the implementation of this system, Hax and Meal noted that the total development costs, including consultant's fees, were $150,000–$200,000. The benefits were smoother production with fewer emergency interruptions, fewer setups, improved service, and a reduction in inventory carrying costs of more than $200,000 each year in each of the plants.

More recently, Bitran and Hax [3] have generalized the procedures and algorithms involved in hierarchical structures similar to that described above. They tested their procedures with data provided by a manufacturer of rubber tires to examine the performance of the system with various levels of forecast error, capacity availability, magnitude of setup costs, and the nature of the planning horizon. They found that increasing forecast errors caused the quality of decisions to deteriorate somewhat, but, even with forecast errors of up to 30 percent, 97 percent service levels were maintained, illustrating that the forecast error effect was moderate. When the costs of setting up for product runs were increased significantly, however, inventory and setup costs increased more than proportionately. This suggests that the particular hierarchical strategy used in this case was inappropriate when extremely high setup costs are encountered. This finding is consistent with the "coupling" logic of Hax and Meal, in that extremely high setups indicate stronger couplings within product groups over time, and suggests that a different hierarchical form may be superior under these circumstances.

Bitran and Hax also tested for the degree of suboptimization inherent in the hierarchical approach when compared to the results of a mixed integer programming model which simultaneously determined optimal solutions for the entire planning problem. The comparisons, shown in Table 6–5, were made under three different sets of conditions. The first, the base case, reflected the costs and capacity conditions experienced by the tire manufacturer. The second comparison reflected runs where abnormally high setup costs were introduced. The third comparison was under tight capacity conditions. The results illustrate that a cleverly constructed hierarchical system results in only slightly higher costs than a computationally ineffi-

Table 6–5
Solution costs for hierarchical and mixed integer
programming systems

	Hierarchical system	Best known integer programming solution
Base case	158,981	158,339
High setup cost	220,535	203,360
Tight capacity	236,991	237,232

Source: G. R. Bitran and A. C. Hax, "On the Design of Hierarchical Production Planning Systems," *Decision Sciences*, vol. 8, no. 1 (January 1977), pp. 28–55.

cient and difficult to administer (although theoretically more elegant) optimizing model when the conditions under which the hierarchical "couplings" were defined remain constant.

The success of the hierarchical systems described here may be attributed to the application of mathematical techniques on the part of Hax and Meal, and Britran and Hax. But, while the cleverness of these researchers in formulating mathematical decision models is clearly one factor affecting their success, it is certainly not all. A major, in fact perhaps the most important, element of their success was the structuring of this large-scale problem so that the model's decision hierarchies reflected and embodied the needs of the organizational hierarchy to intervene in the process of aggregate planning/master scheduling.

SUMMARY

As we look back at the types of techniques that have been described in this chapter we can gain some historical perspectives on the development of formal techniques for aggregate planning and master scheduling, and then use them to extrapolate into the future. Table 6–6 summarizes these developments in roughly the same historical sequence as research into each of the types of procedures began. (It is noteworthy that current research is still proceeding on all four fronts.)

The first attempts to formalize procedures for aggregate planning/master scheduling began with the development of models to which mathematically optimum solutions could be obtained by various methods. While this approach has yielded techniques for obtaining optimal solutions, a basic problem has been that the assumptions are so restrictive that the models are unrealistic, or that realistic models are so

Table 6–6
Developments in formal procedures for aggregate planning/master scheduling

Type of procedure	Advantages	Disadvantages
1. Mathematically optimum (e.g., linear programming, Linear Decision Rule, dynamic programming, etc.)	Provide optimal solutions.	Restrictive assumptions. Computational feasibility.
2. Heuristic procedures (Management coefficients, parametric production planning)	Few restrictions. Incorporates management wisdom and experience.	Do not provide optimal solutions. Use historical data to develop rules (not dynamic).
3. Search Decision Rules	Few restrictions on cost functions	Do not provide optimal solutions. As applied, do not provide decision points for management intervention.
4. Hiearchical procedures	Few restrictions on cost functions. Recognizes organizational needs for intervention.	Do not provide optimal solutions. Considerable judgment required in constructing them.

complex that they are impossible to solve with current computational methods and equipment.

Later developments in heuristic procedures and search methods concentrated in removing restrictions and in increasing the realism of the models. These approaches, embodied in techniques like Bowman's management coefficients model and the Search Decision Rule procedures, have sacrificed optimality for model realism. However, this has been a reasonable sacrifice to make given the current state of the art.

The latest set of developments in hierarchical structures for aggregate planning/master scheduling has again provided a major step forward. These procedures also sacrifice optimality for model realism; they have learned from their predecessors. However, the hierarchical approaches as enumerated by Hax and Meal have also explicitly recognized the organizational needs for management intervention and control of the aggregate planning/master scheduling process. They realized that decision model realism does not refer only to their ability to fit cost structures, but also the organizational and competitive context.

If we project this history of the development of formal models for aggregate planning/master scheduling into the future, we might expect to see a greater emphasis on model realism as it pertains to the task and environment of managers and firms, rather than on model realism in terms of cost structures. This implies decision models with more opportunities for management intervention and control, and demands a greater understanding of the competitive and organizational dynamics of the firm. We might also expect to see some of the past developments in heuristic and analytical decision models successfully applied to more actual industrial situations. This may arise because of a greater sensitivity to an organization's needs on the part of the implementer.

REVIEW QUESTIONS AND PROBLEMS

1. Criticize the utility and the validity of the strict aggregate planning concept; that is, making decisions solely in aggregate terms for W and P.

2. Discuss the validity of a cost minimizing criterion function for the aggregate planning problem.

3. Compare the linear programming model with the LDR in terms of the logic of the linear or quadratic cost relationships required by the two models. Are there any types of cost relationships which might logically enter an aggregate planning problem which neither model can handle?

4. Assuming that beginning values of W_0, P_0, and I_0 are 100 workers, 500 gallons per month, and 320 gallons, respectively, for the paint company, what is the effect of a 20 percent forecast error on decisions for W_t and P_t after the third month for the Linear Decision Rules.

   Assume that demand was forecast originally as 500 gallons per month for the entire 12-month horizon, but actual demand is 500 gallons for the first 3 months and only 400 gallons per month thereafter.

5. What is the meaning of the term "capacity" in aggregate planning models? How does a decision to hire, fire, or subcontract affect capacity? How does physical or limiting capacity affect these decisions?

6. Given a specific enterprise to model, how would you decide between the LDR and the linear programming formats as a vehicle for aggregate planning?

7. Consider the results of the application of the "variable capacity" LDR model of Sypkens: Why should hiring-layoff costs be increased when capacity is introduced as an independent variable? Why should the variable capacity model have reduced inventory costs when the independent decision variable C was not dependent on inventory-related costs?

8. Rationalize the fact that S_{it}, sales, is an independent decision variable in the Bergstrom-Smith extension of the LDR. Can management decide what sales will be?

9. Evaluate the advantages and disadvantages of the management coefficients model.

10. Account for the difference in month-by-month decisions as well as total costs obtained by SDR compared to the optimal LDR for the paint company.

11. Contrast the linear programming formulation of the aggregate planning

problem (Equations 1–5) with Newson's model (Equation 16–20). In what ways are they similar? Different? How might these two models complement one another?

12. Explain why Newson's heuristic approach to master scheduling using the Wagner-Whitin algorithm might achieve good results. Why won't it yield optimal solutions?

13. Refer back to the Perkin Elmer case study. In what ways is the planning procedure described in this case a hierarchical procedure? Does it recognize organizational hierarchies?

14. In what ways could the other methods described in this chapter, e.g., linear programming, LDR, SDR, be used within the context of the hierarchical structure suggested by Hax and Meal?

15. Review the methodologies illustrated by Figure 6–1. What other approaches are possible? Discuss possible advantages and disadvantages. If you were faced with developing and implementing an aggregate planning system which approach would you be most likely to follow?

SELECTED BIBLIOGRAPHY

1. Bergstrom, G. L., and Smith, B. E.   "Multi-Item Production Planning—An Extension of the HMMS Rules," *Management Science*, vol. 16, no. 10 (June 1970), pp. 614–29.

2. Bishop, A. B., and Rockwell, T. H.   "A Dynamic Programming Computational Procedure for Optimal Loading in a Large Aircraft Company," *Operations Research*, vol. 6 (1958), pp. 835–48.

3. Bitran, G. R., and Hax, A. C.   "On the Design of Hierarchical Production Planning Systems," *Decision Sciences*, vol. 8, no. 1 (January 1977), pp. 28–55.

4. Bowman, E. H.   "Production Scheduling by the Transportation Method of Linear Programming," *Operations Research*, vol. 4, no. 1 (February 1956), pp. 100–103.

5. Bowman, E. H.   "Consistency and Optimality in Managerial Decision Making," *Management Science*, vol. 9, no. 2 (January 1963), pp. 310–21.

6. Bradley, S. P.; Hax, A. C.; and Magnanti, T. L.   *Applied Mathematical Programming*. Reading, Mass.: Addison-Wesley Publishing Co., Inc., 1977.

7. Buffa, E. S., and Taubert, W. H.   "Evaluation of Direct Computer Search Methods for the Aggregate Planning Problem," *Industrial Management Review*, Fall 1967.

8. Chang, R. H., and Jones, C. M.   "Production and Work Force Scheduling Extensions," *AIIE Transactions*, vol. 2, no. 4 (December 1970), pp. 326–33.

9. Connors, M. M.; Coray, C.; Cuccaro, C. J.; Green, W. K.; Low, D. W.; and Markowitz, H. M. "The Distribution System Simulator" *Management Science*, vol. 18 no. 8 (April 1972).

10. Damon, W. W., and Schramm, R. "A Simultaneous Decision Model for Production, Marketing, and Finance," *Management Science*, vol. 19, no. 2 (October 1972), pp. 161–72.

11. Dzielinski, B. P., and Gomory, R. E. "Optimal Programming of Lot Sizes, Inventory and Labor Allocations," *Management Science*, vol. 11, no. 9 (1965), pp. 875–90.

12. Ebert, R. J., "Environmental Structure and Programmed Decision Effectiveness" *Management Science*, vol. 19, no. 4 (1972), pp. 435–45.

13. Eisemann, K., and Young, W. M. "Study of a Textile Mill with the Aid of Linear Programming," *Management Technology*, vol. 1 (January 1960), pp. 52–63.

14. Emery, J. C. *Organizational Planning and Control Systems*. New York: Macmillan Co., 1969.

15. Fabian, T. "Blast Furnace Production—A Linear Programming Example," *Management Science*, vol. 14, no. 2 (October 1967).

16. Fetter, R. B. "A Linear Programming Model for Long-Range Capacity Planning." *Management Science*, vol. 7, no. 4 (July 1961), pp. 372–78.

17. Galbraith, J. R. "Solving Production Smoothing Problems," *Management Science*, vol. 15, no. 12 (August 1969), pp. 665–74.

18. Golovin, J. J. "Hierarchical Integration of Planning and Control." Unpublished Ph.D. dissertation, A. P. Sloan School of Management, M.I.T., Cambridge, Mass., August 1975.

19. Goodman, D. A. "A New Approach to Scheduling Aggregate Production and Work Force," *AIIE Transactions*, vol. 4, no. 2 (June 1973), pp. 135–41.

20. Gordon, J. R. M. "A Multi-model Analysis of an Aggregate Scheduling Decision." Unpublished Ph.D. dissertation, A. P. Sloan School of Management, M.I.T., Cambridge, Mass., 1966.

21. Greene, J. H.; Chatto, K.; Hicks, C. R.; and Cox, C. B. "Linear Programming in the Packing Industry," *Journal of Industrial Engineering*, vol. 10, no. 5 (September/October 1959), pp. 364–72.

22. Hadley, G. *Nonlinear and Dynamic Programming*. Reading, Mass.: Addison-Wesley Publishing Co., Inc., 1964.

23. Hanssmann, F., and Hess, S. W. "A Linear Programming Approach to Production and Employment Scheduling," *Management Technology*, vol. 1 (January 1960), pp. 46–52.

24. Hausman, W. H., and Peterson, R. "Multiproduct Production Scheduling for Style Goods with Limited Capacity," *Management Science* (March 1972), pp. 370–383.

25. Hausman, W. H., and McClain, J. O.   "A Note on the Bergstrom-Smith Multi-Item Production Planning Model," *Management Science.*

26. Hax, A., and Meal, H.   "Hierarchical Integration of Production Planning and Scheduling," in M. A. Geisler, ed., *Studies in the Management Sciences, Vol. I, Logistics.* New York: North-Holland Publishing Co., 1975.

27. Holloway, C.A.   "A Mathematical Programming Approach to Identification and Optimization of Complex Operational Systems with the Aggregate Planning Problem as an Example." Unpublished Ph.D. dissertation, UCLA, 1969.

28. Holt, C. C.; Modigliani, F.; and Muth, J. F.   "Derivation of a Linear Decision Rule for Production and Employment," *Management Science*, vol. 2., no.2 (January 1956), pp. 159–77.

29. Holt, C. C.; Modigliani, F.; Muth, J. F.; and Simon, H. A.   *Planning Production, Inventories, and Work Force.* Englewood Cliffs, N.J.: Prentice-Hall, Inc., 1960.

30. Holt, C. C.; Modigliani, F., and Simon, H. A.   "A Linear Decision Rule for Production and Employment Scheduling," *Management Science*, vol. 2, no. 2 (October 1955), pp. 10–30.

31. Hooke, R., and Jeeves, T. A.   "'Direct Search' Solution of Numerical and Statistical Probs," *Journal of the Association of Computing Machinery*, April 1961.

32. Hwang, C. L. et al.   "Optimum Production Planning by the Maximum Principle," *Management Science*, vol. 13, no. 9 (May 1967), pp. 751–55.

33. Jones, C. H.   "Parametric Production Planning," *Management Science*, vol. 13, no. 11 (July 1967), pp. 843–66.

34. Kolenda, J. F.   "A Comparison of Two Aggregate Planning Models." Unpublished Master's thesis, Wharton School of Finance and Commerce, The University of Pennsylvania, 1970.

35. Lasdon, L. S., and Terjung, R. C.   "An Efficient Algorithm for Multi-Item Scheduling," *Operations Research*, vol. 19 no. 4 (1971), pp. 946–69.

36. Lee, W. B., and Khumawala, B. M.   "Simulation Testing of Aggregate Production Planning Models in an Implementation Methodology," *Management Science*, vol. 20, no. 6 (February 1974), pp. 903–11.

37. McGarrah, R. E.   *Production and Logistics Management: Text and Cases.* New York: John Wiley & Sons, Inc., 1963.

38. Moskowitz, H.   "The Value of Information in Aggregate Production Planning—A Behavioral Experiment," *AIIE Transactions*, vol. 4, no. 4 (December 1972), pp. 290–97.

39. Moskowitz, H., and Miller, J. G.   "Information and Decision Systems for Production Planning," *Management Science*, vol. 22, no. 3 (November 1975).

40. Newson, E. P. "Multi-Item Lot Size Scheduling by Heuristic, Part I: With Fixed Resources," "Part II: With Variable Resources," *Management Science*, vol. 21, no. 10 (June 1975), pp. 1186–1203.

41. Peterson, R. "Optimal Smoothing of Shipments in Response to Orders," *Management Science*, vol. 17, no. 9 (May 1971), pp. 597–607.

42. Shwimer, J. *Interaction between Aggregate and Detailed Scheduling in a Job Shop*, Technical Report No. 71, Operations Research Center, M.I.T., 1972.

43. Sikes, T. W. "The Search Decision Rule Applied to Aggregate Planning: Improved Efficiency and Stochastic Extension." Unpublished Ph.D. dissertation, UCLA, August 1970.

44. Silver, E. A. "A Tutorial on Production Smoothing and Work Force Balancing," *Operations Research*, vol. 15, no. 6 (November/December 1967), pp. 985–1010.

45. Sobel, M. H. "Smoothing Start-up and Shut Down Costs: Concave Case," *Management Science*, vol. 17, no. 1 (1970), pp. 78–91.

46. Sypkens, H. A. "Planning for Optimal Plant Capacity." Unpublished Masters thesis, A. P. Sloan School of Management, M.I.T., Cambridge, Mass., 1967.

47. Taubert, W. H. "A Search Decision Rule for the Aggregate Scheduling Problem," *Management Science*, vol. 14, no. 6 (February 1968), pp. 343–59.

48. Taubert, W. H. "The Search Decision Rule Approach to Operations Planning." Unpublished Ph.D. dissertation, UCLA, 1968.

49. Taubert, W. H. "A Case Study Problem in Aggregate Manpower Planning," in M. H. C. Martin and R. A. Denison, *Case Exercises in Operations Research*. New York: John Wiley & Sons, Inc., 1971.

50. Tuite, M. F. "Merging Market Strategy Selection and Production Scheduling," *Journal of Industrial Engineering*, vol. 19, no. 2 (February 1968).

51. Vergin, R. C. "Production Scheduling under Seasonal Demand," *Journal of Industrial Engineering*, vol. 17, no. 5 (May 1966).

52. Wilde, D. J., and Beightler, C. S. *Foundations of Optimization*. Englewood Cliffs, N. J.: Prentice-Hall, Inc., 1967.

53. Zangwill, W. I. "A Deterministic Multi-Period Production Scheduling Model with Backlogging," *Management Science*, vol. 13, no. 3 (1966), pp. 486–507.

54. Zangwill, W. I. "A Deterministic Multi-Product, Multi-Facility, Production and Inventory Model," *Operations Research*, vol. 14, no. 3 (May-June 1966).

55. Zoller, K. "Optimal Disaggregation of Aggregate Production Plans," *Management Science*, vol. 17, no. 8 (April 1971), pp. 533–49.

CASE STUDY
THE GARDEN-TILL MASTER
SCHEDULE

IN EARLY APRIL OF 1975, Dennis Fondy, the general manager of Garden-Till, a manufacturer of power roto-tillers, was concerned over the projected financial results for fiscal year 1975, and particularly with the high levels of finished goods that the firm would have to carry over into the next selling season. Garden-Till's fiscal years ran from May 1 to April 30. The physical inventory had just been completed and on projected sales of $24 million Garden-Till had finished goods inventories of $9 million and WIP (work-in-process) and raw materials inventories of $3 million. The financial statement had also shown that the company had lost money in the last year.

Mr. Fondy had sent out a memo (Exhibit 1) to Garden-Till's staff (Exhibit 2) with 1975's projected financial results. He had requested that the staff get together in three days to discuss the reasons for 1975's poor performance and to discuss alternative manufacturing strategies for fiscal year 1976.

Company and industry background

Roto-tillers were three-, four-, and five-horsepower units, about the size of a rotary lawn mower. They were used to expose and churn up the earth prior to planting crops in small gardens of around two acres or less in size. They were a major segment of the $3.5 billion lawn and garden industry. The average price of a Garden-Till roto-tiller was $250, and the gross margins on all models averaged 20 percent.

The lawn and garden industry could be characterized in several

Exhibit 1

Memo to: Staff
Memo from: Dennis Fondy
Subject: Staff Meeting April 10, 1975

I would like you all to address yourselves to the reasons behind our poor performance in FY 1974. The attached financial statements are the projected results for FY 74. Given our 25 percent inventory carrying costs, 1974's ending inventory levels are a disaster. This represents money we badly need to complete our engineering cost reduction programs that we started last year. Please take a hard look at last year's results and give some consideration to alternative manufacturing strategies for FY 1975. See you all at 1:00 P.M., April 10.

Fiscal year 1975
Projected balance sheet
($000)

Assets

Cash	$ 2,515
Accounts receivable	1,857
Income tax refunds	584
Inventories	11,935
Prepaids	273
Total Current Assets	$17,164
Plant property and equipment	$ 8,005
Accumulated depreciation	1,390
Total Fixed Assets	$ 6,615
Total Assets	$23,779

Liabilities and Equity

Accounts payable	$ 1,983
Accrued liabilities	719
Current debt	1,575
Long-term debt (net of current)	2,000
Retained earnings	222
Stockholders' equity	17,280
Total	$23,779

1975 Projected Income Statement
($000)

Sales		$24,235
Cost of Goods Sold:		19,600
Labor	$ 1,800	
Purchased parts	14,500	
Raw steel	2,000	
Variable overhead	1,300	
	$19,600	
Gross margin		$ 4,635
Interest		970
Sales and administration		4,615
Before tax profit or (loss)		$ (950)

Exhibit 2
Garden-Till's staff

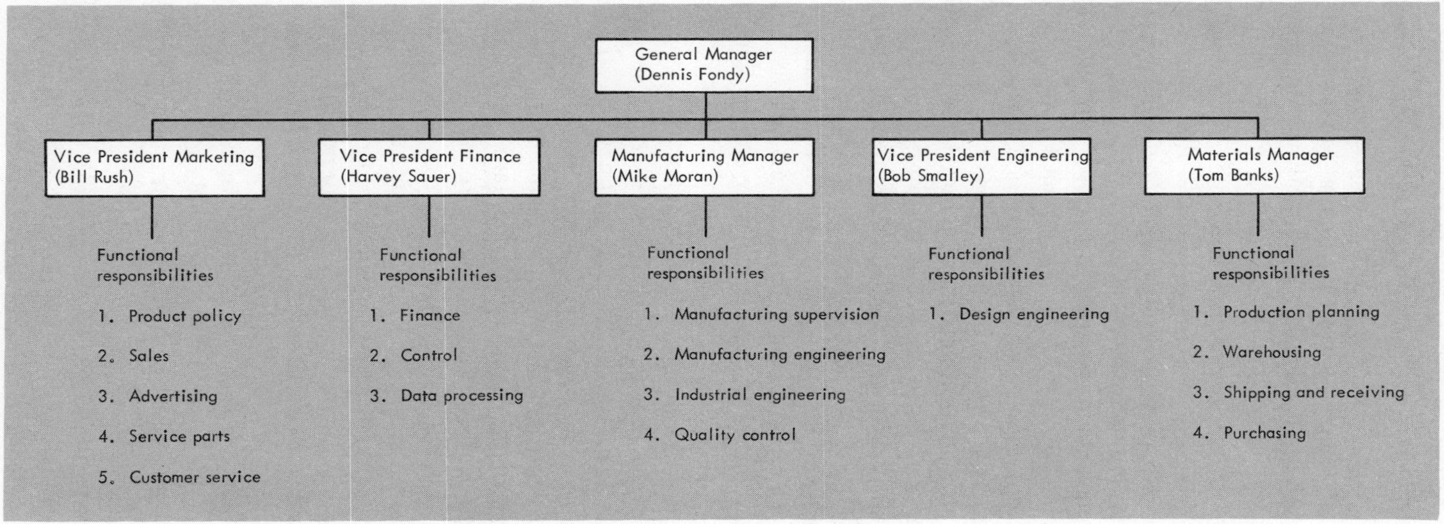

```
                    ┌─────────────────┐
                    │ General Manager │
                    │  (Dennis Fondy) │
                    └────────┬────────┘
        ┌────────────────┬───┴────────────┬────────────────┐
┌───────┴──────┐ ┌───────┴──────┐ ┌───────┴──────┐ ┌───────┴──────┐
│ Vice President│ │Vice President│ │Manufacturing │ │Vice President│
│   Marketing   │ │   Finance    │ │   Manager    │ │  Engineering │
│  (Bill Rush)  │ │(Harvey Sauer)│ │ (Mike Moran) │ │(Bob Smalley) │
└──────────────┘ └──────────────┘ └──────────────┘ └──────────────┘
```

Vice President Marketing (Bill Rush)	Vice President Finance (Harvey Sauer)	Manufacturing Manager (Mike Moran)	Vice President Engineering (Bob Smalley)	Materials Manager (Tom Banks)
Functional responsibilities	Functional responsibilities	Functional responsibilities	Functional responsibilities	Functional responsibilities
1. Product policy	1. Finance	1. Manufacturing supervision	1. Design engineering	1. Production planning
2. Sales	2. Control	2. Manufacturing engineering		2. Warehousing
3. Advertising	3. Data processing	3. Industrial engineering		3. Shipping and receiving
4. Service parts		4. Quality control		4. Purchasing
5. Customer service				

different ways. From a retailing standpoint Sears, Montgomery Ward, and Penney's were the major independent retailers. Sears owned their own manufacturing facilities. Montgomery Ward and Penney's bought from several independent manufacturers. Other kinds of retail outlets included large discount department store chains, hardware stores, building supply houses, farm implement dealers, and a few retailers who specialized in lawn and garden equipment and snowmobiles.

The major manufacturers in the lawn and garden industry were Toro, Lawn-Boy, Yard-Man, Jacobsons, Gilson, AMF, MTD, Murray, Roper, International Harvester, and John Deere. Toro was the largest independent manufacturer with sales of about $200 million.

The industry product lines included lawn mowing equipment, snow removal, leaf removal, and tilling equipment. Lawn mowing equipment accounted for about 80 percent of industry sales, snow removal 10 percent, leaf removal 3 percent, and tillers 7 percent. The equipment varied from a 20 h.p. tractor that sold for well over $2,000 to small hand reel mowers that sold for around $25. The major differentiating features of these products were the horsepower of the engine, the size of the cutting or tilling attachment, electric starters, and whether the unit was self-propelled.

Within the industry there seemed to be several marketing approaches. Some typified the full product line strategy. They offered products in every major market segment, but sold primarily to independent dealers and large department stores. They avoided sales to discounters and attempted to maintain their prices. Some offered their dealers a full product line, price maintenance, national advertising, and local co-op advertising. In general, they required that their dealers have the ability to service their products.

Other manufacturers specialized in only one or two models of lawn mowers. These were high-volume, low-priced, rear-engined riders and rotaries. Their goal was to gain some manufacturing economies of scale while offering a low-priced unit to discounters and dealers. For instance, a dealer of high-priced products might also sell one or two low-priced brands in order to be price competitive with a local discounter. Some manufacturers did not demand that their retailers have the ability to service their units.

Garden-Till followed a third strategy. They produced a premium-priced product in only one market segment of the industry, roto-tillers. They were the leading manufacturers of roto-tillers but ranked only 36th in sales among the 70 lawn and garden equipment manufacturers. With the highest labor rates in the industry,

Garden-Till had attempted to avoid the price competitive segments of the lawn and garden markets. Their standard labor rate was $4.75 an hour. Their high labor rates were due to their location near Toledo, Ohio, an auto parts manufacturing town 59 miles south of Detroit. The second reason for Garden-Till's avoidance of price competitive market segments was its relationship with Taylors, a large chain of department stores. Fifty-five percent of Garden-Till's sales were to Taylors. They would not permit their suppliers to also sell to discounters. They required that they be the lowest-priced retailers of a supplier's product, but they did not price their products to directly compete with discount outlets. This meant that for Garden-Till to distribute its products under its own label, it had to sell to private dealers at prices slightly higher than those offered to Taylors. In the past the only difference between products sold under Garden-Till's label and Taylors' label had been the color of the paint and the decals used on the tillers. Lately, in response to Garden-Till dealer complaints, cosmetic changes had been made to the Garden-Till line. These changes had altered the appearance significantly enough to make it highly unlikely that a Garden-Till and Taylors product would be recognized as being the same thing.

The major events in Garden-Till's history had all centered around attempts to relieve the short-term financial burdens of manufacturing a seasonal product. Garden-Till, as did all its competitors, offered seasonal terms to its customers. The most popular terms offered on tillers stated that if Garden-Till received an order before September 15 for delivery any time after December 1, the dealer's payment was not due until March 30. Garden-Till had similar terms for the fall selling season. These stated that if an order was received by May 1, payment was not due until September 30. Sixty-five percent of Garden-Till's sales were for spring delivery, 30 percent for fall delivery, and the remaining 5 percent was spread evenly throughout the year. Every year around $5 million–$7 million was collected on March 30 and another $3 million on September 30. These terms passed the financial risks of the dealers onto Garden-Till. By assuming the dealer's financial burden, Garden-Till obtained some flexibility in its shipping schedules and gained important information for sales forecasting and production scheduling. All told, around 50 percent of Garden-Till label orders were received prior to September 1. The dealer-specified delivery dates varied between December 15 and February 15 with the majority specifying delivery between January 15 and February 15.

Garden-Till's efforts to reduce their uneven short-term fund's needs had centered around finding a contraseasonal product. They had tried producing and marketing first snowmobiles and then snowblowers. Garden-Till lost money on both products and abandoned them. In retrospect, they felt that their attempts at finding a contraseasonal product had been a mistake. When the products were finally abandoned, over $1 million in tooling investment had to be written off. This was money that was badly needed in 1975. Because of the rapidly rising costs of food, many Americans had been growing their own produce in gardens around their homes. This trend had doubled total industry tiller sales since 1972. It had also encouraged several other lawn and garden equipment manufacturers to add tillers to their product lines. These new competitors had introduced products of equal quality to Garden-Till's and some had reduced their prices 10–15 percent below Garden-Till's prices. Garden-Till had started a cost reduction program, but most of the reductions were to come out of engineering changes which necessitated capital expenditures in retooling. In 1975, Garden-Till was not able to raise the capital needed to fully complete their cost reduction program.

From 1970 to 1975, around 50–55 percent of Garden-Till's annual sales were to Taylors. Garden-Till label products accounted for 35–40 percent of total sales and OEM products equaled 10–15 percent of yearly sales. These were sales to other lawn and garden equipment manufacturers who marketed Garden-Till's products under their own label.

Marketing and product policy

The vice president of marketing, Bill Rush, had received Mr. Fondy's memo requesting a meeting in three days. He knew that the manufacturing manager, Mike Moran, and the materials manager, Tom Banks, would claim that his sales forecasts were largely responsible for Garden-Till's poor performance in 1975. However, he felt that inaccuracy in sales forecasts was a fact of life. For instance, the sales forecasts were very sensitive to a competitor's new products and competitor price changes. These things were impossible to predict with any accuracy. He had also found that weather influenced sales. If there was a late spring or early winter in any of his primary market areas, sales could drop by as much as 20 percent in that area.

Mr. Rush felt that fiscal years 1975 and 1974 had typified his forecasting problems. In 1973, Garden-Till had introduced chain drive versions of its tillers. Prior to 1973, Garden-Till had offered only gear drive tillers. A chain drive tiller worked like a bicycle in transferring the power from the engine to the tines, the digging blades on a tiller. It also used sprockets similar to those on a bicycle to control the speed, whereas a gear drive tiller had a small enclosed gear box that controlled the speed, and the power was transferred by a belt from the engine to the tines. A chain drive tiller cost about $15 less than a gear drive model and could often be repaired by the owner rather than a dealer's service representative. In 1973, the lower price of the chain drive tiller combined with the strong demand for consumer durables resulted in Garden-Till underforecasting sales. When they realized their error in December of 1973, they found that they did not have enough capacity or materials to satisfy dealer delivery requirements in time for the spring selling season. Garden-Till ended FY 1974 with low finished goods and raw materials inventories, but with the knowledge that their profit would have been considerably higher had they been able to supply the market.

In 1974, Garden-Till had announced price increases on all its products in order to keep pace with its own rising costs for materials and labor. All of Garden-Till's competitors had also announced price increases, but unbeknownst to Garden-Till they had significant stocks of finished goods produced in 1973 at 1973 prices. Consumer durables had a bad year in 1974, and this, combined with the competition offering 1973 models at 1973 prices caused Garden-Till and Taylors to overestimate sales. When both Mr. Rush and Taylors discovered their error in December of 1974, it was too late to make any significant cutbacks in the production schedule due to the manufacturing commitment for materials. Fiscal 1975 financial statements had reflected these problems.

Mr. Rush had kept detailed information on his monthly sales forecasts for both fiscal years 1974 and 1975. From them, he plotted out the amount of forecast error for these years. Although he had underestimated demand in 1974 and overestimated demand in 1975, he noted that in absolute terms the error was almost identical. He then graphed the average absolute error per model for each month (Exhibit 3). This showed that his forecasts generally started out with about 50 percent error in them, and by December 1 the error was down to about 10 percent. Garden-Till label forecasts took a big drop in error about September 15 when the early orders were due for billing on March 30. Taylors' label products took a drop in error about November 1 when they finalized their sales forecasts. Mr. Rush knew that both the materials manager and manufacturing manager

Exhibit 3
Timed phased absolute* sales forecast error

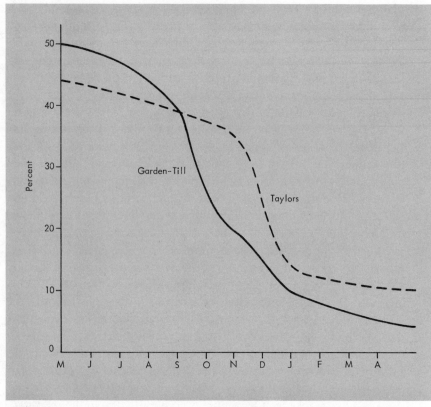

* The error is the average absolute forecast error per model. It does not represent the forecast error in the total demand for tillers. Since the error is absolute it could represent either an underestimation of demand or an overestimation of demand. The following is an example of the calculation of the forecast error.

Tiller model	May forecast for total annual sales	Actual annual demand as of April	Percent error (absolute)
G4C	10,000	15,000	50%
G5C	10,000	5,000	50

had stated that they needed three months' lead time to react to schedule changes. This meant that changes made on December 1 could not actually be implemented until March 1 because of the need to order or reschedule materials. He also felt that it would take the month of March to produce the changes and probably longer. With a two-week delivery time, the dealers would not get their product until somewhere between April 1 and May 1. This was clearly too late since many dealers liked to be sold out of tillers by April 15.

Mr. Rush felt that the meeting with Mr. Fondy was his chance to plead for a better shipping mix earlier in the production season. Garden-Till offered to pay the freight bill if its dealers ordered a full truckload of tillers. If all the tiller models on the order were not available on time, Garden-Till was faced with losing the order or appeasing the dealer by shipping a partial order and the remainder later. In FY 1974, Garden-Till had spent $100,000 over full truckload rates by shipping LTL (less than truckload). In FY 1975, this freight expense variance had been reduced to $35,000.

As many as 15 percent of Garden-Till's orders had been canceled by the dealers and Taylors every year. This usually took place from November 15 to January 15. Mr. Rush had sampled these cancellations and found that about 65 percent were due to overoptimistic sales forecasting on the part of the dealers and Taylors. The remaining cancellations were due to Garden-Till's inability to ship a dealer's order when he required it. The dealer in this case would cancel the order and might even buy tillers from another manufacturer. In fiscal year 1975, Taylors had revised their sales forecast down by 40 percent in January. Taylors had given Garden-Till contracts for their original sales forecast and were legally obligated to accept these quantities. Yet Mr. Rush and Mr. Fondy both knew that they would endanger their relationship with Taylors by forcing them to take all the tillers they had originally ordered. A compromise had been worked out and Garden-Till had been forced to carry heavy inventories of finished goods.

Mr. Rush felt he could sum up his position on manufacturing strategy by requesting faster manufacturing reaction time to proposed production schedule changes and earlier product availability in order to have a good shipping mix. Mr. Rush knew that his task at the meeting with Mr. Fondy would be to convince the staff that the inaccuracy of the sales forecasts was a fact of life. The real payoff for Garden-Till would come by learning to react to sales forecast changes and providing better customer service, not by resisting them and sacrificing customer service for manufacturing efficiency.

The manufacturing process

The manufacturing manager, Mike Moran, regarded the meeting with Mr. Fondy as a good forum to get some troublesome issues resolved. He was particularly interested in pushing for a level production plan. Mr. Moran knew that Garden-Till had sacrificed man-

ufacturing efficiency due to the start-ups and shutdowns that
Garden-Till's seasonal production plans had required.

The basic stages of production were the Press Department, the
Weld Department, prepaint assembly, the Paint Department, and final
assembly. A rule of thumb used at Garden-Till was that the typical
part went through three different press operations and two different
weld operations. It was then sent to prepaint buildup where it was
used as a component to a subassembly. The subassembly was
painted and sent to the final assembly line. Machine setup times
averaged six hours per operation in the Press Department, one hour
per operation in the Weld Department and there were no machine
setups required in the Paint Department, prepaint assembly, or final
assembly. Material handling time averaged 10 minutes per machine
setup in the press department, 15 minutes per setup in the Weld
Department, 8 hours per model changeover in prepaint assembly and
32 hours per model changeover in final assembly.

The company had three assembly lines. Each line was designed to
produce 6,000 units per month per shift, under the current balancing
plan. This called for about 100 people in fabrication, assembly, and
materials handling to support the planned production rate. However, experience had shown that second shift operations only ran at
about 65 percent efficiency. Moran felt that this was due to the fact
that Garden-Till had never been able to hire qualified supervisory
people for the second shift since traditionally, a second shift was
only used for three or four months out of every manufacturing season, and then everyone was laid off. As a consequence, Moran only
planned for 3,900 units per month from second or third shift operations, and as a practical matter, avoided planning the use of second
or third shift operations whenever possible.

He felt that the real savings to Garden-Till from a level production
schedule would come from avoiding the large variances in labor
force requirements projected for fiscal year 1976. Mr. Moran estimated that it cost about $200 to hire and train a new employee. This
cost equaled the reduced efficiency of a new employee while he was
undergoing on-the-job training. He also estimated it cost about $500
to lay off an employee. This cost represented unemployment benefits,
the union negotiated maintenance of the employees health insurance, and the union contract requirement for supplemental unemployment benefits.

In order to make his case for level production, Moran felt that it
would be necessary to review the production process and show the

cost differences between level and seasonal production. He decided to begin by laying out an aggregate production plan for both strategies, and to cost out the factors that influenced these plans. He felt that aggregating the various models into a composite plan was appropriate as a first step, and that deriving a detailed model-by-model master schedule could then be decided as a second step.

Moran began by first making a list of the planning factors (Exhibit 5) that he intended to use in his analysis; he already had the sales forecast, inventory positions, and production requirements (Exhibit 4). Then, he laid out a production plan which reflected Garden-Till's historical mode of operation. He called this plan (Exhibit 6) the "chase" plan since production levels went up and down in accordance with demand levels; i.e., production levels "chased" demand. Once he had determined the number of lines he would run with this plan, calculating employment levels, production, inventories, and hiring and layoff costs was relatively straightforward. Finally, he calculated the total costs associated with this plan.

In formulating the chase plan, Moran took into account the normal May–June extended plant shutdown. During this period of time, the 100 or so production employees that were always the first to be hired and the last to be laid off and thus comprised the "base" work force of the company, were paid vacation pay for the first two weeks, and were temporarily laid off for the next six to eight weeks, depending on the level of finished goods inventory that Garden-Till had ended the year with. While this practice was disgruntling to some employees, many, who were also small farmers, actually planned for this period and looked forward to it. The shutdown also allowed plant maintenance and engineering to prepare for any model changes for the succeeding year. New models were introduced in the fall after existing inventories of old models had been sold off. Mr. Moran also took into account the fact that Garden-Till liked to carry 10,000–15,000 units into the next year as a safety factor and to give a shipping mix during the summer. Thus he planned for an April ending inventory of 15,000 units.

After Moran finished the chase plan, he gave a copy to Tom Banks, who he knew was starting to think about the new year as well. Then, he began to lay out his alternative "level" production plan for comparison (the portion he had completed is in Exhibit 7). As he worked on this plan, he began to think about his upcoming meeting with Fondy. Besides pushing for a level production plan with fewer final assembly model changeovers and fabrication setups, Mr. Moran

Exhibit 4
Garden-Till 1976 total sales forecast (fiscal year)

Catalog item*	Annual sales forecast Dollars (000s)	Units	Monthly sales forecast May	June	July	Aug.
T3G	$2,000	8,000	57	57	57	1,220
T4G	4,500	18,000	128	128	128	2,745
T5G	3,000	12,000	85	85	85	1,830
T3C	2,000	8,000	57	57	57	1,220
T4C	4,000	16,000	113	113	113	2,440
T5C	3,150	13,000	93	92	92	1,980
C3G	1,500	6,000	43	43	43	915
C4G	4,000	16,000	113	113	113	2,440
C5G	2,000	8,000	57	57	57	1,220†
G3C	750	3,000	21	21	21	460
G4C	3,000	12,000	85	85	85	1,830
G5C	2,000	8,000	57	57	57	1,220
O4G	2,000	8,000	57	57	57	1,220
O5G	1,250	5,000	35	35	35	760
Total units	—	141,000	1,000	1,000	1,000	21,500
Total dollars (000s)	$35,250	—	$250	$250	$250	$5,375

  * Taylor models are designated with prefix T in the catalog numbers. Garden-Till model num▮ with the prefix G, and OEM model numbers begin with the prefix O.
  † The inventory currently on hand will cover the cumulative sales forecast from May 1, 197▮ portion of this month.

thought that the meeting with Mr. Fondy was his chance to request a different marketing-production relationship. He felt that the Marketing Department and Taylors should either learn·to forecast sales or at least make the effort to sell their way out of a forecasting error. It seemed to him that given FY 1975's results that it was up to Mr. Fondy to tell Taylors and Mr. Rush that they would have to live with their forecasts rather than try to cover the error with emergency production schedule changes.

Production planning and control

Tom Banks, the materials manager at Garden-Till, was somewhat relieved to receive Mr. Fondy's memo requesting a meeting on manufacturing strategy. In the past, Mr. Banks had been responsible for all production planning, and the production plans essentially dictated Garden-Till's strategy. The plan by necessity usually represented a compromise between Mr. Rush's desire for an early shipping mix and Mr. Moran's desire for long production runs. In trying

Nov.	Dec.	Jan.	Feb.	March	April	Current inventory position (in units)	Annual production plan (in units)
57	57	2,552	2,552	57	57	5,000	3,000
128	128	5,743	5,743	128	128	5,000	13,000
85	85	3,830	3,830	85	85	3,000	9,000
57	57	2,552†	2,552	57	57	4,000	4,000
113	113	5,108	5,108	113	113	4,000	12,000
92	92	4,152†	4,152	92	92	5,000	8,000
43	43	1,913†	1,913†	43	43	4,500	1,500
113	113	5,108†	5,108	113	113	6,000	10,000
57	57	2,552	2,552	57	57	1,000	7,000
21	21	956	956	21	21	1,000	2,000
85	85	3,830	3,830	85	85	3,000	9,000
57	57	2,552†	2,552	57	57	3,500	4,500
57	57	2,552	2,552	57	57	—	8,000
35	35	1,600	1,600	35	35	—	5,000
1,000	1,000	45,000	45,000	1,000	1,000	45,000	96,000
$250	$250	$11,250	$11,250	$250	$250	$11,250	$24,000

to formulate 1976's plan, Mr. Banks had made so many trips between Mr. Moran's and Mr. Rush's offices trying to work out a compromise that he was beginning to feel a little like Garden-Till's version of Henry Clay. He needed some help in defining the marketing-production relationship this year, and Mr. Fondy was the only one who could force a definition. He knew, though, that at the meeting he

Exhibit 5
Planning factors

1. Labor cost: $4.75 per hour
2. Assembly line model changeover cost: $1,482 per changeover
   a. (32 hours of material handling labor) × ($4.75 per hour) = $152.
   b. (20% drop in efficiency first week) × (35 employees) × (40 hours) × ($4.75 per hours) = $1,330
3. Hiring and training cost: $200 per employee
4. Layoff cost: $500 per employee
5. Assembly line production rate:
   a. 300 tillers per day per line (day shift only)
   b. 6,000 tillers per 20 working-day month per line (day shift only)
6. Garden-Till selling price: $250 per tiller
7. Manufacturing cost: (80%) × ($250 per tiller) = $200 per tiller
8. Inventory carrying cost:
   a. (25%)($200 per unit) = $50 per unit per year (or $4.00 per unit per month)
9. The direct labor cost per unit for a single line with 100 employees producing 6,000 units per month is $13.70 per unit ($20.50 per unit on overtime).

Exhibit 6
Garden-Till FY 1976 "chase" production plan

	May	June	July	August	September	October
Sales forecast (in dollars)	250,000	250,000	250,000	5,375,000	5,375,000	250,000
Sales forecast (in units)	1,000	1,000	1,000	21,500	21,500	1,000
Production (in units)	—	—	3,000	6,000	6,000	18,000
Inventory (units) 45,000*	44,000	43,000	45,000	29,500	14,000	31,000
Inventory investment†	$8,800,000	$8,600,000	$9,000,000	$5,900,000	$2,800,000	$6,200,000
Inventory holding cost	$176,000	$172,000	$180,000	$118,000	$56,000	$124,000
Number of assembly lines	—	—	1 shift ½ month	1	1	3
Total employment level#	—	—	50	100	100	300
Direct labor budget§	—	—	$41,100	$82,200	$82,200	$246,600
Hire/layoff cost			$20,000			$40,000

	November	December	January	February	March	April	Total
Sales forecast (in dollars)	250,000	250,000	11,250,000	11,250,000	250,000	250,000	35,250,000
Sales forecast (in units)	1,000	1,000	45,000	45,000	1,000	1,000	141,000
Production (in units)	18,000	18,000	18,000	12,000	6,000	6,000	111,000
Inventory (units) 45,000*	48,000	65,000	38,000	5,000	10,000	15,000	
Inventory investment†	$9,600,000	$13,000,000	$7,600,000	$1,000,000	$2,000,000	$3,000,000	
Inventory holding cost	$192,000	$260,000	$152,000	$20,000	$40,000	$60,000	$1,550,000
Number of assembly lines	3	3	3	2	1	1	
Total employment level‡	300	300	300	200	100	100	
Direct labor budget§	$246,600	$246,600	$246,600	$164,400	$82,200	$82,200	$1,520,700
Hire/layoff cost‖	—	—	—	$50,000	$50,000	$50,000	$210,000

Total sales $35,250,000
Total manufacturing cost§ 20,679,300
Total direct labor   1,520,700
Total inventory carrying cost   1,550,000
Total hire/layoff cost   210,000
Gross margin $11,290,000

* 45,000 units on hand on May 1, 1975.
† In dollars at $200 per unit manufacturing cost.
‡ Factory employment level = 0 on May 1, 1975.
§ Not including direct labor cost.
‖ Plan to force an extended shutdown beginning in May.

Exhibit 7
Garden-Till FY 1975 level production plan

	May	June	July	August	September	October
Sales forecast (in dollars)	250,000	250,000	250,000	5,375,000	5,375,000	250,000
Sales forecast (in units)	1,000	1,000	1,000	21,500	21,500	1,000
Production (in units)	—	3,000	12,000	12,000	12,000	12,000
Inventory (units) 45,000*						
Inventory investment†						
Inventory holding cost						
Number of assembly lines	0	½	2	2	2	2
Total employment level‡						
Direct labor budget§						
Hire/layoff cost						

	November	December	January	February	March	April	Total
Sales forecast (in dollars)	250,000	250,000	11,250,000	11,250,000	250,000	250,000	35,250,000
Sales forecast (in units)	1,000	1,000	45,000	45,000	1,000	1,000	141,000
Production (in units)	12,000	12,000	12,000	12,000	6,000	6,000	111,000
Inventory (units) 45,000*							
Inventory investment†							
Inventory holding cost							
Number of assembly lines	2	2	2	2	1	1	
Total employment level‡							
Direct labor budget§							
Hire/layoff cost‖							

Total sales......................... 35,250,000

Total manufacturing cost‖ ....

Total direct labor ....

Total inventory carrying cost ....

Total hire/layoff cost

Contribution to profit
and overhead _____ _____

* 45,000 units on hand on May 1, 1975.
† In dollars at $200 per unit manufacturing cost.
‡ Factory employment level = 0 on May 1, 1975.
§ $13.70 per unit.
‖ At $186.30 per unit, not including direct labor costs.

would be expected to provide some alternative production scheduling and inventory control approaches.

The production control group had just finished an "ABC" inventory classification program. They had taken the FY 1975 projected production plan and exploded it into the annual gross requirements times the standard cost for each part. They had found that they had requirements for about 2,000 purchased parts. The total cost of these parts was about $14 million with another $2 million being spent on raw steel. Of the 2,000 parts, it was found that 300 accounted for 80 percent of the total purchased parts expenditures. These were classified as "A" items and consisted of such items as engines, gears, wheels, tires, cartons, belts, chains, and handles. Another 1,200 parts accounted for 10 percent of the expenditures, and these were classified as "C" items. They were primarily nuts, bolts, screws, rivets, washers, and decals. The remaining 500 items accounted for 10 percent of the dollar expenditures and were classified as "B" items. These were a miscellaneous group of parts including some very high-usage, low-unit cost items and some very low-usage, high-unit cost items.

The Purchasing Department had just completed the revision of all purchase part lead times. This had been done in response to radically changing supplier conditions between 1974 and 1975. In mid-1974, most durable goods manufacturers were running close to capacity. The majority of Garden-Till's vendors also supplied the auto industry. When the auto industry was going well, Garden-Till found that their lead times often doubled. When the auto industry was in a decline, as it was now, Garden-Till found that parts that formerly had six-month lead times suddenly only had ten-week lead times.

Mr. Banks took the "ABC" inventory classification report and compared it with the lead time listings to see if he could come up with a pattern. The result of this was the "gozinto" tree shown in Exhibit 8. This chart seemed to imply that his real exposure to inventory excess took place about 10 to 12 weeks before the parts were needed on the line.

Procurement at Garden-Till was driven by a master schedule. The master schedule indicated when each model was to be produced, and the size of the production lot. This schedule was then exploded to yield the quantity of each purchased part necessary to support the production level indicated by the master schedule. Thus, if the master schedule called for the plant to produce 1,000 model T3Gs in December, and each model T3G used one T3G sprocket, 1,000 sprock-

Exhibit 8
"Gozinto" tree

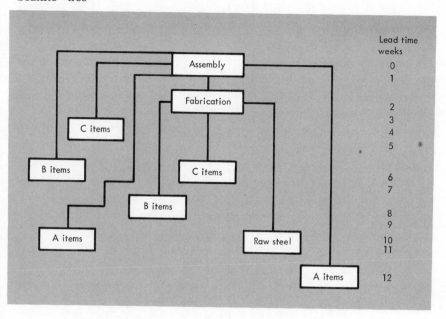

ets, less the amount currently available in raw materials inventory, would be ordered for delivery on the first of December. The plant also used the master schedule as an authorization to begin the production of a model at a specified time.

Although Banks normally derived the aggregate production plan for the company with Moran, he was happy to see that Moran had become involved enough that he had started off on his own. Banks was basically in agreement with the "chase" plan that Moran had evolved, it was in fact quite similar to the production pattern that the company had used for several years. Banks felt that the best thing for him to do for the meeting was to derive a master schedule for the production of each model through the year, within the capacity and inventory limitations set out by the aggregate plan. In doing so, he hoped to accomplish several things. First, he hoped to lay the groundwork necessary to derive purchased part requirements through the year, as described above. Second, he felt that the master schedule was the place to come to grips with the issue of production flexibility, shipping mix, and reaction time that had been raised so often by marketing. Third, he hoped to use the preliminary master

Exhibit 9
Garden-Till FY 1976 master production schedule form (Taylors products only)

Catalog item	Monthly production (in units)												Total production
	May	June	July	Aug.	Sept.	Oct.	Nov.	Dec.	Jan.	Feb.	March	April	
T3G													
T4G													
T5G													
T3C													
T4C													
T5C													
Total production*													
Total production†													

* In units.
† In dollars at $200 per unit.

Exhibit 9 (continued)
Garden-Till FY 1976 finished goods inventory plan (Taylors products only)

| Catalog item | Beginning inventory position (in units) | | | | | | | | | | | | | Total inventory |
	May	June	July	Aug.	Sept.	Oct.	Nov.	Dec.	Jan.	Feb.	March	April	
T3G													
T4G													
T5G													
T3C													
T4C													
T5C													
Total inventory*													
Total inventory†													

* In units.
† In dollars at $200 per unit.

schedule as the basis for forcing some agreement on the process that the company should use in managing the master schedule, such as how often it should be reformulated, who should participate in making it, and how far into the future it should be planned.

A sample of the planning forms Banks currently used to create a master schedule is found in Exhibit 9. In the first master production schedule form, he indicated the quantity of each catalog item that he intended to produce in each month. In the second finished goods inventory plan, he derived the beginning finished goods inventory position for each catalog item that would result if the master schedule were correct, and the sales forecast came to pass.

Chapter 7

Requirements planning: Dependent demand systems

AGGREGATE PLANS AND MASTER SCHEDULES provide a central focus for manufacturing control. They indicate how factory output, inventory, and work force levels should vary over time; and how aggregate factory output should be allocated among the individual products that a manufacturing firm produces. By their nature, however, aggregate plans and master schedules are focused on the end products of the firm. They generally disregard the raw materials, components, and subassemblies that must be managed to ensure that the end products are eventually created. The task of planning and controlling these inputs to the production of finished goods is called *requirements planning.*

Requirements planning is a relevant issue where dependent relationships exist. That is, where the demand for parts, raw materials, components, and subassemblies is dependent upon the demand for finished items. The distinction between dependent and independent demand relationships is an important one. We have already discussed the nature of various kinds of systems that may be employed when the demand for an item is generated by forces outside of the direct control of the firm; that is, independent demand systems. These system approaches are useful for managing inventories of finished goods in distribution warehouses, for example, or for managing spare parts that manufacturers may stock to repair equipment. Suffice it to say at this point that requirements planning systems for managing dependent relationships can be substantially different from independent demand systems. The purpose of this chapter is to show how and why, and to indicate how requirements planning systems may be designed and managed.

Types of systems for dependent demand item control. The product structure diagrams shown in Figure 7–1 illustrate some of the types of dependent relationships that may be found in various industries. Figure 7–1(a), for example, is typical of what one might find in the process industries, say, paper. The finished product here may be sheets, or reams of paper. The semifinished paper whose demand is dependent upon the production of the reams might be jumbo rolls of paper that are sliced to make the individual sheets. The raw material in this case would be pulp, from which the jumbo rolls are made on a papermaking machine.

The product structure in Figure 7–1(b) illustrates the dependencies one might find in a nonintegrated appliance manufacturer which purchases all parts and components, and merely assembles them. The finished product here might be dishwashers, and the various purchased parts and materials whose demand is dependent upon the production of finished dishwashers might include sheet metal stampings, timers, porcelain paint, handles, and so on.

Figure 7–1(c) illustrates the very complex product structure that one might find in an integrated fabrication-assembly operation that makes many of the parts of a piece of machinery, and assembles them as well. The automobile and machine tool industries exhibit such part, subassembly, and finished product dependencies. Figure 7–2 gives a concrete example of this type of product structure for a machine that is used to mark sizes and style numbers on the insides of shoes. It graphically portrays the way in which fabricated parts are used to create several levels of subassemblies which are eventually assembled into a finished marking machine.

There are a number of different types of systems that may be used to plan and control parts and materials whose consumption is de-

Figure 7-1
Dependent demand relationships vary by industry

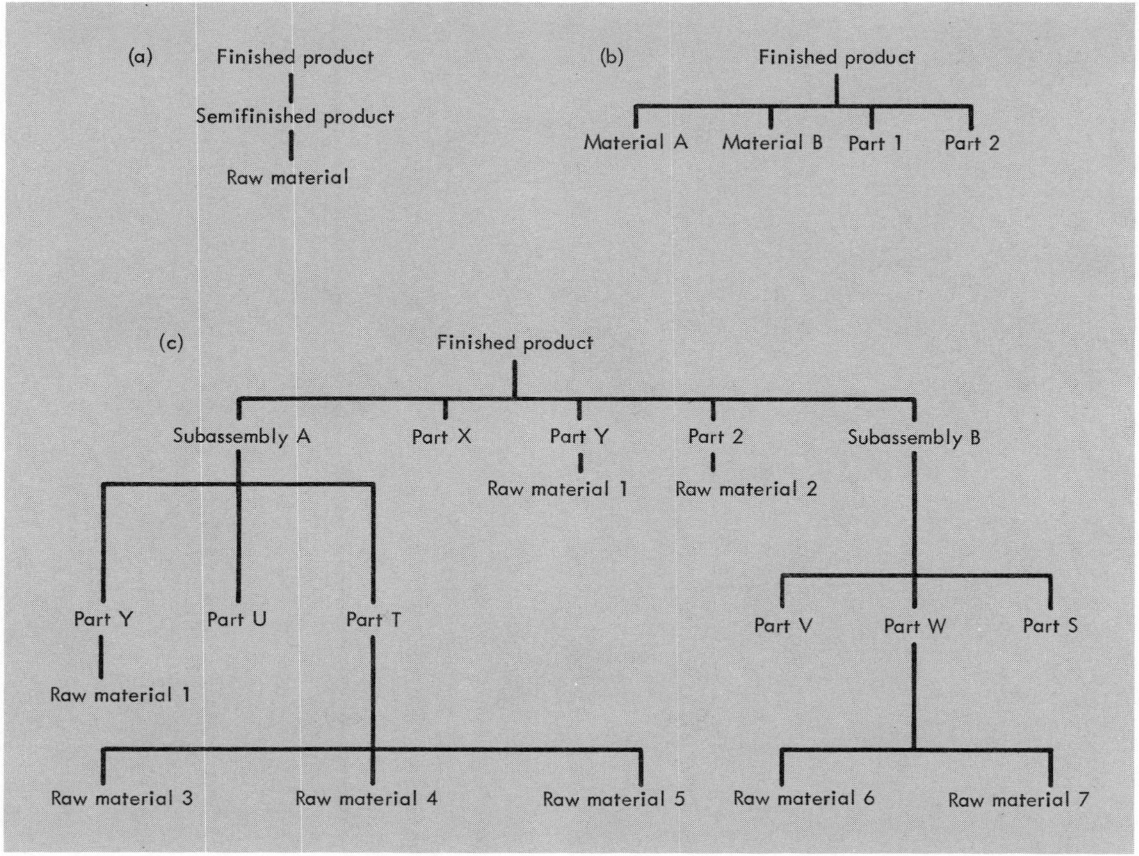

(a)

Finished product
|
Semifinished product
|
Raw material

(b)

Finished product

Material A   Material B   Part 1   Part 2

(c)

Finished product

Subassembly A   Part X   Part Y   Part 2   Subassembly B
                                Raw material 1   Raw material 2

Part Y   Part U   Part T   Part V   Part W   Part S

Raw material 1   Raw material 3   Raw material 4   Raw material 5   Raw material 6   Raw material 7

Figure 7–2
Partial product structure for a marking machine (produced by the Markem
Corporation of Keene, New Hampshire)

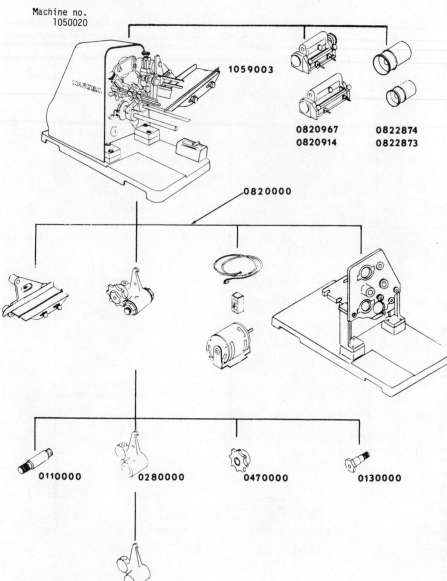

Machine no.
1050020

1059003

0820967
0820914

0822874
0822873

0820000

0110000   0280000   0470000   0130000

Source: Markem Corporation (A) case, by E. W. Davis and W. J. B. Lake, ICH No. 9-673-001, 1972.

pendent upon the output of finished goods. In general, they can be classified into two categories. The first category can be called reorder point-based systems. The common denominator in these types of systems are reorder points. They are used to trigger the production of parts and components in much the same way that they are used with independent demand items. The second major category of systems are explosion-based systems. These types of systems exploit the dependent relationships in product structures by basing the production of parts and components on the need for them as established by a finished goods master schedule. Perhaps the most common variety of explosion-based systems in use today are *material requirements planning* or *MRP* systems. This type of system is described in detail in this chapter. We shall also show how the explosion concept can be used to derive capacity needs in integrated production systems.

REORDER POINT SYSTEMS

The basic logic behind reorder point systems for dependent demand item control is quite similar to that discussed in Chapters 3 and 4. In their most popular form, these types of systems are coupled with economic order quantity logic. Figure 7–3 describes the data used by such systems, the plans and decisions that must be made, and the basic tasks involved in implementing these decisions and feeding their results back into the data base. To illustrate these system relationships, we shall refer to the marking machine whose product structure is illustrated by Figure 7–2. The production of this machine, produced by the Markem Corporation of Keene, New Hampshire, was actually controlled by a reorder point-type system during the 1960s [5]. A number of other case studies document the use of reorder point systems for dependent item control [22, 23].

Data generation/inputs

A reorder point-based system requires that a data base be maintained for each of the dependent items that are used in the production of a finished good. The partial product structure for the marking machine (Figure 7–2) shows 15 different parts and subassemblies, although the actual number of parts is about 100. Assuming for the moment that these 15 items were all that were required to build the

Figure 7–3
The elements of planning and control: Reorder point systems for dependent item control

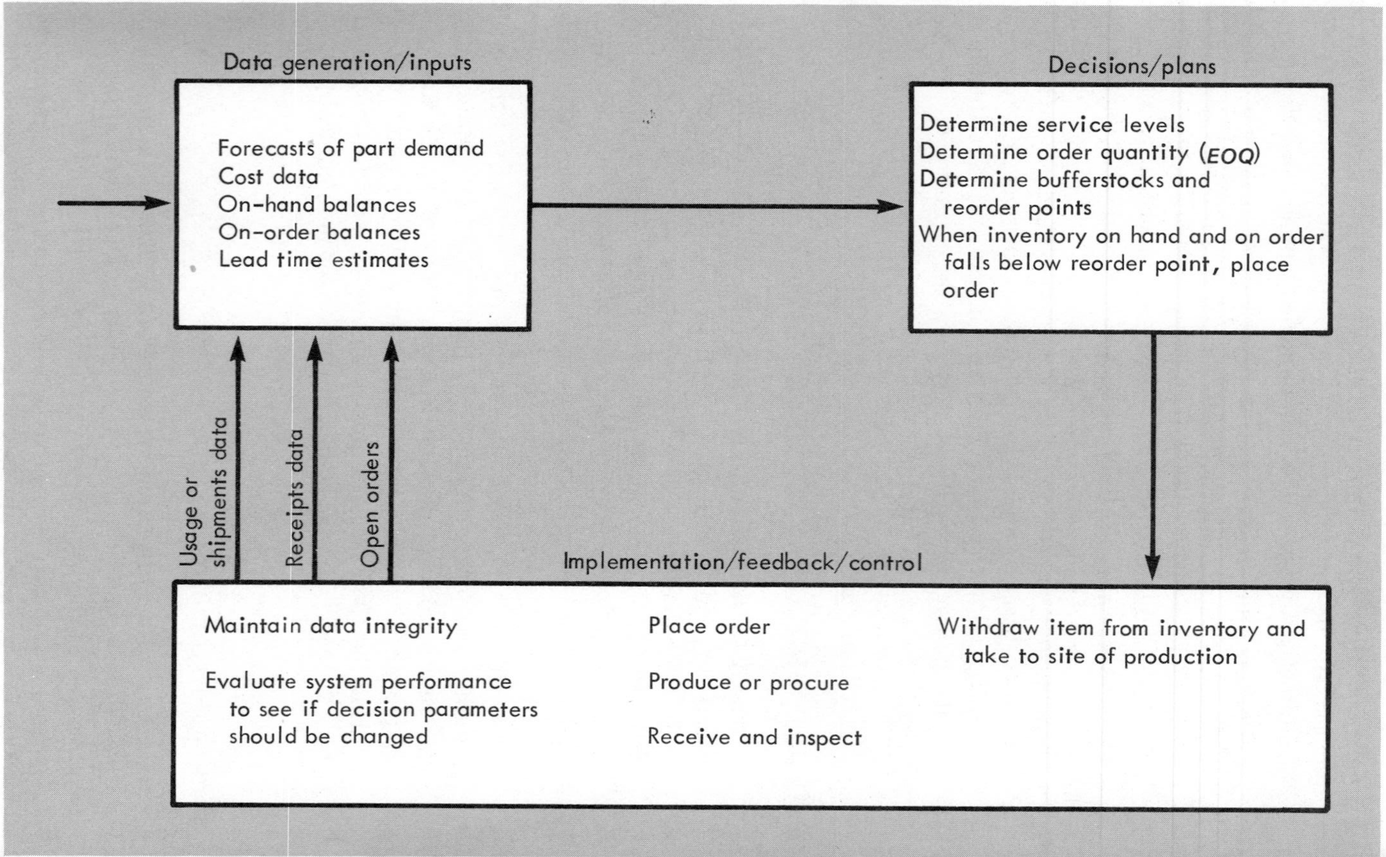

Data generation/inputs

Forecasts of part demand
Cost data
On-hand balances
On-order balances
Lead time estimates

Decisions/plans

Determine service levels
Determine order quantity (EOQ)
Determine bufferstocks and
reorder points
When inventory on hand and on order
falls below reorder point, place
order

Implementation/feedback/control

Place order

Produce or procure

Receive and inspect

Withdraw item from inventory and
take to site of production

Maintain data integrity

Evaluate system performance
to see if decision parameters
should be changed

Open orders

Receipts data

Usage or
shipments data

machine, however, this would imply that records needed to be maintained for each of the 15 items. The data that must be recorded or generated for each of these items would include the following:

1. A forecast of demand for each of the machine parts, including an indication of the variability of demand over the procurement or production lead time. A number of the techniques discussed in Chapter 2 can be used to provide these forecasts, for example, exponential smoothing.
2. The cost data necessary to calculate an economic order quantity, including setup costs and inventory holding costs.
3. Perpetual inventory records indicating the on-hand balance and the quantity of any open orders which have been placed but not yet received.

This data is relatively easy to maintain on either a manual system or on a computer. Cost data is often easily obtained from accounting records. Perpetual inventory records can be maintained on simple file cards or on computer files. The basic requirement for these records, of course, is that each transaction that affects the actual on-hand or on-order quantity be recorded as rapidly as possible after the transaction takes place. From a labor input standpoint, there is usually little difference between recording these transactions on computer files or on manual files since someone usually has to record the transactions manually before they can be entered into a computer file anyway. For most manufacturing companies, reorder point systems absolutely require computerization only when sophisticated forecasting or order point techniques are applied. Assuming that the average manufacturing company has, say, 2,000 dependent demand items to control (probably a conservative estimate), one can imagine the enormous expense of applying exponential smoothing or Fourier series methods, for example, manually. Manual reorder point systems are generally associated with crude but easy to apply forecasting methods such as guessing and using last year's annual usage as an estimate of the next year's demand.

Decisions and plans

The decisions and plans associated with reorder point-based systems are also fairly simple and straightforward. Cost and forecast information is used to compute economic order quantities, buffer stocks, and reorder points for each of the dependent items. The logic applied in deriving these parameters usually takes one of the forms discussed in Chapters 3 and 4, and we will not repeat it here. Once the order quantities and reorder points have been determined, the actual decision making involves checking to see whether on-hand and on-order quantities have fallen below reorder points whenever a transaction is made that affects inventory balances. The reorder points trigger orders for amounts equal to the order quantities associated with each part.

Perhaps the most critical decision that must be made to implement reorder point systems is the determination of service levels. Recall from Chapter 3 that buffer stocks and reorder points should consider uncertainty in demand and lead time estimates. This is accomplished by setting a desired service level that indicates the probability of a stockout that a firm is willing to accept. In previous examples, service levels were set for classes of finished goods. In reorder point requirements planning systems however, a service level applies to the parts used to produce finished goods, and has a slightly different interpretation. The service levels that are set for each dependent item indicate the probability that that part will be available should it be needed in assembly or fabrication. This interpretation reveals the essential philosophy behind reorder point systems; that is, that parts and components are stocked independently just in case they are needed in a higher level intermediate product or the finished product. Service levels are used to determine the required buffer stock which are in turn, used to determine the reorder point for each item. High levels of uncertainty and high service levels result in high reorder points and thus high inventories. The converse is obvious. Thus, the determination of service levels is a prime factor influencing the performance of reorder point systems from both a service and an inventory standpoint.

Implementation, feedback/control

The execution of the decisions made within the context of a reorder point system for dependent item control is theoretically quite as straightforward as generating information for it and making inventory decisions. First, it involves placing orders for the parts which have reached their reorder points, and the consequent activities involved in producing or procuring the item, receiving and inspecting it, and finally, storing it in a stockroom. Second, it involves disbursing parts from the stockroom as the need for them is established. For example, if two of the marking machines (Figure 7–2) were to be produced, the parts necessary to assemble them would be withdrawn from the stockroom and delivered to the assembly area. Coincident with these simple execution steps, other feedback and control tasks that are necessary to keep the system running on an ongoing basis include those that we discussed in Chapter 4. They include maintaining data integrity by recording the inventory transactions that result from executing inventory decisions: receipts, disbursements, and the placing of orders.

System performance

This description of the operation of a reorder point system for dependent item control illustrates several of their main advantages. First, they are extremely simple to operate from the standpoint of all three of the elements of planning and control. Data collection and generation may involve only a few simple records. Decision making and planning is straightforward, and involves only a few of the simplest techniques for determining reorder points and reorder quantities. Execution is confined to the simplest acts of placing orders and issuing parts from stock. The second major advantage of reorder point systems is that they can be implemented without incurring the costs involved in computerization. While manual systems often require that relatively unsophisticated forecasting methods be employed, and make data retrieval for other uses besides inventory control difficult, they can indeed be used, and have been.

The major disadvantages of reorder point systems are essentially the price that must be paid for their operational simplicity. A number of simplifying assumptions are involved in structuring a reorder point system and in making reorder point decisions. They can contribute significantly to the problems that can arise in using this approach. Perhaps the greatest disadvantage associated with them, however, is that reorder point logic essentially treats dependent items as if they were independent of the actual production of finished goods. This can lead to excess inventories, poor service, and high production costs.

Excess inventories can result from the fact that the master schedules that are created at end item levels often result in "lumpy" demand. Recall from Chapter 5 that master schedules are often disaggregated from aggregate plans. They allocate planned production capacity at end item levels to individual products. Figure 7–4 illus-

Figure 7–4
A marking machine master schedule

Item	Time periods								
	1	2	3	4	5	6	7	8	
Machine no. 1104008	10				10				
Machine no. 1050020		3					8		

trates a master schedule as it might appear for two different types of marking machines. It indicates that ten model 1104008 machines should be completed by the beginning of periods 1 and 5, and that two assembly batches of model 1050020 machines are scheduled for completion at the beginning of periods 2 and 7. In contrast to the lumpiness in the demand for parts created by this master schedule, the basic assumption behind order point/economic order quantity models is that demand is smooth and continuous with a stationary statistical distribution of demand over the lead time. The lumpiness of the master schedule or of actual demand, however, often means that demand is not smooth and continuous, and that end item demand is not the result of random forces, but of management decisions in creating the master schedule. Statistically then, the distribution of demand during the lead time is likely to vary, rather than to remain constant.

The result of these differences is that the order quantity for individual parts may be substantially smaller or greater than what is needed to fulfill the master schedule for assembly at any one time. For example, the order quantity for a part based on average demand may be 20, while the master schedule implies that 40 are needed at one time to assemble a machine. Similarly, when an assembly master schedule indicates the need for two parts over a period of three months, the order quantity in a reorder point system may be set at 30 units, or three months *average* usage. This problem was discussed in Chapter 4, and was a critical argument in favor of using time phased inventory plans when lumpy demand occurs, rather than reorder points and economic order quantities. It can result in excess inventories during some time periods, and stockouts during others.

In addition to these factors, poor service or high inventories can result from the use of reorder point systems unless they explicitly recognize the relationships *among* the parts and materials that are used in a particular product. For example, if the service level for each part and raw material was established at 0.90 (that is, reorder points and buffer stocks were determined in such a way that there were only 10 chances in 100 that the part would be out of stock during any one week in a year), then the probability that all of the 15 parts would be on hand when they were required to make a marking machine would be $0.90^{15} = 0.21$. Clearly, if the probability of having all of the parts on hand is to be reasonably high, then the individual service levels for them must be very high indeed. The relevant probability is that of having all the parts necessary to produce a finished machine. Very high service standards, however, are conducive to very high-inventory levels as we saw in Chapter 3.

A third disadvantage of reorder point methods is that they de-couple the management of parts and materials from the aggregate plans and master schedules that may be created for the finished out-put of a factory. Master schedules state explicitly what products are to be produced and when. Yet, instead of deriving the usage of de-pendent items from a known finished goods master schedule, reorder point systems utilize independently derived forecasts of the demand for each part. Thus, if as a result of a rigorous analysis a company decides to increase or decrease demand in their aggregate plans and master schedules, there is no assurance that orders for dependent items will follow.

The fourth disadvantage of reorder point systems is that it is dif-ficult to derive priorities from them for scheduling purposes. We shall discuss priority planning and scheduling rules in detail in Chapter 10. At this point, it is sufficient to note that some set of priority rules must be applied in determining which of the many dependent items that may be produced on the same facilities should be produced first, second, and so on. Certainly one of the determi-nants of such detailed schedules is the urgency with which a depen-dent item is needed. Yet, the only indicator of need in reorder point systems is the proximity of the on-hand and on-order balance to the reorder point. Since reorder points can have little correspondence to the actual needs for the item at the finished product level, this can seriously impair a factory's ability to accurately determine priorities.

MATERIAL REQUIREMENTS PLANNING SYSTEMS

The common denominator in explosion-based systems is that they derive or "explode" forecasts of the demand for dependent items from a master schedule that projects finished goods production into the future. In a sense, they are hierarchical systems much like those discussed in Chapter 6, since the demand at high levels in the production process as indicated by the master schedule, is used to make decisions at lower levels. Thus, explosion-based systems avoid one of the most serious problems associated with most reorder point systems in which dependent item demand is forecasted independently. Material requirements planning (MRP) is industry's current answer to these problems. This system couples explosion logic, associated with forecasts for dependent parts derived from a master schedule, with the inventory planning, or time phased order point logic, that was described in Chapter 4.

Figure 7–5 illustrates the elements of an MRP system. As in the case of reorder point systems, we shall use the marking machine shown in Figure 7–2 to illustrate the data generation/input, decision making and planning, and implementation, feedback, and control elements of this system. The Markem Corporation which makes this machine implemented an MRP system for controlling its production in 1969.

Data generation/inputs

Much of the data that must be generated to operate an MRP system was discussed in the previous section on reorder point systems for dependent items. Cost information, such as setup and inventory carrying costs, is needed to make lot sizing decisions. Production and procurement lead time estimates are required to calculate how far in advance of actual needs items must be ordered. Similarly, perpetual inventory records indicating on-hand and on-order balances and due dates are needed to assess the current inventory position for each item. As in the case of reorder point systems, this information must be maintained for each dependent item. However, unlike reorder point systems, this information is typically maintained on computer files. The particular file in which most of the above-mentioned data is normally maintained is often called the item master file, or the inventory file. We shall soon see why computers are usually used in conjunction with MRP systems.

In addition to cost, lead time, and perpetual inventory data, there are two other primary data inputs to MRP systems. The first is the master schedule, which is usually stated in terms of the planned finished product output of the factory. As Figure 7–4 illustrates, the

Figure 7-5
The elements of planning and control: Material requirements planning systems

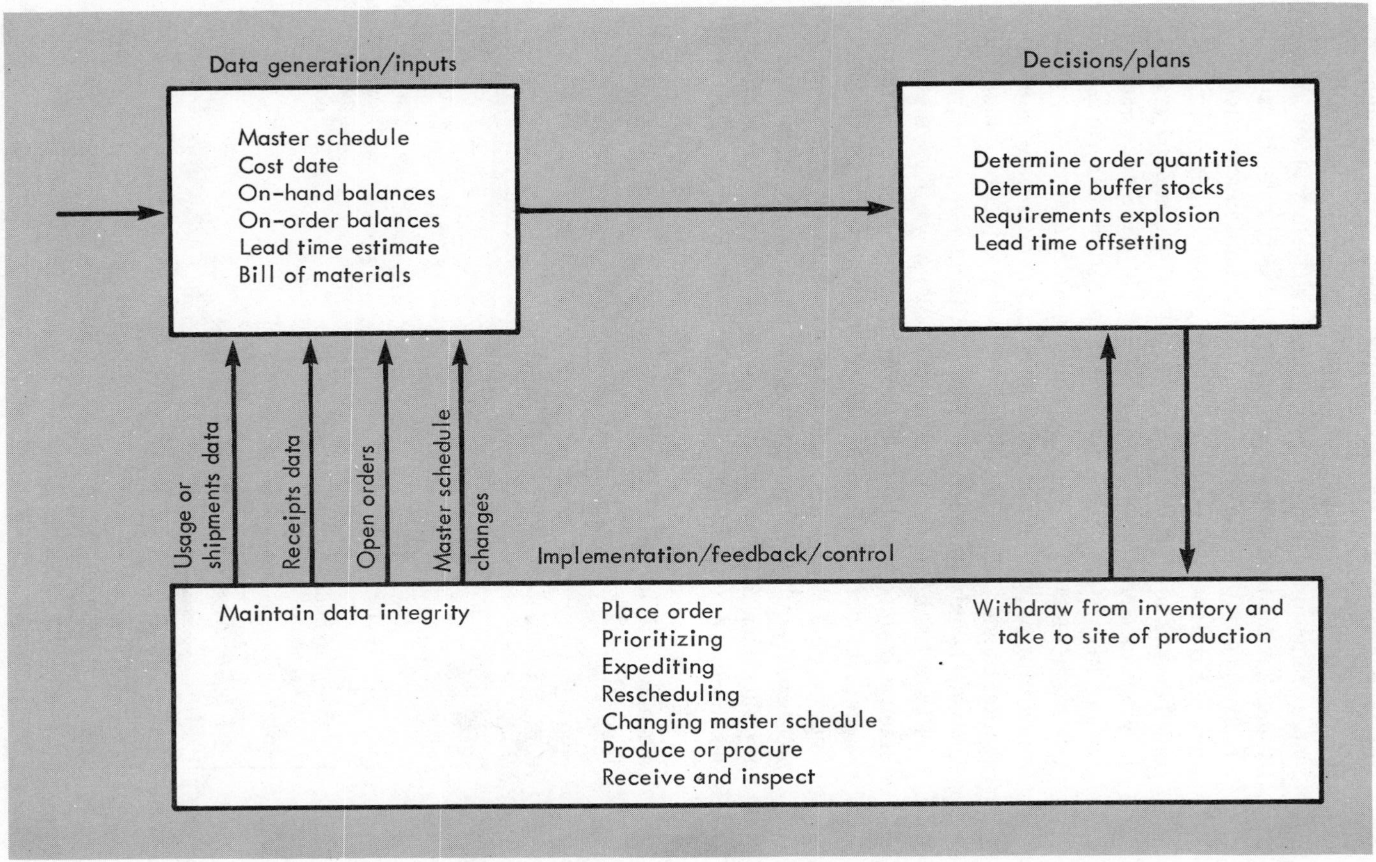

Data generation/inputs

Master schedule
Cost date
On-hand balances
On-order balances
Lead time estimate
Bill of materials

Maintain data integrity

Decisions/plans

Determine order quantities
Determine buffer stocks
Requirements explosion
Lead time offsetting

Withdraw from inventory and
take to site of production

Implementation/feedback/control

Place order
Prioritizing
Expediting
Rescheduling
Changing master schedule
Produce or procure
Receive and inspect

Usage or shipments data
Receipts data
Open orders
Master schedule changes

master schedule is a time phased projection of the products that are actually intended to be produced. It is rarely a projection of the actual demand for finished products. If the factory produces to order, it may deviate from actual demand if custom products are produced in advance of the dates that have been promised to customers. This may occur if the timing of production is moved up in order to smooth out the work load. If the factory produces to a finished goods inventory, the master schedule will not reflect actual demand since it will be met from stock. Here, the master schedule will reflect planned replenishments to this stock, and may also reflect any work load smoothing plans that may have been laid in aggregate plans. In other words, master schedules reflect actual production plans directly. Demand is only indirectly reflected in them.

Master schedules may be stated in two ways. They may be stated in terms of the dates on which the finished goods noted in them are to be completed, or in terms of the date on which the production of the final product is to begin. The difference between these two types of master schedules is the time required to actually make the finished product once the dependent items are available. Either method can be employed, with some modifications. We shall assume the latter.

The second type of data input that is unique to explosion-type systems such as MRP are bills of materials for each of the finished items that a firm may produce. Figure 7–6 illustrates a typical (par-

Figure 7–6
Partial bill of materials for marking machine no. 1050020

```
1  Marking machine no. 1050020
   1  Treadle subassembly ...................................  no. 0820000
      1  Treadle pivot.......................................  no. 0270018
         1  Casting .........................................  no. 0278818
      1  Treadle bracket ....................................  no. 0278819
      4  Caps ...............................................  no. 0118182
   1  Air cyclinder subassembly ............................  no. 0822872
      1  _____
         2  _____
         2  _____
   1  Basic 1050020 subassembly ............................  no. 1350000
      1  _____
         1  _____
            1  _____
            2  _____
         1  _____
         2  _____
            1  _____
```

tial) bill of materials as it might appear for the marking machine shown in Figure 7–2. It shows that a bill of materials (or bill of materials file when computers are used) contains the same information in list form that a product structure diagram shows graphically. That is, it shows which dependent items go into higher level items, such as subassemblies, and ultimately, finished products.

The bill of materials format illustrated in Figure 7–6 is called an indented bill of materials, since it indicates dependency relationships by indentations. For example, the finished item, machine #1050020, is indicated by its beginning closest to the left margin. The notation on this first line indicates first the quantity of machines referred to, then the name of the item, and then its item number. The bill of materials also shows that the finished machine is assembled by bringing together three major subassemblies, item numbers 08200000, 0822872, and 1350000. The fact that these items are directly dependent upon the production of marking machine 1050020 is indicated by the fact that they are next closest to the left margin. The numbers at the beginnings of these lines signify that one treadle, one air cylinder, and one basic subassembly are required to make one marking machine.

Similarly, one treadle subassembly is made up of a number of parts, such as one treadle pivot and four caps, whose demand is primarily dependent on the demand for the treadle subassembly, and secondarily dependent upon that of the finished machine. Each treadle pivot is made from one #0278818 casting and so on. Although many printed reports from an MRP system may use this indented format, "pointers" or locators are used in computer files to indicate which items are dependent upon others to maximize the efficiency of file storage space.

In generating bills of material for MRP systems, care should be taken to make sure that they reflect the way in which a product is actually produced. Bills for requirements planning are not necessarily the same as those that a product design engineering group may produce in the course of their work. Design bills are often only straight lists of the parts or materials used to manufacture a product. They do not reflect that fact that production may proceed through intermediate stages, such as the creation of subassemblies. Later, we shall also discuss *modular bills* and *planning bills*, which can be used to advantage in some MRP systems, but which also deviate somewhat from the description given here.

Decisions and plans

The decisions and plans that must be made within the context of an MRP system parallel in many ways those that must be made in other types of systems. For example, lot size methods and parameters and safety stocks must be established for each identifiable dependent item in the product structure. We have already noted that MRP systems use the time phased order point or inventory planning-type approach defined in Chapter 4. Therefore, the lot sizing and safety stock approaches that were discussed in Chapter 4 are appropriate here. Lot sizing decisions can be placed within the framework of economic order quantity, period order quantity, least total cost, least unit cost, or the Wagner-Whitin methods. Similarly, safety stocks or safety lead times can be employed with each dependent item to buffer the system from supply uncertainties (late deliveries, scrap) and demand uncertainties (poor forecasts, unexpected orders). Once the lot sizing and buffering approach and parameters have been determined, information regarding them may be stored in the item master file with other data. Figure 7–7 illustrates the way that the contents of this file may be displayed for some of the marking machine parts that are shown in the bill of materials in Figure 7–6.

Figure 7–7
Partial list of contents of an item master file

Part no: 0820000	Item: Treadle subassembly
Lead time: 3 weeks	Standard cost: $110
Setup cost: $20	Order quantity: 15 units
Safety Stock: 0	Where used: Model 1050020
On hand: 10	On order: 0

Part no: 0270018	Item: Treadle pivot
Lead time: 3 weeks	Standard cost: $55
Setup cost: $37	Order quantity: 15
Safety stock: 0	Where used: no. 0820000
On hand: 0	On order: 10, due in period 2

Part no: 0278818	Item: casting
Lead time: 6 weeks	Standard cost: $42
Setup cost: 0	Order quantity: 25
Safety stock: 0	Where used: no. 0270018
On hand: 11	On order: 25, due in period 2

The unique feature of MRP systems is the way in which the inventory plans associated with each individual item, subassembly, or finished product are linked together over time through explosion logic. Figure 7–8 indicates how this is accomplished for a few of the items in the marking machine that we have been using as an example. This diagram graphically embodies all of the information and decisions that we have discussed to this point. The hierarchical arrangement of the master schedule and the inventory plans is taken from the bill of materials shown in Figure 7–6. The on-hand, on-

Figure 7–8
Explosion of marking machine dependent item demand within the inventory planning framework

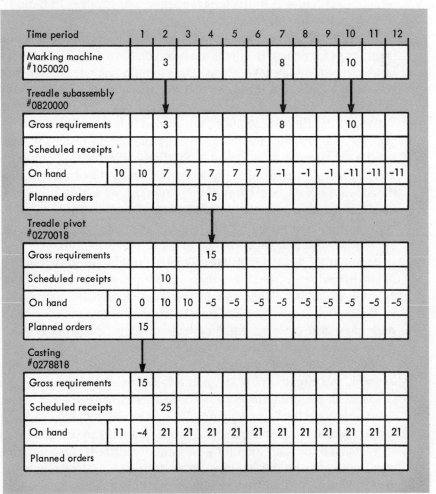

Time period		1	2	3	4	5	6	7	8	9	10	11	12
Marking machine #1050020			3					8			10		
Treadle subassembly #0820000													
Gross requirements			3					8			10		
Scheduled receipts													
On hand	10	10	7	7	7	7	7	-1	-1	-1	-11	-11	-11
Planned orders					15								
Treadle pivot #0270018													
Gross requirements					15								
Scheduled receipts			10										
On hand	0	0	10	10	-5	-5	-5	-5	-5	-5	-5	-5	-5
Planned orders		15											
Casting #0278818													
Gross requirements		15											
Scheduled receipts		25											
On hand	11	-4	21	21	21	21	21	21	21	21	21	21	21
Planned orders													

order, lot size, lead time, and part number information is taken from the inventory file shown in Figure 7–7. The explosion logic is contained in the fact that the gross requirements for a dependent item are directly taken from the upstream item, product, or subassembly which generates demand for it. The term explosion is used to denote that the planned order quantity for an item at a higher level is multiplied by the number of units of the dependent item used to make it. The bill of materials in Figure 7–6 shows that one treadle pivot is required to make one marking machine. Thus, the number of marking machines to be made in period 3 must be multiplied by one to obtain the period three gross requirements for treadle subassemblies. Similarly, since four caps are required to assemble a treadle subassembly (see Figure 7–6) the gross requirements for caps in period 3 would be $4 \times 3 = 12$.

The explosion logic used in MRP systems means that orders and inventories for dependent items are based on the need for them in the production of higher level items. For example, the master schedule shown in Figure 7–8 indicates that the assembly of eight marking machines is expected to commence during period 7. This implies that eight treadle subassemblies are needed before assembly can begin, and thus establishes the gross requirement, or need, for eight treadle subassemblies in period 7. Similarly, after netting out existing inventories, factoring in the lead time required to assemble treadle subassemblies, and using the appropriate lot sizing rules, this need for treadle subassemblies can be established. The need can then be translated into a need for the replenishment of treadle subassembly stocks, which in turn, creates the need for treadle pivots.

A particular dependent item may have "needs," or gross requirements placed on it from more than one source. As shown in Figure 7–9, other marking machines may use the same treadle subassembly as the model 1050020, and some independent demands for spare parts may also enter in. MRP systems combine the gross requirements placed on items regardless of their source.

Conceptually, MRP systems are extremely simple and straightforward, one might almost say, natural. It is hard to believe that the pharaohs in planning the construction of their pyramids did not sit down and say, "lets see, 1 pyramid; I must need 100,000 blocks of stone, 40 caravans of mortar, . . . , and if I want the pyramid built in 20 years, and the lead time for a caravan of mortar is three months, then I need to order the first caravan to start on. . . ." Unfortunately, the implementation of these sytems in most manufacturing environ-

Figure 7–9
MRP systems collect gross requirements from all sources

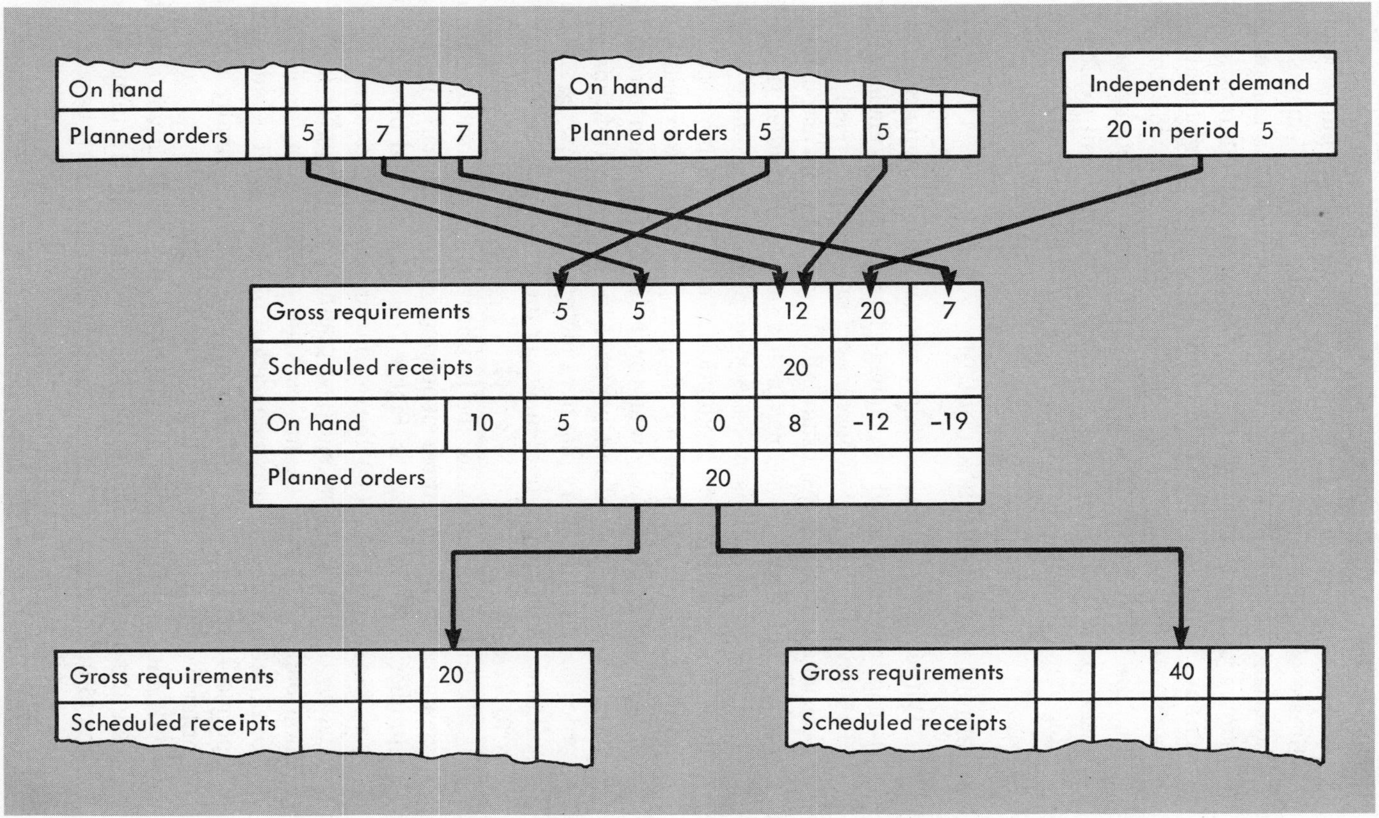
On hand
Planned orders
5
7
7
On hand
Planned orders
5
5
Independent demand
20 in period 5
Gross requirements
5
5
12
20
7
Scheduled receipts
20
On hand
10
5
0
0
8
-12
-19
Planned orders
20
Gross requirements
20
Scheduled receipts
Gross requirements
40
Scheduled receipts

ments had to await the arrival of fast computers to manipulate the vast quantities of data they require. Assuming that our previous estimate of 2,000 dependent items for the "average" manufacturing company is legitimate, one need only multiply the computational effort required to generate Figure 7–8 by about 700 to estimate the amount of data manipulation required to generate material requirements *each time* the master schedule is exploded. Most companies that use MRP reexplode or "regenerate" material requirements each week, or 52 times per year, for reasons that we will explore later. Regeneration serves to increase the computational burden even more.

Implementation, feedback control

While MRP systems are extremely simple conceptually, they pose demanding operational and managerial problems. A glance at Figure 7–5 shows that the list of possible actions that may result from MRP decisions and plans is substantially larger than that associated with reorder point-based systems. In addition to the rather simple and straightforward actions necessary to place and produce an order, these systems also alert production controllers of the need to deal with vendors, marketing, or shop supervisors in expediting, rescheduling, or canceling orders, or revising master schedules. These actions were discussed in Chapter 4 in the context of time phased order point or inventory planning methods. However, the amount of judgment involved in implementing them is considerably greater in MRP systems.

To illustrate, reconsider the implications of the material requirements plans for the three dependent items for marking machine number 1050020 shown in Figure 7–8. The derived inventory plan for item number 0820000, the treadle subassembly, does not indicate the need for any action, since no planned orders appear in the "action bucket" (period 1), and on-hand and on-order (scheduled receipt) inventories appear balanced. A *planned* order is indicated for period 4, but that is three weeks into the future. Normally, a planned order would not be executed this far in advance.

The inventory plan for item 0270018, the treadle pivot, does indicate the need for immediate action. The presence of a planned order for 15 units in period 1 indicates that the order must be placed immediately in order for it to be produced (with a three-week lead time) before the planned on-hand balance falls negative. Otherwise, a stockout will occur, preventing the timely production of the subassembly, and perhaps ultimately, the marking machine. A second potential action is also indicated by this schedule. The presence of a planned scheduled receipt for ten units in period 2 indicates that an order for treadle pivots was released two weeks before. However, an examination of this schedule indicates that none of the incoming ten units are needed until period 4. This raises the question, why not halt production on these units (perhaps freeing up capacity for more urgently needed items) and reschedule their arrival for period 4 when they are needed. A rescheduling decision such as this may not only free up needed capacity, but it will also prevent the firm from carrying ten completed units in inventory for two extra periods.

The ultimate decision on whether or not to reschedule the due date on the outstanding order depends on whether or not the costs and efforts associated with rescheduling, outweigh the costs associated with letting it stand. Some advanced MRP systems are designed to automatically reschedule receipts to correspond to actual needs. The more common approach, however, is to manually intervene and rely on human judgment in rescheduling or expediting decisions. The ability of MRP systems to indicate the potential for rescheduling and expediting, is important, however. Orlicky [20] notes, "In the modern view, the most important function of an MRP system is not inventory control, but its ability to plan and replan priorities; i.e., to schedule and reschedule orders."

The inventory plan for item number 0278818 also indicates the potential for rescheduling. However in this case, the negative projected onhand balance in period 1 and the scheduled receipt in period 2 indicates that the direction of the reschedule should be to get the order in earlier than scheduled (expediting), rather than to delay its receipt. Here again, the production planner is faced with several choices. Expediting the order would involve contacting the foundry which makes the casting (assuming that the casting is a purchased part) and requesting early delivery in order to avoid the stockout, and perhaps delays in the production of the treadle pivot, the treadle subassembly, and the machine in turn. However, since the scheduled receipt for 25 castings is likely to have been placed with the assumption of the standard delivery lead time of three weeks, this will mean that an earlier due date poses some difficulties for the supplier. The expedite request may be refused, or some additional expenses may be incurred in expediting the order.

A second alternative is to essentially admit defeat, assume that the receipt of the order will occur in the second week as scheduled, and change the master schedule so that the eight marking machines scheduled for assembly in period 7 (the order that ultimately generated the need for the casting) are scheduled for assembly in period 8 instead. This change in the master schedule will delay the assembly of the machine, but if this is inevitable, a customer awaiting the delivery of the machine may want to be notified in advance of any delays, or marketing may wish to be notified of potential stockouts at the end item level. Changing the master schedule will also keep the relative needs or gross requirements in context however, and will ensure that actual priorities are maintained.

A third alternative is to allow the receipt of the casting to occur in the second week as scheduled, to take no expediting actions, and to leave the master schedule as it is. This alternative course of action may be based on the hope that production at intermediate stages can be more easily expedited, and that the factory can "catch up" on any delays. Since the treadle pivot and treadle subassembly are produced within the plant, where one would expect the firm to exert greater influence than with vendors, this may be the best course of action assuming that sufficient capacity exists. If de-expediting decisions similar to the one we referred to earlier for the treadle pivot have been made, capacity may indeed be available to expedite at higher levels.

The production planner has yet a fourth alternative course of action. It would not involve expediting the incoming casting order, or changing the master schedule. This alternative would involve violating the lot sizing rules applied at higher levels. Notice that the actual need for treadle subassemblies in period 7 is for one unit. However, the negative on-hand balance projection triggered an order for 15 units, the economic lot size. Only one of these units is really needed to stay on schedule however, and 11 castings are in stock, more than enough to satisfy the minimal need. The fourth alternative then is to change the lot size on the period 4 treadle subassembly planned order. This action will result in additional setup costs (and less inventory) but that is the nature of the trade-off the planner must make for keeping on schedule.

This example of the options that production planners must consider illustrates the need for considerable judgment in operating with an MRP system. The nature of the options to reschedule, expedite, change master schedules, and so on requires that the production planner come in contact with vendors, supervisors, marketing and customer service personnel, and perhaps even customers. Thus, in addition to good judgment, the effective planner must have good interpersonal communications and negotiating skills. To alleviate the work load brought on by these additional responsibilities, it is important that the data generated by an MRP system be presented effectively and efficiently. This can be accomplished by having the system screen inventory plans for exceptions, so that potential actions can be addressed directly.

Figure 7–10 shows the requirements generation report that is used

Figure 7–10
Markem Company requirements generation report

```
  01/25/72                          REQUIREMENTS GENERATION                              PAGE  159

ART NO.  0650400       POLICY CODE D    DESCRIPTION - INK ROLL 1002  STOCK          M/U   19  S/U   71
ITEM TYPE 2   INV. CLASS A   SOURCE M   UNIT OF MEASURE EACH   ORDER QUANTITY  200  SAFETY STOCK     LEAD TIME   6
UNIT COST  1.450   ON HAND    40   MIN.      MAX.      MULT.    ALLOC.   6  B/O    USAGE AVE. 19.1
                   265            270        275        280        285        290        295        300        305
GROSS                            270        275        280        285        290        295        300        305
                                  27         19         11         23         25         29         19         19
OPEN ORD                         200 *
ET
OFFSET                                                             200 *
                                                                  132
BALANCE            34            207        188        155                   107         78         59         40
                   310           315        320        325        330        335        340        345        350
GROSS              25            19         29         19         23         19         29         19         19
OPEN ORD                          4
ET                                29         19          23        19         29         19         19
OFFSET                                                  200 *
BALANCE            15            196        167        148        125        106         77         58         39
                   355           360        365        370        375        380        385        390        395
GROSS              23            19         29         19         19         19         19         19         19
OFFSET
                   23            19         29         19         19         19         19         19         19
BALANCE            16            197        168        149        130        111         92         73         54
```

Explanation:
This exhibit shows an excerpt from one page of the requirements generation report, giving data for one part (No. 0650400), an ink roll type 1002, for the 27 weeks beginning with shop calendar day No. 265 through 395.

The report shows that this part is a Class A item, is a manufactured part as opposed to purchased ("Source M"), is ordered in quantities of 200 according to policy code D, has a lead time of 6 weeks ("Lead Time 6"), and costs $1.45 ("Unit Cost 1.45"). Currently there are 40 in inventory ("On Hand 40"), 6 of which have been allocated to specific orders ("Alloc. 6") and there are no outstanding backorders ("B/O").

The figures in the rows under each week labeled "Gross," "Open Ord," etc., can be read as follows:

In the week of shop day No. 265 there are 40 on hand, but 6 are allocated so the "Balance" is 34.

In the week of day 270 it is anticipated that an open order ("Open Ord") for 200 will be received, raising the stock level to 234; however, there is also a requirement for 27, so the balance on hand is 207.

By the week of day 310 the balance is down to 15 because of intervening gross requirements.

In the week of day 315 a further 19 are required which would reduce the stock level below 0, so an order needs to be placed. The order quantity for the item is 200 units and its lead time is 6 weeks, thus 200 need to be ordered 6 weeks earlier (i.e., the week of day 285) to avoid a stockout. This suggested order is the "Offset" value in the week of day 285 and is marked with an asterisk.

If no order is placed there will be a net requirement of 4 in the week of day 315 (i.e., 15 on hand at the beginning of the week and a gross requirement of 19.) This is indicated in the "Net" row. Note, however, that the program assumes that the order for 200 is placed in the week of day 285 and will be received in the week of day 315 so that the balance on hand will then be 196 as shown.

Source: Markem Corporation (A) case, by E. W. Davis and W. J. B. Lake, ICH No. 9-673-001, 1972.

for each of the 9,000 dependent items that the Markem Corporation uses to produce its many varieties of marking machines. In many respects, the format of this report is similar to that used in a number of companies using MRP systems. The report itself is the computerized counterpart of one of the inventory plans shown in Figure 7–8. While these individual requirements generation reports are useful as backup, the prospect of facing 9,000 of them each week is frightening. Instead of using them to plan and control the production of parts directly, Markem uses several summary reports which indicate the potential for action. Figure 7–11, for example, summarizes all of the planned orders for the upcoming three periods (weeks) of the requirements plans. Orders indicated for the first period are those that are in "action buckets," where action is mandatory. Planned orders for two and three weeks into the future may or may not be acted upon immediately.

Figure 7–12 shows the exception report that Markem uses to indicate when rescheduling, expediting, master schedule changes, and so on, may be needed. It contains the item number, an exception code indicating the type of problem that may exist, and the currently scheduled requirement date and order quantity referred to by the exception condition. For example, code 04 for item number 0320352 indicates that an open order (scheduled receipt) is due in period 481 for 15 units, but that the gross requirements for this part are covered by the projected on-hand balance. This is the type of message that one might expect for the treadle pivot in Figure 7–8, since this condition indicates the potential for rescheduling, or de-expediting.

Figure 7–13 is a summary of the types of exceptions that Markem's MRP system generates each week. Of particular interest here are the total number of exception conditions that may be acted upon, 1,241 in a week. At first glance, this may appear to be an exceedingly high number. However, considering the complexity of manufacturing in a firm with over 9,000 dependent items and hundreds of machine models, it is actually an accurate reflection of the difficulty of planning and controlling production under any type of system. This number of exceptions is indicative of the number of changes that can occur in master schedules as new forecasts are made, and new customer orders are accepted; and of the number of changes in supply conditions caused by scrap, rework, late deliveries, and so on. The fact that an MRP system reflects all of these changes in conditions illustrates their exquisite sensitivity. However, this sensitivity can be a cause for concern in some companies because of the high administrative costs that it implies. We shall discuss some approaches for

Figure 7–11
Markem planned orders list

	1ST PERIOD		2ND PERIOD		3RD PERIOD		
11/14/72			PLANNED ORDERS				
0110366			476	400			SPECIAL STOVE BOLT
0111107	471	1822					RIVETS
0111103	471	10000					RIVET
0210058	471	10					KNURL NUT 5/16-18-7/32
0120080					481	150	PIVOT PIN
0120359					481	50	LOCK NUT
0120734					481	100	FEED ADJUSTING SCREWS
0120840					481	100	KNURLED SCREW 10/32-3/8
0130159	471	13					SHOULDER SCREW
0150026					481	100	CHECK NUT 3/4-16
0171504			476	100			SPACER
0171629					481	10	FELT GUARD STANDOFF
0171690					481	10	FELT GUARD STANDOFF
0180101	471	200					OILITE PSHG 5/16-7/16-5/16
0190206					481	200	SPRING
0190732					481	11	RES POT SPRING
0200382					481	30	DRIVE PINION
0210040					481	300	BEARING NO 77603
0210085			476	1000			BALL BRG NO 77R4A
0210141			476	100			ROD END BRG CFS-6B
0210148					481	100	PILLOW BLOCK
0230373					481	20	PT EXTENSION SHFT
0230517					481	62	CARTRIDGE HEATER 120V 300W
0240037					481	20	PUSHBUTTON SWITCH
0240268	471	30					TAPE END SWITCH
0250274	471	10					GEARMOTOR
0250424	471	7					MOTOR 110/220 50 1 1425
0260097					481	12	MACHINE TABLE

Order
quantity

Number of the
day that begins
the current week
on the shop
calendar

Source: Markem Corporation (A) case, by E. W. Davis and W. J. B. Lake, ICH No. 9-673-001, 1972.

damping the response of MRP systems in later sections of this chapter.

In concluding this segment on implementation, feedback, and control with MRP systems, we should note that in addition to ordering,

Figure 7–12
Markem exception list

RUN DATE - 11/28/72 REQUIREMENTS PLANNING EXCEPTION REPORT

ITEM NUMBER	EXCEPTION CODE	REQUIREMENT DATE	REQUIREMENT QUANTITY
0320352+5	04	481	15
0324966+5	04	486	50
0325128+10	04	491	200
0325149+10	04	501	100
	04	486	6
0330056+5	04	511	40
0330090+10	04	496	100
0330193+10	04	516	10
0330333+10	04	516	200
0330593+5	04	511	50
0331760+5	04	486	15
0332512+10	04	531	30
0339070+15	04	501	80
0339073+15	04	501	40
0339074+15	04	501	40
0339086+15	04	496	40
0339087+15	04	491	40
0339090+15	04	501	40
0339112+10	04	501	100
0339114+10	04	496	100
0339302+15	04	501	100
0339497+15	04	511	20
0339499+10	04	511	200
0339779+10	04	521	500
0339835+15	04	486	200
0340014+5	04	501	32
0340029+10	04	481	24
0340221+5	04	486	600
0350004+10	04	511	12
0350014+10	04	541	10,000
0360003+10	04	481	20
0380273+10	04	551	30
0380277+10	04	486	13
0380326+5	04	506	100
0390023+10	04	511	35
0390195+10	04	536	600
0390202+10	04	526	400
0390359+30	04	506	10
0390511+10	04	491	12

Source: Markem Corporation (A) case, by E. W. Davis and W. J. B. Lake, ICH No. 9-673-001, 1972.

Figure 7–13
Markem Corporation exception report

RUN DATE - 10/17/72   REQUIREMENTS PLANNING EXCEPTION REPORT   PAGE   39

EXCEPTION CODE	EXCEPTION CONDITION EXPLANATION	EXCEPTION COUNT
03	OPEN ORDER EXISTS BUT ALL GROSS REQUIREMENTS COVERED BY ON HAND INVENTORY.	26
04	OPEN ORDER EXISTS THIS PERIOD BUT GROSS REQ. THIS PERIOD COVERED BY ON HAND.	212
05	OPEN ORDER EXISTS THIS PERIOD BUT WILL NOT COVER GROSS REQ. THIS PERIOD.	1
06	NET REQ. EXISTS THIS PERIOD BUT AN OPEN ORDER IS DUE IN A FUTURE PERIOD.	253
07	OPEN ORDER IS DUE THIS PERIOD BUT NO GROSS REQ. EXISTS FOR THIS PERIOD.	179
08	REQ. OFFSET INTO A PAST PERIOD. REQ. HAS BEEN PLACED IN FIRST TIME PERIOD.	105
11	THIS OPEN ORDER NOT IN PLANNING HORIZON, CONSIDERED AVAILABLE IN FIRST PERIOD.	161
15	ALLOCATED QTY EXCEEDS AVAIL. FOR NET. DIFFERENCE ADDED IN 1ST GROSS PERIOD.	78
18	THIS QTY. IS A PAST DUE GROSS REQ. THAT IS INCLUDED IN THE FIRST TIME PERIOD.	53
19	OPEN ORDER IS DUE THIS PERIOD BUT NET REQUIREMENTS EXIST IN A PAST PERIOD.	163

END OF REPORT -   1,241 EXCEPTION CONDITIONS FOUND THIS RUN.

Source: Markem Corporation (A) case, by E. W. Davis and W. J. B. Lake, ICH No. 9-673-001, 1972.

expediting, rescheduling, and so on there are several other more normal, but no less important tasks that must be accomplished. The execution of orders implies the removal of stock from stockrooms and delivery to production areas, procurement, production, and receiving and inspection. The accomplishment of these essential tasks, and reports of their completion, are essential to the operation of this type of system, as with any other. The maintenance of data integrity through accurate and timely transactions reporting is particularly important with MRP systems. A glance at Figure 7–8 illustrates that errors in on-hand or on-order balances can be reflected in all downstream dependent items. In a sense, inventory reporting errors are exploded down through an MRP system, along with good data, compounding the effect of errors at all levels.

Design considerations

MRP systems are not monolithic, standardized entities. The way in which MRP is applied in various kinds of manufacturing operations varies considerably, depending upon the technology, economics, organization structure, and competitive strategy that a firm may exhibit. Unfortunately, this is not always recognized. While there are many optional features that can be used to advantage in some MRP systems, such as firm planned orders [19], and automatic rescheduling, these are essentially technical in nature. At a more general level, the major design considerations that face firms who wish to use MRP include the way in which the firm defines bills of material to fit organizational, technical, and marketing constraints, and the decisions made to inhibit or increase the sensitivity of the system to change.

To illustrate the importance of what many may consider a rather mundane task, structuring a bill of materials, consider a firm whose product structure is similar to that shown in Figure 7–14. This type of product structure might be found in a furniture factory where demand is seasonal, and fabric styles change frequently (See for example [22]). This product structure implies that the furniture operation is composed of two distinctively different types of processes, an assembly/upholstery operation in which fabrics, springs, and so on

Figure 7–14
Production structure for a furniture company

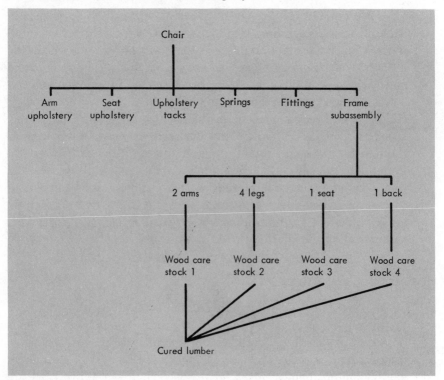

are fitted to a chair frame, and a woodworking shop where chair arms, legs, and so on are formed on saws, lathes, and sanders into various wooden parts for the chair frame. In many such operations, wooden parts are built to stock, while upholstered chairs are finished to customer order. Moreover, the firm may wish to apply a level production strategy with seasonal inventory buildups in the wood-working shop to minimize the training of skilled workers, while the work force of the upholstery/assembly operation may be allowed to vary with demand since the rapid style changes in fabrics would threaten large inventories of finished chairs with obsolescence.

The bill of materials shown in Figure 7–14 could be used as the basis for control in a furniture factory such as this. However, it would be very difficult for such a system to recognize the differences between the two kinds of manufacturing processes that are implied by it. A single master schedule at the finished chair level would cause the seasonal nature of end item production to be transmitted down into the woodworking shop regardless of desires to level production there. Moreover, managing the two types of processes at the central level that this structure implies would not allow managers to distinguish between the types of demands (customer orders versus inventory replenishment orders) they placed on two different classes of workers, and on two different types of process technologies. Administratively, management may wish to run the two processes as if they were separate companies, or to *decouple* their operations. The same situation would apply, but perhaps more clearly, were the woodworking portion of the process located in a separate location 500 miles away.

If a decision is made to decouple operations from the planning and control standpoint, then the bill of materials must be structured in an entirely different way. Two *modular* bills of material must be constructed which recognize the differences *and* the links between the two operations. The first might be an assembly bill, such as that shown in Figure 7–15(a). An assembly master schedule based on actual customer orders would be used to drive the portion of the MRP system that applied here. The output of the system at this level would indicate which wooden parts should be pulled from stock-rooms, and the relative priorities of orders for fabric, springs, and so on. Figure 7–15(b) indicates the second "decoupled" bill that would be used to plan and control wood fabricating. This fabrication bill or M (for manufacturing) bill would be driven by a *second* master schedule defined in terms of basic chair subassemblies instead of

Figure 7–15

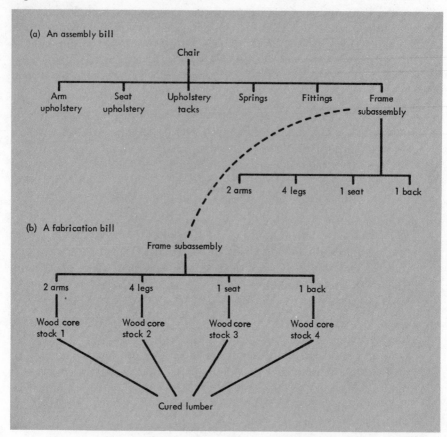

finished chairs. With a second master schedule and bill, there is no problem in leveling out production in the woodworking shop, while maintaining a dotted line informational relationship to assembly operations. The purpose of this second MRP system, if you will, is to pull frame parts up into the stockroom in a manner consistent with the needs of the firm.

Master scheduling for fabrication would recognize that demand for chair parts must be forecasted and built to inventory, rather than to customer order. Master scheduling at the assembly level would be largely concerned with assembly schedules and customer order entry. Thus, decoupling with modular bills of material focuses efforts at each level in on the most important tasks to be accomplished. A second advantage of this approach is that it often results in better forecasts of production needs at lower levels in the product structure. Were a single master schedule and a single bill used to drive the whole system, the master schedule at the end item (finished chair) level would have to project planned output for each chair at least as far out into the future as the sum of the lead times through wood part manufacture. If the firm had 800 basic fabrics which were put on 100 different frame styles this would mean that long-term forecasts for $100 \times 800 = 80,000$ different end item chairs would have to be made. A difficult and time-consuming task that would probably result in forecasts with gross inaccuracies. The reason for forecasting however is so that the 100 chair styles can be built to inventory. With a second fabrication master schedule, only the demand of the 100 chair styles needs to be forecasted. A simpler task, and one which is likely to result in better forecasts.

A related alternative is useful in cases where factories build a large number of end products to stock, but where groups or families of products are quite similar except for one or two minor differences in some dependent materials. In this case, "superbills" [19] can be created to ease the forecasting and master scheduling task, and to increase the firm's flexibility to react flexibly to changes in demand. Figure 7–16 shows bills for two different products that differ only in a minor component that has a very short lead time, and that determines whether the machine can use AC or DC current. If instrument A has 75 percent of the total demand for the product family composed of these two instruments, and instrument B has 25 percent of the demand, then the superbill shown in Figure 7–16(b) can be created. Clearly, a product called an "electronic instrument family" is never actually produced, but this type of *planning bill* can be very useful for longer range material requirements planning purposes. First, it reduces the number of items that must be identified in a master schedule; second, it increases forecasting accuracy since positive and negative forecasting errors for the individual products in the family are likely to be canceled out; and third, it can increase flexibility in the short term. Flexibility can be achieved since the actual product to be produced only needs to be identified at the last moment (before the short lead time AC or DC adapters are ordered). This approach however also implies the need for two master schedules and two sets of bills. A longer range planning bill and master schedule can be used to guide the production of the basic instrument up to the point in time where options are added. A short-range mas-

Figure 7–16
Superbills of material

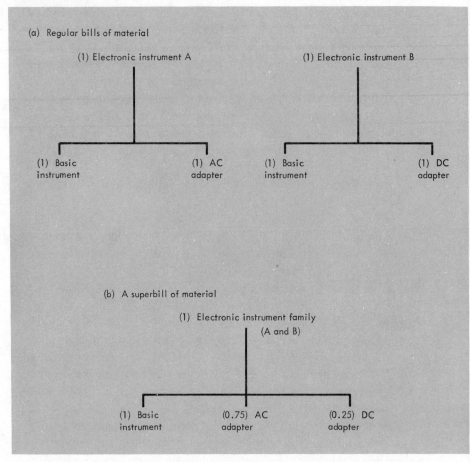

ter assembly schedule and a complete or regular set of bills must be used in the short term to guide the last stages of assembly [10, 19].

The second major design consideration that bears examination by firms who are considering the use of MRP is how much flexibility and responsiveness they would like the system to exhibit. Different firms may make different choices here because of the nature of the markets they serve, their approach to the market, financial and administrative considerations, and the nature of their suppliers. For example, some firms choose to compete largely on the basis of rapid and dependable delivery, but do not have the financial resources to maintain large inventories to support it. For them a net change MRP system, which by its nature is extremely responsive and sensitive may be employed. Net change systems are constructed so that changes in inventory balances or demands are immediately reflected in material requirements plans in an "on-line" mode.

A second firm that also competes on the basis of delivery and service may elect to maintain large finished goods inventories because of different financial, technical, or competitive factors. Finished goods inventories can buffer the manufacturing system from changes in demand, and may mean that a less responsive *regenerative* MRP system can be used. Regenerative systems are not "on line" like net change systems. Here, material requirements plans for dependent items are "regenerated" at periodic intervals, say every week or two weeks.[1] Since plans are updated less frequently, fewer exceptions are reported.

Yet a third firm may consider the minimization of costs and inventories as the most important factor in manufacturing, and will find that excessive and trivial schedule changes and "expedites" cause manufacturing costs to rise. If customer service is of secondary importance, such firms may dampen the responsiveness of MRP systems by "freezing" the master schedule for some fixed interval. This implies that no changes in the master schedule are allowed for, say, ten weeks into the future on a rolling basis. Schedule freezes or "planning fences" protect the factory from variations in demand, but not from uncertainties on the supply side. Reschedules may still be required because of changes in supply conditions, such as late deliveries, and scrap.

A fourth firm may employ schedule freezes to protect their vendors from excessive changes. Some adopters of MRP systems have found that their suppliers have rebelled at their demands to constantly change delivery schedules. Smaller companies in particular, who do not have a great deal of leverage over larger suppliers, have found that the good advice of their system to expedite simply cannot be implemented because of the refusal of major suppliers to cooperate. Many firms [16] have successfully overcome this type of problem by inventing new types of purchase agreements, seeking new vendors, or educating current suppliers about their programs.

Even the choice of lot sizing methods can affect the responsiveness of MRP systems. Biggs, Goodman, and Hardy [2] have reported that

---

[1] Since net change-type systems are often more computationally efficient than regenerative systems, it is not uncommon to find a firm using a net change system in a regenerative mode.

in a series of simulation experiments on an MRP system under uncertainty, the economic order quantity method outperformed more esoteric and theoretically more accurate lot sizing procedures such as the period order quantity and the Wagner-Whitin algorithm. They concluded that the reason was that a fixed order quantity lent some stability to the system, while procedures which could result in changes in the size of an order every time demand forecasts changed were overly sensitive.

Performance characteristics. In one sense, it is difficult to comment on the performance of MRP systems in general, because MRP, as we have shown, is a generic term that is applicable to a broad number of systems. MRP systems have explosion, time phasing, and priority setting characteristics in common. Different bill of materials structuring approaches and different strategies for amplifying or moderating the sensitivity of the basic MRP logic however, result in vast differences in both system applications and resulting performance characteristics.

In general, one would expect that the more that an MRP system's response capabilities are dampened by such devices as master schedule freezes, safety stocks, and prohibitions against vendor schedule changes, the less impact some of the theoretical advantages of MRP will have. However, the logic of planning dependent items on the basis of their real needs, and projecting inventories so that shortages and overages can be predicted before they occur and so that priorities can be changed accordingly, is compelling. In comparison to the reorder point systems that were discussed earlier in this chapter, the advantages of MRP systems are the converse of their disadvantages:

1. MRP systems link dependent demand from one level of the product structure to another providing accurate reflections of the real need for production.
2. Aggregate planning and master scheduling decisions are reflected at lower levels of the product structure, ensuring consistent decisions as the basic directions of manufacturing change.
3. MRP systems recognize "lumpy" demand resulting in lower inventories.
4. MRP systems recognize the relationships *between* dependent items, ensuring better service.
5. MRP systems expose the full range of potential decisions that can be made to management, including expediting, de-expediting, changing the master schedule.

6. MRP systems allow valid priorities to be maintained. This can result in improved capacity utilization.

The disadvantages of MRP systems are inherent in the cost of developing them, and the demands they create for skilled and astute managers to operate them. The initial costs of an MRP system are high when compared with a manual system that does not require computerization. This does not imply that the benefits associated with an MRP system do not outweigh their costs, they often do. The development of planners and managers who can manage with an MRP system is often the greater challenge, however. Orlicky, one of the leading proponents and early developers of the MRP concept calls MRP "a new way of life in manufacturing" [19]. Finding and educating people so that they can work effectively and creatively in this "new way of life" is the key to the successful implementation of MRP systems.

CAPACITY REQUIREMENTS PLANNING

In industries and manufacturing companies that exhibit product structures similar to that shown in Figure 7–1(b), capacity planning can be accomplished at the aggregate planning or master scheduling level alone. This is possible because production activities are focused at a single level, the assembly of purchased parts and components, and on a single process, an assembly line. Manufacturing firms that have vertically integrated production systems, however, face a different problem. For them, aggregate capacity plans and master schedules focused on the end product assembly level disregard the capacity decisions that must be made downstream for "feeder" processes.

The process flows of the Markem Corporation are typical of integrated fabrication/assembly operations. Figure 7–17 is a crude depiction of the two major types of processes that are employed at Markem. The first is an assembly operation where subassemblies and final machines are created. Considered by itself, this portion of the factory would have a dependent product structure much like that shown in Figure 7–1(b). The "feeder" operation into which Markem has integrated is a general purpose job shop where parts are fabricated and machined. Here, parts are produced on a series of different machines, or machine centers. For example, a part may be produced in three steps, sawing, grinding, and drilling. Thus, capacity plans for the company must include plans not only at the assembly level,

Figure 7-17
Process flows in an integrated manufacturing system

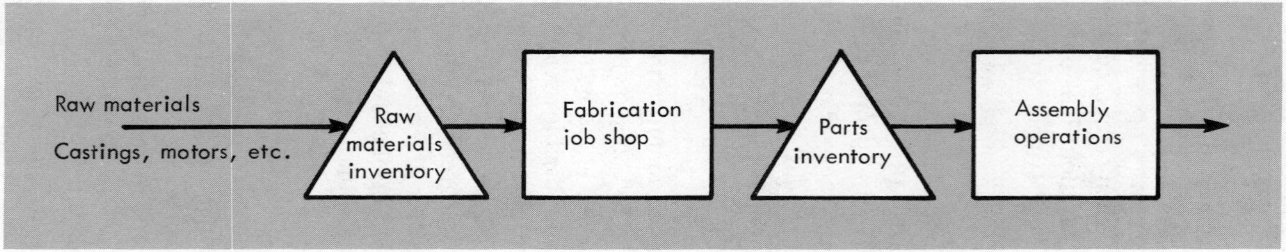

but also at the job shop level, and within it, capacities for machines, such as saws, grinders, and drills, must be considered.

As we noted earlier, one option for operations planning, including capacity planning, is to decouple various manufacturing processes administratively. For Markem, this can be accomplished by creating an aggregate plan and master schedule for each process segment, one for assembly and one for the job shop. When administrative and control considerations indicate that decoupling is undesirable, other capacity planning methods must be considered. Capacity requirements planning techniques offer one solution. These techniques are also useful within the context of decoupled operations. For example, within Markem's job shop, the load on each machine must also be considered. Capacity planning at master scheduling levels here may well obscure potential bottlenecks at one machine or machine center.

Capacity requirements planning involves exploding projected demands on capacity from the data yielded by a material requirements planning system. Conceptually, this is relatively easy, although it usually requires extensive data manipulation and the use of a computer. The basic data input to capacity requirements planning systems is a unit load profile which indicates how much time is required to produce an item at each major processing step. Figure 7–18 illustrates a unit load profile for a part that is produced on a

Figure 7–18
A unit load profile: Part no. 6030744

Weeks after order issued	Operation	Production time per unit (hours)
1	Saw (first operation)	0.30
2		
3	Grinder (second operation)	0.10
4		
5	Drill press (last operation)	0.05

saw, a grinder, and then a drill press. The production time per unit indicates the number of hours required to process the part at each operation. The time denotes the week after a production order for the part is released that the part will be operated on by a particular machine. Thus, part number 6030744 must be operated on by the drill press just before completion, or five weeks after the order is issued. Normally, all of the work on a part at one machine is assumed to be completed during the week that it is assigned, although this is not necessary. The gaps in timing shown in the unit load profile indicate times when a part is not being worked on; queue time, and move time, for example. These time considerations are normally defined when lead times are determined for manufactured parts.

Figure 7–19 shows how unit load profiles are combined with

Figure 7–19
Machine load projections

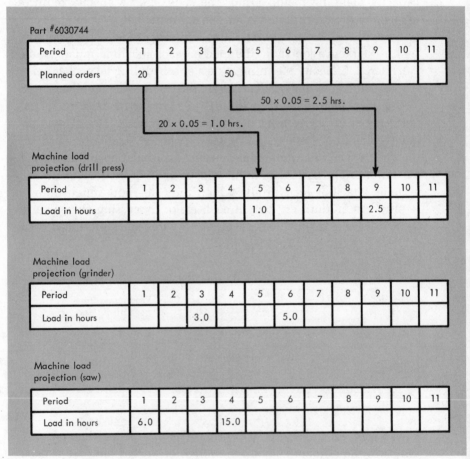

planned order projections from MRP systems to produce a forecast of the load at each machine or processing step. For example, the issuance of an order for part number 6030744 at the beginning of period 1, will create the demand for $20 \times 0.05 = 1.0$ hours of capacity on the drill press (the last operation) five weeks after the order is issued. Similarly, the order will generate a load on the saw (the first operation) in week number 1. The load on these machines can be cumulated for other parts that create demands on them as well. The end result is usually a load report similar to that shown in Figure 7–20, for each machine or process. This report projects the hours of

Figure 7–20

AS OF 294 — PROJECTED WEEKLY MACHINE LOAD REPORT
WORK CENTER 015 050   BLANCHARD   BLANC GRIND   DATE 03/01/72

	299	304	309	314	319	324	329	334	339	344	349	354	359
RELEASED LOAD	69	19	23	51	25	9	19	19	8	12	37	8	4
PLANNED LOAD						1	6	2	21	43	31	47	19
TOTAL LOAD	69	19	23	51	25	10	25	21	29	55	68	55	23
CAPACITY	35	35	35	35	35	35	35	35	35	35	35	35	35
AVERAGE LOAD				41			20				52		
AVAILABLE HOURS	34-	16	12	16	10	25	10	14	6	20-	33-	20-	12

	364	369	374	379	384	389	394	399	404	409	414	419	424
RELEASED LOAD	2		3	12	6					4	6		
PLANNED LOAD	29	11	3	13	42	9	19	34	15	33	8	3	5
TOTAL LOAD	31	11	6	25	48	9	19	34	15	37	14	3	5
CAPACITY	35	35	35	35	35	35	35	35	35	35	35	35	35
AVERAGE LOAD			18				25				25		
AVAILABLE HOURS	4	24	29	10	13-	26	16	1	20	2-	21	32	30

Source: Markem Corporation (B) by B. W. Davis and W. J. B. Lake, ICH No. 9-673-002, 1972.

work that are generated by an MRP system in two ways. First, it projects the planned load from MRP planned orders in much the same way as we have done with the previous example. Second, it also projects the remaining load generated by orders that have been released, but not yet completed. This is the "released" load that is referred to. The value of capacity requirements planning is indicated by a comparison of the total load row with the capacity (in hours). Load reports indicate when serious under- or over-loads are going to develop before they happen. This provides management with the ability, and the time, to plan alternative courses of action, such as subcontracting, expediting or rescheduling to smooth loads, using overtime, or possibly, revising the master schedule.

The methods of capacity requirements planning discussed in this chapter are based on the simplest approach to the subject. Here we have projected capacity requirements purely on the basis of actual and planned materials orders, and have disregarded capacity availability, and the detailed scheduling problems associated with moving work through a series of work centers. This approach is called "*infinite capacity loading*" since it does not explicitly consider actual capacity limitations or sequence restrictions into account. In Chapters 11 and 13 we will discuss more sophisticated *finite capacity loading* techniques [7]. They are based on simulating the effect of planned work while taking priority dispatch rules, and capacity limitations into account in determining process lead times.

SUMMARY

Planning and controlling inventories for dependent demand items requires that some of the familiar tools we have used for independent demand items be applied in substantially different ways. The reorder point/order quantity logic of the fixed reorder quantity systems discussed in Chapter 4 can be applied with some modifications to dependent item control. Several disadvantages accrue to such applications, such as the lack of coordination between dependent items at different levels in a product structure hierarchy, as well as items at the same level destined for use in the same end product. Moreover, it is difficult to link directional decisions regarding end item output made in aggregate plans or master schedules, with decisions for dependent items. The major advantages of these systems are their conceptual simplicity, and the fact that computers are not necessary to implement them in their simplest form.

By way of contrast, MRP systems employ the time phased inventory planning logic discussed in Chapter 4, coupled with the explosion logic suggested by the dependent relationships shown in a bill of materials. MRP systems avoid most of the disadvantages of reorder point systems, and in addition, provide a framework for priority determination on the basis of actual needs. These systems are quite demanding from a managerial standpoint, since they expose many of the options that can be considered to view. The execution of many of these options poses difficult negotiation and communication problems. The design of MRP systems is fraught with important questions regarding bill of materials structuring and the management of uncertainty. The answers to these questions depend upon the technology, financial condition, competitive strategy, and supply constraints of individual firms. As a result, the term MRP systems describes a generic variety of systems which have a few features in common, but which are largely distinctive in practice.

Capacity requirements planning systems are useful for projecting capacity requirements in vertically integrated manufacturing operations, and in job shops where the load on individual machines must be considered to avoid bottlenecks. They use the planned orders generated by MRP systems, together with unit load profiles to project capacity loads. Machine load reports that result can be used to indicate the need for subcontracting, rescheduling, or overtime.

REVIEW QUESTIONS AND PROBLEMS

1. Take a simple product with which you are familiar, such as a mechanical pencil or pen. Using this product as an example of a finished item, draw a product structure diagram that outlines the parts and components that are used to create it. What major manufacturing policy and design decisions are inherent in your assumptions about the way this product is made?

2. Contrast the data generation, decision making and planning, and implementation, feedback, and control elements of reorder point versus MRP systems. Which is the most complex? What are the advantages and disadvantages of reorder point systems? MRP systems?

3. An end product is batch assembled from 48 different parts and components. The parts and components are controlled by a reorder point system, and safety stocks for each have been set with reference to a service level of 0.95. What is the probability that all of the parts and components will be available when it is time to assemble a batch of the finished product?

4. Referring to Figure 7–8, assume that the master schedule has been changed as follows: 4 units in period 2, 6 units in period 7, and 20 units in period 10. Using the data in Figures 7–6 and 7–7, derive new inventory plans for the treadle subassembly, the treadle pivot, and the casting.

5. Given your answer to Question 4, list the decisions that your new plans indicate should be made. What alternatives do you have? How would you go about deciding what to do?

6. Refer back to the Avalon Machinery Company case at the end of Chapter 4. Speculate on how bills of material would be structured in this case. How can independent and dependent demand items be simultaneously considered within the context of an MRP system?

7. Referring to Figure 7–19, derive the additional load in hours associated with planned orders for 100 and 200 units in periods 3 and 7.

8. How can data such as that shown in Figure 7–20 be used in decision making?

SELECTED BIBLIOGRAPHY

1. Berry, W. L. "Lot Sizing Procedures for Requirements Planning Systems: A Framework for Analysis," *Production and Inventory Management*, 2d quarter 1972, pp. 19–34.

2. Biggs, J. R.; Goodman, S. H.; and Hardy, S. T. "Lot Sizing Rules in a Hierarchical Multi-Stage Inventory System," *Production and Inventory Management*, 1st quarter 1977.

3. Chase, R. B., and Acquilano, N. J. *Production and Operations Management: A Life Cycle Approach.* rev. ed. Homewood, Ill.: Richard D. Irwin, Inc., 1977.

4. *Communications Oriented Production and Inventory Control Systems* (COPICS). IBM Corporation, 1972.

5. Davis, E. W., and Lake, W. J. B. "Markem Corporation (A) and (B), ICH No. 9-673-001 and 9-673-002, 1972.

6. Greene, H. J. *Production and Inventory Control.* rev. ed. Homewood, Ill.: Richard Irwin, Inc., 1974.

7. Holstein, W. K. "Production Planning and Control Integrated," *Harvard Business Review*, May–June 1968.

8. Lee, W. B., and McLaughlin, C. P. "Corporate Simulation Models for Aggregate Materials Management," *Production and Inventory Management*, 1st quarter 1974, pp. 56–67.

9. "Material Requirements Planning by Computer," *American Production and Inventory Control Society*, 1971, p. 86.

10. Miller, J. G. "Benson Electronics (B), ICH No. 9-677-013, 1976.

11. Miller, J. G. "Granger Transmission Co. (A), (B), (C)," ICH No. 9-675-201, 9-675-202 and 9-675-203, 1975.

12. Miller, J. G. "The Perkin Elmer Instrument Division," ICH No. 9-676-082, 1975.

13. Miller, J. G.; Berry, W. L.; and Lai, C. F. "A Comparison of Alternative Forecasting Strategies for Multi-Stage Production-Inventory Systems," *Decision Sciences*, October, 1976.

14. Miller, J. G., and Sprague, L. G. "Behind the Growth in Material Requirements Planning," *Harvard Business Review*, vol. 53 (October 1975), pp. 83–91.

15. Moodie, C. L., and Novotny, D. J. "Computer Scheduling and Control Systems for Discrete Part Production," *Journal of Industrial Engineering*, vol. 19, no. 7 (July 1967), pp. 648–71.

16. "Move to MRP Systems Helped Steelcase Boom," *Purchasing*, January 25, 1977.

17. New, C. *Requirements Planning.* New York: Halsted Press, 1974.

18. Orlicky, J. A. "Net Change Material Requirements Planning," *IBM Systems Journal*, vol. 12, no. 1 (1973).

19. Orlicky, J. A. *Material Requirements Planning*. New York: McGraw-Hill Book Co., 1975.

20. Orlicky, J. A. "Rescheduling with Tomorrow's MRP System," *Production and Inventory Management*, vol. 17, no. 2 (1976), p. 38.

21. Orlicky, J. A.; Plossl, G. W., and Wight, O. W. "Structuring the Bill of Material for MRP," *Production and Inventory Management*, vol. 13, no. 4 (1972).

22. Rosenbloom, R., and Dooley, A. R. "Chaircraft Corporation (R)," ICH No. 9-677-092, 1976. (Revisions by W. K. Holstein and S. Wheelwright.)

23. Thurston, P. H. "Pittsfield Manufacturing Company," ICH No. 9-613-068, 1966.

24. Thurston, P. H. "Requirements Planning for Inventory Control," *Harvard Business Review*, May/June 1972.

25. Wight, O. W. "To Order Point or Not to Order Point," *Production and Inventory Management*, vol. 9, no. 3 (1968).

26. Wight, O. W. *Production Planning and Inventory Management in the Computer Age*. Boston: Cahners Books, 1974.

CASE STUDY
HOT LINE, INCORPORATED

EARLY IN THE MORNING OF AUGUST 28, 1972, Mr. Ted Capitani, vice president of manufacturing for Hot Line, was discussing a proposal to adopt a new system for planning and controlling production with Hal Jaskiewicz. Jaskiewicz, manager of production planning and a recent MBA, had proposed the new system in a memo (Exhibit 1), several weeks earlier. As Capitani rose from his desk to end the meeting, he said:

> Hal, I don't know. What you have described makes sense so far. But so did the system that those consultants designed for us three years ago. We paid them $65,000 to design and install our present system and put a lot of our own time and effort into it. But the end result was the same as it always seems to be when we open up this can of worms. Some people are enthusiastic, others get very upset, and in the end it turns out that inventories, stockouts and costs are as high as ever. Our foremen, and other people on the shop floor, have devised their own way of doing things to make up for the deficiencies in our present system, and Jack Wyzicki [VP Marketing] still hasn't forgiven us for all the lost sales which resulted when we went through the start-up phase, and for all the extra work that his people have to do to make it work. I'm going to have to give some more thought to this issue, and its implications for the whole company, before I can commit myself.

Company background

Hot Line began operations in 1956 when they introduced their Hot Line series of monofilament fishing lines. The rapid growth of this product line led to the development and manufacture of a companion line of spin casting reels. More recently, the company had started to manufacture and market a pilot line of spinning rods. These products were marketed through distributors to small sporting goods and

Exhibit 1

Memorandum

August 11, 1972

To: T. Capitani
From: H. Jaskiewicz
Re: Production Planning and Control Systems

Our recent problems with finished goods stockouts and high inventories have been somewhat ameliorated since we began to hold our monthly scheduling meetings. I believe that the improved communications which have resulted are largely responsible for the decline in back orders as a percent of sales from 9 percent to 8 percent, and the improvement in inventory turnover from 4 times per year to 4.5 times per year. However, I do not believe that we have yet uncovered the root of our problems. Clearly, we still have a long way to go before our operating statistics are as good as those of our competitors.

Since I took over as Manager of Production Planning and Control last spring, I have been uneasy about our present system for planning and controlling production. I began to study it closely a few months ago, and I believe that more than anything else, it is the reason for our remaining inventory and stockout problems. It is now easy for me to explain why this is true. Look at the reason for most of our stockouts. It's because we simply don't have all of the *component parts* required to assemble our products at the times that we have scheduled assembly runs to take place. When this happens, we can't produce on time to replenish finished goods inventory, and back orders result. Similarly, if we look at where most of the inventory is in our system, we find that a substantial portion of it is in *component parts*, either those purchased outside or produced from within. Clearly, our problem is that we have *too many* of the *wrong* component parts in inventory.

This occurs because in our present planning and control system, we treat assembly and parts production and ordering as two separate, unrelated entities. For example, last month we had 2,000 Model 1198 spinning reels scheduled for assembly on line number two. But, when we went to get the parts which were to be assembled, we found we only had 1,200 drag gears in stock. Why did we only have 1,200 instead of 2,000? Because under our system we schedule assembly as if we had all the parts we needed, and we schedule parts production and purchases using an EOQ, reorder point rule which acts as if component parts were finished goods items. On drag gears, our rule is to order 4,000 parts (the EOQ) every time our stock levels are drawn down to 1,000 parts (the reorder point). The reorder point is set by determining the average demand for drag gears over the lead time it takes to purchase them. The problem is,

Exhibit 1 (continued)

we never assemble an "average" amount since demand just doesn't behave that way.

I am recommending that we adopt a requirements planning system to
replace our present system. Requirements planning ties together assembly and parts production and will certainly allow us to reduce both inventories and stockouts significantly. Essentially it works like this. First,
we make out our master assembly schedule much as we do now. Then,
instead of hoping that the component parts are there when we expect to
need them for assembly, we "explode" parts requirements using a bill of
materials. Bills of materials are lists of all of the parts required to assemble one unit of a finished product. Explosion means that we multiply the
quantity of items we have scheduled for assembly in a month by the
number of units of each component part which is required to assemble it.
For instance, if we had 2,000 Model 1198s scheduled for production in
two months, by exploding we could see that we need to have 2,000 drag
gears on hand at the time of assembly, no more, no less. Since we know
the purchasing lead time on drag gears is about one month, then we can
plan to order 2,000 one month from now. This way, we'll keep inventories
down since we won't be ordering and holding parts before we need them.
Stockouts will be reduced because we'll have the right parts on hand
when we need them.

I am sure that you can appreciate the beauty of the requirements planning system that I am proposing. It is elegant in its simplicity. Moreover, I
am sure that it will be easy to adapt to. We will need to purchase a larger
computer to handle the explosions for our 123 finished goods items and
3,700 parts, and we will need to construct bills of materials. But after
these tasks are completed, and we have a few training sessions with the
people involved, I am sure that we will have it up and running in no time.

I shall schedule a meeting with you in the next few weeks to define and
discuss this proposal with you further.

hardware stores, and on a direct basis to large retailers. As might be
expected, sales were seasonal, with peaks in the spring, and in December. Hot Line had adopted an aggressive marketing strategy to
complement their high-quality products. Sales and profits (Exhibit
2) had been increasing at a rapid rate.

Manufacturing operations for the three product lines were all carried out in Hot Line's new facility in South Bend, Indiana. Monofilament line and plastic rod blanks were molded in the plastics
department of the plant where plastic reel covers and handles were

Exhibit 2
Financial data

Income Statements
Years Ending December 31, 1970 and December 31, 1971

	1971 ($000)	1970 ($000)
Net sales	$36,300	$28,670
Cost of goods sold		
Direct labor	4,060	2,960
Materials	14,750	10,510
Manufacturing overhead	4,290	3,500
	$23,100	$16,970
Gross profit	$13,200	$11,700
General and administrative	1,930	1,520
Marketing	10,470	8,610
	$12,400	$10,130
Profit before taxes	$ 800	$ 1,570
Provision for income taxes	330	720
Net Profit	$ 470	$ 850

Balance Sheets
As of December 31, 1970 and December 31, 1971

Assets	December 31, 1971 ($000)	December 31, 1970 ($000)
Current Assets		
Cash	$ 60	$ 530
Accounts Receivable	6,460	4,990
Inventory	8,066	7,180
Other	190	240
Total Current Assets	$14,776	$12,940
Fixed Assets		
Net Fixed Assets	2,340	2,260
Total Assets	$17,116	$15,200

Liabilities		
Current Liabilities		
Notes Payable	2,866	3,520
Accounts Payable	4,720	2,980
Accruals	1,760	1,400
Total Current Liabilities	$ 9,346	$ 7,900
Long-term debt	2,030	2,030
Capital stock and surplus	1,500	1,500
Earned surplus	4,240	3,770
Net worth	$ 5,740	$ 5,270
Total Liabilities and Net Worth	$17,116	$15,200

also fabricated. Completed plastic component parts were stored in the manufactured component parts storeroom. These parts were periodically withdrawn from stock, along with parts from the purchased component parts stockroom, and used in one of the three assembly areas of the plant. The first assembly line was devoted to line winding and packaging, the second line to the assembly of spinning reels, and the third line was for spinning rod assembly. Exhibit 3 shows the manufacturing organization in a partial organization chart for Hot Line. Exhibit 4 shows the layout of Hot Line's manufacturing facility.

Exhibit 3
Simplified organization chart

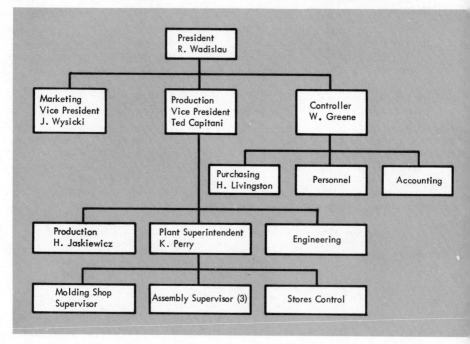

Hot Lines's current production planning and control system

Each month, production planning at Hot Line began with a six-month sales forecast that was prepared by marketing for each final product. The production planning and control department then compared the forecasted demand for each final product with the

Exhibit 4
Plant layout

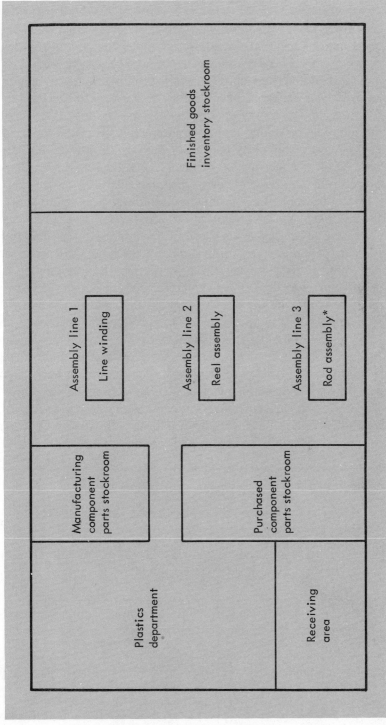

* Note: The capacity of the rod assembly line was 120 rods per day (2,400 rods per month). Two days were required to change over the line for producing a new product.

inventory balance to determine when an assembly lot should be scheduled. Sometimes, when Hal Jaskiewicz thought that marketing was too optimistic or pessimistic in their forecast, he revised them.

The size of an assembly lot was determined by an economic lot size analysis prepared by inventory controllers in the Production Planning and Control Department for each product. This analysis considered a product's annual requirements, the cost of holding inventory (estimated at 24 percent of item cost per year) and the assembly line changeover cost (estimated at $200 every time a line was prepared for the assembly of a different model).

The next step in the production planning process involved the preparation of a master assembly schedule. The master schedule was composed of three separate schedules, one for each assembly line. It indicated the planned starting and completion dates for each assembly lot for each item, for the next six months. Assembly master scheduling was done to ensure that those products in the most danger of stocking out were assembled first, and to check to see if sufficient assembly capacity existed to produce the lots which were scheduled. If the number of lots scheduled for a particular assembly line was greater than the capacity of an assembly line during a month, the start dates for lots were shifted around, or overtime was scheduled. If too few lots were scheduled to keep the assembly line workers busy, the start dates for some assembly lots were shifted forward to balance the work load. Exhibit 5 illustrates a portion of the master schedule for a six-month period.

Exhibit 5
Master schedule

Assembly line 2: Six-month reel production master schedule (in units)						
Model number	September	October	November	December	January	February
1198	1,400		1,640	1,600		1,400
1167		1,100		1,110		1,120
1120		1,240		1,500		1,600
1080	2,750		2,210		3,270	
1010					4,000	
1012	2,000	1,000		1,200	1,110	

The master schedule at this stage was discussed in the monthly scheduling meeting attended by Jaskiewicz, Capitani, Wyzicki, Perry, and Greene. These meetings served to notify those concerned of the current status of production, and plans for the immediate future. Frequently, the meetings resulted in changes in the master schedule, reflecting the desire of the plant superintendent to maintain a balanced work load, or of desires to keep inventories low. Last minute changes in forecasts were also a reason for changes in the master schedule. Jack Wyzicki, was the first to admit that marketing's forecasts were not very good. The three most recent forecasts for one rod model shown below (Table 1) illustrates his point. He felt that he could forecast distributor demand fairly well, but had difficulty forecasting the timing of large orders from major retailers.

Table 1
Forecast

Date of forecast	July	Aug.	Sept.	Oct.	Nov.	Dec.	Jan.	Feb.
June 15	1,000	1,000	900	900	1,300	1,500		
July 20		800	700	700	1,000	1,200	500	500
August 20			600	600	800	900	300	300

The completed master assembly schedule was distributed to the foremen at the start of each month. The foremen were responsible for obtaining the component parts needed to assemble scheduled final products, and for seeing that the assembly lines were set up according to schedule. They were also responsible for assigning their people to the various assembly stations, and for supervising the actual assembly operation.

The component parts for most of the company's products were inventoried in the appropriate stockrooms in the plant (see Exhibit 4). Many of these components were manufactured by Hot Line. Other parts were purchased from outside vendors. Both the manufactured and purchased parts were ordered in economic lot sizes. These lot sizes reflected an average ordering cost of $25, as well as the cost of carrying inventory. The reorder points for these component parts, i.e., the stock levels at which replenishment orders were triggered, were determined using historical demand data.

In spite of the careful attention that Jaskiewicz's inventory controllers paid to determining these reorder points and order quantities, one or more component parts were frequently unavailable on the designated date at which the assembly of an item was scheduled.

Exhibit 6
Spinning rod sales unit forecast (units)

	Inventory balance	September	October	November	December	January	February
Model 1107, 5-foot rod	1,540	600	600	800	900	300	400
Model 1269, 6-foot rod	320	200	200	400	500	500	500
Model 1301, 7-foot rod	500	600	700	900	1,000	800	800

Exhibit 7
Model 1107 bill of materials

Part number	Description	Number required per finished unit	Cost per unit*	Lead time†	Current inventory	On order‡
1107	Assembled rod	1	$3.00	—	1,540	—
610	Rod blank	1	1.00	1 month	300	—
107	Plastic beads§	0.3 lbs.	0.33 per lb.	1 month	3,000 lbs.	—
720	Cork handle and reel holder	1	0.75	2 months	2,890	845
647	Line guides	2	0.05	1 month	6,720	—
648	Line guides	2	0.05	1 month	5,400	—
649	Tip guide	1	0.07	1 month	3,210	—

* The unit costs represent the cost per unit for a component item, not the cost per unit of finished product.
† Note all component parts for spinning rod assemblies are purchased from outside vendors except for the rod blanks, which are molded by Hot Line.
‡ The order of cork handles is scheduled to arrive on October 1.
§ Plastic beads provide the raw material from which the rod blanks are made.

Exhibit 8
Model 1269 bill of materials

Part number	Description	Number required per finished unit	Cost per unit	Lead time	Current inventory	On order
1269	Assembled rod	1	$4.00	—	320	—
611	Rod blank	1	1.50	1 month	2,210	—
107	Plastic beads	0.3 lbs.	0.33 per lb.	1 month	3,000 lbs.	—
720	Cork handle and reel holder	1	0.75	2 months	2,890	845
647	Line guides	3	0.05	1 month	6,720	—
648	Line guides	2	0.05	1 month	5,400	—
649	Tip guide	1	0.07	1 month	3,210	—

Exhibit 9
Model 1301 bill of materials

Part number	Description	Number required per finished unit	Cost per unit	Lead time	Current inventory	On order
1301	Assembled rod	1	$5.00	—	500	—
617	Rod blank	1	2.00	1 month	1,030	—
107	Plastic beads	0.3 lbs.	0.33 per lb.	1 month	3,000 lbs.	—
720	Cork handle and reel holder	1	0.75	2 months	2,890	845
647	Line guides	3	0.05	1 month	6,720	—
648	Line guides	3	0.05	1 month	5,400	—
649	Tip guide	1	0.07	1 month	3,210	—

This resulted in delays in production, idle workers, or partially assembled products that sat in in-process inventory until the required component part could be obtained. The assembly foremen tried to avoid this problem by checking inventory levels themselves in advance of assembly, and, if need be, requesting that the molding shop foremen hurry up the production of required items, or that purchasing expedite the delivery of purchased components.

The walk to Barney's Diner

As Hal Jaskiewicz walked to Barney's Diner for lunch with Hank Livingston, a grizzled veteran from the Purchasing Department, he described his meeting with Capitani that morning, and the plan he had subsequently come up with:

Jaskiewicz: I don't know if I've got Capitani's support for this system or not. But I really believe that we need it if we're going to set things straight. I think I could start using it for rod manufacturing and assembly right now. I've got the latest rod forecast from marketing [Exhibit 6] and I've prepared bills of materials for each rod which contain cost and lead time data for all the component parts [Exhibits 7, 8, 9].

Livingston: Come on, you'll never make any kind of system work here. Look at what happens now. Those dingbats in marketing lie to you each month when they give you their inflated forecasts so they won't miss any sales. You adjust their forecasts and turn them into a master schedule. That's your lie. It's designed to keep the heat off you by making sure that we don't run out of finished goods. You give your lie to the assembly foremen who lie to the molding shop foreman so they can get their parts on time. You all come to me with your lies and get me to expedite purchased parts. So then I lie to a field rep by telling him I need a part in one week when I know I need it in two. He knows I'm lying but compounds it by reporting to his company that I need it in two days. Then their marketing dingbats lie to their production control people and so on and I eventually get the part in two weeks just like I knew I would. That is, unless you then tell me to cancel the order, in which case our vendors don't know whether to believe my lies or not. How do you ever expect to come up with a production control system that will work in a business filled with liars and dingbats?

PART III

PLANNING AND SCHEDULING FOR CONTINUOUS SYSTEMS

Chapter 8

Production planning for high-volume standardized products

SINCE HENRY FORD began to use the automated assembly line to produce high-volume, standardized (any color you want as long as it's black) products, the assembly line has come to represent the epitome of modern mass-production methods. While assembly lines in this pure form are somewhat less frequently encountered than many think, they do account for a sizable proportion of production in the United States. Moreover, many of the planning and control approaches that are appropriate for assembly lines are analogous to those used in other continuous process industries, such as pulp and paper, and chemicals. In all of these instances, the many fragmented, process steps associated with job shops and other intermittent types of production, have been joined together with moving assembly lines to create a single monolithic, production machine.

In the manufacture of most high-volume standardized products a great deal of the detailed scheduling problem is built into the integrated production process which has been designed and built to produce the specialized product in high volume. The sequence of operations, timing, balance, and production rate are all a part of the design of this giant integrated machine. Start a unit at the head end and the detailed scheduling of the sequence of events is largely taken care of by the production system design. It seems simple, just design the production system, set the rate of production, and everything else falls into place.

In fact, of course, it is not quite that simple. We are left with some significant questions: How do we set the production rate? How do we design the production system with the sequences required and with minimum labor requirements? How do we design this production system with enough flexibility that we still can have some control over the production rate and the amount produced? How do we coordinate raw material supplies with the production rate? How do we control inventories throughout the production-distribution system and react to the dynamics of the overall multistage system?

Let us attempt to establish two broad frames of reference, both of which have an impact on the planning for high-volume production. First, we will consider the planning problem in a broad context given the existence of a production system design and its constraints. This follows directly from our previous discussion of aggregate planning and master scheduling. Following from this we will develop general relationships of problems of balance of facilities and manning, product mix, detailed scheduling, and a recognition of the impact of the multistage nature of the system.

Second, we will then develop a broad view of the design of a production system for high-volume products involving the relationships between product design and process planning as well as the sequencing and balance of operations and labor requirements. Bound up in the production system design are some of the constraints which affect planning and scheduling. Coming out of the discussion will be the special problem of assembly line balance, on which a great deal of work has been done. Since it is a special problem we will cover balancing methods separately in Chapter 9. In the remainder of this chapter then, we will return to a discussion of the problems of designing high-volume integrated planning systems. We conclude with a discussion of the interrelationships between production planning and the extensive distribution systems which are characteristic of high-volume, mass-produced products.

Production planning in broad context

We have represented the broad outlines of the planning process in relation to the multistage production-distribution system in Figure 8–1. Note that the flow of material and the set of information time lags correspond to the multistage system of Figure 1–8. Therefore, in planning factory production we are often dealing with a multistage production-distribution system involving time lags which will have a profound effect on the behavior of the system as a whole. Within the "Company System under Managerial Control" and above the dashed line in Figure 8–1 we see the activities which are directly related to scheduling.

In Figure 8–1, forecasts of demand based on information concerning the progress of sales demand at the retail-consumer level, as well as order rates at the factory warehouse, are fed into the "forecasting model." The forecasting model produces period forecasts over the planning horizon for "aggregate planning," and the output of aggregate planning is a basic decision on production rates and work force levels for the upcoming period. Depending on the mode of aggregate planning used, a projected series of decisions for future periods in the planning horizon may also be included. From the basic decisions of aggregate planning then, we can either compute the overtime and subcontracting required, and the projected end of period inventory, or these data will be a part of the output of the aggregate planning procedures, depending on the aggregate planning approach used. To this point, then, we have been discussing the role of the aggregate planning methods developed in Chapters 5 and 6. Translating these aggregate plans into detailed working schedules and materials, facilities, and labor plans is our next task.

A factory cannot run on aggregate schedules. It needs to know what these schedules mean in terms of production rates for each type and size of product aggregated in the total, detailed raw material needs, and how to staff the production lines. Thus we see in Figure 8–1 that the aggregate must be broken down through an allocation of the total to types and sizes of products through knowledge of market trends, or through an analysis of product mix. The latter master scheduling problem is particularly important where the various product types and sizes were produced on time-shared equipment of limited capacity and the profitability of the various items was different.

At any rate a result of the allocation to types and sizes (master scheduling) gives basic information for "detailed scheduling," de-

Figure 8-1
Relationship of forecasts and aggregate and detailed scheduling to production-distribution systems for high-volume standardized products

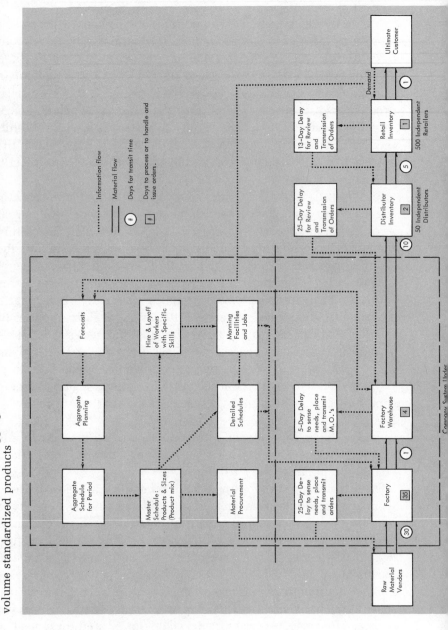

tailed "hiring and layoff" instructions, and "material procurement" schedules as shown in Figure 8–1. Conflicts in master schedules may occur at this point because of capacity limitations for both labor and facilities. Master scheduling involves setting individual type and size production rates and labor force schedules.

Finally, in setting the individual type and size production rates and labor force schedules, the scheduler may be faced with either great rigidity or reasonable flexibility depending on the nature of the processes and the design of the production system. An automotive production line is quite rigid in its nature in that once designed and set up it produces assembled autos at a fairly fixed hourly rate, since all operations have been balanced to coordinate with the preset hourly rate.

What flexibility do schedules then have to obtain a certain target weekly or monthly rate of output? They have basically two alternatives. They can schedule the work force on the line to work shorter or longer hours (including overtime), or they can rebalance the entire line to achieve a somewhat higher or lower hourly rate of output. Obviously, they would use the latter to achieve more drastic changes in output rate, since it involves hiring or laying off workers while simply changing hours worked is usually less expensive. But, the scheduler will be following the basic instructions given by the aggregate plan, which presumably has taken into account the relative costliness of changing production rates through changing hours, using overtime, and rebalancing (hiring and laying off). Thus the aggregate plan establishes the constraints under which the scheduler must perform. This discussion should also point up why assembly line balance is a subject for concern not only for the original design of production systems but for continued operation, since it is through rebalancing that the scheduler can change the basic hourly production rate of the system in high-volume assembly operations. The use of rebalancing in automotive assembly lines to achieve different hourly rates of output is common.

If the assembly line is completely rigid in design, being mechanically paced at a fixed rate, then the scheduler can change total output for the period only by changing the number of hours per period that the worker-machine system is operated. The rigid system is, of course, often used; for example, the gigantic transfer machines used to fabricate engine blocks and other high-volume parts operate at a fixed hourly rate. There are many other situations where the process dictates the rate at which equipment can be used. For example, the brewing process described by Gordon [8] proceeds at a rate determined by the chemical process. This would be generally true of chemical processes.

Design of the production system

Though our focus in this book is on some of the operating problems of production-inventory systems, there is interaction between the design of the production system and the scheduling problems which exist. The basic physical constraints on scheduling imposed by layout, machine capacity, operation sequences, and balance are our central concern in looking at the production system design problem. The overall development of the design of production systems is shown in block diagram form in Figure 8–2. In Figure 8–2 we have shown the general relationships and development springing from product specifications and requirements for performance and sales forecasts, which act as a guide for determining the design capacity. Through what normally would be termed the product design phase, the functional and final production designs are developed which result in drawings and specifications of the product to be produced. The production design actually sets minimum possible costs of production by determining the process alternatives still open for consideration [5, 15]. The production design of the product, then, represents the first major step in the development of the production system design.

In the process planning phase the product is analyzed through the preparation of assembly charts and flowcharts to develop an overall perspective of the manufacturing problem. Decisions based on economics, specialization, and other factors determine which parts and components to purchase from outside vendors and which to manufacture internally [4]. The items for internal manufacture then represent the core around which the production system must be designed. For these items, then, the mode and sequence of operations and processes must be developed in detail.

Given the processes and technological sequence requirements, we still have some degree of flexibility left. That flexibility is in how we sequence and group operations within the requirements and set the basic capacity rate of the system. By breaking tasks down finely, we can achieve relatively high output rates and by grouping tasks together to make up jobs involving several tasks, we can achieve relatively lower output rates. Also, by making even larger groupings of

Figure 8–2
Diagram showing overall development of production system design

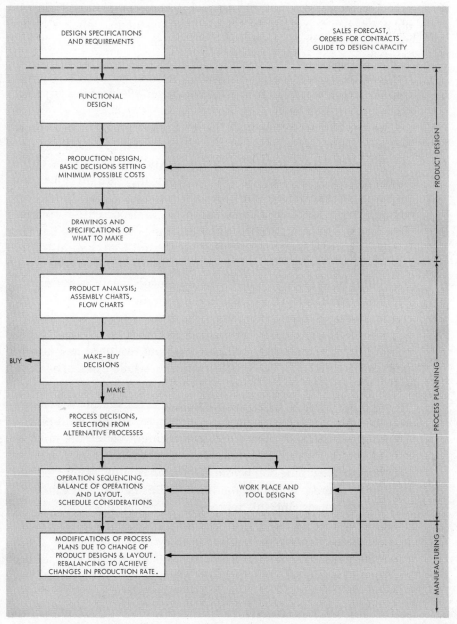

Source: Adapted from E. S. Buffa, *Modern Production Management*, 5th ed. (New York: John Wiley & Sons, Inc., 1977), p. 215.

tasks into jobs, we can develop essentially parallel lines and achieve greater flexibility in setting operating production rates. The process of sequencing tasks into jobs in such a way that a smooth flow is obtained with maximum labor and/or equipment utilization is called line balancing. Because the role of balance is so important to the scheduling process, we will take a few moments at this point to state the basic problem so that it can be understood as an input to scheduling. We will reserve Chapter 9 for a more complete review of methodologies for line balancing.

The line balance problem. The essence of the line balance problem is to group and/or subdivide activities or tasks in such a way that all job stations have an equal amount of work to do in terms of the time required to perform the tasks. When they are all equal, we presume perfect balance and we expect smooth flow. When they are unequal, then the slowest operation in the sequence will restrict the flow for the entire line to the output of the bottleneck station. The result is that the bottleneck station is fully utilized, and all of the other stations are less than fully utilized. We term this underutilization "idle time" even though workers do not sit idly during the equivalent time but tend to work more slowly, balancing their activities to the rhythm of the line.

In order to start with the greatest flexibility in alternatives to *achieve balance for a specified rate of output*, we need to know the performance times for the smallest possible whole units of activity, called tasks, such as tightening a nut, attaching a wire, or soldering a wire. We also need to know the technological constraints which may require certain sequences of these activities. Simple examples of these technological sequence constraints might be: a hole must be drilled before it can be reamed, reamed before it can be tapped; a washer must go on the bolt before the nut; wheel nuts assembled and tightened before placing on the hubcap. But not all tasks have restricted sequences, and this represents the remaining flexibility. An example of a set of tasks with assembly times in seconds and the established sequence requirements is shown in Table 8–1.

In interpreting the sequence requirements in Table 8–1 we see that tasks a and d can take any sequence since no other tasks must precede them. However, task b-1 must follow task a and task c must follow task b. Using the data from Table 8–1 we can construct a chart which summarizes the sequence requirements as well as performance times as shown in Figure 8–3. We can use Figure 8–3 as a basis for establishing a grouping of tasks into job stations to meet some specific production rate for the line as a whole.

Table 8–1
Tasks, assembly times, and technological sequencing requirements for the assembly of a product (total assembly time 125 seconds)

Task code	Time in seconds	Must follow task(s)	Task code	Time in seconds	Must follow task(s)
a	14	—	g	9	e
b − 1	5	a	h	14	e
b − 2	5	a	i	6	fgh
c	30	b	j	7	i
d	3	—	k	3	i
e	5	d	l	4	jk
f	13	e	m	7	l

Let us suppose first that we are asked to balance this sequence of tasks into an assembly line designed to produce 240 units per hour, or a 15-second per unit cycle. Since the total assembly time for all tasks is 125 seconds, the minimum number of job stations possible is then 125/15 = 8.3, or 9 stations. Figure 8–4 shows one solution which does not violate the sequence requirements by grouping the tasks into nine stations. This solution has idle time in several of the stations totaling 10 seconds per cycle.

Figure 8–3
Technological sequence requirements from Table 8–1 (numbers represent element times in seconds)

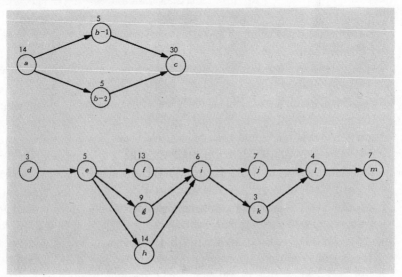

Figure 8–4
A nine-station solution balanced for one line with limiting cycle of 15
seconds per unit or 240 per hour (idle time of 10 seconds per cycle)

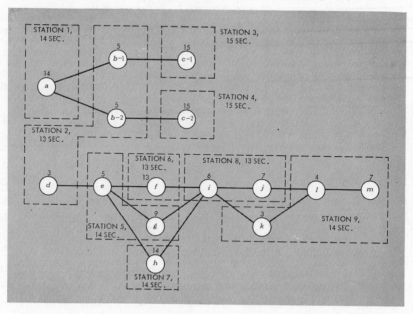

An alternate solution for the same output would be to establish
two parallel lines, each with limiting cycles of 30 seconds per unit.
Figure 8–5 shows a solution involving five stations, the minimum
number possible. Idle time, however, has increased to 25 seconds per
cycle per line. Given the two alternatives for the same design output
rate, a scheduler would find greater flexibility in a solution such as
that in Figure 8–5, but at the cost of an extra worker, since Figure
8–4 requires nine workers to staff the line while Figure 8–5 would
require ten workers to staff the two lines.

Suppose now that the scheduler was directed to reduce output
from the previous 240 units per hour to 144 units per hour. The line
could be rebalanced for the lower output rate as shown in Figure 8–6.
With the 25-second per unit cycle (3,600/144 = 25 seconds per cycle), the minimum possible number of stations is 125/25 = 5 stations.
In order to achieve this minimum number of stations, however, one
would have to find five combinations of the task times which added
perfectly to 25 seconds without violating the sequence requirements.
This is, of course, extremely unlikely for any situation and impossible in the example given. Figure 8–6, however, shows one solution
for a six-station line involving an idle time of 25 seconds per cycle.

Figure 8–5
A five-station solution balanced for two lines each to produce with limiting
cycles of 30 seconds per unit per line, or 240 per hour (idle time is 25
seconds per cycle per line)

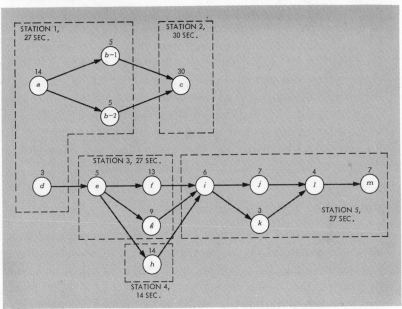

Figure 8–6
A six-station solution balanced for one line with limiting cycle of 25 seconds
per unit or 144 per hour (idle time is 25 seconds per cycle)

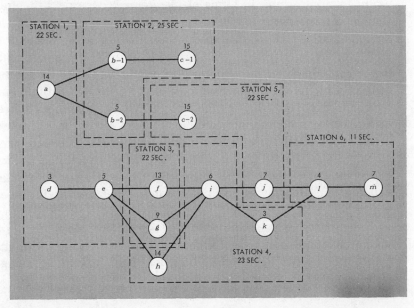

Thus we see the kind of flexibility open to the scheduler through balancing and rebalancing of lines as well as some of the constraints and trade-offs he or she must work with. For specific situations, of course, there may be additional constraints. For example, there may be one station in the sequence which has a long cycle which cannot be subdivided because of the technology involved. Fabrication lines commonly have considerably less flexibility because of fixed machine cycles, and perhaps the only course open to the scheduler is to vary hours worked.

Of course, the line balance problem for large assembly lines, such as those found in auto and appliance plants, is much more challenging, and we will develop and compare in Chapter 9 several imaginative proposals for handling this difficult problem.

Integrated production planning systems

A discussion of production system design gives us information about the nature of the physical constraints imposed on planning and scheduling by the physical characteristics of the system. Now let us return to the issue of integrated systems for production planning and inventory control in high-volume continuous processes. That is, planning systems which integrate aggregate planning, master scheduling, materials control, work force planning and detailed facilities scheduling decisions, and implementation steps.

In describing integrated systems for production planning, it is useful for us to think in terms of hierarchical decision structures similar to those discussed in Chapter 5 and 6. This is because we rarely find firms making all of their plans simultaneously. Rather, we find them laying plans and making decisions in serial fashion; with lower level more detailed plans and schedules being laid within the context of higher order plans and decisions. Figure 8–7 outlines one type of decision and planning hierarchy that we might expect to find in high-volume continuous operations where several facilities are used to produce the same product lines, and where parts and components are purchased (that is, where the product structure is similar to that shown in Figure 7–1(b). Naturally, the decision and planning structure in other types of high-volume operations will differ somewhat.

The process of generating detailed subsidiary plans for high-volume standardized product situations is one of working within the constraints of the aggregate production plan, taking advantage

Figure 8–7
Broad schematic diagram of integrated planning system for high-volume standardized products, given the aggregate production plan

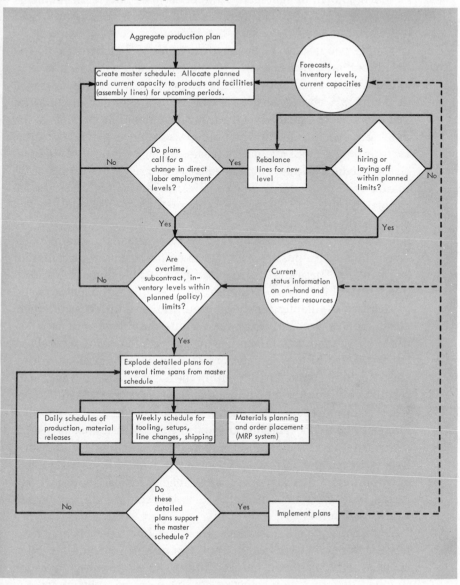

of whatever flexibility there may be to cut and try for practical schedules. Since broad-based planning has already taken place in the development of aggregate production plans, the main problems in creating more detailed schedules involve devising ways to follow it in spirit, and insofar as possible, in fact.

The first step, as we have already mentioned, is to create a master schedule that indicates how each plant's capacity will be allocated to individual products over the planning horizon. As we have seen in Chapters 5 and 6, master scheduling is a complex undertaking that can be accomplished by the intuitive cut and fit methods of the experienced scheduler, or by more sophisticated analytical or heuristic techniques. Once a tentative master schedule is created, an iterative procedure begins which checks back to see if the details of the master schedule, and other more detailed derivative schedules, fit the stated constraints of the aggregate production plan, and are consistent with company policies.

The first "check" question asked in the schematic diagram of Figures 8–7 involves possible changes in employment levels called for by the plans. These changes may call for a rebalancing of labor force to facilities. In the case of complex assembly lines the methods and procedures of Chapter 9 may be used. In many instances alternate staffing plans probably exist for various output rates of facilities based on previous careful studies. At any rate the result of rebalancing will be to hire or lay off personnel in specific skill categories, checking to see if the result is within the aggregate plan. If aggregate planning and master scheduling decisions have been carefully constructed to reflect the relationship between productivity and labor force, it should be possible to adjust staffing assignments within the constraints of the plan. As we recall from Figures 8–4, 8–5, and 8–6, however, the balance solutions must deal with the assignment of whole labor units so that cost and capacity increase or decrease in jumps, or discrete amounts, rather than in a continuous relationship to the work force.

Once capacity considerations involving line balances and work force levels have been worked out, the master schedule is further checked for consistency and feasibility. The second check question involves determining whether or not the overtime, subcontract, and inventory levels for individual products and the aggregate total are consistent with the overall aggregate production plan, and with company labor and customer service policies. If the plan is not consistent with these higher order decisions, another iteration of the master scheduling, or possibly even the aggregate production planning process, may be necessary. If the plan is consistent, it is next checked for feasibility.

The near-term portions of the master schedule may be constrained by decisions made in previous plans. For example, if lead times on raw materials are three months, then the upper limit on next month's production will be constrained by the size of the purchase orders placed two months ago. Similarly, lead times on tooling for line rebalances and for the hiring and training of new employees can constrain the extent of changes in the near-term portions of an aggregate plan, compared to the master schedule that was created in previous planning cycles. If all portions of the master schedule, both in the near term and the long term are consistent and feasible, then more detailed plans based on the master schedule can be laid. If not, then another iteration of the master scheduling/rebalancing/consistency/feasibility checking process may be necessary.

The day-to-day operation of a factory requires a number of detailed schedules. As with the master schedule, these detailed plans must be consistent with the higher order operating structure that they must support. Detailed plans and schedules, a few of which are shown in Figure 8–7, relate to a number of different time spans, and are typically reformulated more frequently than aggregate plans or master schedules. For example, aggregate production plans may be formulated bimonthly, master schedules monthly, and detailed plans on a daily and weekly basis. In this case, the complete *production planning cycle* (the interval between which the highest order plan is active) is two months. Within this total planning cycle, however, various derivative plans are reformulated or recycled on a more continuous basis.

Schedules or plans that are reformulated on a daily basis with very limited planning horizons might include daily production orders authorizing the production of specific products, the release of materials from storerooms to the shop floor, and the assignment of specific workers to specific jobs. Weekly schedules may include tooling order schedules, line changeover and/or setup plans and orders, and shipping schedules. In addition, material requirements plans, perhaps based on the output of an MRP system, will result in orders for materials being placed, expedited, and rescheduled on a daily basis. The planning horizon for these detailed materials plans is typically the same as the planning horizon of the master schedule. The final step before the implementation of the myriad detailed schedules and plans involved in running a high-volume operation is checking to see if they are consistent with the master schedule of production that their implementation is designed to support. Once implemented, the results of these detailed plans and schedules provide the current status information on which later planning cycles are based.

An example. To illustrate the way in which one producer of high-volume standardized products integrates its production planning and control efforts, we will refer to the system employed by the Information Systems Group (ISG), a Division of the Xerox Corporation. The operation of this system, called PPICS (Production Planning and Inventory Control System), in 1976 was reported by Miller and Van Dierdonck in a series of case studies [14].

The ISG Division of Xerox is located in Webster, New York. It produces and sells Xerox copiers and duplicators for North American markets. The ISG manufacturing and distribution network (Figure 8–8) was designed to accommodate three types of products. The first were "new build" machines that were assembled in the ISG manufacturing complex. These machines were manufactured under the control of the ISG Manufacturing Division and shipped to geographically dispersed distribution centers controlled by marketing. Regional refurbishing centers (eight in all) operated under the direction of Manufacturing. They repaired and refurbished used machines into "like new" condition and returned them to the distribution centers for reuse. The third product type included all consumable items such as paper, toner, and fuses. Consumables were fabricated by outside suppliers and by various small ISG plants located around the United States.

Figure 8–8
Xerox Information Systems Group Division manufacturing and distribution network

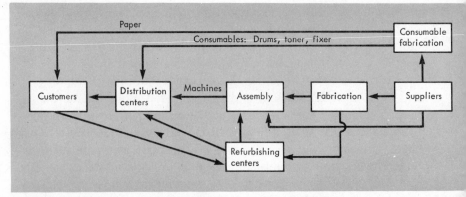

Source: J. G. Miller, and R. Van Dierdonck, "Xerox Corporation: The PPIC's System (A)," ICH No. 9-678-09; 1977.

A typical assembly plant was comprised of one or two major assembly lines and several subassembly lines which fed them. Each plant had its own stockroom and managed its own production planning and inventory control system. Interplant parts orders, or those from refurbishing centers and engineering and service centers, did not go to the Procurement Department or fabrication plant, but to the assembly plant which controlled those parts. Each plant was assigned a set of parts which it "controlled" in interfacing with the needs of other plants or users. Only about 5 percent of the parts were common to all the assembly plants. Purchasing was centralized at the divisional level under the Vice President for Materials Management. The purchasing staff selected vendors, negotiated prices, and set up supply contracts. Material analysts in each plant released orders to purchasing against the requirements indicated by their own version of the PPICS system.

In total, 21 different product lines were manufactured by ISG. These lines consisted of different types of copiers, duplicators, and special-purpose copying systems. Copiers were limited by speed, construction, and technology to applications where only a few copies were required. Duplicators were intended for applications where a large number of copies were required. The ISG Manufacturing Division also made accessory devices, such as automatic input devices, sorters, and slitter-perforators, which increased the productivity of duplicating or copying systems.

The average copier or duplicator contains about 4,000 parts in from 7 to 50 major subassemblies. Two hundred-fifty different models of copiers and duplicators were produced to inventory. The finished goods inventories were stored in the distribution network and thus, were not controlled by Manufacturing. From a Manufacturing point of view, therefore, the products were produced to order. [14]

The planning system used in ISG's assembly plant operations was based on a material requirements planning system. Each assembly plant (at the time of the case study) operated a separate system with its own data base.

The demand input to each plant's system consisted of two parts. On the one hand, there were orders for new machines, as stated in a "Machine Build Schedule", and on the other hand, there were the inter-plant orders for subassemblies or parts produced or carried by that particular plant. The Machine Build Schedule was that portion of the so-called Rolling Production Plan assigned to the particular plant.

The Rolling Production Plan was the result of an elaborate monthly procedure called the supply/demand process. The output of this process was a rolling plan, which specified the quantities to be produced for each product line for each of the 24 months of the plan. The purpose of this process was to make sure that the supply of machines from Manufacturing was in agreement with Marketing's estimate of demand. This process culminated in a series of supply/demand meetings during the last week of each month. These meetings were headed by the president of ISG and attended by the vice presidents of functional areas and by the vice president for long-range planning.

Prior to each of these meetings, a supply/demand group reporting to the Manufacturing Division controller and planning manager received the monthly new demand outlook from marketing. This forecast was one input to this group's supply/demand analysis. Capacity and the inventory of products available in process, the distribution centers, and in the refurbishing centers, together with the previous month's Rolling Production Plan, constituted the other inputs.

The first step that the supply/demand group took was to check whether or not current inventories and work-in-process would provide a sufficient supply to meet the new demand projections. If the new forecasts of demand for a product exceeded the supply available and in the pipeline, then options such as increasing production rates, expediting materials, and shortening the runs of other products were examined. A computer simulation model was used to determine the impact of various alternatives for ameliorating impending shortages (Figure 8–9 illustrates some of the questions that might be asked in such a "what if" analysis). Similarly, if supplies were projected to exceed demand, various options for avoiding excess inventories were examined. Many of the supply/demand mismatch problems that were highlighted in this process were solved through informal negotiations with Manufacturing and Marketing, which also supplied its analysis of various alternatives. There were generally some problems, however, that could not be resolved in this way.

The monthly supply/demand process ended with a supply/demand meeting where the remaining mismatches between supply and demand were resolved. The result of this meeting was the new Rolling Production Plan. The Manufacturing group then derived a Master Build Schedule for each plant from the rolling plan. This procedure involved breaking the rolling plan, which used monthly time buckets, into a more detailed weekly plan, and breaking the plan up according to assembly plants. Each assembly plant was designed to produce a specific group of products.

Through this supply/demand process, ISG coordinated its activities and adjusted its plans to changes in the market. Adjustments were influenced by general economic circumstances, competitive actions, and the group's own marketing strategy. Everybody in the group, particularly Manufacturing, was committed to the Rolling Production Plan. This plan was the basic input for the Production Planning and Inventory Control System (PPICS) for each of the plants.

It is important to note that master build schedules could vary considerably from month to month because of ISG's "hedging" policies. Demand forecasts for each period consisted of two figures. One was the so-called "high case" and the other the "low case" (see Figure 8–10). Supplies, determined by the availability of or commitment to materials and manufacturing

Figure 8–9
Sample questions for "what if" analysis

If an increasing schedule:

Impact on cash flow by month.

Impact on purchase dollar commitment by month.

Inventory level buildup by month.

If a Master Build Schedule increase, what is the impact on spare parts service level performance?

Volume of parts having new net requirements penetrating into X percent of lead time (short lead requisitions).

What additional inventory investment in material hedge would have permitted this change?

Volume of parts requiring rescheduling activity.

Volume of parts requiring expediting by month.

Problem parts list of items with a history of vendor's inability to pull schedule ahead.

Increase in special expediting freight cost.

Interplant dependency impact:

Example: Wire harness demand placed by Webster on Henrietta.

Impact on receiving facilities due to increased volume of purchase material deliveries.

What will the net work-in-process throughput equal?

What will be the increase in work-in-process inventory levels for materials?

If a decreasing schedule:

Dollar value of purchase order cancellation charges.

Total current purchase commitment compared to optimum level with net reduction in forecast.

Increase in months of supply level.

Buildup rate of inventory by month.

Excess inventory bleed-off rate by month. When will the entire effect be netted out?

Exposure to type C surplus material excess increase as an unplanned adjustment.

Additional warehouse space for incoming excess purchase materials.

Volume of rescheduling activity.

Source: J. G. Miller and R. Van Dierdonck, "Xerox Corporation: The PPIC's System (A)", ICH No. 9-678-092, 1977.

capacity, were normally geared to the low case, unless a decision was made in the supply/demand meeting to hedge a certain period. Hedge decisions had to be made six months before completed products were produced because of the six-month cumulative manufacturing and procurement cycle at ISG. They made sure that, if required, the necessary materials would be available to manufacture to the high case instead of the low case. If a decision was made to hedge a certain period, the PPIC's MRP system caused orders to be placed to support its implementation. Three months before the product was to be completed, ISG had to either use the hedge, roll it over, or drop it. The three-month advance notice was dictated by the firm's policy of freezing the master build schedule 13 weeks into the future. If it was decided to use the hedge, commitments were made to increase manpower and other capacity resources accordingly. If it was decided to roll the hedge, then the materials made available by previous commitments were used to provide for a hedge in a future period by rescheduling their delivery or stocking them in inventory. Similarly, if it was decided to drop the hedge, then the materials commitments were netted against future material requirements (see Figure 8–10 for an illustrative example). [14]

The master schedule integrated two demand streams for each end item, and created a more detailed schedule of plant output. The two demand streams included interplant orders for parts and subassemblies, and machine orders from the rolling production plan. Actual shipments of end items were also fed into this module and requirements adjusted accordingly. Any other adjustments to the machine build schedule in the interval between the creation of a build schedule were made at the master schedule level.

Once the machine build schedule has been created, the ISG Division used its PPIC's system as the basis for creating more detailed schedules, plans, and operations procedures. PPICS was conceived of as two back-to-back MRP systems. The first system was designed to bring materials into a plant stockroom by the usual process of exploding materials requirements from a master (build) schedule. Since there were fewer space or materials handling limitations involved in a stockroom operation, compared to on-the-floor assembly storage, this procedure allowed plants to order materials in economical order quantities. The second MRP system allowed Xerox plants to pull materials from the stockroom onto the assembly floor without the expensive and space consuming task of "kitting" found in most low-volume assembly operations. The second MRP system exploded detailed *daily needs* (as opposed to the gross weekly needs reflected in the master schedule) for materials from "continuous" work orders that reflected the current state of affairs on the shop floor. This approach allowed Xerox to adjust the MRP system concept, normally

Figure 8–10
Example hedge tactics at the master schedule level

1. Supply/demand meeting in December. The decision is made to hedge July only.

Rolling Production Plan for January

	Jan.	Feb.	March	April	May	June	July	Aug.	Sept.	Oct.	Nov.	Dec.
Low case	10	10	10	10	10	10	10	12	12	14	14	15
High case							12	14	14	16	17	20
Hedge							2					

2. Supply/demand meeting in January: Do not hedge August
    Supply/demand meeting in February: Hedge September
    Supply/demand meeting in March: Do not hedge October and either
    (a) use the July hedge or

	April	May	June	July	Aug.	Sept.	Oct.	Nov.	Dec.	Jan.	Feb.	March
Low case	10	10	10	10	12	12	14	14	17	20	20	20
High case							16	17	20	25	25	25
Hedge				2	—	2	—					

(b) roll the July hedge into August.

	April	May	June	July	Aug.	Sept.	Oct.	Nov.	Dec.	Jan.	Feb.	March
Low case	10	10	10	10	12	12	14	14	17	20	20	20
High case							16	17	20	25	25	25
Hedge				—	2	2	—					

(c) Drop the July hedge

	April	May	June	July	Aug.	Sept.	Oct.	Nov.	Dec.	Jan.	Feb.	March
Low case	10	10	10	10	12	12	14	14	17	20	20	20
High case							16	17	20	25	25	25
Hedge				—	—	2	—					

Source: J. G. Miller and R. Van Dierdonck, "Xerox Corporation: The PPIC's System (A)," ICH No. 9-678-092, 1977.

used where products were assembled in discrete batches, to a more or less continuous process environment. All in all, the PPIC's system was composed of 12 basic modules, each of which was concerned with either a decision-making function (e.g., materials ordering), a control function (e.g., receiving and inspection), a record-keeping function (e.g., stores inventory balances), or a data processing function (e.g., materials requirements explosions).

Requirement explosions were performed over each weekend and requirements were projected over two years. The system provided a planning status report for each component and intermediate product. These reports were examined by the materials analysts whose task was the key to Requirements Planning. They implemented the material plan suggested on their reports and made any necessary adjustments. Then they placed orders and accelerated or slowed their delivery to make sure that parts were in the stockroom when they were needed. When total material support was achieved, the analysts released work orders to the plant. They monitored material activity and made adjustments to maintain the integrity of the Master Schedule. They also formed a sensitive interface with production control and plant operations in evaluating and executing material plan adjustments to allow short-term load smoothing. Production controllers scheduled plant and subassembly production, and in the fabrication plant, dispatched orders and maintained control over in-shop production priorities. [14].

We can see many parallels between the Xerox ISG system and the generalized decision and planning hierarchy shown in Figure 8–7. The Xerox supply demand process parallels the process of deriving a master schedule (or master build schedule) from an aggregate plan (rolling production plan). It is at this point that specific product production plans are detailed on a weekly basis, and that assembly line balance and capacity decisions are made. The "what if" simulations performed by the ISG division provide the feasibility and consistency checks necessary to ensure that materials are available or are on order to support the near-term portions of the plan, and that projected inventories and overtime requirements are consistent with other plans and company policies. Of particular interest is Xerox' policy of hedging in their master schedule. This practice gives them considerable flexibility to change their schedules as they move through time from one planning cycle to the next. It gives them some assurance that future master schedules will not be rejected because sufficient materials were not ordered in previous periods; i.e., because of infeasibilities.

The detailed scheduling process at Xerox is embodied in their PPIC's system. The first of the two MRP modules in this system works on a weekly time bucket basis, and has a long planning horizon. Its purpose is to provide materials plans so that orders can be placed, rescheduled, and ultimately brought into the assembly plant stockroom. The second MRP system provides an even more detailed short-range plan. Its purpose is to provide instructions as to when items should be pulled from the stockroom for placement along the assembly line. Its daily time buckets not only provide the basis for day-to-day control over the flow of materials in the plant, but they also provide the continuous approximation of material flow necessary to support a continuous process. Other modules within PPIC's, and the actions of individual production controllers provide the basis for other detailed schedules for receiving, shipping, maintenance, tooling, and so on.

Scheduling and the system as a whole

It is important that we try to understand the dynamics of the system as a whole and the impact of activities downstream in the production-inventory-distribution system on the scheduling of factory operations. To do this let us focus our attention on the multistage system diagrammed in Figure 8–11. Figure 8–11 is abstracted from

Figure 8–11
Production-inventory system to manufacture and distribute a consumer durable product (system volume averages 2,500 units per week)

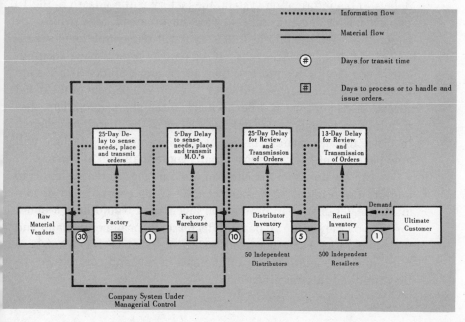

Figure 8–1 to show just the physical flow and the information chain of replenishment reflected back through the system of delays. Though highly idealized and simplified in many respects, this model is sufficient to represent for us some of the important material and information flow aspects of a system to manufacture and distribute a consumer durable product.

We are already familiar with the significance of the time lags in a general way; however, it will be of value now to look more closely at the behavior of the system and to examine its significance for factory scheduling. Our discussion will parallel McGarrah's analysis [12, p. 150]. The general behavior of the system is dependent on the periodic review of inventory needs and on the preparation and transmission of orders for replenishment to the next stage upstream. For example, recall from Figure 1–8 that the retailer had a 10-day review period plus 3 days for communicating needs to the distributor making up a 13-day total delay. The distributor had a 21-day review period plus 4 days for communication, and so on back through the system.

Now let us suppose that consumer demand falls by 10 percent from its previous rate. During the next review of inventory needs the retailer reflects this decrease in orders for replenishment sent to the distributor, but 13 days have elapsed. Similarly, the distributor reflects the decrease in the next orders for replenishment to the factory warehouse, but an additional 25 days have elapsed before the factory warehouse will be aware of the fall in sales. Thus, adding up all time delays in the information system, the factory will not learn of the 10 percent fall in demand until 43 days have passed. Meanwhile, the factory has been producing 1.00/0.90 or 111 percent of the new consumer requirement. An excess of 11 percent would have accumulated each day in inventory at the various stock points. The system inventory will have increased to $11 \times 43 = 473$ percent of the usual normal day's supply. In order to react to the change, retailers, distributors, and the factory warehouse decrease the quantities ordered. In order to take account of the excess inventory, the factory will now have to cut back by substantially more than the 10 percent.

We can see now that the effect of the time lags in the system is to amplify the original 10 percent change at the consumer level to a much greater change in production levels than would have seemed justified by the simple 10 percent decrease in consumer demand and that inventories have increased instead of decreased. Obviously, a more direct communication of changes in demand can reduce the magnitude of this amplification.

Figure 8–12 is identical to Figure 8–11 with the exception that we have added a direct information feedback loop in the form of a system for assessing actual demand and forecasting demand in the immediate period ahead. The 10-day delay in assembling the actual demand and forecast information reduces the total delay by 33 days. A 10 percent decrease in sales under this system would mean that an excess inventory of only 11 × 10, or 110 percent of the normal levels would accumulate before the factory was aware of the change. Obviously, the forecast combined with the aggregate scheduling system shown in Figure 8–1 would stabilize the effects even more.

We can demonstrate the dynamic effects of time lags and changes in system structure more dramatically through the mechanism of a simulation study. Figure 8–13 shows the structure of a production-distribution system which is similar to that in Figure 8–11, but which involves different time values for the overall flow of goods and information. In this instance the solid lines represent physical flow and the lines with small circle dots represent information flow. Forrester [7] developed a dynamic computer simulation model of this system and used it to test a variety of changes in parameters and system organization structure. We will look only at what happens to inventory levels at various points in the system and to factory output when retail sales increase by 10 percent. Figure 8–14 indicates results similar to those shown in connection with our discussion of Figure 8–11, the response in inventory and production levels is not simply 10 percent. Note that there is an amplification of the effect at each stage back through the system and that actual factory production finally increased to a peak of 45 percent above its original level with a time lag of five months. The amplification and oscillating responses are the result of the time lags in the information system.

What happens if we are able to reduce .these time lags through more efficient procedures or by changing the structure of the system? Figure 8–15 shows the result when the entire distributor stage is eliminated. Note that the system response is similar but that the peak values of inventories are considerably reduced. The peak factory output rises to only 26 percent instead of 45 percent. (The curve of factory output based on the original distribution system from Figure 8–14 is included in Figure 8–15 for comparison.) Forrester also tested the effect of simply improving the speed with which information was handled back through the system by reducing the clerical delays of three, two, and one week of sales analysis and reducing purchasing time to one third of these values. The effect was only

Figure 8–12
Production-inventory system with information feedback loop provided by forecasts and up-to-date information of actual customer demand

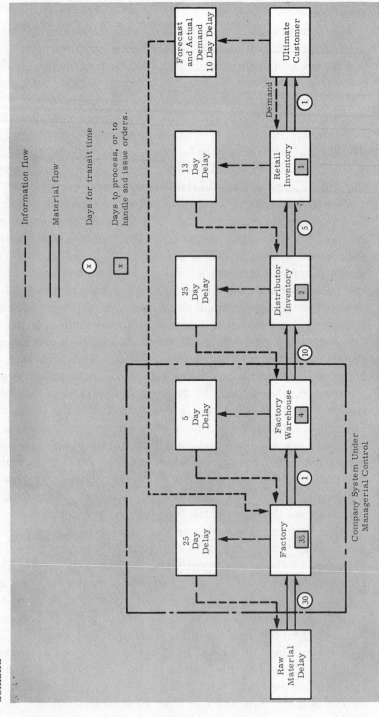

Figure 8–13
Organization of production-distribution system

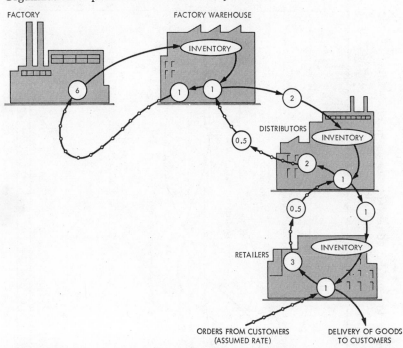

Source: Adapted from J. Forrester, *Industrial Dynamics* (Cambridge, Mass.: M.I.T. Press, 1961), Fig. 2–1.

minor, however. This tends to indicate that improvements in structure, such as those discussed in connection with Figures 8–12 and 8–15, are likely to yield much better results than simply doing what is already being done but doing it faster.

Meaning for scheduling. What impact should this discussion of the dynamics of the system have on the design of scheduling systems for high-volume standardized products? First, it seems evident that a system for tracking the progress of sales at the retail-consumer level is essential, feeding back this information to factory scheduling. This would short-circuit the system of time lags inherent in a multistage production-distribution system. Just this tracking and information feedback in Forrester's results shown in Figure 8–14 would have stabilized the wild oscillations considerably. Second, a forecast based on some smoothing and anticipation of changes in demand would have had a marvelous effect in stabilizing Forrester's system. For example, a 10 percent step increase in demand when smoothed

Figure 8–14
Response of production-distribution system to a sudden 10 percent increase in retail sales

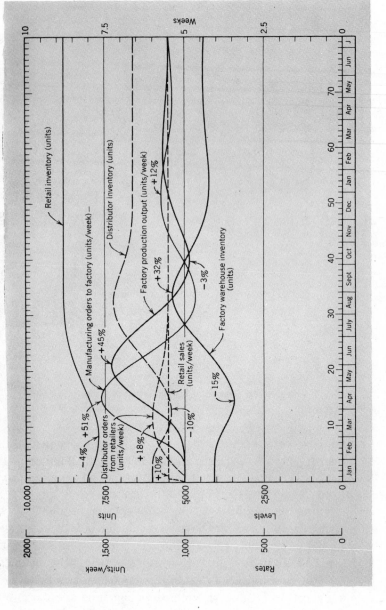

Source: Adapted from J. Forrester, *Industrial Dynamics* (Cambridge, Mass.: M.I.T. Press, 1961), Fig. 2–2.

Figure 8–15
Effect of eliminating the distributor level

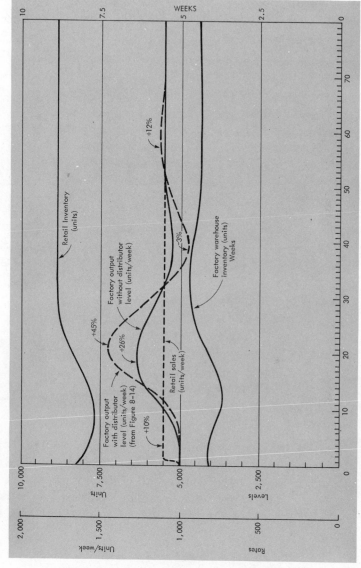

Source: Adapted from J. Forrester, *Industrial Dynamics* (Cambridge, Mass.: M.I.T. Press, 1961), Fig. 2–7.

by an exponential constant of $\alpha = 0.1$ would look like the response shown in Figure 8–16. The smoothed response is letting buffer stocks perform the function they were designed to accomplish. The smoothed function when combined with a forecast, which is forward looking, has the effect of both anticipation and stabilization.

Figure 8–16
Response to a 10 percent step increase in demand when smoothed by an exponential smoothing constant of $\alpha = 0.10$

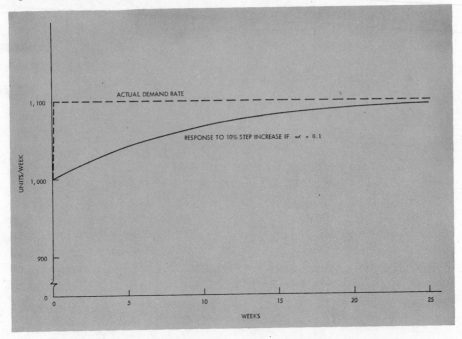

Finally, the incorporation of some aggregate planning system in combination with a presumably smoothed forecast, as shown in the diagram of Figure 8–1, combines all of the features of tracking the progress of sales to provide information feedback, a smoothed forecast, and the stabilizing effect of anticipation and longer range planning.

SUMMARY

Production planning and scheduling for a production system which has been designed for a standardized product might involve mainly aggregate planning and rebalancing of facilities for the simplest situations. When there is a variety of product types and sizes involved, we have a somewhat more complex problem requiring an allocation of the aggregate plan to individual items, but basic planning still focuses on working within the constraints established by the aggregate plan. When a production system has been designed for high-volume standardized products, we recognize immediately that we have traded some flexibility in operation to achieve the cost benefits of the production line type of manufacture. By specializing equipment and layout we can develop a highly efficient system to produce a limited range of products. The result is smooth flow and low cost if there is a large enough sales volume to justify the specialized facility. Usually, however, we must give up a great deal of flexibility to obtain the benefits of specialization. Thus rescheduling of the production facility is under severe constraints, and one cannot simply change production rates without careful reconsideration of the balance or staffing of facilities.

Finally, the scheduling problem needs to be thought of in relation to the system as a whole and designed to be a part of the information flow of that system. Forrester shows that in the unbridled production-distribution system the production facility would be affected most by a change in demand because it is furthest upstream and there is progressive amplification of variation as we proceed upstream in the system. Yet the cost of variations in activity is the most expensive at the level of the production facility, involving the heavy cost of hiring, training, and layoff of employees. Thus information feedback loops short-circuiting the ordinary chain of demand are essential to stabilize the otherwise oscillatory behavior of the system. Also, forecasts and aggregate planning are essential to anticipate seasonal and trend effects in demand rather than simply to respond after the demand changes happen.

REVIEW QUESTIONS AND PROBLEMS

1. Field Study: Locate a case study in the field involving the scheduling of a high-volume standardized product.
   a. Analyze the planning and scheduling system used and describe it in detail with the aid of flow diagrams and other illustrative charts.
   b. Relate the scheduling process found in (a) to the generalized diagram of Figure 8–1:
      (1) What is the source of forecasts, that is, from which point in the distribution process is the information generated?

(2) What is the time lag between demand generation and the availability of forecasts for use?

(3) How is aggregate planning accomplished? What modes of absorbing demand fluctuation are used?

(4) How is product mix in the upcoming production schedule determined?

(5) What degrees of freedom are open to the detailed scheduler, that is, changes in hours worked, hiring and layoff, rebalancing of facilities, expansion or contraction of physical capacity, use of inventory, etc?

(6) Under what constraints does the detailed scheduler work?

c. What techniques are used to rebalance worker and machine assignments if the size of the work force changes?

d. Relate the activities of the detailed scheduler to the schematic diagram of Figure 8–7.

e. What kinds of schedules are developed, that is, to cover which time spans into the future and at what level of detail?

2. Considering the field study work in Question 1, generate the data needed to produce a diagram comparable to Figure 8–11 for your particular project.

a. Given whatever feedback of demand data structure which exists in the organization, compute the reaction at the factory level of a sudden 10 percent decrease in demand.

b. Consider what improvements in the information feedback structure might be effective.

3. Considering all forecasting, and aggregate and detailed scheduling aspects of the production-inventory system of the field study in Questions 1 and 2, draft a management report with recommendations for improvement.

4. Note in the model of the production-inventory system of Figure 8–12 that information concerning demand at the retail level is fed back directly to the factory and that as a result, there is a considerable reduction in the magnitude of oscillations in orders and production activity. What are the implications of this result for organizing and establishing lines of authority and responsibility for a multistage production-inventory system?

SELECTED BIBLIOGRAPHY

1. Bergstrom, G. L., and B. E. Smith. "Multi-Item Production Planning—An Extension of the HMMS Rules," *Management Science*, vol. 16, no. 10 (June 1970), pp. 614–29.

2. Buffa, E. S. *Modern Production Management*, chap. 12. 5th ed. New York: John Wiley & Sons, Inc., 1977.

3. Charnes, A., and Cooper, W. W. *Management Models and Industrial Applications of Linear Programming*. 2 vols. New York: John Wiley & Sons, Inc., 1961.

4. Culliton, J. W. *Make or Buy*. Boston: Graduate School of Business Administration, Harvard University, 1942.

5. Eary, D. F., and Johnson, G. E. *Process Engineering for Manufacturing*. Englewood Cliffs, N.J.: Prentice-Hall, Inc., 1962.

6. Ferguson, R. O., and Sargent, L. F. *Linear Programming*. New York: McGraw-Hill Book Co., 1958.

7. Forrester, J. *Industrial Dynamics*. Cambridge, Mass.: M.I.T. Press, 1961.

8. Gordon, J. R. M. "A Multi-Model Analysis of an Aggregate Scheduling Decision." Unpublished Ph.D. dissertation, Sloan School of Management, M. I. T., 1966.

9. Hodges, S. D., and Moore, D. G. "The Product-Mix Problem under Stochastic Seasonal Demand," *Management Science*, vol. 17, no. 2 (October 1970), pp. 107–14.

10. Mastor, A. A. "An Experimental Investigation and Comparative Evaluation of Production Line Balancing Techniques," *Management Science*, vol. 16, no. 11 (July 1970), pp. 728–46.

11. Marshall, P., et al. *Production-Operations Management: Text and Cases*. Homewood, Ill.: Richard D. Irwin, Inc., 1975.

12. McGarrah, R. E. *Production and Logistics Management: Text and Cases*, chaps. 5 and 6. New York: John Wiley & Sons, Inc., 1963.

13. Miller, J. G. "Hedging the Master Schedule," *Proceedings of the Disaggregation Conference*, Ohio State University, 1977.

14. Miller, J. G., and Van Dierdonck, R. "Xerox Corporation: The PPIC's System (A)," ICH No. 9-678-092, 1977.

15. Niebel, B. W., and Baldwin, E. N. *Designing for Production*. rev. ed. Homewood, Ill.: Richard D. Irwin, Inc., 1963.

16. Sypkens, H. A. "Planning for Optimal Plant Capacity." Unpublished Master's thesis, Sloan School of Management, M.I.T., 1967.

17. Taubert, W. H. "The Search Decision Rule Approach to Operations Planning." Unpublished Ph.D. dissertation, UCLA, 1968.

18. Vazsonyi, A. *Scientific Programming in Business and Industry*. New York: John Wiley & Sons, Inc., 1958.

CASE STUDY
CORNING GLASS WORKS:
ERWIN AUTOMOTIVE PLANT

ONE MORNING in late December of 1974, Mike Jensen, production planner for Corning's Erwin Automotive Plant, had been reviewing a recent *Wall Street Journal* article. The article had discussed the tremendous uncertainties facing the auto industry during the next two quarters and throughout the remainder of the 70s. Those uncertainties had resulted from a changing national environmental policy, a growing economic recession, and the continuing energy shortage. All three of the U.S. auto companies had announced major cutbacks in production during the fourth quarter of 1974 and there were indications that these would continue into the first and second quarters of 1975.

This outlook had not pleased Mike Jensen because the Erwin plant—less than a year old—was highly dependent on the fortunes of the auto industry. Erwin produced only one product, Corning's CELCOR™ brand ceramic substrate, which was used in the catalytic converters required on the exhaust systems of most 1975 cars sold in the United States. Due primarily to the rapidly changing demand for new cars—and thus for converters—the Erwin plant's employment level had jumped from zero in January to 1,500 in June and then had fallen back to 500 hourly workers by October. While Mike had felt that there had been some unusual circumstances surrounding the start-up of the plant which had accentuated these extreme employment shifts, it had been clear that he faced a difficult task in developing aggregate production plans for 1975 that both met corporate objectives and minimized employment fluctuations and layoffs.

As Mike had contemplated his immediate task of preparing an aggregate plan for the 13 four-week periods of 1975, he had wanted to be sure that he had the best information available concerning demand and that the decision rules he applied were those most appropriate to the situation. Additionally, he had wanted to identify opportunities for improving his planning, such as more appropriate performance measures for the plant, more favorable contract terms with the auto companies, or better procedures for generating and evaluating alternative plans.

CELCOR™ product history

The CELCOR™ product was of a type referred to as a monolith. While GM had developed its own catalytic converter concept involving the use of alumina beads coated with platinum, the monolith approach used a ceramic substrate (made of a mix of light colored clays) honeycombed with many different surfaces that could be coated with platinum. The most common substrate produced by Corning was about the size and shape of a large soup can, six inches long and three and one-half inches in diameter. Oval and elliptical shapes were also common and could be produced equally well with Corning's production processes. The base of the substrate looked much like a piece of graph paper with 200–300 cells (small squares or triangles) per square inch. These cells ran the length of the substrate allowing exhaust gases to enter one end and exit at the other. (See Exhibit 1.) While the product could vary in terms of length, base shape, cell pattern (e.g., triangular rather than square), pattern density, and ceramic materials, the production process was essentially

Exhibit 1
Typical CELCOR™ ceramic substrates

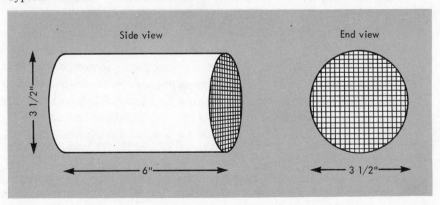

the same in all cases. (In all, the Erwin plant produced 22 different types of substrates.)

The basic substrate produced at the Erwin Automotive Plant passed through two other manufacturing operations after it left Erwin and before it reached the auto assembly plant. The first of these was performed by a company which added the catalyst. This involved a dipping process whereby the catalyst—usually platinum—was applied to all the surfaces of the substrate. The catalyzer company then shipped the units to a "canner," where the substrate was enclosed in a metal can and where all welding and sealing necessary to make the complete tail pipe assembly was done. The tail pipe assemblies were then sent to the automotive plants for use in final assembly.

CELCOR™ had developed into a fully commercial product following a pattern typical of many of Corning's products. In 1971, a Corning development engineer had hit upon an idea for a product that would help the auto industry meet its 1975 emission control requirements. A technical team had been set up to develop an economical production process and to work with the auto industry in demonstrating the product's feasibility and Corning's ability to meet the requirements of individual auto companies.

Once Corning had been convinced that it possessed a usable product it had begun negotiating with the major U.S. auto companies to obtain contracts for supplying a sufficient volume of substrates to justify building a new plant. That commitment had been realized in 1973 and construction of the plant at Erwin, New York, had started immediately. By January of 1974, the plant had been sufficiently completed to install production equipment; within two months substrate production had begun. In April the Erwin plant had shipped 50,000 substrates (production levels for the remainder of 1974 are shown in Exhibit 2).

Under the contract terms with the auto companies, Corning, the catalyzer, and the canner each were to keep two weeks of raw material inventory and two weeks of finished goods inventory on hand. This was required to minimize the chances of an automotive assembly plant having to close down due to a lack of finished tail pipe assemblies. Because of the substantial intermediate inventories and the pipeline throughput time of 13 weeks,[1] the Erwin plant was

---

[1] Pipeline throughput time for a unit was the time it took from when Corning shipped a given substrate until that substrate was part of a tail pipe assembly and ready to go onto a finished auto.

Exhibit 2
Inventory, production and shipments (actuals for last six months of 1974)

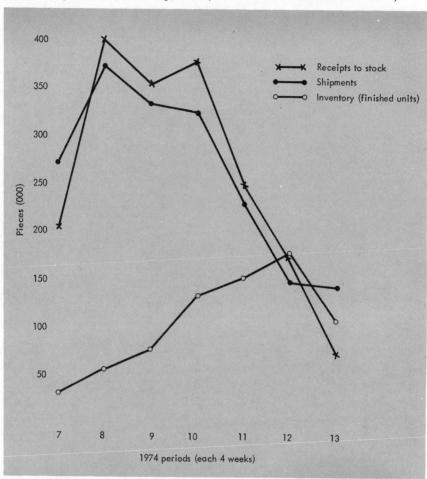

subject to wide swings in demand. As a practical matter, the auto companies with whom Corning had supply contracts—Ford, Chrysler, and Volkswagen—issued ship orders every couple of weeks which told Corning exactly how many substrates to ship in the coming period. Unfortunately, Corning's initial contracts with the auto companies had not anticipated the extent of shipping order fluctuations. In fact, the plant had realized only from recent experience that the auto companies tended to cut off shipments for several weeks at a time to draw down their own inventories when demand slumped.

Exhibit 3
Organization chart

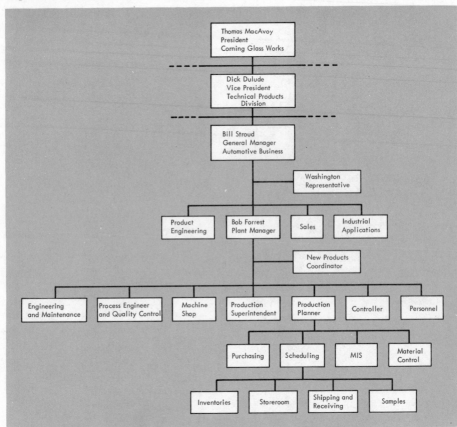

Early 1974 had been a much more hectic period in the plant's development than anyone had anticipated. The auto companies had been extremely nervous about the EPA certification needed to sell 1975 model cars. This certification required most cars to be fitted with catalytic converters, so the auto companies had brought tremendous pressure on Corning to gear up quickly to preclude delay in final assembly of 1975 model cars (due to go on sale in September 1974). In addition, substantial initial production had been required simply to fill the catalytic converter pipeline. These start-up requirements and future potential had largely dictated the amount of production capacity installed at the outset.

An indication of the concern felt by the Erwin plant management had been the tension apparent at daily planning meetings held during the spring and summer of 1974. These meetings had involved the general manager of the Automotive Business, Bill Stroud, and three vice presidents from the corporation. On occasion, Tom MacAvoy, president of Corning Glass Works, had joined the meetings to keep abreast of the latest production progress (see organization chart, Exhibit 3). Ford and Chrysler had also sent their own people to the plant during that period to insure getting their required share of the CELCOR™ production. Due to the pressures of that start-up period, little thought had been given to the plant's steady state production level. Rather, every effort had been concentrated on increasing the output of the plant and meeting the customers' requirements as quickly as possible.

CELCOR™ market

Corning's assessment of the substrate market had been extremely favorable from the outset. Even without GM as a customer, Corning had felt that it would be able to sell a substantial volume of substrates annually. The dollar volume had been expected to grow both as the number of units sold and as the unit price increased.[2] (Corning's competitors had used a different production process which Corning's engineers had felt in the long run would be more costly and difficult to control than its own.) There had been some chance that a delay or postponement of pollution standards for 1977 might enable other processes to be developed, but Corning had felt that the opportunities greatly outweighed that risk.

Corning had felt it commanded a competitive advantage in the substrate business due to its materials expertise and its innovative production process. The company's extensive background in ceramics had enabled it to identify the most appropriate mix of materials for making substrates, and its production and engineering skills had led to the design of manufacturing processes superior to those generally available. While the company in late 1974 had not had protective patents on all aspects of its substrate manufacturing, it had been felt that its superior experience and knowledge as a company made it extremely difficult for a competitor to copy the pro-

---

[2] Management had felt that there was some chance that as pollution standards were tightened GM might have to go to a monolithic converter, in which case the Erwin plant would very likely become a supplier to GM. Tighter pollution standards would also require larger or more dense substrates, resulting in higher unit prices.

cesses and materials mix and obtain the same results at comparable cost.

In late 1974 Corning had been investigating industrial uses of substrates with the hope of opening substantial new markets for CELCOR™. The most promising area had appeared to be utilization of the honeycombed substrate in a large circular heat exchanger. Corning had been building such units with a slightly different production process, but there had been indications that adaption of the CELCOR™ approach would provide substantial improvements and cost reductions in the product.

The CELCOR™ production process

Production of the individual substrates was to tight specifications to ensure that the completed catalytic converter would have a life of 50,000 miles and use a minimum amount of platinum. Substrate porosity had to be closely controlled in manufacturing so the unit would not absorb excess platinum and cost considerably more than was necessary. The object from the auto company's point of view was clearly to meet the standards but to minimize costs in so doing.

Substrate production at the Erwin plant was a three-step process. The initial step was the extrusion operation. In this phase ceramic materials were mixed, prepared, and extruded to obtain various lengths of substrate. These lengths were referred to as "green" logs and were placed in a green log inventory following inspection. The second step was the kiln operation. Green logs were batched and placed in one of the kilns where they remained for some number of days in order to be properly cured. Following firing they were referred to as "fired" logs and held in inventory for the next operation. The third step was the finishing operation where fired logs were cut into the appropriate lengths needed for the finished substrate, inspected, and packed in cartons for shipment to the catalyzer.

During the production operation workers had to keep close track of each individual kiln loading. Samples were taken from each lot and given an ID number and held for future reference. If at some time in the future an automotive company was forced to make a product recall, Corning could determine whether or not the defect was lot related.

A major management concern in the production of substrates at the Erwin Automotive Plant had been that of selection or yield. In the three-step production process 100 percent inspections were carried out by quality control immediately following the first step of extrusion and then again toward the end of the finishing step. During plant start-up the yield at these points had been extremely low, but toward the latter part of 1974 they had improved substantially. Plant management had been confident that the yields could be further increased as direct labor personnel and management gained more experience in the production operations and control of the processes involved.

As a basis for monitoring the operation, plant management had established a standard cost system that assigned a full cost to each good unit produced. These costs included depreciation and overhead as well as direct material and labor. In December 1974 the standard cost of a good finished substrate had averaged $8.40. Of this cost about 10 percent represented depreciation charges, another 15 percent represented materials, direct hourly labor was 30 percent to 35 percent, and the balance represented contribution to overhead. (The high depreciation charges had been due to the substantial excess capacity at the plant.)

The weighted average selling price per unit in late 1974 had been $8.90 per piece (prices had been predetermined by the terms of the contracts). While this had been a concern to plant management, their focus had been on managing gross margin and contribution margin since in the short run the plant did not have much control over the volume being shipped or the price per unit.

The average standard cost of a finished substrate held in inventory in late 1974 had been $9.80. This had exceeded the weighted average cost of units shipped because a disproportionate amount of inventory had been in the slower moving items which tended to be more expensive and were run less frequently due to high set-up costs.

The Erwin plant had maintained four basic inventories—raw materials, green logs, fired logs, and finished pieces. (The logs in a kiln were considered part of the green log inventory until firing was completed.) Historically, Corning's corporate policy had been to set a maximum dollar level for all its combined inventories and then to divide that up by plant. For example, in 1974 the Erwin Automotive Plant had been assigned a maximum inventory level of approximately $3 million. However, late in the year the corporation had been looking at the possibility of changing that criterion to one which measured inventory turnover. For a plant like Erwin, turnover would be measured by computing the standard cost of the units in the four inventories; this total would be divided into the total standard cost of

budgeted sales for the year. If the company adopted this criterion for
all its plants, which in December had appeared likely, corporate
management would specify the desired number of inventory turns
for Erwin. (Turns of 8–10 had been mentioned in some of the initial
discussions with corporate management.)

Plant operating constraints and decision rules[3]

In the first stage of production—extrusion—the Erwin plant had a
number of separate production lines. Because of the high start-up
costs associated with initiating production on any one line, the plant
attempted either to run a given line for five days, 24 hours per day, or
not at all. Operation of a single extrusion line required over 100
hourly workers and produced 1,000 to 2,000 green logs per 24-hour
day. All of the extrusion lines were generally closed down at the end
of the five-day week because of the high overtime costs of running on
the weekend.

As green logs came off the extrusion lines they were 100 percent
inspected. All good product was placed in large wire baskets and
kept in inventory ready for firing. The plant had ample physical
space and even the peak 1974 inventory had not caused any storage
problems. The plant tried to keep a minimum of 15,000 logs in green
log inventory so that kiln firings would not be interrupted or have to
be carried out with only a partial load.

The several identical kilns each had a batch capacity of 1,800 to
2,500 logs per firing, depending on the size and material mix of the
product involved. Kiln firings were scheduled in a specific sequence
due to technical requirements, energy costs, and energy availability.
After firing, logs were placed in a fired log inventory and held for
finishing. As with the green log inventory, a minimum of 15,000 fired
logs had been felt to be needed in order to ensure a smooth production flow in finishing. Kiln operations continued seven days per week
due to scheduling sequence requirements and needed 15 employees
to monitor the kilns regardless of the number of firings per week.

The finishing process was scheduled by kiln lot in order to keep
track of the ID number for each unit. Finishing capacity was measured in terms of the number of good units produced per line shift
and completed units were referred to as receipts to stock (RTS) when

---

[3] Given the depressed state of the U.S. auto industry in late 1974, management had
felt that the Erwin plant had ample equipment capacity for the next few years in all
three of its production stages.

they entered the finished goods inventory. The plant had several fully equipped finishing lines. Each could be run one, two, or three line shifts per day on a five-day week. Finishing output ranged from 1,500 to 2,300 good substrates per line shift. Approximately 30 people were required to operate a single line shift.

The plant production planner

Mike Jensen, Erwin's production planner, had joined the CELCOR™ operation in July 1974. Mike's previous experience had included running his own small manufacturing firm, working as a research engineer for a substantial oil firm, working as a staff assistant in a recreational firm, and two years as an MBA student at the Harvard Business School. Since receiving his initial assignment as planner for the Erwin plant, Mike's responsibilities had evolved to their present scope and included the following tasks:

a. Development of an overall aggregate manufacturing plan for the 13 periods of 1975 and a detailed production schedule for the most immediate three periods (12 weeks).
b. Control of all plant inventories.
c. Development of improved inventory control procedures.
d. Interfacing with the CELCOR™ sales department in obtaining demand forecasts and meeting customer shipping requirements.
e. Management of samples production for the sales department.
f. Budget preparation and control.

In addition to these major areas of responsibility, Mike had recently been given responsibility for data processing at the plant level. As shown in the organization chart in Exhibit 3, Mike had four areas reporting to him—purchasing, material control, MIS, and scheduling.

During the past six months Mike had developed a number of decision rules to assist him in planning. His objective had been to improve the plans and schedules on an incremental basis as quickly as possible. He had anticipated that by early 1975 things would be running smoothly and that then he could take time to review those decision rules and determine how they could be better tuned or perhaps even replaced with a more useful set of rules. The existing set of rules which Mike intended to apply to his immediate task of preparing an aggregate plan for 1975 included the following:

1. In-process inventories. Mike's experience had shown him that to keep production flowing smoothly and to avoid shutdowns or slowdowns caused by lack of product, a minimum of 15,000 green logs should be in inventory waiting for firing and a minimum of 15,000 fired logs needed to be in inventory waiting for finishing. The combined green and fired inventories needed to total 40,000 logs to provide sufficient flexibility so that kiln firings could be altered to balance the two in-process inventories.

2. Kiln firings per week. The energy conservation and technical considerations necessitated a certain sequence of kiln firings and required that the kilns be operated seven days a week with an average of 2.3, 4.6 or 6.9 kiln firings per week. (These three rates of firings were based on experience and used for both planning and operating purposes. The firing rate had to be set at one of these three levels for any given week, but did not have to be held constant for an entire period and in fact there was no advantage to keeping firings per week at a constant level over time.)

3. Product mix. Experience had shown that it was best not to mix the production of substrates requiring different combinations of ceramic materials. Thus, even if more than one extrusion line were running, Mike would schedule all of the lines to produce products that used the same set of input materials. Similarly, in firing and finishing Mike tried to batch identical products to maximize production efficiency.

4. Five-day plant operation. Because of the high cost of overtime for weekend work, Mike tried to plan five-day workweeks for all operations but the kilns.

5. Maintaining stability. Any changes in the work force level or production output rates was disruptive and costly, so Mike tried to minimize the number of such changes.

Existing planning procedures

As a first step in preparing an aggregate plan for 1975, Mike had decided to outline the procedures he had used recently for a somewhat shorter time horizon.

The starting point for Mike's aggregate plan was the shipments forecast that he and the Sales Department had developed. While they had developed a pessimistic and optimistic set of forecasts, Mike felt that as a first cut he would stick with the most likely set. (These shipment forecasts are shown in Exhibit 4.)

Exhibit 4
Sales forecast for calendar 1975*

	Substrate sales (shipments) by 4-week period		
	Optimistic	Realistic	Pessimistic (worst case)
1	160,000	150,000	130,000
2	165,000	145,000	120,000
3	190,000	145,000	115,000
4	245,000	170,000	140,000
5	300,000	210,000	150,000
6	340,000	230,000	150,000
7	360,000	225,000	155,000
8	375,000	230,000	160,000
9	340,000	225,000	165,000
10	315,000	215,000	150,000
11	305,000	210,000	160,000
12	300,000	215,000	165,000
13	275,000	230,000	160,000
Total	3,670,000	2,600,000	1,920,000

* Based on marketing's estimates of demand from existing automotive customers for CELCOR™ substrates and on customers' estimates of seasonal factors affecting shipment rates. (Optimistic, realistic, and pessimistic forecasts assumed annual total auto sales of 9.0, 8.0 and 7.5 million cars, respectively.) The estimates considered auto assembly requirements only and did not include the status of pipeline inventories between Erwin and the assembly plants.

Following agreement on a most likely shipment forecast, Mike had reviewed the present level of operations. One of Mike's goals had been to maintain the status quo as long as possible because of the substantial disruption caused by changing the size of the work force and the level of plant output. Thus he would first project the receipts to stock (RTS) based on the existing level of operations and assuming shipments matched the forecasts.

As a practical matter Mike used a form like Exhibit 5 in his aggregate planning. He selected the number of finishing line shifts for a period, used that and a weighted average output of 2,000 good substrates per line shift to compute RTS for the period, and then used the shipments forecast and the previous ending inventory to determine that period's ending inventory. The procedure was repeated for each subsequent period, remembering that the number of finishing line shifts could be altered whenever ending inventory was tending to get out of line.

With a tentative aggregate plan for finishing, Mike used a form like Exhibit 6 to develop a plan for extrusion. First he converted the "receipts to stock" in Exhibit 5 to equivalent good logs using a factor

Exhibit 5
Aggregate planning form, 1975—Inventory, receipts to stock, shipments

1975 Period	Finishing line-shifts*	Receipts to stock†	Shipments‡	Ending inventory§
1.........	4	160,000	150,000	120,000
2.........	4	160,000	145,000	135,000
3.........			145,000	
4.........			170,000	
5.........			210,000	
6.........			230,000	
7.........			225,000	
8.........			230,000	
9.........			225,000	
10........			215,000	
11........			210,000	
12........			215,000	
13........			230,000	

* Beginning production level, Period 1 = 4 line-shifts per day in finishing.
† Based on weighted average output of 2,000 good substrates per line shift.
‡ From Sales Department shipment forecast (Exhibit 4).
§ Beginning inventory, period 1 = 110,000.

Exhibit 6
Aggregate planning form, 1975—Extrusion log production, total in-process inventory

Period	Extrusion (line-days)*	Green logs produced†	Logs required by finishing‡	Total ending log inventory§
1......	1	30,000	40,000	50,000
2......	1	30,000	40,000	40,000
3......				
4......				
5......				
6......				
7......				
8......				
9......				
10.....				
11.....				
12.....				
13.....				

* Beginning production level, Period 1 = 1 line-day.
† Based on average weighted output of 1,500 good green logs per line-day.
‡ Computed from RTS in Exhibit 5 assuming four good substrates per green log.
§ Beginning log inventory, Period 1 = 60,000. Includes both green and fired logs. This measure is used as a rough cut to determine green log production needs. It is further divided into green and fired log components to calculate kiln firings (see Exhibit 7).

of four good substrates per good green log. (This conversion factor included the appropriate yield factor for the finishing operation.) Next he selected the number of extrusion line-days for a period, used that and a weighted average output of 1,500 good green logs per line day as a standard to compute "green logs produced," and then used the "logs required" and the previous period's ending inventory to determine that period's "ending inventory."

The four factors of no weekend work, no work force reductions, a minimum number of work force expansions, and minimum inventory were used in planning both finishing and extrusion operations. In evaluating his plans, Mike felt it less costly to vary the level of finishing operations than to vary extrusion operating levels because he could vary smaller units of capacity in finishing (line shifts) than in extrusion (line-days) and the extrusion operation presented the more difficult quality control and yield problems.

With a complete plan for finishing and extrusion, Mike used a form like Exhibit 7 to plan kiln firings. This involved taking "green logs produced" from Exhibit 6, using starting inventories of green and fired logs and computing kiln firings and ending fired and green log inventories for each period. As a practical matter, Mike assumed that firings had to be some multiple of 2.3 per week, but not to exceed 27.6 per period, and he assumed an average batch size of 2,100 logs per firing.

Once a plan was completed for all 13 periods, it was evaluated using two rules of thumb. First, as a minimum the contract required that approximately half of the period's shipments be on hand at the beginning of the four-week period. Second, total inventories should be kept under 400,000 equivalent pieces. (Each log was considered equivalent to four good pieces.) If the plan violated these rules then he would alter production levels to correct it. There was considerable judgment involved in deciding how much to alter the output rate of the two main departments and exactly when to do it so that the new level of output could be maintained for as long as possible. While Mike might try half a dozen or more variations in the plan, he realized that he had no way of knowing how close his final plan was to the optimum.

Trade-off considerations

Mike had felt that each of the decision rules he used in planning involved certain trade-offs which always needed to be weighed care-

Exhibit 7
Aggregate planning form, 1975—Kiln firings

Period	Green logs produced*	Fired logs required by finishing†	Minimum required firings‡	Actual number of firings§	Actual number of logs fired‖	Ending green log inventory #	Ending fired log inventory¶
1	30,000	40,000	14.3	16.1	33,810	26,190	23,810
2	30,000	40,000	17.2	18.4	38,640	17,550	22,450
3							
4							
5							
6							
7							
8							
9							
10							
11							
12							
13							

* From Exhibit 6.

† From Exhibit 6.

‡ Based on an average of 2,100 logs per kiln firing. Minimum required kiln firings = (Fired logs required by finishing – Beginning fired log inventory + Minimum desired inventory level) ÷ by 2,100 logs per firing. For Period 1: (40,000 – 30,000 + 20,000) ÷ 2,100 = 14.3.

§ Based on the rule that kiln firings may only occur in multiples of 2.3 per week with a maximum of 27.6 firings per period (see text). To cover Period 1 minimum required firings (14.3), the kilns must be fired 16.1 times.

‖ Actual firings times 2,100 logs per firing.

Beginning green log inventory for Period 1 = 30,000. Ending green log inventory = Beginning green log inventory + Green log production – Actual logs fired. Minimum desired inventory level is 15,000 logs; minimum desired total inventory of green and fired logs is 40,000 logs. For Period 1: 30,000 + 30,000 – 33,810 = 26,190.

¶ Beginning fired log inventory = 30,000. Ending fired log inventory = Beginning fired log inventory + Actual logs fired – Logs required by finishing. For Period 1: 30,000 + 33,810 – 40,000 = 23,810. Minimum desired inventory level is 15,000 logs.

fully. He had summarized the major factors he examined when evaluating these trade-offs as follows:

1. **Maintenance of a five-day workweek.** The economics of overtime had made it unattractive to schedule extrusion or finishing operations for the weekend.

2. **Elimination of work force reductions.** The cost of layoffs had been very high for a number of reasons. First, all hourly workers at Corning had been represented by a single union and the labor contract had provided for bumping. This meant that if a finishing line shift were laid off, senior people on that shift were able to bump anyone else in a Corning area plant with less seniority. Thus, for each person laid off there would on average be two or three job changes, which caused disruptions at other Corning locations as well as at the Erwin plant. Second, motivation of employees remaining always had been extremely low after a layoff. With management continually urging increased production, after a layoff occurred hourly workers—fearing they would run out of work—tended to lower output per man-hour. This made it extremely difficult to produce efficiently and continue to reduce costs through yield improvements.

3. **Minimization of expansions in production levels.** While hourly workers never complained about expansion of the level of output, it did cause considerable disruption. Shift foremen had to learn to deal with a new group of people, different production standards and performance measures had to be established, and worker efficiency tended to decrease even if only temporarily.

4. **Minimization of inventory.** Erwin had to maintain adequate inventory to fulfill contract provisions and balance operations. However, the plant generally had kept inventories as small as possible since inventory was one of the factors by which Corning had evaluated the Erwin plant's performance.

The output of Mike's planning procedure was a set of documents like Exhibits 5, 6, and 7 which he gave to Plant Manager Bob Forrest, General Manager Bill Stroud, production supervisors, and sales personnel. Ending inventory figures went to the plant controller where they were converted into dollar amounts and compared with specified performance measures. From the aggregate plan Mike had his scheduler prepare a detailed 12-week production schedule for each of the plant's 22 substrates.

The aggregate plan provided a helpful detailed guide for materials control and purchasing. It had not been uncommon for the basic ceramic materials and packaging materials to require a two- to three-period lead time in ordering. The aggregate plan allowed scheduling of rail car arrivals to balance production needs against the costs of early arrivals. In the initial months of the plant's operation bulk ceramic materials had often arrived far ahead of production needs and demurrage charges of $50 per day rail car had run at a level of $20,000 to $30,000 per period. (Storage facilities for these materials were limited.) Due partly to better aggregate plans and improvements in Mike's organization, demurrage had recently been brought under control and reduced to about $2,000 per period.

Production planning for 1975

Mike's immediate task had been preparation of an aggregate plan for the 13 periods in 1975. In preparing the plan, he wanted to consider closing the plant for two weeks' vacation during the year if that would better meet his objectives. While at least one of those two weeks would need to occur in the summer so that employees would have part of their vacation when children were out of school, he felt that he could designate the other week almost anytime during the year. For technical reasons, kilns had to continue to be operated during plant close-downs at the minimum of 2.3 firings per week, and could be operated up to the maximum rate of 6.9 per week if so desired.

In recent discussions with the department foreman of the extrusion operation, Mike had learned that the output of good green logs for the current period had been running 30 percent–40 percent above standard due to workers producing at a faster rate than budgeted. (Yield at this point had not changed.) He had felt justified in assuming that this level could be maintained if doing so eliminated the need to lay off a shift in finishing. (There was sufficient group spirit in the plant that extrusion probably could maintain the high level of output if they knew the jobs of people in finishing depended on it.)

For the longer run, Mike had realized that there were several areas in which he might focus his attentions in order to improve his planning procedures and the production operations of the plant. These had included:

Development of more and better cost data. While Mike had felt that the information available to him in December had been adequate for planning, he had not had time during the hectic first nine months of plant operation to analyze the appropriateness of his cost inputs or to develop additional cost data.

Preparation of a computer model that would make it easier to evaluate alternative aggregate plans, to test alternative decision rules and perform sensitivity analyses on the impact of uncertain shipment forecasts and fluctuating production yields.

Development of improved forecasting procedures utilizing auto company sales data, information on inventories in the catalytic converter pipeline and more formal forecasting techniques.

An evaluation of possible alternative contract terms with the auto companies that would provide greater stability for the Erwin plant.

An analysis of the relevant costs for the major trade-offs involved in the aggregate planning task and the conversion of the results into useful decision rules.

Chapter 9

Operations sequencing and balance

AS WE NOTED in discussing the problems of scheduling facilities and workers in the previous chapter, the scheduling of individual operations is normally not necessary for high-volume assembly manufacturing operations because scheduling the line embodies an implicit schedule for all stations on the line. The line is like a giant machine, and once designed and sequenced, internal scheduling is accomplished unless for some reason we rebalance and resequence the operations or stations on the line. So the original design of the line in terms of operation sequencing and balance is related to the broad scheduling problem, since the line must be designed to meet specified output rate requirements. We also noted that part of the flexibility open in adjusting to changes in production requirements can be achieved through rebalancing facilities and manning assignments to new and different output rates. Thus, when an aggregate plan calls for a change in employment levels, it is through this rebalancing procedure that we can absorb more or less labor on the lines.

In Chapter 8 we gave a preliminary statement of the balance problem in order to convey the characteristic nature of rigidity imposed as well as the degree of flexibility open ot us. At this point, however, we would like to indulge in a more careful statement of the actual sequencing and balance problem. We will then follow this problem statement with a review of some of the prominent balancing methodologies and a comparative study which attempts to evaluate them. Finally, we will review some work which lends additional insight into production line operation and develop some criteria for the design of production lines.

The problem of production line design

In simplest terms the essence of the problem is as we stated it in Chapter 8. The product or component to be fabricated or assembled can be represented by a network of work elements or tasks and associated times, some of which must be performed in a given sequence in order to meet the specifications of the product design. In general, the definition of a work element or task is the smallest unit of productive work which is separable from other activity to the extent that it can be performed relatively independently, and possibly in different sequences. But the precedence diagram or network which we showed as Figure 8–3 indicates that many tasks cannot be done in different sequences because of what we generally call technological sequence restrictions. Thus a large number of the possible alternatives for grouping tasks into operations or stations are eliminated as not being feasible solutions. The simplest statement of the problem, then, is to find a grouping of tasks into stations which is feasible and minimizes the number of stations, given a specified desired output rate or cycle time.

In essence, then, the problem is a combinatorial one. "There are $n!$ different sequences of n tasks without precedence constraints. For as few as fifteen tasks $n!$ is 1,307,674,368,000 the enumeration and evaluation of which is beyond the life-span of man or computer" [2]. Fortunately, the technological sequencing requirements reduce the number of *feasible* sequences considerably. Still, we are dealing with a problem for which we cannot consider enumerating all of the possible feasible solutions in order to select the best one. Also fortunately, there normally would be many solutions which are equivalent. They would involve the minimum number of stations for a given specified output rate; otherwise the problem might seem almost hopeless.

Complexities. But, the problem of the design of production lines does not stop when the sequencing and balance have been determined in the simplest form as just stated. There are some other constraints which may enter the problem, and there are some important questions to be raised about aspects of the design other than balance and sequencing. First, there are other physical constraints which can enter the balancing and sequencing problem; for example, should station 3 be located on the front or back side of the line, or below it? An examination of the product to be assembled or fabricated may be required to see how it should be oriented throughout the sequence of processes or if its orientation should be changed at times to facilitate the work to be done. Perhaps a change in sequence (a new sequence restriction) will eliminate the need to reorient. Are there fixed locations for some stations because of equipment which cannot be moved, or moved only at substantial cost?

Other problems in balance occur if one or more of the task times exceed the cycle time for which we are trying to obtain balance. Flexibility of worker position may get around this problem, or sometimes simply adding to the work force assigned to the station can solve it. But sometimes it may be impossible for two sets of hands to accomplish more than one can for a given task. Perhaps the reverse of the latter problem is the task that by its nature requires two workers, one in a supporting role to help lift or guide a part. If the second worker is not fully utilized in the supporting role, then he or she becomes part of the balance and sequencing problem. Can the worker be useful in a supporting role at other stations? Can the workers be assigned tasks of their own to do at the work station in order to utilize available time more fully?

There are a host of other considerations and questions which might have an important impact on the design of a line. Some will interact with balance. Given sequencing, balance, and cycle times, we can run conveyors or other transportation equipment at various speeds to move parts through the process. What are the best speeds? Should parts be attached to conveyors or not? Or stated another way, should workers be mechanically paced by the line or not? Should there be an inventory of items available between stations? What are the physical space requirements? Should workers' locations be fixed or should they range up and down the line? Should workers ride the line while performing their task and then return to some point upstream to begin their cycle over again?

Finally, there are some nagging theoretical and social questions. In the first category there is the question of the use of deterministic time values for tasks and groups of tasks. What would happen to the balancing models if times were more realistically represented as time distributions? Obviously, there is performance time variation, and sometimes the time cycles for two stations in the sequence might both be long ones and sometimes short ones and most often fitting together in varying proportions of long and short cycles. Are the task times additive anyway [3, 4, 10, 26]? If task 1 requires 10 seconds and task 2 takes 15 seconds when done independently, does it require 25 seconds to perform the two tasks together? Balancing models assume that they are additive.

In the second category of nagging questions are those guided by social values. These are related to the feeling often expressed that jobs designed as a result of line balancing are degrading and require the worker to be no more than a link in a giant machine. There is also a related controversy about the economic and social value of job specialization (carried to an extreme in production lines) versus job enlargement. These are extremely important questions in our society, and by evading them here we are simply saying that they are not a part of the focus of this book.

Choice of a cycle time

From the point of view of the overall scheduling problem the cycle time (basic production rate) should be specified according to the requirements established by the aggregate plan, and we must not forget this fact. Balance cannot specify output rate; rather, basic output rate must be derived from the forecasts of the market. But, within the limited range of output rates which might satisfy the aggregate plan, are there certain choices of cycle times for a line which might be better than others or than an arbitrary specification of cycle time? The answer is yes, and the better choices are found through an examination of the balance delay function [18]. The balance delay function shows for a given situation the percent idle time inherent in a range of cycle times which might be selected as a basis for balancing the line.

Suppose, for example, that we are examining a situation in which the sum of all the task times is 360 seconds over the range of possible cycle times of 30 to 60 seconds (range of output rates from 60 to 120 per hour). Perfect balance can occur within certain combinations of cycle time (c) and numbers of stations (n) on the line, such as, $c = 30$ seconds per cycle, $n = 12$ stations; $c = 36, n = 10$; $c = 40, n = 9$; $c = 45, n = 8$; and, $c = 60, n = 6$. All other feasible combinations will have a positive percent balance delay, d, defined by,

$$d = 100(nc - \Sigma t_i)/nc \qquad (1)$$

when n and c are defined as before and the t_i are task times and where n, c, and the t_i are integer numbers. Figure 9–1 shows the balance

Figure 9–1
Typical balance delay function (task times total 360 seconds)

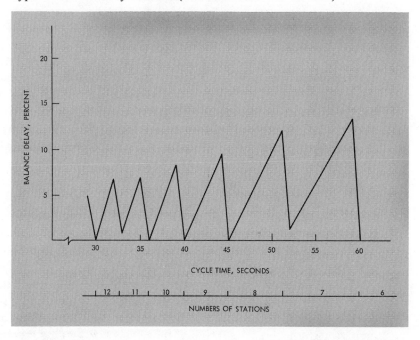

delay function for these conditions. Obviously, some cycle time selections are potentially much better than others. For example, perfect balance is theoretically possible by the selection of c's of 30, 36, 40, 45, and 60 seconds. Also, low values of balance delay occur for cycle times just over the perfect values. On the other hand, selection of cycle times just below the perfect balance values guarantees maximum balance delay. Also note for the example given in Figure 9–1 that perfect balance is not obtainable for 7 and 11 stations because of the discrete nature of the function. We have, of course, chosen a convenient set of numbers for illustration since the sum of task times, 360 seconds, is divisible by a number of the cycle times to produce integer numbers, in the range chosen. Ordinarily it might not work out so conveniently.

Let us note also that the conditions described by the balance delay function are not sufficient for perfect balance. The essential other conditions are that we be able to assign the task times perfectly to the n work stations. That assignment problem is the subject of the following review of operation sequencing and line balance methodologies.

Sequencing and balance methodologies

There have been a large number of proposals for theoretical and practical methods for solving the sequencing and line balancing problem, as may be noted by scanning the bibliography at the end of this chapter. Some of the proposals in the literature have been attempts to deal with the theoretical structure of the problem with a view toward deeper insight and understanding without an attempt to apply the proposed analysis to large-scale balancing problems [14, 16, 30]. Some others, particularly Arcus [1, 2] and Kilbridge and Wester [17, 32] have emphasized the solution of fairly large-scale practical problems and have taken as the definition of the problem the broader statement which we discussed. The broader statement of the problem is, of course, messier and more difficult to deal with and often leads to heuristics in obtaining a solution, but it is more realistic.

Though perhaps implied previously, we make the explicit statement that truly realistic problem definition must include the recognition that the important cases for solution are large-scale ones involving perhaps 75-100 tasks or more and line lengths involving 10-15 or more stations. With this in mind we have selected for presentation the COMSOAL technique developed by Arcus, a computer-based sampling methodology, and "heuristic line balancing" a method developed by Kilbridge and Wester. Later, when we present the results of a comparative study, we will discuss briefly the methodologies of several other techniques, including Dar-El's (Mansoor's) MALB, a new technique with particular promise. We will present the Kilbridge and Wester heuristic technique first, since Arcus compares some of his results to those obtained by the heuristic method.

Heuristic line balancing. The procedure is best described in terms of an example such as the one defined by the precedence diagram in Figure 9–2 which summarizes technological sequencing requirements. As before, the circled numbers represent task or element numbers and the small numbers beside the circles represent

Figure 9–2
Precedence diagram for work elements

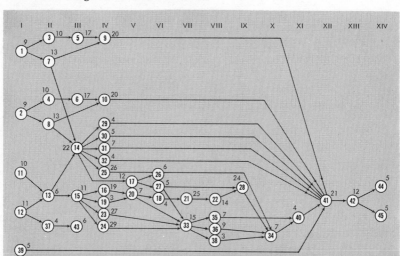

Source: From M. D. Kilbridge and L. Wester. "A Heuristic Method of Assembly Line Balancing," *Journal of Industrial Engineeering*, vol. 12, no. 4 (July–August 1961).

task times in hundredths of minutes. The precedence diagram was constructed by the methods described by Jackson [16], and the diagram constructed in this way is important to the operation of the heuristic method.

The procedure for the construction of the diagram follows. In column I of the diagram list all tasks or work elements which need not follow other tasks. Immediate follower tasks are then listed in columns II, III, and so on, observing precedence relationships. Note that all tasks are as far to the left of the diagram as they can be when sequence restrictions are observed. The sum of all task times is 552, and theoretically perfect balance can be obtained with a cycle time of $c = 552/3 = 184$, or 3 stations (Figure 9–3). The procedure will be described in terms of an objective of balancing the line perfectly for three stations at a cycle time of 184.

Figure 9–2 has been summarized in the more useful tabular form shown in Table 9–1. The most important new information in Table 9–1 is in column (C) which summarizes the flexibility in assignment of tasks to columns of the precedence diagram. For example, task 39 could be moved to the right to any of the columns of the precedence diagram up to column XI without changing basic precedence rela-

Figure 9–3
Precedence diagram balanced for three stations

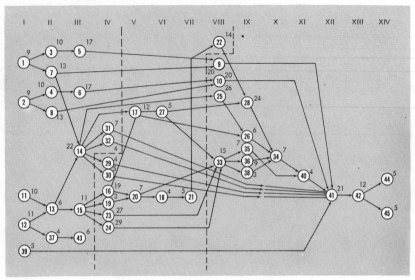

Source: From M. D. Kilbridge and L. Wester, "A Heuristic Method of Assembly Line Balancing," *Journal of Industrial Engineering*, vol. 12, no. 4 (July–August 1961).

tionships. This flexibility in moving tasks horizontally will be useful in the procedure which follows. Note that some tasks, such as task 3, are listed in column (B) Table 9–1 with the notation (w. task number). This is meant to indicate that the task in question can be moved horizontally on the precedence diagram only if the associated task moves ahead of it. For example, task 3 can move to the right only if tasks 5 and 9 move ahead of it. Other data in Table 9–1 which will be of value are the time durations of elements by columns in the original precedence diagram shown in column (E) and the cumulative time sums shown in column (F). Given all of these data we proceed as follows:

Step 1. Since $c = 184$, scan column (F) of Table 9–1 to find the cumulative sum which brackets 184. The cumulative sum for column III comes close, being 173. The task times in column I, II, and III fall short of satisfying the needs of station 1 by only $184 - 173 = 11$ time units.

Step 2. Scan the task times in column IV of the precedence diagram. Is there a combination of task time which adds exactly to 11? Yes, tasks 31 and 32 have task times of 7 and 4, respectively.

Step 3. Move tasks 31 and 32 to the top of the column IV list, thus

Table 9–1
Tabular representation of precedence diagram of Figure 9–2

(A) Column number of diagram	(B) Task identification number	(C) Remarks	(D) Task time dura- tion t_i	(E) Sum of time dura- tions	(F) Cumu- lative time sums
I	1 2 11 12 39	 → II, . . . , XI	9 9 10 11 5	 44	 44
II	3 (w. 5, 9) 7 4 (w. 6, 10) 8 13 37 (w. 43)	→ III, . . . , IX → III, . . . , IX → III, . . . , XIII	10 13 10 13 6 4	 56	 100
III	5 (w. 9) 6 (w. 10) 14 15 43	→ IV, . . . , X → IV, . . . , X → IV, . . . , XIV	17 17 22 11 6	 73	 173
IV	9 10 29 30 31 32 25 16 19 23 24	→ V, . . . , XI → V, . . . , XI → V, . . . , XI → V, . . . , XI → V, . . . , XI → V, . . . , XI → V, . . . , VIII → V, VI → V, VI	20 20 4 5 7 4 26 19 3 27 29	 164	 337
V	17 20		12 7	 19	 356
VI	26 27 18	→ VII, . . . , IX	6 5 4	 15	 371
VII	21 33 (w. 35, 36, 38)	 → VIII	55 15	 70	 441
VIII	22 35 36 38	 → IX, X → IX → IX	14 7 9 3	 33	 474
IX	28		24	24	498
X	34		7	7	505
XI	40		4	4	509
XII	41		21	21	530
XIII	42		12	12	542
XIV	44 45		5 5	 10	 552

Source: From M. D. Kilbridge and L. Wester, "A Heuristic Method of Assembly Line Balancing," *Journal of Industrial Engineering*, vol. 12, no. 4 (July–August 1961).

assigning them to station 1. All tasks in columns in I, II, and III plus tasks 31 and 32 of column IV are now assigned to station 1. The status of solution is now shown by Table 9–2.

Step 4. Scan column (F) of Table 9–2 to find the cumulative sum which brackets $2 \times 184 = 368$. The cumulative sum for column VI is 371.

Step 5. Scan the list of unassigned tasks which can be moved horizontally beyond the 368 total in column VI or to column VII. They are tasks 9, 10, 29, 30, and 25 (w. 26).

Step 6. Is there a combination of task times which can be moved and totals $371 - 368 = 3$? No.

Step 7. Augment the column number in step 4 and repeat. Cumulative sum for column VII in precedence diagram is 441.

Step 8. Scan the list of unassigned tasks which can be moved horizontally beyond the 368 total in column VI or to column VII. They are tasks 9, 10, 29, 30, 25 (w. 26), and 33 (w. 35, 36, 38).

Step 9. Is there a combination of movable task times which totals $441 - 368 = 73$? No.

Step 11. Scan the list of unassigned tasks which can be moved horizontally beyond the 368 total in column VIII, or to column IX. They are tasks 9, 10, 29, 30, 25 (w. 26), and 33 (w. 35, 36, 38).

Step 12. Is there a combination of movable elements which adds to $474 - 368 = 106$, or conversely, since the task time in the movable set totals 115, is there a combination in the movable set totaling $115 - 106 = 9$ which can be retained in station 2? Yes there is, the task times for 29 and 30 are $4 + 5 = 9$ and the balance of these movable tasks have times which total 106.

Step 13. Move task numbers 9, 10, 25 (w. 26), and 33 (w. 35, 36, 38) beyond the 368 total in column VIII or beyond as required by precedence relationships. Station 2 is now made up of the tasks in column IV (not including 31 and 32), V, VI, VII, and 22 in column VIII.

Step 14. Station 3 is made up of the balance of the unassigned tasks whose times also total 184. The final assignment is shown in Table 9–3 and in the precedence diagram of Figure 9–3.

The 14-step procedure just outlined is not a general procedure but is specific to the explanation of this example. Kilbridge and Wester [17] give the following generalizations and suggestions as assistance in applying their heuristic method.

1. Permutability within columns is used to facilitate the selection of elements [tasks] of the length desired for optimum packing of the work

Table 9–2
Modified Table 9–1 after assignment of work elements to station 1 only

(A) Column number of diagram	(B) Task identification number	(C) Remarks	(D) Task time duration t_i	(E) Sum of time durations	(F) Cumulative time sums
I	1		9		
	2		9		
	11		10		
	12		11		
	39		5		
II	3		10		
	7		13		
	4		10		
	8		13		
	13		6		
	37		4		
III	5		17		
	6		17		
	14		22		
	15		11		
	43		6		
IV	31		7		
	32		4	184	184
	9	→ V, . . . , XI	20		
	10	→ V, . . . , XI	20		
	29	→ V, . . . , XI	4		
	30	→ V, . . . , XI	5		
	25 (w. 26)	→ V, . . . , VIII	26		
	16		19		
	19		3		
	23	→ V, VI	27		
	24	→ V, VI	29	153	337
V	17		12		
	20		7	19	356
VI	26	→ VII, . . . , IX	6		
	27		5		
	18		4	15	371
VII	21		55		
	33 (w, 35, 36, 38)	→ VIII	15	70	441
VIII	22		14		
	35	→ IX, X	7		
	36	→ IX	9		
	38	→ IX	3	33	474
IX	28		24	24	498
X	34		7	7	505
XI	40		4	4	509
XII	41		21	21	530
XIII	42		12	12	542
XIV	44		5		
	45		5	10	552

Station 1

Unassigned Work

Source: From M. D. Kilbridge and L. Wester, "A Heuristic Method of Assembly Line Balancing," *Journal of Industrial Engineering*, vol. 12, no. 4 (July–August 1961).

Table 9–3
Modified Table 9–2 after assignment of work elements to all three stations

(A) Column number of diagram	(B) Task identification number	(C) Remarks	(D) Task time duration t_i	(E) Sum of time durations	(F) Cumulative time sums	
I	1		9			
	2		9			
	11		10			
	12		11			
	39		5			
II	3		10			
	7		13			
	4		10			
	8		13			
	13		6			Station 1
	37		4			
III	5		17			
	6		17			
	14		22			
	15		11			
	43		6			
IV	31		7			
	32		4	184	184	
	29		4			
	30		5			
	16		19			
	19		3			
	23		27			
	24		29			
V	17		12			
	20		7			Station 2
VI	27		5			
	18		4			
VII	21		55			
VIII	22		14	184	368	
	9		20			
	10		20			
	25		26			
	33		15			
IX	28		24			
	26		6			
	35		7			
	36		9			Station 3
	38		3			
X	34		7			
XI	40		4			
XII	41		21			
XIII	42		12			
XIV	44		5			
	45		5	184	552	

Source: From M. D. Kilbridge and L. Wester, "A Heuristic Method of Assembly Line Balancing," *Journal of Industrial Engineering*, vol. 12, no. 4 (July–August 1961).

stations. Lateral transferability helps to deploy the work elements [tasks] along the stations of the assembly line so they can be used where they best serve the packing solution.

2.   Generally the solutions are not unique. Elements [tasks] assigned to a station which belong after the assignment is made in one column of the precedence diagram, can generally be permuted within the column. This allows the line supervisor some leeway to alter the sequence of work elements [tasks] without disturbing optimum balance.

3.   Long-time elements [tasks] are best disposed of first, if possible. Thus, if there is a choice between the assignment of an element of duration, say, 20, and the assignment of two elements of duration, say, 10 each, assign the larger element first. Small elements are saved for ease of manipulation at the end of the line. The situation is analogous to that of a pay master dispensing the week's earnings in cash. He will count out the largest bills first. Thus, if the amount to be paid a worker is $77, the pay master will give three $20 bills first, then one $10 bill, one $5 bill and two $1 bills, in that order.

4.   When moving elements laterally, the move is best made only as far to the right as necessary to allow a sufficient choice of elements for the work station being considered.

More complex application.   Wester and Kilbridge applied the heuristic technique to a television assembly line which introduced complexities of worker position with respect to the assembly line and with respect to the orientation of the television set on the line. Figure 9–4 shows a schematic drawing of the assembly line, which we see has been broken down into two main components, line A and line B. Line A involved chassis assembly and testing while line B involved the console assembly. We will discuss only line A, though Wester and Kilbridge present the results for both lines [32].

The precedence diagram for line A shown in Figure 9–5 indicates the nature of the additional complexities. Some tasks had to be performed from the front side of the line, some from the back side of the line, but most tasks could be performed from either side. Also, in order to perform some tasks the front of the television set needed to be facing the operator, in some the back of the set needed to be facing the operator, and for some tasks the orientation of the set could be either way. Notice that the testing station divides the network into two groupings. The tasks were categorized into four sets as follows: The α set involved those where the operator faced the front of the television set from the backside of the line. This included tasks 1, 2, 3, 4, 5, 6, and 23, but excluded 16 and 17. Tasks 16 and 17 were isolated by task 14, which required the operator to face the back of the set. The β set then included tasks 16 and 17. The γ group of

Figure 9–4
Schematic drawing of a television assembly line

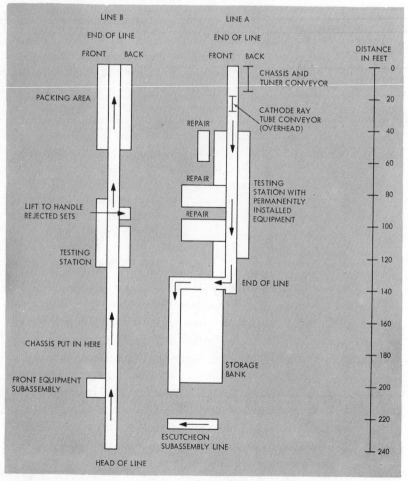

tasks comprised all of the rest prior to testing. These tasks could be performed on the front side of the line facing the back of the television set. Similarly, the tasks following testing could be located on the front side of the line and were coded as the δ set.

The construction of the balance delay function is complicated by the four mutually exclusive groupings of tasks, since for a given cycle time the minimum number of stations required must be computed separately for each of the four groupings of tasks. Figure 9–6

Figure 9–5
Precedence diagram for tasks on line A

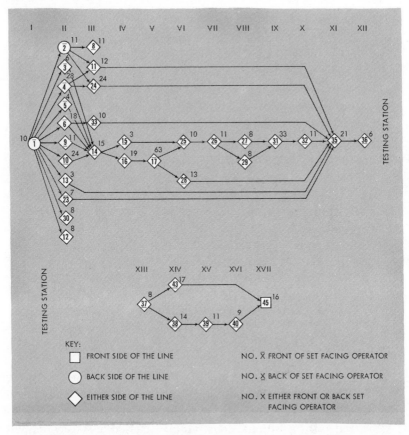

Source: From L. Wester and M. D. Kilbridge, "Heuristic Line Balancing: A Case," *Journal of Industrial Engineering*, vol. 13, No. 3 (May–June 1962).

shows that in the range of cycle times from 0.63 minutes to 1.02 minutes there is a unique opportunity to develop balance at a cycle of 0.84 minutes with a minimum possible balance delay of 2.58 percent. This cycle time was taken as the objective and balance of line A was developed for six stations, actually achieving the minimum balance delay of 2.58 percent. Table 9–4 shows the resulting assignment of tasks to stations which takes into account all of the technological sequencing constraints as well as the positional constraints discussed. In the far right column of Table 9–4 the coding of the operator assignments as B and F refers to their positional assignment to either the back or the front of the line.

Figure 9–6
Balance delay function for line A

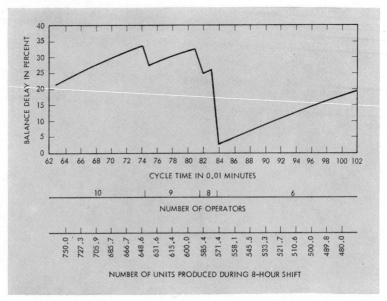

Source: From L. Wester and M. D. Kilbridge, "Heuristic Line Balancing: A Case," *Journal of Industrial Engineering*, vol. 13, no. 3 (May–June 1962).

The present authors can attest to the fact that the heuristic procedure is a tedious one, but it is apparently effective with complex problems involving the usual technological sequencing constraints as well as the positional constraints discussed in connection with the balance of line A of the television assembly problem. Line B was even more complex than line A, involving 133 tasks and the same range of positional constraints as in line A. The complete development of the balance delay functions and the resulting solutions for both lines are shown in [32].

Thomopoulos [27, 28] has developed a mixed model application of the same general heuristic method involving some modifications. This formulation applies to problems involving balance of lines which assemble several models intermixed on the same line.

COMSOAL (Computer Method of Sequencing Operations for Assembly Lines). We might characterize Arcus' COMSOAL [1, 2] as a method by which a fairly large number of feasible solutions are generated rapidly by a biased sampling method. The best solutions in the set become alternate solutions to the line balance problem. The

Table 9–4
Balance of line A: Assignment of Task ($c = 84$)

(A) Column number of precedence diagram	(B) Task identification number	(C) Task time duration t_i	(D) Sum of time duration	(E) Cumulative time sum	
I	1	10			
II	2	11			
	3	6			← Operator 1B →
	4	28			——Tasks α——
	5	4			
	6	18			
	23	7	84	84	
IV	16	19			← Op. 2B →
V	17	63	82	82	— Tasks β —
II	9	11			
	10	24			
III	24	24			← Oper. 1F →
	33	10			
	14	15	84	84	
IV	15	3			
V	—	—			
VI	25	10			
VII	26	11			— Operator 2F —
VIII	27	8			— Tasks γ —
	29	8			
IX	31	33			
X	32	11	84	168	
	8	11			
	11	12			
	13	3			
	30	8			— Operator 3F —
	12	8			
	28	13			
XI	35	21			
XII	36	6	82	250	
XIII	37	8			
XIV	43	17			— Operator 4F —
	38	14			— Tasks δ —
XV	39	11			
XVI	40	9			
XVII	45	16	75	75	

Source: From M. D. Kilbridge and L. Wester, "A Heuristic Method of Assembly Line Balancing," *Journal of Industrial Engineering*, vol. 12, no. 4 (July–August 1961).

universe from which we are sampling is, of course, all of the possible feasible solutions to the particular line balance problem, and there is a finite probability that we can turn up optimal solutions in this fashion, a slightly larger probability of turning up the next best solutions, and so on. The probability of developing excellent solutions is, of course, related to the size of the sample we generate. Obviously, the trick will be in generating feasible solutions rapidly and biasing the generation of these solutions toward the better ones rather than simply generating feasible solutions at random.

The theory behind COMSOAL is illustrated by the simple example shown in Figure 9–7. In Figure 9–7 (a) a precedence diagram is shown for an eight-task assembly job which is to be balanced for a 10-minute cycle time. Arcus manually enumerated all of the 112 feasible combinations of the tasks which involved four, five, or six stations, and the result is shown in the histogram of Figure 9–7(b). There were 25 solutions which utilized four stations, 84 which utilized five stations and only 3 which utilized six stations. Obviously there are additional feasible solutions involving seven and eight stations, but they are not very interesting.

COMSOAL generates feasible solutions by the following general procedure:

Step I. First, by scanning precedence information, list A is formed. This list simply tabulates the total number of tasks which immediately precede each given task. For the example of Figure 9–7 (a) we have:

List A	Task	Total number of immediately preceding tasks
	a	0
	b	1
	c	1
	d	1
	e	1
	f	2
	g	2
	h	2

Step II. The computing routine then scans list A to identify all tasks which have no preceding tasks and places them in list B, the "available list." For our simple example only task a meets these requirements so list B is,

(Available) List B	Task
	a

Figure 9–7
(a) An eight-task precedence diagram, and (b) the
histogram representing the distribution of the 112
feasible solutions for a 10-minute cycle time, involving
four, five, or six stations

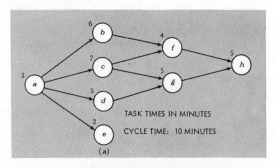

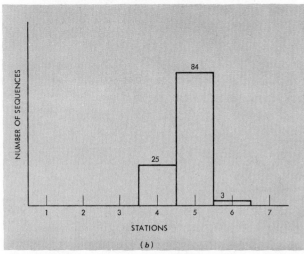

Source: From A. L. Arcus, "COMSOAL: A Computer Method of
Sequencing Operations for Assembly Lines" [1, 2].

Step III. The available list, B, is then partitioned by placing in list
C those tasks which have times no greater than the time left available
at the station being assigned work. List C is called the "fit list" since
only elements that fit the time left to be assigned within a station are
listed. In our example the available time at station 1 is 10 since no
assignments have yet been made, and the time for task a in list B is
only three, so it is transferred to list C,

(Fit) List C   Task
a

Step IV. In the simplest form of COMSOAL, the assignment is now made by selecting at random from the fit list a task to be assigned to station 1. Since only task a is in the fit list at this point, it is selected and assigned to station 1.

Step V. Eliminate task a from lists B and C (leaving them empty at this point for our example).

Step VI. Update list A by scanning the immediate followers of task a and deduct 1 from the tally of the "total number of preceding tasks" as follows:

List A	Task	Total number of immediately preceding tasks
	a	0
	b	$1 - 1 = 0$
	c	$1 - 1 = 0$
	d	$1 - 1 = 0$
	e	$1 - 1 = 0$
	f	2
	g	2
	h	2

Step VII. Update the tasks available in list B by transferring from list A all tasks now listed as having no preceding tasks. List B becomes:

(Available) List B	Task
	b
	c
	d
	e

Step VIII. Transfer from list B to list C those tasks which *fit* the remaining time to be assigned to station 1, or, $10 - 3 = 7$. Since in this instance all of the task times in list B are 7 or less, the fit list becomes,

(Fit) List C	Task
	b
	c
	d
	e

Step IX. Select at random from list C a task to assign to station 1.

Step X. Eliminate the selected task from lists B and C. Repeat Step VI through X until station 1 has been as fully assigned as it can be and continue the procedure, station by station, until all tasks are assigned. As a solution is completed its station count is compared to the station count of the previous best sequence. If there is an improvement, the new solution is stored in memory and the old one discarded. The result is that the computer memory holds no more than two solutions at any one time.

As mentioned, the COMSOAL procedure just outlined was simplified to facilitate the overall grasp of the routine. Actually, instead of selecting a task at random from the fit list, C, as mentioned in both Steps IV and IX, the program biases the selection of the tasks by weighting the tasks in the fit list. A second variation from the procedure outlined provides for aborting a solution as soon as it becomes apparent that the accumulated idle time of the incomplete solution exceeds the total idle time of the previous best solution, since the solution being generated cannot be an improvement. The result of the aborting procedure is to save computer time and have that time spent examining potentially better solutions.

The weighting procedure developed by Arcus is the product of the weights computed by the following five rules:

Rule 1. Weight tasks that fit in proportion to task time. The effect of this weighting is to give large tasks a greater probability of being assigned than small ones.

Rule 2. Weight tasks that fit by $1/X'$, where X' is equal to the total number of unassigned tasks minus 1 less the number of all of the tasks that follow the task being considered. The effect of Rule 2 is to give those tasks that have a large number of followers a greater probability of being assigned than tasks with a small number of followers.

Rule 3. Weight tasks that fit by the total number of all following tasks plus 1. The effect of this rule is to prefer tasks which, when selected, will be replaced and therefore expand the available list.

Rule 4. Weight tasks that fit by the times of the task and of all following tasks. The effect of this rule is to combine the advantages of rules 1 and 3 by selecting large tasks early at each station in the entire sequence, or alternatively by preferring tasks which, although small, tend to expand the available list.

Rule 5. Weight tasks that fit by the total number of following tasks plus 1, divided by the number of levels which those following tasks occupy plus 1. The effect of this weight is to give work elements in the longest chains the greatest probability of being assigned first.

Results. The computer program designed to operate in the form just described with the weighting and aborting procedures is described by Arcus as being applicable to the sequencing and assembly line balance problem in simple form. Arcus applied the program to the 45-task example used by Wester and Kilbridge [32], and summarized earlier in this chapter, and produced optimal assignments in an average of 32 seconds of IBM 7090 computer time. Arcus also applied the program to Tonge's [30, 31] 70-task example (22 stations) in 0.7 seconds and to a 111-task industrial example (27 stations) in 0.7 seconds.

COMSOAL for the balance problem in complex form. Having found a computing procedure that produced optimal or near optimal solutions for basic line balance problems, Arcus proceeded to provide for a series of other more realistic constraints on the program. In essence, these constraints affect the fit list which must satisfy the new constraints in addition to those stated earlier. We will not attempt to describe these additional constraints in detail, but the following list should serve to describe their general nature:

1. Tasks larger than the cycle time.
2. Tasks that require two workers.
3. Tasks fixed in location.
4. Space for parts.
5. Time to obtain a tool.
6. Time for the worker to change position.
7. Time to change the position of a unit. (Orientation of the unit being worked on.)
8. Grouping tasks by criteria.
9. Wages related to tasks.
10. Worker movement between units being assembled.
11. Mixed production on the same line.
12. Stochastic task performance times.

Arcus states that the earliest model of COMSOAL has already been implemented by the Chrysler Corporation, and that a hypothetical line with 1,000 tasks and a known optimum of 200 stations with zero idle time has been run. In addition, a sequence requiring 203 stations resulting in 1.48 percent idle time was computed, and a line with 111 tasks, five mixed products, and all of the complexities just listed had been run.

One of the obvious advantages of a program like COMSOAL for the production scheduling function in an enterprise is the rapidity with which we can call for alternate balance solutions in an attempt to provide the best possible way to adjust to changes in employment level called for by aggregate plans. COMSOAL could also help in building the cost model required for the aggregate plan. It could evaluate the realistic cost effects of decisions for different production levels. Since employment levels are not a continuous function of production rates, we need the actual number of employees required so we can determine the actual hiring and layoff costs which would be associated with decisions to change levels.

Evaluation of alternate line balance methods

Mastor [22] made a comparative study of some of the most prominent line balancing techniques and thereby has performed an invaluable service. In the 1960's, no less than 16 different proposals for line balance systems were made. The picture presented to the practitioner has been a confusing one, since the intercomparisons between methods were not usually clear. Some methods were proposed only as research insights and not to solve practical problems. Mastor's study helped to evaluate the relative power of some of the major proposals, as well as to point out some of their outstanding strengths and weaknesses.

Mastor's study systematically varied three factors, problem size as measured by the number of tasks to be assigned, line length as measured by the number of stations, and order strength of the precedence diagram as measured by the ratio of the number of ordering relations present to the possible number. Computations were made for 20- and 40-task problems at three different order strengths, 0.25, 0.50, 0.75, and at various line lengths. For each problem there could be established a *lower bound* cycle time so that measured average cycle times for each technique represented idle time for the solution, and comparisons between techniques were made on this basis.

Mastor either wrote special computer programs for a given technique or obtained programs from their original authors. In establishing bases for comparison, he constructed certain benchmark rules for assigning tasks to stations. We will discuss briefly the nature of the benchmark rules as well as the other rules for line balancing used for comparison.

The benchmark rules used in the experiments were called the Lexicographic Order Rule, the Number of Immediate Follower Tasks Rule, the Random Sampling Rule, and the Work Element Time Ordered Rule.

1. Lexicographic Order Rule. The search for available tasks is made in lexicographic order, and the tasks are placed in the available list in the order in which they become available. The first task in the available list is assigned to a station first unless the task time exceeds the remaining time in the station. If the task time exceeds the remaining time in the station, an attempt is made to assign the next task in the available list, and so on. The Lexicographic Order Rule does not attempt to determine the best tasks for an initial assignment to stations or to adjust or improve any assignment made. This rule is similar to a rule that randomly assigns work tasks from the available list. Mastor included the Lexicographic Order Rule as a benchmark representing the type of production line that might result if no attempt was made to obtain good results.

2. Number of Immediate Follower Tasks Rule. This rule assigns a task to a station according to the number of tasks that immediately follow it. The number of immediate follower tasks for each task is recorded in an order of assignment table. Assignments are then made from the available list according to the number of immediate follower tasks, the tasks with the largest number of immediate followers being assigned first. The use of the Number of Immediate Follower Tasks Rule is based on the idea that a large number of available tasks makes it possible to utilize more fully the available time in a station than a small number of available work elements.

3. Random Sampling Rule. This rule was first proposed by Arcus [1]. The main difference between this rule and the other Arcus rule described previously is that the Random Sampling Rule does not attempt to introduce a bias into the selection of feasible sequences.

4. Work Element Time Ordered Rule. This rule assigns tasks to stations on the basis of the time that is required to perform the task or work element. The largest task in the available list is assigned first. If the task time exceeds the remaining time in the station, an attempt is made to assign the next largest task. If all of the task times in the available list exceed the remaining time in a station, the number of stations is increased by 1 and the process repeated. The Work Element Time Ordered Rule is based on the idea that the early assignment of large work elements to stations gives greater flexibility by allowing smaller work elements to be assigned as the remaining time in the station decreases.

Line balancing techniques proposed in the literature. In addition to the benchmark rules just discussed, Mastor made computations and comparisons for several proposed techniques, which are briefly described as follows:

1. *Ranked positional weight technique* [13]. This technique es-

tablishes the order for assigning tasks to stations by summing the task times for a task plus all of the tasks which follow it. Tasks with the largest sums are assigned first.

2. *The Hoffman technique* [14]. This technique enumerates every feasible combination of tasks that may be assigned to a station and selects the combination of tasks that minimizes the idle time for the station.

3. *Column Rule (based on the heuristic line balancing method of Kilbridge and Wester* [17]. This technique was discussed earlier in this chapter.

4. *The Arcus technique* [1, 2]. The Arcus technique was described previously in this chapter.

5. *Held, Karp, and Sharesian* [12]. The algorithm developed by Held, Karp, and Sharesian uses a dynamic programming formulation and a heuristic incorporating dynamic programming for solving subsections of problems.

Results of Mastor's main experiments. We will discuss results only for the 40-task problems. There is some truncating of the results for both the Held and Hoffman techniques because of the very large amounts of computer time required for the low-order strength problems. Figures 9–8 through 9–11 summarize the results. In Figures 9–8, 9–9, and 9–10 considerable overlapping occurs among the results of several techniques so they are not shown individually but as a shaded area to indicate the boundaries within which they were all located. Similar results are shown in all of the graphs. The Held and Arcus techniques consistently stand out as requiring the least idle time for any line length and for all order strengths. As noted previously, the Held technique seems to have limitations in terms of the size of problem to which it is applicable; otherwise it is consistently the best performer. The best computations for the Arcus technique involved sample sizes of 80 feasible sequences. Even larger sample sizes probably would have improved the operating results of that technique. The Lexicographic Order Rule was consistently the worst, as it should have been. The poor showing of the column rule based on the heuristic line balancing method of Kilbridge and Wester is undoubtedly affected by the fact that the intuition of the user could not be programmed.

Computing time. The average computing time for the Held technique was about ten times that required for the Arcus technique on the 40-element problem. Still, the time is modest even for the

Figure 9–8
Idle-time curves for 40-element problems, order strength 0.25

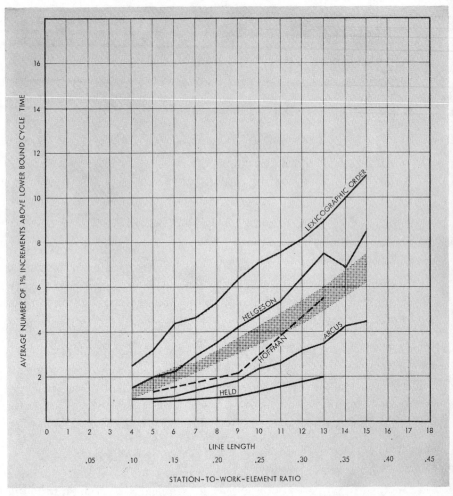

Source: From A. A. Mastor, "An Experimental Investigation and Comparative Evaluation of Production Line Balancing Techniques" (unpublished Ph.D. dissertation, UCLA, 1966), also *Management Science*, vol. 16, no. 11 (July 1970), pp. 728–46.

Held technique ranging from 1.8 seconds for a high-order-strength problem to 32.4 seconds for a low-order-strength problem. The comparable figures for the Arcus technique were 0.8 to 2.7 seconds.

Mastor also compared performance on five actual industrial problems ranging in size from 21 to 111 tasks. For the large problems (70, 92, and 111 tasks) the Held and Arcus techniques performed almost identically when the Arcus technique was run for 999 sequences.

Figure 9–9
Idle-time curves for 40-element problems, order strength 0.50

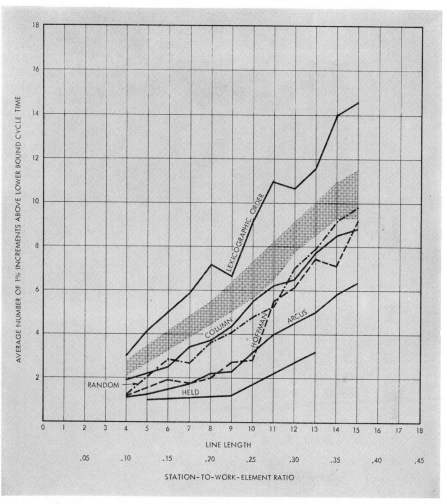

Source: From A. A. Mastor, "An Experimental Investigation and Comparative Evaluation of Production Line Balancing Techniques" (unpublished Ph.D. dissertation, UCLA, 1966), also *Management Science*, vol. 16, no. 11 (July 1970), pp. 728–46.

Still, the Arcus computing time was less, being 20 seconds compared to 34.2 for the 70-task problem, and 56 seconds compared to 94.3 for the 111-task problem.

Model for assembly line balancing (MALB)

The original ranked positional weight technique [13] was one of those included in Mastor's [22] comparative study. However, it did

Figure 9–10
Idle-time curves for 40-element problems, order strength 0.75

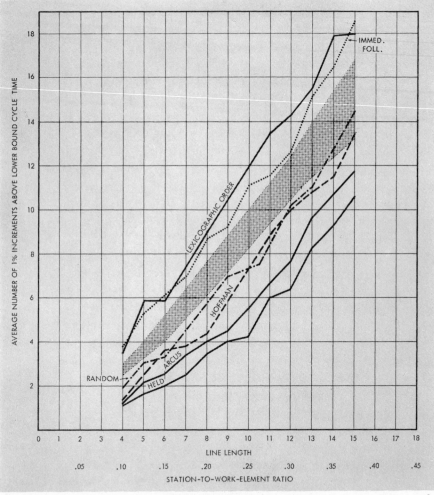

Source: From A. A. Mastor, "An Experimental Investigation and Comparative Evaluation of Production Line Balancing Techniques" (unpublished Ph.D. dissertation, UCLA, 1966), also *Management Science*, vol. 16, no. 11 (July 1970), pp. 728–46.

not perform well compared to COMSOAL and the heuristic method incorporating dynamic programming of Held, Karp, and Sharesian.

Mastor did not include in his comparative study an improvement on the ranked positional weight technique developed in 1964 by Mansoor (Dar-El) [21], however, the improvement went relatively unnoticed until it was computerized (MALB) for large-scale prob-

Figure 9–11
Idle-time curves for 40-element problems, all order strengths

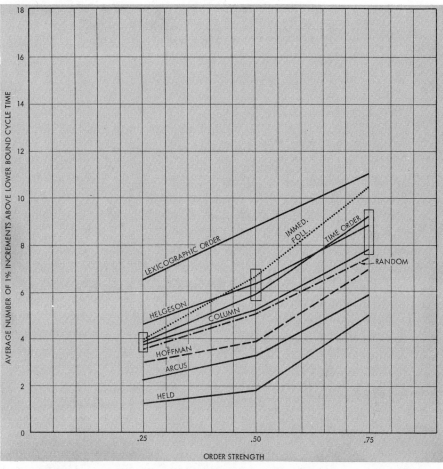

Source: From A. A. Mastor, "An Experimental Investigation and Comparative Evaluation of Production Line Balancing Techniques" (unpublished Ph.D. dissertation, UCLA, 1966), also *Management Science*, vol. 16, no. 11 (July 1970), pp. 728–46.

lems in 1973 by Dar-El [9]. Dar-El compared the performance of MALB against that of Arcus' COMSOAL, thus providing a link of comparison with the other methods examined in the Mastor study. The comparison was based on the average balance delay achieved by both techniques on a number of test problems with from 50 to 140 tasks. The results showed that the average balance delay associated with MALB line balances was from 0.50 percent to over 2 percent lower than the average balance delay achieved by COMSOAL. Moreover, the average computer time to balance a line with MALB was less than one sixth of that required by COMSOAL. Thus, the computerized version of the improved ranked positional weight technique appears to perform extremely well when compared to the best previously known method. MALB is most easily explained by first presenting the basic ranked positional weight technique, including the method by which it has been improved.

Ranked positional weight technique. The basis of the assignment of tasks to stations for this rule is to determine weightings for each task based on the sum of the time to perform that task plus the performance times of all of the tasks which follow it in the precedence chart. The tasks are then listed in descending order of the weights, together with corresponding immediate predecessor tasks. Tasks with the largest weights are then assigned to station 1, taking account of precedence constraints. When station 1 has assignments which fill the cycle time, then assignments are made to station 2 in the same way, and so on. Successive iterations may be made to determine the minimum cycle time for a given number of stations; this solution will give the most even distribution of work across stations.

An example will serve to explain the basic ranked positional weight technique, and the nature of the MALB improvement. Let us assume the balance problem posed by the precedence diagram of Figure 9–12. The numbers inside the circles are the task numbers, and those outside are the task performance times in seconds. Below the diagram we have calculated the positional weights, taking advantage of the fact that the weight for a task is its own task time plus the positional weight of the tasks which follow, and are dependent on it. (Any duplications are eliminated.) Therefore, hand computing time is reduced by computing positional weights from right to left in the precedence diagram. Table 9–5 shows the positional weights in rank order with immediate predecessors indicated.

Next, let us consider the range of possible solutions. Note that the largest task time is $t = 45$ seconds for task 3, and the sum of all task times is 185 seconds. Therefore, the maximum number of stations to consider is $185/45 = 4.1$, or 4. We could have, then four, three, two, or one stations. Figure 9–13 shows the balance delay graphs for four, three, and two stations. Note that the minimum possible balance delays are 1.6, 0.5, and 0.5 percent for four, three, and two stations, respectively. Assume that output requirements are for approximately 50 units per hour, therefore, a cycle time in the range of 60 to 70 seconds would provide the needed capacity. From Figure 9–13,

Figure 9–12

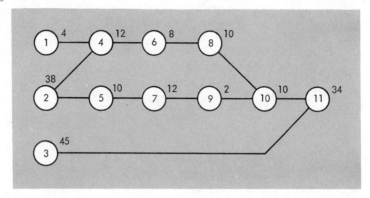

Task number	Task time	Plus positional weight of task number	Positional weight
11	34	—	34
10	10	11	44
9	2	10	46
7	12	9	58
5	10	7	68
8	10	10	54
6	8	8	62
4	12	6	74
1	4	4 .	78
2	38	4, 5(less times for tasks 10 and 11)	136
3	45	11	79
	185 seconds		

Precedence diagram showing tasks required (circles with numbers), and technological sequence requirements. Numbers outside circles are task times in seconds. Positional weights are calculated below the diagram as the sum of the task times plus the positional weights of the tasks which immediately follow (less any adjustments for duplications. For example, the times for tasks 10 and 11 are duplicated in the positional weights of tasks 4 and 5, therefore, in computing the positional weight for task 2 we have, 38 + 74 + 68 − (10 + 34) = 136). Example based on Mansoor (Dar-El) [21].

we see that a cycle time of 62 seconds will in fact produce a minimum balance delay with three stations. We will therefore determine balance for three stations with a minimum cycle time.

The basic procedure is then as follows:

1. Select the work time with the highest positional weight and assign it to the first work station.
2. Calculate the unassigned time for the work station by calculating the cumulative time for all tasks assigned to the station and subtract this sum from the cycle time.

Table 9–5
Tasks in rank order of positional weight, with immediate predecessors
indicated

Task number	Time required, seconds	Positional weight	Immediate predecessors
2	38	136	—
3	45	79	—
1	4	78	—
4	12	74	1, 2
5	10	68	2
6	8	62	4
7	12	58	5
8	10	54	6
9	2	46	7
10	10	44	8, 9
11	34	34	3, 10

Figure 9–13
Balance delay graphs for the balance problem of Figure 9–12.

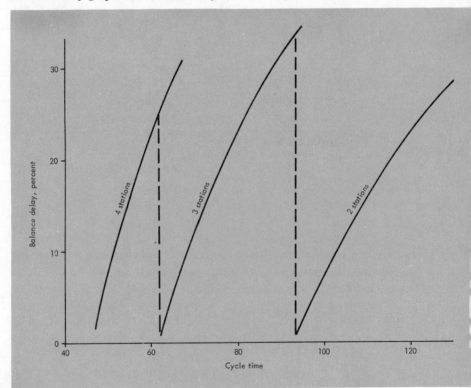

3. Select the work unit with the next highest positional weight and attempt to assign it to the work station after making the following checks:

a. Check the list of already assigned units. If the "immediate predecessor" tasks have been assigned, precedence will not be violated; proceed to Step 3(b). If the immediate predecessor tasks have not been assigned, proceed to Step 4.

b. Compare the task time with the unassigned time. If the task time is less than the station unassigned time, assign the task and recalculate unassigned time. If the task time is greater than the unassigned time, proceed to Step 4.

4. Continue to select, check, and assign if possible until one of the two conditions has been met:

a. All tasks have been assigned.

b. No unassigned work unit remains that can satisfy both the precedence requirements and the "less than the unassigned time" requirement.

5. Assign the unassigned task with the highest positional weight to the second work station, and proceed through the preceding steps in the same manner.

6. Continue assigning tasks to stations until all tasks have been assigned.

Using these assignment rules, we generate Table 9–6 as a solution to the problem. This is the best solution possible with these assignment rules. If one attempts solution at $c = 63$ seconds by the assignment rules, it is impossible to assign all tasks to only three stations. Referring to Figure 9–13, this solution for $c = 64$ seconds has a balance delay of 3.5 percent and slack units not assigned of $S = 7$ seconds.

MALB Assignment Rules. Dar-El (Mansoor) improves on the solution presented in Table 9–6 by allowing backtracking after the initial assignments have been made to test other combinations of task times to see if they yield improvement. Dar-El's modified rules are as follows:

1. Begin by selecting the lowest cycle time corresponding to each of the number of work stations possible, for example, by reference to the balance delay graphs. Record the slack units available.

2. Select the task with the highest positional weight and assign it to the first work station.

Table 9–6
Assignments of tasks to stations by ranked positional weight technique, for three stations, and a cycle time of $c = 64$ seconds (slack time is $S = 7$ seconds)

				Assignment to station 1		
Task number	Weight	Prede- cessors	Time	Cumu- lative station time	Unas- signed time	Remarks
2	136	None	38	38	26	Assigned
~~3 ....~~	~~79~~	~~None~~	~~45~~	~~83~~		>c
1	78	None	4	42	22	Assigned
4	74	1, 2	12	54	10	Assigned
5	68	2	10	64	0	Assigned
			Assignments to station 2			
3	79	None	45	45	19	Assigned
6	62	4	8	53	11	Assigned
~~7 ....~~	~~58~~	~~5~~	~~12~~	~~69~~	11	>c
8	54	6	10	63	1	Assigned
			Assignments to station 3			
7	58	5	12	12	52	Assigned
9	46	7	2	14	50	Assigned
10	44	8, 9	10	24	40	Assigned
11	34	3, 10	34	58	6	Assigned

3. Calculate the unassigned time for the station by calculating the cumulative time for all tasks assigned to the station and subtract this sum from the cycle time.

4. Select the task with the next highest positional weight and attempt to assign it to the station after making the following checks:

   a. Check the list of already assigned tasks. If the immediate predecessor tasks have been assigned, precedence will not be violated; proceed to Step 4(b). If the immediate predecessor tasks have not been assigned, proceed to Step 5.

   b. Compare the task time with the unassigned time. If the task time is less than the station unassigned time, assign the task and recalculate unassigned time. If the task time is greater than the unassigned time, proceed to Step 5.

5. Continue to select, check, and assign if possible until one of the two following conditions are met:

   a. A combination is obtained where the remaining unassigned

time is less than, or equals the slack units available (proceed to Step 8).

b. No unassigned task remains that can satisfy both the precedence and the unassigned time requirements (proceed to Step 6).

6. Cancel each assigned task in turn, starting with the one having the lowest positional weight (the last one assigned) and eventually working back, go through steps 4 and 5 until either:

a. A combination is obtained where the remaining unassigned time is less than or equals the slack units available (proceed to Step 8).

b. All combinations possible have unassigned times in excess of the slack units available so that no solution is possible (proceed to Step 7).

7. Select a cycle time having one more unit and start again with Step 2.

8. Assign the unassigned task with the highest positional weight to the second station and proceed through the preceeding steps in the manner.

9. Continue assigning tasks to stations until all tasks have been assigned.

Note that rules 2, 3, 4, 5, 8, and 9 are the same as the rules for the basic procedure with a minor modification to rule 5. The important modifications are in rules 1, 6, and 7. Applying these rules to the same problem, Dar-El produces the solution shown in Table 9–7 with a cycle time of $c = 62$ seconds with one slack unit assigned and a balance delay of only 0.5 percent. Dar-El shows similar results for four stations and two stations. The comparative results are shown in Table 9–8.

Table 9–7
Assignment of tasks to stations resulting from application of Dar-El's rules ($c = 62$ seconds, $S = 1$ second in station 2)

Station 1		Station 2		Station 3	
Task number	Time, seconds	Task number	Time, seconds	Task number	Time, seconds
2	38	3	45	6	8
5	10	1	4	8	10
7	12	4	12	10	10
9	2			11	34
Totals	62		61		62

Table 9–8
Comparative results between basic and MALB assignment rules for the
sample problem in Figure 2

	Basic positional weight rules			MALB assignment rules		
	Number of stations			Number of stations		
	2	3	4	2	3	4
Minimum cycle time, seconds	97	64	52	94	62	48
Balance delay, percent	4.5	3.5	11	1.5	0.5	3.5
Unassigned slack time, seconds	9	7	23	3	1	7

Other aspects of production line design

While the general methods for balance just discussed are the most important, there are auxiliary balancing techniques which can be used also. These involve careful methods study, selection of operators, artificial subdivision of tasks, and an examination of layout. If the limiting station is subjected to careful methods study in order to integrate the group of tasks assigned to it, it is quite often true that effective methods design can reduce the overall station time requirement. Since the station involved is the limiting one, such improvements increase the output for the line as a whole and reduce idle time. Also, compensations for imbalance can be accomplished through the careful selection and assignment of operators. By assigning operators with high manual skills to the limiting operations an additional degree of balance in practice is obtained. Another technique is to bank materials ahead of the limiting station so that the operator never has to incur idle time because of a lack of material supply. If the supply of material to the limiting operation is metered from the next operation upstream, there may be interference delays because of the work-time distributions of the two operators involved. We will have more to say about this situation later.

Conceptually, of course, the balance of either assembly or fabrication lines is the same. Nevertheless, the fixed machine cycles common in fabrication operations limit the flexibility open to us in achieving balance. It may not be practical to divide a machine operation into two or more tasks as is easily done with assembly work. This partially accounts for the fact that fabrication lines are generally not economical unless we are dealing with extremely high volumes, as is true with some automotive fabricated parts, since good balance probably cannot be achieved for low levels of output. In fabrication lines long machining operations are sometimes artificially divided in order to achieve balance. For example, the drilling of deep holes would require a long cycle; however, drilling can be divided into two or three steps to balance with the overall cycle and to distribute tool wear.

Banks and line speeds. Should parts be rigidly attached to a conveyor at intervals or should they ride freely so that it is possible for them to accumulate in a bank ahead of operations? Some light is shed on this point through a series of experiments dealing with work paced by a machine or conveyor. Conrad [7] compared the output for the same task when the operator was rigidly paced and when queues were allowed to build up ahead of the operator. The result of these experiments was that the critical determinant of output was the time that the assembly unit was available to the operator. Thus, when the operator was rigidly paced (the equivalent of assembly units being attached to the conveyor), the time available was minimized. Of course, the operator's work time is not a deterministic value but is in fact a distribution of work times. If the operator happens to be occupied with a long cycle, the assembly unit might bypass unprocessed, thus reducing effective output below line capacity. However, when queues of assembly units were allowed to build up, full line capacity was realized in Conrad's experiments. Of course, the reason was that the operator could counterbalance long cycles with shorter cycles so that average output could match that of the conveyor or machine. The assembly units would not bypass the worker unprocessed but would wait to be worked.

Hunt [15] confirms the logic of Conrad's experiment through a theoretical examination of an equivalent waiting line model. Hunt assumed Poisson arrival and service rates and computed the maximum possible utilization of the line and average banks for different cases of banking limitations and different numbers of stages or stations. Table 9–9 shows the maximum utilization possible for several possible limitations of banks of material between the two stations of a balanced line. Note that full utilization is possible only for case 1, where infinite queues are allowed to build up in front of each station. In case 2, which corresponds to Conrad's rigid pacing, utilization falls to the lowest level. In case 3, where different levels of finite queues between the stations are allowed, we note that there is a continuous improvement in the maximum utilization factor as the

Table 9–9
Calculated values of ρ_{max}, the maximum possible utilization for a
two-station line and the indicated banking limitations

		2. In front of first station (none at others)	3. In front of first station with other stations having finite queues				
	1. In front of each station		(a) $q = 2$	(b) $q = 3$	(c) $q = 4$	(d) $q = 8$	(e) $q = 18$
		Infinite queues allowed:					
ρ_{max}	1.0	0.6667	0.75	0.80	0.8333	0.90	0.95

Source: Adapted from G. C. Hunt, "Sequential Arrays of Waiting Lines," *Operations Research*, vol. 4 (1956), pp. 674–75.

allowable bank increases. This, of course, agrees with Conrad's conclusion that the time that the assembly unit is available to the
operator is the critical factor.

If there is some reason why the assembly units must be rigidly
attached to conveyors, then the system should be designed so that the
units are available to operators for the maximum possible period of
time. When the conveyor and the unit are large, for example, automobiles or larger appliances, this is often accomplished by letting
workers ride the line while performing their portion of the work, or
walk along with the unit as it moves. This tends to add flexibility to
the operator's cycle time. For smaller units where the worker may be
seated, time available depends on conveyor belt speed and the spacing between units on the conveyor [5].

Summary

The design of production lines can have a marked effect on the
degree of flexibility of output rate that is left open. If a high value is
to be placed on flexibility of output rate, then the physical design of
the system needs to take account of the kinds of things we just
discussed in the last section. For the scheduling function, flexibility
of output rate means being able to increase or decrease hours worked
as well as to change the more fundamental output rate of the
facilities by increasing or decreasing employment levels. The latter
means rebalancing so that one possibly important tool for the
scheduling function is to have a balance or rebalancing system. One
of the balance techniques discussed earlier in this chapter can be

used to generate new plans for work force assignments quickly. Alternately, one might have already prepared basic schedules of work force assignments for several levels of basic output rate. Theses prepared plans could be invoked to implement a change of output rate.

Within the details of production line system design, we have generated some broad criteria which help in realizing the output rates for which the line may have been designed. In summary, these are: Design for maximum time available of the assembly unit at stations by providing banks between operations and avoiding rigid pacing. Where rigid pacing is thought to be necessary, use combinations of belt speed and spacing that provide relatively long times available. Given a basic grouping of tasks resulting from sequencing and balancing models, it ordinarily would be worthwhile to subject the station work to careful methods study to integrate the tasks into a job design, particularly for the limiting or bottleneck operations. As a part of the methods study a careful examination of layout is ordinarily justified to obtain smooth flow of all related activities. Finally, in actual operation there is usually some residual imbalance. Astute selection of operators and their assignments to the line can help to counterbalance these residual imbalances.

REVIEW QUESTIONS AND PROBLEMS

1. Given the line balance problem illustrated by Figure 9–2 and Table 9–1, construct a graph of the balance delay function in the range of $3 \leq n \leq 8$.

2. Given the following data on the precedence relationships required of an assembled product, construct a precedence diagram by the Jackson method.

Task	Time in seconds	Must follow task	Task	Time in seconds	Must follow task
a	14	—	g	9	e
b − 1	5	a	h	14	e
b − 2	5	a	i	6	fgh
c	30	b	j	7	i
d	3	—	k	3	j
e	5	d	l	4	k
f	13	e	m	7	l

3. The demand for the product being assembled by the balanced line illustrated by Figure 9–2 is forecast to increase substantially and the new

aggregate plan calls for a production rate of 53 units per hour. Planners are now considering whether to establish two parallel lines or a line with double capacity. Consider the advantages and disadvantages of the two ways of achieving the production rate and rebalance the line to achieve the desired output by the heuristic method of Kilbridge and Wester. Task times in Tables 9–1 to 9–3 are in seconds.

4. Use the ranked positional weight technique to answer Question 3. Will the *improved* ranked positional weight technique result in a better answer?

5. Using the precedence diagram of Figure 9–2 as an example:
   a. Generate the initial lists A, B, and C for the COMSOAL procedure.
   b. Assign a task at random to station 1 from the (fit) list C and update lists, A, B, and C.
   c. Assign a second task at random from the updated fit list C and again update lists A, B, and C.

6. Based on the comparative experimental study by Mastor, and the additional data on MALB, evaluate the alternate line balancing methods. Which would you recommend as a practical procedure and why?

SELECTED BIBLIOGRAPHY

1. Arcus, A. L. "An Analysis of a Computer Method of Sequencing Assembly Line Operations." Unpublished Ph.D. dissertation, University of California, Berkeley, 1963.

2. Arcus, A. L. "COMSOAL: A Computer Method of Sequencing Operations for Assembly Lines, I—The Problem in Simple Form, II—The Problem in Complex Form," in *Readings in Production and Operations Management* (ed. E. S. Buffa). New York: John Wiley & Sons, Inc., 1966. Also published in slightly different form as, "COMSOAL: A Computer Method of Sequencing Operations for Assembly Lines," *International Journal of Production Research*, vol. 4, no. 4 (1966).

3. Buffa, E. S. "The Additivity of Universal Standard Data Elements," *Journal of Industrial Engineering*, vol. 7, no. 5 (September-October 1956).

4. Buffa, E. S. "The Additivity of Universal Standard Data Elements, II," *Journal of Industrial Engineering*, vol. 8, no. 6 (November-December 1957).

5. Buffa, E. S. "Pacing Effects in Production Lines," *Journal of Industrial Engineering*, vol. 12, no. 6 (November-December 1961).

6. Burgeson, J. W., and Daum, T. E. "Production Line Balancing." 650 Program Library, File 10.3.002. Akron, Ohio: International Business Machines, Inc., 1958.

7. Conrad, R. *Setting the Pace*. Medical Research Council, APU 232–55. London, England: Applied Psychology Research Unit, 1955.

8. Conrad, R., and Hille, B. A. "Comparison of Paced and Unpaced Performance at a Packing Task," *Occupational Psychology*, vol. 29, no. 1 (January 1955), pp. 15–28.

9. Dar-El, E. M. (Mansoor), "MALB—A Heuristic Technique for Balancing Large-Scale Single Model Assembly Lines," *AIIE Transactions*, vol. 5 (4) (December 1973).

10. Davidson, H. O. "On Balance—The Validity of Predetermined Elemental Time Systems," *Journal of Industrial Engineering*, vol. 13, no. 3 (May-June 1962).

11. Gutjahr, L., and Nemhauser, G. L. "An Algorithm for the Line Balancing Problem," *Management Science*, vol. 11, no. 2 (November 1964).

12. Held, M.; Karp, R. M.; and Sharesian, R. "Asembly-Line Balancing—Dynamic Programming with Precedence Constraints," *Operations Research*, vol. 11, no. 3 (May-June 1963).

13. Helgeson, W. B., and Birnie, D. P. "Assembly Line Balancing Using the Ranked Positional Weight Technique," *Journal of Industrial Engineering*, vol. 12, no. 6 (November-December 1961).

14. Hoffman, T. R. "Permutations and Precedence Matrices with Automatic Computer Applications to Industrial Problems," Ph.D. dissertation, University of Wisconsin, Madison, June 1959. Also, "Assembly Line Balancing with a Precedence Matrix," *Management Science*, vol. 9, no. 4 (July 1963).

15. Hunt, G. C. "Sequential Arrays of Waiting Lines," *Operations Research*, vol. 4 (1956), pp. 674–75.

16. Jackson, J. R. "A Computing Procedure for a Line Balancing Problem," *Management Science*, vol. 2, no. 3 (April 1956).

17. Kilbridge, M. D., and Wester, L. "A Heuristic Method of Assembly Line Balancing," *Journal of Industrial Engineering*, vol. 12, no. 4 (July–August 1961).

18. Kilbridge, M. D., and Wester, L. "The Balance Delay Problem," *Management Science*, vol. 8, no. 1 (October 1961).

19. Kilbridge, M. D., and Wester, L. "A Review of Analytical Systems of Line Balancing," *Operations Research*, vol. 10, no. 5 (September–October 1962).

20. Klein, M. "On Assembly Line Balancing," *Operations Research*, vol. 11, no. 2 (March–April 1963).

21. Mansoor, E. M. (Dar-El) "Assembly Line Balancing—An Improvement on the Ranked Positional Weight Technique," *Journal of Industrial Engineering*, vol. 15, no. 2 (March–April 1964).

22. Mastor, A. A. "An Experimental Investigation and Comparative

Evaluation of Production Line Balancing Techniques." Unpublished Ph.D. dissertation, UCLA, 1966, also *Management Science*, vol. 16, no. 11 (July 1970), pp. 728–46.

23. Moodie, C. L., and Young, H. H. "A Heuristic Method of Assembly Line Balancing for Assumptions of Constant or Variable Work Element Times," *Journal of Industrial Engineering*, vol. 16, no. 1 (January–February 1965).

24. Prenting, O., and Battaglin, M. "The Precedence Diagram: A Tool for Analysis in Assembly Line Balancing," *Journal of Industrial Engineering*, vol. 15, no. 4 (July–August 1964).

25. Salveson, M. E. "The Assembly Line Balancing Problem," *Journal of Industrial Engineering*, vol. 6, no. 3 (May–June 1955).

26. Schmidtke, H., and Stier, F. "An Experimental Evaluation of the Validity of Predetermined Elemental Time Systems," *Journal of Industrial Engineering*, vol. 12, no. 3 (May–June 1961).

27. Thomopoulos, N. T. "Mixed Model Line Balancing with Smoothed Station Assignments," *Management Science*, vol. 16, no. 9 (May 1970), pp. 593–603.

28. Thomopoulos, N. T. "The Mixed Model Learning Curve," *AIIE Transactions*, vol. 1, no. 2 (June 1969), pp. 127–32.

29. Thomopoulos, N. T. "Some Analytical Approaches to Assembly Line Problems," *The Production Engineer* (July 1968), pp. 345–51.

30. Tonge, F. M. "Summary of a Heuristic Line Balancing Procedure," *Management Science*, vol. 7, no. 1 (October 1960).

31. Tonge, F. M. "Assembly Line Balancing Using Probabilistic Combinations of Heuristics," *Management Science*, vol. 11, no. 7 (May 1965).

32. Wester, L., and Kilbridge, M. "Heuristic Line Balancing: A Case," *Journal of Industrial Engineering*, vol. 13, no. 3 (May–June 1962).

33. Young, H. H. "Optimization Models for Production Lines," *Journal of Industrial Engineering*, vol. 18, no. 1 (January 1967), pp. 70–78.

PART IV

PLANNING
AND
SCHEDULING
FOR
INTERMITTENT
SYSTEMS

Chapter 10

Job shop scheduling

INTERMITTENT PRODUCTION brings forth the traditional image of the job shop with its broad capability to fabricate a wide range of parts and products to custom order. This general concept of the jobbing machine shop carries over as a model to a broad range of intermittent production facilities where the basis of layout and departmentalization is functional. As we discussed in Chapter 1, the job shop system often does not produce for inventory but instead holds in readiness a flexible producing system. Because of the great flexibility required of such a system the internal complications of job shop systems are much greater than for the production lines discussed in Part III. To help set the frame of reference for our discussion we have reproduced as Figure 10–1 the schematic representation of job shop systems which we presented in Chapter 1. Here we see the broad picture of information flow and the order of magnitude of time delays involved. Contrasting the time delays with those expected in the high-volume standardized product system, we can see that the biggest delays are internal, whereas for the high-volume systems the biggest delays seem to be involved in the distribution chain. In Figure 10–1 there is a minimum 74-day internal delay after a request for bid is received before material starts to flow from vendors. Another 130 days of delay are required for raw material transit, fabrication, and assembly. The time delay for delivery is a relatively minor one.

Open versus closed job shops. Figure 10–1 actually presents the most difficult or general case; that is, a shop which is *open* to job

485

Figure 10–1
System for job shop (information and material flow, time delays, and problems)

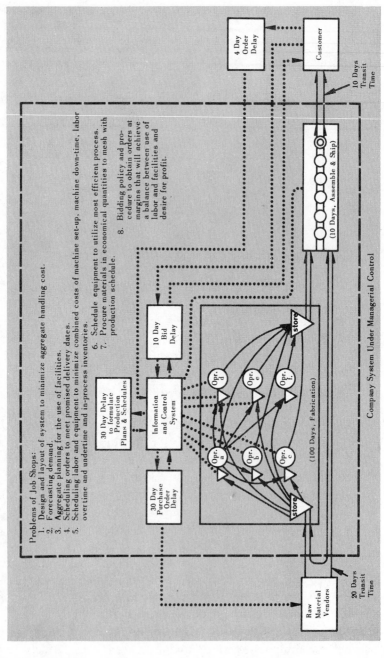

Problems of Job Shops:
1. Design and layout of system to minimize aggregate handling cost.
2. Forecasting demand.
3. Aggregate planning for the use of facilities.
4. Scheduling orders to meet promised delivery dates.
5. Scheduling labor and equipment to minimize combined costs of machine set-up, machine down-time, labor overtime and undertime and in-process inventories.
6. Schedule equipment to utilize most efficient process.
7. Procure materials in economical quantities to mesh with production schedule.
8. Bidding policy and procedure to obtain orders at margins that will achieve a balance between use of labor and facilities and desire for profit.

Company System Under Managerial Control

orders from virtually anyone. Under such circumstances one must forecast, design the physical facility, make aggregate plans, schedule, procure materials, and bid with the greatest uncertainty. Actually, however, we should make a distinction between the open shop and the job shop system which is *closed* to outside order. (We still call it a job shop because of the nature of the physical layout.) The closed job shop is the captive shop of some concern and manufactures for its own internal use in its own product line. Its product line usually has a degree of predictability, although the captive shops may also receive internal one-time orders. Note also that some captive job shops have the characteristics of the open shop if they are essentially experimental or prototype shops. Every automotive company maintains its own very large machine shops (perhaps several) laid out on a functional or job shop basis. But these captive job shops are not open to job order from outside customers. They do in fact produce a largely forecastable line of parts, components, and products. In fact, most of the "job shops" we know of are closed job shops. This is an important distinction because if we know in advance what our product line mix will be, then the eight problems listed in Figure 10–1 can take on a considerably different hue. A search of the literature indicates that we have viewed the intermittent system as being typified by the traditional open job shop model when in fact the closed job shop may be more common and perhaps somewhat easier to deal with.

In organizing our attack on job shop systems we will first discuss generally the problems of job shops as listed in Figure 10–1, attempting to maintain the distinction we have just established between the open and closed job shops. Then we will specialize our treatment of the balance of this chapter to discuss some of the important aspects of job shop scheduling. Integrated manufacturing information and scheduling systems will be discussed in Chapter 11.

Problems of job shop systems

The most obvious physical characteristic of the job shop system is in its functional layout where equipment of the same generic type is grouped together in the same general location. The most obvious information and control characteristic is the need for information and control of individual operations. There are both economic and technological reasons for the functional layout. Since we are dealing with situations where normally most items or products do not have sufficient volume to utilize equipment fully, it becomes economical for the entire set of products to collect the fractional usage demands for various products and let them time-share common equipment. Second, since the sequence of operations and equipment use is likely to be different for different items, so that no one sequence of operations fits a large fraction of the products, equipment is grouped on a generic basis. Departments then become centers of capability and skill to perform a certain class of operations. The basic departmental structure and layout are similar for both open and closed job shops.

Layout and facility design. Layout and facility design can, of course, be considered at several levels of complexity and detail. Our biggest concern is at the broad level of determining the best relative departmental locations and their area requirements in block form (Figure 10–2). Since there are numerous process sequences, or routes, taken through the facility by the various orders, no one sequencing in the layout will be good for all orders. On the other hand, past research indicates that neither is the process sequencing of orders a random one. The problem, then, is to choose a set of relative locations for which the costs associated with location are a

Figure 10–2
Typical block layout for a machine shop

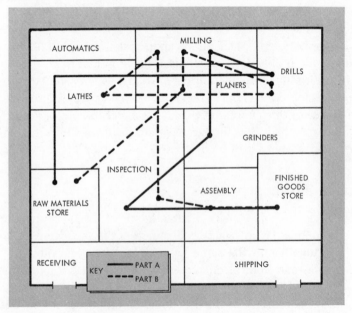

minimum. The costs involved are mainly material transportation but involve personnel transport also in trips to tool cribs, personnel or engineering offices, and so on. The relative location of a department's problem is not trivial, for with only 20 departments there are over 608×10^{12} different combinations of layouts possible. The layout has an effect on average order flow time through the shop and therefore has an impact on production scheduling in the sense that it establishes the general level of expected flow time.

The contrast in expected layout solutions for open and closed job shops is probably very subtle if any difference exists. If one were to examine the interdepartmental flow matrices (material transported in loads per unit of time between all combinations of departments or work centers), it is possible that the open shop would exhibit greater variability of flow path or that the flow matrix would be more unstable from period to period. We have no evidence of this, however. If either or both of these phenomena were present, the effect would be mainly to flatten the ∪-shaped cost criterion function so that unique minimum cost layout solutions would be less likely. Also, of course, total incremental transportation costs should be less for the closed job shop if the flow matrix is in fact less variable and more stable. A number of techniques for designing job shop layouts have been developed [2, 6, 43, 50].

Forecasting demand and aggregate planning. To be meaningful for the use of the planning, scheduling, and control functions, forecasts need to be finally translated into forecasted hours for equipment classes, such as lathes, drills, and mills with allowances included for processing of scrap as well as good product and allowances for expected plant efficiency. Plant efficiency is the percentage of equipment time available which is actually utilized for productive work after deducting time losses due to scheduling delays, machine breakdowns, preventive maintenance, and so on.

Forecasting loads for an open job shop has a different focus than for the closed job shop. In the nearest term the open shop has firm job orders for which fairly detailed process plans and time estimates have been made. Therefore, loads by departments can be developed based on a good data processing and control system, utilizing, for example, the capacity requirements planning approach outlined in Chapter 7. One of the significant decision problems involved in determining quantities to be produced on job order is to determine overage allowances for scrap. If the order is for ten items, what is the most economical size run considering that some scrap may result? If the scrap is larger than expected, there may be significant costs to reset-up equipment for an additional production run. Forecasts beyond the firm orders, however, become more uncertain.

The bid rate and its translation into probable firm orders provides a basis for aggregate planning in the next period beyond the one established by firm orders. The basic forecasting techniques covered in Chapter 2 are applicable to the smoothing and forecasting of expected orders based on the bid rate. Projected department loads can again be generated based on forecasts and used as a basis for hiring and training, or possibly for layoffs. Since the really salable thing for an open job shop is its capability, however, there will be reluctance to lay off highly skilled labor (and a job shop is characterized in part by the rare skills of the labor force) unless there has been a persistent decline in business. Longer term forecasting is somewhat more uncertain but may be tied to forecasts of general business conditions, or if the open shop operates in a particular industry, such as the aerospace industry, longer term forecasts may be based on industry forecasts.

Forecasting load and aggregate planning for a closed job shop should be a direct result of product forecasting and basic inventory policies. A captive job shop can make decisions concerning lot sizes and cycling of parts and products to satisfy demands. For example, if the closed job shop is attempting to use basic economic production lot concepts, it can establish a basis for part or product cycling on time-shared equipment. It can develop aggregate plans and master schedules in a way similar to those we discussed in Chapters 5, 6, and 7, and use material requirements planning systems to explode the requirements for parts being placed in the closed job shop.

Scheduling and control of orders, labor, and equipment. Job shop scheduling is universally regarded as the most complex and difficult industrial scheduling problem. The complexity stems from the fact that each order may require a processing sequence that is different, so that the scheduling department must be capable of dealing with the tremendous variation of sequence, processing requirements, time requirements, priorities, number of operations, and so on. In the open shop these problems are the most extreme since presumably each order is unique and may never be repeated. Actually, however, the detailed scheduling and control for both open and closed job shops seems to be similar. There are differences in detail, however. Obviously, basic documents on process plans and sequences, and time requirements, can probably be reused for closed job shop situations. Also, the determination of the size and timing of production runs is slightly different. The determination of the size of the production runs for job orders in open shops must take into account the overage allowance problem to which we alluded previously. On the other hand, production runs for cycled orders in closed shops may be determined by other lot sizing formulas. In both cases, however, the efficient determination of sequencing priorities for the jobs waiting in a queue to be processed is of paramount importance.

Job shop scheduling research has attempted in large measure to view the job shop system as a network of queues, using the simulation methodology to cope with the complexity of equivalent job shop networks. A great deal of effort has gone into the evaluation of various queue disciplines which might result in more effective priority dispatching systems. Also, more recently, recognition has been given to the fact that in many, if not most, situations we have an excess of machine capacity with skilled workers scheduled to use various pieces of equipment. Equipment is normally scheduled for the most economical process based on an analysis of the product and estimated setup and run-time costs. Labor is then the more flexible component being assigned to use various machines for different requirements as called for by process plans. Labor is therefore often the limiting resource. Nelson has carried on simulation experiments with "labor limited" systems in order to learn more about their behavior. The machine-limited case would occur at or near full machine capacity for the plant.

Materials control often follows many of the concepts that we discussed in Chapter 7, under material requirements planning. Within the context of MRP systems, raw materials and components can be ordered according to one of many different lot sizing procedures that we have discussed. As we shall see in later chapters, MRP systems are also used for the fundamentally important purpose of transmitting global due date priority information for shop floor control use.

Bidding is a critical problem for open job shops, though it is a problem which we will not discuss in detail. Bidding strategies must be somewhat different depending on the nature of business conditions. An organization might cut its margins or even bid at prices involving a degree of loss in order to maintain its skilled labor force intact.

Bidding is also a sensitive interfacing factor in the creation of master schedules in open job shops. One of the main problems here involves reserving capacity for bids which may be accepted for delivery within certain time periods, while ensuring that other work is done on a timely basis. Certain hedging strategies similar to those employed by high-volume standard product producers like Xerox (Chapter 8), can be employed to minimize bidding risks [30].

JOB SHOP SCHEDULING RESEARCH

Job shop scheduling research has centered on the sequencing problem for a number of years. The sequencing problem is easily stated, but clear answers to the basic problem have not been easily found. The problem is to determine the sequence in which units (jobs or orders) are to be processed at each of a series of machine centers. The sequencing problem is, of course, only a part of the overall production control problem in a job shop. The production planning of the technological processing and routing requirements, material procurement, and other planning precedes the sequencing problem. Follow-up or control to ensure on time completion of orders, or at least to minimize the lateness of orders, follows the sequencing problem.

Traditional production control procedures used either the Gantt chart or its concepts to represent the system in deterministic fashion. The scheduler, using graphic aids, produced an hourly schedule in which the projected work load for each machine or work center was charted, hour by hour, order by order. Unfortunately, the Gantt chart model does not conform to some of the most important aspects of reality. New orders entering the system as a whole as well as those entering individual work centers arrive according to some stochastic process. Processing times are not fixed times but actually follow some probability distribution. All orders are not equally urgent or equally important from other points of view. For example, some orders may be of inherently high value because of the nature of raw materials or of previous value added by manufacture so that longer flow time means higher in-process inventory cost.

The recognition that a job shop could be represented as a system or network of queues was an important one, and it triggered off a great deal of fundamental research which is still going on. Jackson [19, 20, 21, 22, 23, 24], Nelson [36, 37, 38, 39, 40, 41, 42], Evans [11, 12, 13, 14], Smith [49], and others did early work which focused on the job shop as a queuing system. The early queuing research pointed up the queue discipline as being an important variable which could be manipulated in sequencing models, and much of the research has been focused on various comparative studies of queue discipline (priority dispatch decision rules) through the mechanism of computer simulation.

Rowe [45, 46, 47] came forth with the first large-scale evaluation of six dispatching decision rules in 1958, using a job shop simulation of a General Electric plant as a vehicle for study. Though the Rowe study involved the dual resources of both labor and machines, and involved no assumptions concerning arrival rates, most of the work which followed by Baker and Dzielinski [3] in 1960, Conway and Maxwell [8] in 1962, Nanot [35] in 1963, and Carroll [7] in 1965 has been in the context of a machine-limited shop involving assumptions of Poisson arrival rates and exponential service times. The conceptual framework involving the dual resources of machines and labor appeared again in 1962 with a study by Allen [1] of General Electric and Nelson's more recent studies [40, 41, 42]. Studies using actual operating data for machine and labor-limited systems have been carried out at General Electric by Rowe [45] and Allen [1], and at the Hughes Aircraft Company by LeGrande [26]. Harris [17, 18] made an extensive investigation in a Los Angeles plant to examine the assumptions involved in the queuing models of much of the research which had been done. We will organize our analysis of job shop scheduling research by considering separately some of the studies made on machine-limited systems and on labor-limited systems, followed by an appraisal of assumptions based on the Harris study.

MACHINE-LIMITED SYSTEMS

The simple meaning of machine-limited systems is that labor is always assumed to be available and that the critical resources are the machines. The result is that order waiting time occurs only because machines are tied up. We will discuss this assumption later in connection with the Harris empirical study. Early theoretical work by Smith [49] in 1956, working at the Management Sciences Research Project at UCLA, had pointed to the shortest operation time rule (SOT) as having minimum possible order flow and waiting time for single-stage systems. The SOT rule sequences orders according to the processing time required, taking those with the shortest times first. Since Smith was able to prove mathematically that the SOT discipline was optimal for single-stage systems, the real question remaining seemed to be how the SOT rule and others would behave in the much more complex and realistic network systems.

Mathematical analysis fails at this point and simulation studies take over. The first simulation studies were largely exploratory, designed to screen a large number of possible priority dispatching rules (queue disciplines). Both the simulation studies of Rowe in 1958, and Baker and Dzielinski in 1960 had turned up the superiority of the SOT rule for network systems on the basis of certain criteria. These preliminary findings were interesting enough to encourage two massive studies to screen a wide range of possible priority dispatch decision rules. The Conway study at RAND Corporation was massive in that it tested 92 different rules (some with changes in parameters only), and the Nanot study was massive in that it involved sample sizes as high as 145,000 and typically in the 40,000 to 60,000 range, for ten rules in eight different job shop structures.

In general, there are at least two bases for classifying priority dispatching rules. The first is on the basis of information availability. A *local rule* determines priorities entirely on the basis of the information available about the order in question at the time it is initiated, for example, its processing time or due date. More *global* rules might take into account overall job load, the status of the load on work centers downstream, or changes in due dates. The second basis of classification is *static* versus *dynamic* rules. In static rules relative priorities remain the same once assigned. With a dynamic priority rule, however, the relative priority position changes through time as, for example, with a due date priority where a new order entering the queue might go to the head of the line. Orders waiting in queues gain in relative status with time, since the longer they wait the less likely it is possible that a new arrival will have an earlier due date. We will discuss the Nanot study followed by more detailed investigations of two specific rules.

The Nanot study [35]

The Nanot study involved six different job shop structures, testing ten different priority dispatching rules with over 2.44×10^6 orders processed through these systems. The six shop structures were as follows:

Job Shop 1—four centers, medium load, pure job shop routing.
Job Shop 2—four centers, high load, pure job shop routing.
Job Shop 3—eight centers, low load, quasi flow shop routing.
Job Shop 4—eight centers, medium load, quasi flow shop routing (two routings).

Job Shop 5—two centers, medium load, pure job shop routing.
Job Shop 6—eight centers, low load, pure job shop routing.

A pure job shop routing is one in which an order leaving one machine is equally likely to go to any other machine in the shop. A pure flow shop is one in which there is only one routing that all orders follow.

The ten static and dynamic rules tested by Nanot were:

Rule 1 (FCFS)—first come, first served.
Rule 2 (SOT)—shortest operation time.
Rule 3 (SS)—static slack; that is, due date less time of arrival at machine center.
Rule 4 (SS/PT)—static slack/remaining processing time.
Rule 5 (SS/RO)—static slack/remaining number of operations.
Rule 6 (FISFS)—due date system; first-in system, first served.
Rule 7 (LCFS)—last come, first served.
Rule 8 (DS)—dynamic slack (time remaining to due date less remaining expected flow time).
Rule 9 (DS/PT)—dynamic slack/remaining processing time.
Rule 10 (DS/RO)—dynamic slack/remaining number of operations.

When applied to the problem of selecting which job or order awaiting processing at a machine is to be worked on first, these rules indicate the way orders should be ranked in priority. For example, the SOT rule indicates that the next job to be selected for processing is the one that takes the least time to complete, followed by the next shortest job, and so on.

The study involved a number of explicit assumptions. The arrival of orders in the system followed a Poisson process, and the service times were exponential. There was only one queue for each machine center, and labor was assumed to be available. No lot splitting was permitted, and transportation time between machine centers was zero. No subcontracting or overtime was allowed, and machine breakdowns, scrap, and other interruptions were not allowed to occur. Setup time was considered to be a part of the processing time for each operation.

Results. A summary of the mean flow times and associated standard deviations for the ten decision rules in the six shop structures is shown in Table 10–1. The first line of the table includes the mean flow times based on theoretical calculations. The SOT rule consistently has the lowest mean flow time. The standard deviations of the FCFS and FISFS rules are in general lower. The significance of the standard deviation measure of performance is shown better in Fig-

Table 10–1
Comparison of mean flow times and standard deviations

| | Shop number | | | | | | | | | | | | | |
| | 1 | | 2 | | 3 | | 4 (Route 1) | | 4 (Route 2) | | 5 | | 6 | |
Rule	Mean	Std. dev.	Mean	Std. dev.	Mean	Std. dev.	Mean	Std. dev.	Mean	Std. dev.	Mean	Std. dev.	Mean	Std. dev.
Theoretical FCFS	1.60	—	7.60	—	3.05	—	3.02	—	3.76	—	0.80	—	1.17	—
1. FCFS	1.67	1.96	6.41	7.31	3.55	1.93	2.77	1.32	3.73	2.17	0.75	0.89	1.19	1.26
2. SOT	0.99	1.87	2.13	9.20	2.26	2.11	1.75	1.58	1.94	3.10	0.46	0.88	0.86	1.24
3. SS	1.71	2.10	6.35	11.30	3.37	1.60	3.24	2.12	3.60	2.30	0.76	0.98	1.24	1.71
4. SS/PT	2.53	3.96	17.97	37.84	3.86	3.25	3.83	3.09	6.89	12.65	1.36	2.70	1.62	2.64
5. SS/RO	1.99	2.92	10.06	20.38	3.65	2.74	3.18	2.25	3.70	2.25	0.88	1.38	1.32	1.88
6. FISFS	1.69	1.55	6.30	—	3.35	1.62	3.07	1.38	3.54	2.00	0.76	0.73	1.22	1.17
7. LCFS	1.68	3.52	—	—	3.34	3.68	2.72	3.18	3.63	8.11	0.76	1.79	1.19	2.18
8. DS	1.86	1.62	—	—	3.33	1.47	2.93	1.35	3.65	1.93	0.83	0.77	1.26	1.16
9. DS/PT	2.54	5.43	—	—	4.54	5.77	3.44	3.74	6.06	13.29	1.18	2.77	1.61	3.17
10. DS/RO	1.78	3.66	—	—	3.84	4.77	2.79	2.54	3.86	8.11	0.77	1.72	1.19	2.08

Source: From Y. R. Nanot, "An Experimental Investigation and Comparative Evaluation of Priority Disciplines in Job Shop-Like Queueing Networks (unpublished Ph.D. dissertation UCLA, 1963).

ures 10–3 and 10–4 where typical flow time curves are plotted versus fractiles of orders processed. The flow time curves were strikingly similar for all shop conditions. Figure 10–3 shows the flow time curves up to the 0.90 fractile. The shaded area includes Rules 1,

Figure 10–3
Typical flow time curves for alternate priority dispatching decision rules

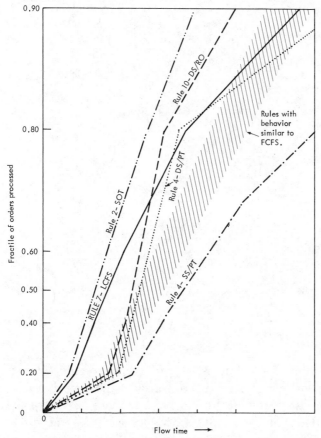

Source: From Y. R. Nanot. "An Experimental Investigation and Comparative Evaluation of Priority Disciplines in Job Shop-Like Queueing Networks" (unpublished Ph.D. dissertation, UCLA, 1963).

3, 5, 6, and 8 (FCFS, SS SS/RO, FISFS, and DS). The SOT rule performs consistently the best in the zero to 0.90 range and is almost linear. Rule 4 (SS/PT) is consistently the worst performer. Up to the 0.80 fractile, Rules 7 and 10 (LCFS and DS/RO) and between the shortest operation rule and the shaded area, but beyond 0.80 they veer sharply to the right reflecting their very large variance. Rule 7

Figure 10–4
Typical flow time curves for alternate priority dispatching
rules at higher fractiles

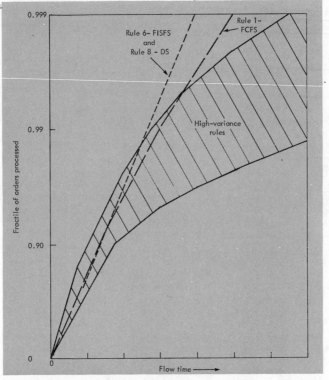

Source: From Y. R. Nanot, "An Experimental Investigation and Comparative Evaluation of Priority Disciplines in Job Shop-Like Queueing Networks"
(unpublished Ph.D. dissertation, UCLA, 1963).

(LCFS) exhibits some interesting properties. For the single-server
Poisson-exponential system this rule leads to the same expected flow
time as the first-come, first-served rule but can be shown to have
greater variance in flow time [35]. This appears to be true also for the
network systems studied by Nanot. For the lower fractiles in Figure
10–3, the LCFS rule flow times are consistently smaller than those
obtained by FCFS for at least 80 percent of all orders. From a practical point of view this dispatching rule is widely used. For example,
in machine shops, orders waiting to be served at a machine center
are often located in tote boxes which are stacked. When the machine
is ready for the next order, it is quite natural and much easier to
remove the top box rather than attempt to get at the one on the
bottom.

Figure 10–4 shows flow time performance beyond the 0.90 fractile. Rules 1, 6, and 8 (FCFS, FISFS, and DS) are plotted individually. The other rules fall into the shaded area, the upper limit of which is the SOT rule. The high-variance rules cause about 1 percent of the orders to have flow times averaging from 4 to 15 times the mean flow time under the FCFS rule.

Nanot investigated the influence of system configuration through the mechanism of an analysis of variance. The results showed that the differences due to the use of different priority dispatching rules was highly significant but that the differences due to system configuration (effect of shop size and differences in routing) were very much less significant. The hypothesis of a configuration effect was not fully conclusive, being rejected at significance levels of 0.02 and 0.01 but accepted at a significance level of 0.05. Rather than reject the hypothesis of a configuration effect, Nanot felt, "a more sensible conclusion is to note the relative importance of the two effects, and not to apply a statistical test whose validity is, after all, subject to the many assumptions of normality."

Nanot also subjected the dynamic priority rules to additional critical examination and gives a great deal of additional information concerning their behavior, thus building on the previous work of Grindlay [16].

The shortest operation time rule (SOT)

Because of its excellent performance characteristics as well as its basic simplicity in operation, the SOT rule is of further interest. Based on the Nanot study, the SOT rule is superior for almost 99 percent of orders, but, of course, it is possible for a few orders to require long flow times. The high flow time variance for the SOT rule is regarded as one of its basic disadvantages, though the estimates of variance produced by Nanot's study based on huge sample sizes seems to indicate that the values are not as high as thought previously. Conway and Maxwell [8] subjected the SOT rule to detailed examination because of its superior performance and in an attempt to find ways of dealing with the high-variance disadvantage. They performed simulation experiments to test the effectiveness of two variants of the SOT rule that might retain the advantage of low mean flow time without the corresponding high variance. These variants of the SOT rule were: (a) alternate the SOT rule with a low variance rule to periodically "clean out the shop," and (b) truncate the SOT rule by imposing a limit on the waiting time that will be tolerated for individual jobs. They also performed experiments to test the sensitivity of the SOT rule to errors in the forecast of processing, to shop load, and to shop size.

Alternating SOT and FCFS produced the results shown in Table 10–2. The cycle of alternation was held constant at 400 time units, which was equivalent to 40 times the mean processing times, with the intention of representing a 40-hour week for a shop in which the mean processing time was one hour. Table 10–2 shows the strong

Table 10–2
Results of experiments where the SOT and FCFS were alternated for varying proportions of time*

Proportion of time using SOT	Mean idle time, %	Mean flow time	Mean flow time/ operation	Variance, flow time	Variance, flow time/ operation
0 (FCFS)	16.59%	244.5	50.7	30,423	7,896
0.20	13.82	230.3	48.6	67,375	45,550
0.40	12.33	223.7	47.1	60,550	40,577
0.60	10.60	215.8	45.7	67,757	48,120
0.80	8.43	211.3	44.1	85,072	67,880
1.00 (SOT)	6.89	205.9	43.4	88,695	71,212

* Transition matrix: pure job shop. Number of machines: 6. Number of jobs in shop: 4N. Sample size: 2,000 jobs, except 20,000 for FCFS.
Source: From R. W. Conway and W. L. Maxwell, "Network Scheduling by the Shortest-Operation Discipline," Operations Research, vol. 10 (1962), pp. 51–73.

effect of the progressive introduction of the SOT rule on both mean flow time and variance. Using the SOT rule only 20 percent of the time more than doubled the variance of flow time and increased the variance of flow time per operation by more than five times. "Apparently in introducing the shortest operation discipline in this manner one secures the disadvantages more rapidly than the advantages." [8]

Truncation of the SOT rule produced the results shown in Table 10–3. Conway and Maxwell judge the severity of truncation by comparing the truncation number (which is approximately equal to the maximum waiting time in a single queue) for the SOT rules under truncation to the expected waiting time per queue for the FCFS rule. From Table 10–3 the average flow time per operation under FCFS is 50.7. The mean processing time is 10 time units so that the mean waiting time per queue is approximately 40 time units as compared to the mean waiting time for the basic SOT rule of 35 time units. A truncation number of 100 means that a job can at most wait about 2.5

Table 10–3
Performance of the truncated SOT rule (TS, C; C = truncation number)*

Rule	Mean idle time, %	Mean flow time	Mean flow time/ operation	Variance, flow time	Variance, flow time/ operation
TS, 0 (FCFS)	16.59	244.5	50.7	30,423	7,896
TS, 100	13.36	236.1	49.1	36,264	14,791
TS, 300	11.98	229.3	48.3	51,417	—
TS, 1,000	7.60	220.4	45.9	75,984	24,557
TS, ∞ (SOT)	6.79	218.2	45.5	125,461	23,069

* Transition matrix: pure job shop. Number of machines: 6. No. of jobs in shop: 4 N. Sample size: 20,000 jobs.
Source: From R. W. Conway and W. L. Maxwell, "Network Scheduling by the Shortest-Operation Discipline," *Operations Research*, vol. 10 (1962) pp. 51–73.

times as long in a single queue as its expected waiting time would be under the FCFS rule. The truncated SOT rule reduces idle time 3.23 percentage points as compared to a reduction of 9.80 for the untruncated rule. The variance is 1.19 times the variance for the FCFS rule. Table 10–4 summarizes the comparisons.

Table 10–4
Effect of truncation number on the performance of the SOT rule

	Truncation number C				
	0	100	300	1,000	∞
Approximate ratio maximum waiting time under TSOT, C to expected waiting time under FCFS	—	2.5	7.4	25.00	∞
Fraction of advantage secured	0	0.34	0.47	0.92	1.00
Variance of TSOT, C/ variance of FCFS	1.00	1.19	1.69	2.50	4.13

Source: From R. W. Conway and W. L. Maxwell, "Network Scheduling by the Shortest-Operation Discipline," *Operations Research*, vol. 10 (1962), pp. 51–73.

One can find grounds for either optimism or pessimism in these results. On the pessimistic side, if the shortest-operation rule is subjected to "reasonable" truncation, say on the order to 300 time units, it loses half of its advantage. On the other side one could note that replacing the FCFS rule with a severely truncated shortest-operation (the maximum waiting time under TS, 100 would be the same order of magnitude as the *maximum* waiting time under FCFS) would yield one-third of the potential benefit without a prohibitive increase in variance. [8]

The sensitivity experiments indicated in general that there was virtually no effect due to shop size for either pure flow or pure job shops. The SOT rule also maintained its advantage over a wide range of shop load. The results of experiments with regard to the sensitivity of the SOT rule to errors in estimating processing times is shown in Figure 10–5. Percent idle time increases with increased errors as might be expected. Two reference levels are shown in Figure 10–5,

Figure 10–5
Sensitivity of shortest operation rule to forecast errors

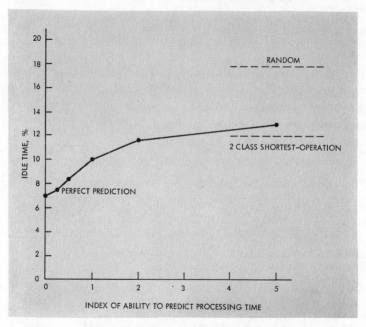

Source: From R. W. Conway and W. L. Maxwell, "Network Scheduling by the Shortest-Operation Discipline," *Operations Research*, vol. 10 (1962), pp. 51–73.

the performance of a random rule for assignment and a two-class SOT rule where orders are classified as either short or long, preference being given to short jobs. Conway and Maxwell conclude that process time errors of estimation are not a serious problem with the SOT rule, since very crude estimates, that is, the two-way classification, achieve fully half the advantage of the SOT rule over the random rule.

It would appear that the SOT rule is an excellent local rule from most points of view. It has the best performance over almost the entire range of fractiles of orders as indicated by the Nanot study.

Perhaps truncation can eliminate the undesirable effects for the minority of orders which might otherwise require inordinately long processing times. Finally, the rule is relatively insensitive to errors in estimating process times. It would seem that a priority dispatching decision rule superior to the SOT rule would probably have to be one of broader horizon which might "look ahead" to anticipate bottlenecks which might produce long waiting times.

COVERT rules

Carroll [7] investigated a family of priority dispatching decision rules characterized in general by the ratio of delay cost to processing time; that is, c/t, or mnemonically COVERT. The basic objective was to find a rule which retained the performance values of the SOT rule but which tended to minimize the extreme lateness of a few orders. The reasoning behind the operation of the COVERT rule and its variants is to establish a trade-off between potential delay costs and the processing time for the tasks. Carroll reasons that the cost of delay is simply the incremental change in order tardiness and assumes that all orders incur the delay cost penalties at the same rate. Thus the rule builds on Jackson's [22, 24] dynamic priority concepts as well as on the SOT rule. In general, then, to implement such a priority rule one would give the highest priority to orders with the largest ratio of expected tardiness to operation time, c/t.

The priority numbers range between zero and one, the extreme value zero being easily classified. If the slack time for an order exceeds its expected waiting time in the system, its priority index is zero, since there should be no difficulty in meeting its due date. The computations of the index numbers are slightly complex though not difficult. The following definitions taken in relation to the flowchart shown in Figure 10–6 indicate how the computation of the priority indexes is carried out:

t = Present time; i.e., time at which the decision is being made.
d = Due date.
i = A subscript to identify the operation number.
t_i = Operation process time.
q_i = Waiting time for an operation.
n_i = Normal scheduled start date for an operation; i.e., due date less aggregate processing and waiting time, $\left[d - \sum_i (t_i + q_i) \right]$.

Figure 10–6
Flowchart for computing priority indexes for the COVERT decision rule

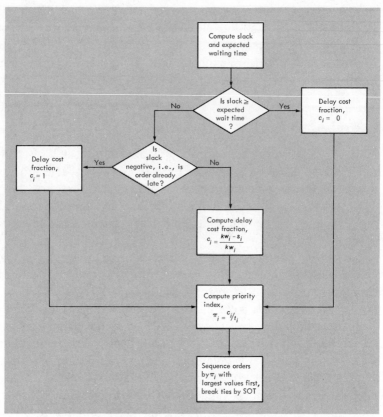

u_i = Urgent scheduled start date for an operation; i.e., due date
less aggregate processing time, $\left(d - \sum_i t_i\right)$.

s_i = Slack or allowable waiting time, or, $u_i - T$.
kw_i = Expected order waiting time, $k(u_i - n_i)$.
k = An approximating factor.
c_i = Expected delay cost for an operation = Incremental change in
Tardiness = $\dfrac{\text{(Wait time-slack)}}{\text{Wait time}}$.

Following the flowchart one first computes the normal and urgent
scheduled start dates, n_i and u_i. The slack for an operation is simply
the difference between the urgent start date and the present time. The
expected waiting time for an operation is the difference between the

urgent and normal start dates modified by the approximating factor k; $k = 1$ in the example which follows. If slack is equal to expected waiting time or more, there should be no problem in meeting the due date, and therefore the delay cost fraction is zero and the priority index is zero. If slack is less than expected waiting time, then there is urgency in some degree, and priorities are important. If the order is already late (i.e., negative slack) then the delay cost fraction is $c_i = 1$ and the priority index may be computed directly. If slack is still positive, the delay cost fraction and the priority index are computed. Orders are then sequenced by the priority numbers, taking those with the largest indexes first. If two orders have the same index number, ties are broken by giving priority to the order with the lowest processing time. An example is shown in Table 10–5 in which the prior-

Table 10–5
Example showing computations of priority indexes for the COVERT rule (present time, $t = 200$, $k = 1$)

	Order number				
	1.	2	3	4	5
Normal start date n_i	194	216	184	96	185
Urgent start date u_i	224	280	196	120	215
Slack $s_i = u_i - 200$	24	80	−4	−80	15
Expected waiting time,					
$kw_i = k(u_i - n_i)$	30	64	12	24	30
$s_i - kw_i$	−6	16	−16	−104	−15
Cost of delay,					
$c_i = \dfrac{kw_i - s}{kw_i}$	0.2	0	1.0	1.0	0.5
Operation processing time ...	8	1	7	12	3
Priority index π_i	0.025	0	0.143	0.083	0.167
Rank order of					
processing	4	5	2	3	1

Source: Adapted from D. C. Carroll, "Heuristic Sequencing of Single and Multiple Component Jobs," (unpublished Ph.D. dissertation, M.I.T., 1965).

ity indexes for five orders are computed assuming present time to be 200. Order number 2 is one in which the slack time exceeds expected waiting time so that the estimated delay cost is zero. Orders 3 and 4 are examples of orders which are already late; that is, they have negative slack and their estimated delay cost is maximum at $c_i = 1$.

Experiments and results. Carroll tested the COVERT rule with two main variations against six other rules in a set of simulation experiments that involved both single- and multiple-component orders (multiple-component orders are assembled units). For single-component order runs he used approximately 3,000 orders involving about 40,000 tasks and for multiple-component order runs 2,000 orders involving 30,000–60,000 tasks. Sample results are shown in Table 10–6 and Figure 10–7 for a run with single-component-type

Table 10–6
Mean tardiness and wait times for six rules. Pure job shop, eight machines, single-component orders, utilization = 0.80 (3,072 orders)

Rule	Mean tardiness per order	Mean wait times
FCFS	36.6	14.4
FISFS (first-in system)	24.7	14.2
SS/RO (static slack per remaining operation)	16.2	13.9
SOT	11.3	7.0
TSOT (truncated SOT)	4.6	8.0
COVERT ($k = 1$)	2.5	10.3

Source: From D. C. Carroll, "Heuristic Sequencing of Single and Multiple Component Jobs" (unpublished Ph.D. dissertation, M.I.T., 1965).

orders and a pure job shop configuration with eight machines. Table 10–6 shows the mean tardiness of the COVERT rule to be superior to even the truncated SOT rule, and the mean wait time to be between the first three benchmark rules and SOT. Figure 10–7 shows the lateness distributions for the six rules and indicates dramatically the effectiveness of COVERT in skewing the distribution so that orders completed on the due date are the mode of the distribution with very few late orders.

In sensitivity tests at other utilization levels Carroll found no significant difference in performance of the COVERT rule except that at low utilization levels the differences between rules tended to blur, but with the COVERT rule maintaining its superiority. This suggests that the sequencing function is less vital with a light shop load. Sensitivity experiments with different flow allowances (time allowed between start and due dates) showed that the COVERT rule could cope with both extremes. Finally, sensitivity experiments dealing with changes in the value of k, the arbitrary approximating constant, showed considerable variation in the performance of the COVERT rule depending on the value of k selected. For example, the performance shown in Table 10–6 and Figure 10–7 could be improved to a mean tardiness per order of 1.4 with a value of $k = 0.5$.

Figure 10–7
Lateness distributions for six rules, pure job shop, single-
component order, 3,072 orders, utilization = 0.80

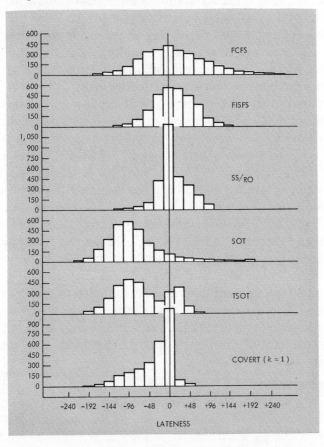

Source: From D. C. Carroll, "Heuristic Sequencing of Single and Multiple Component Jobs," (unpublished Ph.D. dissertation, M.I.T., 1965).

Other experiments.   Carroll tested the COVERT rule in other settings such as shops with more than one machine per machine center
and multiple-component orders in both kinds of shops with similar
general results. It appears that the COVERT rule has a great deal to
offer in maintaining the benefits of the SOT rule while dealing effectively with its defects.

LABOR-LIMITED SYSTEMS

As noted previously much of the job shop scheduling research has
involved the assumption that the machine was the critical resource,

labor being available when an order was assigned to a machine. This assumption does not generally fit reality in job shops. The more usual situation is that not all machines are staffed simultaneously, labor being used as a flexible resource assigned to operate different machines at different times depending on the needs of different orders. In a very real sense, then, labor is usually the dominant limiting resource. Studying the more realistic dual resource situation will provide insight into the behavior of such systems and reveal how best to take advantage of the inherent flexibility of a job shop system with two basic resources. To this point we have considered priority dispatch decision rules for sequencing orders on machines. A labor-limited system raises other basic questions, for example: "What are effective labor assignment procedures and how do these procedures interact with sequencing rules? What are the effects of various degrees of centralized control?"

Nelson [42] has developed an ingenious general model for studying labor- and machine-limited systems. Nelson was motivated in part by conclusions of the Harris [14] field study of job shops which we will review in the last major section of this chapter. The Nelson model is small but efficient in terms of the number of variables one can work with in assessing the effects and interactions of a wide variety of alternate policies and procedures. Figure 10–8 is a schematic diagram of the general model. The design and control parameters of the model are:

Design parameters:

m = The number of machine centers in the system.

c_i = The number of identical machines in machine center i, $(i = 1, 2, \ldots, m)$.

n = The number of laborers in the labor force.

e_{ji} = The relative efficiency of laborer j on any machine in machine center i, $(i = 1, 2, \ldots, m; j = 1, 2, \ldots, n)$.

Control parameters:

l = The machine center selection procedure used in central control.

q_i = The queue discipline used at machine center i, $(i = 1, 2, \ldots, m)$.

d_i = The degree of centralized labor assignment control exercised at machine center i, $(i = 1, 2, \ldots, m)$.

Work load parameters of the model are the arrival and service probability density function and their parameters, and the job rout-

Figure 10–8
General model schematic diagram

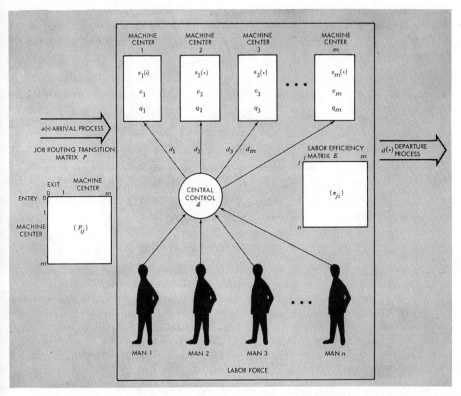

Source: From R. T. Nelson, "Labor and Machine Limited Production Systems," *Management Science*, vol. 13, no. 9 (May 1967), pp. 648–71.

ing transition matrix which can be specified as pure job shop, pure flow shop, and all intermediate degrees. The assignment of laborers to the processing of jobs is dependent on the degree of centralized control over each of the machine centers. A value $d_i = 1$ represents completely centralized control wherein each laborer on completing a service operation at machine center i is given the next work assignment by "central control." The value $d_i = 0$ represents the extreme inertia effect where on completing an operation at machine center i the worker remains in that work center as long as there is any job in its queue, returning to central control for assignment only when there is no work remaining. Intermediate values of the degree of centralized control may also be specified. The assignment of workers to machine centers in central control is governed by a machine center selection procedure l, which operates in conjunction with the queue discipline q_i at the machine centers to form the complete labor assignment procedure.

Initial experiments. In a series of initial experiments Nelson established a simple specific version of his general model where the system consisted of two machine centers each with two identical machines, and a variable number of laborers. The arrival process was Poisson with unit mean arrival rate. A pure job shop configuration was used, and service rates followed identical exponential distributions for all machines. The mean service rate was adjusted to the number of laborers in the system in order to establish comparable work loads for all experiments. Average labor utilization was set at 8/9. The experimental design involved a systematic variation of the number of laborers in the system n, the central control machine center selection procedure l, and the machine center queue disciplines q_i. The number of laborers was varied from one through four, and when $n = 4$ there was a laborer for each machine in the system, resulting in only machine limitation. Three different queue disciplines were used:

$q = 1$, first come, first served (FCFS).
$q = 2$, first in system, first served (FISFS).
$q = 3$, shortest operation time (SOT).

Five different machine center selection procedures l were used for centralized labor assignment:

$l = 0$, random assignment of idle labor among machine centers with work in queue (RAND).

$l = 1$, assignment of labor according to the labor- and machine-limited system counterpart of the FCFS queue discipline for machine-limited systems.

$l = 2$, assignment of labor according to the labor- and machine-limited systems counterpart of the FISFS queue discipline for machine-limited systems.

$l = 3$, assignment of labor according to the labor- and machine-limited systems counterpart of the SOT queue discipline for machine-limited systems.

$l = 4$, assignment of idle labor to the machine center with the most jobs in queue (LNGQ).

The degree of centralized labor assignment control over each of the machine centers was fixed at its maximum level ($d_i = d_2 = 1$)

corresponding to completely centralized control. The labor efficiency matrix set all laborers at full efficiency.

Results of initial experiments.   The rank order of combinations of l and q, machine center selection procedure and queue discipline for order sequencing, are shown in Table 10–7 for mean flow time,

Table 10–7
Rank order of combinations of machine center selection procedure and queue discipline (l, q) for flow time statistics $(n = 3$ laborers)

Rank order	Mean flow time		Variance of flow time		Maximum flow time	
	Machine center selection procedure*	Queue discipline for order sequencing†	Machine center selection procedure	Queue discipline for order sequencing	Machine center selection procedure	Queue discipline for order sequencing
1	LNGQ———SOT		LNGQ———FISFS		LNGQ———FISFS	
2	SOT———SOT		FISFS———FISFS		FISFS———FISFS	
3	LNGQ———FISFS		FCFS———FCFS		FCFS———FCFS	
4	FCFS———FCFS		RAND———FCFS		RAND———FCFS	
5	FISFS———FISFS		LNGQ———SOT		LNGQ———SOT	
6	RAND——— FCFS		SOT———SOT		SOT———SOT	

   * Machine center selection procedure code: RAND—random; FCFS—first come, first served; FIFS—first in system, first served; SOT—shortest operation time; LNGQ—longest queue.
   † Queue discipline code: FCFS—first come, first served; FISFS—first in system, first served; SOT—shortest operation time.
   Source: Adapted from R. T. Nelson, "Labor and Machine Limited Production Systems," *Management Science*, vol. 13, no. 9 (May 1967), pp. 648–71.

variance, and maximum flow time for the system involving three laborers. Similar results were obtained for the systems with two and four laborers. The complete assignment procedure LNGQ-SOT is superior for mean flow time but LNGQ-FISFS has better variance and maximum flow time performance. Table 10–8 shows the rank performance of combinations of l and q for selected fractiles of orders processed. The SOT-SOT combination was best through the 80th fractile and LNGQ-SOT through the 95th fractile.

   Figure 10–9 is useful for examining the independent effects of changes in size of labor force, machine center selection procedure, and queue discipline for order sequencing. Figure 10–9 does not contain a plot for all of the data but only selected values for three and four laborers. Note that with four laborers there is no machine center selection procedure required, since all machines are staffed. Changes in queue discipline for order sequencing showed substantial effects. Nelson notes that the results for the variance of flow time give increasing values for the queue disciplines FISFS, FCFS, and

Table 10–8
Rank order of flow time for combinations of machine center
selection procedure and queue discipline (l, q) (n = 3 laborers)

Fractiles of orders processed	Rank order		
	1	2	3
0.20	SOT–SOT	LNGQ–SOT	RAND–FCFS
0.40	SOT–SOT	LNGQ–SOT	FCFS–FCFS
0.60	SOT–SOT	LNGQ–SOT	FCFS–FCFS
0.80	SOT–SOT	LNGQ–SOT	FCFS–FCFS
0.90	LNGQ–SOT	SOT–SOT	LNGQ–FISFS
0.95	LNGQ–SOT	SOT–SOT	LNGQ–FISFS
0.99	FISFS–FISFS	LNGQ–FISFS	LNGQ–SOT
0.999	LNGQ–FISFS	FISFS–FISFS	RAND–FISFS

Source: From R. T. Nelson, "Labor and Machine Limited Production Systems,"
Management Science, vol. 13, no. 9 (May 1967), pp. 648–71.

Figure 10–9
Mapping of mean flow time versus variance to show independent effects of
changes in size of labor force, machine center selection procedure, and
queue discipline

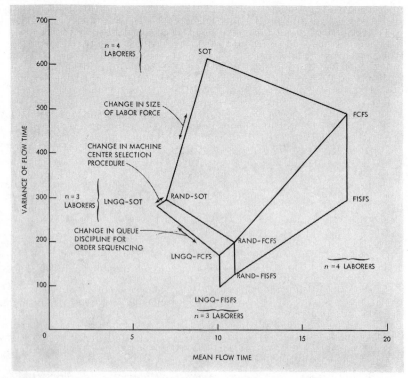

Source: From R. T. Nelson, "Labor and Machine Limited Production Systems," *Management
Science,* vol. 13, no. 9 (May 1967), pp. 648–71.

SOT, respectively, and that these results conflict with those obtained in Conway's study at RAND Corporation.

Conway's experiments with a machine limited network were conducted with the same utilization level and job routing structure as these. One difference between the two sets of experiments is that Conway employed shorter (10,000 versus 32,000 jobs) simulation runs with a larger network (9 machines versus 4 machines). Experimental evidence was provided by the current experiments to support the conjecture that the sample sizes do, in fact, account for the observed difference in results. By looking at sub-sample reports from the simulation runs, it was discovered that sub-samples of 8,000 jobs did not reflect the consistent variance relationships exhibited in the complete 32,000 job runs. [40].

Perhaps the most startling effect indicated in Figure 10–9 is that attributed to changes in the size of the labor force. For all three queue disciplines large increases in mean and variance resulted from increases in the labor force from three to four laborers. We focus on a more complete analysis of this effect in Table 10–9, which shows the

Table 10–9
Effect of changes in the size of labor force on flow time

Size of labor force n	Mean flow time, f'	Job flow time distribution-fractile,							
		0.20	0.40	0.60	0.80	0.90	0.95	0.99	0.999
4	9.4	1.63	3.48	6.09	11.70	18.97	28.74	76.42	101.2
3	6.4	1.08	2.26	3.99	7.79	12.85	20.25	51.45	68.94
2	5.0	0.80	1.60	2.86	5.38	9.24	15.84	51.49	67.32
1	4.2	0.62	1.24	1.85	3.76	7.20	13.90	53.65	122.4

Source: From R. T. Nelson, "Labor and Machine Limited Production Systems," *Management Science*, vol. 13, no. 9 (May 1967), pp. 648–71.

mean flow time and flow time for selected fractiles of orders processed in relation to size of work force. In each case the values given are those obtained by the use of the most effective labor assignment procedure (l, q) for the fractile and work force size. The average utilization of the labor force was maintained at the same level for each value of n, so that we have a measure of physical flexibility. The results indicate that the mean value of flow time decreases as the size of work force decreases. The same behavior is exhibited up to the 0.98 fractile. In other words the labor-limited systems offer a degree of flexibility not inherent in the machine-limited system. Not only that, as the ratio of machines to work force increases, flexibility increases with the exception of the extreme upper tail for a work force of size 1. Reasoning backwards from the observed phenomenon, a machine-limited system loses its flexibility, since labor cannot be reassigned to machine centers where the load is heavy. The queues at some work centers will be empty at times, and thus the average utilization of labor will decrease and flow time will increase. Nelson gives the following example of how the advantage of the flexibility of labor limited systems might be used.

We consider the models used in the experiments with a single machine in each machine center and a work force consisting of two laborers. For the sake of this example we shall assume a FCFS queue discipline. The mean time in system (flow time) for this machine limited system as computed from queueing theory is $f' = 16$. Suppose now that a decision is made to add one more machine in each machine center identical to the machine previously there. The experimental results of the $n = 2$ experiments with FCFS indicate that f' for the new system is 8.7. The nearly 50% improvement in the average time in system can be expected to result in an increased work load due to improved service to the customer with respect to competitors. The increased work load will increase f' until a new equilibrium is attained. The end result will be a more flexible system offering better service at a higher volume with the original labor force. The only costs incurred in the transition are investment in equipment and training.

The degree of centralized control of labor assignment was studied with the system involving three laborers. In these experiments the machine center selection procedure used by central control was LNGQ in combination with the three queue disciplines. The experimental results for flow time under the limiting cases of complete central control and no central control are given in Table 10–10. With LNGQ-FCFS, the use of full central control as opposed to no central control led to a 7 percent decrease in system flow time and a 14 percent decrease in the variance of flow time. With LNGQ-FISFS, the corresponding decreases were 7 percent and 28 percent, respectively. With LNGQ-SOT, the use of full central control decreased mean flow time by 12 percent; however, the variance increased by 39 percent. The more detailed data of flow time by fractiles indicates that the effects of the degree of central control are quite different for the three labor assignment procedures employed. Nelson concludes that in terms of flow time statistics the LNGQ-SOT labor assignment procedure would be relatively better for systems characterized by less centralized labor assignment control and that the other two procedures might perform better in systems characterized by central control of labor assignment.

Table 10–10
Effect of extreme degrees of centralized control of labor assignment on
flow time

| Job flow distribution-facilities | Queue disciplines with: | | | | | |
| | Complete central control $(d_1 = d_2 = 1)$ | | | No central control $(d_1 = d_2 = 0)$ | | |
	FCFS	FISFS	SOT	FCFS	FISFS	SOT
	10.07*	10.14*	6.37*	10.80*	10.91*	7.26*
	168.84†	97.09†	281.20†	195.52†	134.59†	202.57†
0.10	1.276	1.378	0.569	1.171	1.276	0.633
0.20	2.399	2.754	1.138	2.341	2.576	1.652
0.30	3.542	4.144	1.707	3.506	3.908	1.898
0.40	4.817	5.684	2.407	4.864	5.486	2.732
0.50	6.243	7.452	3.244	6.489	7.356	3.605
0.60	8.077	9.532	4.144	8.642	9.721	4.811
0.70	10.617	12.081	5.606	11.513	12.803	6.457
0.80	14.464	15.677	7.807	15.922	17.108	2.930
0.90	22.629	21.721	12.854	24.707	24.826	15.487
0.95	31.598	27.639	20.254	35.001	32.219	24.876
0.98	48.187	39.239	35.293	52.027	44.689	44.285
0.99	61.512	52.625	56.455	66.795	58.996	64.428
0.999	126.795	68.944	118.192	132.477	89.298	178.384
1.0	286.000	80.000	862.000	310.000	102.000	468.000

* Mean.
† Variance.
Source: From R. T. Nelson, "Labor and Machine Limited Production Systems," *Management Science*, vol. 13, no. 9 (May 1967), pp. 648–71.

Job routing structure and labor flexibility experiments were performed involving a tandem arrangement of two service centers and two laborers. Two different labor efficiency matrices were used as a mechanism for providing complete flexibility in one instance and complete inflexibility in the other. Comparing the results of these experiments with those obtained for job shop routines showed the flexible system to be very much superior to the inflexible one for all queue disciplines. Within the flexible tandem system the labor assignment combinations of SOT-SOT and LNGQ-SOT were approximately equally effective. In another paper Nelson [41] has performed an additional extensive set of simulation experiments on a tandem arrangement of two machine centers with various ways of assigning a single laborer to accomplish the work at both centers.

STUDIES WITH ACTUAL SHOP DATA

Three well-known studies have been made on labor-limited systems in actual shop settings. The original Rowe [45] study used a GE plant as a basis for the model. A closely related study in terms of its objectives was carried out by LeGrande [26] under Rowe's direction at the Hughes Aircraft Company. Finally, an interesting study by Allen [1] carried out at a GE plant examines the performance of alternate decision rules under declining load. We will examine the Allen study, since it raises a number of hypotheses not previously discussed, and conclude our discussion of labor-limited systems with an examination of the multiple-criterion problem for judging the effectiveness of priority sequencing rules through the mechanism of the LeGrande study.

Decision rules under declining load

Allen [1] studied the relative effectiveness of several alternate decision rules under declining shop load, but particularly the SOT rule because it had been shown to be superior under "steady-state" conditions. The SOT rule had consistently yielded excellent utilization levels. Rather than steady-state conditions, however, Allen was interested in the short-run situation when shop load was rapidly declining and therefore wished to reexamine the SOT rule under these conditions.

The General Electric job shop used for study consisted of 78 machines classified into 18 machine groups. It was assumed in the simulation studies that any machine in a machine group could perform the required operations with the same setup and processing time. There was the usual complement of machine shop equipment available. The work force consisted of 40 workers classified into 13 labor classes. All those in a given labor class were regarded as being interchangeable, and the worker-machine relationship, in terms of which labor class or classes could operate certain machine groups, was specified. The system as a whole was labor limited except for certain machine groups, such as the boring mills, where machine capacity was limited relative to normal requirements.

Experiments. The conditions of interest to Allen were those where no additional work was released to the shop after the initial load, so that actual runout of the orders takes place. His primary concern then was to examine alternate priority dispatching decision rules with the objective of finding rules which would maintain labor utilization at as high a level as possible until additional orders would be received. One of the factors considered to be important in improving labor utilization was the possibility of *alternate routing*. For the particular order mix studied, approximately one third of the required operations could be performed at more than one machine group, though there were some machine groups for which no alternate routing was possible. For example, large machines might substitute for small ones, but the reverse is seldom true. On the other hand, some of the large machines were sometimes overloaded and became bottleneck operations. Allen therefore incorporated alternate routing into several of the decision rules tested. The eight decision rules tested are listed in Table 10–11. The alternate routing decision

Table 10–11
Average labor utilization figures for eight priority dispatching rules (under conditions where no additional work was released to the shop after the initial load so that run-out takes place)

Rule number and description	Average labor utilization in percent for weeks:	
	1–10	7–10
1. SOT–AR*	85.1	62.8
2. LOT–AR	81.8	54.5
3. RAND–AR	83.4	58.5
4. RAND	79.5	49.5
5. LOT–SOT†	86.7	66.8
6. SOT B–LOT‡	86.5	66.3
7. TC–SOT§	87.9	69.8
8. TC–SW‖	88.3	70.8

    * AR = alternate routing.
    † LOT until week 6, then SOT.
    ‡ B = bottleneck. Use SOT on bottleneck machines, LOT elsewhere.
    § TC = two class. Jobs divided into two classes, those requiring additional processing beyond the operation in question and those not. Higher priority always given to the first class and jobs ordered within classes by SOT.
    ‖ SW = switching. Two class switching rule. Jobs divided into two classes as in Rule 7, but within classes jobs were ordered by LOT until week 6 and by SOT thereafter.
    Source: Data from M. Allen, "A Detailed Simulation of a Non-Stock Production Leveling Problem (unpublished S.M. thesis, M.I.T., 1962), or from (1).

was deferred until the order became available for the operation in question and was therefore regarded as a part of dispatching. The specific method of alternate routing used by Allen in the simulation was to reexamine each queue once each shift. If the backlog was such that there were orders in a queue which could not possibly be processed in the forthcoming shift, an attempt was made to reroute the order into some other queue which did not have a full shift's worth of work.

Summary results of average labor utilization figures for the eight priority dispatching decision rules are shown in Table 10–11. A comparison of the average utilization figures for Rules 3 and 4 indicates that alternate routing has the effect of increasing labor utilization. Of the first four rules, the SOT-AR rule performs the best.

Allen notes that if complete shop runout occurs one objective would be to expedite the reallocation of labor to other areas, or if necessary, to lay off workers as expeditiously as possible. At least one worker would have to be retained in each labor class for which some work still remains. An objective then might be to reduce as rapidly as possible the number of labor classes with outstanding work. Table 10–12 shows the number of labor classes having no

Table 10–12
Number of labor classes having no remaining work beyond week indicated for last 15 weeks of complete runout (13-labor class shop)

Week	Rule 1, SOT–AR	Rule 3, RAND–AR	Week	Rule 1 SOT–AR	Rule 3 RAND–AR
13	0	0	21	7	1
14	2	0	22	9	4
15	3	0	23	10	5
16	3	0	24	11	5
17	3	1	25	11	8
18	3	1	26	11	10
19	3	1	27	13	13
20	3	1			

Source: From M. Allen, "A Detailed Simulation of a Non-Stock Production Leveling Problem" (unpublished S.M. thesis, M.I.T., 1962).

remaining work beyond the 13th week for Rules 1 and 3. The SOT-AR rule is also effective from this point of view. For example, in the 14th week the SOT-AR rule has already eliminated two labor classes, while the RAND-AR rule will still have eliminated only one class by the 21st week.

Allen's reasoning as an explanation for the superiority of the SOT-AR rule under declining load led to the testing of four additional, more complex rules. Allen's explanation for the superiority of the SOT-AR rule was as follows:

By working on the shortest jobs available, the rate of job flow in the shop is increased. Accordingly, any load imbalances which should develop tend to be dissipated more quickly, thus reducing idle time at the downstream machines. It is equally apparent, however, that the shortest-processing-time rule cannot maintain this advantage indefinitely, since there is no additional work available to be released to the shop. Each week, therefore, the average operation time of the jobs processed is greater than the average of the previous week. For example, with 100% labor utilization, 188 jobs were completed, when the shortest-processing-time rule was used between weeks 1 and 2.

On the other hand, only 58 jobs were completed between weeks 5 and 6, even though the utilization during this period was also 100%. While the average operation time when the shortest-processing-time rule is used is increasing, the average operation time when the longest-processing-time rule is used is, of course, decreasing. At some point in time, the rate of job flow with rule 2 should begin to exceed the rate of job flow with rule 1. At this point, it would be quite reasonable to except higher utilization with the longest-processing-time rule. This is not the case, however. Between weeks 6 and 7, 57 jobs were completed, with 94% labor utilization, when rule 1 was used. In this same interval, 138 jobs were completed when rule 2 was used, even though utilization was only 86%. A similar conclusion can be reached concerning the relative performance of these rules during weeks 8, 9, and 10. A closer examination of the simulation output reports suggested one possible explanation. There was a very large variance in the processing times of the operations performed during this four-week interval, when rule 2 was used. Thus, although the average operation time was quite low and was becoming lower, there were some machine groups at which very lengthy operations were still being performed. This was particularly true among the larger pieces of equipment, such as the boring mills. Sizable backlogs began to develop behind these machines so that the amount of work available elsewhere in the shop began to dwindle rapidly. The result, of course, was idle time.

The preceding analysis suggests the possibility of using the LOT-AR rule as long as possible without hurting utilization. When utilization begins to fall, however, switch to the SOT–AR rule. This is the construction of Rule 5. Another strategy was to use the SOT on bottleneck operations, using the LOT rule at all other machine groups. The idea was to complete as many of the long orders as possible while the shop was heavily loaded and thus to compensate for slow rates of order flow. Rule 6 is constructed on the foregoing basis. A third hypothesis for improving labor utilization was to divide all orders into two classes, those which required additional processing and those for which the present operation was the final one. Higher priority was given to the class of orders requiring additional processing, but within each class orders were sequenced by the SOT rule. Rule 7 was set up on the foregoing basis. Finally, Rule 8 was a two-class switching rule in which orders were divided into the same two classes as for Rule 7, but within each class orders were sequenced by the LOT rule for the first five weeks at which point the sequencing was switched to the SOT rule.

As can be seen by examining Table 10–11, the more complex rules have an effect in increasing average labor utilization when the shop is faced with conditions of decreasing load. Allen repeated the experiments with a second and third set of orders on runs for Rules 1, 2, 5, and 8. Though there were differences in absolute levels in the results, the ranking of the rules remained exactly the same.

Flexibility experiments. Since the shop configuration was basically labor limited, Allen performed additional simulation experiments to determine the degree of additional labor flexibility which might result if it was assumed that the entire work force of 40 were pooled into one extremely versatile labor class which could operate all machines within the shop. Table 10–13 summarizes the

Table 10–13
Comparison of average labor utilization in percent and weeks to empty the shop for shops with 13- and 1-labor classes

	Rule			
	SOT–AR Rule 1	LOT–AR Rule 2	RAND–AR Rule 3	RAND Rule 4
13-Labor class shop:				
Utilization, weeks 1–10	85.1	81.8	83.4	79.5
Utilization, weeks 7–10	62.8	54.5	58.5	49.5
Weeks to empty shop	27.0	27.0	27.0	27.0
1-Labor class shop:				
Utilization, weeks 1–10	91.9	93.8	93.6	89.5
Utilization, weeks 7–10	79.8	84.5	84.0	73.8
Weeks to empty shop	20.0	19.0	19.0	19.0

Source: Data from M. Allen, "A Detailed Simulation of a Non-Stock Production Leveling Problem" (unpublished S.M. thesis, M.I.T., 1962).

average labor utilization figures and the number of weeks to empty the shop for the assumed 1-labor class setup in comparison with the previously obtained 13-labor class shop results. The advantages of greater labor flexibility are apparent for all four rules tested. The average difference in labor utilization for the first ten weeks is nearly 10 percentage points, ranging from a difference of 6.8 percentage points for the SOT–AR rule to 12 percentage points for the LOT–AR rule. The number of weeks to empty the shop drops from 27 to 19 or 20. Though a 1-labor class shop may be regarded as impractical,

Allen also made a simulation run where it was assumed that 5 of the 40-person work force could operate all machines in the shop, the other 35 remaining in the 13-labor class structure. It appears that much of the advantage of the one-class shop was retained, since the number of weeks to empty the shop remained at only 19. No average labor utilization figures were reported. Another direct advantage of the shop with greater flexibility is, of course, a reduction in in-process inventory, since average flow time will have been reduced.

Table 10–13 also makes it possible to compare the relative merits of labor versus machine flexibility. By comparing the relative performance of Rules 3 and 4, RAND-AR and RAND, for both the 13- and 1-labor class shops, we see that the average improvement in the ten-week utilization due to alternate routing was only 4 percentage points compared to 10.1 percentage points due to labor flexibility. The alternate routing flexibility effect seems to be relatively independent of the labor flexibility effect, though no statistical analysis is available to establish independence.

One final observation regarding the impact of flexibility is of interest. Note from Table 10–13 that Rule 1, SOT–AR has lost its dominance for the single-labor class shop. Both Rules 2 and 3 yield higher average utilization figures and cut one week off the number of weeks required to empty the shop.

Though he did not investigate in detail, Allen also looked at labor flexibility effects under conditions of a heavy shop load. Simulations for both the 13- and 1-labor class shops were conducted using a due date rule without alternate routing. Although both shop configurations achieved essentially 100 percent labor utilization, the more flexible shop reduced the standard deviation in job lateness from 16 to 12 days. Allen comments that the increased shop flexibility might reduce the need for overtime when the shop is heavily loaded.

Conclusions. Under conditions of declining shop load it appears that the SOT rule is the best simple rule but that a combination of simple rules such as Rules 5, 6, 7, and 8 can result in improvements in average labor utilization. In addition, where complete runout is to take place, the SOT rule is effective in reducing the number of labor classes with outstanding work as rapidly as possible. The introduction of labor flexibility appears to have a substantial effect on labor utilization under conditions of declining load and may be important for heavy load as well. The effects of labor flexibility seem somewhat larger than those due to machine flexibility and may be independent.

Multiple criteria for the effectiveness of priority dispatching decision rules

One of the difficulties of judging the relative effectiveness of different priority dispatching decision rules is that the aggregate criterion function involves some judgmental weighting of the importance of different factors. Which is most important, average flow time, percent of late orders, average waiting time of orders, in-process inventory costs, labor utilization, machine utilization, or what? It is entirely possible that for a given shop the criteria have different weights. For example, in some shops it may be more important to have orders be on time than to have high utilization of labor and equipment. In other situations the reverse could be true. LeGrande [26] developed a labor-limited job shop simulation using actual data at the Hughes Aircraft Company in which he compared six different priority dispatching decision rules on the basis of ten criteria. Briefly the six rules (most of which are identical to previous rules we have discussed) were as follows:

Table 10–14
Relative ranking of the performance of six decision rules based on ten criteria

Equally weighted criteria*	Rule					
	SOT	DS/RO	FCFS	MINSD	FISFS	RAND
1	1.00	0.87	0.86	0.84	0.94	0.84
2	0.83	1.00	0.54	0.48	0.62	0.68
3	1.00	0.63	0.54	0.46	0.64	0.79
4	0.20	1.00	0.20	0.22	0.24	0.20
5	1.00	0.73	0.73	0.68	0.84	0.67
6	1.00	0.52	0.38	0.36	0.51	0.66
7	0.76	0.96	0.84	0.91	1.00	0.80
8	0.91	0.99	0.98	1.00	0.99	0.93
9	1.00	0.92	0.93	0.91	0.87	0.92
10	1.00	0.92	0.93	0.91	0.97	0.91
Total relative rank	8.70	8.54	6.93	6.77	7.62	7.40

* Key to criteria:
  1. Number of orders completed.
  2. Percent of orders completed late.
  3. Mean of the distribution of completions.
  4. Standard deviation of the distribution of completions.
  5. Average number of orders waiting in the shop.
  6. Average wait time of orders.
  7. Yearly cost of carrying orders in queue.
  8. Ratio of inventory carrying cost while waiting to inventory cost while on machine.
  9. Percent of labor utilized.
  10. Percent of machine capacity utilized.

Source: From E. LeGrande, "The Development of a Factory Simulation System Using Actual Operating Data," *Management Technology*, vol. 3, no. 1 (May 1963).

SOT—shortest operation time.

DS/RO—dynamic slack per remaining operation.

FCFS—first come, first served.

MINSD— minimum planned start date per operation.

FISFS—first in system, first served.

RAND—random sequencing.

Table 10–14 shows the relative rank of the different rules when the ten criteria listed below Table 10–14 are weighted equally. The SOT rule has the highest overall ranking. On the other hand, when Le-Grande weighted order completion criteria more heavily, as indicated in Table 10–15, the relative positions of SOT and DS/RO were reversed.

Table 10–15
Relative ranking of the performance of six decision rules based on ten criteria (when order completion criteria are most heavily weighted)

		Rule					
Criteria*	Weighting	SOT	DS/RO	FCFS	MINSD	FISFS	RAND
1	2	2.00	1.74	1.72	1.68	1.88	1.68
2	5	4.15	5.00	2.70	2.40	3.10	3.40
3	5	5.00	3.15	2.70	2.30	3.20	3.95
4	5	1.00	5.00	1.00	1.10	1.20	1.00
5	1	1.00	0.73	0.73	0.68	0.84	0.67
6	1	1.00	0.52	0.38	0.36	0.51	0.66
7	4	3.04	3.84	3.36	3.64	4.00	3.20
8	2	1.82	1.98	1.96	2.00	1.98	1.86
9	3	3.00	2.76	2.79	2.73	2.61	2.76
10	2	2.00	1.84	1.86	1.82	1.74	1.82
Total relative rank		24.01	26.56	19.20	18.71	21.06	21.00

* See Table 10–14 for list of criteria.
  Source: From E. LeGrande, "The Development of a Factory Simulation System Using Actual Operating Data," *Management Technology*, vol. 3, no. 1 (May 1963).

The job shop as an Erlang model queuing system—
An empirical study

In all of the machine-limited studies reported and in some of the labor-limited studies, the job shop was idealized in structure to fit the assumptions of Poisson arrival rates and exponential service times in a network of queues in conformance to general Erlang models. Harris [17, 18] performed an extensive empirical study directed toward three specific questions: (a) How well do the Erlang structural assumptions fit the work center? (b) How well do the Erlang model parameters fit the work center? and (c) How well does the Erlang model predict the observed behavior?

The site of the study was the machine shop of the Los Angeles division of a national aerospace company. The company's stated policy was to maintain itself as a custom designer and manufacturer of electronic and electromechanical devices. Quoting from a private management memorandum on the manufacturing planning and control system [17]:

XYZ's manufacturing system must cope with hundreds of customer orders in concurrent production. Contract value ranges from a few dollars to multi-millions. Deliverable item complexity ranges from simple piece parts and subassemblies to complex systems made up of many thousands of parts. Deliverable item quantities range from single items to a few hundred. The needs of the customer, and consequently the basis for contract award, may vary. In one instance, item price may govern. In another, confidence in the supplier's technical competence may be the prime consideration. Ability to make quick delivery may be the determining factor. To deal with the range, a manufacturing planning, scheduling and control system is needed which will insure proper attention to each proposal and each order, with the dual objective of satisfying the customer and obtaining a profit for the company. Such a system must be well defined in general terms, yet must be flexible, lending itself to improvisation to permit efficient handling of orders in keeping with the particular combination of factors that apply.

There are 164 individual machine tools in the shop organized in 18 groupings plus two additional departmental groupings which involve workers only. The departmental groupings are in turn broken down into 59 machine centers. The sample for study included a seven-month period during which 90,000 individual observations were made and the processing of approximately 10,000 job lots was described.

Structural assumptions.   Harris found that much of the general structure paralleled that of a network of queues, but some of the implications of actual practice did not fit assumptions. Measurement or definition of the exact time of arrival of an order from outside the machine shop was difficult. It was difficult to translate service duration into service rate because of the interruption of service and the rapidly fluctuating capacity of the machine center. At some machine centers the single-channel concept had to be expanded to a multiple-parallel assumption. A queue did in fact exist in front of most of the machine centers; however, the reasons for the queue appeared more complex than in the usual assumption that jobs are simply waiting their turn for service. The jobs may be waiting for the service channel to "open" for business or to satisfy other management requirements.

The queue discipline is thus more complex than normally assumed. In actual operation the service rate could be increased or decreased by changes in effective capacity. Harris listed in the rough order of importance the following capacity changing techniques actually used: overtime, switching operators between job classifications, hiring new operators, subcontracting work, tooling up idle machines, and splitting lots. Harris' conclusion was that the structural assumptions imposed by the general Erlang model did not fit the work center very well.

Job shop model parameters. Harris analyzed the 90,000 observations classified by machine center to test if the arrival and service rates corresponded to a Poisson process. Based on an analysis of mean arrival rates, standard deviations of arrival rates and chi-square fit tests, Harris concluded: (a) The observed distribution of arrivals shows wide variety in the arrival rate, variability, and general shape of the distribution. (b) The Poisson-type distribution is not sufficient to explain or fit all the observed distributions. Only a few machine centers with small amounts of data show reasonable agreement with the Poisson distributions. With regard to service time Harris came to similar conclusions, rejecting the negative exponential distribution even more strongly.

Performance predictions. Harris examined the observed queue length and waiting time actual data and again subjected these data to statistical analysis with the following conclusions: (a) The observed waiting times and queue lengths are longer than predicted by the Erlang model. (b) The observed standard deviations are different from those predicted by the Erlang model. The variation in queue length is less and the variation in wait time is greater. (c) Parametric changes in the Erlang model do not appear able to generate a single distribution which can predict all of the observed distributions.

Proposals. Based on his empirical study Harris recommends a revision of the structure of models used to study job shops. The basic structural assumptions of his proposal are as follows: (a) The service center unit is the "manpower group." The manpower group consists of a specified number of men and a specified number of machine centers, each machine center consisting of a specified number of identical machines. (b) Jobs arrive at the manpower group according to some specified statistical process, each requiring service at some machine center within the manpower group. The particular choice of the required machine center is modeled as a probability choice among the machine centers in the manpower group. (c) *Service*—to complete an order's processing it is necessary to provide the order with a machine from the machine center and a worker from the group. (d) *Queue*—there are specified rules for selecting orders when a queue exists and for allocating workers among the machine centers. The rules are modeled as the policy variables open for evaluation in the model.

MRP and job shop scheduling

Much of the job shop scheduling research that we have discussed preceded the widespread usage of MRP systems for material and priority control. More to the point, it preceded the widespread use of rapid and comprehensive computerized shop floor control systems of many kinds. As a consequence, this research stressed *static* rules rather than *dynamic* ones. When dynamic rules were applied, they tended to use *local* information rather than information from *global* sources. For example, the so-called dynamic slack rule tested by Nanot was only dynamic in the sense that the amount of slack reflected in the rule changed as a job progressed through a shop. Since the due date remained constant from the beginning of any work on the job however, this rule used only static information—that is, information that did not change, as the job progressed. By way of contrast, a truly dynamic global rule would reflect the fact that due dates very often change within the context of MRP systems as master schedules are replanned, and as parts are expedited and rescheduled.

Integrated job shop control systems provide firms with the ability to immediately transmit global information on data such as due date changes back to the shop floor so that current priorities will reflect it immediately. This capability is particularly important in the "closed" job shops one finds in conjunction with integrated fabrication-assembly operations. Since these firms assemble perhaps 100 parts produced in a closed job shop together into a product, it is very important that all of the parts be available for assembly (or unavailable) at the same time. The ability of an information system, such as MRP, to rapidly transmit global information on expediting and rescheduling needs to the shop floor is very important here, lest unnecessary inventories of parts build up while awaiting the one late part, or delivery reliability suffers.

While priority dispatch rules such as SOT may be appropriate when only local information is available in a manufacturing setting, they are antithetical to the operation of MRP systems. MRP systems thrive on their ability to indicate when the due dates of final products, components, subassemblies, or raw materials change, and make sense when a firm is willing to expedite or reschedule in order to make operations consistent with realistic due date needs. The SOT rule, for example, precludes expediting, however. If the SOT rule is in operation and a part needs expediting, then manual intervention, and the usurpation of the SOT discipline, is necessary to enforce it. As a consequence, one finds dynamic, global, due date-oriented priority dispatching rules in use with MRP systems. Examples include earliest due date priority dispatching rules (where global information is available to change the due dates as necessary) such as modified dynamic slack rules, the dynamic slack per remaining processing time rule, and the dynamic slack per remaining number of operations rules, in addition to the simple earliest due date rules.

One particularly important variant of the dynamic slack per remaining operations time rule that is found in use with MRP systems is the "critical ratio" rule [44, 51]. The critical ratio is defined as the ratio of the time remaining until the due date to the standard hours of work and queue time remaining to be performed on the part. That is:

$$\text{Critical ratio} = \frac{\text{Due date} - \text{Current date}}{\text{Standard work and queue time remaining}}$$

An order with a low critical ratio (less than one) would probably be late and should be processed first. Orders with high critical ratios (over one) are ahead of schedule, and not critical.

Figure 10–10 illustrates the way in which the Markem Corporation, whose MRP system was described in Chapter 7, employs global MRP information in generating "daily dispatch reports" for each of its machine centers. This report lists the date (in shop calendar form) on which each job should be started at a work center in order for the total job to be completed on time. In addition, it lists in priority sequence the jobs in queue at the work center. The priorities are determined by computing the slack available for each job at that machine center on the day before the report is made. In this report, positive slack implies that the job is ahead of schedule. This information is both global and dynamic. It is dynamic in that priorities

Figure 10–10
Priority dispatch report for the Markem Corporation

	WORK CENTER 011			AS OF 313			MARCH 28,1972		
SHOP ORDER NUMBER	PART NUMBER	SEQUENCE NUMBER	OPERATION	SCHEDULED START DATE	STANDARD HOURS REQUIRED	VARIANCE	OPERATION SHEET	SET-UP CODE	SKILL LEVEL
608132	C780194	065	052	319	3.7	5			
610079	0311111.	040	052	420	3.9	6			
34608	0310605	040	052	321	2.1	7	100		
610099	0339107	050	052	322	1.5	8			
610087	0332642	030	052	323	2.9	9			
225255	0261627	035	052	325	.7	11			
225255	0323919	030	052	328	1.5	14			
36327	C339767	030	052	328	10.8	14			
36834	0080808	040	052	329	.7	15			
36834	0880807	040	C52	329	.7	15			
36834	0080784	030	052	331	1.2	17			
36832	0343339	050	052	331	2.3	17			
206594	0283774	030	052 H	334	1.5	20			
206594	0334647	030	052 H	334	1.2	20			
206594	0334646	030	052 H	334	1.2	20			
206594	1040364	030	052 H	334	1.0	20			
35256	0942422	040	052	335	.9	21			
206594	1040344	030	052 H	336	1.0	22			
206594	0334636	030	052 H	336	1.0	22			
206594	0334645	030	052 H	336	1.5	22			
206594	0334644	030	052 H	336	1.5	22			
206594	0264759	030	052 H	336	2.0	22			
206594	0264759	030	052 H	336	2.5	22			
206594	C315319	040	052 H	336	1.2	22			
206594	1001554	030	052 H	336	2.0	22			
206594	0334923	030	052 H	336	2.0	22			
611062	0310046	040	052	336	11.7	22			
224082	0611102	030	052	337	.7	23			
206594	0283772	030	052 H	333	.7	24			
206594	0334632	030	052 H	338	1.0	24			
206594	0334633	030	052 H	338	1.0	24			
206594	0335315	030	052 H	338	.7	24			
206594	0335603	030	052 H	338	.7	24			
206594	0335318	030	052 H	338	1.5	24			
206594	0263773	030	052 H	340	.7	26			
34737	0590109	050	052	343	2.2	29			

Source: E. W., Davis, and W. J. B. Lake, "Markem Corporation (B)," ICH No. 9-673-002, 1972.

change continually as new reports are issued each day. It is global in that any change in the ultimate due date of the completed item is immediately reflected in the due date and slack for the relevant operation at remaining work centers.

To this point, little formal research has been done on the performance of various priority dispatching rules used in conjunction with MRP systems. Berry [4] has experimented with the critical ratio rule in a job shop environment where parts were controlled by a reorder point system. In a series of simulation experiments he came to several interesting conclusions. First, he found no significant difference in the performance of two variants of the critical ratio rule, one in which standard queue time was not included in the denominator, and another in which it was. Second, he found that a static critical ratio rule significantly outperformed the slack time per remaining operations rule mentioned in the Nanot study. A static critical ratio rule is one in which new due date information is *not* automatically incorporated in the calculation of the priority index; that is, one in which *local* information is used. Third, and most interesting, he found that static critical ratio rules significantly outperformed dynamic ones; that is, rules in which due dates were changed as new data on inventory status became available. While this finding has not been tested in an MRP environment per se, it may indicate that overly "nervous" MRP systems, such as those that tend to be associated with net change information systems, produce disfunctional results at the shop floor level.

SUMMARY

The early emphasis in job shop scheduling research was largely exploratory in the hope of finding classes of decision rules which might have promise. The result of much of this exploration has been to isolate the SOT rule for its low mean flow time characteristics and others such as the first in system and slack rules for their performance on tardiness and inventory cost criteria. Attempts to meet the important disadvantages of poor tardiness performance of the SOT rule through truncation have been partially successful, but it appears that other basic rules which give weight to future delays, such as COVERT, or weight to finished goods inventory position, where that is appropriate, have greater promise as effective, practical rules when only local information is available.

One problem with the research done to date has been the apparent disagreement between investigators concerning appropriate criteria. Mean flow time and flow time variance, tardiness, and labor utilization have all been used. With the exception of the Allen study, where labor utilization was specifically a focus of interest in a declining load situation, it would appear that tardiness as a criterion is somewhat more in tune with the usual industrial environment. The quotation from the company memo in the Harris study lends some credence to this belief, and the personal experience of these authors adds weight to the same view. As we will see in the installations of actual systems discussed in Chapter 11, the tardiness criterion was the one emphasized.

More recent work on labor-limited systems has provided deeper insight into the inner workings of job shop systems and in particular has helped to define the real meaning of flexibility in the context of job shop systems. The work on labor-limited systems has also brought to light the fact that a complete labor assignment procedure involves both a procedure for machine center selection and a queue discipline.

The advent of MRP type systems has brought a new dimension to the problem of job shop scheduling. These systems have the ability to rapidly transmit priority information relating to end item demands down to part, and ultimately, the individual operation level. This means that much more complete, global, due date information can be used to set priorities. Since MRP systems are due date oriented, they require that due date-related priority dispatch rules be used, however. While there is some evidence indicating that dynamic slack rules such as the critical ratio method perform best in stable or static environments, more work needs to be done in clarifying their effectiveness in environments where due dates are dynamic.

REVIEW QUESTIONS AND PROBLEMS

1. Contrast the nature and difficulty of the "Problems of Job Shops" listed in Figure 10–1 for closed versus open job shops.

2. What is the impact of physical layout on the production scheduling problem? Are there differences in the layout effect on scheduling for open versus closed job shops?

3. Machine-limited systems assume that labor is always available and that the critical resource is machines. Is the assumption generally valid? What other factors might cause order waiting time?

4. Job orders are received at a work center with the characteristics indicated by the following data. In what sequence should the orders be processed at the work center if the priority dispatch decision rule is:
   a. FCFS (first come, first served).
   b. SOT (shortest operation time).
   c. SS (static slack; that is, due date less time of arrival at work center).
   d. FISFS (due date system, first in system, first served).
   e. SS/RO (static slack remaining number of operations).
   Which decision rule do you prefer? Why?

   Compute priorities for each rule and list the sequence in which orders would be processed.

Order number	Due date	Date and time received at center	Operation time, hours	Remaining operations
1.	May 1	April 18, 9 A.M.	6	3
2.	April 20	April 21, 10 A.M.	3	1
3.	June 1	April 19, 5 P.M.	7	2
4.	June 15	April 21, 3 P.M.	9	4
5.	May 15	April 20, 5 P.M.	4	5
6.	May 20	April 21, 5 P.M.	8	7

5. What is a local priority dispatch rule? A global priority rule? A static rule? A dynamic rule?

6. Based on the Nanot experiments which two priority rules would perform best if on-time completion of orders were the dominant criterion?

7. Is the COVERT rule simply a modification of the SOT rule? By what rationale does it achieve excellent order tardiness?

8. Using the data of Table 10–5 calculate the effects on priority indexes and rank order of processing of setting $k = 0.5$. Does the smaller value of k place a smaller or larger value on tardiness of orders?

9. Again using the data of Table 10–5, calculate the effects on priority indexes and rank order of processing, of determining the delay cost fraction strictly by the formula $kw_i - s_i/kw_i$ rather than setting $c_i = 1$ for orders where slack is negative. If priorities are computed by this revised method, what is the priority sequencing of orders with positive slack? For orders with negative slack what is the effect? Is COVERT really a two-class rule, processing all orders with negative slack first by one rule and all orders with positive slack second by a different rule?

10. If the COVERT rule were being used, what basis for establishing priorities do you think would dominate if the shop were operating under extremely heavy load conditions?

11. Discuss the significance of Nelson's experimental result which indicated that the normalized mean value of flow time decreased as the size of the work force decreased.

12. Based on the Nelson experiments what degree of central control of labor assignment seems appropriate?

13. Referring to Allen's experiments concerned with declining load, the SOT-AR rule performed best among single-class rules, with average labor utilization as a criterion. Do you think that SOT-AR would dominate SOT in general? Under declining as well as normal loads? Judged by other criteria such as mean flow time, variance of flow time, and tardiness?

14. Account for the superiority of all of the complex rules compared to the best simple rule in Allen's experiments concerning declining load.

15. When Allen combined the 13 labor classes into one he found substantially improved labor utilization for each of the four rules tested, indicating the value of increased flexibility. Speculate on comparative results had he progressively dismantled the plant, selling machines, and laying off workers, as rapidly as possible while maintaining a machine-limited system.

16. Using the LeGrande study as a frame of reference, argue pro or con the statement, "The basic error in job shop scheduling research has been the search for dominance in simple rules with simple criterion functions

when in fact there is a multiplicity of criteria which interact in a complex way."

17. What adaptations would be necessary in order to use the COVERT rule with an MRP system?

18. What evidence can you collect from this chapter to support the thesis that Nanot's dynamic slack per remaining operation time rule will outperform other rules in an MRP environment?

SELECTED BIBLIOGRAPHY

1. Allen, M. "The Efficient Utilization of Labor under Conditions of Fluctuating Demand," chap. 16 in J. F. Muth and G. L. Thompson, eds., *Industrial Scheduling.* Englewood Cliffs, N.J.: Prentice-Hall Inc., 1963.

2. Armour, G. C., and Buffa, E. S. "A Heuristic Algorithm and Simulation Approach to Relative Location of Facilities," *Management Science,* vol. 9, no. 2 (January 1963), pp. 294–309.

3. Baker, C. T., and Dzielinski, P. B. "Simulation of a Simplified Job Shop," *Management Science,* vol. 6, no. 3 (April 1960), pp. 211–23.

4. Berry, W. L., and Rao, V. "Critical Ratio Scheduling: An Experimental Analysis," *Management Science,* vol. 22, no. 2 (October 1975), pp. 192–201.

5. Bowman, E. H. "The Schedule Sequence Problem," *Operations Research,* vol. 7 (September 1959), pp. 621–24.

6. Buffa, E.; Armour, G. C. and Vollmann, T. E. "Allocating Facilities with CRAFT," *Harvard Business Review,* March–April 1964.

7. Carroll, D. C. "Heuristic Sequencing of Single and Multiple Component Jobs," Unpublished Ph.D. dissertation, Sloan School of Management, M.I.T., 1965.

8. Conway, R. W., and Maxwell, W. L. "Network Scheduling by the Shortest Operation Discipline," *Operations Research,* vol. 10, no. 1 (1962) pp. 51–73. Reprinted as Chap. 17 in J. F. Muth and G. L. Thompson, ed., *Industrial Scheduling.* Englewood Cliffs, N.J.: Prentice-Hall, Inc., 1963.

9. Davis, E. W., and Lake, W. J. B. "Markem Corporation (B)," ICH 9-673-002, 1972.

10. Emery, J. "An Approach to Job Shop Scheduling Using a Large-Scale Computer," *Industrial Management Review,* vol. 3 (Fall 1961), pp. 78–96.

11. Evans, R. V. *Numerical Methods for Queues with Complex Service Rates.* Western Management Science Institute, Working Paper No. 29. UCLA, 1962.

12. Evans, R. V. *Queueing When Jobs Require Several Services Which Need Not Be Sequenced*. Western Management Science Institute, Working Paper No. 17. UCLA, September 1962.

13. Evans, R. V. *The Structure of Some Two Dimensional Queueing Systems*. Western Management Science Institute, Working Paper No. 36. UCLA, July 1963.

14. Evans, R. V. *The Structure of Production and Processing Systems*. Western Management Science Institute, Working Paper No. 56. UCLA, December 1964.

15. Gere, W. S., Jr. "Heuristics in Job Shop Scheduling," *Management Science*, vol. 13, no. 3 (November 1966), pp. 167–90.

16. Grindlay, A. A. *Tandem Queues with Dynamic Priorities*. Western Management Science Institute, Working Paper No. 14. UCLA, September 1962.

17. Harris, R. D. "An Empirical Investigation of a Job Shop as a Network of Queueing Systems." Unpublished Ph.D. dissertation, UCLA, 1965.

18. Harris, R. D. *An Empirical Investigation and Model Proposal of a Job Shop-Like Queueing System*. Western Management Science Institute, Working Paper No. 84. UCLA, July 1965.

19. Jackson, J. R. *Scheduling a Production Line to Minimize Maximum Tardiness*. Management Sciences Research Project, Research Report No. 43. UCLA, 1955.

20. Jackson, J. R. "Networks of Waiting Lines," *Operations Research*, Vol. 5 (August, 1957), pp. 518–21.

21. Jackson, J. R. "Simulation Research on Job Shop Production," *Naval Research Logistics Quarterly*, vol. 4 (December 1957).

22. Jackson, J. R. "Some Problems of Queueing with Dynamic Priorities," *Naval Research Logistics Quarterly*, vol. 7 (September 1960), pp. 235–50.

23. Jackson, J. R. "Job Shop-Like Queueing Systems," *Management Science*, vol. 10, no. 1 (October 1963), pp. 131–32.

24. Jackson, J. R. "Queues with Dynamic Priority Disciplines," *Management Science*, vol. 7, no. 1 (1961), pp. 18–34. Reprinted as chap. 19 in J. F. Muth and G. L. Thompson, eds., *Industrial Scheduling*. Englewood Cliffs, N.J.: Prentice-Hall Inc., 1963.

25. Johnson, S. M. "Optimal Two- and Three-stage Production Schedules with Setup Time Included," *Naval Research Logistics Quarterly*, Vol. 1 (1954), pp. 61–68. Reprinted as Chap. 2 in J. F. Muth and G. L. Thompson, eds., *Industrial Scheduling*. Englewood Cliffs, N.J.: Prentice-Hall, Inc., 1963.

26. LeGrande, E. "The Development of a Factory Simulation System Using Actual Operating Data," *Management Technology*, vol. 3, no. 1

(May 1963). Reprinted as Chap. 9 in E. S. Buffa, ed., *Readings in Production and Operations Management*. New York: John Wiley & Sons, Inc., 1966.

27. Maggard, M. J. "An Evaluation of Labor and Machine Limited Parallel Queueing Systems," Unpublished PH.D. dissertation, UCLA, 1968.

28. Malouin, J. "Comparative Analysis of the Scheduling Rule Shortest Processing Time Truncated with Four Other Due Date-Oriented Scheduling Rules in a Simulated Job Shop." Unpublished Ph.D. dissertation, UCLA, 1970.

29. Mann, A. S. "On the Job Shop Scheduling Problem," *Operations Research*, vol. 8 (October 1960), pp. 219–23.

30. Miller, J. G., "Hedging the Master Schedule," *Proceedings of the Disaggregation Conference*, Ohio State University, 1976.

31. Miller, J. R. "Parametric Priority Rules in Dual Resource Limited Service Systems." Unpublished Ph.D dissertation, UCLA, 1969.

32. Mitten, L. G. "Sequencing *n* Jobs on Two Machines with Arbitrary Time Lags," *Management Science*, vol. 5 (April 1958), pp. 299–303.

33. Moodie, C. L., and Roberts, S. D. "Experiments with Priority Dispatching Rules in a Parallel Processor Shop," *International Journal of Production Research*, vol. 6, no. 4 (1968), pp. 303–12.

34. Moore, J. M., and Wilson, R. C. "A Review of Simulation Research in Job Shop Scheduling," *Production and Inventory Management*, vol. 8, no. 1 (1967).

35. Nanot, Y. R. "An Experimental Investigation and Comparative Evaluation of Priority Disciplines in Job Shop-Like Queueing Networks." Unpublished Ph.D. dissertation, UCLA, 1963. Also Management Sciences Research Project, Research Report No. 87, UCLA, 1963.

36. Nelson, R. T. *Priority Function Methods for Job Shop Scheduling*. Management Sciences Research Project, Research Report No. 51. UCLA, February 1955.

37. Nelson, R. T. "Waiting-Time Distributions for Application to a Series of Service Centers," *Operations Research*, vol. 6 (November–December 1958), pp. 856–62.

38. Nelson, R. T. *An Empirical Study of Arrival, Service Time and Waiting Time Distributions of a Job Shop Production Process*. Management Sciences Research Project, Research Report No. 60. UCLA, June 1959.

39. Nelson, R. T. "A Simulation Study and Analysis of a Two Station, Waiting Line-Network Model." Unpublished Ph.D. dissertation. UCLA, 1965. Also Management Sciences Research Project Research Report No. 91, UCLA, January 1965. Also published as "Queueing Network Experiments with Varying Arrival and Service Processes," *Naval Research Logistics Quarterly*, vol. 13, no. 3 (September 1966).

40. Nelson, R. T. "Labor and Machine Limited Production Systems," *Management Science*, vol. 13, no. 9 (May 1967), pp. 648–71.

41. Nelson, R. T. "Dual Resource Constrained Series Service Systems," *Operations Research*, vol. 16, no. 2 (March–April 1968). Also published as Western Management Science Institute Working Paper No. 113. UCLA, February 1967.

42. Nelson, R. T. "A Simulation Study of Labor Efficiency and Centralized Labor Assignment Control in a Production System Model," *Management Science*, vol. 17, no. 2 (October 1970), pp. 97–106.

43. Nugent, C. E.; Vollmann, T. E.; and Ruml, J. "An Experimental Comparison of Techniques for the Assignment of Facilities to Locations," *Operations Research*, vol. 16, no. 1 (January–February 1968), pp. 150–73.

44. Putnam, A. O., and Everdall, R. et al., "Updating Critical Ratio and Slack Time Priority Scheduling Rules," *Production and Inventory Management*, vol. 12, no. 4 (1971), pp. 51–72.

45. Rowe, A. J. "Application of Computer Simulation to Sequential Decision Rules in Production Scheduling," *Proceedings: Eleventh Annual Industrial Engineering Institute*, UCLA, February 1959.

46. Rowe, A. J. "Sequential Decision Rules in Production Scheduling," Unpublished Ph.D. dissertation, UCLA, August 1958.

47. Rowe, A. J. "Towards a Theory of Scheduling," *Journal of Industrial Engineering*, vol. 11 (March 1960), pp. 125–36.

48. Schussel, G. "Workload Balancing and Inventory Minimization for Job Shops," *Journal of Industrial Engineering*, vol. 19, no. 4 (April 1968), pp. 194–202.

49. Smith W. E. "Various Optimizers for Single Stage Production," *Naval Research Logistics Quarterly*, vol. 3 (March 1956), pp. 59–66.

50. Vollmann, T. E., and Buffa, E. S. "The Facilities Layout Problem in Perspective," *Management Science*, vol. 12, no. 10 (June 1966, pp. 450–68.

51. Wassweiler, W. "Material Requirements Planning—The Key to Critical Ratio Effectiveness," *Production and Inventory Management*, vol. 13, no. 3 (1972), pp. 89–91.

Chapter 11

Job shop planning, scheduling, and control systems

THE PRIORITY DISPATCHING RULES discussed in the previous chapter should not be confused with an integrated job shop planning and control system. They focus on but one very important part of a production control system, the scheduling function. We must relate the important work that has been done on loading and scheduling to an overall *system* for planning, scheduling, and control. In order to do this we will first examine the nature of work flow structure and its implications for planning and control. Then, we will visualize the broad information requirements of an integrated planning, scheduling, and control system. With the information system as a broad frame of reference we will then discuss actual systems of two kinds: (a) *infinite loading* systems where sequencing rules are used as a mechanism to prioritize the flow of orders, but where capacity is ignored, and (b) systems which compute an operational schedule which prescribes the time of starting and finishing every operation to be performed, taking account of the availability of equipment and of the work to be done. These systems are termed *finite loading* systems [11].

Work flow structure

In broad aggregate terms the work flow structure of a job shop can be represented by an interdepartmental flow matrix.

A flow matrix shows the physical flow of work per unit of time between all combinations of work centers or departments for a sample of job orders. The flow matrix in physical terms has a significance for plant layout, however, for planning, scheduling, and control purposes, our interest shifts to the job order as a unit of measurement. This was the unit of measure used throughout the job shop scheduling research reported in the previous chapter.

Berry and Holstein [2, 12] used the job order transfer matrix concept to examine work flow structures in the machine shop of a large electrical equipment manufacturer. They point out that these matrices are useful for (a) determining the extent of work flow concentration, (b) characterizing the pattern of work flow, and (c) locating important paths of work flow linking individual work centers. Overall measures of matrix density, or flow dominance measures, are useful in making gross comparisons between two or more shops. However, insight into the functioning of a particular shop is more likely to be obtained by analyzing component network diagrams prepared from the job order transfer matrix.

Network diagrams. Berry and Holstein developed the diagram shown in Figure 11–1 from the job order transfer matrix data for an electrical equipment manufacturer. The data were reduced from 7,000 individual orders representing more than 50,000 separate machine operations. The 250 machines in the shop were organized into 30 work centers. Only 17 of the 30 work centers appear in Figure 11–1. The remaining centers were not major flow paths in the structure by the criterion defined; that is, no flow links are shown which account for less than 0.9 percent of the total job order transfers. Thus, Figure 11–1 shows system flows which are of importance to planning, scheduling, and control by virtue of the fact that they are the dominant flows. Berry and Holstein also define multiple-link paths through networks as paths involving three or more work centers in sequence, together with methods for identifying them.

Product or raw material effects. No shop is a pure job shop in the sense that it has a broad capability to process anything. Some kind of specialization by product, raw material, or process is invariably involved. Berry and Holstein examined the job order data for the electrical equipment manufacturer by product and by raw mate-

Figure 11–1
Shop work flow structure for the machine shop of a large electrical equipment manufacturer

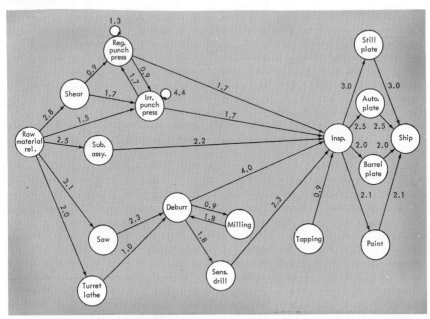

Note: Figures on arrows represent the percent of total job transfers. Sixty-three percent of all job transfers in the sample are accounted for by the links shown on the diagram. No links which account for less than 0.9 percent of the total job transfers are shown.
Source: From W. L. Berry, "Labor Assignments in Job Shops: An Application of Work Flow Analysis" (unpublished doctoral dissertation, Harvard Business School, 1968), p. 118. See also [12].

rial form. All job orders were coded by one of five major raw material types and by one of three major product types. The percent of job orders related to each was then determined with the results shown in Table 11–1. Note that the three most important products account for

Table 11–1
Percent of job orders for different raw material forms and product types

Raw material form	Percent of job orders	Product type	Percent of job orders
Bar stock	28.8	Device products	10.9
Plate stock	2.0	Brake products	6.8
Sheet stock	36.4	Switch products	5.2
Castings	7.5		
Weldments	7.2		
Other	18.1	All other product types	77.1

Source: From W. L. Berry, "Labor Assignments in Job Shops: An Application of Work Flow Analysis" (unpublished doctoral dissertation, Harvard Business School, 1968), pp. 92, 93. See also [12].

only 23 percent of the total job orders, but two raw material forms, bar and sheet stock, account for 65 percent of the job orders. These figures suggest that specialization by raw material form is somewhat more important than specialization by product in characterizing that particular shop. Other shops might well be described better by their products, or some other factors such as material composition, product size or weight.

Berry and Holstein then prepared component job order transfer matrices for each raw material form and product type. Large differences between the matrices were noted in terms of density and the values of corresponding elements in the matrices. The data of Table 11–2 summarizes the differences in structure for the five major raw material forms and three major product types related to six work centers. Note, for example, that the automatic lathe center works largely on bar stock jobs but does not work on sheet stock, plate stock, castings, or weldments. Similarly, the regular punch press center is dominant for sheet stock orders. For product types, the vertical turret lathe dominates as a work center for brake products.

Raw material network diagrams.   The differences in flow structure show up clearly in graphical form. Figure 11–2 shows the network diagram for bar stock. Comparing Figure 11–2 with the overall shop work flow structure of Figure 11–1, note that six work centers are not used sufficiently by bar stock orders to justify the inclusion of links in the diagram; that is, if links exist at all they do not represent major flows. Also, one new work center (automatic lathe) appears as being important for bar stock. The network diagram for sheet stock indicates a quite different structure.

Knowledge of work flow structure provides insight into the functioning of a specific job shop system. Thus, changes in demand for specific products, or changes in product mix, may not be expected to affect all work centers equally.

INTEGRATED JOB SHOP PLANNING AND CONTROL SYSTEMS

An integrated job shop planning and control system must tie together information requirements, and decisions and plans, and provide the basis for feedback and control. It must integrate the various levels in decision hierarchies so that low-level plans are both feasible, and consistent with, higher level master schedules and aggregate production plans. Figure 11–3 presents a rough schematic of an

Table 11–2
Percent of job orders processed by work centers for different raw material forms and product types

	Raw material form						Product type			
Work center	Bar stock	Sheet stock	Plate stock	Castings	Weld-ments	Other raw material forms	Device products	Brake products	Switch products	Other products
Regular punch press ...	4.25*	72.04	0.00	0.00	0.00	23.71	13.87	0.00	1.79	84.34
Vertical turret lathe	0.00	0.00	1.09	85.87	3.26	9.78	0.00	81.52	3.26	15.22
Blanchard grinding	13.16	0.00	16.67	17.54	5.26	47.37	29.87	20.18	4.38	45.57
Automatic lathe	95.24	0.00	0.00	0.00	0.00	4.76	9.52	3.17	3.17	84.14
Sensitive drill press no. 2	36.04	20.99	2.03	5.25	4.69	31.00	11.34	5.11	9.31	74.24
Batch annealing furnace	40.98	26.69	5.26	2.26	3.76	21.05	21.43	3.38	6.02	69.17

* Body of table indicates the percentage of jobs processed by a given work center in each raw material form or product type category; e.g., 4.25 percent of the jobs processed at the regular punch press work center use bar stock for raw material.

Source: From W. L. Berry, "Labor Assignments in Job Shops: An Application of Work Flow Analysis" (unpublished doctoral dissertation, Harvard Business School, 1968), p. 128. See also [12].

Figure 11–2
Work flow structure for bar stock

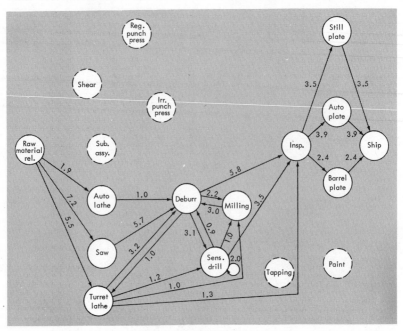

Note: Figures on arrows represent the percent of total bar stock job transfers. Seventy percent of all job transfers in the sample of bar stock jobs are accounted for by the links shown in this diagram. No links which account for less than 0.9 percent of the bar stock job transfers are shown.
Source: From W. L. Berry, "Labor Assignments in Job Shops: An Application of Work Flow Analysis (unpublished doctoral dissertation, Harvard Business School, 1968), p. 117. See also [12].

integrated system for job shop planning and control for a typical open job shop. This schematic indicates the many functions that must be coordinated in an integrated system: aggregate production planning, master scheduling, material and capacity requirements planning, purchase order and shop floor control systems, order entry, engineering, and bill of materials, routing, and inventory file maintenance. To put the topic of much of our discussion in Chapter 10 and thus far in this chapter in perspective, the use of priority dispatching rules for detailed job shop scheduling is normally a part of what is called the shop floor control subsystem in Figure 11–3.

In some respects, the decision structure implied by Figure 11–3 is similar to the one used to demonstrate integrated systems for high-volume standardized products (Figure 8–7). The similarities are reflected in the fact that the master schedule is derived with respect to the framework laid out in the aggregate production plan. Moreover,

Figure 11–3
An integrated system for job shop planning and control

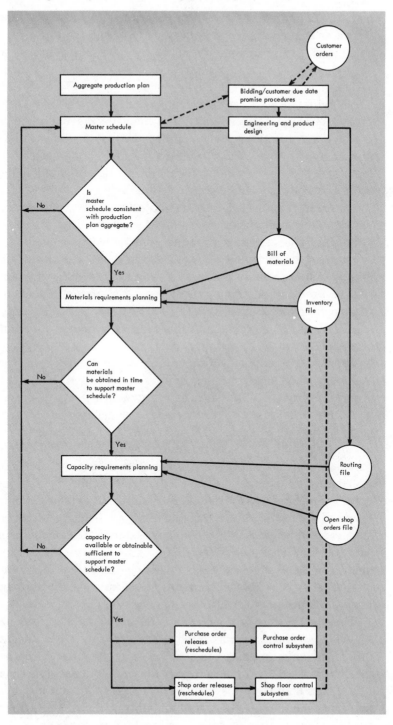

both depict iterative processes for ensuring that the master schedule which drives the system is both consistent with the aggregate plan and feasible from the standpoint of capacity and materials availability.

The major differences in the flowchart shown in Figure 11–3 compared to that for high-volume standardized products are reflected in the sequence in which capacity plans are made, the requirement for a job shop floor control system, and the way that customer order data and engineering functions relate to the rest of the system. These features reflect the job shop process technology orientation and the order positioning strategy characteristic of open job shops.

We see in Figure 11–3 that the master scheduling process is intimately tied in with the process of order entry, bidding, and due date promising. The customized products most often associated with job shops must be designed in detail. Design and manufacturing engineering specifications that result form the basis for the bill of materials and routing data that indicate how the product is to be made, what parts are to be fabricated, the operations to be performed in fabricating parts, and the items that must be procured from outside sources. The feasibility of the due date for the customized product can be checked by using an MRP planning system to check on whether materials are on hand, or can be ordered or expedited on time to meet order commitments. Similarly, capacity requirements planning can be employed to check on the availability of capacity at affected machine centers, or to ensure that sufficient additional capacity can be obtained. If neither of these feasibility checks are passed, the master schedule, and ultimately the customer due date, must be changed.

It is important to note that detailed capacity requirements planning occurs quite far down the decision structure, rather than initially as a result of aggregate production planning as in many high-volume standardized product companies. This is due to the custom nature of such job shop operations. Here, the product to be produced must be defined in the master schedule, bills of materials, and routing information before capacity can be planned because capacity requirements vary as the product mix changes.

The MRP system will generate parts and component orders destined for one of two sources. If the part is purchased from outside, the order will have to go through purchasing channels. If the part is produced internally, in the job shop, the order will pass to the control of the shop floor control system. It generates shop floor information, and is used in the process of applying priority dispatch rules as parts pass through various operations or machine centers.

Infinite versus finite loading

As we indicated earlier, there are essentially two kinds of shop floor control and loading system techniques that are applied in job shop environments. Infinite loading systems do not explicitly consider capacity or sequence at the detailed shop floor scheduling level. Rather, they employ *standard* process and queue times in both capacity requirements planning and in calculating priority dispatch rules. By way of contrast, finite loading systems predict *actual* process and queue times in both capacity requirements planning and in calculating priorities by simulating the flow of work through operations with fixed capacity.

To illustrate the differences between finite and infinite kinds of loading and shop floor control systems, consider the case of three jobs waiting to be processed at a machine center with a capacity of eight processing hours per day. The operating characteristics of the three jobs are shown in Table 11–3. The standard processing and

Table 11–3
Operating characteristics for three jobs awaiting processing at a single machine center

Job no.	Units	Standard setup time (hours)	Standard run time per unit (hours)	Standard setup and run time for job (hours)	Standard process and queue time	Due date*
1	50	8	0.16	16	6 days (48 hours)	10 days (beginning of period 3)
2	100	16	0.24	40	15 days (120 hours)	20 days (beginning of period 5)
3	25	8	0.32	16	6 days (48 hours)	20 days (beginning of period 5)

* The due dates refer to the number of days into the future that the job is due to be completed; these due dates can also be expressed in terms of time buckets or periods.

queue times indicated in this table are computed by the rather common formula $K(S + QR)$, where K is a factor reflecting standard queue time allowances, and S and R are the standard setup and run time per unit for a particular job, respectively. Q designates the lot size. Thus, if K is 3, the standard processing and queue time for job 1 is 3(8 hours + 50 × 0.16 hrs/unit) = 48 hours, or six 8-hour days.

Infinite loading capacity requirements planning procedures include the unit load profile technique discussed in Chapter 7. If it were applied in projecting the workload at a machine center, capacity

needs would be forecasted by offsetting work and queue time requirements from job due dates. Thus, if the work center being examined in Table 11–3 is the last operation for each of the three jobs
indicated, and if weekly (5-day weeks, eight-hour days) time buckets
were being used, the work load for the first job (16 hours) would have
been offset into period 2, the week preceding the due date. Similarly,
since job two is due at the beginning of period 5, its workload of 40
hours would be offset back into period 4, and the work of job three (16
hours) would have also been offset back into period 4. As a result, the
total projected workload would appear as shown in Table 11–4. Using

Table 11–4
Projecting work loads for the three jobs in Table
11–3 using infinite loading techniques

Time period	1	2	3	4	5
Job 1		16			
Job 2				40	
Job 3				16	
Total load in hours	0	16	0	56	0

the standard queue time allowances implied by Table 11–3, the same
jobs could be scheduled backward to determine the scheduled due
date for the completion of these jobs at previous work centers. For
example, job three has an estimated standard queue time of
(48 -- 16) = 32 hours, or by rounding off, one period. This implies
that the due date for this job at the previous work center is the
beginning of period two. By successively scheduling jobs back
through their standard set-up, run, and queue times, (rounding off to
the nearest whole period as necessary), the load at preceding work
centers can be determined in a manner similar to that which was
applied to derive Table 11–4.

By applying this type of infinite loading technique, one can obtain
a *rough* estimate of the workload by time period for each machine
center. The word rough must be emphasized however. First, the
infinite loading technique is apt to result in overloaded work centers
as shown in Table 11–4. Here, 56 hours of work are scheduled in
period 4 while only 40 hours of regular time capacity are available. If
this notification occurs far enough in advance, extra capacity might be
obtained by scheduling overtime, subcontracting, or adding an extra
shift. However, in the near term, many of these options may not be
available. Second, there is no assurance that the amount of time a job

awaits processing is always the same. This simplifying assumption is not generally true. The priorities at the time of processing and the size of the load on the machine center derived by competing jobs can and generally will change the actual queue time from one instance to another. For example, if all three jobs arrived at the machine center of Table 11–3 at the same time at the beginning of period 1, the actual schedule and load would vary significantly. The critical ratios (see p. 527) for jobs 1, 2, and 3 would be 1.67, 1.33, and 3.33 respectively. If the critical ratio priorities were actually followed, job 2, not job 1, would be worked on first, thus shifting its load to an earlier period.

Finite loading systems would handle capacity requirements planning in a somewhat more detailed manner. Rather than projecting shop loads from due dates with standard process and queue times with the presumption of infinite capacity, finite loading techniques would simulate actual queue times and loads based on the amount of capacity that is available. For example, a finite loading technique might first project the workload for the machine center of Table 11–3 back in a manner similar to that shown in Table 11–4. However, on recognizing the overload in period four (Table 11–4), a finite loader would seek to relieve the overload by shifting jobs back and forth. If the particular shifting rule applied is one that seeks to equalize the load as much as possible, the work of job three might be shifted back to period three so that the load appeared as in Table 11–5. Working

Table 11–5
Projecting capacity utilization for the three jobs in
Table 11–3 using finite loading techniques

Time period	1	2	3	4	5
Job 1		16			
Job 2				40	
Job 3			16		
Total capacity utilization in hours	0	16	16	40	0

backward from this, we can see that the time that job three is required to finish at the preceeding workcenter is actually at the beginning of period 3, rather than at the beginning of period 2 as implied by the assumption of standard queue times.

At this point, there may be a temptation to declare finite loading techniques superior to infinite loading techniques, since the former yield much more precise and detailed information about shop floor schedules and capacities. However, such judgments would be premature. Finite loading techniques are much more complicated and difficult to implement, offsetting some of the gains one might hope to acquire from greater precision. Moreover, long-term simulations of shop utilization are usually substantially in error. Machine breakdowns, differences in the efficiencies in operators, and other random effects can cause simulated schedules to rapidly deviate from actual shop floor conditions.

Moreover, the two different types of systems provide different kinds of information, both of which can be useful. The infinite loading methods show loads at machine centers that *can be* worked on. Bottlenecks or uneven loads are quickly pointed out so that action to increase, decrease, or smooth loads can be taken. In other words, infinite loaders indicate how much capacity is needed. Simple finite loaders such as the one illustrated above, on the other hand, indicate how a predetermined level of capacity may be used. While this may provide useful scheduling data for the short term, where capacities tend to be fixed, in the long term, we also need a clear picture of capacity needs.

Finally, some finite loading procedures are much more sophisticated than the simple example procedure discussed above. The example we have worked with here relied upon loading to finite schedules by working backward from a due date. More sophisticated techniques may apply both forward and backward passes to obtain capacity needs, while simultaneously scheduling resources and making cost and schedule tradeoffs. Since these more sophisticated approaches rely on networking and/or "critical path" methodologies, we will discuss them in Chapter 13 after discussing critical path techniques. In the remainder of this chapter, we will limit our discussion to the simple type of finite and infinite loading-based systems above, and concentrate on developing a picture of how these and many other techniques can fit into an integrated job shop planning, scheduling, and control system.

INFINITE LOADING SYSTEMS

The basic characteristic which distinguishes an infinite loading system is simply that central, detailed, capacity constrained schedules for the use of workers and machines are not made up in advance. Rather, the shop is paced by one of the kinds of priority dispatching decision rules discussed in Chapter 10. This does not mean that no one ever makes up a capacitated schedule or plan for the use of workers and machines. It does mean, however, that such schedules are made up only locally at machine centers as the load develops. In this sense, then, an infinite loading system depends on more decentralized control, where machine center supervisors or machine operators make up detailed schedules. In the loading systems used by Nelson [17] discussed in Chapter 10, varying degrees of control were applied, ranging from complete central control (where on completing an order at one machine center the worker was given the next work assignment by central control) to complete local control (where on completing an order at a machine center the worker stayed at that center as long as there were any orders left to do in the queue, returning to central control for assignment only when the queue was empty).

The Markem Corporation, which we have used as an example in several chapters, provides us with a view of an infinite loading system [6]. Much of the description of this system is embodied in the latter half of Chapter 7, where Markem's capacity requirements planning system was described. The priority dispatching list generated by Markem's shop floor control system is shown in Figure 10–10. The overall structure of the system in which this shop floor and capacity requirements planning system is embedded is similar to that shown in Figure 11–3.

Davis and Lake [6] describe Markem's shop floor control system in the following terms:

A critical input for the Shop Floor Control system (installed in 1968) was the routing information for each component. When a new component was designed at the company, the drawing was forwarded to the Manufacturing Engineering Department, where the sequence and times of the manufacturing operations were determined. These were entered on a standard form and entered on the computer master files to be accessed through the "Item Master File." The first operation on any component was the processing of the order by the Production Control Department. The second operation was the requisitioning of raw material; if this was steel bar stock, 10 days were allowed for this operation. There could be up to 20 different operations on any one component. If any alterations were made to the routing on a component, the details were entered on a "Routing Master Maintenance" form and the files were updated on a daily file maintenance run.

When the inventory control section decided that an order for the manufacture of a part needed to be generated, they entered the details, such as the part number, the order quantity and the due date, on a form that was then keypunched and entered into the daily stock and order processing run on the company's IBM 360 Model 30 computer. During this run, as well as entering the new order on the order file, the computer generated a set of documentation for the order that was forwarded to the Machine Shop Loading section of the Production Control Department. This set included a routing sheet, showing all the operations on the component with their times and due dates, together with cards to report the start, the finish and the time spent on each operation. The due dates for each operation were determined by working backwards from the required completion date and allowing standard times between operations.

At any one time there were as many as 2,000 orders for machining of components, either in progress or waiting to be started, with the possibility of up to 20 operations on any one of these orders.

In addition to all the reports shown in Figures 7–20 and 10–10, Markem's shop floor control system also provides the basis for several other kinds of information, as shown in Figures 11–4 and 11–5.

Figure 11–4
Markem open shop orders report

AS OF 264   OPEN SHOP ORDERS   01/18/72

SHOP NO	PART NO	TYPE	QTY												
34135	0000051	2	2	R 39	R 56	R 15	R 11	R 36	R511	M 43	42	25	42	28	57
				249	259	269	271	276	273	275	277	279	281	233	284
34138	0000077	2	2	R 39	R 56	R 15	R 11	M 43	42	28	57				
				263	273	275	279	279	281	283	284				
30953	0000927	1	1	R 15	R 11	R 36	R 15	M 43	42	35					
				278	282	283	285	282	283	284					
35431	0001157	3	50	M 25	42	310									
				260	261	262									

Source: E. W. Davis, and W. J. B. Lake, "Markem Corporation (B)." ICH no. 9-673-002, 1972.

Figure 11–4 shows a daily open shop orders report. The purpose of this report is to provide information about the status and location of orders. Job order location is very important in job shops where the seemingly confused flow of materials representative of this type of process can easily result in "lost" work. Davis and Lake [6] describe this report as follows:

In this daily report, which was printed out in part number sequence, each operation to be carried out on a component was printed out in a horizontal row, with the work centers (e.g., "42," "25," etc.) on the top line and the due date (by shop calendar day number) for the operation immediately below. When an operation was completed, the foreman of the relevant work center sent a prepunched reporting card to the computer center. Other cards were used for the start of an operation or when an order was moved on to the next work center. The effect of an operation completion card was to print an "R" by the operation on the "Open Shop Orders" report while a move card

Figure 11-5
Markem input-output report

WORK CENTER 015 050 BLANCHARD					INPUT/OUTPUT REPORT			BACKLOG	27.2		02/16/72 - 285		
	285	290	295	300	305	310	315	320	325	330	335	340	345	350
PLANNED INPUT	42.4	19.2	7.2	26.7	9.5	17.6	49.8	12.5	17.8	18.3	14.7	13.3	23.8	55.3
AVE. PLANNED INPUT	16.1	16.7	14.8	17.2	15.7	16.1	22.8	20.7	20.1	19.7	18.7	17.6	18.8	26.1
ACTUAL INPUT	60.1													
AVE. ACTUAL INPUT	39.8													
CUM. DEV. INPUT	660.7-													
PLANNED OUTPUT		35.0	35.0	35.0	35.0	35.0	35.0	35.0	35.0	35.0	35.0	35.0	35.0	35.0
ACTUAL OUTPUT	49.0													
AVE. ACTUAL OUTPUT	63.6													
CUM. DEV. OUTPUT	1177.0-													

	355	360	365	370	375	380	385	390	395	400	405	410	415
PLANNED INPUT	43.3	50.4	24.3	9.4	7.9	25.1	47.1	11.5	13.1	17.5	3.1	4.0	9.4
AVE. PLANNED INPUT	29.5	33.7	31.8	27.3	23.4	23.7	28.4	25.0	22.6	21.6	17.9	15.1	14.0
PLANNED OUTPUT	35.0	35.0	35.0	35.0	35.0	35.0	35.0	35.0	35.0	35.0	35.0	35.0	

Source: E. W. Davis, and W. J. B. Lake, "Markem Corporation (B)," ICH no. 9-673-002, 1972.

would print an "M" by the following operation. Thus in [Figure 11–4], part number 0000051, on shop order 34135, had passed through the first six operations and was in work center 43 awaiting the seventh, at the time of the report.

Figure 11–5 illustrates Markem's weekly input-output report. Input-output reports, an innovation of Wight [6, 24], are designed to indicate when the weekly input to a work center is likely to exceed weekly output; that is, when bottlenecks, or extra capacity is indicated. By using historical input and output figures, these reports also track the actual (as opposed to the standard or planned) capacity of a work center. They can also be used to spot drops in labor efficiency.

FINITE LOADING SYSTEMS

Some of the earliest work in job shop scheduling by Gantt attempted to work out detailed schedules for each order, maintaining detailed order backlog records on each machine or other critical resources by "Gantt charts." These systems, though often thought to be the epitome of careful planning and control, usually were finally abandoned in favor of some kind of loading system which decentralized detailed scheduling and control. The usual reasons given for abandoning Gantt-type systems were that the complicated manual methods were costly to maintain and often the information represented on the charts was either inaccurate or out of date anyway. We can add in the light of present-day knowledge of queuing networks that the old Gantt systems were also static models attempting to represent a dynamic problem. They were deterministic in nature where realism demanded a stochastic model. Finally, the information time lags in a manual system were bound to reduce the planning and control value of the Gantt-type systems.

Are conditions still such that a detailed finite loading scheduling system is bound to fail? It would seem likely that present-day concepts and knowledge of the basic problem coupled with the power of rapid computing and data processing systems could make it possible to construct a practical detailed scheduling and control system. Reiter [20] has developed such a system and installed it in a large gear-manufacturing job shop. In describing his system and distinguishing it from infinite loading systems, Reiter states:

The most important differences derive from the fact that this system computes operational shop schedules which prescribe the time (to the minute if desired) of starting and finishing every operation to be performed in the shop, taking full account of the availability of equipment and of all work to be done. I know of no operating job shop scheduling system that attempts this task; almost all systems currently in operation are based on machine—or shop—loading methods. Such methods do not produce feasible operational shop schedules. Therefore, the shop schedule is in practice determined by the decisions of various production supervisors or foremen, or in some cases by the workers themselves. These decisions are made more or less independently of one another on the basis of the information available to each foreman and in view of his own skills and objectives. The resulting shop schedules are not necessarily those that management would prefer. A second difference derives from the fact that this system calculates dates of delivery in such a way as to reflect the effect in time units of the amount of congestion or interference in the shop due to the presence of other orders and to the work-force allocation decisions affecting the capacities of work centers.

We shall discuss two finite loading systems, giving considerable detail concerning the Gear Shop system [20] and the Western Electric Interactive system [10].

The Gear Shop

The Gear Shop used by Reiter for the development and testing of the system had approximately 1,000 machines and produced high-quality gears ranging in size from gears with diameters of less than 1 inch to very large gears approximately 4 feet in diameter. Most gears are made from forgings purchased from outside suppliers or provided by customers, and only a small fraction are made from bar stock.

Depending on the gear and its complexity, between 7 and 50 operations were required on many different machines. These operations would include cleaning, sizing, and shaping, heat-treating the raw materials, cutting and grinding gear teeth, and final heat treatment to obtain the desired characteristics.

Orders varied from 1 to 5,000 pieces with a large number of orders in the range of 50 to 300 pieces. The company had a relatively large number of customers and a shifting mix of orders. High-quality gears are of relatively high value, and the important criteria for performance were technical quality, reliability, and on time delivery.

Reiter divided his job shop planning, scheduling, and control system into four major subsystems: (a) the order status subsystem, (b) the planning and promised-date subsystem, (c) the shop-scheduling subsystem, and (d) the production and schedule control subsystem. We will summarize the operation of each of the subsystems followed by a discussion of the operation of the system as a whole.

Order status subsystem. Figure 11–6 summarizes the major elements of the order status subsystem and shows its major connections to two of the other subsystems. The order status subsystem involves all of the preproduction planning required to determine processes, their routing, the tooling that must be designed and ordered, the raw materials that must be determined and ordered, and so on. This is accomplished through an "inquiry card" system in which cards containing the necessary order information are sent to the various organizational units. After making the necessary inquiries or analyses these organizational units respond with an estimate of the date by which it expects its portion of the work to be completed or delivered. These estimated dates are recorded in the order status file. As a later second response, each organizational unit notifies the order status file for updating when the actual work is completed, for example, when shop routing has been prepared. When all of the necessary preplanning operations have been completed, the order is ready for release to the shop. When issued to the shop, the order leaves the order status file and enters the sum-

Figure 11–6
Order status subsystem

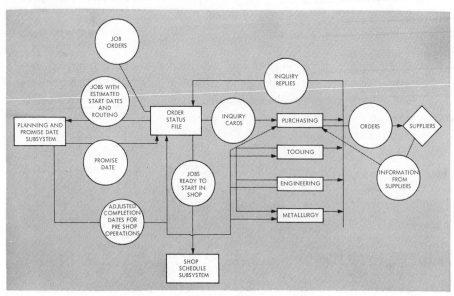

Source: Adapted from S. Reiter. "A System for Managing Job Shop Production," *Journal of Business*, vol. 34, no. 3 (July 1966), pp. 371–93. By permission of The University of Chicago Press.

mary file in the shop-scheduling subsystem, to be discussed under that heading.

Planning and promised-date subsystem. When an order in the order status file (just discussed) enters the planning and promised-date subsystem, it has already gone through some of the preproduction planning so that it has available process routings (and alternate routings), estimates of the completion times of all preproduction planning, and a schedule of dates requested by the customer. The planning and promised-date subsystem, shown in Figure 11–7, performs the following:

1. It decides or provides information and presents alternatives for a management decision on how many sublots the order should be divided into.

2. It selects the actual routing to be used.

3. It decides whether a production lot shall be "streamed," including which operations will involve streaming and the number of sublots involved. (Certain operations may have long processing times followed by operations with short processing times. Lot

Figure 11–7
Planning and promised-date subsystem

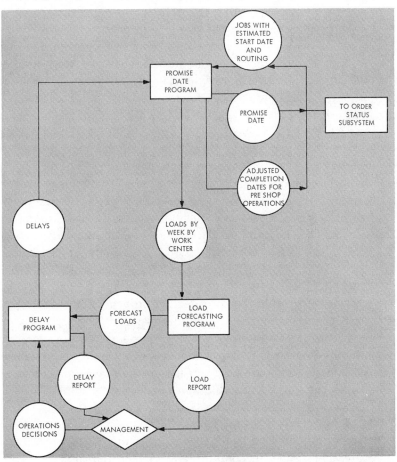

Source, Adapted from S. Reiter, "A System for Managing Job Shop Production," *Journal of Business*, vol. 34, no. 3 (July 1966), pp. 371–93. By permission of The University of Chicago Press.

streaming involves dividing the total job order into sublots which can be moved to the short operation as completed, rather than in batches, thus shortening overall flow time.)

4. It calculates a promised-delivery date for each production lot and calculates the number of days the estimated completion time of each preproduction planning operation is early or late in relation to the release dates specified by customers for delivery. Two reports are prepared, one presenting the information by order number and the second by vendor. The report shows the number of days each order

from each supplier of material, tools, and so on, can be delayed
without endangering meeting the promised date, or specifies the
number of days the order from the vendor should be advanced in
order to meet the promised date.

5. It calculates for each work center the contribution made by
each production lot to the load during the weeks in which the order
will appear in that work center. The contribution is computed both
in terms of the number of jobs and the hours of processing time.

6. It updates forecasts of future work loads in each work center
in each week for 52 weeks in the future. Based on these forecasts and
on decisions concerning the allocation of labor among work centers
(capacity), it calculates the expected waiting time or delay of orders
in each work center in each future week. "These delays are a representation of the state of the entire shop. The state of the shop is thus
given by a matrix of delays, the dimensions of which are the number
of weeks by the number of work centers—in our case, 52 × 230."

7. It produces periodic reports showing the anticipated state of
the shop (in terms of the preceding item 6) for several periods in the
future as a basis for planning the allocation of labor among work
centers and evaluating prospective orders. These reports may be
used in connection with sales efforts and pricing practices.

The work of the order status subsystem, and the planning and
promised-date subsystem completes all of the preproduction planning for an order so that it is ready to enter the shop. At this point it
leaves the order status file and enters the "summary file" in the
shop-scheduling subsystem.

Shop-scheduling subsystem. The broad outlines of the shop-
scheduling subsystem are shown in Figure 11–8. It has two basic
subsystems, one for computing slack, and the shop scheduler. All
orders listed in the summary file are given priorities termed a relative
slack priority. The computation of the priority index is as follows:

$$\text{Priority index} = \frac{\text{Promise date} - \text{Remaining processing time}}{\text{Promise date} - \text{Current date}}$$

Since the priority index changes with time, we might term it a relative dynamic slack priority rule; it is not identical to any of the
priority rules discussed in Chapter 10. Provision is made for special
priorities to be made based on direct management decisions for
specific orders. All operations to be scheduled are then listed by
order in the sequence of decreasing priority in the condensed schedule input file. This file is the basic input to the shop scheduler. The

Figure 11–8
Shop-scheduling subsystem and production and schedule control subsystem

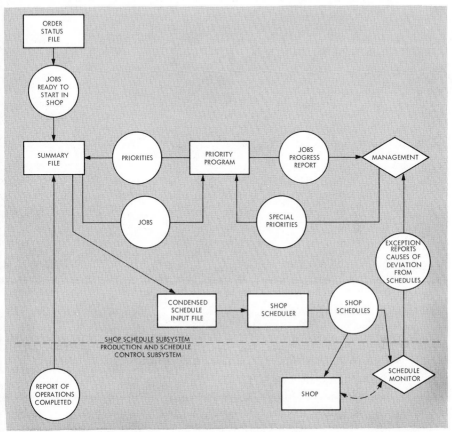

Source, Adapted from S. Reiter, "A System for Managing Job Shop Production," *Journal of Business*, vol. 34, no. 3 (July 1966), pp. 371–93. By permission of The University of Chicago Press.

shop scheduler generates a schedule for each work center which shows start and finish times to the nearest hour. A typical page from a shop schedule is shown in Figure 11–9. The column headings in Figure 11–9 are largely self-explanatory. The fourth column gives the number of the operation to be done at this work center; for example, the first order shown indicates that the operation to be performed is the 12th in the routing of the order. The start and finish times list the hour of the day, the day, and the date. The schedule also shows the work center and finish time of the previous operation, and the work center and start time of the following operation. It is important to note that the priority system is not used by the supervisor to select

Figure 11–9
Sample page from shop-scheduling printout

WORK CNTR	PART NUMBER	SHOP ORDER	SEQ NO.	OPER CODE	LOT SIZE	C P	S U	START TIME	FINISH TIME	PREV FINISH + WORK CNTR	NEXT START + WORK CNTR	ORDERED QUANTITY	CUST CODE
2235	1079	273202	12	007R	49			1TH 0R	1TH 12		2RR3 1TH 12	107	042
2235	1R3R	52R901	15	007R	117			1TH 0R	1F 04		2R45 1TH 20	117	11R
2235	1164	304001	10	0024	111			1TH 14	2R 00	2333 1TH 14	2235 2R 02	111	060
2235	5055	556301	06	0050	2R			1F 06	1F 0R	2654 1TH 14	2235 1F 10	2R	043
2235	5055	556301	07	0052	2R			1F 10	1F 12		2R45 1F 15	2R	043
2235	9220	519R01	10	002R	47			1F 14	2R 03	2351 1F 0R	2341 2R 06	47	CR5
2235	1164	304001	11	0027	111			2R 02	2R 10		2342 2R 07	111	060
2235	360R FORGING- 360R1	513901	05	0034 ANALYSIS-	25			2R 05	2R 06	2633 1F 11	251R 2R 10	25	02R
2235	325719 FORGING- 325719	693101	10	0042 ANALYSIS-	105 1045			2M 0R	2M 14	2522 1F 22	2645 2M 15	105	1R3
2235	9220	519R01	12	0050	47			2M 12	2R 15	2341 2R 09	2359 2TU 05	47	0R5
2235	2224	570401	10	0024	100			2TU 00	2TU 11	2333 2R 03	2342 2TU 05	100	074
2235	3623	609501	10	0050	26			2TU 00	2TU 00	2216 2R 12	1611 2TU 04	26	043
2235	2224	570402	0R	0050	97			2TU 02	2TU 13	2234 2TU 02	2359 2TU 10	101	074
2235	2710 FORGING- 2774C	611701	09	0073 ANALYSIS- R620	20			2TU 13	2TU 15	2522 1F 03	2641 NT SCD	21	069
2235	1164	304001	14	0032	111			2TU 15	2R 12	2342 2R 01	2442 NT SCD	111	060
2235	5012	56R901	32	0131	25			2R 00	2R 05	3053 1TH 14	1614 NT SCD	26	087

Source: Reprinted from S. Reiter, "A System for Managing Job Shop Production," *Journal of Business,* vol. 34, no. 3 (July 1966), pp. 371–93. By permission of The University of Chicago Press.

a job to work on, but is used by the computer scheduling routine as a part of the overall scheduling algorithm which determines the detailed schedule shown in Figure 11–9.

The shop scheduler routine uses lot streaming when advantageous, and schedules the sublots to be streamed as called for by previous decisions, or by a built-in decision criterion, scheduling desirable sequences of setups in work centers where lot streaming is taking place.

Production and schedule control. The reporting system used provides, first, for reports at specified times of all operations completed or partially completed. Second, a job progress report identifies those jobs which have fallen behind schedule and may not meet promised dates in spite of the dynamic priority. Finally, the schedule monitor system compares actual performance with scheduled performance on a sampling basis and reports situations which represent large departures from the original schedule.

Operation of the system as a whole. Figure 11–10 shows the four subsystems assembled into the system as a whole. At any one point in time there are available all of the data which define the state of the system. Based on these data the system performs the following:

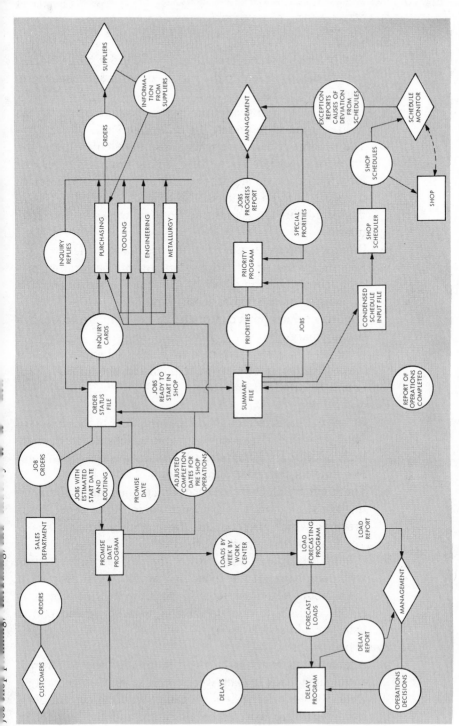

Source: Reprinted from S. Reiter, "A System for Managing Job Shop Production," *Journal of Business*, vol. 34, no. 3 (July 1966), pp. 371–93. By permission of The University of Chicago Press.

1. Each day:
   a. Newly arrived orders are entered in the order status file and inquiry cards are sent to the various departments engaged in preproduction planning.
   b. Inquiry cards returned from preproduction planning activities are used to update the order status file.
   c. The promised date program is used to calculate promised dates for all orders not already having promised dates and for which the requisite information is available. The delays currently in force are used. The orders are added to the orders and hours totals in the appropriate weeks in respective matrices.
   d. Promised dates are entered in the order status files.
   e. Reports are issued to various departments performing preproduction planning activities showing allowable variation in dates of completion of those activities.
   f. Reports of operations completed in the shop are entered in the summary file.
   g. If the date is one on which a new shop schedule is calculated, the number of pieces completed on operations in process is reported from the shop.
2. Every third day:
   a. Relative slack is recalculated for every order in the summary file. Management decisions to give some jobs extraordinarily high priority are given effect by entering a fictitious promised date for the order in question.
   b. The summary file is sorted according to the newly calculated relative slack, and a new condensed schedule input file is prepared which also contains the operations in process.
   c. The job progress report is issued.
   d. A shop schedule is prepared for the next six days, starting with completion of the scheduled operations in process. If there should be a breakdown in the computer, the shop thus could continue to operate for one more scheduled period using the old schedule.
3. Every two weeks:
   a. Accumulated loads in jobs and hours are used to forecast anticipated loads in each work center in each of the next 52 weeks. These forecast loads together with the current decisions regarding work force allocation and the number of

shifts operated are used to calculate revised delays for each work center in each of the next 52 weeks.

b. All information referring to past weeks is dropped from the load files but may be retained for a time in another form to provide a historical record.

c. The current estimates of future delays are entered as the delay parameters in the promised date program. For the next two weeks all promised dates will be calculated on the basis of the revised delays.

d. Delay reports are issued to management to be used to help guide work force allocations and longer term operations decisions in the future. Some changes in work force allocation are likely to be planned more than two weeks in advance.

Results of installation.   At the time of Reiter's report his system had been operating in the Gear Shop for about a year. While Reiter observes that a controlled experiment to judge and identify effects was not possible he makes the following statement about results.

While we cannot yet have firm scientific evidence, experience with the system so far shows such a sharp break with the past that the effects of the system seem quite clear. What we have observed so far is (a) a reduction in the number of orders not meeting due dates to a value regarded by the management as very near the irreducible minimum; (b) a remarkable reduction in lead time per order, which is equivalent to a very large increase in shop through-put, with no substantial change in the number of machines or of men; (c) greatly increased control of shop operations and significantly smoother day-to-day operations; (d) a considerable reduction in overtime work; and (e) the emergence of routinely available information as a basis for planning such things as outside subcontracting of certain operations, something not ordinarily done by this company. In general, the problem areas have shifted from the shop to procurement and other pre-shop paper work. The problem used to be to get the product out on time; it is now to get the material and the blueprints and tooling in on time.

It appears that the integrated system developed and installed by Reiter has made a detailed scheduling system feasible through the use of a dynamic and realistic conceptual framework and the use of rapid data processing. Reiter states:

For each type of shop and type of business there is a size beyond which the shop becomes unmanageable using the usual methods. When job shops exceed that size, they have chronic problems symptomatic of the difficulty.

With an effective computerized management system like this one, the size of shop that a given management can control is significantly larger than its former limiting size.

Western Electric interactive system [10]

An interesting development which uses the capabilities of time-shared computing has promise for the job shop-scheduling problem. Jones and co-workers [9, 10, 13] developed interactive scheduling systems which use either typewriter or display terminals and thereby places the production supervisor, or a scheduler, in a loop with a computer program. By interacting with the computer program the scheduler develops and/or alters a schedule. Schedules are generated by making choices from among sets of decision rules, for example, rules for the acceptance or rejection of orders, rules for sequencing orders, and rules for allocating the use of overtime. The scheduler develops a schedule by testing the effects of various combinations of possibilities, and simulating various alternate assignments and their effects.

Godin and Jones developed a small-scale application of the interactive scheduling concept in one of the coil winding shops of the Western Electric Company. Of the 200 types of coils manufactured, approximately 65 are active at any point in time and each type is usually being produced for three or four different orders. There are 20 of one type winding machine and 2 of a second type, and the work force consists of from 20 to 35 machine operators working on two or three shifts depending on shop load. Because of differences in skills not all operators can wind all types of coils and performance against standard varies considerably for various combinations of operators and coil types. Similarly, some machines cannot be used to wind some types of coils. The production supervisor must assign workers and machines to each order in a way which balances pressures for on-time deliveries against the other factors which make for production effectiveness.

The system allows for the production supervisor to consider seven variables in constructing schedules:

1. Skill levels of workers.
2. Skill needs of products.
3. Capability of machines.
4. Availability of workers, machines, and materials.
5. Quantities required.

6. Completion dates.
7. Existing machine setups.

Conversational language.   The system functions through a main program and 23 subroutines. To communicate with the program through the terminal, a simple conversational language was developed. A single key stroke indicates a whole series of commands. The keys are identified by a plastic overlay on the keyboard, for example, the overlay shows "Load" over the exclamation point key. When this key is depressed, the computer understands it as a request to print the winding shop load on the printer.

Figure 11–11 is an illustration of how the supervisor can converse with the computer program through simple commands which evoke

Figure 11–11
How the supervisor and the computer converse. Each computer message begins with 00 and is followed by the supervisor's response beginning with REPLY 00. Some symbols represent function buttons such as the Q, which represents the command GO, and the + sign, which represents the command PRINT THE CURRENT SHOP STATUS.

```
00   TYPE CURRENT DAY,WEEK,MONTH,END DAY,WEEK,MONTH
REPLY 00,'1,2,6,2,2,6'
00   TYPE NUMBER OF WEEKS IN EACH MONTH
REPLY 00,'5'
00   TYPE NUMBER OF DAYS IN EACH WEEK
REPLY 00,'5,5,5,5,5'
00   TYPE IN THE DECISION RULE YOU WISH TO USE
REPLY 00,'6'
  START OF SHIFT   1         ON DAY   1        OF WEEK   2
  PHASE 1......INDICA             MACHINES DO
00   READY,    R
```

Source: From V. Godin, and C. H. Jones, "The Interactive Shop Supervisor," *Industrial Engineering*, November 1969.

responses or questions from the program. The supervisor answers questions with the information requested. For example, in the seventh line of Figure 11–11 the program requests, "TYPE IN THE DECISION RULE YOU WISH TO USE." The supervisor responds with the code "6," which calls a preprogrammed decision rule.

The language used in the interactive process is designed to emphasize the computer's subordinate role. The computer speaks in the first person in a helpful manner as follows: "SORRY, I CANNOT UNDERSTAND YOUR REQUEST. TRY AGAIN." Or, "I SUGGEST SMITH, M. ON CODE 2588AB ON MACHINE NO. 2." Or, "I NEED HELP ASSIGNING GREGG, F."

Simulation and reports.   The computer program can carry out simulations of shop schedules so that the supervisor can test various alternate assignments and try to anticipate future problems. Simulations can be run in a completely automatic mode with no human intervention but it is more likely to simulate in interactive mode. When the interactive mode is used the supervisor enters two parameters which set the guidelines for the system. The first parameter tells the computer how long it may keep an operator on the same coil type before manual reassignment is necessary, and the second tells what region the computer program may search when suggesting assignments for operators. In addition to these two parameters a normal daily run includes the open-order file and the operator-machine job assignments already in existence. The latter input is generated through the use of a small prepunched card deck.

Given the current operator-machine job assignments, the computer program starts to simulate shop activity, automatically reassigning an operator to a new job on the same coil type whenever possible. If the range of the first guideline parameter would be exceeded by such a reassignment, the program informs the supervisor that a new assignment must be made manually. At the same time, the program uses the second parameter to search the open-order file

Figure 11–12
Simulation shows what happens as jobs begin and end

```
TIME IS    7.90
13338  GILLINGHAM, G        FINISHED ON MACHINE    15
    18  TYPE  2596E  COILS MADE IN    0.8  HOURS WITH    100 PERCENT EFF
GILLINGHAM, G           ASSIGNED TO   2596E  ON MACHINE    15


TIME IS   11.00
13338  GILLINGHAM, G        FINISHED ON MACHINE    15
    66  TYPE  2596E  COILS MADE IN    3.0  HOURS WITH    100 PERCENT EFF
GILLINGHAM, G           ASSIGNED TO   2596E  ON MACHINE    15


TIME IS   11.50
20654  SKORONSKI, B        FINISHED ON MACHINE    11
    26  TYPE  2507BA  COILS MADE IN    4.2  HOURS WITH     65 PERCENT EFF
SKORONSKI, B            ASSIGNED TO   2507BA ON MACHINE    11


TIME IS   11.70
26756  NITSCHKE, R        FINISHED ON MACHINE    21
   181  TYPE  1555C  COILS MADE IN    4.6  HOURS WITH    100 PERCENT EFF
NITSCHKE, R             ASSIGNED TO   1555C  ON MACHINE    21


TIME IS   12.20
17021  DALE, C             FIN
    65  TYPE  2
```

Source: From V. Godin and C. H. Jones, "The Interactive Shop Supervisor," *Industrial Engineering,* November 1969.

and the history file for a high-efficiency job for the operator in question. Based on this search, the supervisor is offered one or two suitable assignments for the operator.

The length of the simulation run is normally two to four days, however, the length of run is not restricted. When the simulation run is complete a summary of activity over the simulated period is typed out as shown in Figure 11–12.

Various reports can be called for at any time that the system is in operation such as shop status, a history of work by operator or by machine, load summarized by standard hours, and so on. Figure 11–13 shows an example of a shop status report.

Figure 11–13
This display of shop status can be obtained from the computer any time the system is in operation

MACHINE	CODE	E.NO.	NAME
1	2588S	15982	DOWLER, B
2	2588L	20654	SKORONSKI, B
3	2588BM	13338	GILLINGHAM, G
4	2588AS		
5	2588C	34149	HYLAND, B
6	2588BY		
7	2588AN	30264	KRAMER, J
8	2588BT	13989	GREGG, F
9	2507AJ	10460	FLEMING, M
10	2588CM		
11	0		
12	2588CH	26499	STARR, B
13	2588BF	18884	MERCEIN, C
14	2596C	23979	ANDERSON, D
15	2596A		
16	2588AF	17021	DALE, C
17	1535G	88868	JETER, B
18	2507AK	11631	ALDRIDGE, L
19	2588BW	25448	JORDAN, H
20	2588AP		
21	1535F	26736	NITSCHKE, R

Source: From V. Godin and C. H. Jones, "The Interactive Shop Supervisor," *Industrial Engineering*, November 1969.

MIXED SYSTEMS

Finite loading systems have advantages for short-term operations scheduling; e.g., their ability to give forward visibility to upcoming work and to simulate detailed start and completion dates. Infinite loaders have advantages in providing longer term perspectives of capacity needs. It seems inevitable that someone would try to mix the two approaches. Curiously, the mixed finite/infinite loading approach was not recently developed as an outgrowth of improvements in both areas. Rather, a mixed system was developed in the late 50s and early 60s at the Hughes Aircraft Company.

The Hughes Aircraft Company job shop control system

In the following discussion of the Hughes Aircraft Company job shop control system one must keep in mind the fact that some of the activities discussed in connection with Figure 11–3, are being assumed. The control system is imbedded in a broader system involving bidding, product definition, operational planning, operations, and operational control, not unlike the generalized system described by Figure 11–3.

Hughes is a large aerospace firm which bids on the design, development, and manufacture of complex electronics systems. The shop was characterized by a diverse product mix of machined and sheet metal parts, machine assemblies, waveguides, and etched circuit boards flowing through functionally grouped work centers. There were 2,000 to 3,000 orders being processed at any one time, with an average of seven operations per order. The average operation required 2½ hours of processing time. The shop consisted of approximately 1,000 machines and/or workplaces, which were grouped into 120 functional machine or work centers. The work centers were manned by 400 direct workers so that the entire system was labor limited. At this labor force level the average order cycle time was between three and four weeks.

The loading system for planning, scheduling, and control described here was reported at different stages of development by Le-Grande [15], Steinhoff [22], and Bulkin, Colley, and Steinhoff [3], a summary of the end operating system being described in the latter reference.

The system was developed around a Weekly Shop Load Forecast for each machine group and a Job Shop Simulation Scheduler routine which produced a Daily Order-Schedule Report and a Daily Hot-Order Visibility Report. The two daily reports and the weekly load forecast were based on daily updated fabrication open-order master files. The entire system was computer based.

System as a whole. Figure 11–4 shows the broad outlines of the

Figure 11–14
Hughes Aircraft Company's production planning and control system

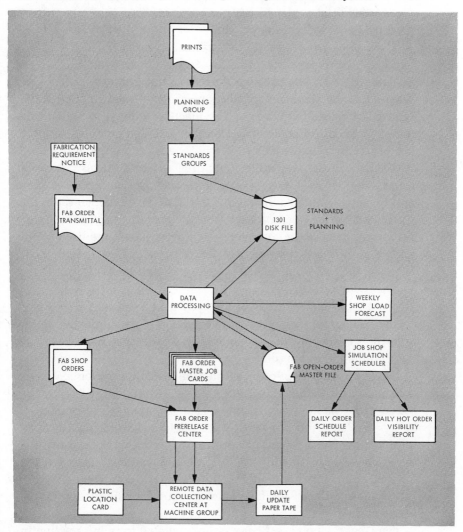

Source: Adapted from M. H. Bulkin, J. L. Colley, and H. W. Steinhoff, "Load Forecasting, Priority Sequencing, and Simulation in a Job Shop Control System," *Management Science*, vol. 13, no. 2 (October 1966), pp. 29–51.

system as a whole. On release of engineering prints, operational process planning is performed followed by the addition of standard process times and the flow allowances. These data are placed in the disk file. On receipt of a fabrication requirement notice from one of the assembly product-line departments, a fabrication order is trans-

mitted to data processing, which initiates the preparation of a fabrication shop order and establishes an open order in the fabrication
open-order master file. In addition, a deck of master job cards is
produced which accompanies the order in the shop.

The fabrication order and the master job cards are then sent to a
fabrication order control prerelease center from which orders are
dispatched to the shop. Once the fabrication shop order has been
released to the shop, the master job cards are used in conjunction
with plastic location cards at the machine groups to actuate the
remote data collection devices. Data transmission provides for locating orders into the various functional machine groups in the shop.
At the end of each day a file containing all order moves transacted
during the day's activity is used to update current order locations
and to code completed operations in the fabrication open-order file.

The fabrication open-order master file contains the critical information (updated daily) on every open order and is the heart of the
system. It produces three critical documents, the Weekly Shop Load
Forecast, the Daily Order-Schedule Report, and the Daily Hot-Order
Visibility Report.

Given the broad outlines of the system as a whole, we will now
concentrate our attention on the information in the fabrication open-
order master file and the key operating reports which are based on
the information in the file.

The fabrication open-order master file is maintained on magnetic
tape and contains the basic information shown in Figure 11–15. The
file contains the information shown for every open fabrication order.
In the header section of the file are contained fixed identification
information plus the items of information shown on the right which
are updated daily. In addition, the "open operations" data is listed
for each open fabrication operation necessary to complete the order.
Finally, the trailer of the file contains summary information on the
status of the order.

The Weekly Shop Load Forecast is generated from information in
the fabrication open-order master file for each machine group as
shown in Figure 11–16. The Weekly Shop Load Forecast projects the
anticipated load for each machine or work center for 10 weeks in
advance. The shop load forecast shown in Figure 11–16 is for a
milling machine center with six machines. The projected work load
in standard hours is divided into total active load and preshop load
(not yet released to the shop) and further subdivided into orders
which are on schedule, behind schedule, or held due to lack of

Figure 11–15
Fabrication open-order file information for each open order

Header:

Work order number	Part number	Project code	Procurement code	Bill of material	Cost account	Make span	Due date	Order Quantity	Current location			Previous location		Held code	Level of effort
									Dept.	Mach. group	Oper. no.	Dept.	Mach. group		

|← Fixed →|← Updated daily →|

Open operations: Data on all fabrication operations to complete order

Work order number	Operation number	Make location		Setup standard hours	Run-time standard hours	Setback	Completion code
		Dept.	Mach. group				

Trailer:

Work order number	Part number	Number moves remaining	Days in current location

Source: From M. H. Bulkin, J. L. Colley, and H. W. Steinhoff, "Load Forecasting, Priority Sequencing, and Simulation in a Job Shop Control System," *Management Science*, vol. 13, no. 2 (October 1966), pp. 29–51.

production plans, material, tooling, and so on. The shop load forecast can be used in each machine group to establish labor force and machine needs for the present and future weeks.

Order scheduling

The Daily Order-Schedule Report and Hot-Order Visibility Report are developed by the Job Shop Simulation and are used by shop supervisors and expediters in the daily sequencing of orders at the machine groups in the shop. The simulation scheduler was developed by Steinhoff [22] as a computing routine used to simulate one shift of shop activity and to generate the two daily reports. The priority dispatching decision rule used in the simulation scheduler is the dynamic slack time per operation rule (DS/RO). Dynamic slack time is computed as the number of days remaining to the due date less the remaining number of days of processing time. The priority index is then computed by dividing dynamic slack by the number of remaining operations. Actually, the priority rule is a two-class rule, since hot orders are segregated and processed first in the sequence of the priority index followed by the processing of all other orders in the sequence of the priority index.

Simulation scheduler. The operation of the simulation scheduler involves, first, the computation of the slack time per operation

Figure 11–16
Weekly Shop Load Forecast for one machine group. "Preshop load" represents orders not yet released to shop. "Held" orders are not available to be worked on due to lack of production plans, material, or tooling. "In machine group" portion of active load are orders already physically located at the machine group

SHOP LOAD FORECAST
M-DAY 605 CALENDAR DAY 01-06-65
MACHINE GROUP LOAD IN STANDARD HOURS

DEPT-MG 71-43 MILLS 6 MACHINES

	Week of Performance										Greater Than 10	Total
	1	2	3	4	5	6	7	8	9	10		
TOTAL LOAD	208	175	227	204	126	116	42	52	28	23	53	1254
ON SCHEDULE	138	122	211	186	126	114	34	52	25	14	53	1075
BEHIND SCHEDULE	70	53	16	18		2	8		3	9		179
HELD	37	44	12	18	2							113
TOTAL ACTIVE LOAD	123	115	102	64	46	53	21	6	15	23	53	621
ON SCHEDULE	85	76	98	58	46	51	13	6	12	14	53	512
BEHIND SCHEDULE	38	39	4	6		2	8		3	9		109
HELD	11	21	4		2							38
IN MACHINE GROUP	96	37	26		8							150
TOTAL PRESHOP LOAD	85	60	125	140	80	63	21	46	13			633
ON SCHEDULE	53	46	113	128	80	63	21	46	13			563
BEHIND SCHEDULE	32	14	12	12								70
HELD	26	23	8	18								75

Source: From M. H. Bulkin, J. L. Colley, and H. W. Steinhoff, "Load Forecasting, Priority Sequencing, and Stimulation in a Job Shop Control System," Management Science, vol. 13, no. 2 (October, 1966), pp. 29–51.

for every order in the fabrication open-order master file. Contained in the system is a table of machine group capacities and labor force capacities. The labor force is divided into labor classes which can be assigned to one or more machine groups, and this capacity table is updated as needed. The simulation program then makes an initial assignment of each order in the open file to the machine group indicated in the current location in its header record (see Figure 11–15). When all orders in the file have been assigned to their respective "current location" machine groups, the orders in each machine group are ranked in priority sequence, hot orders first. The priority-sequenced orders for each machine group are then assigned sequentially until either all available machines or workers have been exhausted. For those machine groups serviced by a common labor pool, and for which the availability of workers is the capacity limitation, the machine group with the highest priority job will be serviced.

After the initial order assignment the actual simulation begins. An event clock is used to record operation completions at the machine groups based on the estimated run times. On the completion of an operation in the simulation, a new priority index is computed for the order, and it is moved to its next operation location, where it is placed in the queue in the proper priority sequence or actually processed if a worker and a machine are available. At the machine group where the operation completion occurred, the job at the head of the queue is processed. This continues for one shift, and all activities taking place during the dynamic simulation are recorded and used to generate the daily operating reports.

The Order-Schedule Report for one machine group is shown in Figure 11–17. The report shows the orders in the machine group at the beginning of the shift followed by the orders expected to arrive (incoming orders) during the shift. Within these two categories the orders are further subdivided into hot orders (those marked with the number 1 in the column headed "Effort") and other orders. Within these two categories the orders are sequenced in terms of the DS/RO priority sequencing rule. Those orders which are listed with negative priority numbers are already behind schedule; hence they have negative slack. The "Special" column uses a code which indicates that an order may lack production planning (U), is being worked on out of sequence (X), or that the operation is a "write-in" operation (W) added over and above the standard production plans. A "held" code

Figure 11–17
Daily Order-Schedule Report for one machine group

ORDER SCHEDULE REPORT

REPORT NUMBER	M-DAY	DATE	PAGE	MACHINE GROUP
3659-94	517	10-28-64	1	71-91

EFFORT	PRIORITY	PART NUMBER ENG.	PART NUMBER PRE	PART NUMBER BASIC	PART NUMBER DASH	WORK ORDER PRE	WORK ORDER BASIC	WORK ORDER SPLIT	PROC. CODE	PROJ. CODE	PROD. LINE	PREVIOUS LOCATION	ARRIVAL TIME	ORDER QUANTITY	ESTIM. ACTUAL HOURS/OP.	SPECIAL	HELD FOR	OPS. LEFT	ESTIM. RUN-TIME LEFT	DATE PROMISED
	ORDERS-IN-STATION																			
1	- 5.4			443209		21	487403		11	03		71-15	INSTA	4322	18.5			03	15.2	
1	.9			834445	098	21	364409		11	32		71-23	INSTA	400	12.2	X		04	85.8	
1	1.9			486191	002	21	494429		46	69		71-43	INSTA	1	.1			05	2.3	
	- 6.5		902	401961		21	393484	01	40	352		71-43	INSTA	35	5.3	X		14	229.0	
	- 3.3			221066		26	501700		11	53		71-43	INSTA	75	2.5	W		03	41.0	510
	- 2.4			417212		21	489618		11	177		71-11	INSTA	290	2.3	W		03	16.2	
	1.8		420	990283		21	499111		11	177		71-11	INSTA	10	.0			06	1.9	
	2.0		1	506481		26	514301		11	08		71-43	INSTA	17	.0	U		00	.0	519
	2.0			529093		26	514305		11	08		71-43	INSTA	60	.0	U		00	.0	519
	2.0		1	513229		26	514313		11	08		71-16	INSTA	14	.0	U		00	.0	519
	3.6			415666		21	506615		11	051		71-43	INSTA	15	.2			05	.3	
	4.1		2	401957		21	393474		40	353		71-61	INSTA	109	3.6	M		02	1.3	
	7.0			421090		21	495108		11	17		71-11	INSTA	63	1.5	X		07	11.8	
	INCOMING ORDERS M-DAY 517																			
1	- 9.7		2	259446	001	21	442638		11	69		71-61	10 00	85	1.7			03	46.2	523
1	- 8.2		2	259443	001	21	442636		11	69		72-31	12*30	59	1.2			04	64.1	528
1	- 7.6		2	259446	001	21	442638	01	11	69		37-32	07 30	75	1.5			05	88.1	
	- 65.0		902	479392		21	394101	01	41	352		71-92	10 00	10	.0			00	.0	
	- 9.5			423953	009	21	506607		11	052		71-21	11 00	16	.2			01	.0	
	- 4.0			402535		21	508600		11	17		71-31	11 00	20	.1			01	.1	
	1.6			464465		21	516401		66	71		79-11	08 00	4	.1			07	7.4	
									AVG EST HRS			2.5		TOTAL EST HRS				51.8		
	LAST PAGE																			

Source: From M. H. Bulkin, J. L. Colley, and H. W. Steinhoff, "Load Forecasting, Priority Sequencing, and Simulation in a Job Shop Control System," *Management Science*, vol. 13, no. 2 (October 1966), pp. 29–51.

indicates that an order is held for material, planning, or tooling, and the promised date indicates an order completion estimate.

The supervisor uses the information in the Order-Schedule Report to plan the work of the shift. Supervisors know which orders are in their machine groups, their relative priorities, and work content, and also know how many hot orders will arrive during the day.

The Hot-Order Visibility Report segregates all orders for a given department that are in the "rush" classification. Figure 11–18 is an example of a Hot-Order Visibility Report for one department. This report assists expediters in performing their jobs.

Figure 11–18
Daily Hot-Order Visibility Report for one department

HOT ORDER VISIBILITY REPORT

REPORT NUMBER	M · DAY	DATE	PAGE	DEPARTMENT
3699-03	517	10-28-64	4	72-00

EFFORT	PART NUMBER				WORK ORDER			PROC. CODE	PROJ. CODE	PROD. LINE	OPERATION LOCATION	SPECIAL	ARRIVAL TIME	PREVIOUS LOCATION	ORDER QUANTITY	ESTIM. ACTUAL HOURS/OP.	HELD FOR	OPS. LEFT	ESTIM. RUN-TIME LEFT	PRIORITY	DATE PROMISED
	ENG.	PRE	BASIC	DASH	PRE	BASIC	SPLIT														
1								60	00		72-31	X	1-S1	72-14	1-	1.5		06	7.1 - 12.0		
											71-21		06 53	72-31		5.4		05	5.1 - 15.0		
											72-32		01*30	71-21		0.2		02	3.0 - 20.0		
											72-31		01*30	72-32		0.7		01	2.3 - 30.0		
1			2		21			11	66		72-31		1-STA	72-14	220	4.1		03	10.4 - 4.7	532	
											71-21		11 00	72-31		10.3		02	0.6 - 12.0		
1			2 441753 001		21 44161			46	64		72-41	H	INSTA	72-46	39	3.4		06	5.1 - 5.9		
											72-24		10 30	72-41		2.0		05	3.1 - 6.8		
											72-47		01*00	72-24		0.3		04	2.4 - 8.1		
											72-42		01*00	72-47		0.5		03	2.4 - 10.0		
											72-46		01*30	72-42		0.7		02	1.7 - 13.0		
1			2 441766 001		21 441620			46	64		72-46		INSTA	72-31	20	0.4		07	2.0 - 5.0	539	
											72-47		07 30	72-46		0.1		06	1.9 - 5.7		
											72-42		07 30	72-47		0.3		05	1.7 - 6.7		
											72-44		08 00	72-42		0.9		04	0.7 - 8.0		
1			10 18		26 651			41	53		72-31	H	INSTA	37-12	22	1.2		03	38.3 - 14.0		
											78-00		08 30	72-31		2.0		02	36.3 - 19.0		
1			1 11 18		26 717 00			41	53		72-41		INSTA	72-14	2	0.1		03	72.3 - 11.0		
											78-00		07 30	72-14		4.0		02	68.3 - 15.0		
1			40 446 164		21 455104			11	17		72-31		1-S1	37-32	26	7.8		01	20.3 - 13.0		
1			40 161 460		21 463625			11	55		72-21	X	1-STA	37-30	23	12.0		02	3.7 - 5.0		
1			40 177800 112		21 442108			41	64		72-33	0	1-STA	72-31	1	0.0		00	0.0 - 28.0		
1			90 487 468 161		27 470108			16	03		72-07	0	1-STA	72-05	545	0.0		00	0.0 - 38.0		
1			40 460 424 101		27 460762			16	04		72-05	0	1-STA	78-22	400	0.0		00	0.0 - 3.0		
1			40 486413 163		27 443152			16	03		72-05	0	1-STA	74-11	150	0.0		00	0.0 - 7.0		
1			40 485104 101		27 502114			16	03		72-05	0	1-STA	74-11	50	0.0		00	0.0 - 3.0		
1			402 297 476 001		21 432600			41	44		72-33		INSTA	74-25	1	1.4		02	1.4 - 11.0		
											75-14		07 30	72-33		1.4		01	0.0 - 18.0		
											75-45		10 00	75-15		0.0		00	0.0 - 33.0		
1			902 297 476 001		21 432601			41	64		72-33	H	INSTA	74-25	1	0.4		02	1.1 - 11.0		
											74-32		07 31	72-33		1.1		01	0.0 - 15.0		
											75-45		08 31	75-32		4.4		00	- 53.0		
1			484700 002		21 482602			41	64		72-32		INSTA	72-14	1	0.4		04	6.9 - .0		
											75-52		08 30	72-32		2.3		07	4.6 - .0		
		LAST PAGE																			

Source: From M. H. Bulkin, J. L. Colley, and H. W. Steinhoff, "Load Forecasting, Priority Sequencing, and Simulation in a Job Shop Control System," *Management Science*, vol. 13, no. 2 (October 1966), pp. 29–51.

Comments on the Hughes system. While the Hughes system is essentially a loading system, it incorporates the daily simulation scheduling which has the effect of providing the department supervisor with a feasible daily schedule. If the backlog of work for a given machine group indicated a bottleneck problem developing, alternate routing can be considered to relieve the problem in the short run, or additional worker or machine capacity in the longer run. It is interesting that the DS/RO priority dispatching decision rule was used in the light of Nanot's study reported in Chapter 10. The DS/RO rule was one of the high-variance (flow time criterion) rules. Undoubtedly, the priority rule was used because of the results of LeGrande's study [15], which indicated that if order completion criteria were weighted more heavily, the DS/RO rule was best of those tested (see Table 10–15). But the rule actually being used in the Hughes system is a two-class DS/RO rule, and we have no data on the relative performance of this specific rule.

Extensive data on the performance of the Hughes system is given in reference [3]. Among other data given, the first six months of operation showed a 10 percent increase in the number of orders completed by their scheduled due dates. This improved performance reduced the average order cycle time by one week, from the earlier stated three to four weeks, thus effecting a significant reduction of in-process inventory and an increase in machine and labor force utilization. Simultaneously, there was a 60 percent reduction in expediting effort.

SUMMARY

We are not in a position to make a comparative evaluation of the potential performance of the Hughes and Gear Shop systems particularly since the Reiter study states results in only general terms. Both deal with the problem of large-size shops by computerized methods. The mixed system at Hughes Aircraft Company provides a feasible (capacity constrained) schedule to each machine center on a daily basis by simulating the operations of the entire shop each day. Thus the daily schedule takes account of current work in progress at each machine center as well as the relative priorities of incoming orders. The Reiter system provides a detailed schedule for each operation to be performed and calculates dates of delivery in such a way as to reflect the effect in time units of the amount of congestion or interference in the shop due to the presence of other orders and due to work force allocation decisions.

What does seem clear at this point is that both simple finite and infinite loading systems have their advantages. Perhaps from this perspective, mixed systems offer the best opportunities for future development. A study by Moodie and Novotny (Table 11–6) has illustrated the tremendous diversity that exists in the structure of job shops and the systems and dispatching rules that they employ. It does not seem quite realistic to presume that one pure system type is

Table 11–6. Summary comparison between three loading and three detailed schedule systems

Type of system and company	Shop size statistics	Periodic simulation used as a basis for scheduling	Output reports	Priority dispatching rule used	Type of computer used	Interval between job status update	Direct interrogation of computer possible?	Benefits claimed for system
Loading Systems:								
Hughes	2,500 orders in process 120 work centers 1,000 machines	Each day	Shop load forecast location report Coordination report; order schedule; hot order visibility report	Slack Time/operation $P = \dfrac{DS}{RO}$	IBM–1410 IBM–1301	Once daily	No	Reduces cycle time Increases productivity Meets more due dates Reduces expediting
Texas Instruments	5,000 orders in process	Not used		None	IBM–1440 IBM–1301 and 1311	Every three hours	Yes	Reduces cycle time Reduces expediting Increases productivity Meets more due dates Reduces late penalty costs
Western Electric	500 orders in process	Not used	Load report Shop schedule Shop station report Job status report Station priority listing Shipping report	Slack Time $P_t\left(D_t - D_o - \left[\dfrac{Hij(k) + A(k)}{8}\right]\right)$	Monrobot	Once daily	Yes	Reduces cycle time Increases productivity Reduces in-waiting inventories
Detailed Schedule Systems:								
Gear Shop	1,000 machines	Every three days	Shop schedule Load report Delay report Job progress report	$P = \dfrac{\text{Promise date} - \text{Remaining process time}}{\text{Promise date} - \text{Current date}}$		Every three days	No	Increases throughput with same resources Less overtime Gives more information for planning Helps supervision
Western Electric Interactive System	65 orders in process	As needed	Load report Shop schedule History Shop status Summary statistics	Various rules available for use	IBM– 360/50 IBM–1052 consoles	As needed		Increases productivity Provides better balance between on-time delivery and shop efficiency

Source: Modified from C. L. Moodie and D. J. Novotny, "Computer Scheduling and Control Systems for Discrete Part Production," *Journal of Industrial Engineering*, vol. 19, no. 7 (July 1968).

the best for all of the types of firms that have need of job shop scheduling, planning, and control. Moreover, many of the more advanced limited resource schedulers discussed in Chapter 13 contain features that seem to combine the best of the simpler system types that we have reviewed in this chapter.

REVIEW QUESTIONS AND PROBLEMS

1. Why is the knowledge of the work flow structure of a job shop important in designing a planning, scheduling, and control system?
2. Contrast the decision structure for an integrated job shop planning and control system (Figure 11–3) with that for a typical high-volume standardized product (Figure 8–7).
   a. In what ways are they similar? different?
   b. How do the system differences reflect differences in the product and process technologies?
   c. How do various common system elements, such as aggregate planning, vary in importance between the two types of systems?
3. Refer to Table 11–3.
   a. Project work loads on the machine centers using finite loading techniques assuming the following changes in the number of units being produced:

Job number	Number of units
1	100
2	50
3	25

   b. What if any action does this projection imply?
   c. Assuming the same changes in job quantities as in 3(a), what would a critical ratio scheduling rule indicate the priorities were? Project capacity utilization for the machine centers by loading to infinite capacity.
   d. What if any action does the capacity projection in 3(c) imply?
4. What are the strengths and weaknesses of finite versus infinite loading systems for job shops?
   a. How does one choose between the two alternatives?
   b. When are mixed systems appropriate?

SELECTED BIBLIOGRAPHY

1. Bedworth, D. D. "Discrete Part Manufacturing Control by Digital Computer," *Journal of Industrial Engineering*, vol. 18, no. 2 (February 1967).

2. Berry, W. L. "Labor Assignments in Job Shops: An Application of Work Flow Analysis." Unpublished doctoral dissertation, Harvard Business School, 1968.

3. Bulkin, M. H.; Colley, J. L.; and Steinhoff, H. W., Jr. "Load Forecasting, Priority Sequencing, and Simulation in a Job Shop Control System," in E. S. Buffa, ed., *Readings in Production and Operations Management*, chap. 11. New York: John Wiley & Sons, Inc., 1966. Also published in similar form in *Management Science*, vol. 13, no. 2 (October 1966), pp. 29–51.

4. *Capacity Planning and Operations Sequencing System-Extended (CAPOSS-E)*; General Information Manual, IBM Corporation, April 1977.

5. Carlson, J. G. "How Management Can Use the Improvement Phenomenon," *California Management Review*, vol. 3, no. 2 (Winter 1961). Reprinted as Chap. 32 in E. S. Buffa, ed., *Readings in Production and Operations Management*. New York: John Wiley & Sons, Inc., 1966.

6. Davis, E. W., and Lake, W. J. B. "Markem Corporation (B)" ICH No. 9-673-002, 1972.

7. Elmaghraby, S. E., and Cole, R. T. "On the Control of Production in Small Job Shops," *Journal of Industrial Engineering*, vol. 14, no. 4 (July–August 1963), pp. 186–96.

8. Emery, J. "Approach to Job Shop Scheduling Using a Large-Scale Computer," *Industrial Management Review*, vol. 3 (Fall 1961), pp. 78–96.

9. Ferguson, R. L., and Jones, C. H. "A Computer Aided Decision System," *Management Science*, vol. 15, no. 10 (June 1969), pp. 550–61.

10. Godin, V., and Jones, C. H. "The Interactive Shop Supervisor," *Industrial Engineering*, November 1969, pp. 16–22.

11. Holstein, W. K. "Production Planning and Control Integrated," *Harvard Business Review*, May–June 1968.

12. Holstein, W. K., and Berry, W. L. "Work Flow Structure: An Analysis for Planning and Control," *Management Science*, vol. 16, no. 6 (February 1970), pp. 324–36.

13. Jones, C. H.; Hughes, J. L.; and Engvold, K. J. "A Comparative Study of Computer Aided Decision Making from Display and Typewriter Terminals," IBM Technical Report TR 00.1891, Poughkeepsie Lab, June 1969.

14. Kusnick, A. A. "Management and Engineering Information Systems," *Industrial Management Review*, Spring 1966, pp. 3–16.

15. LeGrande, E. "The Development of a Factory Simulation System Using Actual Operating Data," *Management Technology*, vol. 3, no. 1 (May 1963). Also reprinted as Chap. 9 in E. S. Buffa, ed., *Readings in Production and Operations Management*. New York: John Wiley & Sons, Inc., 1966.

16. Moodie, C. L., and Novotny, D. J. "Computer Scheduling and Control Systems for Discrete Part Production," *Journal of Industrial Engineering*, vol. 19, no. 7 (July 1968), pp. 336–41.

17. Nelson, R. T. "Labor and Machine Limited Production Systems," *Management Science*, vol. 13, no. 9 (May 1967), pp. 648–71.

18. O'Malley, R. L.; Elmaghraby, S. E.; and Jeske, J. W. Jr. "An Operational System for Smoothing Batch-Type Production," *Management Science*, vol. 12, no. 10 (June 1966), pp. 433–49.

19. Parkinson, G. "Simplified Computer Control—The Mechanics of the New Production Control System," *Factory*, October 1966.

20. Reiter, S. "A System for Managing Job shop Production," *Journal of Business*, vol. 34, no. 3 (July 1966), pp. 371–93.

21. Schussel, G. "Workload Balancing and Inventory Minimization for Job Shops," *Journal of Industrial Engineering*, vol. 19, no. 4 (April 1968), pp. 194–202.

22. Steinhoff, H. W., Jr. "Daily System for Sequencing Orders in a Large-Scale Job Shop," in E. S. Buffa, ed., *Readings in Production and Operations Management*, Chap. 9. New York: John Wiley & Sons, Inc., 1966.

23. Thomas, E. D., and Covaleski, D. P. "Planning Nuclear Equipment Manufacturing," *Interfaces*, vol. 3, no. 3 (1973), pp. 18–29.

24. Wight, O. W. *Production and Inventory Management in the Computer Age*. Boston: Cahners Books, 1974.

CASE STUDY
GRANGER TRANSMISSION (A)

IN EARLY 1974, concern about the increasing requirements for working capital, and the increase in the number of late deliveries was building at Granger Transmission. Expressions of this concern were most often directed toward Jim Tillich, vice president of materials management.

Tillich, a veteran of 18 years of experience in the company, had previously held positions as foreman, engineer, supervisor, plant manager, and materials manager after having received an MBA from a well-known eastern business school. His response to these concerns about inventory turnover and missed deliveries is summed up in the following quote:

We're living through hell!

We call a forging company where we have had an order on the books for two years that's supposed to be delivered in March and say—how's it look? The guy on the other end says, "how the hell do I know. I haven't even had an acknowledgment from the steel mill on the order I placed for the steel that goes into your order." Then, he calls you back after calling the steel mill and says it doesn't look like March, it looks like August.

Now, that order for forgings may be necessary to complete the assembly of maybe 200 orders that we have promised to deliver to our customers in June and July.

We've got the same situation on ball bearings where order lead times are 101 weeks and on foundry castings where lead times are 99 weeks. Even little things, like cotter pins, must be ordered a year in advance.

At the same time, we get over 100 requests each day to change the delivery dates on our customers' orders, most of them requests for early deliveries. Since our average product has over 200 parts, that means up to 20,000

Exhibit A-1
Delivery performance

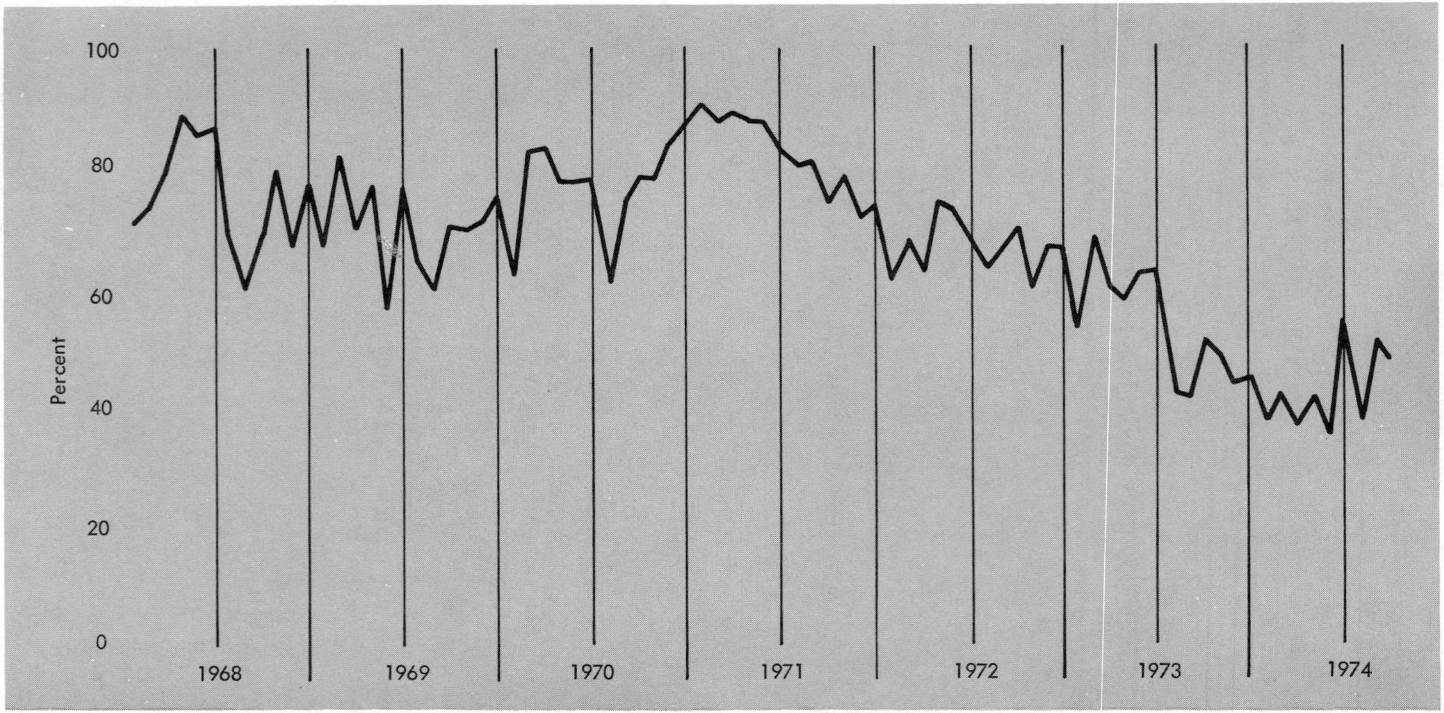

Note: Percent of deliveries made on time = $\dfrac{\text{Shipments}}{\text{Past due orders} + \text{Shipments}}$.

Source: Company files.

part schedule changes each day, if we agree to the change, and that's getting rare. Is it any wonder that our delivery performance doesn't look so hot? [see Exhibit A–1.]

As for inventory turnover, well, we're not a retail grocer. That's for sure. But our domestic inventories turn almost three times a year, and that's not bad for our kind of business. You can see that when you compare our inventory performance against that of companies with similarly complex operations, although I really believe that none is as complex as ours. You see, in a job shop operation you need in-process inventory out your ears to keep loads balanced from machine center to machine center. Whenever our turnover gets over three, we have severe problems. We become very inefficient and sporadic, productivity goes down, and the number of missed deliveries goes up.

Company background

Granger Transmission Company was a multinational producer and marketer of small-volume, heavy-duty transmissions for use in extractive industrial, marine, and construction equipment. Although founded as an independent firm, the company was acquired in 1935 by a large heavy equipment manufacturer. It has been operated as an independent subsidiary since that time.

Granger Transmission's products were designed to customer specifications, and produced in small lots. The price of these products ranged from several hundred dollars to over $10,000 per unit. Sales of over $93 million in fiscal 1974 represented a 20 percent increase in sales over 1973. One third of the sales of Granger Transmission were to the parent company, another one third to three other large OEM manufacturers, and the balance to numerous smaller accounts. It was estimated that 90 percent of the customers of Granger Transmission accounted for 10 percent of the total volume. Approximately two thirds of all sales were manufactured in the company's domestic facilities.

The product line was divided into eight basic categories of assembled transmissions and clutches. An additional category of products was comprised of spare parts, which accounted for about 30 percent of the company's total dollar volume. The eight categories of assembled products were classified by function and in no way implied that the products in each line were standardized. Each product was assembled to customer order and specification. About 50 percent of the orders used some standard components and subassemblies, however.

Demand for these components could be produced before an actual order was received for an assembly that used them.

Granger Transmission competed largely on the basis of being able to offer high-quality, highly engineered special purpose products. In the words of John Bonhoeffer, president of the firm, "Our products are the result of a total systems engineering approach whether they are sold as an individual component or part of an integrated transmission package. We have the capability to design and manufacture a complete driveline from the engine to the wheels. Our engineers work closely with customers in new product development, and extensive use is made of our multimillion dollar research and testing facility."

In addition to quality and engineering excellence, however, customers also expected other things of the company. A recent experience with a major account highlighted these factors.

We've had four due date changes from one of our good customers for the same order in the last two weeks. They beat on us to stay flexible and to be able to react to these changes, but if we deliver two weeks early, they return the goods. If we're one week late, their assembly line shuts down. For the last year or so, demand has been very strong. With the materials shortage situation that means that we're telling our customers *when they can have* our products rather than them telling us when they want them. We're not very popular with some of our customers anymore.

Manufacturing

Granger Transmission's domestic manufacturing facilities were concentrated in two plants about 90 miles apart in central Ohio. The largest plant complex was at Dayton. The smaller plant at Columbus had a similar layout and produced the same products. About two thirds of the productive floor space in the Dayton plan was devoted to a general-purpose machine shop. Parts and components were finished and fabricated here from bar stock, castings, and forgings.[1]

The machine shop was composed of about 320 different machine centers, where general-purpose equipment was used to perform specific operations, such as boring, grinding, heat treating, and turning. The typical part traveled through 10 to 15 of these machine

---

[1] About 75 percent of purchased materials cost was for completed parts and components purchased from outside vendors. The balance of materials cost was for raw materials (bar stock, and so on) which was processed through the machine shop to make parts.

centers as it was being fabricated. When a part reached a particular machine center, the machine operator first set up the machine so that it would work the part according to specifications. The operator stayed with the machine while it was running.

Company reports indicated that the capacity of the machine shop was used in the following way: setup time—22 percent; run time—52 percent; and miscellaneous indirect labor activities (including material handling, getting tools,)—26 percent. The numbers of parts which were worked on together in a batch (the lot size) was determined by the Production Control Department. They used their judgment in setting these lot sizes. Frequently, the lot size was determined by the lot size used to obtain the raw material from which the part was made. Thus, if a semifinished part was purchased in lots of 100 because this was the "minimum buy," or because 100 qualified the company for a quantity discount, the size of the lots put into the machine shop for finishing the part was also 100.

Part production in the machine shop typically took a substantial amount of time, averaging about 16 weeks in process. The exact amount of time depended upon the priority of the item (how badly it was needed), the number and type of operations to be performed on it, and the lot size. For instance, part 203149A had an average usage of 1,000 pieces per month. If the lot size was maintained at the current level of 1,000 (one setup per month), the standard time to process it through the machine shop was 72 days, including 12 days to move the part from machine center to machine center. Lots of 2,000 pieces, on the other hand, would require a standard time of 110 days to process from bar stock to finished parts. If the part was urgently needed, however, it could be fabricated in 15 days by hand carrying it through the shop, and breaking setups on machines where other parts are being manufactured. Such rush jobs were avoided if possible because of their disruptive effect on the shop and the consequent losses of productivity. Sometimes, rush jobs were subcontracted instead. On balance, though, subcontracting was kept to a minimum because of the additional expense involved, and because there was difficulty in getting subcontractors to meet Granger's quality standards.

The other one third of productive floor space in the Dayton plant was devoted to assembly and testing. The typical product was hand-assembled in a stationary location from about 200 parts and components. As many as 20 or 30 different products were being assembled at any one time. The average time to complete the assembly of one product was about two days. However, the demand for any one product was very small. For example, one of Granger's big sellers was one type of special clutch for oil well drilling rigs. They produced and sold about 200 per year.

In addition to productive floor space, about one half of the total floor space was used for inventory storage.[2] There was a storage area for raw materials which were used to produce parts in the machine shop. In early 1974, the value of this inventory in the Dayton plant was $700,000. There was also a storage area for finished parts which separated the machine shop from the assembly area. This inventory ($8.5 million worth) was comprised of finished parts for use in assembly which were obtained both from the machine shop (about one third of the total number of parts) and from outside vendors. The last storage area was for finished assemblies waiting for shipment. The total value of this inventory in Dayton was $300,000. Included in the inventory value of these finished products was the total cost of purchased materials (about 40 percent), the value added by direct labor (20 percent), and factory overhead (40 percent). An additional inventory of $5.6 million was on the machine shop floor as in-process inventory. In May of 1974, about $5 million of the inventory in the Dayton plant was destined for use in orders which were already past due.

Through 1974, most of Granger Transmission's operations in both the fabrication and assembly areas were worked three shifts per day, for six or seven days each week.

Planning and control

Domestic planning and control activities were the responsibility of Bill Buber, materials manager. He supervised both the Production Control Department, the Purchasing Department, and with the head of Industrial Engineering, was responsible for determining and justifying capital expenditures to top management. Purchasing was centralized for domestic operations, and was operated with eight buyers, eight assistant buyers, a purchasing agent, and his assistant. The Production Control Department was composed of eight product planners, who worked closely with Marketing in determining when orders for the eight basic product lines would be scheduled, and for monitoring their progress. In addition, production schedules and

---

[2] Including space for work-in-process.

stock chasers were located at the manufacturing locations to release and control specific parts orders. The Stores Control group, which disbursed, received, and recorded inventory transactions, was also a part of Production Control.

Domestic production planning and control activities at Granger Transmission revolved around computerized Materials Requirements Planning and Shop Floor Control systems installed in 1964 and 1969, respectively. The materials requirements planning system depended on data maintained in two computer files, and on requirements inputs, to operate. The bill of materials file contained product structure data; i.e., a list of which parts went into which subassemblies, and which subassemblies went into which final products. The file was analogous to a recipe book in a kitchen in that given the quantity of final products to be produced, say ten omelets, a complete list of input components could be derived; e.g., 40 eggs, ten pounds of cheese, two pounds of bacon, 20 tablespoons of salt, and so on. Engineering had the responsibility for maintaining an accurate bill of materials for each product or part they designed.

The other computer data file was an inventory file. This file contained current (updated daily) information on each of the company's 60,000 parts, materials, subassemblies, and products. This information included on-hand balances, open purchase or shop orders, lead times, order quantities, safety stocks, unit costs, and so on. Many people provided information for this file: purchasing provided lead time and order quantity data; stores control recorded inventory transactions; accounting provided costs; and production control provided expected lead times for fabrication.

Purchasing obtained lead time data from the company's suppliers. Lead times for fabricating parts were constructed by adding together (1) the sum of the standard setup times for each of the machines in the shop that the part would be processed on; (2) the sum of the standard unit run times for the part on each machine times the number of parts in a batch; (3) the sum of the standard times for moving the lot of parts from machine center to machine center, the standards allowed one day for each move; and (4) the sum of the queue times for each machine center the lot of parts would be processed through. The expected queue time for each machine center was the anticipated length of time a lot of parts waited once it got to a machine center to be processed. Typically, the expected queue time was three times the sum of the standard setup and run times for a lot at each machine center.

Given the data in these two files, the planning of materials requirements was a straightforward operation. For example, a production planner might accept an order for five Model X transmissions for delivery in week 356 (using a numbered week calendar). The requirements and consequently the orders for all the parts that went into this product, could be determined by exploding from the bill of materials file and offsetting lead times and quantities obtained from the inventory file. Exhibit A–2 shows two of the exception report sheets which might be generated as a result of this process. The first is for a plate (A3773) that goes into this transmission, as well as many other models. This status report indicates that 115 of these parts are required in week 355. Thus, 110 parts will be needed for other products or for spare parts in addition to the five parts needed for the Model Xs. These are scheduled for completion in week 355 since the lead time to assemble the five transmissions is one week. The requirements can then be compared with scheduled receipts for orders already made, and projected on-hand balances to indicate when orders should be planned. For example, the projected on-hand balance here drops to -22 in week 355. Since the part has a shop lead time of four weeks, an order can be planned for week 350.

By referencing the bill of materials file, the planned orders for part A3773 can be projected as the future requirements for the materials that go into it. For example, part A3774 is purchased from an outside vendor whose lead time is currently six weeks. Here, the derived requirement for 22 part A3774s in week 350 triggers an order for 500 pieces (the order quantity) in week 343, after offsetting the lead time of six weeks.

Requirements for parts came from several sources other than from exploding the requirements for higher level parts, subassemblies, and assemblies. For high usage parts, for example, a forecast of part usage derived with another computer program was also used. Part A3773 again provides an example. Here, the forecast quantity is 36 units. This usage is subtracted from projected on-hand balances but is not shown as a requirement so that firm orders and forecast orders are not confused. The reason for forecasting requirements is so that Granger would be able to promise delivery faster than they would if they only used firm orders for delivery in future periods. This was particularly important for items used as spare parts as well as in assembly, since the company wished to be able to respond immediately to customer needs for many of these products.

Another kind of forecast was used for a few final products (most were not forecasted). These were called management stock orders,

Exhibit A-2. Material status report

and were orders issued in anticipation of the receipt of an order from a good customer. Because of the high risk involved in committing the company to these, they originated from the highest levels of the company after preliminary negotiations with the customer. Safety stocks were yet another kind of requirement. These were set by marketing service and/or production control using the NRN (nice round number) method. They were used to protect against stockouts on important service parts and for parts which had high scrap rates or unreliable delivery problems. Safety stocks and management stock orders accounted for about $1 million of total domestic inventories in 1974.

All of the daily materials status reports issued by the materials requirements system were reviewed by Bill Buber before he passed them on for action by Production Control or Purchasing. Essentially four kinds of action were indicated in these exception reports: order, cancel an order, reschedule an order, and expedite. Ordering was indicated whenever the planned on-hand balance fell to a negative value over the lead time. Order cancellations for parts were generated whenever requirements were reduced because of order cancellations for assembled components, or when new parts were designed to replace an order. Order rescheduling was indicated whenever there was a delay in expected requirements. For example, when a customer moved the order due date out into the future. Expediting indicated that an order needed to be processed faster than the standard lead time because an order due date had been moved up or parts had been scrapped in the shop. Sometimes, orders for good customers were accepted with promised delivery dates that were less than the standard lead time into the future. This would trigger an expedite order if the appropriate parts were not already in stock.

Other exception and control reports issued by the system were the Open Purchase Order Buyer Fail-Safe Report and the Order Acceptance Report. The Open Purchase Order Buyer Fail-Safe Report (Exhibit A–3) was issued weekly to the Purchasing Department, and sometimes sent on to the appropriate vendor. This report listed all open purchase orders, the quantity ordered, and the due date. In addition, it listed a fail-safe week which indicated the latest date that a fail-safe quantity (also indicated) could arrive before threatening to make an order for an upstream part or assembly late. Thus, if buyers anticipated problems in getting a complete order on time, they could try to negotiate with vendors for at least the delivery of the fail-safe quantity by the fail-safe week.

Exhibit A–3
Open Purchase Order Buyer Fail-Safe Report

02/05/71		OPEN P.O. BUYER FAIL-SAFE REPORT.		Dayton			WEEK – 343	
BUYER	VENDOR#	PART #	ORDER#	WEEK#	QTY.	FWEEK	FQTY.	CUT.
D	52487	# 9670A	791930	345	5	345	1	
D3	52487	# 9670B	819371	360	50			
D1	52487	# 9682	789410	344	50	338	19	
D1	52487	# 97008	808601	347	35	347	31	
D3	52487	# 9753A	819380	352	100			
D3	52487	# 9791A	789561	345	25	348	25	
D3	52487	# 9791A	810201	351	65	351	1	
D1	52487	# 9813	810211	354	50			
D3	52487	# 98158	788760	343	15			
D3	52487	# 9824	819390	350	25			
D3	52487	# 9825	793490	346	50	349	15	
D1	52487	# 9841	793730	345	50			
D3	52487	# 9870A	758611	347	50			
D1	52487	# 9957	810220	348	25			
D1	52487	# 201522	825880	352	1000			
D3	52487	# 203717A	822100	354	250			
D1	52487	# 205826	819330	349	100	349	38	
D3	52487	# 205896	826850	358	25			
D3	52487	# 205896L	825890	357	50			
D3	52487	# 206207	793770	348	200	346	108	
D1	52487	# 206331	791841	351	50	350	13	

Source: Company files.

The Order Acceptance Report (Exhibit A–4) was also issued weekly to the product planners, so that they could review the status of orders that had been accepted. This report indicated whether or not the delivery to a customer would have to be rescheduled for a later date. It also indicated the most critical (most past due) part or component that went into the product that was expected to be late. In most cases, the most critical part was the one which was going to make the entire order late. A late order was indicated whenever the standard lead time that remained to complete production and assembly of a part exceeded the time remaining until the order was due. The due date on all orders from Granger's customers had to be approved by the product planners before marketing could accept the order. Product planners could determine whether a due date was

Exhibit A–4
Order Acceptance Report

```
                    ORDER ACCEPTANCE REPORT                                    PAGE #    2

            CURRENT WEEK#  342- DATE OF RUN 01/25/71
```

ORDER NUMBER	CUST. NUMBER	WEEK# REQUIRED	WEEK# ALLOCATED	PART NUMBER	QUANTITY	RESCH.	MOST CRIT. PART NUMB.
28972C	0002	349	349	29965	5		
28972C	0002	353	353	29965	5		
28973C	0002	349	?49	6875	5		
28974C	0002	357	357	A 6914	5		
28974C	0002	362	362	A 6914	5		
28974C	0002	366	366	A 6914	10		
28974C	0002	370	370	A 6914	5		
28975C	0002	353	355	33586	17	YES	2815 K
28975C	0002	357	357	33586	25		
28975C	0002	362	362	33586	35		
28975C	0002	366	366	33586	35		
28975C	0002	370	370	33586	20		
28976C	0002	349	355	33591	1	YES	O 5499 E
28976C	0002	353	355	33591	5	YES	O 5499 E
28976C	0002	357	357	33591	15		
28976C	0002	362	362	33591	10		
28976C	0002	366	366	33591	15		
28976C	0002	370	370	33591	10		
28977C	0002	366	366	33593	10		
28978C	0002	353	355	33596	3	YES	OA 6070 F
28978C	0002	362	362	33596	5		
28978C	0002	370	370	33596	5		
28979C	0002	353	357	33594	5	YES	M 2780

Source: Company Files.

feasible by examining the standard lead times required to obtain the materials and components that went into the order on video consoles which had access to the computer files. Most of Granger's best customers placed orders six to nine months in advance of their needs. Other customers often requested shorter lead times, but were often given longer ones than they required.

Granger's shop floor control system was an important adjunct to the materials requirements planning system. It was used to maintain the relative priorities of the orders being processed by manufacturing. A key data file for this system was the routing file. It contained information on the sequence of manufacturing steps required to produce each part which Granger manufactured. When the materials requirements planning system released an order for the fabrication shop (which it would only do when all the materials required to produce the part were on hand or expected with some certainty) a computer program would print out a route sheet (Exhibit A–5) and a

Exhibit A–5
Route sheet

OPER NO	PART NUMBER		DESCRIPTION	PART NUMBER		WORK ORDER NO
000-1	.A..3773..	FLOATING PLATE		*A-3773*		*342 B 42*
	ROUTING DATE	MADE FROM/SPEC INSTRUCTIONS		QUANTITY *612*		
000-2	05/26/70	#A-3773		LOAD	OF	
	USED ON			LOAD QUANTITY		
	CL6					
	RANGE			VENDOR *Brillion*		
	50			HEAT NO		

OPER NO	PLANT DEPT CENTER	%.	HOURS/C	PIECES/HOUR	%.	DESCRIPTION	PIECES GOOD	SCRAP	CLOCK NO
010-0	1- 3-BH		1.25	40.0	X	TURN,FACE,BORE,CHAM & U.C.			
020-0	1- 3-HE		1.67	30.0	X	FACE TO LENGTH,CTBR & CHAM			
030-0	1- 3-J		.524	190.	X	BROACH TEETH			
040-0	1- 4-RW					WASH			
045-0	1- 3-FC		2.70	37.0	X	GRIND FRICTION SURFACE			
050-0	1- 6-EA		2.08	48.0	X	DRILL 24 HOLES			
060-0	1- 6-EA		1.20	83.0	X	DRILL FOUR HOLES			
070-0	1- 4-RW					WASH			
080-0	1-15-NB					INSPECT			

Source: Company files.

packet of reporting cards for that order. The route sheet showed the sequence of operations, by work center, for producing the part along with other data such as the standard time to produce it, and directions. The reporting cards (one for each operation/work center) were standard computer cards with some prepunched data which would be sent to data processing whenever an operation was completed at the appropriate work center.

The data acquired from this reporting system was used in several ways. First, shop foremen would receive a daily schedule (Exhibit A–6) listing all of the parts waiting for work at each work center, and their priorities. These priorities were based on a "critical ratio," which was the ratio of the time remaining (in days) before the job was

Exhibit A–6
Daily schedule

DATE 02/06/73			DAILY WORK CENTER JOB SCHEDULE			WEEK 446	DAY WEDNESDAY			
PLANT 03		DEPT 05		MACH.CTR. BH		SHIFTS WORKED 2.0		CAPACITY 110.9		
				-PRIORITY-		QTY	QTY	NEXT	WORK	TIME
PART #	PART NAME	ORDER#	OP#	OPER DESC	PO	PI	OF OP	AT OP	HOURS	LOCATION	REM.	REM.
					1	2					
209335H	IMP WHL	a 438C34	020	FIN	.436		142	142	11.1	0316NB	18.3	8.0
216140A	SPINNER	445C22	010	TURN	1.236		88	88	6.4	0305BQ	18.6	23.0
209308C	IMP WHL	445C67	020	FACE		.430	212	212	16.7	0316NB	18.5	8.0
A 4639A	CARRIER	445B45	010	TURN		2.675	54	54	5.4	**SAME**	8.5	23.0
A 4639A	CARRIER	445B45	020	FACE		2.675	54		5.4	0305YE	6.3	23.0
B 1640A	RETAINER	441B22	010	FACE		4.106	108	108	7.3	0305EG	10.4	43.0
TOTAL HOURS IN THIS MACHINE CENTER									52.3			
PARTS IN PREVIOUS WORK CENTER										PREVIOUS		
208346	IMP WHL	443C31	010	TURN	.437		27	27	4.7	0316NBR	18.2	8.0
203587E	FW PILOT	a 444C98	010	SEMI-TURN	.462		28	28	4.3	0316NBR	17.3	8.0
203346C	IMP WHL	446A09	010	TLRN	.742		250	250	15.4	0316NBR	24.2	18.0
208346A	IMP WHL	446A07	010	TURN	.907		1234	1234	62.2	0316NBR	36.3	33.0
209335H	IMP WHL	a 446A10	010	TURN	1.388		141	141	11.1	0316NBR	20.1	28.0
# B 5164	RETAINER	445C90	020	TURN		2.006	98	98	6.1	0305BQ	11.4	23.0
A 4639B	CARRIER	446B17	010	TURN		2.215	255	255	12.6	0316NBR	10.3	23.0
208457B	IMPELLER	444A44	010	TURN		3.632	10	10	4.1	0316NBR	10.4	38.0
208346C	IMP WHL	446A08	010	TURN		4.105	50	50	5.8	0316NBR	20.2	83.0
TOTAL HOURS FOR THIS MACHINE CENTER IN PREVIOUS CENTERS									126.3			

[1] PO = Priority for items for which firm customer orders existed.

[2] PI = Priority for items which were being made to forecast and which were not tied to specific customer orders (as yet).

Source: Company files.

scheduled to be completed, to the standard hours (including queue time) of work remaining on the part. Thus, an order with a low critical ratio (less than one) would probably be late, and should be processed first. Orders with high critical ratios (over one) were ahead of schedule, and not so critical. This report also indicated the parts which were at other work centers, which would go to this work center upon completion. This helped the shop foreman to schedule orders on his machines with some foresight.

In February of 1973, this report was a considerable source of agitation to Herb Hegel, a foremen for the gear manufacturing section of the Dayton plant, as he talked to the plant production controller on the phone.

Hey, you guys are causing me a lot of problems. You aren't keeping me supplied with work down here. I've only got 50 hours of work for the BH work center, and damn little coming in from feeder work centers this week. What are we supposed to do when we run out of work? Sit on our hands?

Exhibit A–7
Location list

PART #	PART NAME	W.O. #	OPER.	OPER DESC.	WORK CTR	QTY	P.O.	P.I.	COMP.
			030	WASH	1- 4-RW	1	7.750	7.750	344
			040	INSPECT	1-15-NB	1	9.073	9.073	345
.A..3771..	H&B PLT	342A95	020	TURN	1- 6-BC	35	1.412	.551	344
			050	FACE	1- 3-HE	35	1.578	.615	344
			060	FIN	1- 3-YB	35	1.721	.671	345
			075	CUT	1- 6-CRC	35	1.885	.735	346
			080	DRILL	1- 6-EA	35	2.410	.940	346
			090	FIN	1- 3-Y	35	2.742	1.070	347
			100	BROACH	1- 3-JA	35	3.213	1.254	347
			110	WASH	1- 4-RW	35	3.822	1.491	347
			120	DRILL	1- 3-IAA	35	4.180	1.631	348
			130	NUMBER	1- 3-Z	35	5.981	2.334	348
			140	DEBURR	1- 4-NB	35	7.018	2.738	348
			150	WASH	1- 4-RW	35	10.468	4.085	348
			160	INSPECT	1-15-NB	35	12.000	4.682	349
.A..3771A.	H&B PLT	342B43	020	TURN	1- 6-BC	20	99.999	1.506	344
			050	FACE	1- 3-HE	20	99.999	1.695	344
			060	FIN	1- 3-YB	20	99.999	1.859	345
			075	CUT	1- 6-CRC	20	99.999	2.051	346
			080	DRILL	1- 6-EA	20	99.999	2.567	346
			090	FIN	1- 3-Y	20	99.999	2.946	347
			100	BROACH	1- 3-JA	20	99.999	3.703	347
			110	WASH	1- 4-RW	20	99.999	4.532	347
			120	DRILL	1- 3-IAA	20	99.999	5.043	348
			130	NUMBER	1- 3-Z	20	99.999	7.909	348
			140	DEBURR	1- 4-NB	20	99.999	9.830	348
			150	WASH	1- 4-RW	20	99.999	15.870	348
			160	INSPECT	1-15-NB	20	99.999	19.680	349
.A..3773..	FLTPLT	342B42	010	TURN	1- 3-BH	612	1.436	1.236	344
			020	FACE	1- 3-HE	612	1.722	1.482	345
			030	BROACH	1- 3-J	612	2.034	1.752	346
			040	WASH	1- 4-RW	612	2.566	2.210	346
			045	GRIND	1- 3-FC	612	2.678	2.306	347
			050	DRILL	1- 6-EA	612	4.087	3.519	347
			060	DRILL	1- 6-EA	612	7.284	6.273	348
			070	WASH	1- 4-RW	612	9.000	7.750	348
			080	INSPECT	1-15-NB	612	10.536	9.073	348
.A..3774B.	H&B PLT	340B64	130	NUMBER	1- 3-Z	104	7.840	6.884	344
			140	DEBURR	1- 4-NB	104	9.742	8.554	344
			150	WASH	1- 4-RW	104	15.870	13.935	344
			160	INSPECT	1-15-NB	104	19.680	17.280	344

DATE 02/04/71   LOCATION LIST   WK # 343   FRIDAY

Other reports generated by the shop floor control and reporting system were the daily location list (Exhibit A–7) which showed the present and anticipated location of released orders. The long-range machine load report (Exhibit A–8) projected the total hours of work at each machine center by forecasting both actual (orders already in the shop) and planned (unreleased) orders. Since Granger released orders as if they had "infinite capacity" in the shop, this report could be used to see where overtime, additional shifts, or machinery should be added for future business. In commenting on this report, Bill Buber said,

Exhibit A–8
Long-range machine load report

DATE 01/14/71		LONG RANGE MACHINE LOAD		WEEK 339	
PLANT 01	DEPT.# 03		MACH.CENTER 8H	CAPACITY	504.0
PERIOD		PLANNED	ACTUAL	TOTAL	
339 TO 342		186.9	363.5	550.4	
343 TO 346		386.3	.0	386.3	
347 TO 350		620.4	.0	620.4	
351 TO 354		794.9	.0	794.9	
355 TO 358		662.5	.0	662.5	
359 TO 362		622.7	.0	622.7	
363 TO 366		622.2	.0	622.2	
367 TO 370		627.0	.0	627.0	
371 TO 374		637.0	.0	637.0	
375 TO 378		627.4	.0	627.4	
379 TO 382		626.5	.0	626.5	
383 TO 386		639.3	.0	639.3	
387 TO 390		633.5	.0	633.5	

This report is losing its usefulness. For one thing, machine tools now have lead times far in excess of the time period spanned by this report, so it's not much good for telling us when to add capacity, except after the fact. We've tried to use it to reschedule orders, too (delay delivery to a customer to free up capacity). But, we just seem to succeed in causing bottlenecks at other work centers, or collosal underloads develop.

May 1974

TILLICH: I don't know how we're going to do it! Bonhoeffer wants me to commit to a goal of an inventory turnover of 3½ for the next year's plan, and four for the year after. I know that the capital crunch is hitting us, but I just don't think it's possible for us to do it in this kind of business.

BUBER: Well, we've got the extended materials planning program working pretty well at the Arco Foundry.[3] If we can extend that to our other long

---

[3] *Extended materials planning* was the name of the program Granger was presenting to its vendors which had very long lead times. With it, the company would commit to buying a certain amount of the vendor's capacity each year, rather than placing individual orders for specific products one to two years in advance of when they would be

Exhibit A–9

B111-159				INVENTORY TURNOVER EXCEPTION REPORT						PAGE---152			

ONHAND WILL BE REDUCED BY 050% OF SAFETY STOCK.
LOOKING FOR LESS THAN 1.0 TURNS.
FIRST 12 MONTHS OF ORDERS USED.

PROD. CODE	PART NUMBER	ONHAND QTY.	SAFETY STOCK	SCHED. REC.	TOTAL AVAIL.	ORDERS 1ST 12	ORDERS 2ND 12	TURN OVER	STANDARD COST OF EXCESS IN DOLLARS LABOR	MATERIAL	BURDEN	PRODUCTION YTD.	PYTD.	SERVICE YTD.	PYTD.
08265	..212743..	1						.0		21					
08265	..213754..	4			4	3	3	.7		21		2	5		
08265	..213354..	1			1	3	3	1.0					5		
08265	..225270..	5			5	3	3	.6	7	25	2		5		
08265	..225-79..	5			5	3	3	1.0					5		
08265	..228359..	6			6	3	3	.5	48	142	15		5		
08265	.A..242541.	13			13	13	13	1.0					20		
08265	.A..2916FV	100			100	12	12	.1		10			20		
08265	A-2200 SER.								55	325	21				
08280	..204952..	87	5		84	27		.3		25		21	6		
08280	..204952A.	90	5		87	27		.3		32		21	6		
08280	..204952B.	87	5		84	27		.3		56		21	6		
08280	..212710..	78			78	27		.3		150		17	16		
08280	..213660..	118	20		118	27		.3		157		31	6		
08280	..213668A.	121	20		111	27		.2		120		21	5		
08280	..213668B.	120	20		110	27		.2		145		21	5		
08280	..213671..	47			47	9		.1	121	266	76	5	6		
08280	..213673..	53			53	9		.1		485		7	3		
08280	..213688..	45	10		40	15		.4		5		10	12		
08280	..213702..	21			21	9		.4		342		7	2		
08280	..213718..	23			22	9		.4		425		7	2		
08280	..225184..	18			18	6		.5	71	85	80	7	2		
08280	..225186..	33			33	9		.2	155	144	64	7	3		
08280	..225187..	61			61	9		.2	216	191	55	7	3		
08280	..225214..	11			11	9		.8	11	11	3	5	6		
08280	..225221..	15		7	12	9		.7	40	68	13	7	2		
08280	..225237..	5		19	24	9		.3	56	50	25	5	2		
08280	..225243..	4			4	9		1.0				5	4		
08280	..225245..	1		18	19	9		.4	234	167	177	5	10		
08280	..220093B.	18			18	6		.5	60	66	66	7	2		
08280	..228130A.	26			26	10		.3	50	313	28	7			
08280	..228161..	7		15	22	9		.4	1258	2234	1451	7	3		
08280	..228162..	17		9	16	9		.5	609	1235	644	7	3		
08280	..228355A.	7			10	9		.9	7	20	5	7	2		
08280	.A..2669F8	68			68	13	3	.1		220		10	3		
08280	.M..1945V.	17			17	9		.5		22		7	3		
08280	.P..2007AG	700			700	171		.2		215		133	38	2	2
08280	.P..2032BA	12			12					33			2		
08280	.M..2051BP	15			15			.0		8			25		
08280	.M..2451DC	44			44	16		.4	15	1	5	10	12		
08280	.M..2071F.	100			100	22		.2		122		17	14		
08280	.M..2483AS	87			87	36		.4		22		34	14		
08280	.MA..251..	14			14			.0		1			5		
08280	.MA..379A8	22			22	9		.4		37		8	8		

Note: Turnover is defined here as the ratio of the number of parts for which there are firm orders for delivery in the next twelve months, divided by the number of parts currently available in inventory (excluding safety stocks.)

lead time vendors that might help some. Maybe that with some more fine tuning on our production planning system we'll get turnover up some. One thing I can do for sure is to review that list of items with turnovers of less than one that we got from accounting. (Exhibit A–9)

TILLICH: I doubt if those things will give us anywhere near as much help as we need though, Bill. For one thing, we're running into a lot of vendors who don't want anything to do with extended materials planning. I think it helps them as much if not more than us, but they can't conceive of running a business without a fat order backlog behind them. As for the system, I don't know. Maybe it's time we started out with a fresh sheet of paper instead of just adding more Band-Aids and patches here and there. But I can't conceive of a better basic system than the one we've got. Sure, our performance doesn't look so hot, but without the system we'd really be in trouble. I think that we'll have to do something drastic than fine tuning to get inventories down.

needed. Since vendors usually didn't enter these orders into production until a month or so before the due date, Granger could enter its orders a month or two in advance of their needs once they had reserved the capacity. They applied this concept of the Arco Foundry by treating the portion of Arco's capacity committed to them as their own in the Materials Requirements Planning System.

CASE STUDY
GRANGER TRANSMISSION (B)

IN SEPTEMBER 1974 Bill Buber, materials manager for Granger Transmission, was describing the new master scheduling and resource planning methods he and his staff had developed for domestic operations.

In early 1974 we felt that we had just run out of capacity in this company. Even the new 40,000 square foot addition to our Dayton plant and all the new machine tools we bought didn't help. We went through a lot of grief in terms of late orders and a lot of scrambling around until it became apparent to us that we needed a master schedule that reflected capacity—because that was our constraint. But then the question was how to do it. We had several consultants in to advise us, and they were helpful to some degree, but we just couldn't do things the way other companies could because our product line is so unstable.

So then we got the idea of going back to the Sales Department and saying, "What do you want us to make? What do you want us to sell? Give us a product mix!" Because the availability of capacity is going to be based on a product mix.

I got marketing to give me a listing that gave me product specifications for groups of essentially similar products. Like, for example, a marine gear that is in the 50-horsepower range but maybe has ten different types of products where the only difference is in gear ratios. Once I got these groups identified we had the basis for forecasting product families, and subsequent demands on capacity (Exhibit B–1). This was helpful because we could forecast for large groups of products better than for individual ones, and because the machining requirements for the individual products in a family were essentially the same. Now we glossed over a lot of the very specific options that might make a product different from the rest in the family. These would be important if we were trying to make plans for specific materials. But, we could ignore them because what we were really after was a fix on long-range capacity requirements.

Exhibit B–1
Product line forecast

Product line	FY 1974–75 forecast*
A	200
B	300
C	150
D	50
E	125
F	100
G	15
H	10
I	5

* Product family units shipped per month.

We developed a "bill of capacity" for each of these product families with engineering. It told us how many machine-hours were required at each machine center to produce one unit from each product family. Then, marketing made an annual forecast of shipments by month for each of these product families. With this data, we were in a position to do some meaningful planning.

Resource profiles

The marketing forecast of product family shipments was used by Bill Buber and his staff to develop a resource profile for the year. To accomplish this, they first gathered data on capacities by determining the average actual *output* (in hours of work per week) for each of the machine centers in the Dayton plant. Then, using the "bill of capacity," and marketing's product family forecast for each of the nine product lines (A–I), total resource requirements in terms of both labor and machines could be exploded. Exhibit B–2 illustrates the net result of this planning method, a resource profile where the hourly requirements for each product line at each machine center has been converted to a percent of presently available capacity.

The resource profile made it apparent that the total plant was not out of capacity, but that certain work centers through which almost all of the product lines flowed, formed major bottlenecks. For example, the CJ-Barber Coleman Hobber would have to run at 180 percent of capacity to meet fiscal year 1974–75 requirements. Such overloads at bottleneck work centers were relieved by one of two methods. In some cases, additional shifts or half shifts were planned to increase capacity. Half shifts could be added by working weekends or by having workers work on four-hour shifts. In others, where the machine

Exhibit B–2
Resource profile

FY /15

CENTER	TYPE	QUANTITY	# OF SHIFTS	CAPACITY hrs/wk	A	B	C	D	E	F	G	H	I	TOTAL %	REMARKS
05-05															
BD	2AC CHUCKER	4	3	1561	22	22	16	3	8	11	11	2		95	
BR	3AC WARNER & SWASEY	8	3	2966	3	16	46	1	13	2	1	2	-	84	
CA	REISHAUER GEAR GRINDER	2	3	900		38			22	-	12			72	
CAB	REISHAUER GEAR GRINDER	2	3	950		10	43		13	2			1	69	
CD	P. & W. GEAR GRINDER	1	3	544		59			4					63	
CEA	MAAG GEAR GRINDER	4	3	3044		10	76		14	5		8		113	OFF LOAD TO CAB 3:1 RATIO
CO	P. & W. GEAR GRINDER	4	3	1190			120		8					128	OFF LOAD TO CA, CD
CI	PFAUTER HOBBER	5	3	2374	6	22	41		9	2	4		2	86	
CJ	BARBER COLMAN HOBBER	1	3	620	27	39	50	1	29	25		8	1	180	OFF LOAD TO CI, CW
CN	GEAR SHAVER	3	2.5	700	14	37	15		8	9	4			87	
CQ	GEAR POINTER	1	1	22	13	56	-		12	3				84	
CS	FELLOWS SHAPER	1	3	549		37			8	-				45	
CW	BARBER COLMAN HOBBER	3	3	1530	7	12	26	2	8	9	6			70	
CX	BARBER COLMAN SHAPER	1	3	546	-	38	25	7	6	2	24			102	OFF LOAD TO CS
CY	FELLOWS SHAPER	1	3	514	15	77	17		10	12			2	133	OFF LOAD TO CS
FD	INTERNAL GRINDER	1	3	285	8	8	10	5	8	4	6			49	RELIEVE FI
FI	INTERNAL GRINDER	1	3	275	25	59	32	11	25	10	9			171	MOVE MACHINE FROM PLT2
FJ	SURFACE GRINDER	1	1	328	6	44	20	1	11	14				93	
FM	VERTICAL INTERNAL GRIND.	1	2	368		38	57	1	16	1		3		116	ADD ½ SHIFT
FY	GEAR HONE	2	2	528	19	28	11		12	9	5			84	
H	ENGINE LATHE	1	3	427	26	42	29	-	15	8	6		-	126	OFF LOAD TO HES
HES	W. & S. LATHE-SPECIAL	2	2	234	5	43	18		11	12				89	ADD 1 SHIFT
JA	HORIZONTAL BROACH	1	1	90	14	3	53	2	12	3				87	
NH	GEAR CHAMFER	1	3	337	18	42	10		12	11	5			98	
~	MARMAFLEX	1	1	240	3	35	48		12	2	2		-	102	ADD ½ SHIFT

was fully utilized around the clock, the excess load was relieved by off-loading some of the work to other machine centers which could also perform the work, although perhaps not as efficiently. In one instance, a second machine was added. By making a number of these changes, the resource profile was adjusted so that the capacity of the plant both in terms of labor and equipment, matched forecast shipment requirements (see the remarks in Exhibit B–2).

Master scheduling

Once the resource profile had been adjusted to reflect the anticipated product mix in the coming year, the problem became one of accepting orders and promising due dates in such a way that promises did not exceed the company's ability to fulfill them. This was accomplished with a master schedule.

The master schedule (Exhibit B–3) indicated the capacity allocated to each product line in accordance with the resource profile. Capacity here was expressed in product family units. Thus, for example, an output of 200 "family units" of product line A could be produced in each month. The master schedule also indicated the firm orders that the company currently had in hand for future delivery. By keeping track of these and new firm orders as time progressed, the production planners could see how much of the capacity allocated to a particular line was being sold. Thus, they had two checks for reasonableness that they could make before agreeing to a promise date for a customer order. The first check was the master schedule. If the orders already in hand exceeded the capacity, then no other orders could be accepted, unless the due date on existing orders was moved out. For instance, if a customer requested delivery of 100 units of product line A in June of 1975, the product planner could readily see

Exhibit B–3
Master schedule

Customer / Master number	Model Spec	CAP	Past Due	JAN 1975	FEB	MAR	APRIL	MAY	JUNE	JULY	AUG	SEPT	OCT	NOV	DEC	JAN 1976	FEB	MAR	APRIL	MAY	JUNE	JULY	AUG	SEP
A		200		200	200	198	200	200	150	125	145	50	15	10	10			15		50				
B		300		300	300	295	290	290	290	275	240	190	125	37	90	82	75	62		40				
C		150		150	150	150	135	120	120	110	95	60	35	18	11		10		5					
D		50		50	45	45	50	50	40	38	30	25	15	9	9		5			5				
E		125		125	125	125	125	125	120	115	115	110	90	83	77	70	50	20		5				
F		100		100	100	100	98	98	95	95	88	75	75	70	70	69	50		25		10			

that Granger would have problems in meeting such a request. As an alternative, 50 units in June and the balance in July might suffice.

The second check the production planner could make for due date reasonableness, after establishing whether or not sufficient capacity existed, was whether the appropriate materials could be acquired in time. This was done by querying the bill of materials and inventory files on the video display unit. If the inventory of parts was insufficient to fill the order, and the lead time to acquire them longer than the time remaining until the proposed due date, the due date would have to be negotiated. This latter type of check on due date reasonableness had existed at Granger for some time.

In commenting on the new procedures for resource planning and master scheduling, Bill Buber said:

> I think master scheduling will be a real help in keeping us out of trouble. But now that we've committed to this approach it's raised a lot of questions that I'm not sure how to answer.
>
> For instance, what happens when we're all booked up in a month and a good customer who has placed an order for a later period wants to move delivery into that month? By the same token, what happens if a customer wants to change the due date to a later period? Or, what if a critical part for an order will be late? Should we try to reschedule the due date for the whole order? You know, some of our customers play the same games with us that we play with our vendors. On long lead time items that we can't forecast well on, we'll order twice as much as we'll need earlier than we need it so that we can be assured of a place in line at their factory. Then, when we finally get close enough to figure out what we need we cancel orders and move due dates around. How do we handle these situations in master scheduling?
>
> Perhaps the biggest question I have now though is how do we handle changes in product mix. The original marketing forecast was for 200 per month for product family A and 300 per month for family B. But family A products are sold mainly to the construction equipment industry which is doing much worse than expected this year. We'll probably only sell 50 per month. But, B-type products are sold to the oil rig equipment industry which is doing much better. They might demand as much as 400 units per month instead of 300. Should we go back and change our resource profile to reflect these possible changes in mix?
>
> I guess what I'm really asking is how do we manage the master schedule?

CASE STUDY
GRANGER TRANSMISSION (C)

MEMORANDUM TO: Mr. J. Bonhoeffer
FROM: Mr. J. Tillich
SUBJECT: Inventory Turn
DATE: December 4, 1974

I firmly believe that an inventory turn for Granger between 3½ and 4 per year is a possibility. However, to achieve such a turn, Granger will be required to make some rather major changes in its method of doing business and its relationships with its customers. Therefore, I think the most thoroughly possible exploration of the problem needs to be made, and a specific program, if it is deemed desirable, be implemented.

I think, first, we should examine closely where we are in our inventory turn at the present time. I have attached, as Exhibit C–1, the relevant inventory turn figures for Granger's various divisions in the year ended June 30, 1974. You will note, with the exception of Granger–Dayton, all of our divisions have inventory turns of approximately two per year. Our overseas divisions do not have the tools at the present time to establish materially better inventory turns than they presently have. Granger–Columbus has got the same tools to manage its inventory which Dayton does, and should be expected to turn its inventory approximately the same number of times per year. I base this statement on the consulting study of a few years ago, which indicated that the product lines and improvements were roughly comparable. I feel that substantial improvements in the Columbus inventory situation are under way, and I further feel the inventory turn rate in Columbus will show substantial improvement in the course of this fiscal year.

Exhibit C–1
1974 inventory turn for Granger

Granger–Dayton	2.73
Granger–Columbus	2.09
Granger–Belgium	2.08
Granger–Australia	2.06
Granger–Great Britain	1.96

The goal for the rest of the company, therefore, could very well be expressed as the need to equal the results already being achieved by Dayton. We, therefore, should examine Dayton's inventory turn in relationship to other companies of similar complexity. I have attached as Exhibit C-2, a list of roughly similar companies and the inventory turn achieved in 1974 by these companies. You will note that the Dayton Division ranks higher than Clark and lower than International Harvester, about at the middle of the list.

Exhibit C–2
1974 inventory turn for selected other companies

Dana	3.8
Modine	3.6
Cummins	3.5
Borg Warner	3.3
Cat	3.1
A.C.	2.9
Emerson Electric	2.8
IH	2.8
Clark	2.5
Rexnord	2.5
Warner Electric Brake & Clutch	2.2
Koehring	2.1
Sunstrand	1.7
Gardner Denver	1.6
Giddings & Lewis	1.5
Snap-On Tools	1.3

Since it is pretty generally acknowledged, by people who know, that Granger has an extremely difficult inventory management problem (we are trying to maintain an inventory effectiveness on more part numbers than is Detroit Diesel, Allison), I do not think that it is appropriate or accurate to say that inferior results are being obtained. Certainly an inventory turn of 3.0 times per year would rank Granger among the most effective companies in this measurement in American industry. I think you will agree that none of the companies, which have inventory turns substantially more than three, are really directly comparable to our company.

Therefore, it logically follows that a program, which will produce more than 3½ and perhaps 4 inventory turns per year, must entail features that are not commonly accepted American business practice.

To achieve a high inventory turn in our company, therefore, it is my opinion we need a four-point program. These four points are:

1. A conservative, realistic master schedule.
2. A policy of periodically rolling the order board.
3. A policy to purchase more parts and make fewer.
4. A reduction of the number of products manufactured.

The first two of these are the more important of the four. At the present time, we are carrying, between Dayton and Columbus, approximately an $8 million past due. This past due must have in it an inventory content of approximately $5 million. Therefore, it will be possible to reduce Granger's inventory by $5 million by elimination of the past due. A master production schedule that is kept at something less than the theoretical capacity of the plant to produce will help to reduce the past due. I would suggest that a master production schedule of approximately 95 percent of theoretical capacity would be nearly the correct one for maximum inventory turn. This would provide the flexibility to make up almost any lost time inasmuch as we hadn't scheduled our entire capacity. Therefore, any vendor delivery slowdowns could be made up and any scrap, rework or machine break- downs could be compensated for. This would be the major step in keeping the past due at a low figure. It is much more important than control of the inventory on any single part number because it controls the inventory of the many part numbers which go to make up an assembly. There is a multiply- ing effect of past due which does not exist for individual part numbers.

Rolling of the order board will contribute the other part of keeping the past due at zero. When some set of circumstances has been reached wherein there is no possible way that recovery can be made from a past due situation, the order board must be rolled in order to eliminate this past due. By rolling the order board I do not mean that the past due orders are rescheduled, I mean that the past due orders are scheduled into a future date and the future orders are also rescheduled to keep from overloading the master schedule.

The final two points, although not as significant as the first two, neverthe- less, will make a major contribution. At the present time, we have about $200,000 of inventory to support Dayton's punch press and screw machine operations. There is, almost undoubtedly, another $200,000 worth of mate- rial and labor as a work-in-process inventory resulting from these two ma- chine centers. If we were to completely eliminate these two machine centers, naturally our vendors would be required to carry the financial burden of the raw material and work-in-process inventory, and all that Granger would be required to carry would be the finished material inventory. These two ma- chine groupings alone, therefore, would eliminate between $400,000 and $500,000 worth of inventory. If other machines were considered, it would make further reductions. Of course, it is to be understood that this might have an unfavorable effect on the Profit and Loss Statement inasmuch as we could be expected to pay more for the parts involved than our in-house costs would be. Obviously, these machines were purchased in the first place in order to reduce the product cost.

Because of such things as minimum order quantities (many ball bearing companies now require a $500 minimum order), it is nearly impossible to turn the inventory on slow-moving product lines at the rate of 3½ or 4 times per year. Product lines, such as the 2600 transmission, the 2800 transmission, the 27 inch hydraulic coupling, and our air sheaves and pump mount boxes, will not support the kind of inventory turn we are trying to achieve. In many cases, on these parts, the minimum buy amounts to an annual supply.

Therefore, we are getting only one inventory turn per year on them, and to improve to the 3½ to 4 benchmark, it will be necessary to eliminate these product lines from our product structure. A program of this nature will take much careful thought and consideration, and it cannot be done by product code; it will have to be done by product specification. In addition, there is one caution. Those product lines with heavy service parts requirements turn somewhat more slowly than those product lines with minimal service parts requirements. This is exemplified by the comparison between inventory turn of machine tool clutches and inventory turn on marine gears. It will do little or no good for inventory turn to drop a product line from the program if we must continue to service that product line. Therefore, dropping the machine tool clutches, without dropping the service parts for the machine tool clutches, will hurt the inventory turn, rather than help it. Because of the profitability of service parts, I think we want to be very sure we are doing the right thing before we undertake to trim down our product lines in order to enhance our inventory turn. But, it should be noted that this issue is directly related to our current total resource planning problem. As the 1977 resource plan we discussed last week shows (Exhibit C–3), our shopping list for new equipment and consequent floor space needs, indicates a level of financing that we probably cannot support at this time. As you know, a capital investment of about $5 million is required to obtain this level of capacity. Moreover, it is still not clear that our vendors will be able to develop sufficient capacity to be able to supply us with materials to meet our 1977 plan.

In summary, therefore, I believe that the types of inventory turns under discussion are achievable, but they will take a radical departure from the theories practiced by us in doing business in the past. Whereas we have done our very best to satisfy our customers by trying to produce to their schedules, we can no longer afford to do that. We can produce only to a schedule which we set. We will be backing off from maximum customer service, also, in the areas of making less parts and buying more because our product will cost more. And we will be backing off on customer service if we cut down on the number of products offered because many of these products were offered in order to give a customer a complete line. I believe changes such as these are completely beyond the scope of the Production and Inventory Control Departments and indeed beyond the scope of the entire Manufacturing Department. They must be decided at the very highest level in the company and instructions issued for the implementation of whatever program is thought to be appropriate.

                                                                    J. Tillich

Exhibit C–3
Resource plan 1977

CENTER	TYPE	QUANTITY	# OF SHIFTS	CAPACITY	A	B	C	D	E	F	G	H	I	TOTAL	REMARKS
03-06 BD	2AC CHUCKER	4	3	1561	15	18	26		12	10	13	2		96	
BR	3AC WARNER & SWASEY	8	3	2966	4	20	56	11	18	2	1	2	-	114	-564 HRS = 1½ MACHINES
CA	REISHAUER GEAR GRINDER	2	3	900			74		6	-	16			96	
CAB	REISHAUER GEAR GRINDER	2	3	950		22	76	46	17	4			5	170	-713 HRS = 1½ MACHINES
CD	P. & W. GEAR GRINDER	1	3	544			78	18						96	
CEA	MAAG GEAR GRINDER	4	3	3044	14		71		21	3			17	126	-944 HRS =3⅓ MACHINES
CO	P. & W. GEAR GRINDER	4	3	1190			137		39					176	-964 HRS =3⅓ MACHINES
CI	PFAUTER HOBBER	5	3	2374	2	26	49	10	13	1	5		3	109	-332 HRS } = 2 MACHINES
CJ	BARBER COLMAN HOBBER	1	3	620	25	64	73		45	20		13	2	242	-911 HRS
CN	GEAR SHAVER	3	2.5	700	7	41	12	15	10	6	4			95	
CQ	GEAR POINTER	1	1	22	15	60	1		12	5				93	
CS	FELLOWS SHAPER	1	3	549		30			10					40	+302 HRS RELIEVE CX, CY
CW	BARBER COLMAN HOBBER	3	3	1530	7	25	34	17	9	5				97	
CX	BARBER COLMAN SHAPER	1	3	546	1	35	52	47	9	2	29			175	-437 HRS } OFF LOAD TO CS
CY	FELLOWS SHAPER	1	3	514	13	158	22		22	27			4	246	-776 HRS } +2 MACHINES
FD	INTERNAL GRINDER	1	3	285	5	27	25	10	15	5	7			94	
FI	INTERNAL GRINDER	1	3	275	24	50	40	23	29	6	12			184	-245 HRS = 1 MACHINE
FJ	SURFACE GRINDER	1	1	328	7	60	31	3	16	12	5		4	138	-141 HRS = ADD 1 SHIFT
FM	VERTICAL INTERNAL GRIND.	1	2	368		30	31	14	11				6	92	
FT	GEAR HONE	2	2	528	9	40	19	21	9	7	6			111	-84 HRS = ADD 1 SHIFT
H	ENGINE LATHE	1	3	427	21	59	43	9	19	8	7		2	168	-312 HRS } = 1 MACHINE
HES	W. & S. LATHE-SPECIAL	2	2	234	2	49	41	21	13	11				137	-101 HRS }4 1 SHIFT HES
JA	HORIZONTAL BROACH	1	1	90	4	20	50	17	2					93	
NH	GEAR CHAMFER	1	3	307	11	45	12	6	12	7	5			98	
PC	MAGNAFLUX	1	1	240	5	47	62	11	15	1	2		1	144	-118 HRS = ADD 1 SHIFT

As John Bonhoeffer read Tillich's memorandum, he recalled the previous week's meeting of the top officers of the company where Granger's future had been the topic of discussion. The basic question had been: How fast can we really expect to grow and what kind of company will we end up being? Can we really grow to a sales volume of $107 million in 1977 as planned, and maintain a 10 to 12 percent growth rate thereafter?

Cash was certainly a problem. Although both Granger and its parent company had been consistently good performers and generators of funds, company borrowing to fund expansion, the growing needs for working capital, and to meet environmental regulations, had made interest a substantial drain on profitability. It did not appear likely that interest rates would decline in the long run, nor that stock prices would increase to the point where a public offering of stock would be prudent. Moreover, Bonhoeffer was mindful of a luncheon meeting he had had with the parent company's principle banking connection the day before. Most of the discussion had centered around financial considerations, such as leverage, the cost of money, and the depressed condition of the stock market. However, they had also spent considerable time exploring the notion that it was necessary to be assured that there would be materials available for a plant to consume if an expansion were to be made. Bonhoeffer knew that capacity was a serious problem in some of the industries that were key suppliers to Granger. Almost one half of the foundries in existence in 1951 for example, had shut down by 1974 due largely to environmental problems and regulations.

As Bonhoeffer considered these problems, however, he was also mindful of the fact that the nation was probably entering a period of deep recession. He wondered what effect this turn in the national economy would have on the company's dilemma, at least in the short run.

Chapter 12

Network planning and scheduling

THE LARGE-SCALE ONE-TIME PROJECT has been a mode of production systems since the beginnings of civilization, but its recognition as a managerial problem of great significance is fairly recent. The recognition came as a result of the postwar emphasis on the design, development, and production of very large-scale systems in the aerospace industry, such as the Polaris missile, where a complicated product was to be developed and manufactured, usually in small numbers or even only one. Though volume is usually small in terms of numbers of completed products to be manufactured, the overall volume in terms of labor hours, dollars expended, and facility requirements may be huge. Since its recognition and the development of its methodology, the value of the concepts associated with project management have been applied to large-scale construction; to the design, construction, and installation of new manufacturing plants; to the design, development, and construction of missiles like the Polaris; and to other situations where the basic conditions of the one-time project apply.

Viewed as a production system a one-time project is very much like a job shop in many respects, since products, processes and their sequences are custom in nature. In fact, a large fraction of systems such as missiles are produced in jobbing-type machine shops. The range of processes required for all components, however, normally transcends the process capabilities of the usual shop, and the result is a great deal of subcontracting of specialized work. Such large-scale systems are actually produced by a combine of shops.

Planning, scheduling, and control problems

The special problems of large-scale one-time projects stem from their characteristic multiple parts and components, and custom design. First, in planning what must be done, the very complexity of the project makes process sequences of extreme importance, for operations performed out of sequence can cause delays and extra costs. Thus, compared with the entire set of modern project management techniques, the development of the production plan as a network of operations probably yields the greatest net improvement over old traditional managerial methods. To prepare the network chart requires planning, questioning, and preparations. What operations are required? How will they be performed? What equipment is required? What kinds of labor skills? What are the operation sequencing requirements? Which operations can go on simultaneously? What are the estimated time requirements of the various activities? If one can just produce answers to these questions, then the basic information which makes it at least possible to perform effectively is available.

A second focus of problems centers on scheduling and the effective use of the available resources. Given the network of required operations, there will be a careful timing and sequencing of required operations to complete the project in minimum time, called the critical path schedule. Perhaps even more important will be a knowledge of permissible slack or schedule slippage of certain operations. This slack gives management flexibility in achieving the schedule. This flexibility can also be used to level the labor requirements somewhat over the entire project or make it possible to use limited equipment for several operations in a way that does not conflict, and still does not extend the project time. Heuristic scheduling computer programs have been designed which handle this limited resources problem.

Given a feasible schedule of activities, workers, and equipment, there remains the problem of controlling operations and rescheduling where necessary. Again, due to complexity and the large number of activities going on simultaneously, the information and control problem is also complex. Computer-based reporting and control systems have become common in meeting these problems and in developing updated schedules to reflect the latest conditions in new feasible schedules.

The inventory problem at first seems direct and simple, yet there are some important inventory problems. Inventory cost is in general directly related to overall project time. To minimize the investment in inventories during the project, material receipt schedules must be carefully coordinated with the schedule of operations. If orders for raw material supply were released in a block at the beginning of the project, a large fraction of inventories would be held for a much longer period than necessary and would probably create a physical storage problem as well. An inventory decision problem centers on the generation of waste and scrap during the production process. If material is wasted or scrapped so that a certain operation cannot be completed, then the entire project may be delayed if the activity is on the critical path schedule. Thus a relatively inexpensive item of material could cause large idle-labor costs, inventory costs, or possibly penalties for not meeting project delivery dates. Therefore in ordering materials an important decision problem centers on the overage allowance. One-time purchase inventory models provide a basis for balancing these costs [2].

A brief historical note

The planning, scheduling, and control techniques commonly used for large-scale projects are known as network planning and scheduling and by the more common names of PERT (program evaluation and review technique, or performance evaluation and review technique), and CPM (critical path methods). There is also a multitude of other variants and trade names for various proprietary approaches.

The application of network analysis to problems of planning and control occurred in 1957, apparently independently by two different groups. The initial development may be traced to a joint project of the Du Pont Company and the Univac Division of Remington Rand Corporation (now Sperry Rand). Du Pont was interested in achieving better control of its engineering function and for that purpose created the integrated engineering control group (IEC) under the direction of J. S. Sayer. In 1956, M. R. Walker of Du Pont and J. E. Kelley, Jr., of Remington Rand started a project designed to control the maintenance of chemical plants. The outgrowth of this project was the critical path scheduling method. This technique of planning and controlling maintenance was widely used by Du Pont for many engineering functions. In fact, it proved so successful that Du Pont seems to have declared the method to be confidential, and neither Du Pont nor Remington Rand made disclosures about its existence.

Apparently independently of the Du Pont effort, the Navy undertook in 1957 the task of planning and controlling the Polaris project. The magnitude of the task was enormous, involving approximately 3,000 separate contracting organizations. Due to the high-priority nature of the Polaris, the Navy set up a team comprised of the Navy Office of Special Projects, the Booz-Allen and Hamilton Company, and the Missiles Systems Division of Lockheed Aircraft Company, to develop a special control technique. The result was the PERT technique, which was used to plan and control the Polaris project with outstanding success [17]. The project was so successful that use of PERT is now required in some form for all prime government defense contractors.

When the effectiveness of PERT was publicized in 1959, the CPM technique was released to the public by Du Pont. The basic conceptual framework and methodology of PERT and CPM are the same with some differences in detail which we will point out.

PERT/CPM planning methods

As with any planning model one must first define the objectives of the project and its limits as well as the relationship of the project to the overall enterprise objectives. There must be stated a definite starting and ending time whether derived internally or imposed by the customer. Each activity (or operation) must also have a definite beginning and end point, and these points in time are called "events." An event has no time duration, while "activities" occur between events and require measurable performance time. A project then is a collection of interrelated activities connected by events and leading to the end accomplishment of the project activities. What we will refer to as the PERT/CPM planning phase involves only the activities and events of the project and their interrelationships without regard to time or schedule. We divide this planning phase into (a) activity analysis, (b) construction of an arrow diagram, and (c) node numbering.

Activity analysis is the process planning phase of PERT. While it is comparable functionally to what a production planner or production engineer does in specifying operations, methods, and tooling for fabricated parts and products, the differences for large-scale projects stem from complexity. Due to the extremely large number of components it is easy to miss the need for certain activities and relationships. Thus, while professional planning personnel are used, it is not uncommon to base at least some of the activity analysis on meetings and round table discussions including managerial and operating personnel. These sessions produce the lists of required activities, such as the one shown in Table 12–1 which indicates the activities

Table 12–1
Activities required to renew a pipeline

Identification code	Activity	Immediate predecessor activities
A.	Assemble crew for job	None
B.	Use old line to build inventory	None
C.	Measure and sketch old line	A
D.	Develop list of materials	C
E.	Erect scaffold	D
F.	Procure pipes	D
G.	Procure valves	D
H.	Deactivate old line	B, D
I.	Remove old pipe	H, E
J.	Prefab new pipe	F
K.	Place valves	E, G, H
L.	Place new pipe	I, J
M.	Weld pipe	L
N.	Connect values	K, M
O.	Insulate	K, M
P.	Pressure test	N
Q.	Remove scaffold	N, O
R.	Clean up and turn over to operating crew	P, Q

required to renew a pipeline. We will develop the data in Table 12–1 as an example throughout our discussion of network planning and scheduling.

The development of the *arrow diagram* which follows must be based on an activity list which is complete, verified, and approved. The arrow diagram is a pictorial representation of the activity list together with the interrelationships required. Unlike a Gantt chart the arrow diagram makes no attempt to relate the project to a time scale but concentrates on showing the interrelationships between different activities. These interrelationships are derived solely from the nature of the different activities and not from any scheduling considerations. Every activity in the list will be represented by an arrow. The arrow is not drawn to scale; that is, neither its length nor orientation and direction have any particular significance. The tail of the arrow represents the start of the activity and the head its completion. They correspond to the events that bound the activity. An alternate formulation represents activities as occurring at the nodes. It will be discussed later in this chapter.

The sequence of arrows will represent the sequence of activities, but not in the sense of a schedule at this point. The nodes are represented by small circles and symbolically define the events. A typical node is shown in Figure 12–1 where activities A, B, and C have

Figure 12–1
Typical node in a PERT
arrow diagram

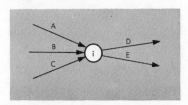

(a) The event *i* marks the end of activities A, B, and C, and the beginning of activities D and E.
(b) Neither D nor E can start until all of the activities defined by A, B, and C have been completed.

the node *i* as an ending event and activities D and E have the same event as their starting point. The logical relationship established by a node is that none of the arrows (activities) leaving a node may start until *all* of the arrows entering the node have been completed. In Figure 12–1 all three of the activities A, B, and C must be finished before either D or E may begin.

The main guide in constructing an arrow diagram is in observing the sequencing requirements. In relating a given activity (arrow) to the diagram one might ask three questions:

1.   What activities must be completed *before* this activity can be started?
2.   What activities may be carried out in *parallel* with this activity and are also dependent on completion of the same preceeding activities?
3.   What activities immediately succeed this activity?

The precedence relationships will sometimes produce the following situations: Suppose that a project has activities A, B, C, and D such that both A and B must be completed before C starts, and that B must be completed before D starts, as shown in Figure 12–2. But, Figure 12–2 cannot be used as a part of the arrow diagram because it shows

Figure 12–2
Logical relationship to be represented in an arrow
diagram

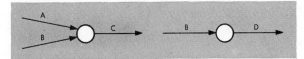

C depends on the completion of A and B, but D depends
only on the completion of B.

two arrows labeled B, indicating two activities where in fact there is
only one. One might be tempted to represent this set of relationships
as shown in Figure 12–3 (a), but it is, of course, not correct because it
specifies the beginning of D as being dependent on the completion of A
and this is not true.

Figure 12–3

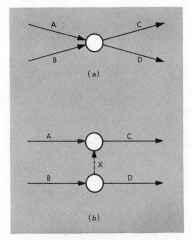

(a) Fails to represent the required
sequence relationships since the beginning of activity D is shown to be
dependent on A as well as B.
  (b) Inclusion of dummy activity X
at zero times makes C dependent on
the completion of both A and B, but D
dependent only on the completion of
B.

The solution to this problem in PERT/CPM arrow diagramming is to
insert a "dummy," activity using an arrow with a dashed line, as shown
in Figure 12–3 (b). This arrow does not represent a real activity and will
be given a performance time of zero in the scheduling phase and a cost
of zero in the costing phase. The dummy activity has no net effect on

either the project time or cost but allows us to establish the proper logical interrelationships. In Figure 12–3(b) note that D now depends only on the completion of B, and the activity C depends on the completion of A and X. Since X is an instantaneous activity occurring immediately on the completion of B, the activity C depends on the completion of both A and B, which meets the original precedence requirements stated. Dummy activities can also be used which require significant time in order to ensure the proper phasing of activities in the resulting schedule, such as when approvals or releases must be obtained in order for the project to proceed beyond a certain point.

Figure 12–4 shows an arrow diagram based on the activities required to renew a pipeline as shown in Table 12–1. Figure 12–4

Figure 12–4
Arrow diagram for the activities required to renew a pipeline

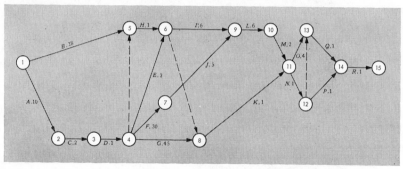

Activities are listed in Table 12–1. Circles represent numbered nodes or events, arrows represent activities. Arrow 1–5 representing activity B requires 28 days.

contains additional information which we will discuss. Our immediate interest is in the structure of the diagram. Activities A, C, and D can proceed while activity B (use old line to build inventory) is proceeding independently. But activity H (deactivate old line) is dependent on the completion of both branches through the dummy activity connecting nodes 4 and 5. The other sequencing requirements are similarly shown.

The *node numbering* represented in Figure 12–4 is based on simple but important rules. An arrow is designated by the numbers of the nodes it connects, ij, where i represents the tail and j the head of the arrow. The nodes are then numbered such that for every arrow, i is always less than j ($i < j$). This practice of node numbering is effective in computing routines both to construct all of the logical relationships of an arrow diagram and to prevent the occurrence of closed loops.

A great deal of the total benefit derived from modern project management technique comes from the preparation of the arrow diagram. It provides a disciplined basis for planning the entire project and results in a clear picture of the scope of the project in a form which can be easily read and understood. It tends to prevent the omission of activities which might be easily overlooked in large projects involving thousands of activities. The arrow diagram may provide an excellent vehicle for refining the overall conception of the project and for training project personnel. Finally, the arrow diagram forms the basis for evaluating alternate strategies, objectives, and schedules. We will consider first the topic of critical path scheduling.

CRITICAL PATH SCHEDULING

Given the arrow diagram for a project, such as Figure 12–4, we wish to know the longest time path through the network. We will first consider this problem with deterministic process times, such as those shown in Figure 12–4, and develop the associated critical path schedule. Later we will also consider the effect of uncertainty in the time estimates and compute a probabilistic critical path schedule.

Deterministic critical path schedule

It will be helpful to look at the scheduling problem through the eyes of the Gantt chart graphical model. To do this we will follow the procedures of Burgess and Killebrew [4] and start with a list of activities for the pipeline renewal project in ascending order of the j numbers. Table 12–2 shows such a list with the tail numbers i listed in order if there are repetitions of head numbers. Arranging the data in the order of head numbers simplifies the process which follows. We wish to construct a Gantt bar chart which takes account of the sequence relationships of the arrow diagram such as the one shown in Figure 12–5, constructed with data taken from Table 12–2. We proceed as in the following steps:

1. The first activity in Table 12–2 is A, the 1–2 activity. It is established as a ten-day activity from the beginning of the time scale, numbering the left and right ends according to the tail and head numbers.

Table 12–2
Pipeline renewal data listed in the order of arrow
head number

Activity code	Node number		Expected activity time, days
	Tail, i	Head, j	
A	1	2	10
C.................	2	3	2
D.................	3	4	1
B.................	1	5	28
Dummy	4	5	0
E	4	6	2
H	5	6	1
F.................	4	7	30
G.................	4	8	45
Dummy	6	8	0
I	6	9	6
J	7	9	5
L.................	9	10	6
K.................	8	11	1
M	10	11	2
N	11	12	1
O	11	13	4
Dummy	12	13	0
P.................	12	14	1
Q	13	14	1
R.................	14	15	1

2. The next activity is C, which is a 2–3 activity. It begins immediately after the 1–2 operation so that the 2s line up on the same vertical line.

3. Continue by taking the activities in the order of their head numbers, placing them on the chart in such a way that the tail numbers line up vertically with the right-most previous matching head number.

Grouping activities according to their head numbers makes it possible to make a quick determination of the earliest time each subsequent activity can be started. Figure 12–5, then, gives us a picture of the earliest starting and earliest completion times for each operation as well as the earliest possible completion time for the project, assuming that there are no other restrictions at this point.

The critical path in relation to the Gantt chart, shown in Figure 12–6, was obtained in the following way: Beginning with the last activity, 14–15, match tail numbers with head numbers above which are coterminous, or are the right-most head numbers which are limiting. The critical path schedule defines the activities which must be performed according to the schedule shown in order to meet the

Figure 12–5
Gantt chart representation of the earliest starting times for the activities
required for the pipeline renewal project

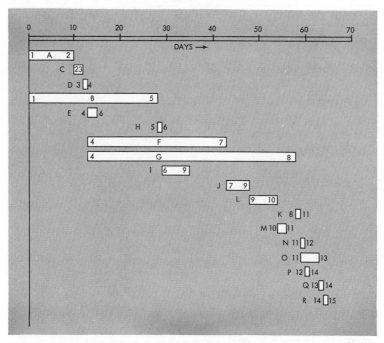

overall project schedule. If any of the critical activities do not meet their schedules, then the entire project schedule slips by the same amount, since other activities are dependent on the completion times of the critical ones. Thus the critical activities for the pipeline renewal project are A, C, D, G, K, O, Q, and R. The schedule for the critical activities contains no slack, whereas all other activities have schedules which can be slipped to some degree without affecting other activities; that is, they have slack. We will discuss two kinds of slack: total slack and free slack.

The concept of *total slack* is shown in Figure 12–7. Below the Gantt chart we show, first, the slack in the original schedule for activities B, H, I, L, and M. We see, for example, that activity B can be delayed up to a maximum of 16 days without affecting the project completion time. Note, however, that in order to accomplish the delay of activity B the starting times of activities H, I, L, and M must also be delayed. Total slack means then that an activity has slack which is shared with other activities. For example, activities B, H, and I all have a maximum of 16 days slack shared between them. If

Figure 12–6
Gantt chart for pipeline renewal project with critical path schedule
superimposed

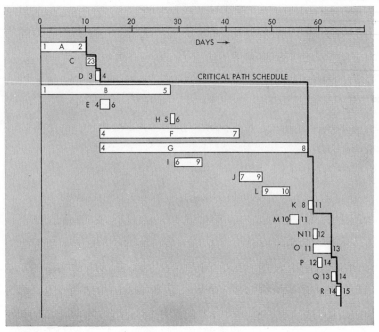

Activities A, C, D, G, K, O, Q, and R are on the critical path.

one uses all or part of it, the other activity cannot use it, as is shown in the second and third bars at the bottom of Figure 12–7 where activity B uses all of the slack in one instance and activity I uses all of it in the second instance. Note that activities L and M have only three days total slack, which is shared with activities B, H, and I, but the 13 days slack which preceeds activities L and M is not available to either of them. The only way it could be available would be if L and M could be started earlier, but this is impossible since L is limited in its starting time by the finish of activity J which is in turn limited in its starting time by the finishing of activity F, and so on. Note that activity M occupies a unique position with respect to its three-day slack. While in one sense this is total slack since it is shared with the preceding three operations which can also use it, on the other hand it is unique since if it is still available at the time we might wish to use it for activity M, that activity can be delayed by three days without affecting the starting times of any other activity. This is the definition of "free slack."

Figure 12–7
Illustration of total slack in the schedules of activities B, H, I, and L

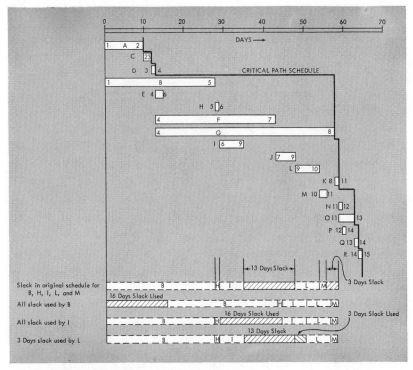

Three examples of schedule slippages which do not affect project completion are shown.

Free slack in the pipeline renewal project schedule is shown in Figure 12–8. Noting again that free slack makes possible the delay of an activity without affecting the starting times of any other activity, we see that activities E, I, M, and P all have varying degrees of free slack. For example, activity E can be delayed up to 14 days without affecting the starting time of activity I. Since I also has slack, however, activity E could be delayed another 13 days by utilizing the slack of I and delaying I's starting time. Thus, activity E has both free slack (14 days) and total slack which it shares with other activities (30 days including its free slack). The concepts of both total and free slack will be very important in arranging variations of the original critical path schedule which take account of the best use of labor force and equipment as well as in adjusting to upsets in original plans such as equipment breakdowns or simply incorrect time estimates of performance.

Figure 12–8
Illustration of free slack in pipeline renewal project schedule

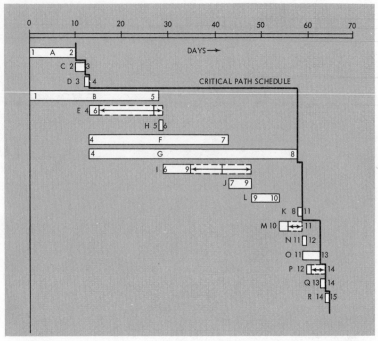

Shown are examples of free slack in activities whose schedules can be slipped by the amounts indicated without affecting the scheduled start times of any other activity or the project completion time. E has free slack of 14 days; I, 13 days; M, 3 days; and P, 3 days.

Critical path determination by network methods

The equivalent important statistics concerning starting and finishing times, total and free slack, and the critical path can be determined graphically by using the Gantt chart. However, the main value of showing the Gantt chart was to visualize the ideas of total and free slack in relation to the critical path schedule. All of the computations can be performed automatically, with existing computer routines yielding early and late starting and finishing times of activities and total and free slack, as well as the critical path through the network. The critical input data would be the activities, their performance time requirements, and the precedence relationships established by the *ij* numbers of the tails and heads of the arrows which result from the node numbering process. Figure 12–9 represents a sample output for such a computer computation for the pipeline project. We

Figure 12-9
Sample output for machine composition of activity statistics and critical path for the pipeline project

CRITICAL PATH	SEQUENCE CODE I	J	DESCRIPTION OF JOB	JOB COST	JOB TIME	EARLIEST START – FINISH		LATEST START – FINISH		SLACK TOTAL – FREE	
*	1	2	A ASSEMBLE CREW		10	0	10	0	10	0*	0
	1	5	B BUILD INVENTORY		28	0	28	16	44	16	0
*	2	3	C MEASURE AND SKETCH	300	2	10	12	10	12	0*	0
*	3	4	D DEVELOP MATERIAL LIST	100	1	12	13	12	13	0*	0
	4	5	DUMMY			13	13	44	44	31	15
	4	6	E ERECT SCAFFOLD	300	2	13	15	43	45	31	14
	4	7	F PROCURE PIPE	850	30	13	43	16	46	3	0
*	4	8	G PROCURE VALVES	300	45	13	58	13	58	0*	0
	5	6	H DEACTIVATE LINE	100	1	28	29	44	45	16	0
	6	8	DUMMY			29	29	58	58	29	29
	6	9	I REMOVE OLD PIPE	400	6	29	35	45	51	16	13
	7	9	J PREFAB SECTIONS	1200	5	43	48	46	51	3	0
*	8	11	K PLACE VALVES	100	1	58	59	58	59	0*	0
	9	10	L PLACE NEW PIPE	800	6	48	54	51	57	3	0
	10	11	M WELD PIPE	100	2	54	56	57	59	3	3
	11	12	N FIT UP	100	1	59	60	62	63	3	3
*	11	13	O INSULATE	300	4	59	63	59	63	0*	0
	12	13	DUMMY			60	60	63	63	3	3
	12	14	P PRESSURE TEST	50	1	60	61	63	64	3	3
*	13	14	Q REMOVE SCAFFOLD	100	1	63	64	63	64	0*	0
*	14	15	R CLEAN UP	100	1	64	65	64	65	0*	0

5200

Source: Courtesy of Cesar Toscano.

will illustrate the necessary relationships established in the computer program by the manual computation of the activity statistics for the pipeline project.

Earliest start and finish times. From the basic expected activity times we first calculate earliest start and finish times. If we take zero as an arbitrary starting time for the project, then for each activity there is a relative earliest starting time (ES), which is the earliest possible time that the activity can begin assuming that all of the preceding activities are also started at their ES. Then for that activity its earliest finish time (EF) is ES + activity time. The procedure for computing ES and EF manually from the network is as follows:

1. Place the value of the project start time to the left of the beginning activities, such as A and B, in the position shown for the early start time in Figure 12–10. In Figure 12–10 we see a zero for both of these activities as the ES. The early finish time for these activities is then simply ES + activity time, or 10 for activity A and 28 for activity B, shown in the early finish locations in Figure 12–10.

2. Now consider any new unmarked activity, all of whose predecessors have been marked with their ES and EF, and mark to the left of the new activity in the ES position the largest number in the EF position of its immediate predecessors. This number is

Figure 12–10
Arrow diagram with early and late start and finish times, critical path, and slack indicated

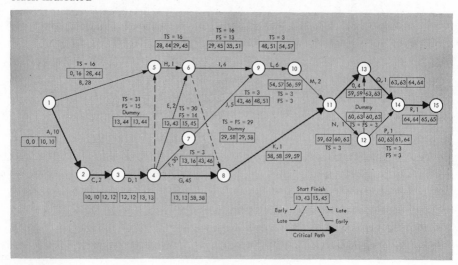

the ES time for the new activity. For activity C the ES time is 10 since that is the EF time of the preceeding activity.

3. Add to this number the activity time and mark the result in the EF position. For activity C, $ES + 2 = 12$.

4. Continue through the entire network until the "finish" activity has been reached. As we showed previously in Figure 12–6, the EF for the finish activity R is 65.

In order to complete the computations accurately one must take careful note of the effects at nodes where several arrows feed in. The activity which follows will take its ES from the largest EF of any of its immediate predecessors, including dummy activities. For example, following node 5, activity H must consider both activity B and the dummy. The largest EF of the two is 28, which becomes the ES for activity H.

Latest start and finish times. Let us assume for this example that the target time for completing the project is the EF time of 65 days. In other words, there is no slack whatsoever in the project as a whole; it must be completed as soon as it possibly can be. Therefore, $LF = 65$ for the finish activity, and the LS time for that activity is LF − activity time. The LS and LF times for each activity can now be determined by working backwards from activity R as follows:

1. Mark the values of LF and LS in their proper positions for the finish activity, R. For the pipeline project shown in Figure 12–10, $LF = 65$, and $LS = 64$.

2. Consider any new unmarked activity, *all of whose successors have been marked*, and mark in the LF position for the new activity the *smallest LS* time marked to the left of any of its immediate successors. In other words, LF for an activity equals the earliest LS of the successors for that activity. In Figure 12–10, then, activity P takes its $LF = 64$ from the LS time of activity R.

3. Subtract from this number the activity time which becomes the LS for the activity. For activity P, $LS = 64 - 1 = 63$.

4. Continue backwards through the chart until all LS and LF times have been entered on the chart in their respective positions.

Computation of slack and critical path. The total slack (TS) of an activity represents the maximum amount of time that it can be delayed beyond its ES without delaying the project completion time. ($TS = LS - ES$, or $LF - EF$.) Since the critical activities are those in the sequence of the longest time path through the network, it follows that the activities on this path will have the minimum possible TS. In our example the target date coincides with the LF for the finish activity so that all critical activities have zero total slack. If the project target date were later than the EF of the finish activity, then all activities on the critical path would have exactly this amount of TS. Similarly, all noncritical activities will have greater TS than the critical ones. All of the activities on the critical path have zero slack and all of the noncritical activities, including the dummy activities, have at least some TS and may have free slack FS.

Free slack is the amount of time that an activity can be delayed without delaying the ES of any other activity. Free slack for an activity never exceeds the TS for that activity and is computed as the difference between EF for that activity and the earliest of the ES times of all of its immediate successors. For example, activity M has FS = 3 since the earliest ES time for its two successors is 59 and its own EF is 56.

Probabilistic network planning and scheduling

Because the very nature of large-scale one-time projects makes time estimates of activities highly uncertain, the original PERT methodology attempted to take uncertainty into account by assuming that the activity time estimates were probability distributions. Then the critical path was a probabilistic critical path and the schedules for all of the activities reflected the uncertainty of the activity times.

Three time estimates are developed for each activity as a basis for specifying the probability distributions of activity times. The three different time estimates are:

The optimistic time, designated a is the shortest possible time in which the activity may be accomplished if all goes well. The estimate is based on the assumption that the activity would have no more than one chance in 100 of being completed in less than this time.

The pessimistic time, designated as b, the longest time that an activity should take under adverse conditions, but barring acts of nature. This time estimate is based on the assumption that the activity would have no more than one chance in 100 of being completed in a time larger than b.

The most likely time, designated by m, is the modal value of the distribution.

The PERT computational algorithm reduces these three time estimates to a single average estimate, t_e, the mean of a Beta distribution.
The estimates of the mean and variance of the distribution may be
computed by the following:

$$\bar{x} = 1/6[A + 4M + B]$$
$$s^2 = [1/6(B - A)]^2$$

where A, B, and M are estimates of the values of a, b, and m, respectively, and $\bar{x}$ and s^2 are estimates of the mean and variance, t_e and σ_t^2.
Figure 12–11 shows the general relationship of the specified time
values for two distributions.

Figure 12–11
PERT time estimates

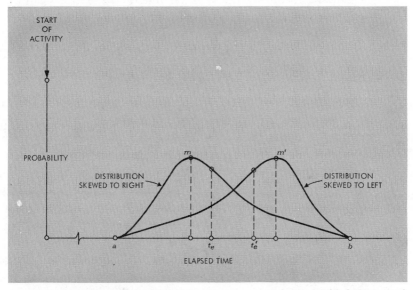

a = optimistic time, b = pessimistic time, m = modal or most likely time, and
t_e = expected time.

It is easy to understand why the origins of PERT produced a system based on the recognition of a high degree of uncertainty. In a
project such as the Polaris or Apollo programs, a planner would find
it very difficult to make a single time estimate before even knowing
whether it is even feasible to design such a system. The engineers
involved might reason that if no major technological breakthroughs
are required, then an optimistic time might be three months. If a
major engineering problem arises so that basic new research efforts

are required, then perhaps a pessimistic time may be 12 months. It should be noted, however, that the extreme times are not meant to be wild guesses but should be based on logical reasons.

Probabilistic critical path. In the standard PERT algorithm the computation of early and late start and finish times are similar to those already discussed for deterministic time values, since the three time values specifying the distribution are reduced to the expected time t_e. The basic theoretical assumption in PERT is that each activity has a probability distribution, but since it is assumed that the actual deviations from the expected time values for any one path is the sum of the many individual activity deviations, the total accumulated deviation of a path will be a random variable with normal probability distribution. In other words, even though each activity has its own particular probability distribution function, the sum of all of the deviations along any one path is such that the resultant deviation has a normal probability distribution. The assumption is that since there are many activities the individual differences in distributions cancel each other out.

The fact that any one path has an associated probability distribution allows management to associate a particular date with any node in the diagram. This date is then compared to the probability distribution of the critical path up to that node, and a probability of completion by that date is obtained. This probability measure is, of course, obtainable for the project completion node as well as for any intermediate node. This assignment of probabilities to completion dates is a very powerful planning and control tool. Management can plan, reschedule, or even renegotiate contracts on the basis of expected outcomes and stated risk levels. Obviously, however, the output is no better than the input data, and there is a danger that the very existence of the precise probability statements tends to give an aura of accuracy which may not necessarily be justified.

Criticism of the PERT methods and statistics have raised fundamental questions, though practitioners acclaim the successes of PERT even if its theoretical base may be shaky. Grubbs [10] shows that the mean and variance values used by PERT for the Beta distribution are for individual values of time selected at random and not for some average of random variables. Fulkerson [9] shows that the expected critical path length in PERT networks are always optimistic and generates an improved estimate which has been added to and commented on by Clingen [5]. In addition, Elmaghraby [6, 7, 8] and Klingel [13] have also analyzed the problem of the expected time path through a network.

Monte Carlo methods have been used by Van Slyke [20] to simulate the time through networks, plotting cumulative probability time distributions of the results. Thus he could assign an index of criticality to each and every activity which indicated the probability that the activity in question would be on the critical path.

Finally, MacCrimmon and Ryavec [16] made an extensive analytical study of PERT assumptions which should be read by all those who plan to use the technique.

ACTIVITIES ON NODES REPRESENTATION

An alternate network procedure represents activities as occurring at the nodes, and the arrows represent the sequences of activities required to carry through the project. There is an advantage in this mode of arrow diagramming in that it is not necessary to use dummy activities. Figure 12–12 is the arrow diagram for the pipeline renewal project which may be compared with the comparable activities on arrows diagram shown in Figure 12–10. The analysis developing the early and late starting and finishing times as well as slack times is identical with the procedure described previously.

Between the two representations of activities there seems to be no overwhelming advantage of one over the other. Either methodology can use the deterministic as well as the probabilistic model. Computer programs exist for both methodologies which make them computationally feasible for large-scale projects. As originally developed the PERT methodology was probabilistic and the CPM methodology was deterministic. It is understandable when one considers the origins of the two methodologies why each emphasized its own unique qualities. Since CPM was developed in an environment dominated by maintenance and construction engineering activities where time estimates are fairly well defined, the deterministic model was more logical. The PERT technique, however, was developed in the environment of research and development activities where time estimates are very much less reliable so that some way of taking into account extreme uncertainty was important.

SUMMARY

PERT/CPM provides an effective conceptual framework and techniques for project scheduling. The determination of the critical path through the network represented a new concept when these methods were developed, and formalizing the concepts of total and

Figure 12-12
CPM chart for the pipeline renewal project

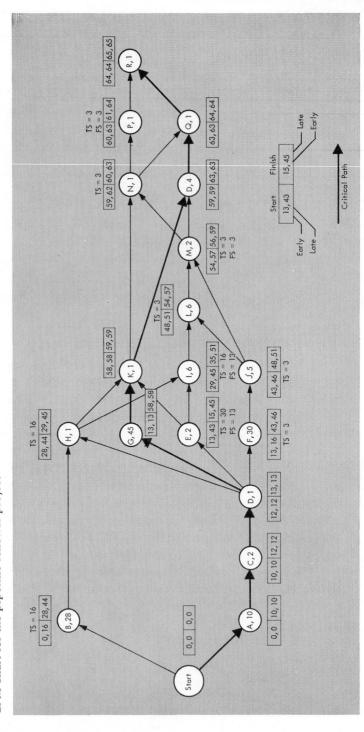

free slack has provided a basis for developing the network schedule into a workable project schedule. With a known degree of flexibility defined by the slack in activity schedules we can consider alternatives in realistic schedules from the viewpoint of the best use of skilled labor in the project and the effective use of limited equipment. Simulation of alternatives is a feasible approach to these problems. When properly used the probabilistic schedules provided by the three time estimates are of immense managerial value in preparing flexible plans and in achieving a managerial mental set which is in tune with the uncertain nature of most large projects.

The network schedule concepts and techniques when coupled with modern data processing capability also provide a viable framework for the development of managerial control procedures. As work on the activities progresses, actual performance will vary from plans, using up available slack and in some instances resulting in the change of the critical path. With present-day computing programs, the effects of these deviations from plans can be quickly reflected in revised schedules.

Apparently, however, the Department of Defense (DOD) has not had satisfying experience with the probabilistic estimates for they have abandoned them for most contracts. One type of incident was rumored to have taken place in some Navy yards where schedulers were taking their most likely estimates and adding and subtracting arbitrarily determined amounts to obtain optimistic and pessimistic time estimates, thus defeating the purposes of the probabilistic estimates. There have also been difficulties in applying the techniques to very large projects. For example, it was found that the Minuteman missile program was too large for existing computers.

REVIEW QUESTIONS AND PROBLEMS

1. Inventory problems in the planning and execution of large-scale projects are of minor significance! Discuss.

2. Why is it that deterministic methods of network planning developed in the environment of maintenance operations at the Du Pont Company while probabilistic network planning methods developed in the aerospace industry?

3. Justify the rule that arrow diagrams cannot be cyclic.

4. Rationalize the rules for node numbering.

5. What are the functions of dummy activities in PERT/CPM networks?

6. Why is the Gantt chart representation of the pipeline renewal project

shown in Figure 12–5 inadequate for understanding the options open to management for developing the most effective schedule?

7. Define the terms: total slack, free slack, critical path.

8. Define the terms: earliest start, earliest finish, latest start, latest finish.

9. In calculating schedule statistics, why is the latest of the EFs of the immediate predecessors the ES for the following activity?

10. In calculating schedule statistics, why is the earliest of the LSs of successor activities the LF for the immediately preceding activity?

11. Define the terms: optimistic time, pessimistic time, most likely time.

12. What is the nature of the probability distribution when m and t_e are the same for an activity?

13. What is the managerial value of a probabilistic critical path?

14. Summarize the criticisms leveled at current network planning methods.

15. Table 12–3 summarizes the activities, sequence requirements, and time requirements for an organization to prepare a new product for production.
    a. Prepare an "activities on arrows" network for the project.
    b. Prepare an "activities on nodes" network for the project.
    c. Calculate the schedule statistics for the project; i.e., ES, LS, EF, LF, TS, and FS.
    d. Identify the critical path for the project.

Table 12–3
Activities required to prepare a new product for production

Identification code	Activity	Immediate predecessor activities	Most likely time, days
A.	Review preliminary layouts	None	3
B.	Prepare tool orders	A	1
C.	Prepare raw material requisition	A	2
D.	Prepare final layouts	A	3
E.	Design and make tools	B	10
F.	Test quality of tools	E	1
G.	Review gage requirements	None	2
H.	Obtain gages	F, G	5
I.	Obtain purchased parts and raw materials	C	10
J.	Deliver tools to manufacturing	F	1
K.	Deliver raw material and purchased parts to manufacturing	I	1
L.	Deliver final layouts to manufacturing	D	1
M.	Deliver gauges to manufacturing	H	1
N.	Manufacture parts	J, K, L, M	10

16. Referring to Problem 15 some difficulties in the schedule arose shortly after the project started. First, due to illness of key people, activity D, "Prepare Final Layouts" has been delayed a full week (five working

days). The project leader has authorized overtime at a total cost of $500 on Saturday, Sunday, and every night of the following week to make up the time and minimize effects on the project completion time. Also, activity I, Obtain Purchased Parts and Raw Materials, has been potentially delayed six days. The supplier cannot ship by the agreed date but two days can be saved by the use of air freight at an extra cost of $200. Penalties for delaying the project completion time are estimated to be $150 per day due to lost sales in missing optimum market timing. Evaluate the effects of the delays.

17. Table 12–4 gives additional information concerning the pipe renewal project discussed in the text (see Table 12–1 and 12–2 and Figures 12–5 through 12–10) in the form of optimistic, most likely, and pessimistic time estimates. Compute expected times and variances. Which activities have the greatest uncertainty in their completion schedules? Which have the least?

Table 12–4
Three time estimates for pipe renewal project

Activity code	Optimistic time, estimate of a	Most likely time, estimate of m	Pessimistic time, estimate of b
A	7	10	13
B	24	26	40
C	1	2	3
D	0.5	1	1.5
E	1	1.5	5
F	16	26	60
G	30	40	80
H	1	1	1
I	4	6	8
J	2	4	12
K	0.5	0.9	1.9
L	3	5	13
M	1	2	3
N	0.5	1	1.5
O	2.5	3	9.5
P	1	1	1
Q	0.5	0.5	3.5
R	1	1	1

SELECTED BIBLIOGRAPHY

1. Archibald, R. D., and Villoria, R. L. *Network-Based Management Systems*. New York: John Wiley & Sons, Inc., 1967.

2. Buchan, J., and Koenigsberg, E. *Scientific Inventory Management*. Englewood Cliffs, N.J.: Prentice-Hall, Inc., 1963.

3. Buffa, E. S. *Modern Production Management*, chap. 8. 5th ed. New York: John Wiley & Sons, Inc., 1977.

4. Burgess, A. R., and Killebrew, J. B. "Variation in Activity Level on a Cyclical Arrow Diagram," *Journal of Industrial Engineering* vol. 13, no. 2 (March–April 1962), pp. 76–83.

5. Clingen, C. T. "A Modification of Fulkerson's PERT Algorithm," *Operations Research*, vol. 12, no. 4 (July–August 1964), pp. 629–31.

6. Elmaghraby, S. E. "On Generalized Activity Networks." *Journal of Industrial Engineering*, vol. 17, no. 11 (November 1966), pp. 621–31.

7. Elmaghraby, S. E. "On the Expected Duration of PERT Type Networks," *Management Science*, vol. 13, no. 5 (January 1967), pp. 299–306.

8. Elmaghraby, S. E. "The Theory of Networks and Management Science, II," *Management Science*, vol. 17, no. 2 (October 1970), pp. 54–71.

9. Fulkerson, D. R. "Expected Critical Path Lengths in PERT Networks," *Operations Research*, vol. 10, no. 6 (November–December 1962), pp. 808–17.

10. Grubbs, F. E. "Attempts to Validate Certain PERT Statistics or 'Picking on PERT,'" *Operations Research*, vol. 10, no. 6 (November–December 1962), pp. 912–15.

11. Kelley, J. E., Jr. "Critical Path Planning and Scheduling, Mathematical Basis," *Operations Research*, vol. 9, no. 2 (May–June 1961), pp. 296–320.

12. Kelley, J. E., Jr. "The Critical Path Method: Resources, Planning and Scheduling," J. F. Muth and G. L. Thompson, eds., *Industrial Scheduling*, chap. 21. Englewood Cliffs, N.J.: Prentice-Hall, Inc., 1963.

13. Klingel, A. R., Jr. "Bias in PERT Project Completion Time Calculations for a Real Network," *Management Science*, vol. 13, no. 4 (December 1966), pp. 194–201.

14. Levin, R. I., and Kirkpatrick, C. A. *Planning and Control with PERT/CPM.* New York: McGraw-Hill Book Co., 1966.

15. Levy, F. K., Thompson, G. L., and Wiest, J. D. "The ABCs of the Critical Path Method," *Harvard Business Review* (September–October, 1963), pp. 98–108.

16. MacCrimmon, K. R., and Ryavec, C. A. "An Analytical Study of the PERT Assumptions," *Operations Research*, January–February, 1964, Reprinted as Chap. 30 in E. S. Buffa, ed., *Readings in Production and Operations Management.* New York: John Wiley & Sons, Inc., 1966.

17. Malcolm, D. G.; Roseboom, J. H.; Clark, C. E.; and Fazar, W. "Application of a Technique for Research and Development Program Evaluation," *Operations Research*, vol. 7, no. 5 (September–October 1959). Reprinted as Chap. 29 in E. S. Buffa, ed., *Readings in Production and Operations Management.* New York: John Wiley & Sons, Inc., 1966.

18. Moder, J. J., and Phillips, C. R. *Project Management with CPM and PERT*, 2d ed. New York: Reinhold Publishing Corp., 1970.

19. Shaffer, L. R.; Ritter, J. B.; and Meyer, W. L. *The Critical Path Method*. New York: McGraw-Hill Book Co., 1965.

20. Van Slyke, R. M. "Monte Carlo Methods and the PERT Problem," *Operations Research*, vol. 11, no. 5 (September–October 1963), pp. 839–60.

21. Wiest, J. D. "Heuristic Programs for Decision Making," *Harvard Business Review* (September–October, 1966), pp. 129–43.

22. Wiest, J. D., and Levy, F. K. *A Management Guide to PERT/CPM*, 2d ed. Englewood Cliffs, N.J.: Prentice-Hall, Inc., 1977.

Chapter 13

Project scheduling and control

THOUGH THE NETWORK PLANNING AND SCHEDULING METH-
ODS just discussed produce a critical path schedule, the schedule
is but an input to the final scheduling process. The reasons for
this are that the critical path schedule in its raw form has made no
attempt to consider some other extremely important possibilities.
One such possibility might center on the time-cost trade-off where
additional effort selectively allocated might shorten the schedule
and reduce its cost. The other is that the raw schedule might be very
poor from the viewpoint of labor and equipment utilization. Thus,
in this chapter we will take the raw critical path schedule and
generate final schedules which may be compatible with these
broader objectives, and set up procedures designed to provide information feedback and control for the schedules that are adopted.

We will divide our discussion into the unlimited resources case
followed by the limited resources situation and conclude with a discussion of control procedures.

Unlimited resources scheduling models—Least costing

In general, the techniques of least costing when resources are not
limited are centered on the control of the allocation of money to each
activity. The concepts are based on the cost versus time curve for an
activity such as those shown in Figure 13–1. The curves are convex

Figure 13–1
Typical activity time-cost curves

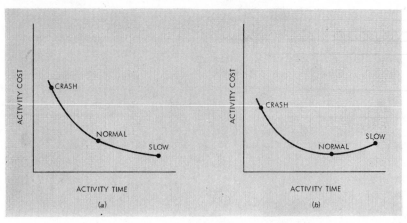

in form and reflect the fact that under some circumstances activity time can be reduced by pouring in more resources on a "crash program" to complete the activity quickly; or that restricting the flow of resources below normal levels may produce a "slow" schedule in time, which may be lower in cost, as in Figure 13–1(a), or even higher, as in Figure 13–1(b), than the normal cost. The time-cost curves for different activities vary considerably, with the time for some activities being drastically affected by the application of additional resources. For example, in large construction projects the time for carpenters to complete the forms for the concrete foundations is closely related to the number of carpenters used. As the number of carpenters increases, however, our ability to use them effectively decreases to the point finally where they may be stumbling over each other. On the other hand, the reduction of resources below normal levels could have either of the effects shown in Figure 13–1(a) or 13–1(b). The slow schedule for an activity could produce a higher than normal cost if the smaller resources enforced a change in work methods which was less efficient. For example, masons that mix their own mortar and lay and carry bricks are less efficient than teams in which the labor is divided between brick carriers and brick layers. Finally, we can easily conceive of situations where increased resources would extend activity time by causing extensive interference.

Given the time-cost curve concept and the critical path schedule, management would wish to allocate resources within the project in the most effective way, and this will mean draining off resources from some activities, producing slow schedules for them, and pouring these resources into activities where they will be most effective.

Shorten critical path. First, we may wish to use resources in a way which would shorten the critical path. If the critical path length exceeds the allowable time for the project, and there is a penalty for not meeting the deadline, management would have a strong incentive to shorten the overall schedule. The emphasis would be placed on activities along the critical path, drawing resources from noncritical activities and allocating these resources to the critical ones. The activity with the time-cost curve having the smallest slope, that is, change in cost per unit change in time, will be the most fruitful activity to receive additional allocations of resources. Once the activity time has been changed, the schedule would have to be recomputed to detect any possible shifts in the critical path. If the project is still too long, the cost of an additional decrease in project time is compared to the decrease in penalty, and if there is a reduction in marginal cost, the critical path activity with the smallest slope is shortened. This marginal analysis would be continued until it is no longer economical to reduce project length.

Decreasing total cost. Either as a part of the objective of shortening the critical path or independently, we can use the differential time-cost characteristics of the noncritical jobs to minimize total project cost. We would decrease the cost allocations to noncritical jobs, increasing their activity times, by selecting the noncritical activity with the highest slope; that is, the largest change in cost per change in unit activity time. These general concepts of the relationships between time-cost curves for activities together with a recognition of their differential slope characteristics form the basis for formal analytical methods, which we will now discuss.

Formal methodologies. Kelley [13] and Fulkerson [8] developed linear programming models which idealized the convex cost functions shown in Figure 13–1 by assuming a linear function connecting the crash and normal points. The total project cost is taken as the sum of the linear activity cost functions, and this total project cost function is minimized by the linear program. The dual of the linear programming model in combination with the network flow algorithm developed by Ford-Fulkerson is used to develop the least costly schedule for any project duration. This produces a piecewise linear project cost curve which may be used as a basis for decision purposes involving a trade-off between project completion time and possible late penalties. Clark [4] developed a methodology which achieves similar results but with a modified rule for selecting the activities whose resources will be increased.

Berman [2] developed a model for minimizing product cost for a given project duration which utilizes continuous activity cost functions. He showed that for serial activities the time-cost slopes of all activities on the serial path should be equal to each other and less than, or equal to, zero. The latter point means that the activity time should be to the left of the minimum point on the cost curves, such as those shown in Figure 13–1. Further, for a complex junction or node Berman showed that the suboptimal time location of a junction, when the time locations of all other junctions are fixed, is defined by the condition that the sum of the time-cost slopes of activities immediately preceding the junction should equal the sum of the time-cost slopes of activities immediately following the junction. Berman then extended these concepts to the balancing of an entire network and outlines an iterative algorithm for achieving time-cost balance within the network.

Other analytical approaches have been proposed by Jewell [10] and Moder and Phillips [18], and these and still others are summarized in a most excellent survey by Davis [6].

Limited resource scheduling models

The unlimited resource case just discussed is of interest, especially in terms of gaining insight into some of the possible trade-offs. However, the limited resources situation is the more general one and can include unlimited resources as a special case. In analyzing the problem of project scheduling under conditions of limited resources a distinction must be made between the objectives of resource leveling, resource allocation, and cost minimization. Resource leveling is the simplest form of the problem where the project completion date is considered fixed and an attempt is made to reduce peak resource requirements and smooth out the period-by-period variations. The resource allocation form of the scheduling problem is more complex as it involves the allocation of limited project resources to each activity with the objective of finding the earliest possible completion date consistent with the fixed resource constraints. Cost minimization is the most difficult scheduling objective as it involves minimization of the sum of the cost elements associated with the execution of the project including: payroll, overtime, hiring and layoff, early completion rewards, late completion penalties, etc.

The simplest approach to the resource problem is one of leveling the demand for the resource in question, using the flexibility made available by slack to shift the timing of activities. The demand for resources based upon the early start schedule would commonly have sharp peaks such as the profile of daily expenditures for labor for the pipeline renewal project shown in Figure 13–2. The flexibility of-

Figure 13–2
Profile of daily labor expenditures for the pipeline renewal project

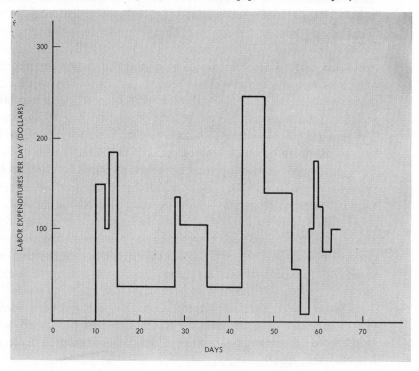

fered for leveling in the pipeline project is not great, however, in many more complex projects, the alternatives available are ample. Simulation methodologies may be used to generate the alternatives. The starting solution could be the early start schedule for which a profile similar to Figure 13–2 may be developed. The first attempt at leveling could then set a maximum of the resource to be used below the highest peak level.

The execution of the simulation program would then proceed as indicated by the arrow diagram, setting the simulated calendar date at zero, beginning all activities leaving node 1, and keeping track of the amount of the resource used and available. As the calendar is advanced and as activities are completed, resources are returned to the "available" pool. As new activities are started, resources are drawn from the pool. Simulation would proceed until an activity requires resources from a pool which is temporarily exhausted. When this happens the next step depends on the decision criteria used by the simulator. Some will delay the activity, even past its latest starting time, until resources are available. Others, when the latest starting time is reached, will "bump" noncritical jobs and reassign the resources to the delayed job. Whatever decision rule is used, the simulator will reflect the bottlenecks that actually occur when the project is carried out. On the basis of the simulation, management may take appropriate corrective action, which may require hiring more personnel of a certain skill classification and less of another, or possibly the revision of the expected completion date of the project. The general simulation approach is useful to management, since it can point out in advance where resource bottlenecks will occur.

A number of rigorous approaches to the resource leveling problem have been proposed. Burgess and Killebrew [3] propose a method which compares alternate schedules which have been generated by sequentially moving activities which have slack, computing the resulting resource profile. They propose as a criterion the sum of the squares of resource requirements, selecting schedules which minimize this measure. Their computer program is set up to handle a maximum of two different resources.

Dewitte [7] of Hughes Aircraft Company developed a computerized leveling program, similar to the one just discussed, which attempts to minimize the absolute magnitude of resource fluctuation from a mean level.

Levy, Thompson, and Wiest [15] developed a workforce smoothing program designed to level labor requirements in several projects simultaneously. After computing a labor profile for each project based on the early start schedules, the computer program sets trigger levels at one unit below peak requirements and attempts to reschedule activities with slack so that peak requirements are below the trigger level. On completion of a cycle the trigger level is reset again and the process repeated. When a trigger level is reached which cannot be reduced, then each product independently is subjected to the same procedure.

The leveling procedures assume that resources can be made available in the amounts needed and implicitly are assuming that there is a cost advantage to minimizing fluctuations in load. Though the criterion functions do not express these costs, they are the costs of hiring and firing, overtime costs, and idle-labor costs, similar to the costs associated with the change of production levels and rates incorporated in aggregate planning and scheduling models discussed in Chapters 5 and 6. In some instances the critical resources may be available in limited quantities so that they must be viewed as constraints on the project schedule. This might be true for certain special items of equipment and for certain labor force skill classifications.

The remaining material on limited resource scheduling models will first discuss the special properties of resource limited schedules in order to show that the traditional concepts of slack and criticality lose their normal CPM/PERT meanings. This will be followed by a description of Wiest's SPAR approach to resource allocation scheduling and Jones's and Taubert's SDR/CPM approach to cost minimization scheduling.

Properties of resource constrained schedules

Wiest [21] discusses the schedule properties in the context of a schedule chart, which shows time phasing more clearly than an arrow diagram, since the lengths of arrows are proportional to activity times. Figure 13–3 is a simple schedule chart. It combines the characteristics of the arrow diagram, which shows required activity sequences, with the Gantt chart, which utilizes a horizontal time scale. Figure 13–3 shows eight activities in their sequence and time relationships but includes as well the *crew size requirement* for each activity. As we will see, the latter information will be important in a redefinition of the meaning of slack for resource constrained schedules. Wiest presents the following definitions which are helpful in examining the special properties he discusses.

Local left shift—A left shift of an activity accomplished by a series of one day left shifts each of which maintains the feasibility of the schedule *both* in terms of sequence requirements and resource constraints. In Figure 13–3 if the total resource constraint is a crew size of ten workers then no activities shown can be locally left shifted.

Figure 13–3
Schedule chart showing sequence requirements, activity times in days,
and crew size requirements for eight activities

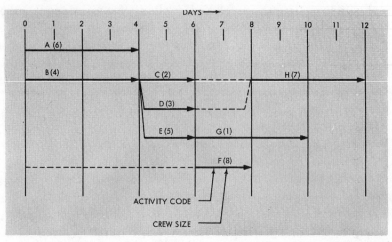

Source: Based on J. D. Wiest, "Some Properties of Schedules for Large Projects with Limited Resources," *Operations Research*, vol. 12, no. 3 (May–June 1964), Figure 1.

Local right shift—Definition is similar to local left shift. In Figure 13–3 activity G can be locally right shifted if the resource limit is ten workers but no other activities can be locally right shifted unless other activities move first.

Global shift—A left or right shift of more than one day.

Left-justified schedule—A feasible schedule in which no activity can be started at an earlier date by local left shifting of that activity alone because of either sequence or resource constraints. Figure 13–3 is a left-justified schedule if the resource limit is ten.

Right-justified schedule—Definition similar to left-justified schedule.

Slack. Wiest shows that for a resource constrained schedule slack is dependent on a specific set of left- and right-justified schedules and is therefore dependent on the rules used for generating these specific schedules. As we will see, there are possible several sets of left- and right-justified schedules when resources are limited. For example, Figure 13–4 shows the unique left- and right-justified schedules for a specific case when resources are unlimited. Note that there are no alternate left- and right-justified schedules and that slack in the left-justified schedule is continuous, that is, the schedule for activity A, for example, can be slipped *either* one or two days and not delay any other activity or delay the project completion time.

Figure 13-4
Unique left- and right-justified schedules for six
activities with sequence requirements shown
(left-justified schedule shows slack in activities
A, C, and D)

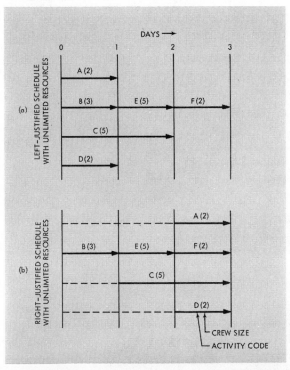

Source: Based on J. D. Wiest, "Some Properties of Schedules for
Large Projects with Limited Resources," *Operations Research*, vol. 12,
no. 3 (May–June 1964), Figure 4.

Note, however, that when total crew size for the project is limited
to ten workers there are several left-justified schedules possible all of
which fit the definition. In Figure 13–5(a) neither activities A nor D
can be locally left-shifted because the necessary crew would not be
available during the second day. In Figure 13–5(b) activity C cannot
be locally left-shifted because the crew requirements during the first
day are already at seven. The question is immediately raised, of
course, why not forget about local left-shifting and left-shift either
activity A or D two days (a global shift in Wiest's terminology)
thereby producing the left-justified schedule shown in Figures 13–
5(c) and (d)? The answer is that there are some advantages to restrict-

ing moves to local shifting in the design of heuristics to develop project schedules. Note that in the schedules of (a) and (b) of Figure 13–5 all activities are critical, i.e., there is no slack, but schedules (c) and (d) provide one day of slack for activity C.

Figure 13–5
Four left-justified schedules when crew size is limited to ten (schedules (c) and (d) allow slack for activity C, but schedules (a) and (b) have no slack)

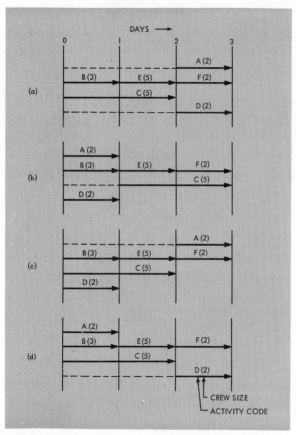

Source: Based on J. D. Wiest, "Some Properties of Schedules for Large Projects with Limited Resources," *Operations Research*, vol. 12, no. 3 (May–June 1964).

Thus the rules and procedures used to generate resource limited schedules can provide rigidity as in Figures 13–5(a) and (b) or may facilitate the possibility of smoothing as in Figures 13–5(c) and (d). Retaining the concept of local shifting only, also retains the continuous nature of slack found in the unlimited resource schedule of Figure 13–4(a).

Schedule-generating rules. Wiest considers rules for local right-shifting of activities which tend to distribute slack in ways that do not preclude further local right-shifting. Beginning with a left-justified schedule of activities, the Wiest heuristic rules locally right-shift all activities as far as possible, thus deriving a right-justified schedule by the following priority rules:

1. Right-shift jobs in descending order of their EF (early finish); i.e., move jobs with the latest EF first.
2. If several jobs have the same EF, calculate for each job in this set an LS (late start), assuming in each case that no other jobs in the set have been right shifted. Then right-shift the jobs in descending order of their LS.
3. In the case of a tie in LSs, right-shift the tied jobs in ascending order of labor force requirements, that is, the smallest crew size jobs first.
4. In case of a tie in crew sizes, move the tied jobs in ascending order of their identifying numbers.

The rules then define a procedure for obtaining a related right-justified schedule from a given left-justified schedule which defines the continuous slack between the two related schedules.

If the generating procedure is an effective one, the sequence of local shifts made will tend not to preclude further local shifts. Let us see why these rules accomplish this objective. The rules move first the shortest activity and/or those which can be right-shifted the farthest. "We would expect that this would tend to distribute potential slack to the largest number of jobs, rather than distributing larger amounts of slack to fewer jobs." This is shown in Figure 13–6 where Figure 13–6(a) is a left-justified schedule. If Wiest's rules are followed, the right-justified schedule in (b) is generated, and the related pair of left- and right-justified schedules have slack in activities A, B, and C of two, four, and two days, respectively. If activity C is locally right-shifted first, however, the resulting right-justified schedule in Figure 13–6(c) results, and the related pair of left- and right-justified schedules (a) and (c) have only four days slack in activity C and no slack elsewhere.

Thus, using Wiest's ideas, the amount and distribution of slack among activities in a resource limited situation is dependent on the schedule-generating procedures and is defined by the pair of related left- and right-justified schedules generated by the rules. The slack values are continuous yet shared in the same sense discussed for total slack in Chapter 12, that is, the two days slack in activity C of the

Figure 13–6
Left-justified schedule (a) and two right justified schedules
(b), (c)

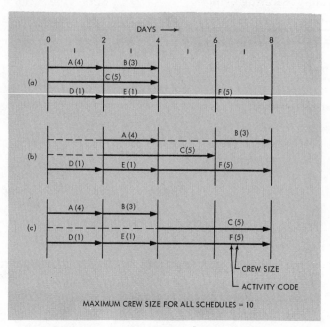

Schedule in (b) is generated by Wiest's rules showing that the related
(a)–(b) schedules provide slack as follows: A—two days, B—four days,
C—two days.
   Schedule in (c) is generated by right local shifts moving activity C first.
Resulting related (a)–(c) schedules provide slack only for activity C of four
days.

schedule in Figure 13–6(b) is dependent on the prior move of B. If B
locally right-shifted only three days, then C could locally right-shift
only one day.

Critical sequence—A redefinition of critical paths. With a resource limited schedule the concept of critical paths being an unbro-
ken sequence of technologically ordered activities must change. The
analogous concept is a critical sequence of activities which may
alternate between resource constraints and technological constraints
or be constrained by both simultaneously. The schedule in Figure
13–3 with a resource limit of ten has a critical sequence in it. It is
defined by the set A–B, C–D–E, F–G, H. The technological sequence is
B, D, H, but it is broken for the sixth and seventh days by activity F
strictly because of resource limitations. The sequence and timing of
A, E, and F are dictated by resource constraints. Activities C and G

have two days slack each if right-shifted by Wiest's rules. Wiest defines critical sequence rigorously so that the concept can be incorporated into heuristic scheduling programs.

SPAR—A heuristic scheduling program for resource allocation

Wiest applies some of the properties of resource limited schedules just discussed, and others, in a heuristic scheduling model called SPAR (scheduling program for allocation of resources) [22]. Wiest describes the basic operation of the heuristic model as follows:

In its basic approach, the model focuses on available resources, which it serially allocates, period by period, to jobs listed in order of their early start times. Jobs are scheduled, starting with the first period, by selecting from the list of those currently available and ordered according to their total slack (which is based on technological constraints only and normal resource assignments). The most critical jobs have the highest probability of being scheduled first, and as many jobs are scheduled as available resources permit. If an available job fails to be scheduled in that period, an attempt is made to schedule it the next period. Eventually all jobs so postponed became critical and move to the top of the priority list of available jobs. [22]

The basic flow diagram for SPAR is shown in Figure 13–7. The operation of the basic program just described is modified by a number of scheduling heuristics designed to increase the use of the available resources and/or to decrease the length of the schedule. These scheduling heuristics or subroutines are related to (a) *crew size* in which the program selects from three different crew sizes associated with each activity; (b) a subroutine designed to *augment critical activities* which have crew sizes less than their maximums; (c) *multi-resource activities* in which separate activities are created for each resource and the activities are constrained to start on the same day with the same level of resource assignment; (d) a subroutine designed to *borrow from active activities* when resources available are insufficient for scheduling some critical activity; (e) *rescheduling of active activities* in order to schedule a critical activity; and (f) an *add-on unused resources* routine which increases the crew sizes of activities with the smallest slack from the pool of unused resources.

Wiest reports the results of a number of laboratory-type tests as well as field tests of actual cases to which SPAR has been applied. The laboratory tests used projects which were small enough that predetermined optimum schedules could be computed for compari-

Figure 13–7
Flow diagram for SPAR

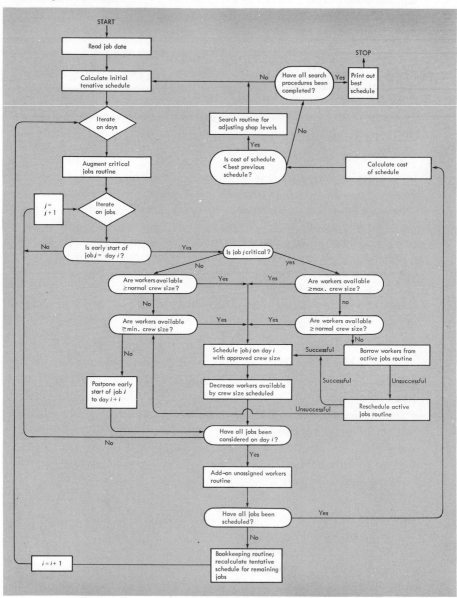

Source: From J. D. Wiest, "A Heuristic Model for Scheduling Large Projects with Limited Resources," *Management Science*, vol. 13, no. 6 (February 1967), pp. 359–77.

son. Although the SPAR program does not produce a provable optimum program, it was capable in many instances (though not all) of generating an optimum schedule. Wiest reports field tests in a small construction project, a large construction project, the month-end closing of accounting records project, a space vehicle project, and two job shop projects. Also, the concepts of SPAR are incorporated in the Babcock and Wilcox case study at the end of the chapter.

Small construction project. This project involved 12 different resource groups containing approximately 100 multiresource activities or the equivalent of 181 single-resource activities. Table 13–1

Table 13–1
Peak resource requirements for the small construction project

Resource schedule	Resource number											
	1	2	3	4	5	6	7	8	9	10	11	12
Unlimited*	12	3	20	7	8	12	14	8	4	2	4	1
Limited†	7	3	13	4	7	7	12	4	5	2	2	1

* All jobs scheduled at early start times and with normal crew size.
† Based on resource limits from tenth iteration.
Source: From J. D. Wiest, "A Heuristic Model for Scheduling Large Projects with Limited Resources," *Management Science*, vol. 13, no. 6 (February 1967), pp. 359–77.

compares the peak resource requirements for the best schedule generated by SPAR and the results obtained from conventional CPM techniques. The comparative smoothing effects of the SPAR program are obvious, the ninth resource being the only one in which conventional CPM schedules produced lower peak requirements. The total length of the construction project was reduced from 93 days in the CPM schedule to 80 days in the SPAR schedule. The reduction in the total length of the project resulted from the above-normal alloction of available resources to critical jobs through the "add-on unused resources" subroutine of SPAR.

Space vehicle project. The space vehicle project involved many activities which required multiple resources. The project required large block engineering activities which required the talents of up to five different types of engineers, involving 300 activities. Figure 13–8 shows a composite workforce loading chart for the program. The unlimited resources line resulted from a conventional PERT-type schedule with all activities at their early start times. The limited resources line results from the SPAR schedule where peak labor force requirements were considerably reduced. The total length of the

Figure 13–8
Labor force loading schedule for the space
vehicle project

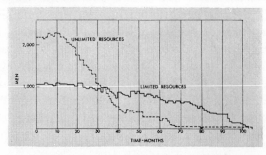

Source: From J. D. Wiest, "A Heuristic Model for Scheduling Large Projects with Limited Resources," *Management
Science*, vol. 13, no. 6 (February 1967), pp. 359–77.

project was shortened by five months through the SPAR schedule.
Obviously the unlimited resources schedule involves the immense
difficulties of near peak resource requirements at the beginning of
the project which quickly begin to drop off to fairly low levels
involving large hiring and layoff costs. The SPAR schedule also
reduced by 30 percent the number of unit increases in resource
requirements, that is, the month-to-month changes in the resource
schedule. For the unlimited resource schedule the total positive
changes in resource levels was 2,406, representing gross hirings,
but only 1,683 for the SPAR schedule.

SDR/CPM—A cost minimization scheduling program

The SDR/CPM scheduler is a program developed by Jones and
Taubert for project scheduling which attempts to minimize total
overall project cost. Its flexibility is such that it can handle the objectives discussed earlier of unlimited resources with least costing, resource leveling with a fixed completion date, and/or resource allocation for the earliest possible completion date. In addition, it can
schedule using overtime if desired.

The SDR/CPM scheduler represents an application of the Search
Decision Rule concepts of Chapter 6 to project scheduling. It utilizes
traditional CPM concepts with one important difference. Activities
are defined in terms of the number of worker-days of a particular resource required for activity completion, rather than in terms of a
fixed time interval requiring the uniform application of the resource.

Under SDR/CPM activity X, for example, might be defined as consisting of a 30-worker-day effort of labor class 1 employees with the stipulation that the activity could be performed by no less than one, and no more than five employees working as a team, with a typical average work crew consisting of three workers. The traditional CPM specification of the same activity would be a fixed ten-day activity requiring three workers of labor class 1 for each of the ten days. Thus it can be seen that the duration, and hence daily labor force requirements of each SDR/CPM activity are considered to be variable within specified limits. In the previous example activity X could be performed by 1 person working for 30 days, 5 workers working for 6 days; or any combination in between which provides a total of 30 worker-days of effort. It is felt that the SDR/CPM specification is closer to the real-world practicalities of project scheduling where management is simultaneously allocating scarce resources to various activities from several labor pools.

The number of components (independent variables) in the SDR decision vector depends on the nature of the scheduling decisions desired. At the minimum, the vector consists of one component for each activity to be scheduled. This is necessary in order to represent the straight-time (eight hours per day) labor force allocation decision for each activity. If overtime is an important decision variable then a second set of decision components must be added in order to specify the overtime to be worked on each activity. Finally, if resource leveling is important then a third set of decision components must also be added in order to specify when the activity should start. In other words, the number of components in the SDR decision vector will be one, two, or three times the number of activities in the project. The number of components determines the dimensionality of the cost response surface which will be explored by the search routine.

The SDR/CPM cost model computes the cost of operating the project with a given set of trial decisions determined by the search routine. This involves making a CPM network forward and reverse pass to determine the completion date and slack, computing labor force requirements by labor class as a function of time. The impact of the decisions in terms of straight-time payroll, overtime, hiring/layoff expenses, penalties for late project completion, incentives for early completion, and so on, are costed out.

In order to illustrate this approach, the basic structure of the pipeline project given in the last chapter has been modified to construct an expanded SDR/CPM example which represents the problem of allocating limited resources from four labor pools. The cost model contains six cost elements including highly nonlinear relationships represented by seventh and eighth order polynomials. The basic structure of the SDR/CPM project is shown in Table 13–2. Activities

Table 13–2
SDR/CPM example adopted from the pipeline project (data given in Figure 12–9)

Activity number	From–to (i)–(j)	Worker/days	Labor class	Crew Max-imum	Min-imum	Average
1	1–2	30	1	5	1	3
2	1–5	140	4	15	2	5
3	2–3	4	3	4	1	2
4	3–4	2	1	3	1	2
5	4–5	0	5	0	0	0
6	4–6	4	3	3	1	2
7	4–7	30	5	0	0	0
8	4–8	45	5	0	0	0
9	5–6	2	4	2	2	2
10	6–8	0	5	0	0	0
11	6–9	18	4	8	1	3
12	7–9	15	1	7	2	2
13	8–11	2	1	3	2	2
14	9–10	24	1	7	3	4
15	10–11	4	2	4	2	2
16	11–12	2	1	3	2	2
17	11–13	20	1	6	2	5
18	12–13	0	5	0	0	0
19	12–14	2	1	3	2	2
20	13–14	2	3	3	1	2
21	14–15	2	4	3	1	2

5, 10, and 18 represent the dummy activities shown in Figure 12–9 of Chapter 12. They have been assigned to labor class 5 which has been established for the purpose of representing activities which require no direct labor resources. Activities 7 and 8 (procure pipes and procure valves in Figure 12–9) have also been assigned to labor class 5. They represent 30- and 45-day fixed duration activities which do not require any labor resources. This example was structured specifically to illustrate the flexibility of the SDR/CPM method in handling dummy activities, time-consuming zero resource activities and multiple-labor pools with different resource costs.

The cost elements of the model are given below and are illustrated in Figure 13–9.

Figure 13–9
Cost relationships of the SDR/CPM example

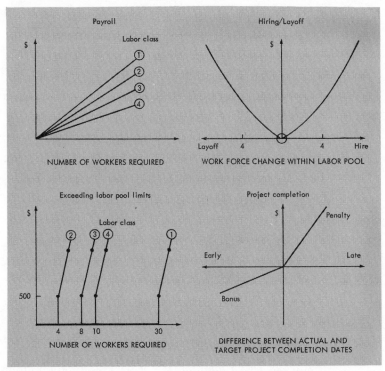

1. **Straight-Time and Overtime Pay:**

Labor class	Straight-time pay ($ per hour)	Overtime pay ($ per hour)
1	$5.00	$7.00
2	4.00	6.00
3	4.50	6.50
4	3.50	5.50
5	0	0

Note: Overtime pay does not necessarily have to be set at 1.5 times the straight-time rate.

2. **Hiring Cost (M = Number of workers hired)**

$$= 8.93 \times 10^{-2} + 2.86 \times 10^{2}M - 2.42 \times 10^{2}M^{2}$$
$$+ 2.54 \times 10^{2}M^{3} - 1.31 \times 10^{2}M^{4} + 3.55 \times 10^{1}M^{5}$$
$$- 5.21M^{6} + 3.90 \times 10^{-1}M^{7} - 1.17 \times 10^{-2}M^{8}$$

Note: Applies to hiring within each labor class. Equation obtained by polynomial cruve fitting.

3. *Layoff Cost* (M = *Number of workers laid off*)

$$= -1.51 \times 10^{-6} + 5.63 \times 10^{2}M - 6.27 \times 10^{2}M^{2}$$
$$+ 5.54 \times 10^{2}M^{3} - 2.37 \times 10^{2}M^{4} + 5.25 \times 10^{1}M^{5}$$
$$-5.78 \times M^{6} + 2.50 \times 10^{-1}M^{7}$$

Note: Applies to layoffs within each labor class. Equation obtained by polynomial curve fitting.

4. *Cost of Exceeding Labor Class Personnel Limits*

= $500/worker-day

where the maximum labor class limits are given by:

Labor class	Maximum workers available per day
1	˙30
2	4
3	8
4	10
5	0

5. *Late Project Completion Penalty*

= $200/day based on a 65-day project completion target

6. *Early Project Completion Bonus*

= $100/day based on a 65-day project completion target

The cost model was optimized and scheduling decisions computed with and without the overtime, and with and without the resource leveling decision options discussed earlier. Without the resource leveling decision option in effect all activities are scheduled to start at their earliest CPM computed start dates.

The results of the test are summarized in Table 13–3 and contrasted with the costs associated with a straightforward CPM scheduling solution without cost optimization. It can be seen from this table that not only did the SDR/CPM method reduce total overall project costs by a significant percentage (almost 20 percent), but it also produced scheduling decisions which permitted the project to be completed a day and a half ahead of schedule.

Most of the savings produced by this particular SDR/CPM example are derived from scheduling decisions which reduce hiring and

Table 13-3
Cost element comparison of SDR/CPM scheduling of CPM scheduling

Cost element	CPM only	SDR/CPM scheduling without personnel leveling		SDR/CPM scheduling with personnel leveling	
		Without overtime	With overtime	Without overtime	With overtime
Straight-time pay	8,904	8,904	8,455	8,904	8,839
Overtime pay	—	—	684	—	100
Hiring within labor class	6,663	4,791	4,703	4,625	4,611
Firing within labor class	9,700	7,333	7,061	7,072	6,924
Exceeding labor class limits	—	—	—	—	—
Late completion penalty	—	—	—	—	—
Early completion reward	—	−148	−148	−150	−150
Total	25,267	20,880	20,755	20,451	20,324
Percent improvement		17.4%	17.9%	19.1%	19.6%

layoff costs. These costs are computed by the seventh and 'eighth order polynomial expressions given earlier. These expressions were derived by applying mathematical curve-fitting techniques to hand-drawn hiring and layoff curves. The curves are approximately linear for personnel changes of one to four workers and specify a hiring cost of $200 per worker and a layoff cost of $300 per worker. Beyond this point the cost per worker increases sharply in order to represent the increasing costs associated with hiring or laying off a larger number of workers. Replacing the polynomials by their linear equivalents does not significantly alter the results of Table 13-2 since most personnel changes happen to fall in the one- to four-worker range. One of the advantages of the SDR/CPM scheduling approach is that it does not depend on a particular pre-specified type of cost relationship such as linear and quadratic for its operation. In addition, other cost elements, or cost curve shapes can be easily added to fit the particular application.

The SDR/CPM tests reported above were performed using the adaptive pattern search program. The search was initiated using a starting vector based on the average crew size for each activity shown in Table 13-2. The search was terminated after 1,000 evaluations of the objective function.

Control of large-scale one-time projects

The control phase of large projects is not a separate and distinct one. It is actually a complementary part of the other phases of planning and scheduling. Control will occur during the arrow diagram development phase, during the scheduling phase, and perhaps most important, during the performance phase of the project through reports of progress and the revision and updating of estimated times and schedules. Network analysis does not provide automatic control nor does it provide automatic planning for that matter. It does, however, provide a highly efficient managerial tool for planning and control. The basic performance of these two functions rests on management. Control may be divided into control of the planning function and control of the performance of the project.

Control of planning. Planning for a one-time project is, of course, a one-time function. The first point where control needs to be exercised by management is in the definition of project objectives, and this needs to occur before the list of project activities is developed. The activity list must be agreed upon by all management personnel involved in a particular project, since an incomplete list of activities will completely invalidate the subsequent phases of network planning and scheduling. A common practice seems to be to delay approval of the activity list until the arrow diagram has already been developed. The justification for this is that the arrow diagram will in itself provide a check on the activity list.

Approval of the arrow diagram is probably the key control function in the entire managerial technique. An erroneous arrow diagram could create so many problems in the performance of the project that the whole network concept might be abandoned.

Where the project is not internal, it is considered of basic importance to bring in the customer on the approval of the arrow diagram. The advantages of involving the customer in the approval of the arrow diagram come during the execution phase of the project. Since the arrow diagram is meant to be a complete description of the project, showing logical relationships, customer approval in effect means approval of a fairly detailed action plan. If modifications or changes are introduced later on, they can always be related to the original arrow diagram. Contract modification then ceases to be a matter of straight bargaining, since the arrow diagram can pinpoint exactly what the change involves and, more important, pinpoint the effects these changes will have on the schedule and on costs.

As with other kinds of control programs, different levels of responsibility and authority may require different degrees of detail in the arrow diagram and schedule. Thus a master arrow diagram, fairly small in size, can be constructed for top managerial personnel where each arrow of the master diagram will represent a small arrow diagram in itself with the duration of the master arrow being the length of the critical path of the detailed diagram. Each level of management involved can then exercise control at a different level.

Control of performance. Control of performance is dynamic and cannot be accomplished as a one-time project. Different reports may be generated during the course of the project to control performance. With the basic data provided in the schedule of earliest and latest start and finish times, slack times, and the critical path, there are many possible variations of report forms of the data. In one project a "daily list" was prepared by the computing center for each manager, showing a list of the critical activities to be started or completed each day and for the upcoming week.

The strategic factor in controlling performance is in the maintenance of an up-to-date schedule. The information feedback system needs to be rapid and accurate so that the critical schedule produced daily or weekly reflects the latest revisions in time estimates and the latest actual times for completed activities. One such system used by a utility company for major construction and project work involved circulating to operating managers in addition to the usual data on early and late start and finish times, slack, criticality, and an indication of the progress against the schedule. The schedule also had four blank columns to be marked by the managers if applicable as follows:

Column A—Activity just started and should be shown as "in progress" in the next schedule.

Column B—Activity just completed and should be shown as such in the next schedule, actual time for completion being entered.

Column C—Activity not to be started by its early start time but would be delayed by an amount specified.

Column D—Modification of the estimated activity time for an activity not yet started.

Individual managers marked the four blank columns thus providing daily information feedback to the data processing system. Updated schedules then reflected these revisions.

SUMMARY

Project planning, scheduling, and control combine aggregate planning with the details of the planning and scheduling of individual activities. The planning horizon is the entire project. The overall objectives are basically similar to those of the aggregate planning methods which we discussed in Part II but the emphasis is different because of the peculiar nature of one-time projects. In the resource leveling and resource allocation models an implied criterion is the cost of the changes in resource level (hiring and layoff), though there is no explicit cost function to be minimized. The Jones and Taubert SDR scheduling approach shows that it is now feasible to schedule small projects on a cost minimization basis by utilizing computerized search routines. Unlike the high-volume standardized product case, one cannot use inventories as a trade-off for change costs. Rather, inventories are in-process inventories and are related to the project duration and the details of the schedule. When several projects are going on simultaneously, the utilization of existing resources and schedule coordination between projects becomes important, and models like Wiest's SPAR and Jones's and Taubert's SDR/CPM schedules become even more important and valuable.

It is interesting to note that network planning and scheduling techniques in a sense combine both aggregate and detailed scheduling. That is, out of the entire process which involves aggregate planning comes a disaggregated schedule. Now that it has been possible to optimize a cost model for this entire process a logical direction for future research would be to concentrate on the combination of aggregate and disaggregate planning and scheduling into one integrated system.

REVIEW QUESTIONS AND PROBLEMS

1. Suggest examples of activities (other than those given in this chapter) whose time-cost curves would be represented by Figure 13–1(a) and Figure 13–1(b).

2. A construction organization has an opportunity for a contract worth $45,000 but the contract calls for penalty for late performance of $2,000 per week after the projected completion time of eight weeks from the start time of the project. Given the data in Table 13–4 concerning the network of activities and associated costs, should the contractor sign the contract?

3. Problem 17 of Chapter 12 gives data for estimates of a, m, and b for all

Table 13–4
Network of activities and costs for a construction project

Activity	Immediate predecessor activity	Normal schedule		Crash schedule	
		t_e, Weeks	Cost	t_e, Weeks	Cost
A	None	2	$4,000	1	$6,500
B	None	3	3,500	1	9,500
C	None	6	5,500	5	6,750
D	B	4	3,000	3	5,000
E	B	2	4,500	1	5,000
F	B	7	4,250	6	5,750
G	A, D	4	5,250	3	8,000
H	C, E	3	2,500	2	3,500

activities required for the pipeline renewal project. The project is in progress with all activities scheduled to begin according to their ES times. A problem has developed in the completion of activity G, procure valves. New estimates of the valve delivery as of $T = 45$ are $A = 13, M = 15$, and $B = 23$ days. All other activities to this point have been started and finished according to their ES and EF times.

Penalty clauses in the contract require the contractor to forfeit $500 per day for each day that project completion is delayed beyond $T = 65$ days. A careful analysis of the remaining activities yields the following data regarding slow and crash schedules. Which if any of the activities should be expedited?

a. Activity G can be expedited by using air freight at a cost of $500. Given delivery by air freight the supplier will guarantee delivery within $T = 61$ days. Based on the revised delivery guarantee it is estimated that the earliest delivery possible would be $T = 57$ days and that the most likely delivery times would be $T = 59$ days.

b. Activity M, weld pipe, can be expedited in its expected time by one day by doubling the crew for that activity, drawing resources from activity K.

c. The estimate of b for activity O, insulate, can be shortened to 3.5 days by the rental of a lift truck so that the work can be done from normal working positions, at a cost of $200.

4. Define the terms: local shift, global shift, left-justified schedule.

5. Using Wiest's heuristic rules generate a right-justified schedule for the left-justified schedule shown in Figure 13–10. Maximum crew size is 15 workers. Your answer should document the sequence of local right-shifts in order to prove that the Wiest rules have been followed. How much slack is available to each activity for the related left- and right-justified schedules?

Figure 13–10
Left-justified schedule for a project with a
maximum crew size of 15 workers

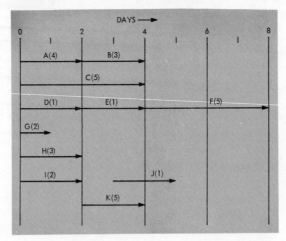

6. Define the term "critical sequence." How is a critical sequence different from a critical path?

7. We now have additional data on crew size requirements for the pipeline renewal project. Original data for the project is given in Tables 12–1 and 12–2 together with the network diagrams shown in Figures 12–10 and 12–12. The contractor maintains a maximum size crew of 25 workers and the various activities require the following crew sizes per day:

Activity	Crew, workers/day	Activity	Crew, workers/day
A	—	J	25
B	—	K	10
C	—	L	25
D	—	M	5
E	15	N	10
F	—	O	10
G	—	P	5
H	8	Q	10
I	5	R	10

a. Develop a graph of total crew requirements versus project days, assuming that all activities start according to the ES times.

b. Given the ES schedule deployment of labor what percent of the time is the total crew utilized after the first activity requiring the crews begins?

c. Using only available schedule slack develop an improved labor deployment which tends to maximize labor utilization once the first activity requiring crews begins. Develop a graph of the labor deployment in your improved schedule.

d. What is the percent utilization of the crew after the first activity requiring labor begins for your improved schedule?

e. If unplanned-for workers are laid off and if the layoff of one worker for more than five days costs an average of $300, compare labor turnover costs for the schedules developed in (a) and (c). Labor turnover costs are due to worker's compensation insurance premiums and hiring and training costs.

8. Contrast the concepts of resource leveling, which assumes unlimited resources, with those used by Wiest in his heuristic program for limited resources.

SELECTED BIBLIOGRAPHY

1. Archibald, R. D., and Villoria, R. L. *Network-Based Management Systems.* New York: John Wiley & Sons, Inc., 1967.

2. Berman, E. B. "Resource Allocations in a PERT Network under Continuous-Time Cost Functions," *Management Science,* July 1964.

3. Burgess, A. R., and Killebrew, J. B. "Variation in Activity Level on a Cyclical Arrow Diagram," *Journal of Industrial Engineering,* vol. 13, no. 2 (March–April 1962), pp. 76–83.

4. Clark, C. E. "The Optimum Allocation of Resources among the Activities of a Network," *Journal of Industrial Engineering,* vol. 12, no. 1 (January–February 1961).

5. Crowston, W., and Thompson, G. L. "Decision CPM: A Method for Simultaneous Planning, Scheduling and Control of Projects," *Operations Research,* vol. 15, no. 3 (May–June 1967), pp. 407–26.

6. Davis, E. W. "Resource Allocation in Project Network Models—a Survey," *Journal of Industrial Engineering,* vol. 17, no. 4 (April 1966), pp. 177–88.

7. Dewitte, L. "Manpower Leveling in PERT Networks," *Data Processing for Science/Engineering,* March–April 1964.

8. Fulkerson, D. R. "A Network Flow Computation for Project Cost Curves," *Management Science,* vol. 7 (1961).

9. Heuser, W. A. Jr., and Wynne, B. E., Jr. "An Application of the Critical Path Method to Job-Shop Scheduling—A Case Study," *Management Technology,* vol. 3, no. 2 (December 1963), pp. 128–44.

10. Jewell, W. S. "Risk Taking in Critical Path Analysis," *Management Science,* January 1965.

11. Johnson, R. A.; Kast, F. E.; and Rosenzweig, J. E. *The Theory and*

Management of Systems. 2d ed. New York: McGraw-Hill Book Co., 1967.

12. Johnson, T. J. R. "An Algorithm for the Resource Constrained Project Scheduling Problem." Unpublished Ph.D. dissertation, M.I.T., 1967.

13. Kelley, J. E. "Critical Path Planning and Scheduling: Mathematical Basis," *Operations Research,* vol. 9, no. 3 (1961).

14. Levin, R. I., and Kirkpatrick, C. A., *Planning and Control with PERT/CPM.* New York: McGraw-Hill Book Co., 1966.

15. Levy, F. K.; Thompson, G. L.; and Wiest, J. D. "Multi-Ship Multi-Shop Workload Smoothing Program," *Naval Research Logistics Quarterly,* March 1963.

16. Levy, F. K.; Thompson, G. L.; and Weist, J. D. "The ABCs of the Critical Path Method," *Harvard Business Review,* September–October 1963, pp. 98–108.

17. Malcom, D. G.; Roseboom, J. H.; Clark, C. E.; and Fazar, W. "Application of a Technique for Research and Development Program Evaluation," *Operations Research,* September–October 1959, pp. 646–69. Reprinted as chap. 29 in E. S. Buffa, ed., *Readings in Production and Operations Management.* New York: John Wiley & Sons, Inc., 1966.

18. Moder, J. J., and Phillips, C. R. *Project Management with CPM and PERT,* 2d ed. New York: Reinhold Publishing Corp., 1970.

19. Shaffer, L. R.; Ritter, J. B.; and Meyer, W. L. *The Critical Path Method.* New York: McGraw-Hill Book Co., 1965.

20. Wiest, J. D. "Heuristic Programs for Decision-Making," *Harvard Business Review,* September–October 1966, pp. 129–43.

21. Wiest, J. D. "Some Properties of Schedules for Large Projects with Limited Resources," *Operations Research,* vol. 12, no. 3 (May–June 1964). Reprinted as Chap. 31 in E. S. Buffa, ed., *Readings in Production and Operations Management.* New York: John Wiley & Sons, Inc., 1966.

22. Wiest, J. D. "A Heuristic Model for Scheduling Large Projects with Limited Resources," *Management Science,* vol. 13, no. 6 (February 1967), pp. 359–77.

23. Wiest, J. D. and Levy, F. K. *A Management Guide to PERT/CPM.* 2d ed. Englewood Cliffs, N.J.: Prentice-Hall, Inc., 1977.

CASE STUDY: BABCOCK & WILCOX COMPANY: THE NUCLEAR DIVISION

DURING THE LATE 1960s, the Babcock & Wilcox Company (B&W) experienced numerous problems in the management of their nuclear manufacturing operations. These problems, which were focused on the production of a new nuclear product at the existing Barberton, Ohio plant as well as the new Mt. Vernon, Indiana plant, were largely responsible for the drastic reduction in company profits from 1968 to 1971 (see Exhibit 1).

On the surface the exact nature of these difficulties seemed to have revolved around labor difficulties, the inability of manufacturing to get new machinery debugged, and some plain bad luck. All of these problems resulted in late deliveries on multimillion dollar contracts which, in turn, resulted in contract cancellations and court proceedings regarding financial penalties.

Looking back on the 1968–71 era in 1975, many B&W managers felt that another fundamental problem had been that the company had tried to plan and control the production of a new product (nuclear components) with a new process technology, with old planning and control systems and assumptions—systems and assumptions that were appropriate for other B&W products but not nuclear components manufactured in a job-shop environment. These same managers now pointed with pride to a sophisticated computerized manufacturing planning system called the Long-Range Planning System (LRPS) that was developed at B&W during this period of difficulty, and whose implementation accompanied financial recovery.

Exhibit 1

BABCOCK & WILCOX COMPANY: THE NUCLEAR DIVISION
Ten-Year comparison
($000)

Income and Retained Earnings

For the calendar year

	1974	1973	1972
Sales (on percentage of completion method for long-term contracts) .	$1,277,168	$1,063,741	$ 955,885
Costs and expenses except depreciation	1,177,094	999,024	890,895
Depreciation	24,850	21,640	19,403
	1,201,944	1,020,664	910,298
Income from operations	75,224	43,077	45,587
Income from investments	5,731	3,783	3,157
Interest expense	(22,082)	(10,203)	(6,446)
Income before taxes and minority interests	58,873	36,657	42,298
U.S. and foreign taxes on income	24,650	14,450	17,780
	34,223	22,207	24,518
Income applicable to minority interests	(88)	(124)	(82)
Net income for the year	34,135	22,083	24,436
Cash dividends declared	9,685	9,684	6,833
Remainder, to retained earnings	24,450	12,399	17,603
Retained earnings at beginning of year	240,593	228,194	210,591
Retained earnings at end of year	$ 265,043	$ 240,593	$ 228,194

Changes in Financial Position

For the calendar year

	1974	1973	1972
Working capital at beginning of year	$ 134,496	$ 151,250	$ 144,452
Financial resources were provided by:			
Net income	34,125	22,983	24,486
Add or (deduct) items not affecting working capital:			
Depreciation	24,850	21,640	19,403
Deferred income taxes, noncurrent	1,330	1,170	1,110
Income applicable to minority interests	88	124	82
Equity in undistributed earnings of affiliated companies ..	(3,242)	(2,710)	(625)
Working capital provided by operations for the period	57,161	42,307	44,406
Fair market value of common stock issued for purchase of			
minority interests in subsidiary			6,383
Additional noncurrent borrowings	6,855	14,554	14,586
Conversion of current debt to noncurrent	155,000		
	219,016	56,861	65,375
Financial resources were used for			
Additions to property, plant, and equipment	61,629	36,836	41,897
Cash dividends declared	9,665	9,684	6,833
Reductions of noncurrent indebtedness	1,634	6,548	3,691
·Purchase of interest in B&W Ltd.		10,458	
Purchases of and other changes in minority interests	64	(329)	3,805
Purchase of Treasury stock		12,172	
Change in noncurrent receivables	566	223	(1,133)
Other, net	1,912	(1,977)	3,484
	75,490	73,615	58,577
Net increase (decrease) in working capital	143,526	(16,754)	6,798
Working capital at end of year	$ 278,022	$ 134,496	$ 151,260

1971	1970	1969	1968	1967	1966	1965
$ 959,092	$ 826,424	$ 718,566	$ 647,613	$ 624,723	$ 561,627	$ 481,600
895,697	782,779	690,111	584,522	545,935	485,628	412,487
18,396	16,417	13,439	10,934	16,436	14,778	13,519
914,093	799,196	703,550	595,456	562,371	500,406	426,006
44,999	27,228	15,016	52,157	62,352	61,221	55,594
1,931	1,459	505	928	305	2,095	1,461
(8,344)	(11,449)	(9,022)	(3,391)	(1,412)	(838)	(715)
38,586	17,238	6,499	49,694	61,245	62,478	56,340
17,170	6,390	190	23,710	27,260	28,710	26,030
21,416	10,848	6,309	25,984	33,985	33,768	30,280
(752)	(827)	(584)	(742)	(770)	(766)	(330)
20,664	10,021	5,725	25,242	33,215	33,002	29,450
6,168	8,810	16,752	16,726	16,681	15,313	13,458
14,496	1,211	(11,027)	8,516	16,534	17,689	15,992
196,095	194,884	205,911	197,395	180,861	163,172	147,180
$ 210,591	$ 196,095	$ 194,884	$ 205,911	$ 197,395	$ 180,861	$ 163,172

1971	1970	1969	1968	1967	1966	1965
$ 128,355	$ 141,205	$ 214,728	$ 180,735	$ 156,721	$ 163,400	$ 137,710
20,664	10,021	5,725	25,242	33,215	33,002	29,450
18,396	16,417	13,439	10,934	16,436	14,778	13,519
3,510	3,900	5,015	3,925			
752	827	584	742	770	766	830
43,322	31,165	24,763	40,843	50,421	48,546	43,799
72,386	13,500	22,000	59,000	28,000		
115,708	44,665	46,763	99,843	78,421	48,546	43,799
24,283	25,340	50,523	37,388	33,509	34,807	19,610
6,168	8,810	16,752	16,726	16,681	15,313	13,458
62,200	12,200	53,200	14,200	2,200	2,200	
	9,499					
4,771	237	204	320	320	278	(40)
218	(157)	(669)	(1,612)	1,547	1,695	(13,535)
1,971	1,586	276	(1,172)	150	932	(1,384)
99,611	57,515	120,286	65,850	54,407	55,225	18,109
16,097	(12,850)	(73,523)	33,993	24,014	(6,679)	25,690
$ 144,452	$ 128,355	$ 141,205	$ 214,728	$ 180,735	$ 156,721	$ 163,400

Exhibit 1 (continued)

	1974	1973	1972
Income from operating: % of sales	5.9%	4.1%	4.8%
Net income for year: % stockholders' equity first of year	10.8%	7.0%	8.3%
Orders received (thousands of dollars)	$2,103,331	$1,884,344	$1,475,326
Unfilled orders (thousands of dollars)	$4,114,714	$3,288,551	$2,467,948
Common shares issued end of year..........................	12,604,906	12,604,906	12,604,906
Per average number of shares outstanding; 1974—42,105,748, 1973—12,146,573, 1972—12,406,339; 1965–71—12,366,626			
Income for year	$ 2.82	$ 1.82	$ 1.97
Cash dividends declared	80	80	55
Stockholders' equity	28.22	26.11	35.54

	1974	1973	1972
Assets			
Current asets			
Cash	$ 47,903	$ 30,014	$ 21,259
Marketable securities..................................	400	598	18,291
Accounts receivable....................................	187,741	177,022	141,041
Unbilled sales	177,486	123,337	103,445
Inventories	307,915	221,587	170,243
Total Current Assets	721,445	552,558	454,279
Noncurrent receivables	1,065	499	276
Investments	27,698	24,169	11,719
Property, plant and equipment	291,554	253,117	238,279
Prepaid expenses and other assets	14,212	11,125	12,026
Total Assets	$1,055,974	$841,468	$716,579
Liabilities and Stockholders' Equity			
Current liabilities			
Notes payable	$ 23,403	$ 72,939	$ 11,671
Accounts payable and accrued liabilities	272,559	217,965	192,988
Provision for warranty expense..........................	40,839	42,421	33,803
Cash dividends payable	2,421	2,421	1,733
U.S. and foreign income taxes	104,196	82,316	62,834
Total Current Liabilities	443,423	418,062	303,029
Noncurrent indebtedness	249,704	86,385	78,380
Deferred income taxes...................................	19,960	18,630	17,460
Minority interests in subsidiary companies	1,278	1,255	801
Total Liabilities...................................	714,365	524,332	399,670
Stockholders' equity			
Preferred stock authorized and unissued			
Common stock including capital surplus	88,716	88,715	88,715
Retained earnings......................................	265,043	240,593	228,194
	353,759	329,308	316,909
Less: Treasury stock, at cost	12,150	12,172	
Total Stockholders' Equity	341,609	317,136	316,909
Total Liabilities and Stockholders' Equity..............	$1,055,974	$841,468	$716,579

1971	1970	1969	1968	1967	1966	1965
4.7%	3.3%	2.1%	8.1%	10.0%	10.9%	11.5%
7.4%	3.6%	2.0%	9.0%	12.6%	13.4%	12.8%
$ 867,938	$1,118,298	$ 812,758	$ 911,082	$1,099,295	$ 840,064	$ 651,195
$1,948,507	$2,039,661	$1,747,787	$1,653,595	$1,390,127	$ 915,555	$ 637,118
12,366,626	12,366,626	12,366,626	12,366,626	12,366,626	12,366,626	12,366,626
$ 1.67	$ 81	$ 46	$ 2.04	$ 2.69	$ 2.67	$ 2.38
50	72	1.36	1.36	1.36	1.20	1.10
23.69	22.51	22.42	23.31	22.62	21.25	19.85

1971	1970	1969	1968	1967	1966	1965
$ 24,829	$ 26,521	$ 13,549	$ 16,199	$ 12,839	$ 15,830	$ 14,641
949	496	1,912	1,266	5,297	16,580	79,117
138,178	131,452	113,878	98,985	85,525	75,671	10,301
101,007	95,779	84,578	67,071	47,841	35,136	16,683
157,198	162,001	170,152	160,300	138,625	119,396	98,936
422,161	416,249	384,069	343,821	290,127	262,613	249,678
1,409	1,191	1,348	2,017	3,629	2,082	387
11,246	9,851	340	340	341	447	961
216,472	211,291	202,648	165,638	139,415	122,392	102,476
7,702	6,421	4,567	4,217	5,157	4,851	3,292
$658,990	$645,003	$592,972	$516,033	$438,669	$392,385	$356,794
$ 11,647	$ 81,930	$ 86,340	$ 6,761	$ 3,658	$ 5,776	$
182,957	153,409	126,762	90,237	76,860	72,101	59,512
32,530	23,029	12,605	7,992	4,431	4,955	4,354
1,544	1,540	4,188	4,184	4,176	3,824	3,368
49,030	27,986	12,969	19,919	21,277	19,236	19,044
277,708	287,894	242,864	129,093	109,392	105,892	86,278
67,486	57,300	56,000	87,200	42,400	16,600	18,800
16,350	12,840	8,940	3,925			
4,523	8,542	7,952	7,572	. 7,150	6,700	6,212
366,067	366,576	315,756	227,790	158,942	129,192	111,290
82,332	82,332	82,332	82,332	82,332	82,332	82,332
210,591	196,095	194,884	205,911	197,395	160,861	163,172
292,923	278,427	277,216	288,243	279,727	263,193	245,504
292,923	278,427	277,216	288,243	279,727	263,193	245,504
$658,990	$645,003	$592,972	$516,033	$438,669	$392,385	$356,794

Exhibit 1 (concluded)

Property, Plant, and Equipment

For the calendar year

	1974	1973	1972
Cost			
At beginning of year	$ 494,099	$460,539	$426,381
Expenditures during year	61,629	36,836	41,897
Other additions—initial consolidation of subsidiaries	3,344		
Retired or sold during year	(6,025)	(3,276)	(7,739)
At end of year	553,047	494,099	460,539
Accumulated depreciation			
At beginning of year	240,982	222,260	209,909
Charged to operations during year	24,850	21,640	19,403
Other additions—initial consolidation of subsidiaries	613		
Retired or sold during year	(4,952)	(2,918)	(7,052)
At end of year	261,493	240,982	222,260
Net Book Value	$ 291,554	$253,117	$238,279

By 1975, B&W had become a leader in the manufacture of major components for nuclear power systems. They had been successful in regaining creditability in the eyes of their customers, and consequently a sizable share of the market.

Company background

The Babcock & Wilcox Company was founded in 1867 when George Babcock and Stephan Wilcox developed a new concept in steam-boiler design. The firm supplied these boilers to the first electrical generating station which was built in Philadelphia in 1881. Also, in 1887, B&W built the steam generator for Thomas Edison's first central power station.

Over the years, B&W followed a growth strategy of expanding and diversifying into areas which augmented its major commitment to supplying the power generation industry, where the company had always had an excellent reputation as a supplier of fossil-fired steam systems. Growth came through continual technological advancement provided by an emphasis on engineering know-how. By 1967, sales had reached $625 million with profits of $33.2 million and the company was listed 141 on Fortune's list of the 500 largest companies in the United States.

As the partial organization chart in Exhibit 2 illustrates, the company in 1975 was composed of a number of closely related operating divisions reflecting the individual characteristics of related groups of

1971	1970	1969	1968	1967	1966	1965
$406,685	$383,355	$334,556	$298,317	$266,404	$232,858	$214,948
24,283	25,340	50,523	37,388	33,509	34,807	19,610
		131		444		119
(4,587)	(2,141)	(1,724)	(1,149)	(2,040)	(1,261)	(1,819)
426,381	406,685	383,355	334,556	298,317	266,404	232,853
195,394	180,707	168,918	158,902	144,012	130,382	118,583
18,396	16,417	13,439	10,934	16,436	14,778	13,519
		119		247		29
(3,881)	(1,849)	(1,650)	(918)	(1,793)	(1,148)	(1,749)
209,909	195,394	180,707	168,918	158,902	144,012	130,382
$216,472	$211,291	$202,648	$165,638	$139,415	$122,392	$102,476

products or customers. For example, the Tubular Products Division manufactured specialty steel tubing, steel extrusions, and welded fittings. The Refractories Division produced firebrick and ceramic fibers. The Automated Machine Division produced metalworking and metal-cutting machinery, some industrial machinery, and broaching machines. Bailey Meter manufactured analog and digital combustion control systems for the steam generation market. Control Components Inc. built specialty control valves. Diamond Power Specialty Corp. produced boiler cleaning equipment, nuclear control-rod drives, and insulation for nuclear power plants. The Navy Nuclear Fuel Division supplied the special fuel needs of the U.S. Navy.

In 1975, revenues from the sale of steam-generating equipment accounted for 73 percent of total sales. Included in this category were the sales by divisions belonging to the Industrial Products Group, whose products and customers were closely associated with those of steam-generating equipment. The Tubular Products Division, which supplied tubing for both internal use and sale to independent customers, accounted for 21 percent of total sales.

In terms of sales, personnel, and capital investment, the Power Generation Group was the largest organizational unit in the company. As a practical matter, however, this group was involved in two distinct businesses which served many of the same customers. The Fossil Power Generation Division engineered, manufactured, constructed, and sold steam-generating equipment which used fossil

Exhibit 2
Partial organization chart

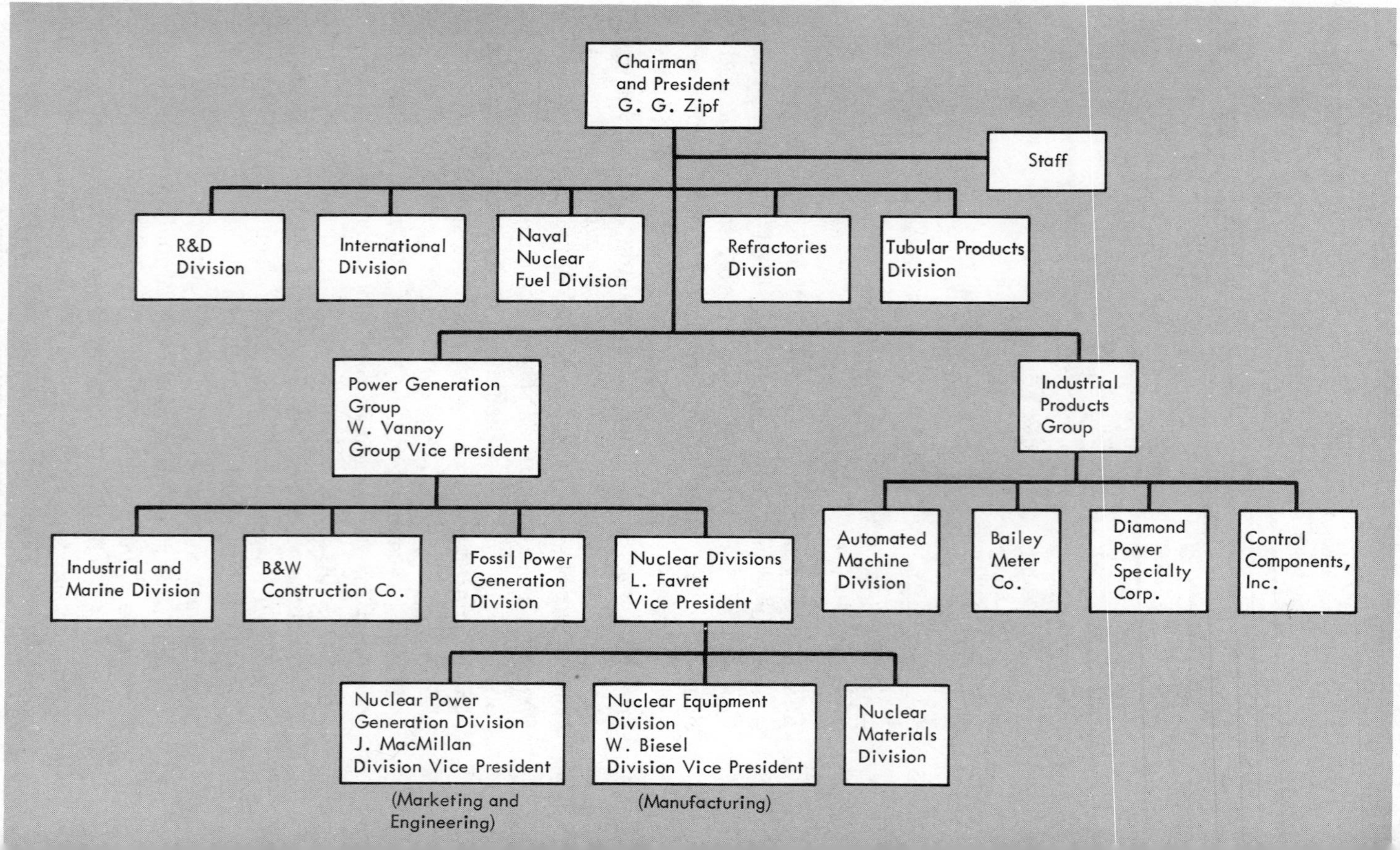

fuels as a power source. The Nuclear Power Generation Divisions engineered, manufactured, constructed, and sold steam-generating equipment which was powered by nuclear fuels.

Nuclear-powered equipment was sold to three types of customers. The Navy had long used B&W equipment and fuel in its submarines and aircraft carriers, and was an important customer. During the period between 1972 and 1974, an average of nearly $250 million in orders for Navy nuclear hardware and fuel were received each year. Another class of customers were the utility companies for whom B&W designed, manufactured, and constructed complete commercial nuclear power plants. In 1975, B&W nuclear power systems accounted for 15 percent of the installed nuclear-generating capacity in the U.S. commercial power generation industry. The third class of customers were the other major suppliers of commercial nuclear power systems, such as Westinghouse and General Electric, to whom B&W occasionally sold system components that these firms were either unwilling or unable to manufacture. Nuclear pressure vessels manufactured in the Mt. Vernon works were a good example of the type of component this class of customer was likely to procure from B&W. In 1975, the total nuclear business was profitable, although that portion of the business that catered to commercial (nonmilitary) customers was still running in the red.

An unusual aspect of B&W's business was that sales (shipments) could be accurately forecast for several years in advance. This was due to the fact that most of the company's products took several years to engineer and manufacture. In 1975, orders for sales of $1.678 billion for all products were received, and by the end of the year the total undelivered backlog was worth $4.227 billion. The company expected to ship 28 percent of this backlog in 1976, 49 percent in 1977 through 1979, and 23 percent thereafter. Approximately 50 percent of the total backlog was for nuclear business, although the financial and regulatory uncertainties facing B&W's utility customers had forced the cancellation of three nuclear systems and the extension or indefinite postponement of others in 1974. A severely depressed market for nuclear steam systems produced only three orders in 1975, totaling 3,100 megawatts of capacity for the industry.

The nuclear business

During the early 60s, it had become clear to B&W top management that nuclear energy would play a major role in fueling steam-generating plants in the future. B&W had considerable knowledge in the nuclear field, having operated an extensive nuclear research center since 1956. Also, the company had obtained the contract for the nation's first privately financed nuclear power system, Consolidated Edison's Indian Point Station, and had supplied the reactor for the world's first nuclear merchant ship, the *Savannah*. In addition, the company furnished components for the Nuclear Navy Submarine Program. As a result of these successes, the decision had been made to enter the market for Commercial Nuclear Power Generation Systems.

A nuclear steam system was composed of eight major components. These included the reactor vessels, the core structure, pressurizer, closure head, steam generator, primary piping, internals, and the core flooding tank. While from a contract and marketing point of view the basic product of the division was generally a "system," for control purposes manufacturing viewed each of the eight types of components as a product. Each component was, in itself, composed of a number of different subcomponents, manufacturing steps, and parts and materials.

Nuclear division manufacturing operations were located in Barberton, Ohio, and Mt. Vernon, Indiana. The Mount Vernon plant was constructed for the sole purpose of manufacturing and assembling large nuclear components. Portions of the older Barberton site were converted to nuclear products after the decision to enter the business was made. Many of the smaller parts of a nuclear system component were produced at Barberton. Many of these parts were shipped to Mt. Vernon where the very large major components of the system were built (primarily heads, reactor vessels, steam generators, and pressurizers).

The production process organization of these plants was very accurately described by the term "job shop." The plants were multibay facilities designed to accommodate the very large size of many of the components, and the general-purpose machines designed to work on them (see Exhibit 3). The term "job shop" also described the fact that the process flow of a component in the course of fabrication was exceedingly complex. In marked contrast to fossil fuel steam system production, in which components moved from one special-purpose operation to the next in serial or "assembly line" fashion, nuclear components moved in an almost random pattern from one work center to another—often to revisit previous work centers again.

Exhibit 3

Exhibit 4 illustrates the basic job shop flow in simplistic form. The exhibit represents a shop consisting of four Work Stations numbered one through four. Each Work Station represents one or more machines with unique capabilities. The four lines, representing components to be manufactured, enter at the top and leave at the bottom. As shown, each component follows a unique path through the shop. The complexity of the actual situation in comparison to this example can be gauged by noting that contracts for nuclear systems at a given time may represent over 340 components each of which involve thousands of separate work activities, and travel across hundreds of machines in various shops. B&W had opted for the job shop approach to process organization for nuclear components since it allowed many different components to be worked on in the same work center, thus avoiding the necessity of duplicating expensive pieces of equipment. Adding to the arguments for the job shop type of process at these plants was the fact that each nuclear system was, to

Exhibit 4
Nuclear equipment manufacturing

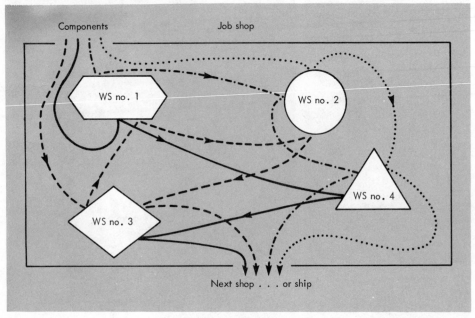

some extent, uniquely designed for its customer. The use of general-purpose equipment gave the firm a great deal of flexibility in producing to a customer's specifications.

The total time required to obtain materials for the system components ranged from one to three years, and the time to fabricate and assemble units, once the materials were available, took another one to three years. The total cost of a set of components was roughly composed of 50 percent purchased materials and 50 percent labor and overhead. However, B&W managers felt that over 70 percent of the overhead allocation was fixed. Hourly workers were highly skilled, and were represented by the International Union of Boilermakers. Wages were competitive with prevailing rates in the Barberton and Mt. Vernon areas.

Management philosophy focused the plants on three operating criteria; cost, quality, and on-time delivery. Elden Thomas, manager of production systems, and one of the original inventors of LRPS, described the work of the division as rather like producing a "500-ton Swiss watch," due to the exacting quality standards of the company, its customers, and federal regulations. The importance of on-time deliveries was indicated by the fact that very large penalties (up to $119,000 per week) for late deliveries were sometimes part of the terms of sales contracts.

Long range planning system (LRPS)

Although the company had successfully conceived, developed, and manufactured a multitude of new products during its more than 100 years of existence, it found that it was unable to meet its commitments to customers for the delivery of nuclear systems in 1968. The decline in earnings during 1968 through 1971 were largely due to the extra costs the company had incurred as a result of these events.

The first reasons that were advanced to explain the inability to meet delivery commitments were that certain start-up problems, especially at the Mt. Vernon facility, had delayed production, and prevented the plant from achieving anticipated output rates. Starting up any new manufacturing facility in the capital goods business is an arduous task. However, these problems are compounded when the product to be manufactured is in effect a prototype, and the plant organization, work force, and machine tools are new and untested in an actual production situation. This was evidenced by the delays and lost production that were associated with work force training and labor difficulties, late deliveries of production machinery from vendors supplying the new plant, and equipment engineering problems that plagued the start-up of the Mt. Vernon plant. Additionally, a minor earthquake in the normally geologically stable southern Indiana region upset the balance of delicate machinery causing further delays in production and losses in capacity. Thus, the forces of nature, perversely timed to coincide with anticipated start-up problems, contributed to the company's tribulations.

Upon reflection, however, it became apparent to some that an important contributing factor to the problems of the new nuclear business was the lack of a planning system for developing customer due date promises that reflected the new form of process organization employed at the Barberton and Mt. Vernon plants. Due dates had previously been determined with rules of thumb developed from years of experience with fossil fuel steam system manufacturing. In fossil manufacturing operations, the work stations were usually arranged in proper sequence to allow materials to enter one end of the shop and flow sequentially to completion. The normal work mix required that some work be performed at each work station, but seldom required the product to pass over any of the work stations more than once. All jobs followed essentially the same path from one work station to another. Consequently, it was relatively easy to regulate throughput by balancing the expenditures of machine-hours or labor-hours at each work station, to "line up" or "load" each shop with a high degree of certainty as to work content, schedule requirements, and fabrication completion, and thus to project shipment capabilities with ease. The job shop form of process organization employed at Mt. Vernon and Barberton was clearly different, and the recognition that new techniques were needed to promise shipment dates, determine equipment requirements and regulate production in this situation led to the development of LRPS by B&W's Corporate Operations Research Group.

The Operations Research (OR) function had anticipated the potential usefulness of a long-range planning system for determining customer due date commitment feasibility in the nuclear business as early as 1966. The OR group had been formed in 1966 and was specifically charged with the responsibility for performing all OR work for company divisions and subsidiaries. In the words of one B&W manager, "As one might expect, turning OR personnel loose in a 100-year-old company to look for opportunities for improvement resulted in the discovery of many areas with the potential for achieving quick financial returns, and several long-term problems, including the need for an improved method for planning nuclear equipment manufacturing operations."

After developing a clear understanding of the nuclear job shop process, OR personnel began in 1966 to review the progress toward developing solutions which fit the company's needs. It took little time to determine that only scant progress had been made toward what B&W managers felt were practical solutions. Many studies had been reported where simulation was used to test various kinds of scheduling (sequencing) rules to determine which maximized the probability of meeting due dates, reducing costs, or meeting other criteria. However, B&W managers felt this kind of work was theoretical in nature and could not be applied due to the general assumptions which were necessary. During that time, however, several researchers were investigating approaches using heuristic decision rules in scheduling algorithms incorporated in job shop simulation models. The works of J. D. Wiest and Stanley Reiter appeared most useful.

Wiest was contacted and provided with "live data" for testing his experimental computer program called SPAR (scheduling program for the allocation of resources). After several months of working with Wiest, the SPAR program was purchased and expanded for further "in-house" research using "live data" from a portion of the Mt. Vernon facility. By the end of 1967, it was satisfactorily shown that using heuristic scheduling rules to simulate the company's nuclear job shop operation was practical and extremely useful. Since SPAR was written for purposes of conducting research, it, therefore, had severe limitations. However, the OR group felt that SPAR had served several valuable functions: (1) in upgrading OR personnel's knowledge of resource allocation concepts, (2) in demonstrating simulation scheduling to Production Control management, and (3) in assisting OR personnel in designing the ultimate tool (LRPS) required to solve B&W's nuclear manufacturing planning problem.

The fundamental LRPS approach that grew from the OR group's early efforts is illustrated in Exhibit 5. As shown, data describing the

Exhibit 5
Computer Simulation

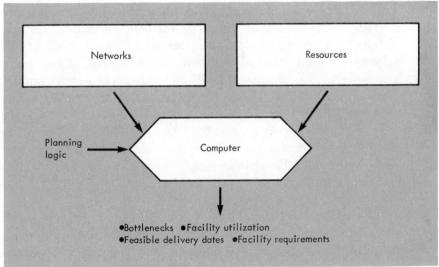

sequence of work to be done (routings) in PERT or CPM *network* form, along with desired completion dates, and information regarding resource availability, would be fed into the computer. The heuristic scheduling rules incorporated in the LRPS planning logic would then use this data to generate a simulated resource constrained schedule of nuclear manufacturing operations. The heuristic rules could best be described as scientific "rules of thumb." These rules were referred to in the simulation whenever a "decision" had to be made about which job to schedule at each machine center during its next available period. The rules were designed to maximize the productivity of B&W's facilities subject to the constraints that all contracts were to be completed on time if sufficient capacity was available. The output of this simulation was designed to provide management with information about scheduling bottlenecks that might develop; facility utilization over the duration of all nuclear contracts; feasible delivery dates for firm or potential contracts; and ultimately the facility requirements needed to meet various mixes of contractual obligations. (See Appendix for a detailed description of the LRPS logic.)

Depending upon the results of any one simulated schedule, additional simulations could be made to evaluate specific alternatives, or questions. For example, the effects on the overall operation of the acquisition of a specific piece of equipment for installation at some future date could be evaluated quickly by altering the resource capacity information going into the computer and generating a new simulated schedule. Many other tactics could also be examined, such as: (1) subcontract arrangements, (2) changes in Work Station capacity, (3) alterations in the sequence of fabrication, (4) changes in required contract completion dates, (5) addition of a new contract, (6) loss of a contract, (7) overtime policies, (8) effects of potential contracts prior to bid submission, and (9) trade-offs between work stations. It was also apparent to the OR group that finding an acceptable overall plan of operation would involve an iterative process whereby management would have to review simulated results, develop alternate strategies, and then resimulate operations, repeating this process until a satisfactory plan was derived.

In designing LRPS, the OR group felt that it was very important to address two issues. The first was to find ways to reduce the immense amount of simulation data to manageable proportions. The second was to find ways to identify and realistically represent critical Work Stations in manufacturing. Work Stations were groups of machines or workers with a similar purpose, and were the "resources" over which work had to be scheduled.

The first way that data requirements were reduced was to define classes of "networks" for each major component that identified the basic sequence of manufacturing activities involved in producing it.

Exhibit 6
Nuclear equipment components

Components	Type	Units	
Reactor	10	50	~113
Core structural	4	48	contracts
Pressurizer	5	29	
Closure head	10	94	3–4 years
Steam generator	8	87	
Primary piping	1	11	Several $100
Internals	1	11	million
Core flooding tank	1	11	
	40	341	

The names of the components produced for nuclear contracts are shown in Exhibit 6. Also shown for each component are the approximate number of types, and the total number of units, of each component which might have been on order at any given time in the early 1970s. For example, there might have been as many as 50 of 10 different types of reactor vessels on order. The significance of this example is that only 10 "basic" networks might be needed to represent the work activities required to build 50 reactor vessels, thus reducing data requirements immensely. It was found, after looking at all components, that approximately 40 "basic" networks could be used to represent the required manufacturing activities to build 341 individual components; however, each of the "basic" networks had to be slightly modified to accurately represent an individual component of a contract. In order for LRPS to take advantage of this analysis, a separate part of the system was dedicated to network data analysis and storage. This portion of the system was designed so that modifications to original networks could be easily made. Both the original, as well as any modified networks, could be stored for further use in simulating manufacturing schedules.

Critical Work Stations (the resources) were defined in a detailed study, which showed that there were approximately 125 Work Stations which involved important equipment or skills used in nuclear manufacturing. Further investigation revealed that in most instances the equipment or skills were either extremely expensive, required a long procurement lead time, or were one of a kind. These three criteria became the major guidelines for determining which Work Stations had to be capacity constrained to properly generate a simulated schedule. In designing LRPS, provision was made for identifying up to 150 capacity constrained Work Stations. Each Work Station could, however, contain any number of machines or workers.

Another characteristic of the critical Work Stations that was identified in this study was the capability of making "trade-offs" of work from one Work Station to another. Trade-offs would occur if an originally assigned Work Station was not available to perform required work because it had been scheduled to capacity. In this case, the work could be done by an alternate (although often less efficient) Work Station. This necessary and desirable practice had to be fully understood and taken into consideration when producing simulated

Exhibit 7
Manufacturing process plan
FABRICATION OUTLINE

PAGE __2__ OF __2__   ISSUE DATE _____   SEQ. PAGE _____ OF _____

SC 620	ORDER 0015	CP 60	UNIT	PART. NO. GP / MARK 1,2 A 0,0,0,1		CONTROL	PCS	OUTLINE BY	REV.	NEXT ASSEMBLY

DRAWING NO.	ITEM OR PART DESCRIPTION UPPER SECTION CORE SUPPORT CYLINDER		ESTIMATE			ESTIMATE BY
		PROP	DETAIL PRELIM	DETAIL	

MATERIAL SIZE & SPECIFICATION	INDICATE P.	INDICATE D	INDICATE X	APPROVED BY

START	FINISH	SEQ.	SHOP	W.C.	OPER. NO.	OPERATION DESCRIPTION	NO. DAYS	CUM DAYS	NO. MEN	E/S	EST. HRS.	FACT HRS.
*		230	ncl	005	02	FIT (2) TABS	1	65				
		240	ncl	145	02	WELD O.D. L.S. PER WC-1	3	68				
		250	ncl	008	03	ARC AIR RUN OFF TABS	1	69				
		260	ncl	008	01	GRIND FOR P.T. & REROLLING	2	71		s		
		270	103	161	06	P.T.	2	73		s		
		280	ncl	413½	32	WELD REPAIR	2	75				
		290	117	018	01	CLEAN FLOOR PLATES & ROLLS	4	79				
		300	117	128	10	FORM (REROLL)	3	82				
*		310	ncl	005	02	FIT (2) 17385 STRUTS	3	85				
		320	ncl	008	03	ARC AIR (2) LIFTING LUGS	1	86				
		330	ncl	008	01	GRIND LIFTING LUG AREA	1	87		s		
		340	125	107	48	VBM MACHINE	15	102				
		350	125	008	01	GRIND WELD PREP	2	104				
		360	103	161	06	P.T.	2	106		s		
		370	ncl	413	32	WELD REPAIR	1	107				

capacity constrained schedules. That is, the simulated schedules had to reflect Work Station "trade-off" capabilities and the cost penalties involved in trading work from the preferred resource (specified in a "Manufacturing Process Plan" as shown in Exhibit 7) to a secondary resource.

As the detailed development of LRPS proceeded, it became evident that even with the data reduction tactics that had been identified, the simulation scheduler would perhaps be called upon to schedule as many as 100,000 activities in order to properly evaluate the company's nuclear manufacturing operations at any given time. Any of the known techniques available in 1968 for handling this volume of data on the company's IBM 360/50 computer made solving this problem economically unfeasible. But, Operations Research personnel were convinced that if just 10,000 activities per hour could be scheduled, the computer costs would be justified and the "turnaround time" required to answer questions regarding manufacturing plans would be acceptable. Extensive research yielded computer techniques which allowed up to 18,000 activities per hour to be scheduled on an IBM 360/50 computer.[1] It was estimated that the system cost $225,000 to develop and program. In 1975, the annual operating costs were approximately $200,000, including computer and personnel costs necessary to support its maintenance.

LRPS reports

LRPS was designed in such a way that large amounts of data regarding specific contract component schedules, resource utilization, and contract completion dates could be generated by the simulation scheduler, and held for later use. Much of this data could be presented to management through means of formalized reports, including:

1. **Gross Resource Utilization Report.** A sample of this report is shown in Exhibit 8. The basic purpose of this report was to show the amount of work traded from one Work Center to another over the duration of the simulated schedule (perhaps as long as ten years). Also shown is the total number of jobs delayed, and the average delay days incurred at each Work Station during the simulated schedule for each delayed activity.

---

[1] By 1975, this was increased to 50,000 activities per hour on the company's new IBM 370/155 computer.

Exhibit 8

B & W - PUC - INFORMATION SYSTEMS DEPARTMENT - PROGRAM   222 - VERSION   2 - TIME 071H - DATE 10/31/72 - PAGE   1

G R O S S   R E S O U R C E   U T I L I Z A T I O N   R E P O R T   SIMULATION DATE   8/ 4/72

------------RESOURCE------------		RESOURCE VERSATILITY SUMMARY			ACTIVITY DELAY SUMMARY		RESOURCE DELAY SUMMARY	
SHP A/C OPR	IDENTIFICATION	SCHEDULED	TRADED TO	TRADED FROM	NO DELAYS	DAYS/DELAY	NO DELAYS	DAYS/DELAY
999 999 999	- PSEQUE	33823	0	0	9	0.0	0	0.0
999 999 83	- HOT WIRE TIG	5	5	0	3	13.9	0	0.0
999 999 82	- CULT WIRE TIG	2	0	5	9	0.0	0	0.0
999 999 81	- KELLERING CANTON	60	0	10	74	4.2	0	0.0
999 999 80	- MORE CLAD	0	0	6	0	0.0	0	0.0
999 999 78	- WELD MACH	2	2	0	9	0.0	0	0.0
999 999 77	- WELD MACH	9	0	2	9	0.0	0	0.0
999 999 72	- SUBLET CONTOUR	90	90	0	62	48.2	0	0.0
999 999 75	- SKICA MT VERSION	16	0	0	1	8.3	0	0.0
999 115 10	- ROLINE DRILL	168	0	0	114	176.0	0	0.0
123 116 999	- PIT CRRML INTERN	12	0	0	2	0.0	0	0.0
123 116 918	- PIT RAD DRL 528	7	0	0	2	24.6	0	0.0
123 164 34	- HBM FLR MITSUBIS	407	160	129	133	33.6	0	0.0
123 164 32	- HBM FLR MITSUBIS	337	227	65	141	25.5	0	0.0
123 164 31	- HBM FLR GLL	339	138	336	132	29.2	0	0.0
123 164 30	- HBM FLR GL	329	227	42	129	21.2	0	0.0
123 164 29	- HBM FLR GL 9%	343	105	90	139	45.4	0	0.0
123 164 24	- HBM FLR G&AY	237	102	11	122	36.8	0	0.0
123 164 22	- HBM FLR G&AY	361	136	287	122	26.8	0	0.0
123 164 23	- HBM FLR 5. TX GR	488	183	342	129	21.5	0	0.0
123 164 21	- HBM FLR 1.5 TON	191	69	0	122	61.3	0	0.0
123 164 13	- HBM TABL 6 SP TC	58	51	5	13	8.1	0	0.0
123 164 10	- FFR LGSEAM SINGL	275	75	173	131	52.5	0	0.0
123 164 40	- VAM 1 X X/21. TR	575	310	0	2.2	39.0	0	0.0
123 164 45	- VAM 144 X/270 TR	191	156	55	115	46.5	0	0.0
123 167 42	- VAM 120 X/270 TR	298	134	84	147	39.3	0	0.0
123 167 20	- VAM 144 X/270 TR	298	152	76	134	51.7	0	0.0
123 167 12	- VAM 121-144 TR	283	113	237	137	46.4	0	0.0
117 145 22	- FFR LGSEAM KILT	54	18	1	9	0.3	0	0.0
117 145 40	- FFR LGSEAM SINGL	103	103	0	15	29.7	0	0.0
117 145 2	- FFR LGSEAM SINGL	123	78	9	11	49.7	0	0.0
117 145 8	- PLASMA ARC	395	0	0	9	0.0	0	0.0
115 145 15	- ALS LGSEAM SINGL	437	0	0	64	2.9	0	0.0
123 145 40	- FFR LGSEAM SINGL	100	10	157	11	6.4	0	0.0
103 119 15	- GUN DRL 11N 3SPN	131	0	6	93	59.7	0	0.0
103 119 4	- GUN DRL 1/4-2.5	7	7	0	1	0.1	0	0.0
103 119 2	- GUN DRL 1/4-1.5	119	6	7	3	5.1	0	0.0
103 116 914	- PIT RAD DRILL	1	0	0	3	0.0	0	0.0
103 109	- HBM NAVY REMOVED	0	0	72	0	0.0	0	0.0
103 104 5	- HBM FLR 6 SPIND	345	72	64	73	19.5	0	0.0
103 104 10	- HBM TABL 6 SP TC	298	121	45	71	9.9	0	0.0
103 104 8	- HBM TABL 5 SPIND	86	68	0	33	10.7	0	0.0
103 104 5	- HBM TABL 6 SPIND	83	0	25	1	8.0	0	0.0
103 104 4	- HBM TABL 5 SPIND	418	0	170	66	6.9	0	0.0
103 167 23	- VGM 108 X/270 TR	196	185	8	129	41.4	0	0.0
103 167 37	- VAM BARNES 3AXIS	67	0	0	16	10.1	0	0.0
103 167 24	- VGM 144 X/360 TR	250	203	15	142	43.9	0	0.0

① ② ③   ④   ⑤   ⑥   ⑦   ⑧   ⑨

Key:
1. Shop number.
2. Work center number.
3. Operation number.
4. Operation description.
5. Number of jobs assigned to this operation.
6. Jobs that were traded to this Work Center from other Work Centers that were capacity limited.
7. Jobs that should have been assigned to this Work Center and were traded to other less efficient job centers because of capacity limits.
8. Number of jobs that are expected to be late.
9. Average number of days late for jobs that will be late.

2. LRPS Contract Completion Diagram.

Exhibit 9 shows a sample of this report. The plot consisted of plus or minus weeks plotted on the y-axis and the years in which contracts were due plotted on the x-axis. Any dot plotted above the zero location on the y-axis indicated the simulated completion of a component and the given number of weeks ahead of the required schedule date that it would be completed. The opposite was true for the dots below the zero location on the y-axis. This plot provided an easily understood graphic portrayal of the ability to meet shipment dates with a

Exhibit 9
Projected contract completion date

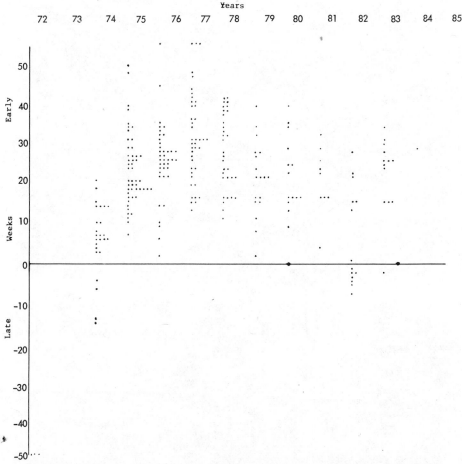

Note: The late jobs shown in this graph would be delivered late *if* no action were taken. Thus, this report stimulated further efforts to add capacity or take other actions which would improve delivery performance.

specific resource configuration. A supplemental report would specifically identify the potentially late units.

3. LRPS Work Center Load Reports. Exhibit 10 is a graphic portrayal of the simulated work load for a given Work Center over time. Normally a simulation would be made assuming all Work Centers were operative five days a week and three shifts a day, excluding holidays. If the results of the simulation were not satisfactory, additional simulations could be run assuming overtime, subcontracting

Exhibit 10
Required machining days per quarter—LRPS run no. 120, machine no. 10

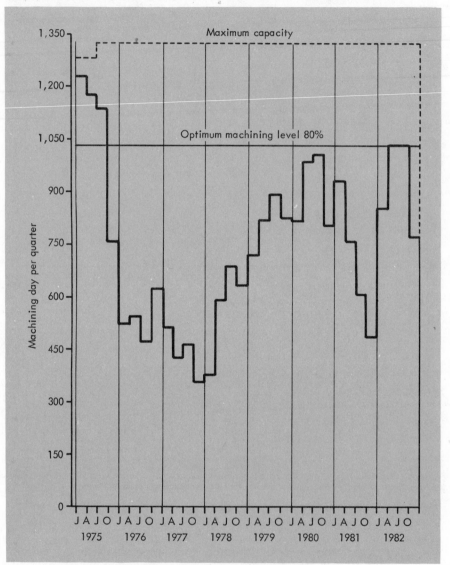

some of the work, or the procurement of additional Work Center
capacity.

4. **Resource Utilization Chart.** Exhibit 11 shows the simulated
utilization of a given Work Station as well as the amount of work
queued-up behind the Work Station over time. This particular ex-

Exhibit 11

B AND W - PGU - INFORMATION SYSTEMS DEPARTMENT - PROGRAM 222 - VERSION 2 - TIME 0807 - DATE 10/31/72 - PAGE 369

R E S O U R C E   U T I L I Z A T I O N   C H A R T

SHIP 123   WORK CENTER 109   OPERATION 026   -   HI M FLX CONTOUR

INTERVAL --- ENTIRE WORK CENTER

WK BEG	RESOURCE WEEKS SCHEDULED		RESOURCE WEEKS QUEUED	
	0 5 10 15 20 25 30 35 40 45 50 55 60 65 70		0 5 10 15 20 25 30	
??/ ./7 ?	•	1	U	1
1?/ ?/7 ?	•	1	0	1
1 ?/ ./7 ?	•	1	0	1
1?/ ?/7 ?	•	1	0	1
10/ ?/7 ?	•	1	0	1
10/ ./7 ?	•	1	0	1
11/ ?/7 ?	•	1	00	2
11/1?/7 ?	•	1	0	1
11/ ?/7 ?	•	1	0	1
11/ ?/7 ?	•	1	00	2
12/ ?/7 ?	•	1	000	3
12/ ./7 ?	•	1	00	2
12/11/7 ?	•	1	0000	4
12/24/7 ?	•	1	00000	5
12/31/7 ?	••	2	0000	4
1 ?/ ?/7 ?	•• ◄ — — — — ADD MACHINE	2	000	3
01/1 ?/7 ?	••	2	0000	4
01/21/7 ?	••	2	00000	5
01/2 ?/7 ?	••	2	0000	4
0 ?/ 4/7 ?	••	2	0000	4
0?/11/7 ?	••	2	0000000	7
0?/1 ?/7 ?	••	2	00000	5
0?/2?/7 ?	••	2	000	3
0?/ ?/7 ?	••	2	00000	5
03/11/7 ?	••	2	0000000	7
03/1 ?/7 ?	••	2	0000000	7
03/2 ?/7 ?	••	2	0000000	7
0?/31/7 ?	••	2	0000000	7
04/ ?/7 ?	••	2	00000000000	11
04/15/7 ?	••	2	000000000000	12
04/22/7 ?	••	2	0000000000000	13
04/2 ?/7 ?	••	2	00000000000000	14
05/ ?/7 ?	••	2	0000000000000000	16
05/1 ?/7 ?	••	2	00000000000000000000	20
05/2 ?/7 ?	••	2	0000000000000000000000	22
05/27/7 ?	••	2	0000000000000000000000	22
06/03/7 ?	••	2	0000000000000000000000	22
06/1 ?/7 ?	••	2	000000000000000000000	21
06/17/7 ?	••	2	00000000000000000000000	23
0?/ ?/7 ?	••	2	00000000000000000000	20
07/0 ?/7 ?	••	2	00000000000000000000	20
07/0 ?/7 ?	••	2	000000000000000000000	21
07/1 ?/7 ?	••	2		
0?/2 ?/7 ?	••	2		

WORK IN QUEUE

hibit shows that an additional machine was assumed available on a given week during the simulation. By comparing this same report with that from a previous simulation without the additional machine, decisions could be made regarding the advisability of adding additional real capacity to the manufacturing operation at a specific time. By making proper use of all of the available reports, "what if" questions could be answered and appropriate specific long-range actions could be taken.

5. Resource Utilization Report. Exhibit 12 represents a sample report showing the detailed simulated schedule for a given Work Station. Information shown on the report for each activity scheduled includes the *Available* Start Date (date predecessor activity was completed), Simulated Start Date, and Simulated Finish Date.

In addition to the above types of reports, LRPS also produced numeric data and graphical illustrations showing the amount of floor space required for each shop for the simulated schedule. To achieve this, it was necessary to provide input data giving the amount of floor space required by each piece of work as it progressed through

Exhibit 12

B AND W - PGDIV - INFO SYSTEMS AND COMPUTER SERVICES - PROGRAM 222 - VERSION 1 - TIME 2C27 - DATE 12/19/71	PAGE 157

R E S O U R C E   U T I L I Z A T I O N   R E P O R T

WK BEG	SHP	W/C	OPR	AV DATE¹	ST DATE²	FN DATE³	SC	ORD	NUM	TYP	REV	UNT	GP1	MRK1	SQ1	GP2	MRK2	SQ2
03/08/76 •	108	107	C20	03/10/76	03/11/76	03/16/76	600	00027	059	S6G	018	004	024	00018	290	024	00018	30C
•	108	107	C20	03/14/76	03/16/76	03/18/76	600	00030	054	S6G	000	005	C46	00001	010	046	00001	020
03/15/76 •	108	107	020	03/16/76	03/18/76	04/02/76	600	00027	059	S6G	018	004	024	00003	050	024	00003	070
03/29/76 •	108	107	C20	03/30/76	04/02/76	04/07/76	600	00030	054	S6G	000	002	025	00001	400	025	00001	410
04/05/76 •	108	107	C20	04/09/76	04/09/76	04/24/76	600	00017	059	S6G	017	009	025	00004	050	025	00004	070
04/26/76	108	107	C20	05/01/76	05/01/76	05/06/76	600	00030	054	S6G	000	003	025	00001	400	025	00001	410
05/03/76	108	107	C2C	05/07/76	05/07/76	05/11/76	600	00016	054	S6G	001	011	C32	A0001	140	025	A0001	150
05/10/76 •	108	107	C20	05/12/76	05/12/76	05/13/76	600	00016	054	S6G	001	014	C32	A0001	050	032	A0001	080
•	108	107	C20	05/12/76	05/13/7A	05/15/76	600	00030	054	S6G	000	002	C25	A0001	140	025	A0001	150
05/17/76	108	107	C20	05/22/76	05/22/76	05/26/76	600	00016	054	S6G	001	014	C46	00001	010	046	00001	020
05/31/76	108	107	C20	06/04/76	06/04/76	06/09/76	600	00024	054	C1W	003	002	010	00154	110	010	00154	170
06/07/76	108	107	C20	06/10/76	06/10/76	06/15/76	630	00005	055	NSS	001	002	010	00065	080	010	00065	090
06/14/76	108	107	C20	06/17/76	06/17/76	07/08/76	600	00016	054	S6G	001	012	C32	A0001	200	032	A0001	210
07/12/76	108	107	C2C	07/14/76	07/14/76	07/21/76	600	00016	054	S6G	001	016	C24	A0001	690	024	A0001	700
07/26/76	108	107	C20	07/29/76	07/29/76	07/31/76	600	00030	054	S6G	000	004	C25	A0001	140	025	A0001	150
•	108	107	C20	07/31/76	07/31/76	08/17/76	600	00017	059	S6G	017	006	029	A0001	290	029	A0001	30C
08/02/76 •	108	107	C20	08/09/76	08/17/76	08/28/76	6CC	00027	059	S6G	018	004	029	00016	010	029	00016	02C
08/30/76	108	107	C20	C9/02/76	09/04/76	09/04/76	6C0	00016	054	S6G	001	015	C32	000C3	C50	032	00003	08C
09/13/76	108	107	C20	09/17/76	09/17/76	10/01/76	600	00027	059	S6G	018	005	024	00003	050	024	0CC03	07C
10/04/76	108	107	C20	10/06/76	10/06/76	10/12/76	6C0	00025	054	C1W	003	001	C20	00070	800	020	00070	81C
10/18/76	108	107	C20	10/22/76	10/22/76	10/26/76	630	00005	055	NSS	0C1	001	C10	00070	C8C	C1C	00070	C9C
•	108	107	C20	10/23/76	10/26/76	10/27/76	6CC	00025	054	C1W	0C3	004	010	00152	220	010	00152	23C
10/25/76	108	107	C20	10/28/76	10/28/76	11/10/76	600	00017	059	S6G	017	008	C29	00016	C10	029	00016	02C
11/31/76 •	108	107	C20	11/04/76	11/10/76	11/12/76	600	00025	054	C1W	003	001	C10	00154	110	010	00154	12C
11/08/76 •	108	107	020	11/11/76	11/12/76	11/18/76	600	00026	054	C1W	003	001	010	00151	250	010	00151	26C
11/15/76 •	108	107	C20	11/17/76	11/23/76	11/26/76	600	00016	054	S6G	001	015	C25	000C1	400	025	00001	41C
	108	107	020	11/19/76	11/19/76	11/23/76	600	00016	054	S6G	001	017	032	A0021	050	032	A0021	06C
11/29/76	108	107	C20	11/30/76	11/30/76	12/04/76	600	00016	054	S6G	001	017	C46	00001	010	046	00001	020
•	108	107	C20	11/30/76	12/04/76	12/10/76	600	00C26	054	C1W	003	002	010	00151	250	010	00151	26C
01/10/77	108	107	C2C	01/12/77	01/12/77	01/18/77	600	00026	054	C1W	003	003	010	00151	25C	010	00151	260
01/24/77	108	107	C20	01/26/77	01/26/77	01/28/77	600	00C16	054	S6G	0C1	018	C32	A0021	05C	032	A0021	06C

¹ Allowed start date.
² Expected start date.
³ Finish date.

the manufacturing process. Using this data and the amount of usable floor space existing in each shop, the system logic could generate data showing the resulting floor space utilization for any specific time period desired.

The primary purpose of LRPS was to function as a long-range capacity planning device. It also came into play as a tool for helping to plan material need dates, need dates for detailed engineering drawings, dates for manufacturing processing, need dates for quality assurance specifications, and as an aid in planning the overall level of manpower required. This type of planning has been done by interfacing LRPS data with other systems.

LRPS implementation

In describing his view of the situation as he saw it in 1968, Elden Thomas said:

> While the company was struggling with the problems it encountered in starting up nuclear manufacturing, each manufacturing manager had his own understanding and interpretation of what he thought were the major problems. Each was, therefore, making every attempt to correct the problems which he perceived. This resulted in improvement in some areas, often at the expense of creating complications in others. The real difficulty, however,

was that no tool existed which was capable of assessing the impact of individual problems or their solutions on the overall shipment schedules or facility requirements. Management was convinced all possible actions were being taken. Hence, only a few lower level manufacturing people were interested in pursuing the development and use of LRPS.

It was extremely difficult to convince manufacturing management that LRPS could be a useful tool. Many of these men had had previous experience with a computer-based "loading-system" (not resource or network constrained) which had not helped them solve their problems. They had little confidence that another tool employing a computer could help them solve their current crisis. To change this attitude, a great deal of time and effort was expended giving presentations, day-long in some cases, which included: (1) demonstrating that the OR team had a good understanding of their operations; (2) presenting a logical (formalized) description of their problem; (3) presenting a description of the proposed solution with supporting reasons for its selection; (4) discussing the cost of the proposed solution, and (5) obtaining suggestions and critical comments regarding the proposed solution.

The basic formulation of LRPS was completed by the end of 1968. Manufacturing personnel who worked directly with the OR group during the formulation period were convinced approval and funding for development of LRPS should be provided, but they were unable to persuade upper level manufacturing management. During the first six months of 1969, at least 30 presentations were made to all levels of management and other interested functions for the purpose of obtaining approval and funding for LRPS. Functions covered during this period included Production Control, Manufacturing Engineering, Industrial Engineering, Material Control, Manufacturing Management, Facilities Control, Manufacturing Systems, Systems and Data Processing, Division Finance and Accounting, Division Management, Corporate Finance and Accounting.

Although time consuming, this work proved vital for final acceptance and approval. While the basic design of LRPS as originally defined remained, many "fine-tuning" adjustments had to be made because of knowledge gained during these sessions. Even more important, these sessions gave a larger number of people a chance to contribute their thoughts and achieve a basic understanding of the approach. It also allowed each person to feel he had an important part in the formulation of the solution.

After obtaining funding for the development of LRPS in mid-1969, a concentrated effort was made to complete the job as rapidly as possible. By February of 1970 LRPS was being tested using data from the Mt. Vernon plant. By mid-1970 LRPS was implemented for use in Mt. Vernon. For the larger Barberton plant, implementation did not occur until mid-1971.

In thinking over what he had just said, Thomas added:

You know, this tool has a unique history. As in other companies, we had pursued this idea for years, but just couldn't seem to get anywhere with the concept. Then, of course, we ran into our start-up problems. After going through several managers, each of whom failed to turn things around, Mr. Favret, our current Nuclear Divisions vice president, finally took things in hand. He took a strong position that we could never really turn things around without the assistance of a sound long-range planning tool which would allow identification of potential capacity problems far enough in advance to allow corrective action to be taken. This was the kind of management support and leadership, backed up by actual use of the tool in decision making, which made implementation of such a new manufacturing planning concept successful.

Besides having the support of management, maybe the two smartest things that we did that ultimately made LRPS successful was that we created a special group charged with the responsibility of operating the system, from defining programming modifications to gathering data, generating reports, interpreting output reports and developing recommendations for management actions. These weren't Operations Researchers or programmers, but people who had manufacturing experience and could identify with the users of the system, as well as the complex computer aspects of LRPS. The second smart thing we did was to keep the scope of LRPS fairly confined in the beginning. We constantly had to guard against attempting to tie it into a global planning and control system that did everything for everybody. If we would have attempted this, we probably would have failed to achieve anything. As it was, we succeeded with LRPS, and this had gained us the kind of credibility needed to implement a lot of things that followed.

Now, LRPS is rather an institution. People supply it with data and use the output in the normal course of their work, and in my view, the impact of the system on the company has been immeasurable. To cite just a few instances:

At one time manufacturing had tentatively agreed to purchase a $1 million machine which was believed needed to improve delivery on four partially fabricated components. There were also indications that current firm contracts would cause such congestion at one machine that the company would be unable to provide adequate completion dates for another large contract that was being bid. Upon evaluating the situation using LRPS, it was determined that buying the additional machine would provide little improvement in the firm work and have no effect on the delivery dates for the contracts being bid. The end result, after much consideration, was a decision not to buy the machine.

Another example involved finding that an additional stress relief furnace, valued at $500,000, was required to eliminate a bottleneck operation. As a result of this information, the company purchased the furnace. LRPS further ascertained that despite the new furnace, more stress relief capacity would be necessary if other contracts were to be obtained during a specific time frame.

An unanticipated benefit from being able to use LRPS to accurately predict time of performance in fulfilling contracts has been a dollar saving in contract terms, dealing with escalation. The prices stated in B&W contracts are firm. A portion of the price, however, is variable and dependent upon the values of specific indicators for material prices and labor rates. The term used to describe this variable function is escalation. The escalation allowed in a contract is fixed by the values of the indicators during specific calendar months, which depend on the start and completion dates as specified in the contract. As a result of being able to accurately determine when the company could successfully start and complete work on a number of bids, the company was able to include in contracts correct escalation clauses. These were dollars which the company would not have been able to recover if it had accepted the originally requested contract start and completion dates.

During 1972, an upturn in noncommercial nuclear business was anticipated and the resources needed to satisfy the current and expected work load for the next eight years was determined. LRPS indicated that approximately $6 million worth of additional facilities would be required. This amount of capital was included in B&W's capital plan and was used to fund expansions as needed.

In commenting on LRPS, Lew Favret said:

Front-end control is essential in managing any business, especially one as complex as the fabrication and assembly of nuclear equipment. Without having the ability to perceive the long-range manufacturing situation, it is virtually impossible to predict schedules or resource requirements for the operation. LRPS definitely gives us the kind of overall perspective required to make sound decisions on manufacturing schedules and buildings and machine tool requirements. It provides a road map that allows management to make firm commitments for schedules and capital resources requirements for both the backlog business as well as new orders. Without this visibility, management runs the chance of either overloading or underloading their resources and cannot operate at their fullest capacity. During the past three years, our facilities have been able to operate at full capacity and long-term sublet contracts could be negotiated to optimize the facilities throughput.

APPENDIX

LRPS has incorporated in it a limited-resource, network-constrained, multi-network, heuristic, simulation module. This enables the company to simulate nuclear equipment manufacturing operations over the duration of all firm and proposed nuclear contracts. While the simulation module is of primary importance, other modules permit the user to efficiently edit, create, maintain, and modify data, and to easily and selectively generate desired output information regarding simulated manufacturing operations.

Exhibit A-1 shows an LRPS "Conceptual Flowchart" illustrating the major aspects of the computerized system. There are currently 40 computer programs incorporated in the total system. Some of the programs are executed in "phases" or as a unit, but others are "stand-alone" programs.

There are also four major LRPS files, which are referred to as "banks." These are: the resource bank, the component bank, the contract bank, and the work bank.

The system is designed in modular form. Each "bank" and its associated computer programs perform certain functions. The function performed determines which module will be employed. Therefore, in reviewing Exhibit A-1, the reader will not be able to identify start and end points as one would if all the programs had to be executed each time the system was used.

Resource bank

The *resource bank* is designed to contain data describing resources (Work Stations) identified as being critical or of major importance. For each resource included, the following information must be specified:

Resource identification number.

Quantity of resource.

Resource performance factors.

Hours per day and hours per week available.

Identification of logical trade-offs to other resources.

Penalty factors associated with logical trade-offs, etc.

This information is used extensively for data editing while using the component bank, and during execution of the resource allocation program. The resource bank must be built prior to construction of the other "banks." But, after it is built, logical modifications or revisions can be made without affecting any other portions of the system. This feature allows the user to modify resource data to reflect actual resource limits as they occur or are planned to occur.

Exhibit A–1
LRPS conceptual flowchart

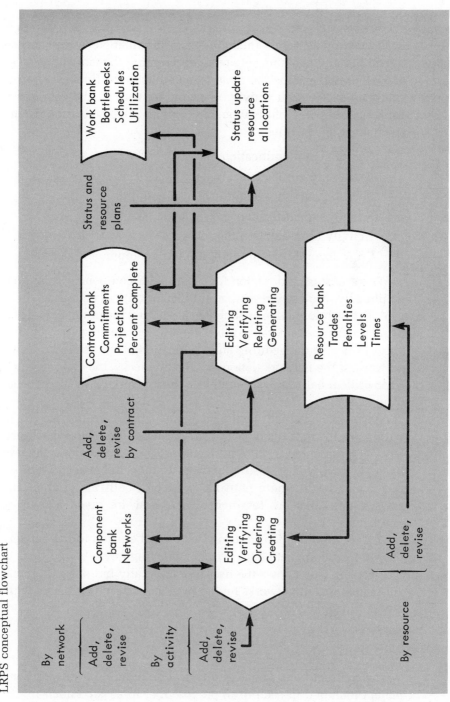

Component bank

The *component bank* functions as an information storage and retrieval file and contains networks representing the fabrication steps or activities that must be done to manufacture a finished nuclear component. For each activity of every network in the component bank the following information, plus various other codes and parameters, must be specified:

Component identification.
Activity identification (I node).
Successor activity identification (J node).
Resource identification.
Activity time duration (hours).
Crew size information (minimum, maximum, and normal).

When routing information for a particular component is laid out graphically, it closely resembles a PERT or critical path diagram.

With this information available in card form, the program logic for using the component bank is executed. It contains logic which provides extensive data editing and verification of the "soundess" of a network. If the network data pass all edit checks, the logic required to do critical path analysis and place the network on the component bank is executed.

Networks contained on the component bank are not associated with specific contracts or with start or completion dates. Each network is represented in CPM form and program logic allows the user to easily modify any existing network to reflect changes in fabrication plans. Each time a network is altered, both the original and revised networks are retained on file and are given a revision number.

Logical modifications and revisions can be made to the network data in the component bank without affecting any other portions of the system. This allows the user to continually build, modify, and verify component networks for use in other parts of the system without executing any other functions.

Contract bank

The *contract bank* contains information pertaining to each component included in each firm, proposed, or forecasted nuclear contract. For each component on the contract bank the following information, plus various other codes and parameters, must be specified:

Contract identification.

Component identification.

Contract unit identification.

Component (network) revision number.

Required (contract) completion date.

With this basic information available in card form (one card per component-unit of each contract) the program logic revises the contract bank. Also, networks representing the fabrication of components are retrieved from the component bank, and placed in the work bank when the contract bank is revised. During this process, the networks from the component bank are time-oriented to the required contractual completion dates, as well as oriented to all other work, and then merged on the work bank.

This scheme provides a fast and flexible method for generating and modifying any real or assumed work load since program logic allows the user to easily add new contracts, delete contracts or components of contracts, add to contracts, substitute new or revised components for existing components of contracts, or any combination of the above. Another advantage of this approach is that when one network is used for components of several different contracts, considerable data preparation time (manual) and network analysis time (computer) is saved.

Work bank

The *work bank* contains the detailed future work load which comprises the activities required to manufacture the components of every contract, whether designated as firm, proposed, or forecasted work. Each activity has associated with it the network-analyzed information provided from the component bank, and the contract completion date information supplied from the contract bank. This work load included in the work bank can be acted on by three major system functions: a status function, a resource allocation function, and a reporting function.

The status function enables users to maintain a current description of progress toward finished components and contracts on an activity by activity basis in the work bank. The detail status information is then summarized and stored in the contract bank to reflect the more general status of the components and contracts.

The resource allocation function (simulation program) allows the user to develop resource-constrained, feasible schedules for activities, components, contracts, and resources. It additionally indicates the time and magnitude of queue buildup behind resources and the time and extent of delays projected for any activity, component, or contract.

The schedule information produced by the resource allocation program is stored on the work bank in detail form (by activity and resource) and on the contract bank in summary form (by contract and component) as the schedule is generated. Report generation programs are then used to retrieve selected output information from these files regarding simulated contract completion dates, resource utilization, the buildup of queues behind resources, and so on. Depending upon the acceptability of the overall simulated plan, additional simulations may or may not be made. For example, when unacceptable contract completion dates result from a bottleneck caused by a particular Work Station, the user can assume that an additional machine will be available at some time in the future, and rerun the simulation to determine what effect the additional capacity would have on the overall schedule for all contracts and resources.

LRPS was designed with the objective of maximizing the speed, flexibility and accuracy of manufacturing planning capability, while minimizing the need for input data preparation and manual intervention. For this reason, a large part of the system consists of data handling logic. By maintaining a file on resources, by reusing analyzed networks, and by separating summary and detail information in the system, this goal was achieved.

To recognize how LRPS reduces data preparation time, a few examples of its capabilities in this area are described below:

Users need to supply entirely new network information about a component to the component bank only when a new component of a completely different design from an existing component is conceived. Even then it needs to be supplied merely once—regardless of how many times the new component network will subsequently be used in the various contracts. Assuming a new component contains 500 activities and is to be used in 20 contracts, just 500 cards need to be prepared instead of 10,000. Normally, the changes to fabrication networks for a component are described by adding, deleting, or substituting activities. When this occurs, the system then assumes the function of revising and reanalyzing the changed component network. Likewise, assuming a component network contains 2,000 activities and a change in fabrication methods involves only five activities, then only 5 cards instead of 2,000 are prepared to develop the revised component network.

When developing or revising work loads in the work bank, the user can add, delete, or substitute components in contracts on a one-card-per-component basis. If, for example, a contract is added that contains ten components, the user states the "names" of the ten components and causes thousands of activities to be added to the work load, thus eliminating equivalent manual data preparation time.

Prior to performing the simulation, it is necessary to establish presimulation priorities for each activity included in the work bank to be simulated. This involves working back from the due date on each contract component and establishing the latest date that each of the operations specified in the work bank for that contract can be started in order to meet the contract date. Since the fabrication time plus slack time required to perform each operation involved in making a component is found in the work bank, the early start date for each operation can also be determined. With all of this data available for each contract, the next step is to relate these early and late start dates by contract to all other contracts in order to provide proper priorities when contention for a resource occurs during simulation. With this data available the scheduling algorithm is used to simulate the manufacturing operation, including appropriate trade-offs from one resource to another when congestion occurs.

LRPS schedules at the rate of approximately 50,000 activities per CPU hour on an IBM 370/155 computer. In addition, the scheduling rate remains approximately linear regardless of the number of activities to be scheduled. Also, there are no constraints on the number of activities that can be scheduled. To date, the largest schedule simulated with the system has been approximately 100,000 activities, while the normal schedules contain approximately 70,000.

PART V

MANAGING THE PRODUCTION INVENTORY CONTROL SYSTEM

Chapter 14

Designing and managing production planning and inventory control systems

It is said, a fanatic is one who, having lost sight of his objectives, redoubles his efforts. There is plenty of room for fanaticism in the field of production and inventory control. That firm whose objective has become "installing an MRP system," or "installing a sales [forecasting] system," or "putting in shop floor control," is in trouble. These are all very good means to certain ends. [But] these ends need to be stated clearly by the management of the firm and reviewed frequently by all who manage inventory.

—Frank S. Gue,*
Westinghouse Canada, Ltd.

* "Lets See Now—What Was It We Were Trying to Do?" *Production and Inventory Management*, vol. 18 (4), 1977.

A MAJOR PORTION OF THIS BOOK has been devoted to the tools and techniques of planning and control for production-inventory systems. This has reflected one of our primary objectives in writing the book, and has been made possible by the tremendous theoretical and practical developments in the field in the last few decades. As noted in the preface however, another important objective of the book has been to increase the level of understanding of the personal, organizational, strategic, and management implications of planning and control. We have relied on case studies and descriptions of actual operating systems in trying to transmit these perspectives. With reference to Gue's quote above, we have attempted to transmit information about both the "means" (tools and techniques) and the "ends" (their purpose, setting, and implications). Therefore, it is fitting that we conclude the book with a chapter which attempts to place these ends and means in final perspective.

This chapter is divided into two major sections. The first is concerned with the design of planning and control systems. We presume that the reader that has progressed this far has an understanding of the basic techniques and types of systems that can be employed to plan and control production and inventories. Our discussion then will focus on the key considerations that must be taken into account in weaving these techniques and systems into the fabric of an ongoing organization. The second major section is concerned with the management of the production/inventory control process. We will not attempt here to boil practice down to a few "principles" of management. Our approach will be to identify some of the key areas of the process that are particularly susceptible to error and problems.

DESIGNING THE SYSTEM

Referring back to Chapter 1, and Part II in its entirety, we have seen that systems for planning and control are procedures which define the relationships between the elements of planning and control: data generation, decision making and planning, and implementation, feedback, and control. Data generation includes the preparation of cost data for decision making, the maintenance of inventory and open order records, estimating production and procurement lead times, and the preparation of forecasts (Chapter 2). Decision making and planning includes making basic inventory decisions (Chapters 3 and 4), master schedules and aggregate production plans (Chapters 5 and 6), and detailed materials plans and schedules

(Chapters 7, 8, 11, 12, and 13). Implementation, feedback and control is embodied in the record keeping, ordering, expediting, rescheduling, dispatching, manufacturing, and overall monitoring of the tasks described in Chapters 4, 5, 7, 8, 11, and 13.

In reviewing the chapters that deal with the various elements of planning and control, and that describe different kinds of systems for integrating these elements, a striking feature is that there are so many alternative tools and techniques that can be applied. While some of these approaches are clearly superior to others, this would have been a very short book indeed were this always the case. It is not. There are a variety of industrial situations, each of which requires some particular combination of techniques for the best results. The trick in designing systems for planning and control is in recognizing where some special tailoring is required, where standard solutions apply, and how to incorporate the two in a meaningful way.

One way to ensure that the means (tools and techniques) applied in a particular company, match the ends in terms of effectiveness, is to use the following checklist in evaluating various system alternatives:

1. Does the system fit the process technology?
2. Does the system fit the positioning strategy?
3. Is the system consistent with the organization structure and with the abilities of the people in the organization?
4. Is the system consistent with basic priorities?
5. Does the system recognize important differences in processes? Product lines? Item value?
6. Do the benefits of the system outweigh its costs?

While this checklist of questions is not all inclusive, it does direct one to some issues that are central to the design and implementation of planning and control systems.

Fit with technology. By contrasting the types of systems generally appropriate for high-volume standardized products (Chapter 8) and those for job shops (Chapter 10), we can clearly see that process technology impacts the types of tools and systems that are appropriate. For example, high-volume assembly lines subsume many detailed scheduling problems in the design of the line itself; thus, capacity planning can occur at the aggregate production planning level. By way of contrast, the scrambled flows associated with job shops require lower level capacity requirements planning approaches that recognize the impact of a changing product mix on capacity utilization. Similarly, an examination of the dominant flows in job shops may indicate that bills of capacity stated in aggregate terms can be applied in aggregate production planning in job shops.

At another level, we can observe product technology (as opposed to process technology) affecting the product structure associated with different products and firms. At the least, product structure will indicate whether dependent or independent demand-type systems are needed. Moreover, a closer look at complex product structures often indicates the necessity of structuring bills of materials in different ways, and identifying various control points in a system. For example, a firm that offers a standard product with numerous options may require a modular or planning bill of materials approach rather than, or in addition to, more straightforward bills.

Fit with positioning. Asking whether or not a system fits with a process technology may appear on the surface to be a rather obvious question. However, the experience of some of the firms described in case studies in this book illustrates how easy it is to fail to perceive the obvious. Similarly, checking whether or not a system is consistent with the demands created by a particular positioning strategy is seemingly simple and naive. However, at the detailed level, positioning strategies that indicate whether a firm produces to stock or to order or somewhere in between can strongly influence the design of a system.

For example, a firm that produces to order must have very strong links between the order entry, engineering, master scheduling, and bill of materials and routing file maintenance functions as shown in Figure 11–3 (Chapter 11). Firms that produce to stock on the other hand must have well-developed finished goods inventory control and stock reporting procedures (Chapters 4 and 8). At the master scheduling level, we might also find that planning bills must be relied on more in systems that produce to semifinished state, rather than purely to stock or to order.

Organizational needs. In the same way that an integrated system must be consistent with the demands placed on it by a technology and positioning strategy, it must also be consistent with the needs and constraints placed on it by the organization that makes it work. These needs and constraints can be wide and far ranging. They include the need for the system to present information to managers on a timely basis, and in a manner that is meaningful to them. Priority dispatching reports, for example, must be presented to shop supervisors *before* jobs are processed. Afterwards is too late for the report to be meaningful, and the credibility of the whole system can be endangered. Similarly, a priority dispatch list need not always be presented in terms of "critical ratios" or other sometimes confusing and esoteric numerical indicators. While the critical ratio can be used to prioritize jobs, machinists might be much more content to work with a simple priority listing that shows job numbers, preferred sequences, and due dates.

Even the physical organization of the information that is presented must be considered. For example, one firm has printed priority dispatch data horizontally rather than vertically as we have often seen it displayed in earlier chapters (Chapter 11, for example), so that supervisors will have more room for note taking, and in one instance, so the computer form could be folded at a convenient point to facilitate displaying the data on the front of a machine. This may appear to be a rather picayune point. But, the output of systems is to be used by people, it does not exist for its sake alone. What may appear a minor point to the system designer may be a major source of irritation to the user.

In terms of the entire system, an extremely important aspect of the fit between systems and organization is transparency. Transparency refers to the ability of the people involved to clearly see and understand how various decisions and plans affect their performance and responsibilities. In Chapters 5 and 6 we discussed at some length the importance of hierarchical decision structures in production planning systems. This concept is important because it provides a way of making systems transparent by defining logical decision points where managers can solve their problems within the constraints of higher order decision processes, or even recognize the necessity of renegotiating these constraints. The need for transparency clearly exists at high levels in decision processes, at the interface between aggregate production plans and master schedules for example. It applies at lower levels too, however. For example, job shop supervisors and lead workers are often measured on both cost efficiency and on delivery performance. As often however, these two performance measures are antagonistic—when setup labor can be saved by doing jobs in one sequence, but where due dates dictate another. These situations require that enough information be present on priority dispatch lists for supervisors to make judicious trade-offs, or to recognize the need to negotiate the final decision with other affected parties.

Fit with priorities. There is a widespread feeling on the part of many system designers that the ultimate objective of manufacturing, and hence of systems, is to minimize costs. There is evidence to the contrary however. Skinner [11], and others [7, 12] have recognized that while cost minimization is generally a very important goal, its importance is often superceded by other strategic priorities, priorities that are consistent with the more global goals of maximizing profits, return on investment, or ensuring corporate survival. Some firms, for example, do not attempt to compete on the basis of low-cost/low-price products. Their primary basis for competition, that is their formula for success, is quality, for example, or customer service. These formulae for success reflect the fundamental priorities of a business in terms of what it attempts to accomplish and how; that is, its corporate strategy. Corporate strategy, however, is often a difficult and cumbersome concept to work with in directly assessing the appropriateness of detailed operating decisions, or in our case, planning and control systems. Wheelwright [12], offers a more indirect framework for assessing this fit:

Unfortunately, simply giving manufacturing management a statement of the corporate objectives and strategy is not particularly effective in achieving this desired consistency in decision making. The gap between operating decisions and their impact on corporate strategy is just too great. Some intermediate step is needed.

Manufacturing decisions reflect tradeoffs among different performance criteria. Thus, identifying these criteria and prioritizing them has proven effective in bridging this gap. Four performance criteria that are generally most important are:

1. Efficiency: This criterion encompasses both cost efficiency and capital efficiency and can generally be measured by such things as return on sales, inventory turnover and return on assets.
2. Dependability: Included here are such things as product dependability and dependability of the firm's promises (delivery promises and price promises). This is often extremely difficult to measure, although many companies attempt to measure it in terms of the "percent of on-time deliveries."
3. Quality: Product quality and reliability, service quality, speed of delivery, and maintenance quality are important aspects of this criterion. For many firms this is easy to measure by internal standards, but as with the other criteria the key is how the market evaluates quality.
4. Flexibility: The two major aspects of this criterion are changes in the product and the volume. Special measures are required for this criterion, since it is not generally measured. [12]

These four performance measures can be used to assess alternative system designs once they have been prioritized in rank order by the management of a firm. For example, we have seen in Chapter 10 that various priority dispatching rules perform differently along different dimensions. LeGrande's study (Table 10–14) shows that the SOT rule maximizes labor efficiency, but has a wide flow time variance, while the dynamic slack per remaining operations (DS/RO) rule minimizes the number of orders completed late, but does not maximize labor efficiency. Thus, it is reasonable to expect that a firm that rank orders its strategic performance measures as (1) efficiency, (2) quality, (3) flexibility, and (4) dependability might apply the SOT rule. By way of contrast, a firm that ranks dependability first in its strategic priorities may choose to apply the dynamic slack per remaining operations rule.

Similarly, a major issue in designing an MRP system is identifying how much "nervousness" or sensitivity to change is appropriate. A firm that competes largely on the basis of flexibility (that is, its ability to react swiftly to customer orders or design changes) may require a very sensitive net change system. On the other hand, another firm that ranks efficiency high and flexibility low, may be content to use a less responsive regenerative approach, and freeze its master schedule for some period of time. These examples serve to illustrate the importance of assessing the fit between alternative system designs, and the needs of the company they may serve.

Recognizing differences. The system design task is often complicated by the fact that a plant may produce several different product lines with different priorities, employ several positioning strategies, and use more than one type of process technology. These "unfocused factories" [10] offer particular problems to the system designer because of the conflicting demands that are placed on the system. In such cases, the designer has two choices, the first is to build a single system around the dominant product. But this presents obvious difficulties for other product lines. The second alternative is to attempt a compromise by differentiating the system, or even creating dual systems at important junctures. This is often the preferable course of action since the system may be one of the few tools that managers have to "focus" in on the special needs of product lines or process segments.

We have discussed several ways of focusing systems in on particular areas of concern in previous chapters. In Chapter 4, we discussed

ABC classifications as a means of identifying where different kinds of
systems or decision rules may be applied to items with different
volumes or values. In Chapter 7, we discussed how an MRP system
can be designed to buffer the two different kinds of operations (assembly and wood parts fabrication) that existed in a furniture manufacturing company. This differentiated system allowed the assembly portion of the process to chase demand and react to a "to order"
positioning environment, and allowed the wood parts fabrication
process to level out production and produce to stock. Yet, this differentiated system also tied the two parts of the process together at
important junctures. In the Perkin Elmer case, we saw how a firm
differentiated its forecasting methods and control procedures for different product types. One approach was taken for finished machines,
another for service parts, and yet a third for new products that represented the "major risks" in the company. These examples illustrate
the importance of evaluating system alternatives in terms of their
ability to recognize important product and process differences.

Costs versus benefits.   As a final step in the design of systems for
planning and controlling production and inventories, it is clearly
important to see whether or not they pay for themselves economically or strategically. This step ensures that a firm does not go
through the expensive, often tedious and trying, and time-
consuming, task of erecting a set of procedures and disciplines without gaining a just return on this effort. The dangers, of course, are
that the system is either too sophisticated, or not sophisticated
enough. In the former case, the added benefits of a high-powered
system may not justify its incremental benefits to the firm. In the
latter case, the danger is that the system is so simpleminded that it
does not add anything to what is currently being achieved.

The process of measuring costs versus benefits is conceptually
straightforward. It involves measuring the (hopefully) positive difference between the costs of designing, implementing, and maintaining the system over time and the value of the benefits received as a
result. If the benefits of the new system outweigh the costs sufficiently to indicate that the planning and control system project represents a better use of corporate time and money than alternative
projects, the decision to proceed becomes obvious. This analytical
approach is similar to that which firms often require in analyzing
capital appropriations for new plants and machinery. In fact, return
on investment and discounted cash flow calculations can be prepared to obtain a measure of the financial impact of proposed new

systems. Such formal approaches are desirable because of the rigor they impose upon the evaluation process. There are problems, however, and they center on the difficulties of measuring costs, and particularly, benefits.

Many of the costs involved in designing, implementing, and maintaining planning and control systems can be estimated with relative ease. Figure 14–1 outlines some of the costs, sorted according to their impact on profits, the balance sheet, or on the strategic side, that might be expected for a firm planning to move from a manual informal system to a more formalized computer-based planning and control system. Among the costs that can be fairly easily quantified are the investments in new data processing equipment, system designed and programming costs, data base maintenance and computer processing costs, the costs associated with initially developing an accurate data base (routings, bills of material, inventories, and so on), and the balance sheet impact of the temporary inventory level increases that usually occur when better inventory decisions result in a rebalancing of inventories. The latter is a consequence of reallocating inventories among parts and goods so that the firm has the right amount for each, rather than too much of what is unneeded (often slow-moving items) and too little of what is really needed (often fast-moving items). Temporary increases in inventory levels can occur when the inventories of fast-moving items are increased before the complete depletion of slow-moving item excess inventories has a chance to occur.

Among the developmental and long-run costs that are more difficult to numerically quantify are start-up and debugging costs, and training costs. These costs are associated with the implementation of the system into the firm's "culture"—a process that can be quite trying and time consuming. Similarly, the "costs" associated with being vulnerable to errors and serious problems during the transition into a new system, and to the potentially stultifying impact of excessive formalization on certain types of organizations must also be qualitatively considered.

On the benefits side of Figure 1–14, we can also see a number of nonquantifiable benefits along with those that can be numerically estimated. The strategic benefits associated with the implementation of improved systems are particularly hard to quantify, but can in total be the major force in stimulating their development. For example, the ability to respond to changes in demand, product design, or marketing tactics, can allow firms to seize opportunities that slower

Figure 14–1
The impact of planning and control systems

Long-run benefits

Profit Impact:
*Reduction in writeoffs of obsolete inventories.
*Reduction in inventory-related interest costs.
*Reduction in direct labor idle time and overtime premiums.
*Reductions in materials scrap.
*Increased sales from improved customer service.
*Reductions in administrative costs.
*Reduction in public warehousing costs.
*Reduction in premium transportation costs.
*Fewer returned shipments.

Balance Sheet Impact:
*Reduction in inventories.
*Reduction in working capital needs.
*Reductions in capital expenditures due to:
   *Need for less warehouse and storage space.
   *More effective utilization of existing capacity.
*Reduction in debts.
*Increased debt capacity

Strategic Impact:
*Cost and service advantage over competition.
*Faster response to changes in demand, product designs, and marketing tactics.
*Ability to introduce new products faster.
*Capital freed up for use in new or developing businesses.
*Increased ability to focus in on needs of different product lines and process segments.
*Improved morale of work force and managers.

Developmental and long-run costs

Profit Impact:
†System design costs.
†Costs of developing data base.
†Costs associated with training personnel to use system.
†Start-up and developing costs.
*Increased computer processing costs.
†Data base maintenance costs.

Balance Sheet Impact:
†Temporary increases in inventory levels.
*Increased investment in data processing equipment.

Strategic Impact:
†Vulnerability during transition to new system.
*Potentially more rigid organization develops.

* Long-run continuing costs.
† One-time developmental costs.

competitors may miss, or to avoid costly problems that could not otherwise be averted. The capability to introduce new products quickly and efficiently can also be of strategic importance. Mr. Dan Carroll, president of Gould, Inc., a $1.6 billion corporation, recognized this in a statement he made to his management group in 1973. After discussing the importance of effective planning and control within the context of a broader discussion of materials management, he said:

> Then I told the management group that if they really wanted to get scared, they should remember that we spend $25 million a year on new product R&D. Do you know the easiest way to bomb a new product? Poor materials management—you can't get the right materials, or the quality is off, or you can't get the product through the factory, or you can't coordinate transportation and distribution to get the product into the hands of the customer. I would be willing to bet that substantially greater than half of all new product failures are not because the technology or market strategy are deficient, they're because people don't pay enough attention to materials management. [9]

Judiciously, weighing the costs and benefits of a new production planning and control system is an important part of the design and evaluation process. It involves considering the quantifiable and the difficult to measure. The costs and benefits associated with effective systems impinge upon almost every component of the physical production-inventory system, and a large portion of the enterprise of which it is a part.

MANAGING THE PLANNING AND CONTROL PROCESS

Once the planning and control system has been designed there is no assurance that it will take over and simply run by itself. It won't. Like an automobile, it is necessary to feed it with the appropriate imputs, to lubricate it with the motivation necessary for people to keep it moving, to make periodic maintenance checks and repairs, to tune it to run under varying conditions, and occasionally, to make major overhauls. In other words, it is necessary to manage the planning and control process. This is a large and complex process to monitor. But, if a manager waits until inventories rise out of control, stockouts or due dates begin to slip, or manufacturing costs rise to signal that the process is not working, it is too late. A proactive approach implies that periodic 10,000 mile checkups be used as well. One simple way to do this is to periodically evaluate the major elements of planning and control shown in Figure 14–2 and discussed throughout this book.

Data collection and generation. Planning and control systems operate on the basis of accurate and timely information. Thus, a logical first check is to see whether the data is in fact sound. With some data inputs, such as forecasts and lead time estimates it is usually unrealistic to expect perfect accuracy. These data generally represent single point estimates of probablistic variables. One can reasonably expect them to be inaccurate in a single instance. It is not unreasonable, however, to expect such probabilistic data to be unbiased over a number of instances. If forecasts, for example, are consistantly 30 percent higher than actual demand over a long period of time, there is a strong likelihood that there is something systematically wrong with the forecasting process.

Persistent biases in probabilistic data often reflect serious problems in the assignment of responsibility to the people who interface with different parts of the system. Someone in marketing may be consciously forecasting 30 percent high in order to ensure that the firm does not encounter extraordinary stockouts, not necessarily a problem. But if someone in production control is also planning safety stocks to cover such exigencies, the result will be double coverage and excess inventories. In managing the production control process, it is important that the responsibilities for handling uncertainties be clearly defined, and that probabilistic input data be monitored for systematic biases that are inappropriate given these responsibility assignments.

A second class of data inputs are those which are not probabilistic, such as bills of material or inventory records. An inventory record which purportedly tells how much of a particular item is in stock is either right or wrong. In order for any planning and control system to work effectively, however, they must almost always be right. For example, general rules of thumb for computerized systems are that 95 percent of the inventory records and 99 percent of the bills of material must be correct at any one time. An inventory record which reports inventories as lower than actual can trigger an unneeded order; needlessly driving up inventories and wasting capacity. An inventory record that is higher than actual can result in stockouts and perhaps work stoppages. Similarly, inaccurate bills of material can result in unneeded parts being ordered and needed parts not

Figure 14–2
The elements of planning and control

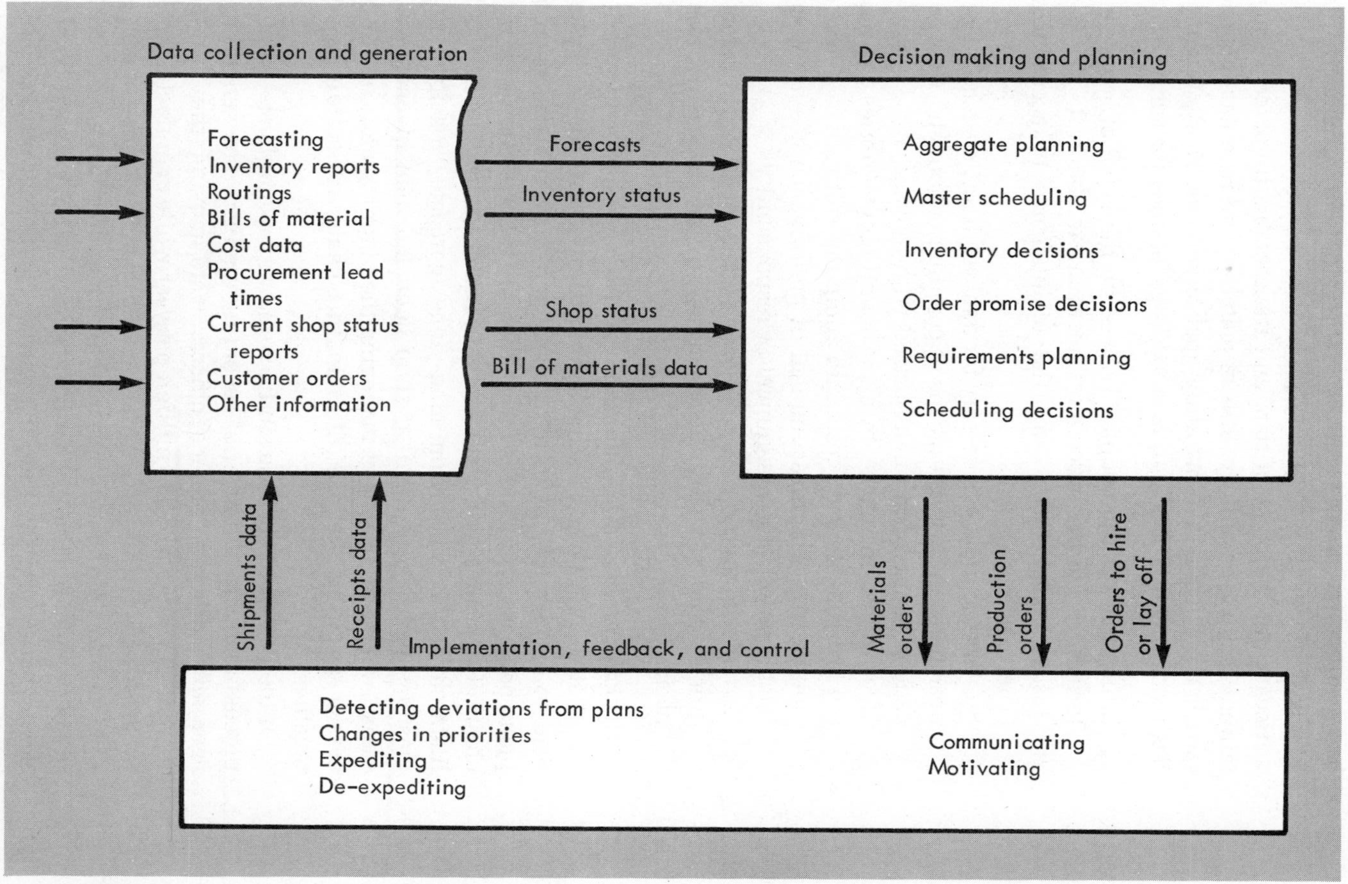

being ordered, or worse still, in the product being made with the wrong parts, leading to quality problems.

Because of the mass of data and transactions involved in maintaining accurate inventory, bills of material, and records, data accuracy is a particularly demanding goal to achieve. O. W. Wight [13] has recommended five simple steps as guidelines for achieving it:

1. *Education*—of the people involved on the value of accurate information and the procedures necessary to obtain it.
2. *Assign responsibility*—for the maintenance of accurate and timely data.
3. *Provide the tools*—necessary for data accuracy, such as properly designed forms, rapid means of communication, and storage locations secure from unauthorized withdrawals.
4. *Measure performance*—by cycle counting inventories and building "reasonableness" tests into computer software to detect obvious errors. The measurement of performance has an obvious relationship to the assignment of responsibility.
5. *Correct the causes of problems*—when errors are detected, quickly find out why they occured so that the basic cause of problems can be removed.

Decision making and planning.   As we have discussed and illustrated at several points in this book, planning and control systems tend to be hierarchical in nature. We generally find decisions and plans being made in series rather than all at once. Each link in the chain of decisions and plans tends to become more detailed as the hierarchy is traversed—from long-range aggregate capacity plans to master schedules, to detailed shop floor and item inventory decisions. An important part of managing the planning and control process is ensuring that the links in this chain are solidly welded together.

In the Perkin Elmer case study, we saw an example of a planning process that was in danger of becoming unglued. The general manager and corporate finance officers were moving the firm at a manufacturing rate of $93 million per year while manufacturing was progressing at the rate of $112 million per year. Regardless of who was right in terms of the appropriate rate of manufacturing, neither part of the organization had a chance of achieving their objectives alone. Somewhere along the line, the master scheduling process had become inconsistent with the overall aggregate plan. Fortunately, Gaynor Kelly, the general manager of Perkin Elmer Instrument Division, had the foresight to include a simple procedure in the planning process that allowed him to check on the consistency between the ongoing and fluid master scheduling process and the periodic, more stable, aggregate capacity and financial planning processes. This procedure, which involved pricing out the sales value of the products currently being manufactured, is typical of the kind of process monitoring that is critically important in ensuring that the different parts of a planning and control hierarchy are consistent with one another.

Implementation, feedback, and control.   The basic output of the decision-making and planning element is a set of action messages that indicate how the flows through the production-inventory system should be initiated and regulated. These action messages—expedite, order, produce a part, assemble, ship, reschedule—indicate what must be done to achieve the plans that have been laid. Obviously, it is fundamentally important that these actions be executed, and that their completion (or noncompletion) be reported back to close the system's feedback loop. This is the realm of the implementation, feedback, and control element of planning and control.

Managing the implementation, feedback and control portion of the planning and control process is very close to actually managing the business itself. Thus, many of the problems and caveats that apply here in terms of labor and personnel relations, cost accounting, and interpersonal communication and leadership, are well beyond the scope of this book. It is axiomatic however that unless "doing" follows "planning," planning is a futile exercise. This does not mean that plans and instructions must always be followed to the letter regardless of the course of intervening events, although there may be some organizational levels at which this discipline may be preferable to allowing wide latitude. What we mean is that for any series of plans to be useful, the organization must attempt to execute them until new plans based on data and information fed back through the system indicate that new courses of action should be taken. In complex production-inventory systems, any one organizational unit, such as a work center, that deviates from the directions provided by the current plan affects not only its own performance, but also the performance of other organizational units that are dependent upon its planned outputs.

Perhaps the most insidious problem in implementation, feedback, and control is the development of an "informal" system whose directives supercede those of the formal planning system. The inevitable result of this unfortunate happenstance is that "doing" is not guided by the formal plan but by something else. The confusion, excess inventories, and slipping due dates that initially follow the development of an informal system can ultimately result in the collapse of the entire system as less and less faith is placed in its ability to cope. There are a number of reasons why informal systems develop; among them:

1. The formal system produces plans that are unrealistic and unobtainable.
2. The formal system does not produce revised plans in time to maintain valid priorities.
3. The performance measurement system rewards other things besides achievement of the plan.
4. The responsibility for implementation is not defined.

The first two reasons for the development of an informal system follow from either poor system design, deteriorating data integrity, or inconsistencies in the planning hierarchy. For example, an aggregate capacity plan that reduces capacity and a master schedule that increases output demands beyond capacity levels is one type of impossible plan that can be presented for implementation. A series of infeasible plans such as this can quickly destroy the faith in those changed with their implementation, and result in the development of underground or informal plans. Similarly, inaccurate instructions that result from faulty data are quickly disregarded in favor of data that is trustworthy, although perhaps much more limited in scope. Inaccurate shop priorities lists that indicate what should be produced may thus be ignored in favor of the list of real needs that an assembly supervisor may give the fabrication superintendent over lunch. In this case, the supervisor is running the factory, not the factory manager.

Similarly, if responsibility for the execution of plans and the measurement of results is not properly assigned, informal systems can quickly develop. For example, one firm [8] developed a planning and control system that developed shop orders and priorities in such a way that inventories would be minimized and planned delivery due dates would be met. However, the shop supervisors assigned to execute them were measured on labor efficiency—due date performance was largely ignored. The result was predictable, the supervisor ignored the directives of the formal system and produced parts in a sequence that maximized efficiency—costs were low but delivery performance was terrible and the system was an effective waste of resources.

In order to manage the implementation, feedback and control process effectively, the system must produce realistic and believable plans and orders. This can be ensured by designing the system carefully, and monitoring the data collection, decision-making, and planning elements to make sure that they are working properly. Beyond this, it is necessary to assign responsibility for the execution of the plans and orders, and to measure performance against plan, as well as against other factors.

SUMMARY

We began this book with the observation that one function of systems is to relate the parts of something to a larger whole. We then began the process of relating the physical parts (materials, warehouses, factories) to the whole production-inventory system, and the less tangible parts of the elements of planning and control to the whole production planning and inventory control system. Viewed from a larger perspective however, the production-inventory system and the planning and control system are but parts of an even larger whole—the business itself.

Our purpose in this final chapter has been to indicate some of the very strong linkages between the overall business and the processes of designing and managing the planning and control system. These linkages exist in designing the system so that it recognizes the unique technology, market position, organization, strategic priorities, economics, and product line and process differences of the business, and in managing the planning and control process so that the basic needs of the business are satisfied. Our examination of these relationships has been motivated by our strong belief that planning and control systems are not ends unto themselves. The future development of effective planning and control systems must be accompanied by a firm understanding of the relationship of these means to the achievement of higher order ends—the successful management of the enterprise.

SELECTED BIBLIOGRAPHY

1. Anthony, R. N. *Planning and Control Systems: A Framework for Analysis.* Boston: Division of Research, Graduate School of Business Administration, Harvard University, 1965.

2. Emery, J. C. *Organizational Planning and Control Systems.* New York: The Macmillan Company, 1969.

3. Freeland, J. R., and Baker, N. R. "Goal Partitioning in a Hierarchical Organizational," *OMEGA,* vol. 3, no. 6 (1975).

4. Galbraith, J. *Designing Complex Organizations.* Reading, Mass.: Addison-Wesley Publishing Company, 1973.

5. Gomersall, E. "The Backlog Syndrome," *Harvard Business Review,* September–October 1964.

6. Gue, F. S. "Let's See Now—What Was It We Were Trying to Do?" *Production and Inventory Management,* vol. 18, no. 4 (1977).

7. Hayes, R. H., and Schmenner, R. W. "What's the 'Right' Manufactuıing Organization," *Harvard Business Review,* January–February, 1978.

8. Miller, J. G. "Benson Electronics (B)," ICH 9-677-013, 1976.

9. Miller, J. G., and Gilmour, P. "Gould Corporation (A)," ICH 9-678-184, 1978.

10. Skinner, W. "The Focused Factory," *Harvard Business Review,* May–June 1974.

11. Skinner, W. "Manufacturing-Missing Link in Corporate Strategy," *Harvard Business Review,* May–June 1969.

12. Wheelwright, S. "Reflecting Corporate Strategy in Manufacturing Decisions," *Business Horizons,* February 1978.

13. Wight, O. W. *Production-Inventory Management in the Computer Age.* Boston: Cahners Books, 1975.

CASE STUDY
BENSON ELECTRONICS: THE
SAN JOSE PLANT

AS BILL BERLIN, director of manufacturing, described the inventory problems at the San Jose Plant over the past year, he continually tapped the stack of computer-generated "should-have/should-take" reports in front of him:

In October of 1974, our total floor inventory here reached almost $53 million at cost.[1] That wouldn't have been so bad, considering that we were shipping at the rate of almost $240 million per year at the time. But then two things happened. First, it became apparent to us that we would be lucky to ship $170 million in the coming year because of a general business downturn. Second, financing, which had never been tremendously difficult, became increasingly expensive. That meant one thing, we had to cut back on inventories.

Our inventories were already higher than usual because of a few misjudgments on new products. But I am pleased that we have been able to correct for that, and more. Last month (October 1975) our floor inventories were down to $35 million and our stockroom inventories had been cut as well. Much of the credit for this goes to our should have/should take reporting system. I think we still have room for improvement, though. We are still carrying more inventory than our system tells us we "should have" and so we must continue to drive out excess stock. Moreover, I think there are some improvements we can make in our systems that will make this easier to accomplish in the future.

---

[1] In-process inventory at the San Jose Works was divided into two categories, floor inventory and stockroom inventory. Floor inventory was located in the factory in work areas, while stockroom inventory was located in the factory stockroom.

The San Jose Works

Benson Electronics was a multibillion-dollar integrated manufacturer of consumer, industrial, and military electronic devices. The San Jose Plant, one of the company's seven major manufacturing centers, produced computers, the company's largest and most successful product line. It produced standard computers, computers built to the individual specifications of large customers, and many of the components and subassemblies from which these computers were assembled.

The plant, which employed 6,000 hourly workers at its peak, was controlled as a cost/investment center. All of the output of the plant was sold to a separate marketing distribution division at standard cost. The general manager of the San Jose Works was measured on her ability to meet standard cost goals established every two years, on the investment in equipment and inventories it took to run the operation, and on service. Service was measured as the percentage of orders shipped by the date that had been promised to marketing.

Works personnel thought of the products of the division as being divided into two types. The first was called equipment. Equipment referred to completed computers and major subassemblies such as the panels and wiring boards. This class of products was assembled only after a firm or "hard" order, which contained a complete list of specifications for the product, was received. Even the "standardized" products of the division had so many options that it was impossible to predict the exact configuration of equipment in advance.

In contrast, the second category of products, called apparatus, referred to the standardized components that were required to assemble equipment. These items, which numbered over 30,000, were produced in anticipation of demand for two reasons. First, this strategy reduced the lead time between the receipt of a hard customer order and delivery from approximately 26 weeks to 15 weeks. Second, many types of apparatus, such as coils and printed circuit boards, were purchased directly by customers for spare parts or to upgrade existing computer installations. The marketing organization expected the San Jose Works to have them available for immediate shipment. Exhibit 1 is a simplistic portrayal of the relationship between equipment, apparatus, and the individual parts and materials that went into them.

The organization of the San Jose Works is depicted in Exhibit 2. It shows five organizational levels. The first level is the general manager of the works to whom two individuals at the director level

Exhibit 1
Simplified product structure diagram

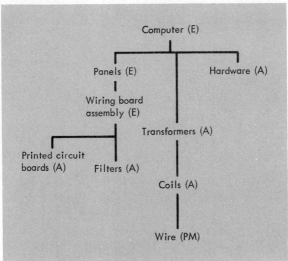

Key:
E—Equipment; produced to order.
A—Apparatus; produced to stock.
PM—Purchased materials.

(manufacturing and engineering) reported. The personnel manager and comptroller also reported to the general manager but Purchasing and Quality Control were centralized in the company, and reported to corporate groups.

The director of manufacturing supervised the manager of apparatus manufacturing and equipment manufacturing as well as the manager of stores and forecasting. This latter function was concerned primarily with production planning, expediting, and stockkeeping. As the product structure diagram in Exhibit 1 implies, the manager of equipment manufacturing oversaw most of the operations that involved the *assembly* of components, while the manager of apparatus manufacturing supervised the operations that were involved in *fabricating* components.

Organizationally, the two "factories within the factory" represented by the equipment and apparatus shops were further broken down into ten subbranches.[2] Equipment manufacturing, for exam-

---

[2] It should be noted that these "divisions" were purely organizational and not geographical. That is, assembly areas were intermingled with fabrication areas and vice versa.

Exhibit 2
Organization

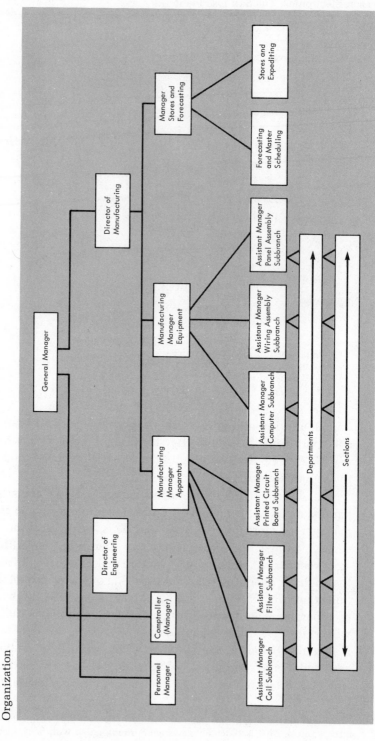

ple, was composed of a computer assembly subbranch, a panel assembly subbranch, a wiring board assembly subbranch, and others. Similarly, apparatus manufacturing was broken down into a printed circuit board subbranch, filter subbranch, integrated circuit subbranch, and so on. The subbranches, each of which might employ as many as 800 people, were further divided into departments. Department categories were based on differences in process technology or in the type of product produced. For example, the panel subbranch was composed of several departments that differed in the type of panel they assembled. The integrated circuit subbranch was separated into hybrid and monolithic departments because of the differences in the process technology applied to either. Departments were further divided into sections, each of which might specialize in a particular process step.

In 1975, there were roughly 80 departments in the San Jose Works. As the subbranches of which they were a part, the departments were cost centers, and the supervisors in charge of them were measured primarily on their efficiency. Efficiency was defined as the ratio of standard hours to the actual number of hours required to produce something. Efficiency was usually expected to be 100 percent or better. There was strong pressure in the organization to maintain high efficiencies as indicated by the statement of one supervisor: "Around here, you get two kinds of messages—Attaboy and Aw Shucks. You get an Attaboy when you achieve 100 percent efficiency and an Aw Shucks when it drops a tenth of a percent. The problem is that it takes 100 Attaboys to balance out one Aw Shucks."

Manufacturing control

The flow of the labor and materials inputs to and between the various shops, departments, and areas of the San Jose Works was controlled with a computerized system. This system was an explosion, or material requirements planning type system, that exploded the net requirements for individual parts and components from a master schedule by referencing a bill of materials file and an inventory file. The master schedule was also used as the basis for exploding labor requirements.

Master scheduling. The master schedule at Benson was a list of the products the San Jose Works planned to have completed at various time periods in the future. As a practical matter, there was no single document called a master schedule; since the data were aggregated at different levels to suit the needs of various organizational entities, and to reflect the uncertainty of future projections of plant output. Conceptually, however, this collection of data was of primary importance in running the plant.

One way to think of the master schedule is represented in Exhibit 3. It shows the typical table of output units categorized by product

Exhibit 3
Master schedule

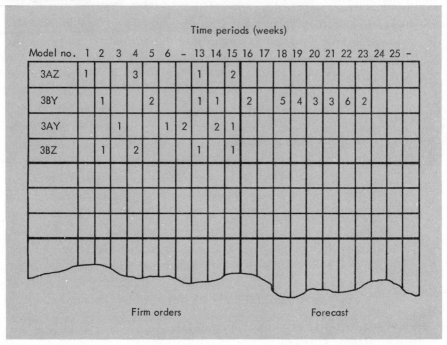

Time periods (weeks)

Model no.	1	2	3	4	5	6	–	13	14	15	16	17	18	19	20	21	22	23	24	25	–
3AZ	1			3				1		2											
3BY		1			2			1	1		2		5	4	3	3	6	2			
3AY			1			1	2		2	1											
3BZ		1		2				1		1											

Firm orders   Forecast

model number, and the number of the week in which these units of product were to be completed. It also shows that conceptually, the master schedule was split into two parts. The first part, covering the first 15 weeks in the future, usually contained firm orders for individual model numbers. The second portion, covering time periods further in the future, was at a higher level of aggregation. It grouped similar models together.

The first, or "firm" portion of the master schedule indicated where order entry interfaced with production control in specifying major equipment assembly needs. Recall that major equipment was assembled only after the receipt of particular orders, because the options and specifications that a customer would require could not be accurately predicted in advance. Order entry personnel, who knew that it took roughly 15 weeks to assemble a major piece of equipment, would thus book orders in the current week for delivery 16 weeks hence. For example, the order for one Model 3AZ in week 1 shown in the exhibit, was accepted 14 weeks before, and had been in the process of being assembled for 14 weeks. It would be shipped at the end of week 1. Order entry personnel had a rough idea of the capacity of the assembly area that put together Model 3s and generally avoided accepting more orders for a period than could be constructed. They implicitly assumed, however, that all of the parts, materials, and subassemblies (apparatus) required to assemble the equipment they accepted orders for, would be available when needed.

The forecast of needs for the last part of the master schedule was supplied to the San Jose Works by the marketing division monthly. Because marketing did not have any basis for predicting whether future Model 3 shipments would require the A, B, Z, or Y options, these forecasts were not broken down by individual product. As might be expected, the forecasts in this portion of the master schedule changed frequently, as marketing obtained new information and revised their forecasts monthly. The firm part of the master schedule remained fairly constant once it was made, except for rare instances when orders were canceled. When an order was canceled, usually as a result of lengthy negotiations with the marketing department and the customer, it was taken from the master schedule.

Materials explosions and selects. The master schedule, along with a bill of materials file and an inventory file, was used to project, and reproject, materials needs each week for the departments and shops in the San Jose Works in such a way that the shipment goals laid out in the master schedule could be met. Exhibit 4 shows graphically four bills of material used to determine component requirements for the first four example products shown in the master schedule in Exhibit 3.

Production planning used this data to move jobs through the assembly or equipment shops in the following way. First, the computer was used to explode the firm part of the master schedule. Thus, if a Model 3AZ was to be shipped in week 15, the explosion would show that one component A and one subassembly Z (see bill of materials in Exhibit 4) would be needed in the assembly shop at the beginning of week 1 to give assembly the 15 weeks they needed to assemble these components into the product. Second, production control would

Exhibit 4

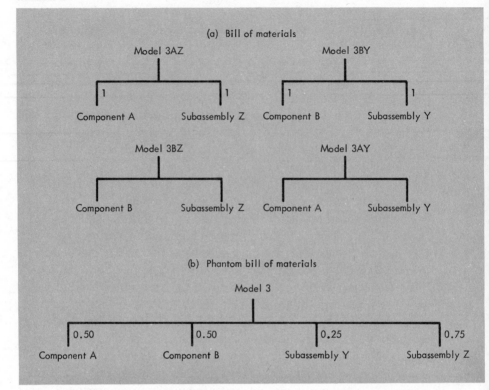

issue job select orders. These orders implemented the results of the explosion by giving the stockroom the authorization to "select" one component A and one subassembly Z from the stockroom shelves, and deliver them to the assembly area so that they could begin work. Even if one of the two components was out of stock in the stockroom, say component A, the other part, subassembly Z, would still be delivered to the assembly area. Production control felt that if they did not do this, the subassembly might be used later to provide materials for another order. Moreover, plant management felt that having one component present and the other missing gave the assembly shop supervisor some motivation to pressure whatever other department was late in delivering the missing part. If an order for a piece of equipment was canceled, the shops were supposed to return any material associated with it to the storeroom, although this was not always done.

The forecast portion of the master schedule was exploded to ensure that the parts and components (apparatus) used to assemble equipment would be fabricated far enough in advance to make sure that these parts were in the storeroom when they were needed. A special kind of bill of materials, called a "phantom bill" was used to accomplish this. The phantom bill (see Exhibit 4) was a bill of materials which did not correspond to any product the company actually made, but which had all of the elements of a family of products. This enabled planners to overcome the problem of forecasting individual product options by using probabilistic data.

The phantom bill in Exhibit 4, for example, shows that 50 percent of the Model 3 shipments used component A and 50 percent component B, and that 75 percent used subassembly Z and 25 percent used subassembly Y. Thus, if the master schedule projected shipments of four Model 3s in week 19, the computer would calculate from the phantom bill that two components A, two components B, 3 Zs and 1 Y, would be needed in the stockroom 15 weeks in advance of this date. If a check of the projected inventory status[3] during the lead time (say four weeks) required to fabricate these components showed that fewer than this amount would be on hand unless a new manufacturing order were issued, a manufacturing order would in fact be issued along with a select order which provided the affected apparatus shop with all (they hoped) of the materials and parts it needed to fill the order. If sufficient capacity existed, and there were no stockroom shortages for the apparatus selects, the four components would be available in the stockroom 4 weeks later when week 19 was 15 weeks in the future. No attempt was made to determine whether or not sufficient capacity existed to fill these apparatus orders within the planned manufacturing lead times at the time orders were placed. However, if the long-range capacity and labor plans were correct, sufficient capacity would be available when needed.

In the process of exploding apparatus requirements from the master schedule, two additional factors were considered. The first was the need to produce apparatus in lots of an economical size. The actual size of the lots produced was based on the technique described in Exhibit 5, which was designed to balance the costs of setting up to produce a part, and the cost of holding inventories. The second consideration was the inclusion of extra buffer stocks to pro-

---

[3] This check was accomplished by comparing the number of units of material on hand and on order (from the inventory file) with the anticipated demand over the procurement lead time.

Exhibit 5
Calculating economic lot sizes

The San Jose Works used two methods for calculating economic lot sizes. One method was applied when the demand for a type of apparatus or purchased part was relatively constant throughout a year. The second, more complex method, was used when demand varied significantly throughout a year. Both methods, however, strove to achieve the same goal: balancing the costs of placing an order for the production or procurement of a batch of parts, and the cost of holding these items in inventory.

The cost of holding items in inventory was calculated by the accounting department as a percentage of the cost of a unit of production. This percentage, typically 30 percent of item value, was calculated by summing the expected costs associated with holding inventory, and dividing by the expected total cost of goods produced in a year. The costs associated with holding inventory included: fire protection, insurance, materials handling costs, depreciation in storage areas, taxes on inventory, spoilage and obsolescence costs, the clerical costs of financing and accounting, and the target percentage return on investment for money tied up in inventory.

The cost of placing an order depended on where the order was placed. If the part or apparatus in question was manufactured locally, the cost of placing an order included clerical costs, storeroom handling costs, and the cost of setting up equipment or arranging the workplace to produce the item in question. If the item was purchased from outside vendors, the ordering costs included the clerical costs associated with placing the order, and the cost of receiving, handling, and placing the unit in the storeroom.

Method I

The explosion of the master schedule resulted in the projection of materials requirements week by week into the future. Thus, the projected net requirements for a part with a two-week lead time might look like those shown in Table I. In this example, the requirements are the quantity of an apparatus needed to complete the projected assembly of equipment from the master schedule. If it takes, say, two weeks to assemble the equipment after the apparatus is available, the apparatus requirements are offset two weeks to reflect this fact. In this case, the ten units of apparatus required in week 1 would be used in building a piece of equipment that the master schedule indicates should be completed at the beginning of week 3. Outstanding orders due indicates orders for the apparatus placed in previous weeks (remember that the item here has a two-week manufacturing lead time) and due to be completed at the beginning of the week indicated. The net requirements row indicates the net projected need for the apparatus that must be filled by future production.

Since this net requirements "plan" indicates that the usage of this type of

Exhibit 5 (*continued*)

Table I

Week	Requirements	Outstanding orders due	Net requirements*
1	10	10	0
2	10	10	0
3	10		−10
4	10		−10
5	10		−10
6	10		−10
7	10		−10
8	10		−10
9	10		−10
10	10		−10
11	10		−10
12	10		−10
13	10		−10

* Since net requirements are obtained by subtracting requirements from outstanding orders due and beginning inventory (assumed to be 0), a negative value indicates future run-outs of material.

apparatus is fairly constant, the economic order quantity model is used to determine the best order quantity. This model is based on the formula:

$$Q_o = \sqrt{\frac{2Rc_P}{ic}}$$

where

R = Annual requirements.
Q_o = Lot size.
i = Percentage cost of holding inventory (in decimal form).
c = Standard cost of the unit.
c_P = Cost of ordering.

Thus, since the annual requirements of the type of apparatus in the example above is likely to be $52 \times 10 = 5{,}200$ per year, and if the cost of ordering is $5, the cost of the unit is $5 and the inventory holding cost percentage is 30 percent the lot size should be approximately 60 units, instead of the ten used in past periods. With this new information, a projection of planned orders and inventory balances can be made (see Table II).

The planned orders that appear within the manufacturing lead time of the department producing these parts are then included in the promise sheet of that department.

Method II

In many cases, the requirements for a part or piece of apparatus are not as evenly spread throughout the year as they were in the previous example.

Exhibit 5 (continued)

Table II

Week	Requirements	Outstanding orders due	Net requirements	Planned order releases	Projected inventory balance
1	10	10	0	60	0
2	10	10	0		0
3	10	60	−50		50
4	10		−40		40
5	10		−30		30
6	10		−20		20
7	10		−10	60	10
8	10		0		0
9	10	60	−50		50
10	10		−40		40
11	10		−30		30
12	10		−20		20
13	10		−10		10

(□) designates the anticipated receipt of planned orders.

Since constant demand is one of the basic assumptions behind the derivation of the formula for Q_o, this means that this method for determining lot sizes cannot be used. Rather, an iterative approach for determining the least total cost of various lot sizes is applied.

The net requirements schedule shown in Table III is typical of those with uneven demands.

Table III

Week	Requirements	Outstanding orders due	Net requirements
1.....................	10	10	0
2.....................	10	10	0
3.....................	70		−70
4.....................	30		−30
5.....................	0		0
6.....................	100		−100
7.....................	0		0
8.....................	0		0
9.....................	200		−200
10.....................	0		0
11.....................	0		0

To determine the best ordering quantities to use in this situation, the computer system at the San Jose Works evaluates alternative lot sizes in the following way (assuming a $25 ordering cost):

1. Compute the unit cost of producing just enough to satisfy the needs for the next period in which a net requirement appears. Using the require-

Exhibit 5 (*concluded*)

ments shown in the example above (70 in the first period of need), and the cost data from the previous example, the cost of this alternative would be:

Ordering cost $25
Inventory cost = 0
  (because just enough made to meet requirements)   0
      Total cost $25
Unit cost = $25/70 units .... $ 0.36

2. Compute the unit cost of producing just enough to satisfy the needs for the next two periods in which a net requirement exists.*

Ordering cost $25
Inventory cost (from above) = 0 + cost of holding 30 units
  1 week = 0 + 30 × $50 × 0.006 × 1   9
      Total cost $34
Unit cost = $34/100 units .... $ 0.34

3. Compute the unit cost of producing just enough to satisfy the needs of the next three periods in which a gross requirement exists:

Ordering cost .... $ 25
Inventory holding cost = $0 + $9 (from above) + cost of holding
  100 units 3 weeks = $0 + $9 + 100 × $50 × 0.006 × 3 99
      Total cost $124
Unit cost = $124/200 .... $ 0.62

4. Obviously, the plan which yields the least unit cost is to produce 100 units for period 3, and to use 30 of them to satisfy the requirements for period 4. It does not pay to produce period 6 requirements with this batch. The computer program continues in this manner to plan lot sizes for periods beyond period 4.

---

* Note that the annual inventory percentage holding cost is converted to a weekly basis by dividing 30 percent by 52 weeks = 0.6 percent. To convert to decimal form, 0.60 ÷ 100 = 0.006.

tect against unexpected demands or late deliveries. The technique used to calculate buffer stocks is described in Exhibit 6.

Shop loading and scheduling. The current and forecast work load for a particular apparatus department was projected into the future as the production planning system exploded material requirements from the master schedule. The result was a weekly pro-

Exhibit 6
Calculating buffer stocks

Often, the projected net requirements for a part or piece of apparatus were more or less than the amount actually needed when the time came to use them. This, obviously, was due to the fact that requirements were based on a master schedule, much of which was in turn based on imperfect (by nature) forecast information. When more was produced than was eventually needed, the result was extra inventory. This was costly, but given the values of the company, this eventuality was much less important than not having enough, and thus endangering the plant's ability to deliver products quickly. To protect against this possibility, the system in use at the company was designed to incorporate "protective" or "buffer" stocks into the requirements for an item, over and above planned requirements.

The need for a protective buffer stock was determined by calculating the ratio of the difference between planned and actual usage, and planned usage. Thus, if the actual usage of a part in a week was projected to be 20 units, and actual usage was 15, the ratio would be $(20 - 15)/20 = 0.25$. If the ratio was positive, actual usage was less than planned, hence protective stock was not required in that period. If the ratio was negative, planned usage was less than actual, indicating the need for protective buffer stocks in that period.

These ratios were used to calculate a moving average ratio over time. If the moving average was negative, the amount of protective buffer stock in use was determined by multiplying future projections of demand by the moving average ratio. For example, if the moving average was based on an equal weighting of the past three weeks experience in which the ratio was $- 0.42$, $+ 0.25$, and $- 0.70$, respectively, it would equal $- 0.29$. Thus, the projected usage in future periods would be increased by 29 percent.

mise sheet (Exhibit 7) which the department or shop supervisor used to schedule individual jobs. The promise sheet was analogous to a master schedule for each shop. It extended six weeks into the past and six weeks into the future. The past due or "back scheduled" jobs listed on the promise sheet were jobs that had not been completed on time, either because of a materials shortage, insufficient capacity, or some other reason. The jobs which were scheduled for completion in future weeks were generated from the requirements explosion process. Shops were authorized to work on those future scheduled jobs that were within the lead time of the shop. For example, the shop whose promise sheet is shown in Exhibit 7, had been assigned a lead time of four weeks by production control. Thus it was authorized to

Exhibit 7
Shop load

WEEKLY PROMISE SHEET

CODE AND DESC	CUST OWNER	TOTAL BACK SCHEDULED	6 & OVER (011)	5 (012)	4 (013)	3 (014)	2 (021)	1 (022)	CURRENT WEEK (023)	1 (024)	2 (031)	3 (032)	4 (033)	5 (034)	6	MON	TUE	WED	THU	FRI	SAT
C2280 Cir Pack	LOAD								870	613	602	627	625	625	618						
C2281 Cir Pack	LOAD									79	57	238	.04	236							
C2281D Cir Pack	LOAD								107	347	242	256	256	256	268						
C2281E Cir Pack	LOAD	152						152	123	180	148	144	150	156	144						
C2281F Cir Pack	LOAD								12	98	76		41	16							
R 473	LOAD	655	300	72	156	133															
R 582	LOAD	394	102	100	148	44							24								
R 583	LOAD								3	73	38	20	64								
RFZ 413	LOAD												61								
RFZ 104	LOAD									320	1003		457								
RFY 173	LOAD								241	214	92	197	156	193	194						
RFQ 248	LOAD	13925			1350	3980	4788	3807	4206	4010	2742	3942	2643	4835	3273						
RFT 687	LOAD	25921	3524	3931	7642	3179	3994	3651	4071	4008		2171	3952	4820	3330						
S 99	LOAD								239	153	965	75	65		98	BACK					
S 104	LOAD								88	126	111	128	52	73							
S 105	LOAD											32		418							
S 106	LOAD	150					157	137	129		443	226	74	71		BACK					
S 307	LOAD										29	225	75	72							
S 340	LOAD									301	284	79	74	71							
Z 290	LOAD	818						818	919	919	811	895		655		PCT					
Z 290A	LOAD	17					15	2	2	1	2		4	3							
TOTAL LOAD		148710	13981		23095		51986		85738		57452		67104								
		21903		9553		22192		66904		65101		50522		63606							
TOTAL SURPLUS									50												

work on all of the jobs which were back scheduled, plus the first four weeks of the future scheduled load. The select system would work to ensure that in the week the promise sheet was issued, the materials associated with jobs due four weeks later were issued. Thus enough materials to complete 625 units of the C2280 circuit pack in Exhibit 7 would be issued the week the promise sheet came out.

Lead times (manufacturing intervals) were assigned to individual shops on the basis of the estimated time required to set up and run a job, plus slack time for scheduling. Almost any job in the apparatus shops could be completed within a week if it were the only job to be worked on. But because each shop was required to work on numerous jobs, extra slack scheduling time was added to the lead time so that the supervisors would have the flexibility to smooth out work loads, change lot sizing decisions, and implement mix changes. On the average, any one job was only being worked on a total of about one week, even though four weeks were allowed.

In determining which jobs to work on at a particular time, the shop supervisor had to consider a number of factors, such as the priority of the job, the availability of materials, setup costs, and the size and productivity of the work force in the shop. The way in which this was accomplished is illustrated by the methods used in the coil shop. The coil shop wound copper wire of various types on different sized spools to produce over 200 different coils. These coils then were used in transformers and inductors that went in final products. The 20 winding machines in the department were operated by 20 first-shift operators, 9 second-shift operators, and 1 third-shift operator. When the shop was busy, there were typically over 60 different types of coil on the promise sheet waiting to be wound. But only about half of the winding machines could make all of the coils. The rest were special-purpose machines and could only be used to produce certain types. Moreover, there were wide differences in the skills of the operators. Some were much more efficient at winding some types of coils than others. It took an operator about 30 minutes to set up a machine to produce a typical coil and another hour or so during which the operator averaged 50 percent efficiency. After an hour of "learning," efficiency rose to expected levels. This learning effect, plus the setup time, meant that long production runs resulted in much higher efficiencies than short runs.

The coil shop supervisor scheduled by first making a list of the coils that were waiting to be wound from the promise sheet. This list consisted of five categories; in order of their importance they were, critical orders, back scheduled orders, current orders, future orders, and no materials. Critical orders were orders that the supervisor's supervisor or colleagues were urging him to complete. Back scheduled, current, and future orders were specified on the promise sheet. No materials orders were orders that could not be worked on because the select system failed to provide all the materials needed to complete a job.

The second scheduling step was to make a list of the orders currently being processed. This list was compared to the first one to determine if any high-priority items were not being run while low-priority items were. If, for example, a future order was being wound and a back scheduled order was not, the first was usually dropped, and replaced with the latter. Sometimes, even when the load was heavy, there would not be enough work to keep one of the more specialized machines busy. In this case, the supervisor was supposed to avoid low efficiencies by asking the plant manager to authorize the production of coils that were future scheduled beyond the normal four-week cutoff. If the authorization to "move work up" was obtained, a special select order was supposed to be cut to provide the shop with materials.

Should have—Should take

The should-have/should-take system was implemented in 1974 to monitor the in-process floor inventory investment in the various shops and departments at the San Jose Works. This adjunct to the computerized planning and control system used the master schedule and bill of materials information to quantify the amount of floor inventory a shop *should have*. By comparing the should-have amount with actual inventory levels, it was felt that problems could be quickly identified and solved.

An estimate of the floor inventory each shop should have was made monthly. This estimate was built up by first cumulating the value of the materials that had been issued to a shop through the select system, but that had not been returned in the form of a finished part or product, as a canceled order, or as scrap or loss. For example, the first product in Exhibit 7, C2280 circuit packs, had 870 + 613 + 602 + 627 + 625 = 3,337 units worth of raw materials issued at the time the promise sheet was made up. Had any of these jobs been completed previously and returned to the storeroom, they would not have been on the promise sheet. If the cost of the raw materials required to build one circuit pack was $10, the should-have materials floor inventory for current and future scheduled jobs would be $33,370. The amounts shown under the "current materials cost" column in Exhibit 8 reflect this type of calculation. The "back material cost" column in Exhibit 8 is obtained in precisely the same way. However, since jobs may have been back scheduled because of a shortage of one material that was holding up the job, a correction was made. This correction is shown in the column labeled "short." By subtracting the value of the materials not available because of a

Exhibit 8
Should-have—should-take inventory report

SHOULD-HAVE – SHOULD-TAKE INVENTORY
SUB-BRANCH 90500
MONTH ENDING SEP 1975

			LOAD RELATED DATA						ACCOUNTING RESULTS				RATIO CALCULATIONS		
SHOP or DEPT*	$ CUR HOURS	$ BACK SCHED HOURS	CUR MATL COST	BACK MATL COST	TOTAL BACK COST	SHOULD SHORT INVENTORY	SHOULD HAVE INVENTORY	LABOR LOAD RATE	ACCOUNT MATERIAL COST	ACCOUNT TOTAL COST	SHT MATL RATIO (ACC/SHM)	SHT TOT RATIO (ACC/SHT)	SHT TOT RATIO (ACC/STT)
Z43	10303 2	5997	63226	25332	31209								
Z76	2391 6	5432	1625	941	6373								
90510	12339 2	11339	65151	26243	37592	521	114636	77545 17.58	172078	234629	1.89	2.05	3.33
Z55	P64	1968	719	914	2884								
Z50	343	451	3175	441	512								
Z57				24	24								
Z62	9583	21034	39192	39548	60582								
Z67		174	54	2093	2267								
Z69				73	73								
Z73	10344	3054	22293	4013	70A7								
90520	21170	26681	65433	47129	73809	5546	154866	86603 34.71	226448	307353	2.12	1.98	3.55
Z84	5779	3448	44728	8061	11509								
Z86	5327	5874	103348	139101	145065								
90530	11106	9332	148476	147252	156574	3030	313126	159592 23.78	729879	832254	2.49	2.65	5.22
Z47	24463	54687	203563	118325	173012								
Z89	1103	3006	27149	34654	36660								
Z90	2148	6924	14373	13393	20317								
90540	27650	63617	245085	166372	229989	29037	473687	272735 28.26	666132	786015	1.74	1.66	2.88
Z49													
90550	247	2418	127C8	21804	24222	2449	34728	12955 27.48	133954	138516	4.18	3.90	13.69
90500	72567	113377	536853	408799	522176	40583	1091013	609420	1928491	2296766	2.13	2.11	3.77

* Numbers starting with Z are sections within a department. Numbers beginning with 9 refer to department totals. All departments beginning with "905---," are parts of the subbranch numbered 90500.

stockout from the "back material cost," the should-have amount of materials on the floor for back scheduled jobs was obtained.

Besides materials cost, the only other component of floor inventory cost was labor and overhead value added. It was possible for the San Jose Works to measure the amount of labor and overhead value added for each job continually. However, this would have entailed an extensive and expensive labor reporting system. Instead, they used a simplifying assumption which gave a fairly accurate estimate. This assumption was that labor (and hence overhead) value was added linearly with the time the job had been in the shop. Returning to our previous example, we might find that the total standard labor and overhead charge for completed C2280 circuit packs was $17.58 per unit. In this case, since the product was expected to be on the floor for four weeks, it was assumed that $17.58/4 = $4.395 in value was added to each unit each week. Thus, the 870 units in the current week would have 870 × $17.58 = $15,294.60 worth of in-process labor and overhead in it. The 613 units due in week one would have $8082.40 worth of in-process labor associated with it and so on. By summing these labor value added amounts for all in-process C2280 circuit packs, the total "$ cur. hours" in Exhibit 8 was obtained. In order to prevent double counting, the "$ back scheduled hours" column was obtained by simply carrying forward the maximum value added estimate from the time these jobs were current.

The total should-have floor inventory was obtained by summing the first four columns in the should-have report in Exhibit 8 and subtracting the sixth column labeled "short." Should-take inventory indicated the amount of in-process inventory the department would have if there were no back scheduled items. It was calculated by subcontracting "$ back sched. hours" and "back matl. cost" from should-have.

The inventory crunch

In discussing the actions taken to reduce inventories at the San Jose Works, Bill Berlin described three basic steps that had been taken.

I. The first step was to reduce the rate at which input materials were acquired, and the size of the work force. A revision of the forecasts in the master schedule was sufficient to ensure that the net requirements for raw materials were reduced, since material needs were directly related to output by the explosion process. In addition, purchasing and manufacturing lot sizes and buffer stocks were slashed. The size of the work force was reduced through layoffs to about 75 percent of November 1974 levels. This occurred in February 1975, immediately after the typical winter surge in shipments. In describing the effects of these decisions, Berlin noted:

> You know, these are moves that have to be made, but what a lot of people don't realize is that it takes quite a while before inventory levels actually drop as a result of them. We have a total manufacturing span of 26 weeks and purchase lead times averaging 10 weeks beyond that. That means that if we shut off the materials faucets completely, and reduce the output faucet 25 percent, it will still take us quite a while to purge the system of unneeded inventories. So to get quick results, we had to do more than just reduce our production and materials procurement rates.

II. The second tactic taken to reduce investment was to examine stockroom inventories. Materials and parts stored in stockroom areas were not accounted for in the should-have/should-take system. It only monitored floor inventories. However, the total actual investment in stockroom areas generally equaled the shop floor in-process inventory investment. In an intensive review of the stockrooms, it was found that they contained approximately $7 million in dead or inactive parts, many of which were subsequently removed and sold

for scrap. It was also found that as a result of the reduced production
plans, $22 million worth of inventory in the stockrooms were made
up of parts and materials for which there was more than a six
months' supply. A program to identify other divisions and factories
which used these parts, and to transfer them, was instrumental in
reducing these excesses.

III. The last step in the inventory reduction campaign focused on
the shop floor in-process inventories. In Berlin's words:

> Should-have/should-take had been around for a little while, but we really
> started to put it to use in the latter part of 1974. The first thing I had to do was
> to gain some credibility for the technique. I started by scanning the should-
> have reports [Exhibit 8], looking for a department where the ratio of actual to
> should-have was way out of line. There were plenty, but I took the worst
> department and invited the department head and his boss in to talk about it.
> I pointed out that their investment in inventory was way too high and that
> they needed to bring it into line. Their reaction wasn't surprising. They
> didn't believe they had any excess inventory and told me that the report was
> useless!
>
> From that point, I got our internal auditors to go down and take a detailed
> physical inventory of what they actually had in that shop, item by item. We
> then exploded their promise sheet to find out what they should have, item by
> item, and compared the two lists. Now I had proof that there was too much
> inventory down there, and we had another meeting. They were much more
> receptive this time. We set some goals to get that department's inventory
> down, and they did.
>
> I've been following the same procedure every month. I pick one or two of
> the worst shops or subbranches, we go through the whole "I don't believe
> it—auditing procedure," and eventually we get someone else on board. I
> don't believe in constantly pressuring everybody all the time on this
> "should-have" business because these shop and subbranch heads have to
> worry about other things too—primarily their costs and efficiencies. My
> hope is that in doing it the way I am, I'll be able to train these people so they
> can balance inventories and costs wisely.
>
> This program is working [see Exhibit 9]. We have been able to chase a lot
> of excess inventory off the floor and back to the stockrooms where we can
> account for it and use it. But the benefits have extended beyond this. For
> example, one of the HIC's (hybrid integrated circuits) shops turned up with a
> million dollar difference between should-have and actual. Those things are
> so expensive and small that you can just about hold that much inventory in a
> desk drawer. When we went down there we found that most of the excess
> was in a new circuit which engineering had pegged for a fairly low yield rate
> of about 50 percent in its initial stages of production and then forgotten
> about. Now these HIC's are repairable. That is, of the 50 percent defective in
> any run, 50 percent of those can be repaired, then 50 percent of those, and so

Exhibit 9
Works total ($000)

	Should-have (material only)	Accounting results (material only)	Accounting minus should-have (material only)	Should have total (including labor)	Accounting total	Accounting minus should-have total
1974:						
November	24,844	39,923	15,079	35,567 14,843*	49,868	14,301
December	21,553	35,361	13,808	31,749 21,402*	44,404	13,655
1975:						
January	24,345	35,729	11,384	35,285 22,827*	46,679	11,394
February	24,009	35,521	11,512	34,366 22,171*	46,734	12,368
March	23,035	34,604	11,569	32,079 17,746*	44,746	12,661
April	20,971	33,159	12,188	29,954 16,692	42,645	12,691
May	17,128	30,540	12,412	24,642 14,022*	39,198	14,556
June	17,268	29,213	11,945	24,494 13,383*	37,578	13,084
July	16,545	27,983	11,438	23,704 14,169*	35,843	12,139
August	16,616	28,135	11,519	23,336 14,013*	36,279	12,943
September	19,003	27,435	8,432	25,534 13,333*	35,619	10,085
October	18,568	27,712	9,144	24,671 14,043*	35,681	11,010

* Should-take total.

on. But our accounting system doesn't give a shop credit in the efficiency reports for repairing defectives. So the shop supervisor just let the defectives pile up until he got far enough ahead on his efficiencies on other items to repair them. The result was a lot of inventory in salvagable circuits. When we found this out, we worked out a program with the supervisor to reduce this inventory. But, more important, it signaled to us that we had to get engineering on the stick to get those yields up, and they did. This illustrates just one of the benefits of the should-have/should-take system that we hadn't expected.

November 1975

In November 1975, Berlin was reviewing his objectives for the following year. The company had encountered even more financial reverses during the year than they had expected, and the forecast of shipments from the San Jose Works remained at $170 million for the following year. The pressure for further reductions in inventories was still there. Moreover, Berlin found that he had two new problems as well. First, labor efficiencies at the San Jose Works had dropped from over 100 percent at the beginning of 1975 to 96 percent. Second, even though the materials shortages and vendor reliability problems had largely disappeared as a reason for delivery service problems, the percentage of equipment deliveries made on time had remained at 86 percent throughout 1975. An increase in competition on the basis of delivery time made it more important that customer service improve in the following year.

Index

Vollman, T. E., 34, 236, 244, 489, 532, 535
Voris, W., 154

W

Wage, S., 103–4
Wagner, H. N., 153–54, 197
Wagner-Whitin algorithm, 176, 181–
    83, 194, 296, 348, 366
Wassweiler, W., 535
Wester, L., 444–57, 465, 481–82
Wheelwright, S. C., 95, 104, 704, 716
White, C. R., 34
Whitin, T. M., 153, 154, 197
Whybark, D. C., 102, 104, 188–89, 197
Wiest, J. D., 16, 632–33, 640–50, 662

Wight, O. W., 34, 197, 375, 551, 578, 716
Wilde, D. J., 310
Williams, J. G., 188–89, 197
Wilson, R. C., 534
Winters, P. R., 62, 104
Work flow structures, 542, 545
Wyckoff, D., 34
Wynne, B. E., Jr., 661

Y–Z

Young, H. H., 482
Young, W. M., 261, 308
Zangwill, W. I., 299, 310
Zimmerman, H. J., 154
Zoller, K., 299, 310

This book has been set in 10 and 9 point
Melior, leaded 3 points. Part numbers and titles and chapter numbers and titles are 30
point Melior. The size of the text area is 26 by
46½ picas.